Southern Living®
ANNUAL RECIPES COOKBOOK

20TH ANNIVERSARY EDITION

Southern Living®

ANNUAL RECIPES COOKBOOK
20TH ANNIVERSARY EDITION

Oxmoor House®

Library of Congress Catalog Number: 97-69573
ISBN: 0-8487-1688-4

Manufactured in the United States of America
First printing 1998

WE'RE HERE FOR YOU!

We at Oxmoor House are dedicated to serving you with reliable information that expands your imagination and enriches your life. We welcome your comments and suggestions. Please write us at:

Oxmoor House, Inc.
Editor, *Southern Living® Annual Recipes Cookbook,*
20th Anniversary Edition
2100 Lakeshore Drive
Birmingham, AL 35209

To order additional publications, call 1-205-877-6560.

We Want Your FAVORITE RECIPES!

Southern Living cooks are the best cooks of all, and we want your secrets! Please send your favorite original recipes for main dishes, desserts, and everything in between, along with any hands-on tips and a sentence about why you like each recipe. We can't guarantee we'll print them in a cookbook, but if we do, we'll send you $10 and a free copy of the cookbook. Send each recipe on a separate page with your name, address, and daytime phone number to:

Cookbook Recipes
Oxmoor House
2100 Lakeshore Drive
Birmingham, AL 35209

SYMBOLS WITHIN THIS BOOK:

QUICK! indicates that a recipe can be prepared quickly or easily.

♥ indicates a light recipe with nutritional analysis or ingredient substitutions that will reduce the amount of calories, fat, cholesterol, or sodium.

Southern Living®

Executive Editor: Kaye Mabry Adams
Foods Editors: Elle Barrett, Susan Hawthorne Nash
Associate Foods Editors: Denise Gee, Jackie Mills, R.D.
Assistant Foods Editors: Cynthia Briscoe, Donna Florio,
    Monique Hicks, Diane Hogan, Andria Scott Hurst,
    Alison Lewis, Patty M. Vann
Test Kitchens Director: Vanessa Taylor Johnson
Assistant Test Kitchens Directors: Judy Feagin, Peggy Smith
Test Kitchens Staff: Margaret Monroe, Mary Allen Perry,
    Vanessa McNeil, Vie Warshaw
Administrative Assistant: Wanda T. Stephens
Editorial Assistant: April Tanner
Senior Foods Photographer: Charles Walton IV
Photographers: Ralph Anderson, Tina Cornett,
    William Dickey, J. Savage Gibson
Senior Photo Stylist: Cindy Manning Barr
Assistant Photo Stylists: Buffy Hargett, Mary Lyn Hill
Photo Services: Tracy Duncan, Tena Payne
Production Manager: Kenner Patton
Assistant Production Manager: Bradford Kachelhofer
Editorial Contributors: Trinda Gage, Telia Johnson, Jan Moon

Oxmoor House, Inc.

Editor-in-Chief: Nancy Fitzpatrick Wyatt
Senior Editor, Editorial Services: Olivia Kindig Wells
Art Director: James Boone

Southern Living® Annual Recipes Cookbook,
20th Anniversary Edition

Senior Foods Editor: Susan Payne Stabler
Foods Editor: Janice Krahn Hanby
Copy Editor: Donna Baldone
Editorial Assistant: Stacey Geary
Production Director: Phillip Lee
Associate Production Manager: Vanessa Cobbs Richardson
Production Assistant: Faye Porter Bonner
Indexer: Mary Ann Laurens
Designer: Carol Middleton

Cover: Nanny's Famous Coconut-Pineapple Cake (page 74)
Back Cover: (clockwise from top left) Cranberry-Cornbread
    Stuffed Cornish Hens (page 288), Antipasto Kabobs (page 20),
    Three-Cheese Soufflés (page 140), and Bow Ties, Black Beans,
    and Key Limes (page 225)
Page 2: Curried Pumpkin Soup (page 364)
Page 5: Summery Chicken Salad (page 319) and Honey Angel
    Biscuit (page 63)

CONTENTS

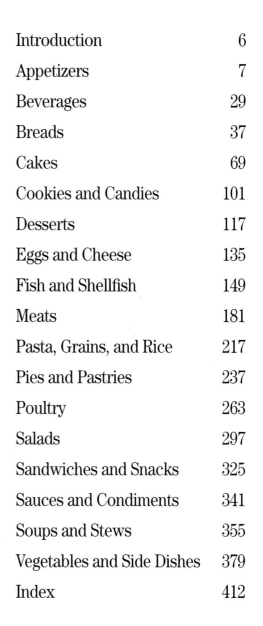

INTRODUCTION

20TH ANNIVERSARY EDITION

We're celebrating the 20th year of publication
of the ever-popular cookbook series,
Southern Living® Annual Recipes,
with this special keepsake edition.

The *Southern Living® Annual Recipes Cookbook, 20th Anniversary Edition* showcases over 1500 of the highest-rated recipes from *Southern Living® Annual Recipes*. Never before have so many exceptional *Southern Living* recipes been gathered into one handsome volume. Plus, by popular demand, the recipes are organized into traditional food chapters to help you find your favorites.

For easy reference, we included these convenient symbols, too:

QUICK! indicates that a recipe can be prepared quickly or easily.

♥ indicates a light recipe with nutritional analysis or ingredient substitutions that will reduce the amount of calories, fat, cholesterol, or sodium.

Take a few moments to get acquainted with the chapters. Preview some of the hearty main-dish recipes that begin on page 181 or the scrumptious desserts that begin on page 117. And don't miss a whole crop of Southern vegetables and other side dishes starting on page 379.

We thank you for sharing your recipes and stories through the years, and we know you'll enjoy this unparalleled collection.

The Editors

At right: Antipasto Kabobs (page 20)

APPETIZERS

Goat Cheese With Sun-Dried Tomatoes and Rosemary

GOAT CHEESE WITH SUN-DRIED TOMATOES AND ROSEMARY
(pictured at left)

6 dried tomato halves
3 cloves garlic, pressed
2 tablespoons olive oil
1 tablespoon chopped fresh
   rosemary or dried rosemary
1 French baguette, thinly sliced
Olive oil
1 (11-ounce) package goat
   cheese
Garnish: fresh rosemary sprigs

● **Cover** tomato with boiling water; let stand 5 minutes. Drain and chop. Combine tomato, garlic, oil, and rosemary; cover and chill up to 4 hours.
● **Brush** baguette rounds with additional olive oil. Place on an ungreased baking sheet, and bake at 350° for 8 minutes or until lightly toasted.
● **Just** before serving, place goat cheese on a serving plate, and top with tomato mixture. Serve with baguette rounds, and garnish, if desired. **Yield:** 8 appetizer servings.

Note: Tomatoes should not be marinated more than 4 hours.

The Lucullan Society
Lynchburg, Virginia

PEPPERED GOAT CHEESE
QUICK!

1 (3-ounce) package goat
   cheese
1 to 2 teaspoons freshly cracked
   pepper
2 to 3 teaspoons olive oil
Garnishes: fresh rosemary sprigs,
   fresh oregano sprigs

● **Roll** goat cheese in pepper to coat; drizzle with olive oil. Garnish, if desired, and serve with French baguette slices. **Yield:** 2 to 4 appetizer servings.

Bill Keller
Birmingham, Alabama

OREGANO CHEESE PUFFS

Fontina cheese contains about 45% butterfat, so it's smooth in texture and is packed with a creamy rich flavor – definitely worth a try.

¾ cup milk
3 tablespoons butter or margarine
¾ cup all-purpose flour
½ teaspoon salt
⅛ teaspoon pepper
3 large eggs
½ cup (2 ounces) shredded
   fontina cheese, divided
1½ teaspoons dried oregano

● **Bring** milk and butter to a boil in a medium saucepan. Reduce heat to low; add flour, salt, and pepper all at once, stirring vigorously until mixture leaves sides of pan and forms a smooth ball. Remove from heat, and let cool 5 to 10 minutes.
● **Add** eggs, one at a time, beating with a wooden spoon after each addition. Stir in ¼ cup cheese and oregano. Drop by level tablespoonfuls onto greased baking sheets.
● **Bake** cheese puffs at 400° for 18 minutes. Sprinkle with remaining ¼ cup cheese, and bake 2 to 3 additional minutes. Serve immediately. **Yield:** 2½ dozen.

Valerie Stutsman
Norfolk, Virginia

SPINACH-ARTICHOKE-TOMATO PUFFS

1 (10-ounce) package frozen
   chopped spinach, thawed
1 (14-ounce) can artichoke hearts,
   drained
1 (8-ounce) jar dried tomatoes in
   oil, drained
1 (3-ounce) package goat cheese
¼ teaspoon salt
¼ teaspoon pepper
1½ (17¼-ounce) packages frozen
   puff pastry sheets, thawed

● **Drain** spinach well, pressing between layers of paper towels to remove excess moisture.

● **Position** knife blade in food processor bowl; add spinach, artichoke hearts, and tomato. Pulse 5 times or until chopped, stopping often to scrape down sides. Add goat cheese, salt, and pepper; process until blended. Set aside.
● **Roll** 1 pastry sheet into a 15- x 12-inch rectangle on a surface sprinkled lightly with cornmeal. Cut into 3-inch squares.
● **Spoon** about 1 tablespoon spinach mixture in center of each square. Fold all corners toward center, slightly overlapping edges.
● **Grease** baking sheets, and sprinkle with cornmeal. Place pastries on baking sheets. Repeat procedure with remaining puff pastry and spinach mixture.
● **Bake** at 400° for 12 to 15 minutes. Serve immediately. **Yield:** 5 dozen.

Chef Jim Napolitano
Cumberland Club
Nashville, Tennessee

ST. LOUIS TOASTED RAVIOLI

2 tablespoons milk
1 large egg, lightly beaten
¾ cup dry Italian-seasoned
   breadcrumbs
½ teaspoon salt (optional)
½ (27.5-ounce) package frozen
   cheese-filled ravioli, thawed ✳
Vegetable oil
Grated Parmesan cheese
Spaghetti or pizza sauce

● **Combine** milk and egg. Place breadcrumbs and salt, if desired, in a shallow bowl. Dip ravioli in milk mixture; coat with breadcrumb mixture.
● **Pour** oil to depth of 2 inches into a Dutch oven; heat to 350°. Fry ravioli, a few at a time, 1 minute on each side or until golden. Drain on paper towels.
● **Sprinkle** with Parmesan cheese, and serve immediately with warm spaghetti or pizza sauce. **Yield:** about 2 dozen.

✳ You can substitute refrigerated fresh ravioli for frozen ravioli. Vary the flavor by using sausage, chicken, Italian, or other filling varieties.

Charlie Gitto Jr.
Charlie Gitto's
St. Louis, Missouri

TORTILLA BITES

Cajun-style blackened seasoning provides the spice accent for this make-ahead appetizer.

1 pound unpeeled large fresh shrimp
¼ cup Cajun blackened seasoning
1 (8-ounce) package cream cheese, softened
½ teaspoon ground red pepper
¼ teaspoon salt
2 cloves garlic, crushed
Vegetable cooking spray
1 large red bell pepper
6 (8-inch) flour tortillas
18 large fresh spinach leaves
1 medium avocado, thinly sliced (optional)
Fresh Salsa

• **Peel** shrimp, and devein, if desired; cut shrimp in half lengthwise. Combine shrimp and blackened seasoning in a heavy-duty, zip-top plastic bag; seal bag, and toss to coat. Chill 1 hour.
• **Combine** cream cheese and next 3 ingredients; set aside.
• **Thread** shrimp onto skewers.
• **Coat** food rack with cooking spray; place rack on grill over medium-hot coals (350° to 400°). Place shrimp and red bell pepper on rack.
• **Cook,** covered with grill lid, about 10 minutes, turning shrimp once and red pepper occasionally.
• **Remove** shrimp from grill when done; remove shrimp from skewers, and set aside.
• **Remove** red bell pepper from grill when skin is blistered and black. Remove and discard skin and seeds, and cut pepper into thin strips. Set pepper strips aside.
• **Spread** cream cheese mixture evenly on 1 side of each tortilla. Place 3 spinach leaves on half of the cream cheese. Top spinach evenly with shrimp, red bell pepper strips, and avocado slices, if desired. Roll each tortilla tightly, starting at spinach side.
• **Cut** each tortilla crosswise into 5 portions, and secure each portion with a wooden pick. Cover and store in refrigerator. Serve with Fresh Salsa. **Yield:** 30 appetizers.

Fresh Salsa

QUICK!

1 small purple onion, quartered
2 jalapeño peppers, seeded and quartered
2 cloves garlic
¼ cup chopped fresh cilantro
2 tablespoons fresh lime juice
1 teaspoon salt
1 (14½-ounce) can diced tomatoes, drained

• **Position** knife blade in food processor bowl; add first 6 ingredients. Pulse 6 times or until vegetable mixture is finely chopped.
• **Combine** onion mixture and tomatoes. Cover and store in refrigerator up to 1 week. **Yield:** 2 cups.

Wendy V. Kitchens
Charlotte, North Carolina

GRILLED HONEY CHICKEN WINGS

10 chicken wings
½ cup soy sauce
¼ cup dry sherry
¼ cup honey
¼ teaspoon garlic powder
¼ teaspoon ground ginger
3 tablespoons butter

• **Cut** off wingtips, and discard; cut wings in half at joint.
• **Combine** soy sauce and remaining 5 ingredients in a small saucepan; cook over medium heat, stirring constantly, until thoroughly heated. Reserve ¼ cup marinade, and chill.
• **Pour** remaining marinade into a large heavy-duty, zip-top plastic bag; add chicken, and seal. Chill 2 hours, turning occasionally.
• **Remove** chicken from marinade, discarding marinade. Cook chicken, covered with grill lid, over medium-hot coals (350° to 400°) 20 minutes, turning once and basting with reserved ¼ cup marinade. **Yield:** 20 appetizers or 2 to 3 main-dish servings.

Sharon Chapman
Aiken, South Carolina

THAI LETTUCE FOLDS
(pictured at right)

2 tablespoons peanut oil
2 cloves garlic, minced
4 skinned and boned chicken breast halves, cut into ¼-inch cubes
⅓ cup chicken broth
2 green onions with tops, finely chopped
1 tablespoon chopped fresh mint leaves
1 tablespoon chopped fresh cilantro
1 tablespoon lime juice
½ teaspoon ground red pepper
¼ teaspoon ground ginger
16 Bibb lettuce leaves
½ pound fresh bean sprouts
Cucumber Dipping Sauce

• **Heat** peanut oil in a large skillet over medium-high heat 1 minute. Add garlic and chicken; cook 3 to 5 minutes, stirring constantly. Add broth, and cook over medium heat until most of liquid evaporates. Stir in green onions and next 5 ingredients.
• **Spoon** 2 tablespoons chicken mixture onto each lettuce leaf; sprinkle with bean sprouts, and fold over. Serve with Cucumber Dipping Sauce. **Yield:** 16 appetizer servings.

Cucumber Dipping Sauce

QUICK!

½ cup water
¼ cup sugar
¼ cup rice wine vinegar
1 tablespoon plum sauce
¼ teaspoon dried crushed red pepper
⅛ teaspoon salt
½ cup finely chopped cucumber
1 tablespoon chopped fresh cilantro
1 tablespoon chopped fresh mint leaves

• **Combine** first 6 ingredients in a small saucepan.
• **Bring** to a boil; reduce heat, and simmer 3 minutes. Remove from heat; cool.
• **Stir** in cucumber, cilantro, and mint. **Yield:** about 1 cup.

Thai Lettuce Folds

CURRIED SHRIMP BALLS

QUICK!

How easy can it get? Just 5 ingredients. Traditional goes tropical when creamy shrimp balls are rolled in toasted, curried coconut.

1 cup flaked coconut
1 teaspoon curry powder
2 (8-ounce) packages cream
   cheese, softened
1 (6-ounce) can shrimp, rinsed,
   drained, and chopped
2 tablespoons finely chopped
   onion

• **Combine** coconut and curry powder; place on a baking sheet, and bake at 325° for 5 minutes or until golden. Set coconut mixture aside.
• **Combine** cream cheese, shrimp, and onion; shape into 1-inch balls, and roll in coconut mixture. Cover and chill. **Yield:** 3 dozen.

Janet Filer
Arlington, Virginia

COCONUT FRIED SHRIMP

1 pound unpeeled medium-size
   fresh shrimp
¾ cup biscuit mix
1 tablespoon sugar
¾ cup beer
¾ cup all-purpose flour
2½ cups flaked coconut
Vegetable oil
Orange-Lime Dip

• **Peel** shrimp, leaving tails intact; devein, if desired, and set shrimp aside.
• **Combine** biscuit mix, sugar, and beer, stirring until smooth; set aside.
• **Coat** shrimp with flour; dip in beer mixture, allowing excess coating to drain. Gently roll coated shrimp in flaked coconut.
• **Pour** oil to depth of 3 inches in a large saucepan; heat to 350°.
• **Cook** shrimp, a few at a time, 1 to 2 minutes or until golden; drain on paper towels, and serve immediately with Orange-Lime Dip. **Yield:** about 3 dozen.

Orange-Lime Dip

QUICK!

1 (10-ounce) jar orange
   marmalade
3 tablespoons spicy brown
   mustard
1 tablespoon fresh lime juice

• **Combine** all ingredients in a small saucepan; cook over medium heat, stirring constantly, until marmalade melts. Cool. Cover and store in refrigerator up to 1 week. **Yield:** about 1¼ cups.

CITRUS-MARINATED SMOKED SHRIMP

Hickory or fruitwood chips
2 pounds unpeeled jumbo fresh
   shrimp
1 (6-ounce) can frozen orange
   juice concentrate, thawed and
   undiluted, divided
¼ cup honey
2 tablespoons water
1 tablespoon chopped fresh basil
1 tablespoon chopped fresh
   thyme

• **Soak** wood chips in water at least 30 minutes.
• **Peel** shrimp, and devein, if desired.
• **Combine** ¼ cup juice concentrate, honey, and remaining 3 ingredients.
• **Place** shrimp in a shallow dish or large heavy-duty, zip-top plastic bag; pour orange juice mixture over shrimp, stirring or shaking to coat. Cover or seal, and chill 1 hour.
• **Prepare** charcoal fire in smoker; let burn 15 to 20 minutes.
• **Drain** chips, and place on coals. Place water pan in smoker; add remaining orange juice concentrate to pan.
• **Remove** shrimp from marinade; pour marinade into water pan. Add water to pan to depth of fill line.
• **Thread** shrimp onto skewers, and place on upper and lower food racks. Cover with smoker lid.
• **Cook** 45 minutes to 1 hour. **Yield:** 8 appetizer servings.

Charlie Gagne
Birmingham, Alabama

VIETNAMESE EGG ROLLS

½ (3¾-ounce) package cellophane
   noodles
½ pound lean boneless pork
1 pound unpeeled large fresh
   shrimp
3 cloves garlic, pressed
1 tablespoon sesame oil
6 green onions, chopped
2 tablespoons chopped fresh
   cilantro
2 teaspoons grated fresh ginger
20 egg roll wrappers
Vegetable oil

• **Soak** noodles in hot water to cover 10 minutes or until soft; drain. Cut into 2-inch pieces; set aside.
• **Trim** excess fat from pork, and cut into 1-inch pieces; set aside.
• **Peel** shrimp, and devein, if desired.
• **Position** knife blade in food processor bowl, and add pork. Process until pork is coarsely chopped. Add shrimp, and process until mixture is finely chopped.
• **Cook** meat mixture and garlic in sesame oil in a wok or large skillet over medium-high heat, stirring constantly, 5 minutes or until meat crumbles and shrimp turn pink.
• **Add** noodles, green onions, cilantro, and ginger; cook 2 to 3 minutes, stirring constantly. Cool completely.
• **Spoon** ¼ cup mixture in center of each egg roll wrapper. Fold top corner of wrapper over filling, tucking tip of corner under filling; fold left and right corners over filling. Lightly brush remaining corner with water; tightly roll filled end toward remaining corner, and gently press to seal.
• **Pour** vegetable oil to depth of 2 inches into a wok or Dutch oven; heat to 375°. Fry egg rolls, a few at a time, until golden, turning once; drain. **Yield:** 20 egg rolls.

Agnes Nguyen
Birmingham, Alabama

At right: *Sweet-Tart Lemonade (page 30)*

BEVERAGES

Brandy Alexanders

SANGRÍA TEA

1 (10-ounce) package frozen
   raspberries, thawed
3 cups water
¾ cup sugar
1 family-size tea bag
2 cups dry red wine
1 lemon, sliced
1 lime, sliced
1 (16-ounce) bottle orange soda,
   chilled
Garnishes: lemon slices, lime slices

• **Place** raspberries in container of an electric blender or food processor; process until smooth, stopping once to scrape down sides.
• **Pour** raspberries through a fine wire-mesh strainer into a pitcher, discarding seeds. Set aside.
• **Combine** water and sugar in a saucepan; bring to a boil, stirring often. Remove from heat; add tea bag. Cover and steep 5 minutes.
• **Remove** tea bag, squeezing gently; cool tea.
• **Pour** tea into pitcher; stir in wine and lemon and lime slices. Chill.
• **Stir** in orange soda just before serving. Serve tea over ice. Garnish, if desired. **Yield:** 2 quarts.

BRANDY ALEXANDER
(pictured at left)

QUICK!

2 cups vanilla ice cream
3 to 4 tablespoons brandy
3 to 4 tablespoons white crème de
   cacao
Garnish: white chocolate shavings

• **Combine** first 3 ingredients in container of an electric blender; process until smooth, stopping once to scrape down sides.
• **Spoon** evenly into glasses. Garnish, if desired. Serve immediately. **Yield:** 2 servings.

Rebecca Salisbury Rice
Murfreesboro, Tennessee

PEACH MELBA SUNDAE SHAKE

⅔ cup fresh or frozen raspberries,
   thawed
2 tablespoons sugar
1 large peach, peeled and sliced ∗
¾ cup milk
2 cups peach ice cream, softened
Peach ice cream
Garnishes: fresh raspberries,
   fresh peach slices, fresh
   mint sprigs

• **Combine** ⅔ cup raspberries and sugar in container of an electric blender; process until smooth, stopping once to scrape down sides. Transfer to a small container, and set aside. Wash blender container.
• **Combine** sliced peach and milk in container of blender; process until smooth. Add 2 cups peach ice cream, and process until smooth, stopping once to scrape down sides.
• **Spoon** about 2 tablespoons raspberry mixture into bottom of two 16-ounce glasses; add peach mixture. Top each with a scoop of ice cream, and drizzle with remaining raspberry mixture. Garnish, if desired. **Yield:** 2 servings.

∗ You can substitute 1 cup frozen peach slices, thawed, for a fresh peach.

Mrs. Harland J. Stone
Ocala, Florida

PINEAPPLE MILK SHAKE

QUICK!

3 cups vanilla ice cream
1 (8-ounce) can crushed
   pineapple, undrained
½ cup milk

• **Combine** all ingredients in container of an electric blender; process just until smooth, stopping once to scrape down sides. **Yield:** 3 cups.

Andy and Mike Karandzieff
Crown Candy
St. Louis, Missouri

PUNCH FOR A BUNCH

8 cups water, divided
1½ cups sugar
1 (7.5-ounce) bottle frozen lemon
   juice, thawed
1 (6-ounce) can frozen orange
   juice concentrate, thawed and
   undiluted
2 (6-ounce) cans unsweetened
   pineapple juice (1½ cups)
1 (2-liter) bottle ginger ale,
   chilled

• **Combine** 2 cups water and sugar in a medium saucepan. Bring to a boil; reduce heat, and simmer 20 minutes. Cool. Stir in remaining 6 cups water and fruit juices.
• **Cover** and freeze at least 8 hours, stirring juice mixture twice during freezing process.
• **Remove** from freezer 30 minutes before serving. Break into chunks; add ginger ale, and stir until slushy. **Yield:** 5 quarts.

Lynn L. Williams
Lexington, Virginia

FRUIT JUICE PUNCH

QUICK!

3 cups pineapple juice
2 cups water
2 cups apple juice
1 (6-ounce) can frozen lemonade
   concentrate, undiluted
1 (6-ounce) can frozen orange
   juice concentrate,
   undiluted
2 teaspoons lemon instant tea
   mix
2 cups ginger ale, chilled

• **Combine** first 6 ingredients in a large bowl, stirring well; cover and chill at least 2 hours.
• **Stir** in ginger ale just before serving. **Yield:** about 2½ quarts.

Fruit Juice and Vodka Punch: Stir in 1½ cups vodka before chilling. **Yield:** 3 quarts.

Liz Randall
Spindale, North Carolina

Beverages 33

CINNAMON WINTER CIDER

QUICK!

1 (12-ounce) can frozen apple
  juice concentrate, thawed and
  undiluted
1 (12-ounce) can frozen
  cranberry-apple juice
  concentrate, thawed and
  undiluted
1 (6-ounce) can frozen lemonade
  concentrate, thawed and
  undiluted
9 cups water
5 (3-inch) sticks cinnamon
6 whole cloves
1 teaspoon ground nutmeg
⅓ cup cinnamon schnapps or
  rum

● **Combine** first 7 ingredients in a Dutch
oven; bring to a boil. Cover, reduce heat,
and simmer 15 minutes. Remove and
discard spices. Stir in schnapps; serve
warm. **Yield:** 3 quarts.

Louise W. Mayer
Richmond, Virginia

TENNESSEE
HOT CHOCOLATE

*For a richer, darker cup of hot
chocolate, use Dutch-processed cocoa.
It has a lower natural acidity, which
is perfect for this recipe.*

3 cups milk
¾ cup half-and-half
½ cup sugar
½ cup cocoa
⅓ to ½ cup bourbon
1 teaspoon vanilla extract
Marshmallows (optional)

● **Combine** milk and half-and-half in a
medium saucepan; cook over medium
heat until mixture is thoroughly heated
(do not boil). Add sugar and cocoa, stirring with a wire whisk until blended. Remove from heat, and whisk in bourbon
and vanilla. Pour into mugs, and top
with marshmallows, if desired. **Yield:**
4½ cups.

Wylene B. Gillespie
Gallatin, Tennessee

ORANGE COFFEE

4 sugar cubes
1 large orange
¼ cup sugar
2 tablespoons butter or margarine
½ cup brandy
¼ cup Triple Sec or other
  orange-flavored liqueur
4 cups brewed coffee
Garnishes: sweetened whipped
  cream, orange zest

● **Rub** sugar cubes over surface of
orange until cubes are light yellow;
place cubes in a large saucepan. Cut
orange in half, and squeeze juice into
saucepan, discarding orange halves; add
¼ cup sugar and butter.
● **Cook** over medium-high heat until
sugar dissolves, stirring often. Stir in
brandy and liqueur, and bring to a boil.
Remove from heat.
● **Ignite** mixture carefully with a long
match, and let burn until flames die. Stir
in coffee, and pour into cups. Garnish, if
desired. **Yield:** about 5 cups.

Mike Singleton
Memphis, Tennessee

SUGAR-AND-SPICE HOT
CHOCOLATE

¼ cup cocoa
⅓ cup sugar
½ teaspoon ground cinnamon
¼ teaspoon ground nutmeg
⅛ teaspoon salt
½ cup hot water
3½ cups milk
1 teaspoon vanilla extract
Garnishes: whipped cream, ground
  cloves

● **Combine** first 5 ingredients in a large
saucepan; stir in hot water.
● **Bring** mixture to a boil over medium
heat, stirring constantly; reduce heat,
and simmer 2 minutes.
● **Add** milk, and cook, stirring constantly, until mixture is thoroughly
heated (do not boil). Remove from heat;
add vanilla, stirring with a wire whisk
until mixture is frothy. Garnish, if desired. **Yield:** 4 cups.

Charlotte Pierce Bryant
Greensburg, Kentucky

MEXICAN COFFEE

½ cup ground dark roast coffee
1 tablespoon ground cinnamon
¼ teaspoon ground nutmeg
5 cups water
¼ cup firmly packed dark brown
  sugar
⅓ cup chocolate syrup
1 cup milk
1 teaspoon vanilla extract
Sweetened whipped cream
Garnish: ground cinnamon

● **Place** coffee in coffee filter or filter
basket; add cinnamon and nutmeg. Add
water to coffeemaker; brew according
to manufacturer's instructions.
● **Combine** brown sugar, chocolate
syrup, and milk in a large heavy
saucepan. Cook over low heat, stirring
constantly, until sugar dissolves. Stir in
coffee and vanilla. Serve immediately
with a dollop of whipped cream; garnish, if desired. **Yield:** 6½ cups.

SPICY TOMATO WARM-UP

QUICK!

1 (46-ounce) can spicy vegetable
  juice
3 beef-flavored bouillon cubes
3 tablespoons lemon juice
1 tablespoon Worcestershire sauce
⅛ teaspoon pepper
¼ to ½ teaspoon hot sauce

● **Combine** all ingredients in a large
saucepan; cook over medium heat until
bouillon cubes dissolve. Serve warm.
Yield: 5½ cups.

*At right: Orange-Pecan Scones (page 45),
Basic Buttermilk Biscuits (page 44), and
Potato-Bacon Biscuits (page 44)*

BREADS

ZUCCHINI LOAVES

You can freeze these loaves up to 1 month; drizzle with glaze after thawing.

3 large eggs, lightly beaten
1½ cups sugar
3 cups shredded zucchini
¾ cup vegetable oil
2 teaspoons vanilla extract
2 cups all-purpose flour
1 cup whole wheat flour
½ cup wheat germ
¼ cup nonfat dry milk powder
1 teaspoon baking powder
1 teaspoon baking soda
1 teaspoon salt
2 teaspoons ground cinnamon
½ teaspoon ground nutmeg
¼ teaspoon ground cloves
1 cup sifted powdered sugar
2 tablespoons milk
½ teaspoon vanilla extract
¼ cup chopped pecans, toasted

● **Combine** first 5 ingredients; stir well.
● **Combine** all-purpose flour and next 9 ingredients, stirring well. Add to zucchini mixture, stirring just until blended. Spoon batter evenly into two greased and floured 8- x 4- x 2½-inch loafpans.
● **Bake** at 350° for 45 to 50 minutes or until a wooden pick inserted in center comes out clean. Cool in pans on wire racks 10 minutes; remove from pans, and let cool completely on wire racks.
● **Combine** powdered sugar, milk, and ½ teaspoon vanilla, stirring until smooth. Drizzle evenly over loaves; sprinkle with pecans. **Yield:** 2 loaves.

Ann Birkmire
Sharon, Massachusetts

CRUNCHY BREAKFAST BREAD

1¾ cups all-purpose flour
2½ teaspoons baking powder
½ teaspoon salt
1 cup sugar
¾ cup nutlike cereal nuggets
½ cup raisins
2 tablespoons grated orange rind
1 large egg, lightly beaten
1 cup milk
¼ cup vegetable oil

● **Combine** first 7 ingredients in a large bowl; make a well in center of mixture.
● **Combine** egg, milk, and oil; add to dry ingredients, stirring just until dry ingredients are moistened.
● **Spoon** into a greased and floured 8½- x 4½- x 3-inch loafpan. Bake at 350° for 1 hour or until a wooden pick inserted in center comes out clean. Cool in pan on a wire rack 10 minutes; remove from pan, and cool on wire rack. **Yield:** 1 loaf.

Jodie McCoy
Tulsa, Oklahoma

COWBOY COFFEE CAKE

QUICK!

2 (11-ounce) cans refrigerated buttermilk biscuits
¼ cup butter or margarine, melted
⅓ cup firmly packed brown sugar
⅓ cup chopped pecans
1 teaspoon ground cinnamon

● **Arrange** biscuits in a lightly greased 9-inch round cakepan, overlapping edges.
● **Combine** butter and remaining 3 ingredients; spread evenly over biscuits.
● **Bake** at 350° for 22 minutes or until golden. Serve warm. **Yield:** 1 (9-inch) coffee cake.

James Michelinie
Louisville, Kentucky

CINNAMON-RAISIN COFFEE CAKE

1½ cups all-purpose flour
1 tablespoon baking powder
½ teaspoon salt
¾ cup sugar
¼ cup shortening
1 large egg, lightly beaten
½ cup milk
1 teaspoon vanilla extract
½ cup firmly packed brown sugar
½ cup raisins or chopped walnuts
2 tablespoons all-purpose flour
2 teaspoons ground cinnamon
2 tablespoons butter, melted

● **Combine** first 4 ingredients; cut in shortening with pastry blender until

mixture is crumbly. Combine egg, milk, and vanilla; add to flour mixture, stirring until blended. Set batter aside.
● **Combine** brown sugar and next 3 ingredients; stir in butter.
● **Spoon** two-thirds of batter into a greased and floured 9-inch round cakepan; sprinkle with brown sugar mixture, and top with remaining batter. Bake at 375° for 25 minutes or until golden. **Yield:** 1 (9-inch) coffee cake.

A Taste of Oregon
Junior League of Eugene, Oregon

NUTTY ORANGE COFFEE CAKE
(pictured at right)

¾ cup sugar
½ cup chopped pecans
2 teaspoons grated orange rind
½ (8-ounce) package reduced-fat cream cheese
2 (11-ounce) cans refrigerated buttermilk biscuits
½ cup butter or margarine, melted
1 cup sifted powdered sugar
2 tablespoons fresh orange juice

● **Combine** first 3 ingredients in a small bowl; set aside.
● **Place** about ¾ teaspoon cream cheese in center of each biscuit; fold biscuit in half over cheese, pressing edges to seal.
● **Dip** biscuits in melted butter, and dredge in sugar mixture; place biscuits, curved side down, in a single layer in curves of a lightly greased 12-cup Bundt pan, spacing evenly (do not stack). Place any remaining biscuits around center tube of pan, filling in spaces, if necessary. Drizzle any remaining butter over biscuits; sprinkle with any remaining sugar mixture.
● **Bake** at 350° for 35 to 40 minutes or until done. Immediately invert onto a serving plate.
● **Combine** powdered sugar and orange juice, stirring well; drizzle over warm coffee cake. Serve immediately. **Yield:** 1 (10-inch) coffee cake.

Barbara Kennedy
Fort Pierce, Florida

Nutty Orange Coffee Cake

RASPBERRY-STREUSEL MUFFINS

The streusel (German for "sprinkle") makes a delicious crown for these sweet muffins. It's a crumbly topping of flour, butter, sugar, and, in this recipe, chopped pecans.

1¾ cups all-purpose flour, divided
2 teaspoons baking powder
½ cup sugar
1 large egg, lightly beaten
½ cup milk
½ cup butter, melted
1 cup frozen unsweetened raspberries
2 tablespoons butter or margarine, melted
¼ cup chopped pecans
¼ cup firmly packed brown sugar

• **Combine** 1½ cups flour, baking powder, and sugar in a large bowl; make a well in center of mixture.
• **Combine** egg, milk, and ½ cup butter; add to dry ingredients, stirring just until moistened. Fold in raspberries. Spoon into greased muffin pans, filling two-thirds full.
• **Combine** remaining ¼ cup flour, 2 tablespoons butter, pecans, and brown sugar; sprinkle over muffins.
• **Bake** at 375° for 20 to 25 minutes. Remove from pans immediately. **Yield:** 1 dozen.

Bill and Tricia Kelly
Greenville, South Carolina

HOT BUTTERED RUM MUFFINS

½ cup butter or margarine, softened
½ cup sugar
2 large eggs
2 cups all-purpose flour
2 teaspoons baking powder
½ teaspoon salt
⅛ teaspoon ground cloves
⅛ teaspoon ground nutmeg
½ cup milk
5 tablespoons rum, divided
3 tablespoons sugar

• **Beat** butter at medium speed with an electric mixer until creamy. Add ½ cup sugar, beating well. Add eggs, one at a time, beating just until blended after each addition.
• **Combine** flour and next 4 ingredients. Combine milk and 3 tablespoons rum. Add flour mixture to butter mixture alternately with milk mixture, beginning and ending with flour mixture. Beat mixture at low speed until blended after each addition.
• **Spoon** into greased muffin pans, filling three-fourths full.
• **Bake** at 375° for 20 to 25 minutes or until golden. Remove from pans immediately; place on a wire rack.
• **Combine** remaining 2 tablespoons rum and 3 tablespoons sugar in a small saucepan; cook over low heat, stirring constantly, until sugar dissolves. Brush over warm muffins. **Yield:** 1 dozen.

Sandra Souther
Gainesville, Georgia

CHEESE MUFFINS

QUICK!

These golden pillowy muffins get top marks for ease, taste, and versatility.

2 tablespoons butter or margarine, divided
½ cup chopped onion
1½ cups biscuit mix
1 cup (4 ounces) shredded sharp process American cheese, divided
1 large egg, lightly beaten
½ cup milk
1 tablespoon sesame seeds, toasted

• **Melt** 1 tablespoon butter in a skillet over medium-high heat; add onion, and cook, stirring constantly, 3 minutes or until tender.
• **Combine** onion, biscuit mix, and ½ cup cheese in a large bowl. Combine egg and milk; add to onion mixture, stirring just until moistened.
• **Spoon** into greased muffin pans, filling half-full. Sprinkle with remaining ½ cup cheese and sesame seeds; dot with remaining 1 tablespoon butter.

• **Bake** at 400° for 13 minutes or until golden. Remove from pans immediately, and serve warm. **Yield:** 1 dozen.

Bill and Tricia Kelly
Greenville, South Carolina

DILLY CHEESE MUFFINS

QUICK!

3 cups biscuit mix
1½ cups (6 ounces) shredded Swiss cheese
1 tablespoon sugar
1 large egg
1¼ cups milk
1 tablespoon vegetable oil
1 tablespoon chopped fresh dill
½ teaspoon dry mustard
Vegetable cooking spray

• **Combine** first 3 ingredients in a large bowl; make a well in center of mixture.
• **Combine** egg and next 4 ingredients, stirring well; add to dry ingredients, stirring just until moistened.
• **Place** paper baking cups in muffin pans; coat with cooking spray. Add batter, filling two-thirds full.
• **Bake** at 350° for 25 to 28 minutes. Remove from pans immediately, and cool on wire racks. **Yield:** 1½ dozen.

Kathy Jones
Montreal, Missouri

SUNNY CORN MUFFINS

2 ears fresh corn in husks
2 tablespoons butter or margarine
¼ cup finely chopped onion
1 cup all-purpose flour
1 cup yellow cornmeal
1½ teaspoons baking powder
½ teaspoon baking soda
1 teaspoon salt
2 tablespoons sugar
1 cup buttermilk
1 large egg
¼ cup butter or margarine, melted
1 cup (4 ounces) shredded Cheddar cheese
1 (4.5-ounce) can chopped green chiles, drained
¼ cup sunflower kernels

- **Remove** husks from corn; tear husks into ½-inch strips. Soak husks in hot water 15 minutes; drain. Cut corn kernels from cobs.
- **Melt** 2 tablespoons butter in a large skillet over medium-high heat; add corn and onion, and cook until tender, stirring often. Set aside.
- **Combine** flour and next 5 ingredients in a large bowl; make a well in center of mixture.
- **Combine** buttermilk, egg, and ¼ cup melted butter; add to dry ingredients, stirring just until moistened. Stir in corn mixture, cheese, and chiles.
- **Arrange** 4 husk strips across each of 12 lightly greased muffin cups to resemble spokes; spoon batter into cups, filling each three-fourths full. Sprinkle with sunflower kernels.
- **Bake** at 375° for 18 to 20 minutes or until muffins are golden (corn husks will brown deeply). Remove immediately from pans; cool on wire racks. **Yield:** 1 dozen.

EASY CARAMEL-CHOCOLATE STICKY BUNS

1 (15-ounce) can coconut-pecan frosting
1 cup pecan halves
2 (10-ounce) cans refrigerated buttermilk biscuits
20 chocolate kisses, unwrapped

- **Spread** frosting in bottom of a lightly greased 9-inch square pan. Arrange pecan halves over frosting. Set aside.
- **Separate** biscuits; flatten each to about ¼-inch thickness. Place a chocolate kiss to 1 side of center of each biscuit. Fold biscuit in half, forming a semicircle; press edges of biscuits gently to seal. Repeat procedure with remaining biscuits and chocolate kisses. Arrange biscuits over pecans, placing flat sides down.
- **Bake** at 375° for 28 to 30 minutes or until lightly browned. Cool in pan on a wire rack 5 minutes; invert onto serving plate, and serve immediately. **Yield:** 20 servings.

Doris J. Phillips
Fayetteville, Arkansas

FRENCH BREAKFAST PUFFS

⅓ cup butter or margarine, melted
½ cup sugar
1 large egg
1½ cups all-purpose flour
1½ teaspoons baking powder
½ teaspoon salt
¼ teaspoon ground nutmeg
½ cup milk
¼ cup sugar
½ teaspoon ground cinnamon
2 tablespoons butter or margarine, melted

- **Beat** first 3 ingredients at medium speed with an electric mixer until creamy and well blended.
- **Combine** flour and next 3 ingredients; add to butter mixture alternately with milk, beginning and ending with flour mixture. Beat at low speed until blended after each addition. Spoon into greased miniature (1¾-inch) muffin pans, filling two-thirds full.
- **Bake** at 350° for 14 to 16 minutes. Remove from pans immediately.
- **Combine** ¼ cup sugar and cinnamon. Dip tops of muffins in 2 tablespoons melted butter, and then in sugar mixture. **Yield:** 28 miniature muffins.

Note: If using regular muffin pans, bake 20 to 25 minutes. Yield: 10 muffins.

Virginia Cookery, Past and Present
Olivet Episcopal Church Women
Franconia, Virginia

HAZELNUT SCONES

2 cups all-purpose flour
2 teaspoons baking powder
¼ teaspoon salt
½ cup sugar
⅓ cup butter
½ cup chopped blanched hazelnuts
2 large eggs, lightly beaten
½ cup whipping cream
1½ tablespoons Frangelico or other hazelnut-flavored liqueur
1 tablespoon sugar
18 whole hazelnuts

- **Combine** first 4 ingredients in a large bowl; cut in butter with pastry blender until mixture is crumbly. Stir in chopped hazelnuts; make a well in center of mixture, and set aside.
- **Combine** eggs, whipping cream, and liqueur; add to dry ingredients, stirring just until moistened.
- **Roll** dough to ¾-inch thickness on a lightly floured surface. Cut with a 2½-inch daisy-shaped cutter, and place on baking sheets. Sprinkle tops evenly with 1 tablespoon sugar, and place a hazelnut in each center.
- **Bake** at 350° for 15 minutes. Serve with Lemon Honey (see recipe on page 354), butter, and strawberry jam. **Yield:** 1½ dozen.

Sharon McCullar
Victoria Room
Shreveport, Louisiana

CRANBERRY SCONES

2½ cups all-purpose flour
2 teaspoons baking powder
½ teaspoon salt
½ cup sugar
½ teaspoon ground cloves
¼ cup butter or margarine
1 cup whipping cream
¾ cup fresh or frozen cranberries, thawed, coarsely chopped

- **Combine** first 5 ingredients; cut in butter with pastry blender until mixture is crumbly.
- **Reserve** 1 tablespoon whipping cream; add remaining whipping cream and chopped cranberries to dry ingredients, stirring just until dry ingredients are moistened.
- **Turn** dough out onto a lightly floured surface; knead 5 or 6 times. Shape into an 8-inch circle. Cut into 8 wedges, and place on a lightly greased baking sheet. Prick wedges with a fork 3 or 4 times, and brush with reserved 1 tablespoon whipping cream.
- **Bake** at 425° for 18 minutes or until lightly browned. Serve warm with whipped cream, if desired. **Yield:** 8 scones.

Mary Bonney
Sterling, Virginia

QUICK CALAS

Pronounced "kah-LAHS," these fried rice cakes, similar to beignets, are named from an African word for rice. They've been popular in New Orleans for more than a century.

2 cups cooked long-grain rice
2 cups biscuit mix
2 tablespoons sugar
1 teaspoon ground cinnamon
1 teaspoon ground nutmeg
2 large eggs, lightly beaten
½ cup evaporated milk
1 teaspoon vanilla extract
Vegetable oil
Sifted powdered sugar

• **Combine** first 5 ingredients in a bowl. Combine eggs, milk, and vanilla; add to dry ingredients, stirring well. Cover and chill 1 hour.
• **Pour** oil to depth of 2 inches into a Dutch oven or electric fryer; heat to 350°. Drop batter by tablespoonfuls into hot oil. Fry calas, a few at a time, 2 minutes or until golden, turning once. Drain on paper towels. Sprinkle with powdered sugar; serve warm. **Yield:** about 4 dozen.

ACORN SQUASH PUPPIES

1 (1¾-pound) acorn squash
2 cups self-rising cornmeal
¼ cup all-purpose flour
1 large egg, lightly beaten
½ cup milk
½ cup finely chopped onion
Vegetable oil

• **Cut** acorn squash in half crosswise; remove and discard seeds. Place squash, cut side down, in a shallow baking dish or pan. Add water to dish to depth of ½ inch.
• **Bake** at 375° for 45 minutes or until tender. Drain and cool slightly.
• **Scoop** out pulp, discarding shells. Place pulp in container of an electric blender or food processor; process until smooth. Measure 1¼ cups squash puree; set aside. (Reserve any remaining puree for another use.)

• **Combine** cornmeal and flour in a large bowl; make a well in center of mixture. Set aside.
• **Combine** squash puree, egg, milk, and onion. Add to dry ingredients, stirring just until moistened.
• **Pour** oil to depth of 2 inches into a Dutch oven; heat to 360°. Drop by tablespoonfuls into hot oil. Cook 2 minutes or until golden, turning once. Drain on paper towels. **Yield:** 2 dozen.

Mary Horton
Moulton, Alabama

BAKED HUSH PUPPIES

QUICK!

1 cup yellow cornmeal
1 cup all-purpose flour
1 tablespoon baking powder
1 teaspoon salt
1 teaspoon sugar
⅛ teaspoon ground red pepper
2 large eggs, lightly beaten
¾ cup milk
½ cup finely chopped onion
¼ cup vegetable oil
Vegetable cooking spray

• **Combine** first 6 ingredients in a large bowl; make a well in center of mixture. Set aside.
• **Combine** eggs and next 3 ingredients, stirring well; add to dry ingredients, stirring just until moistened.
• **Coat** miniature muffin pans with cooking spray. Spoon about 1 tablespoon batter into each muffin cup, filling about three-fourths full.
• **Bake** at 425° for 15 minutes or until golden. Remove from pans, and serve immediately. **Yield:** 3 dozen.

Millie Givens
Savannah, Georgia

♥ Per hush puppy: Calories 55
Fat 2.4g Cholesterol 13mg
Sodium 71mg

CORN-JALAPEÑO FRITTERS
(pictured at right)

2 cups milk, divided
1 cup quick-cooking yellow grits
3 tablespoons butter or margarine, softened
1 teaspoon baking powder
1 teaspoon salt
2 large eggs, lightly beaten
¼ cup finely chopped red bell pepper
½ cup finely chopped green onions
1 to 2 teaspoons seeded, minced jalapeño pepper
2 tablespoons finely chopped fresh basil
1 cup fresh corn, cut from cob (about 2 ears)
¼ cup all-purpose flour
2 tablespoons olive oil, divided
Garnish: sour cream, green onion fan

• **Combine** ½ cup milk and grits; set aside.
• **Heat** remaining 1½ cups milk in a medium saucepan over medium-high heat until boiling. Add grits mixture, stirring constantly with a wire whisk. Cook 2 minutes or until thickened.
• **Remove** from heat, and pour into a large bowl; cool slightly. Add butter and next 9 ingredients, stirring well.
• **Heat** 1 tablespoon olive oil in a large nonstick skillet or griddle over medium heat until hot.
• **Pour** 1 tablespoon batter for each fritter into hot skillet, and cook fritters until tops are covered with bubbles and edges look cooked; turn and cook other side. Repeat procedure with remaining olive oil and batter. Garnish, if desired. **Yield:** 2 dozen.

Helen H. Maurer
Christmas, Florida

Corn-Jalapeño Fritters

ITALIAN CHEESE BREADSTICKS

QUICK!

1 (11-ounce) can refrigerated
   breadsticks
2 teaspoons dried Italian
   seasoning
1½ teaspoons garlic powder
¾ cup (3 ounces) shredded
   mozzarella cheese

• **Twist** breadsticks, and place on a baking sheet. Sprinkle with Italian seasoning and garlic powder.
• **Bake** at 350° for 10 to 13 minutes; sprinkle with cheese, and bake 5 additional minutes or until cheese melts and breadsticks are golden. Serve with spaghetti sauce and Ranch-style salad dressing for dipping. **Yield:** 6 servings.

Jennifer Cobble
Birmingham, Alabama

SEASONED BREADSTICKS

QUICK!

1 (11-ounce) can refrigerated
   breadsticks
Olive oil
1 teaspoon chili powder
½ teaspoon ground cumin

• **Unroll** dough onto a large cutting board; cut dough crosswise into thirds. Separate dough into 24 pieces; stretch each piece to 11 inches, and place ¼ inch apart on cutting board. Brush dough lightly with olive oil.
• **Combine** chili powder and cumin; sprinkle evenly over dough. Twist ends of dough pieces in opposite directions 3 or 4 times. Place breadsticks 1 inch apart on ungreased baking sheets, pressing ends securely.
• **Bake** at 350° for 12 to 14 minutes or until golden. Transfer to wire racks to cool. **Yield:** 2 dozen.

Caryn Hogan
Birmingham, Alabama

QUICK ROLLS

QUICK!

2¼ cups biscuit mix, divided
1 (8-ounce) carton sour cream
½ cup butter, melted

• **Combine** 2 cups biscuit mix, sour cream, and butter, stirring well.
• **Sprinkle** remaining ¼ cup biscuit mix over work surface. Drop dough by level tablespoonfuls onto biscuit mix, and roll into balls. Place 3 balls into each of 12 greased muffin cups.
• **Bake** at 350° for 15 to 20 minutes or until rolls are golden. **Yield:** 1 dozen.

Carolyn W. Olah
Crawfordville, Florida

CRÊPES

French for "pancake," the paper-thin crêpe is one of the most versatile recipes to cross the Atlantic. This savory recipe is perfect for a filling of chicken or vegetables.

1 cup all-purpose flour
¼ teaspoon salt
1¼ cups milk
2 large eggs
⅔ cup butter, melted and divided

• **Beat** first 3 ingredients at medium speed with an electric mixer until smooth. Add eggs, beating well; stir in 2 tablespoons melted butter. Cover and chill at least 1 hour.
• **Brush** bottom of a 6-inch nonstick skillet with melted butter; place over medium heat until hot.
• **Pour** 2 tablespoons batter into pan; quickly tilt in all directions so batter covers bottom of pan. Cook 1 minute or until crêpe can be shaken loose from pan. Turn crêpe over, and cook about 30 seconds. Place crêpe on a dish towel to cool. Repeat procedure with remaining batter. **Yield:** 16 (6-inch) crêpes.

Note: You can make crêpes ahead by stacking them between sheets of wax paper and placing in an airtight container. Store in the refrigerator up to 2 days or freeze up to 3 months.

EASY PANCAKES

QUICK!

1 (5.5-ounce) package or 1¼ cups
   biscuit mix *
1 large egg, beaten
⅔ cup milk
1 tablespoon vegetable oil

• **Place** biscuit mix in a medium bowl; make a well in center. Combine egg, milk, and oil, stirring well; add to biscuit mix, stirring just until dry ingredients are moistened.
• **Pour** about ¼ cup batter for each pancake onto a hot, lightly greased griddle. Cook pancakes until tops are covered with bubbles and edges of pancakes look cooked; turn and cook other side. **Yield:** 8 pancakes.

* You can substitute 1 (7-ounce) package bran muffin mix for biscuit mix.

GINGERBREAD PANCAKES

1 cup all-purpose flour
2 teaspoons baking powder
½ teaspoon salt
1 tablespoon sugar
1 tablespoon ground cinnamon
½ teaspoon ground ginger
¼ teaspoon ground allspice
⅛ teaspoon ground nutmeg
⅛ teaspoon ground cloves
1 large egg, lightly beaten
1 cup buttermilk
3 tablespoons butter or margarine,
   melted
1 tablespoon molasses
Orange Marmalade Syrup

• **Combine** first 9 ingredients in a large bowl; make a well in center of mixture.
• **Combine** egg and remaining 3 ingredients; add to dry ingredients, stirring just until moistened.
• **Spoon** about 2 tablespoons batter for each pancake onto a hot, lightly greased griddle.
• **Cook** until tops are covered with bubbles and edges look cooked; turn and cook other side. Serve pancakes with warm Orange Marmalade Syrup. **Yield:** 10 pancakes.

Orange Marmalade Syrup

⅔ cup maple syrup
⅓ cup orange marmalade

● **Combine** ingredients in a small saucepan, and bring to a boil, stirring constantly. **Yield:** 1 cup.

Joel Allard
San Antonio, Texas

HONEY-BUTTERED PEANUT BUTTER WAFFLES

⅓ cup chunky peanut butter
1 cup pancake mix
2 tablespoons sugar
1 (5-ounce) can evaporated milk
½ cup water
1 large egg
Honey Butter

● **Place** peanut butter in a 1-quart glass bowl. Microwave at HIGH 20 to 30 seconds.
● **Add** pancake mix and next 4 ingredients; beat at medium speed with an electric mixer just until smooth.
● **Bake** in a preheated, oiled waffle iron until golden. Serve with Honey Butter. **Yield:** 8 (4-inch) waffles.

Honey Butter

¼ cup butter, softened
2 tablespoons honey

● **Combine** butter and honey, stirring until blended. **Yield:** ⅓ cup.

Valerie Stutsman
Norfolk, Virginia

BELGIAN WAFFLES

4 large eggs, separated
3 tablespoons butter, melted
½ teaspoon vanilla extract
1 cup all-purpose flour
½ teaspoon salt
1 cup milk
Sweetened whipped cream
Sliced fresh strawberries

● **Beat** egg yolks at medium speed with an electric mixer until thick and pale. Add butter and vanilla, beating until blended. Set aside.
● **Combine** flour and salt. Add flour mixture and milk to egg mixture, beating until smooth. Set aside.
● **Beat** egg whites until stiff peaks form; fold into batter.
● **Bake** in a preheated, oiled Belgian waffle iron until golden. Serve with sweetened whipped cream and strawberries. **Yield:** 8 (4-inch) waffles.

Jane Maloy
Wilmington, North Carolina

ALMOND SUNBURST

1 (16-ounce) package hot roll mix
Vegetable cooking spray
Cornmeal
Fruit Filling
Glaze
Garnish: toasted sliced almonds

● **Prepare** roll mix according to directions up to point of shaping dough.
● **Coat** a 12-inch pizza pan with cooking spray; sprinkle with cornmeal.
● **Turn** dough out onto a floured surface; knead 4 or 5 times. Roll into a 15- x 10-inch rectangle; sprinkle with Fruit Filling to within 1 inch from edge.
● **Roll** up, jellyroll fashion, starting at long side; moisten edge with water, and pinch seam to seal. Place, seam side down, on prepared pan. Shape into a ring; moisten ends with water, and pinch together to seal.
● **Make** cuts in dough at 1-inch intervals, using kitchen shears, cutting from outside edge to, but not through, inside edge. Gently turn each slice on its side, slightly overlapping slices.

● **Cover** and let rise in a warm place (85°), free from drafts, 30 minutes or until doubled in bulk.
● **Bake** at 350° for 25 minutes or until golden. Remove to a wire rack; cool 15 minutes. Drizzle with Glaze. Garnish, if desired. **Yield:** 1 coffee cake.

Fruit Filling

½ cup raisins *
½ cup chopped dried apricot halves *
½ cup dried cherries *
½ cup chopped almonds
⅓ cup firmly packed brown sugar
2 teaspoons ground cinnamon
2 teaspoons grated orange rind
1 teaspoon grated lemon rind

● **Combine** all ingredients, stirring well. **Yield:** 2 cups.

* You can substitute 1 (6-ounce) package dried tropical fruit medley for the raisins, apricots, and cherries.

Glaze

1 cup sifted powdered sugar
2 tablespoons milk
1 teaspoon almond extract

● **Combine** all ingredients, stirring until smooth. **Yield:** ⅓ cup.

Greek Sunburst: Combine 1 (10-ounce) package frozen chopped spinach, thawed and well drained, 1 (4-ounce) package crumbled basil-tomato feta cheese, and ¼ teaspoon salt. Spread mixture over dough. Shape and let rise as directed. Sprinkle with 3 tablespoons grated Parmesan cheese, and bake as directed.

Pizza Sunburst: Spread ½ cup pizza sauce over dough. Brown ½ pound ground pork sausage in a small skillet, stirring until it crumbles; drain. Sprinkle sausage and 1 cup (4 ounces) shredded Cheddar cheese over pizza sauce. Shape dough, and let rise as directed. Sprinkle with 2 tablespoons grated Parmesan cheese, and bake as directed.

YEAST GINGERBREAD MEN

1 (¼-ounce) envelope active dry
    yeast
¼ cup warm water (105° to 115°)
¾ cup milk
½ cup sugar
⅓ cup butter or margarine
1 teaspoon salt
1 large egg
3 cups all-purpose flour, divided
1 cup graham cracker crumbs
½ teaspoon ground cinnamon
½ teaspoon ground cloves
½ teaspoon ground ginger
¼ cup currants or raisins
1 large egg, beaten

• **Combine** yeast and warm water in a 1-cup liquid measuring cup; let stand 5 minutes.
• **Combine** milk and next 3 ingredients in a small saucepan; heat until butter melts, stirring occasionally. Cool to 105° to 115°.
• **Combine** yeast mixture, milk mixture, 1 egg, 1 cup flour, graham cracker crumbs, and next 3 ingredients in a mixing bowl; beat at medium speed with an electric mixer until smooth. Gradually stir in remaining 2 cups flour.
• **Cover** and let rise in a warm place (85°), free from drafts, 1 hour or until doubled in bulk.
• **Punch** dough down, and divide into 6 portions; set 5 portions aside. Form three-fourths of 1 portion of dough into an oblong shape about 5 inches long; place on a lightly greased baking sheet. Cut a lengthwise slit halfway through bottom to form legs. Divide remaining one-fourth of that portion into 3 equal parts. Shape 1 part into a head and remaining 2 parts into arms; gently press each to attach to body. Gently push currants into dough for eyes and buttons. Repeat procedure with remaining dough.
• **Cover** and let rise in a warm place, free from drafts, 40 minutes. Gently brush each with beaten egg.
• **Bake** at 350° for 15 minutes or until golden. Cool on wire racks. **Yield:** 6 gingerbread men.

Louise Smith
Columbus, Georgia

EASTER EGG BREAD

Margie bakes enough loaves to give to her immediate family. If you start baking about a week ahead, you can do it, too.

2 cups sugar
1½ cups milk
1 cup butter or margarine
3 (¼-ounce) envelopes active dry
    yeast
1 tablespoon all-purpose flour
1 teaspoon sugar
⅓ cup warm water (105°
    to 115°)
6 large eggs, lightly beaten
9 cups all-purpose flour
2 hard-cooked eggs, unshelled and
    dyed
1 large egg, lightly beaten
1 teaspoon sesame seeds

• **Combine** first 3 ingredients in a large saucepan; cook over medium heat until butter melts. Cool milk mixture to 105° to 115°.
• **Combine** yeast and next 3 ingredients in a large bowl; let stand 5 minutes. Stir in 6 lightly beaten eggs. Gradually add 9 cups flour alternately with milk mixture, stirring well.
• **Turn** dough out onto a well-floured surface, and knead until dough is smooth and elastic (about 5 minutes). Place dough in a well-greased bowl, turning to grease top.
• **Cover** and let rise in a warm place (85°), free from drafts, 1 hour.
• **Punch** dough down, and divide in half; divide each half into 3 portions. Shape each portion into a 2½-foot rope. Pinch 3 ropes together at 1 end to seal; braid ropes. Place braid on a lightly greased baking sheet, and shape into a circle. Place 1 hard-cooked egg where braids meet, shaping dough around egg. Repeat procedure with remaining 3 ropes of dough.
• **Cover** and let rise in a warm place, free from drafts, 30 minutes.
• **Brush** bread with 1 beaten egg, and sprinkle with sesame seeds.
• **Bake** at 350° for 30 minutes or until golden. **Yield:** 2 loaves.

Margie Spanos
Birmingham, Alabama

CHALLAH

Challah is a traditional Jewish yeast bread that's rich with eggs and light in texture. Though it can be formed in many shapes, the bread is most often braided.

1 (¼-ounce) envelope active dry
    yeast
1 teaspoon sugar
½ cup warm water (105° to 115°)
½ cup vegetable oil
½ cup warm water (105° to 115°)
¼ cup sugar
2 large eggs
2 teaspoons salt
4 to 4½ cups all-purpose flour
Vegetable cooking spray
1 egg white
1 teaspoon water
1 teaspoon sesame seeds or poppy
    seeds

• **Combine** yeast, 1 teaspoon sugar, and ½ cup warm water in a 1-cup liquid measuring cup; let stand 5 minutes.
• **Combine** oil and next 4 ingredients in a large mixing bowl; beat at medium speed with an electric mixer until blended. Add yeast mixture and 2 cups flour; beat until smooth. Gradually stir in enough remaining flour to make a soft dough. (Dough will be sticky.) Cover and let rest 10 minutes.
• **Turn** dough out onto a well-floured surface; knead 5 minutes. Place in a well-greased bowl, turning to grease top.
• **Cover** and let rise in a warm place (85°), free from drafts, 1 to 1½ hours or until doubled in bulk.
• **Punch** dough down; turn out onto a well-floured surface, and knead several times. Divide into thirds. Shape each third into a 14-inch rope. Place ropes on a greased baking sheet (do not stretch); pinch ends together at one end to seal. Braid ropes; pinch loose ends to seal. Spray with cooking spray.
• **Cover** and let rise in a warm place, free from drafts, 30 to 40 minutes or until doubled in bulk.
• **Beat** egg white and 1 teaspoon water; gently brush over bread. Sprinkle with sesame seeds. Bake at 375° for 30 to 35 minutes or until golden. **Yield:** 1 loaf.

Sally Wolfish
Dallas, Texas

PANDORO

This classic Italian bread is traditionally baked in a tall, star-shaped pan. If you can't find one, use an 8-inch springform pan instead.

"Sponge"
1 teaspoon active dry yeast
1 tablespoon warm water (105° to 115°)
6½ cups bread flour, divided
¼ cup sugar
2 large eggs
¼ cup butter or margarine, softened and cut into pieces
4 large eggs
2 egg yolks
1 cup sugar
1 teaspoon salt
2 teaspoons vanilla extract
1½ tablespoons grated lemon rind
1¼ cups butter or margarine, softened and cut into pieces
½ cup chopped candied citron
¼ to ½ cup bread flour
Butter-flavored cooking spray

• **Prepare** "Sponge" according to recipe, and set aside.
• **Combine** yeast and warm water in a 1-cup liquid measuring cup; let stand 5 minutes.
• **Add** yeast mixture, 2½ cups flour, ¼ cup sugar, and 2 eggs to "Sponge"; stir vigorously with a wooden spoon until blended. Gradually stir in ¼ cup softened butter.
• **Cover** and let rise in a warm place (85°), free from drafts, 45 minutes or until dough is doubled in bulk.
• **Add** 4 eggs and next 5 ingredients; beat at medium speed with an electric mixer until smooth. Gradually add 2 cups flour, beating until blended. Stir in remaining 2 cups flour with a wooden spoon. Gradually stir in 1¼ cups butter and citron.
• **Turn** dough out onto a heavily floured surface, and knead until smooth and elastic (about 5 minutes), adding an additional ¼ to ½ cup flour, if necessary. Place in a well-greased bowl, turning to grease top.

• **Cover** and let rise in a warm place, free from drafts, 1½ hours or until doubled in bulk.
• **Punch** dough down, and divide in half; place in two Pandoro pans or 2 (8-inch) springform pans coated with cooking spray.
• **Cover** and let rise in a warm place, free from drafts, 1½ hours or until doubled in bulk.
• **Bake** at 350° for 30 minutes. Cover with aluminum foil, reduce oven temperature to 300°, and bake 20 additional minutes.
• **Remove** from pans, and cool on wire racks. **Yield:** 2 loaves.

"Sponge"

2 (¼-ounce) envelopes active dry yeast
½ cup warm water (105° to 115°)
1 large egg
2 tablespoons sugar
¾ cup bread flour

• **Combine** yeast and warm water in a 1-cup liquid measuring cup; let stand 5 minutes.
• **Combine** yeast mixture, egg, sugar, and flour in a large mixing bowl; beat at medium speed with an electric mixer until smooth.
• **Cover** "Sponge," and let rise in a warm place (85°), free from drafts, 30 minutes or until doubled in bulk. **Yield:** about 1½ cups.

Jim and Sandra Kolka
Marietta, Georgia

PANETTONE

Panettone is a sweet yeast bread that's studded with currants and citron, and baked in a tall cylindrical shape. The bread originated in Milan, Italy, and is traditionally served at Christmastime.

2 (¼-ounce) envelopes active dry yeast
1 cup warm water (105° to 115°)
½ cup butter, softened
½ cup sugar
2 large eggs, beaten
3 egg yolks, beaten
2 teaspoons salt
2 teaspoons grated lemon rind
1 teaspoon vanilla extract
5 to 6 cups bread flour, divided
1 cup chopped candied citron
1 cup currants
2 tablespoons butter, melted

• **Combine** yeast and warm water in a 2-cup liquid measuring cup; let stand 5 minutes.
• **Combine** yeast mixture, ½ cup butter, and next 6 ingredients in a large bowl, stirring with a wooden spoon until blended. Gradually stir in 3 cups flour, mixing well. Stir in citron and currants. Gradually stir in enough remaining 3 cups flour to make a soft dough.
• **Turn** dough out onto a lightly floured surface, and knead until smooth and elastic (about 2 minutes). Place in a well-greased bowl, turning to grease top.
• **Cover** and let rise in a warm place (85°), free from drafts, 1½ hours or until doubled in bulk.
• **Punch** dough down, and place in a greased 2-quart soufflé dish; brush with melted butter. Cover and let rise in a warm place, free from drafts, 1 hour or until almost doubled in bulk. Using a sharp knife, gently cut a deep X in top of bread.
• **Bake** on lower rack of oven at 350° for 8 minutes. Reduce oven temperature to 325°, and bake 1 hour or until bread sounds hollow when tapped. (Cover loosely with aluminum foil after 45 minutes to prevent excessive browning, if necessary.) Remove from dish immediately; cool on a wire rack. **Yield:** 1 loaf.

Jim and Sandra Kolka
Marietta, Georgia

PEANUT LOVER'S BREAD

1 (¼-ounce) envelope active dry yeast
¼ cup warm water (105° to 115°)
¾ cup buttermilk
3 cups all-purpose flour, divided
¾ teaspoon baking powder
¼ teaspoon baking soda
¾ teaspoon salt
¼ cup sugar
¼ cup peanut oil
¼ cup butter or margarine, softened
Peanut Filling
Butter-flavored cooking spray

• **Combine** yeast and warm water in a 1-cup liquid measuring cup; let stand 5 minutes.
• **Heat** buttermilk in a small saucepan; cool to 105° to 115°.
• **Combine** 2 cups flour, baking powder, and next 4 ingredients in a large bowl. Add yeast mixture and buttermilk; beat at medium speed with an electric mixer 1 to 2 minutes. Stir in remaining 1 cup flour. Place dough in a well-greased bowl, turning to grease top. Cover and chill 8 hours.
• **Punch** dough down; turn out onto a floured surface, and knead until smooth and elastic (about 5 minutes).
• **Roll** dough into a 16- x 12-inch rectangle; spread with butter. Sprinkle with Peanut Filling, lightly pressing filling into dough.
• **Cut** into 3 (4- x 16-inch) pieces; fold each portion lengthwise in half over filling, pinching seams together to form ropes. Place ropes, seam side down, on a greased baking sheet (do not stretch); pinch rope ends together at 1 end to seal. Braid ropes; pinch loose ends to seal, and tuck under. Lightly spray braid with cooking spray.
• **Cover** and let rise in a warm place (85°), free from drafts, 45 to 60 minutes or until doubled in bulk. Bake at 375° for 20 to 25 minutes or until golden. **Yield:** 1 loaf.

Peanut Filling

QUICK!

¾ cup finely chopped unsalted peanuts
⅓ cup crushed French fried onions
3 tablespoons real bacon bits
2 teaspoons poppy seeds
2 tablespoons grated Parmesan cheese
¼ teaspoon garlic powder
1 egg white, lightly beaten

• **Combine** all ingredients, stirring well. **Yield:** 1¼ cups.

June Kilgore
Dothan, Alabama

WALNUT BREAD

2 (¼-ounce) envelopes active dry yeast
¼ cup warm water (105° to 115°)
1½ cups milk
2 tablespoons olive oil
2 tablespoons honey
2 teaspoons salt
2 cups unbleached flour, divided
2 cups whole wheat flour
1 cup rye flour
1 cup coarsely chopped walnuts

• **Combine** yeast and warm water in a 1-cup liquid measuring cup; let stand 5 minutes.
• **Combine** yeast mixture, milk, and next 3 ingredients in a large mixing bowl; beat at medium speed with an electric mixer until well blended.
• **Combine** 1½ cups unbleached flour, wheat flour, rye flour, and walnuts; gradually add to yeast mixture, beating after each addition.
• **Turn** dough out onto a lightly floured surface; knead in remaining ½ cup unbleached flour, and continue kneading until smooth and elastic (about 5 minutes). Place in a well-greased bowl, turning to grease top.
• **Cover** and let rise in a warm place (85°), free from drafts, 1 hour or until doubled in bulk.
• **Punch** dough down; divide in half. Shape each portion into a 6-inch ball; place on a lightly greased baking sheet.

• **Cover** and let rise in a warm place, free from drafts, 45 minutes or until doubled in bulk.
• **Using** a sharp knife, gently make a ¼-inch-deep cut in the shape of an X in the top of each loaf; bake at 375° for 20 to 25 minutes or until loaves sound hollow when tapped. Remove to wire racks to cool. **Yield:** 2 loaves.

Dr. Harold Cannon
Birmingham, Alabama

OATMEAL BREAD

1 (12-ounce) can evaporated milk
½ cup water
2 tablespoons shortening
2 cups regular oats, uncooked
⅓ cup firmly packed brown sugar
1½ teaspoons salt
1 (¼-ounce) envelope active dry yeast
½ cup warm water (105° to 115°)
3¾ to 4¼ cups all-purpose flour
2 teaspoons regular oats, uncooked

• **Combine** first 3 ingredients in a saucepan; bring to a boil. Pour mixture over 2 cups oats; stir in sugar and salt. Cool to 105° to 115°.
• **Combine** yeast and warm water in a 1-cup liquid measuring cup; let stand 5 minutes.
• **Combine** yeast mixture and oat mixture in a large mixing bowl. Stir in enough flour to make a soft dough.
• **Turn** dough out onto a floured surface, and knead until smooth and elastic (about 5 minutes). Place in a well-greased bowl, turning to grease top.
• **Cover** and let rise in a warm place (85°), free from drafts, 1 hour or until doubled in bulk.
• **Punch** dough down, and divide in half. Shape each portion into a loaf, and place into two well-greased 8½- x 4½- x 3-inch loafpans. Cover and let rise in a warm place, free from drafts, 30 minutes or until doubled in bulk. Sprinkle with 2 teaspoons oats. Bake at 350° for 35 minutes or until loaves sound hollow when tapped. Remove from pans, and cool on wire racks. **Yield:** 2 loaves.

Betty Czebotar
Baltimore, Maryland

SAFFRON BREAD

Saffron is the world's most expensive spice. To be economical, substitute 2 teaspoons turmeric for ¼ teaspoon saffron in this recipe. We liked both versions.

2½ cups warm milk (105° to 115°), divided
2 (¼-ounce) envelopes active dry yeast
8 cups all-purpose flour, divided
1½ cups sugar
¼ teaspoon salt
¼ teaspoon ground saffron
¾ cup butter, melted
1 large egg, lightly beaten
1 cup slivered almonds
1 cup golden raisins
2 tablespoons butter, melted
2 teaspoons sugar
Slivered almonds (optional)

● **Combine** ½ cup warm milk and yeast in a 1-cup liquid measuring cup; let stand 5 minutes.
● **Combine** remaining 2 cups warm milk, 1 cup flour, sugar, and next 4 ingredients; add almonds and raisins. Stir in yeast mixture.
● **Add** remaining 7 cups flour, 1 cup at a time, stirring after each addition until smooth. Place dough in a large well-greased bowl, turning to grease top.
● **Cover** and let rise in a warm place (85°), free from drafts, 2 hours or until doubled in bulk.
● **Turn** dough out onto a well-floured surface, and knead 5 minutes or until smooth.
● **Divide** dough in half. Divide each half into 3 portions. Shape each portion into an 18-inch rope. Pinch loose ends of ropes at 1 end to seal; braid ropes. Repeat procedure with remaining half of dough. Place braids on greased baking sheets.
● **Cover** and let rise in a warm place, free from drafts, 30 minutes or until doubled in bulk.
● **Brush** braids with 2 tablespoons melted butter; sprinkle with 2 teaspoons sugar and additional slivered almonds, if desired.
● **Bake** at 400° for 25 to 30 minutes, covering bread with aluminum foil after 20

minutes to prevent excessive browning. **Yield:** 2 loaves.

Note: For a variation, shape dough into S-shaped rolls. Bake at 400° for 10 to 13 minutes. Yield: 3 dozen.

Kathy Seaberg
St. Petersburg, Florida

PARMESAN BREAD

1 (¼-ounce) envelope active dry yeast
1 cup warm water (105° to 115°)
3 cups all-purpose flour, divided
¼ cup butter or margarine, melted
1 large egg, beaten
2 tablespoons sugar
2 teaspoons dried onion flakes
1 teaspoon salt
1 teaspoon dried Italian seasoning
½ teaspoon garlic salt
⅔ cup grated Parmesan cheese, divided
1 tablespoon butter or margarine, melted

● **Combine** yeast and warm water in a 2-cup liquid measuring cup; let stand 5 minutes.
● **Combine** yeast mixture, 2 cups flour, ¼ cup butter, and next 6 ingredients in a large mixing bowl. Beat at medium speed with an electric mixer 2 minutes. Gradually stir in ⅓ cup Parmesan cheese and remaining 1 cup flour to make a soft dough.
● **Cover** and let rise in a warm place (85°), free from drafts, 1 hour or until doubled in bulk.
● **Punch** dough down, and place in a greased 2-quart casserole. Brush with 1 tablespoon melted butter; sprinkle with remaining ⅓ cup Parmesan cheese.
● **Cover** and let rise in a warm place, free from drafts, 45 minutes or until doubled in bulk.
● **Bake** at 350° for 30 minutes or until golden. Let bread cool in casserole on a wire rack 10 minutes. Remove bread from casserole, and let cool on wire rack. **Yield:** 1 loaf.

Velma McGregor
Gretna, Virginia

MINI SWISS CHEESE LOAVES

Fill Mini Swiss Cheese Loaves with turkey or chicken for lunch or serve them as a savory bread with dinner.

1 (¼-ounce) envelope active dry yeast
¼ cup warm water (105° to 115°)
2⅓ cups all-purpose flour, divided
2 tablespoons sugar
1 teaspoon salt
¼ teaspoon baking soda
1 (8-ounce) carton plain nonfat yogurt
1 large egg
1 cup (4 ounces) shredded reduced-fat Swiss cheese *
Vegetable cooking spray
2 teaspoons sesame seeds, toasted

● **Combine** yeast and warm water in a 1-cup liquid measuring cup; let stand 5 minutes.
● **Combine** yeast mixture, 1 cup flour, sugar, and next 4 ingredients in a large mixing bowl.
● **Beat** batter at low speed with an electric mixer 30 seconds or until blended. Beat at high speed 2 minutes, scraping bowl occasionally.
● **Stir** in remaining 1⅓ cups flour and cheese, mixing well.
● **Divide** batter evenly among 8 (5- x 3- x 2-inch) loafpans coated with cooking spray; sprinkle evenly with sesame seeds.
● **Cover** and let rise in a warm place (85°), free from drafts, 1 hour. (Batter may not double in bulk.)
● **Bake** at 350° for 25 minutes or until golden. Remove loaves from pans; serve warm or cool on a wire rack. **Yield:** 8 loaves.

* For reduced-fat Swiss cheese, we used Alpine Lace.

Shannon Arrington
Woodland, Alabama

♥ Per loaf: Calories 226
Fat 4.9g   Cholesterol 38mg
Sodium 380mg

French Bread

FRENCH BREAD
(pictured at left)

Crusty French Bread served with seasoned olive oil can double easily as an appetizer – not just the bread for the meal.

2 (¼-ounce) envelopes rapid-rise yeast
2 tablespoons sugar
2½ cups warm water (105° to 115°)
1 tablespoon salt
1 tablespoon butter, softened
6½ to 7 cups all-purpose flour, divided
1 egg white
1 tablespoon cold water

• **Combine** first 3 ingredients in a 1-quart liquid measuring cup; let stand 5 minutes.
• **Combine** yeast mixture, salt, and butter in a large bowl. Gradually stir in enough flour to make a soft dough. Place in a well-greased bowl, turning to grease top.
• **Cover** and let rise in a warm place (85°), free from drafts, 40 minutes or until doubled in bulk.
• **Punch** dough down; turn out onto a lightly floured surface. Knead lightly 5 times. Divide dough in half. Roll 1 portion into a 15- x 10-inch rectangle. Roll up dough, starting at long side, pressing firmly to eliminate air pockets. Pinch ends to seal; turn under.
• **Place** dough, seam side down, on a greased baking sheet sprinkled with cornmeal. Repeat procedure with remaining dough.
• **Cover** and let rise in a warm place, free from drafts, 30 minutes or until doubled in bulk. Make 4 or 5 (¼-inch-deep) cuts on top of each loaf with a sharp knife.
• **Bake** at 400° for 25 minutes.
• **Combine** egg white and water; brush over loaves, and bake 5 additional minutes. **Yield:** 2 loaves.

Nancy P. Mumpower
Bristol, Virginia

DRIED TOMATO FOCACCIA

10 pieces dried tomatoes (about ⅓ cup)
½ cup boiling water
1 cup milk
2 tablespoons butter or margarine
3½ to 4 cups bread flour, divided
2 (¼-ounce) envelopes active dry yeast
2 tablespoons sugar
2 teaspoons salt
1 large egg
3 tablespoons dried chives *
¼ cup olive oil
¼ teaspoon dried oregano *
¼ teaspoon dried rosemary *

• **Combine** tomatoes and boiling water in a saucepan; let stand 30 minutes.
• **Remove** tomatoes, reserving liquid; finely chop tomatoes, using kitchen shears, and set aside.
• **Add** milk and butter to reserved tomato liquid, and heat until mixture reaches 120° to 130°.
• **Combine** 1½ cups flour, yeast, sugar, and salt in a large mixing bowl. Gradually add liquid mixture to flour mixture, beating at low speed with an electric mixer until blended. Add egg, and beat 3 minutes at medium speed. Stir in tomato, chives, and enough remaining flour to make a soft dough.
• **Turn** dough out onto a floured surface, and knead 5 minutes. Place in a well-greased bowl, turning to grease top. Cover and let rise in a warm place (85°), free from drafts, 1 hour or until doubled in bulk.
• **Combine** olive oil, oregano, and rosemary; set aside.
• **Punch** dough down. For round loaves, divide dough in half; shape each portion into a 10-inch round. For sandwich buns, divide dough into 12 balls, and shape each portion into a 3-inch round. Place on lightly greased baking sheets; flatten dough slightly, and brush with half of olive oil mixture. Cover and let rest 10 minutes.
• **Bake** at 350° for 15 minutes. Brush with remaining olive oil mixture, and bake 5 to 10 additional minutes or until lightly browned and bread sounds hollow when tapped. Cool on wire

racks. **Yield:** 2 (10-inch) loaves or 12 sandwich buns.

* You can substitute ¼ cup chopped fresh chives, ¾ teaspoon chopped fresh oregano, and ¼ teaspoon chopped fresh rosemary for the dried herbs.

Eva Royal
Evening Shade, Arkansas

ONION FOCACCIA

3 (¼-ounce) envelopes active dry yeast
2 cups warm water (105° to 115°)
3 tablespoons olive oil
2 teaspoons salt
6 cups unbleached flour, divided
1 large purple onion, chopped
1 tablespoon olive oil

• **Combine** yeast and warm water in a 2-cup liquid measuring cup; let stand 5 minutes.
• **Combine** yeast mixture, olive oil, and salt in a large bowl. Stir in 5 cups unbleached flour to make a stiff dough.
• **Turn** out onto a lightly floured surface, and knead in enough remaining 1 cup flour to make a firm dough. Place in a well-greased bowl, turning to grease top.
• **Cover** and let rise in a warm place (85°), free from drafts, 45 minutes or until doubled in bulk.
• **Cook** onion in olive oil in a large skillet over medium-high heat, stirring constantly, until tender. Set aside.
• **Punch** dough down, and divide in half. Roll each portion into a 12-inch circle, and place in a lightly greased 12-inch pizza pan.
• **Arrange** onion evenly on each round; gently press into dough. Cover and let rise in a warm place, free from drafts, 20 minutes. Using fingertips, press small indentations into dough; let rise 10 additional minutes.
• **Bake** at 400° for 20 to 25 minutes or until golden. Remove loaves to wire racks to cool.
• **Serve** with antipasto meats, olive oil for dipping, and mustards. Yield: 2 loaves.

Dr. Harold Cannon
Birmingham, Alabama

SKILLET PIZZA CRUSTS

3 (¼-ounce) envelopes active dry
    yeast
1 teaspoon sugar
¾ cup warm water (105° to 115°)
3 cups all-purpose flour
1 teaspoon salt
½ cup warm water (105° to 115°)
2 tablespoons olive oil
Vegetable cooking spray

• **Combine** first 3 ingredients in a 2-cup liquid measuring cup; let stand 5 minutes.
• **Combine** yeast mixture, flour, and next 3 ingredients in a large bowl, stirring until well blended.
• **Turn** dough out onto a lightly floured surface, and knead 5 minutes. Place dough in a bowl coated with cooking spray, turning to coat top. Cover and let rise in a warm place (85°), free from drafts, 30 minutes or until dough is doubled in bulk.
• **Punch** dough down; knead lightly 4 or 5 times. Divide into 6 equal portions; roll each portion into an 8-inch circle.
• **Cook** each round on 1 side in a non-stick 8-inch skillet coated with cooking spray over medium heat about 2 minutes or until dough rounds are lightly browned. Cool on a wire rack. Freeze in an airtight container up to 6 months. **Yield:** 6 (8-inch) pizza crusts.

Kathy Piques
Knoxville, Tennessee

♥ Per crust: Calories 286
Fat 5.9g Cholesterol 0mg
Sodium 392mg

PARMESAN PIZZA CRUST

2 (¼-ounce) envelopes active dry
    yeast
2 cups warm water (105° to 115°)
6 to 7 cups all-purpose flour,
    divided
2 teaspoons salt
2 teaspoons sugar
½ cup grated Parmesan cheese
½ cup vegetable oil
Vegetable cooking spray
Cornmeal
Olive oil

• **Combine** yeast and water in a 2-cup liquid measuring cup; let stand 5 minutes. Combine yeast mixture, 3 cups flour, salt, and next 3 ingredients in a large mixing bowl; beat at low speed with an electric mixer until blended. Stir in enough remaining flour to make a medium-stiff dough.
• **Cover** and let rise in a warm place (85°), free from drafts, 45 minutes or until dough is doubled in bulk.
• **Turn** dough out onto a lightly floured surface, and knead 4 or 5 times. Coat two 12-inch pizza pans with cooking spray; sprinkle with cornmeal. Divide dough in half, and pat each portion evenly into a pan; brush with olive oil, and prick with a fork.
• **Bake** at 425° for 10 minutes. Add desired sauce and toppings, and bake 15 to 20 additional minutes; sprinkle with desired cheeses, and bake 5 additional minutes. **Yield:** 2 (12-inch) pizzas.

Variation: For a double-crust pizza, pat half of dough in bottom and up sides of a 14-inch deep-dish pizza pan; set remaining half of dough aside. Bake at 425° for 10 minutes; add desired sauce, toppings, and cheese. Roll out remaining dough, and place over toppings. Fold edges together, and seal. Bake at 425° for 20 to 25 minutes or until golden. **Yield:** 1 (14-inch) double-crust pizza.

Note: To freeze, divide risen dough in half before kneading, wrap in plastic wrap, and place in heavy-duty, zip-top plastic bags; freeze up to 3 months. Thaw overnight in refrigerator.

Debbie Huffman
Woodland, Mississippi

ARMENIAN THIN
BREAD

1 (¼-ounce) envelope active dry
    yeast
1 cup warm water (105° to
    115°)
3¼ to 3¾ cups all-purpose flour,
    divided
1½ teaspoons salt
1 teaspoon sugar
¼ cup butter or margarine,
    melted

• **Combine** yeast and warm water in a 2-cup liquid measuring cup; let stand 5 minutes.
• **Combine** yeast mixture, 2 cups flour, salt, sugar, and butter in a large mixing bowl; beat at medium speed with an electric mixer until smooth. Stir in enough remaining flour to make a stiff dough.
• **Turn** dough out onto a floured surface, and knead until smooth and elastic (about 8 minutes).
• **Place** in a well-greased bowl, turning to grease top. Cover and let rise in a warm place (85°), free from drafts, 1 hour or until doubled in bulk.
• **Punch** dough down, and divide into fourths; roll and stretch each portion of dough into a 14- x 10-inch rectangle. Place dough rectangles on ungreased baking sheets.
• **Bake** at 350° for 15 to 20 minutes or until bread is lightly browned. Break bread into pieces before serving. **Yield:** 4 bread sheets.

Southern Accent
Junior League of Pine Bluff, Arkansas

HONEY ANGEL BISCUITS

1 (¼-ounce) envelope active dry
  yeast
2 tablespoons warm water (105°
  to 115°)
5 cups all-purpose flour
1 tablespoon baking powder
1 teaspoon baking soda
1 teaspoon salt
1 cup shortening
2 cups buttermilk
3 tablespoons honey
Honey Butter

● **Combine** yeast and warm water in a 1-cup liquid measuring cup; let stand 5 minutes.
● **Combine** flour, baking powder, baking soda, and salt in a large bowl; cut in shortening with pastry blender until mixture is crumbly.
● **Combine** yeast mixture, buttermilk, and honey, and add to dry ingredients, stirring just until dry ingredients are moistened.
● **Turn** dough out onto a lightly floured surface, and knead 1 minute.
● **Roll** dough to ½-inch thickness. Cut with a 2-inch round cutter, and place on ungreased baking sheets.
● **Bake** at 400° for 10 minutes or until golden. Serve with Honey Butter. **Yield:** 4 dozen.

Ruth Shirley
Dallas, Texas

Honey Butter

QUICK!

¼ cup honey
½ cup butter or margarine,
  softened

● **Combine** honey and butter in a small bowl, stirring mixture until blended. **Yield:** ⅔ cup.

Note: You can store unbaked dough in the refrigerator in an airtight container up to 1 week.

BASIL BISCUITS

1 (¼-ounce) envelope active dry
  yeast
2 tablespoons warm water (105°
  to 115°)
1 cup buttermilk
2½ cups all-purpose flour
1½ teaspoons baking powder
½ teaspoon baking soda
¼ teaspoon salt
2 tablespoons sugar
½ cup shortening
¼ cup finely chopped fresh basil
2 tablespoons finely chopped
  oil-packed dried tomatoes,
  drained

● **Combine** yeast and warm water in a 2-cup liquid measuring cup, and let stand 5 minutes. Stir in buttermilk, and set aside.
● **Combine** flour and next 4 ingredients in a large bowl; cut in shortening with pastry blender until mixture is crumbly. Add buttermilk mixture, basil, and tomato, stirring with a fork until dry ingredients are moistened. (Dough will resemble cottage cheese and be sticky.)
● **Turn** dough out onto a heavily floured surface, and knead lightly 4 or 5 times.
● **Roll** to ½-inch thickness; cut with a 2½-inch round cutter. Place on a lightly greased baking sheet. Cover and let rise in a warm place (85°), free from drafts, 30 minutes.
● **Bake** at 450° for 10 to 12 minutes or until browned. **Yield:** 1 dozen.

SWEET POTATO ANGEL BISCUITS

3 large sweet potatoes ✻
3 (¼-ounce) envelopes active dry
  yeast
¾ cup warm water (105° to 115°)
7½ cups all-purpose flour
1 tablespoon baking powder
1 tablespoon salt
1½ cups sugar
1½ cups shortening

● **Wash** sweet potatoes; bake at 375° for 1 hour or until done. Let potatoes cool to touch; peel and mash. Set aside 3 cups mashed sweet potato, and keep warm. Reserve any remaining mashed sweet potato for another use.
● **Combine** yeast and warm water in a 2-cup liquid measuring cup; let stand 5 minutes.
● **Combine** flour and next 3 ingredients in a large bowl; cut in shortening with pastry blender until mixture is crumbly. Add yeast mixture and mashed sweet potato, stirring until dry ingredients are moistened.
● **Turn** dough out onto a lightly floured surface; knead 5 minutes. Place dough in a lightly greased bowl, turning to grease top; cover and chill 8 hours.
● **Roll** dough to ½-inch thickness, and cut with a 2-inch round cutter. Place biscuits on ungreased baking sheets; cover and let rise in a warm place (85°), free from drafts, 20 minutes or until doubled in bulk.
● **Bake** at 400° for 10 to 12 minutes or until lightly browned. **Yield:** 7 dozen.

✻ You can substitute 3 cups canned, mashed sweet potatoes for fresh.

Note: You can freeze unbaked biscuits up to 1 month. To serve, let thaw 30 minutes; cover and let rise in a warm place (85°), free from drafts, 20 minutes or until doubled in bulk. Bake as directed.

Therese Reid
Rhodesdale, Maryland

HOT CROSS BUNS

4¼ to 4¾ cups all-purpose flour,
    divided
⅔ cup sugar
1 (¼-ounce) envelope rapid-rise
    yeast
1 teaspoon salt
1 teaspoon ground nutmeg
¼ teaspoon ground cinnamon
1 cup milk
¼ cup water
⅓ cup unsalted butter, cut up
2 large eggs
⅔ cup currants
⅓ cup chopped mixed candied
    fruit
1 tablespoon all-purpose flour
1 egg white, slightly beaten
1 cup sifted powdered sugar
1 to 1½ tablespoons milk
½ teaspoon vanilla extract

• **Combine** 2½ cups flour, sugar, yeast, salt, nutmeg, and cinnamon in a large mixing bowl, stirring well. Set aside.
• **Combine** 1 cup milk, water, and butter in a saucepan; cook over medium heat, stirring constantly, just until butter melts. Cool to 120° to 130°.
• **Add** milk mixture to flour mixture; beat at low speed with an electric mixer until dry ingredients are moistened. Add 2 eggs; beat at medium speed 3 minutes. Gradually stir in enough remaining flour to make a soft dough.
• **Turn** dough out onto a well-floured surface; knead until smooth and elastic (about 8 minutes). Place in a well-greased bowl, turning to grease top.
• **Cover** and let rise in a warm place (85°), free from drafts, 1 hour (dough may not quite double in bulk).
• **Punch** dough down, and turn out onto a floured surface. Combine currants, candied fruit, and 1 tablespoon flour in a bowl, stirring to coat. Knead about one-fourth of fruit mixture at a time into dough until all fruit mixture is evenly dispersed.
• **Divide** dough into 15 equal portions; shape each portion into a ball. Place balls in a greased 13- x 9- x 2-inch pan; cover and let rise in a warm place, free from drafts, 1 hour or until doubled in bulk. Gently brush tops with beaten egg white.

• **Bake** at 375° for 16 minutes or until buns are deep golden and sound hollow when tapped. Cool 10 minutes in pan on a wire rack.
• **Combine** sifted powdered sugar, 1 to 1½ tablespoons milk, and vanilla; pipe evenly on top of warm buns, forming a cross. **Yield:** 15 buns.

Velma Kestner
Berwind, West Virginia

OATMEAL-CINNAMON PECAN ROLLS

1 (¼-ounce) envelope active dry
    yeast
¼ cup warm water (105° to 115°)
1 cup milk
1 cup sugar, divided
1 teaspoon salt
⅓ cup butter
2 large eggs
4 to 4½ cups all-purpose flour
1 cup quick-cooking oats,
    uncooked
⅓ cup butter, melted
⅓ cup dark corn syrup
1¼ cups firmly packed brown
    sugar, divided
¾ cup chopped pecans, toasted
2 tablespoons butter or margarine,
    softened
2 teaspoons ground cinnamon

• **Combine** yeast and warm water in a 1-cup liquid measuring cup; let stand 5 minutes.
• **Combine** milk, ½ cup sugar, salt, and ⅓ cup butter in a saucepan; cook over low heat until butter melts, stirring occasionally. Cool to 105° to 115°.
• **Combine** yeast mixture, milk mixture, eggs, and 1 cup flour in a mixing bowl; beat at medium speed with an electric mixer until well blended. Gradually stir in oats and enough remaining flour to make a soft dough.
• **Turn** dough out onto a well-floured surface, and knead until dough is smooth and elastic (about 10 minutes). Place dough in a well-greased bowl, turning to grease top.
• **Cover** and let rise in a warm place (85°), free from drafts, 1 hour or until doubled in bulk.

• **Punch** dough down; cover and let rest 10 minutes.
• **Combine** ⅓ cup melted butter, corn syrup, and ¾ cup brown sugar, stirring until blended. Spoon evenly into two 9-inch square pans. Sprinkle with pecans.
• **Divide** dough in half. Roll each portion into a 12-inch square. Spread each with 1 tablespoon softened butter, leaving a ½-inch border.
• **Combine** cinnamon, remaining ½ cup sugar, and remaining ½ cup brown sugar; sprinkle over dough.
• **Roll** up dough, jellyroll fashion, pressing firmly to eliminate air pockets; pinch seams to seal. Cut each roll into 12 (1-inch) slices, and place in prepared pans.
• **Cover** and let rise in a warm place, free from drafts, 45 minutes or until doubled in bulk.
• **Bake** at 375° for 20 minutes or until golden. Invert onto plates. **Yield:** 2 dozen.

Donna Campbell
Huntsville, Alabama

OLD-FASHIONED CINNAMON ROLLS

⅓ cup skim milk
⅓ cup reduced-calorie margarine
¼ cup firmly packed brown sugar
1 teaspoon salt
1 (¼-ounce) envelope active dry
    yeast
½ cup warm water (105° to 115°)
½ cup fat-free egg substitute
3½ cups bread flour, divided
¾ cup quick-cooking oats,
    uncooked
Vegetable cooking spray
¼ cup reduced-calorie margarine,
    softened and divided
¾ cup firmly packed brown sugar
¼ cup raisins
2 teaspoons ground cinnamon
1 cup sifted powdered sugar
2 tablespoons water

• **Combine** first 4 ingredients in a saucepan; heat until margarine melts. Cool to 105° to 115°.
• **Combine** yeast and warm water in a 1-cup liquid measuring cup; let stand 5 minutes.

• **Combine** milk mixture, yeast mixture, egg substitute, 1 cup flour, and oats, stirring well. Gradually stir in enough remaining flour to make a soft dough.

• **Turn** dough out onto a lightly floured surface; knead until smooth and elastic (about 8 minutes). Place dough in a large bowl coated with cooking spray, turning to coat top.

• **Cover** and let rise in a warm place (85°), free from drafts, 1 hour or until doubled in bulk.

• **Punch** dough down; cover and let rest 10 minutes. Divide dough in half, and roll each portion into a 12-inch square. Spread each square of dough with 2 tablespoons margarine.

• **Combine** ¾ cup brown sugar, raisins, and cinnamon; sprinkle mixture over each square. Roll up jellyroll fashion; pinch seam to seal (do not seal ends). Cut each roll into 1-inch slices, and place in two 8-inch square pans coated with cooking spray.

• **Cover** and let rise in a warm place, free from drafts, about 30 minutes or until almost doubled in bulk.

• **Bake** at 375° for 15 to 20 minutes or until golden.

• **Combine** powdered sugar and 2 tablespoons water; drizzle over warm rolls. **Yield:** 2 dozen.

❤ Per roll: Calories 169
Fat 3.4g Cholesterol 0mg
Sodium 154mg

SWEET POTATO ROLLS

2 (¼-ounce) packages active dry yeast
1½ cups warm water (105° to 115°)
3 cups whole wheat flour
3 cups all-purpose flour
⅓ cup firmly packed brown sugar
1¼ teaspoons salt
½ cup butter or margarine, softened
2 large eggs
1 (16-ounce) can cut sweet potatoes, drained

• **Combine** yeast and warm water in container of an electric blender, and process 30 seconds. Let yeast mixture stand 5 minutes.

• **Combine** flours in a large bowl. Add 1 cup flour mixture, sugar, and remaining 4 ingredients to yeast mixture in blender; process until smooth.

• **Gradually** stir yeast mixture into remaining flour mixture to make a soft dough.

• **Turn** dough out onto a heavily floured surface, and knead until smooth and elastic (about 5 minutes). Place in a well-greased bowl, turning to grease top. Cover and let rise in a warm place (85°), free from drafts, 1 hour or until doubled in bulk.

• **Punch** dough down, and divide in half; shape each portion into a ball. Roll each portion of dough into a 16-inch circle on a floured surface, and cut into 16 wedges. Roll up wedges, beginning at wide end, and place, point side down, on a greased baking sheet. Cover and let rise in a warm place, free from drafts, 30 minutes or until doubled in bulk.

• **Bake** at 350° for 15 minutes or until golden. **Yield:** 32 rolls.

Note: You can make dough ahead. Knead, place in a greased bowl, and cover securely with plastic wrap. Chill at least 6 hours. Punch dough down; proceed as directed.

Sue Ewing's Supper Club
Richmond, Virginia

CENTERPIECE ROLLS

1 large egg, lightly beaten
1 tablespoon water
1 (25-ounce) package frozen roll dough, thawed
Toppings: poppy seeds, caraway seeds, dillseeds, dried basil, dried thyme, dried marjoram, cornmeal, oats

• **Combine** egg and water. Brush top of each unbaked roll with egg mixture, and sprinkle with desired toppings.

• **Arrange** all but 5 unbaked rolls in a cluster with sides touching on a greased baking sheet. Knead remaining 5 rolls together; divide in half. Form each half into a rope long enough to go around the cluster. Twist ropes together; wrap around cluster, pressing edges to seal.

• **Let** rise in a warm place (85°), free from drafts, 1 hour or until dough is doubled in bulk.

• **Bake** at 350° for 15 minutes or until lightly browned. **Yield:** 1 loaf.

Note: You can bake rolls individually or in clusters of 2 or 3. Bake at 350° for 12 minutes or until lightly browned.

Greg Dowling
Birmingham, Alabama

WHOLESOME WHOLE WHEAT ROLLS

2½ cups milk, divided
2 (¼-ounce) envelopes active dry yeast
½ cup honey
½ cup shortening
2 teaspoons salt
3 cups whole wheat flour
2 large eggs
3½ to 4 cups all-purpose flour
Melted butter or margarine

• **Heat** milk to 110° to 115°. Combine yeast and ½ cup milk in a 1-cup liquid measuring cup; let stand 5 minutes.

• **Combine** remaining 2 cups milk, honey, shortening, salt, and wheat flour in a mixing bowl; beat at medium speed with an electric mixer until smooth. Add yeast mixture and eggs; mix well. Gradually stir in enough all-purpose flour to make a stiff dough. Place in a well-greased bowl, turning to grease top.

• **Cover** and let rise in a warm place (85°), free from drafts, 1 hour or until doubled in bulk.

• **Punch** dough down; turn out onto a well-floured surface, and knead 4 or 5 times. Roll to ½-inch thickness; cut with a 2½-inch round cutter. Place on a lightly greased baking sheet.

• **Cover** and let rise in a warm place, free from drafts, about 30 minutes or until doubled in bulk.

• **Bake** at 400° for 12 to 15 minutes or until browned. Brush rolls with melted butter. **Yield:** 2 dozen.

Heidi Huffman
Woodland, Mississippi

MORRISON HOUSE BRIOCHE

*Don't limit this buttery bread
just to breakfast. It's also delicious
as a sandwich or dinner roll.*

4⅓ cups all-purpose flour
2 tablespoons sugar
½ (¼-ounce) envelope active dry
    yeast (1½ teaspoons)
¼ cup warm water (105° to 115°)
2 teaspoons salt
8 large eggs
1¼ cups unsalted butter, chilled
    and cut into pieces
1 large egg, lightly beaten

• **Combine** flour and sugar in a large mixing bowl. Make a well in center of mixture; add yeast and warm water in center. Let stand 5 minutes.
• **Beat** at low speed with an electric mixer until blended; add salt and 8 eggs, one at a time, beating until blended after each addition. Gradually add butter, beating well (small bits of butter will be visible). Cover and chill at least 8 hours (dough will be sticky).
• **Divide** dough into 12 portions; pinch off a 1-inch ball of dough from each portion, and set aside.
• **Roll** larger pieces into balls on a lightly floured surface; place in well-greased individual brioche molds or muffin pan. Place molds or muffin pan on a baking sheet.
• **Make** a well in center of each ball. Shape remaining dough pieces into balls, and place in wells.
• **Brush** brioche with beaten egg; let stand 30 minutes.
• **Bake** at 350° for 30 minutes. Cool in molds or pans 10 minutes; remove from molds or pan. **Yield:** 1 dozen.

*Morrison House
Alexandria, Virginia*

FRENCH MARKET BEIGNETS

1 (¼-ounce) envelope active dry
    yeast
1 cup warm water (105° to 115°)
¾ cup evaporated milk
¼ cup sugar
1 teaspoon salt
1 large egg, lightly beaten
4 to 4½ cups all-purpose flour
Vegetable oil
Sifted powdered sugar

• **Combine** yeast and warm water in a 2-cup liquid measuring cup; let stand 5 minutes.
• **Combine** yeast mixture, evaporated milk, and next 3 ingredients. Gradually stir in enough flour to make a soft dough. Cover and chill 8 hours.
• **Turn** dough out onto a well-floured surface; knead 5 or 6 times. Roll dough into a 15- x 12½-inch rectangle; cut into 2½-inch squares.
• **Pour** oil to depth of 3 to 4 inches into a Dutch oven; heat to 375°. Fry 3 or 4 beignets at a time, 1 minute on each side or until golden. Drain; sprinkle with powdered sugar. **Yield:** 2½ dozen.

HONEY PUFFS

2 (¼-ounce) envelopes active dry
    yeast
1 cup warm water (105° to 115°)
2 cups warm milk (105° to 115°)
¼ cup sugar
1 teaspoon salt
1 large egg
4 cups all-purpose flour
Vegetable oil
Honey
Ground cinnamon

• **Combine** yeast and warm water in a 2-cup liquid measuring cup; let stand 5 minutes.
• **Combine** yeast mixture, warm milk, and next 3 ingredients; stir with a wooden spoon until well blended.
• **Add** flour, 1 cup at a time, stirring until smooth after each addition.
• **Cover** and let rise in a warm place (85°), free from drafts, 1 hour or until doubled in bulk.

• **Pour** oil to depth of 4 inches into a Dutch oven; heat to 375°. Drop dough by tablespoonfuls into hot oil, and fry until golden, turning once. Drain on paper towels; keep warm. Repeat procedure with remaining dough.
• **Drizzle** with honey, and sprinkle with cinnamon; serve immediately. **Yield:** 4 dozen.

*Jean Voan
Shepherd, Texas*

OVERNIGHT REFRIGERATOR PANCAKES

QUICK!

1 (¼-ounce) envelope active dry
    yeast
¼ cup warm water (105° to 115°)
4 cups all-purpose flour
2 tablespoons baking powder
2 teaspoons baking soda
1 teaspoon salt
2 teaspoons sugar
6 large eggs
4 cups buttermilk
¼ cup vegetable oil

• **Combine** yeast and warm water in a 1-cup liquid measuring cup; let stand 5 minutes.
• **Combine** flour and next 4 ingredients in a large bowl; make a well in center. Combine eggs, buttermilk, and oil; add to flour mixture, stirring just until dry ingredients are moistened. Stir in yeast mixture. Cover and chill 8 hours.
• **Remove** from refrigerator; stir well.
• **Preheat** griddle to 350°; lightly grease griddle. Pour about ¼ cup batter for each pancake onto hot griddle. Cook pancakes until tops are covered with bubbles and edges look cooked; turn and cook other side. **Yield:** 2½ dozen.

Note: You can store pancake batter in refrigerator up to 1 week.

*Dolores Thielermeir
Maynard, Arkansas*

At right: *Orange Butter Cake (page 70)*

CAKES

BUTTERMILK-LEMON PUDDING CAKE WITH BLUEBERRY SAUCE

⅔ cup sugar
¼ cup all-purpose flour
1½ cups buttermilk
½ cup fresh lemon juice
¼ cup butter or margarine, melted
3 large eggs, separated
1 tablespoon grated lemon rind
¼ cup sugar
Powdered sugar
Blueberry Sauce
Garnish: lemon rind curls

• **Combine** ⅔ cup sugar and flour in a large bowl; stir in buttermilk, lemon juice, butter, egg yolks, and lemon rind. Set aside.
• **Beat** egg whites at high speed with an electric mixer until foamy. Gradually add ¼ cup sugar, 1 tablespoon at a time, beating until stiff peaks form and sugar dissolves (2 to 4 minutes).
• **Fold** egg white mixture into batter; pour into a greased 9- x 5- x 3-inch loafpan, and place loafpan in a 13- x 9- x 2-inch baking pan. Add hot water to baking pan to depth of 1½ inches.
• **Bake** at 350° for 1 hour and 10 minutes, shielding with aluminum foil after 40 minutes to prevent excessive browning. Carefully remove loafpan; cool on a wire rack 15 minutes. Dust with powdered sugar. Serve over warm Blueberry Sauce, and garnish, if desired. **Yield:** 6 to 8 servings.

Blueberry Sauce

QUICK!

¼ cup sugar
2 teaspoons cornstarch
¼ cup water
2 tablespoons lemon juice
¼ teaspoon ground cinnamon
2 cups fresh or frozen blueberries

• **Combine** all ingredients in a medium saucepan; cook over medium-low heat, stirring constantly, until mixture boils and thickens. **Yield:** 1 cup.

Linda Magers
Clemmons, North Carolina

ORANGE BUTTER CAKE
(pictured on page 69)

2 cups all-purpose flour
1 cup graham cracker crumbs
1 cup firmly packed light brown sugar
½ cup sugar
1 teaspoon baking powder
1 teaspoon baking soda
¼ teaspoon salt
1 teaspoon ground cinnamon
1 cup butter, softened
1 tablespoon grated orange rind
1 cup fresh orange juice
3 large eggs, lightly beaten
Tropical Cheese Spread (optional)

• **Combine** first 12 ingredients in a large mixing bowl; beat at low speed with an electric mixer until blended. Beat at high speed 3 minutes. Pour batter into two greased and floured 8½- x 4½- x 3-inch loafpans.
• **Bake** at 350° for 45 minutes or until a wooden pick inserted in center comes out clean. Cool in pans on wire racks 10 minutes; remove from pans, and let cool completely on wire racks. Frost with Tropical Cheese Spread, if desired. **Yield:** 2 loaves.

Tropical Cheese Spread

QUICK!

1 cup chopped dried mixed fruit
¾ cup water
2 tablespoons Grand Marnier or other orange-flavored liqueur
2 (8-ounce) packages cream cheese, softened
½ cup orange marmalade

• **Combine** first 3 ingredients in a small saucepan; bring to a boil over medium heat. Cover, reduce heat, and simmer 8 minutes or until fruit is soft. Drain well.
• **Beat** cream cheese at medium speed with electric mixer until creamy; add marmalade, and beat until blended. Fold in fruit. **Yield:** 3½ cups.

Dorsella Utter
Louisville, Kentucky

ACORN SQUASH CAKE

¼ cup butter, softened
¾ cup firmly packed light brown sugar
1 large egg
1 cup cooked mashed acorn squash
½ teaspoon vanilla extract
2 cups all-purpose flour
2 teaspoons baking soda
½ teaspoon salt
1 teaspoon ground cinnamon
1 cup chopped pecans
Streusel Topping

• **Beat** butter and sugar at medium speed with an electric mixer until creamy. Add egg, beating well. Stir in squash and vanilla.
• **Combine** flour and next 3 ingredients; gradually add to squash mixture, beating at low speed after each addition. Stir in pecans. Pour batter into a greased 9-inch square pan, and sprinkle with Streusel Topping.
• **Bake** at 350° for 40 minutes. Cool cake in pan on a wire rack. **Yield:** 9 servings.

Streusel Topping

QUICK!

½ cup firmly packed light brown sugar
⅓ cup all-purpose flour
½ teaspoon ground cinnamon
¼ cup butter, softened
½ cup chopped pecans

• **Combine** all ingredients in a bowl. **Yield:** 1½ cups.

Valerie Stutsman
Norfolk, Virginia

CHEATER'S CARROT CAKE

QUICK!

1 (8.25-ounce) package yellow
   cake mix
1 (8-ounce) can crushed
   pineapple, undrained
1 cup shredded carrot
⅓ cup mayonnaise
2 large eggs, lightly beaten
1 (2-ounce) package pecan pieces
1 teaspoon ground cinnamon
½ (12-ounce) container cream
   cheese frosting

• **Combine** first 7 ingredients in a large
bowl, stirring until blended. Pour into a
greased and floured 9-inch square pan.
• **Bake** at 350° for 30 minutes or until a
wooden pick inserted in center comes
out clean. Cool completely in pan on a
wire rack. Spread frosting on top of
cake. **Yield:** 1 (9-inch) cake.

Bill Jackson
Alpine, Alabama

FROSTED CARROT CAKE

1½ cups all-purpose flour
⅔ cup whole wheat flour
2 teaspoons baking soda
2 teaspoons ground cinnamon
¼ teaspoon salt
1 cup firmly packed brown sugar
¾ cup fat-free egg substitute
¾ cup nonfat buttermilk
1 (8-ounce) can crushed pineapple
   in juice, drained
2 cups grated carrots
⅓ cup raisins
3 tablespoons vegetable oil
2 teaspoons vanilla extract
Vegetable cooking spray
Orange-Cream Cheese Frosting

• **Combine** first 5 ingredients; set aside.
• **Combine** brown sugar and next 7 ingredients in a large mixing bowl; add
dry ingredients, and beat at medium
speed with an electric mixer until well
blended. Pour batter into a 13- x 9- x 2-
inch pan coated with cooking spray.
• **Bake** at 350° for 30 to 35 minutes or
until a wooden pick inserted in center
comes out clean. Cool cake completely

in pan on a wire rack. Spread Orange-
Cream Cheese Frosting over top of
cake. Cover and chill. **Yield:** 18 servings.

♥ Per serving: Calories 208
Fat 4.8g Cholesterol 8mg
Sodium 306mg

Orange-Cream Cheese Frosting

QUICK!

½ cup 1% low-fat cottage cheese
2 teaspoons vanilla extract
1 (8-ounce) package light cream
   cheese, softened
1 teaspoon grated orange rind
1 cup sifted powdered sugar

• **Position** knife blade in food processor bowl; add cottage cheese. Process
about 1 minute or until smooth. Add
vanilla, cream cheese, and orange rind,
and process until smooth. Add powdered sugar, and pulse 3 to 5 times or
until mixture is smooth. **Yield:** 1½ cups.

NO-MOLASSES GINGERBREAD

QUICK!

1 teaspoon baking soda
½ cup cane syrup
½ cup butter, softened
½ cup sugar
2 large eggs, lightly beaten
1½ cups all-purpose flour
1 teaspoon ground cinnamon
½ teaspoon ground ginger
¼ teaspoon ground cloves
¼ teaspoon salt
½ cup water

• **Combine** soda and syrup; set aside.
• **Beat** butter with an electric mixer
until creamy. Gradually add sugar, beating well. Add eggs, one at a time, beating after each addition. Stir in syrup
mixture.
• **Combine** flour and next 4 ingredients;
add to butter mixture alternately with
water, beginning and ending with flour
mixture. Mix after each addition.
• **Pour** batter into a greased and floured
9-inch square pan. Bake at 350° for 30
minutes or until a wooden pick inserted
in center comes out clean. Cool in pan

on a wire rack at least 10 minutes before
serving. **Yield:** 9 to 12 servings.

Louise Smith
Columbus, Georgia

PUMPKIN GINGERBREAD
WITH CARAMEL SAUCE

2¼ cups all-purpose flour
½ cup sugar
⅔ cup butter or margarine
¾ cup chopped pecans
¾ cup buttermilk
½ cup canned pumpkin
½ cup molasses
1 large egg
1½ teaspoons ground ginger
1 teaspoon baking soda
½ teaspoon ground cinnamon
¼ teaspoon salt
¼ teaspoon ground cloves
Caramel Sauce
Vanilla ice cream

• **Combine** flour and sugar; cut in butter
with pastry blender until mixture is
crumbly. Stir in pecans. Press 1¼ cups
mixture in bottom of an ungreased 9-
inch square pan; set aside.
• **Combine** remaining crumb mixture,
buttermilk, and next 8 ingredients; beat
at low speed with an electric mixer until
blended. Pour over crumb mixture;
bake at 350° for 40 minutes or until a
wooden pick inserted in center comes
out clean. Cool in pan on a wire rack.
Cut into squares; serve with Caramel
Sauce and ice cream. **Yield:** 12 servings.

Caramel Sauce

QUICK!

½ cup butter or margarine
1¼ cups firmly packed brown sugar
2 tablespoons light corn syrup
½ cup whipping cream

• **Melt** butter in a small heavy saucepan
over low heat; add sugar and corn
syrup. Bring to a boil; cook, stirring constantly, 1 minute or until sugar dissolves. Gradually add cream; return to a
boil. Set aside. **Yield:** 2 cups.

Linda Magers
Clemmons, North Carolina

Cakes   71

KAHLÚA GINGERBREAD WITH KEY LIME CURD

½ cup butter or margarine, softened
¾ cup sugar
⅓ cup firmly packed dark brown sugar
1 large egg
2 cups all-purpose flour
1½ teaspoons baking soda
1½ teaspoons ground ginger
1 teaspoon ground cinnamon
1 teaspoon ground cloves
½ teaspoon salt
1 cup molasses
⅔ cup hot water
⅓ cup Kahlúa or other coffee-flavored liqueur
2 tablespoons brewed coffee
Key Lime Curd
Whipped cream
Garnishes: fresh mint sprig, Key lime rind

• **Beat** butter at medium speed with an electric mixer until creamy; gradually add sugars, beating well. Add egg, beating until blended.
• **Add** flour and next 9 ingredients; beat at medium speed until smooth. Pour into a greased and floured 13- x 9- x 2-inch pan.
• **Bake** at 325° for 35 minutes or until a wooden pick inserted in center comes out clean. Cut into triangles; serve warm or at room temperature with Key Lime Curd and whipped cream. Garnish, if desired. **Yield:** 12 servings.

Key Lime Curd

2 cups sugar
1 cup butter or margarine, cut up
⅔ cup fresh Key lime juice
1 tablespoon grated Key lime rind (optional)
4 large eggs, lightly beaten

• **Combine** first 3 ingredients, and lime rind, if desired, in a large heavy saucepan; cook over medium heat, stirring constantly, until butter melts. Gradually stir one-fourth of hot mixture into eggs; add to remaining hot mixture, stirring constantly.

• **Cook** over low heat, stirring constantly, 10 minutes or until lime mixture thickens and coats a spoon. Remove from heat; cool. Cover and chill at least 2 hours. **Yield:** 3 cups.

Stop and Smell the Rosemary: Recipes and Traditions to Remember
Junior League of Houston, Texas

GINGERY GINGERBREAD

½ cup butter, softened
½ cup sugar
1 large egg
1 cup molasses
½ cup finely grated fresh ginger
2½ cups all-purpose flour
1½ teaspoons baking soda
½ teaspoon baking powder
1 teaspoon ground cinnamon
1 teaspoon ground ginger
½ teaspoon ground cloves
1 cup hot water
Vanilla ice cream

• **Beat** butter at medium speed with an electric mixer until creamy; gradually add sugar, beating well. Add egg and molasses, beating until blended. Add fresh ginger, beating until blended.
• **Combine** flour and next 5 ingredients; add to butter mixture alternately with hot water, beginning and ending with flour mixture. Beat at low speed until blended after each addition; beat 1 additional minute or until very smooth. Pour into a greased 13- x 9- x 2-inch pan.
• **Bake** at 350° for 40 minutes or until a wooden pick inserted in center comes out clean. Cool in pan on a wire rack 10 minutes; remove from pan, and let cool completely on wire rack.
• **Cut** into squares; serve with vanilla ice cream. **Yield:** 12 servings.

Milton Hurst
Birmingham, Alabama

GRANDMA'S CHOCOLATE CAKE

QUICK!

2 cups all-purpose flour
2 cups sugar
¼ cup cocoa
1 teaspoon ground cinnamon
1 cup butter or margarine
1 cup water
1 teaspoon baking soda
2 large eggs
½ cup buttermilk
1 teaspoon vanilla extract
1 (12-ounce) package miniature chocolate-covered peppermint patties, unwrapped
Chocolate Frosting

• **Combine** first 4 ingredients, and set aside.
• **Combine** butter and water in a large saucepan; bring to a boil.
• **Remove** from heat; stir in soda. Add flour mixture, stirring well.
• **Stir** in eggs, buttermilk, and vanilla.
• **Spoon** batter into a greased and floured 13- x 9- x 2-inch pan.
• **Bake** at 350° for 30 minutes. Top with candy; bake 2 additional minutes. Gently spread melted candy over warm cake. Spread Chocolate Frosting over top. Cut into squares. **Yield:** 15 servings.

Chocolate Frosting

QUICK!

½ cup butter or margarine
⅓ cup milk
1 (16-ounce) package powdered sugar, sifted
¼ cup cocoa
1 teaspoon vanilla extract

• **Combine** butter and milk in a large saucepan. Bring mixture to a boil, and remove from heat.
• **Combine** powdered sugar and cocoa; add to butter mixture. Add vanilla, stirring until smooth. **Yield:** 2 cups.

Carol Boker
Memphis, Tennessee

QUICK CHOCOLATE COLA CAKE

QUICK!

1 (18.25-ounce) package devil's
   food cake mix without
   pudding
1 (3.9-ounce) package chocolate
   instant pudding mix
4 large eggs
½ cup vegetable oil
1 (10-ounce) bottle cola-flavored
   carbonated beverage
   (1¼ cups)
Chocolate-Cola Frosting

• **Combine** cake mix, pudding mix,
eggs, and oil in a large mixing bowl; beat
at low speed with an electric mixer until
blended. Set aside.
• **Bring** cola to a boil in a small
saucepan over medium heat. With mixer
on low speed, gradually pour hot cola
into cake batter. Increase speed to
medium; beat 2 minutes.
• **Pour** batter into a greased and floured
13- x 9- x 2-inch baking pan.
• **Bake** at 350° for 30 minutes or until a
wooden pick inserted in center comes
out clean. Cool in pan on a wire rack 10
minutes.
• **Spread** warm Chocolate-Cola Frosting over top of warm cake; let cake cool
completely in pan on wire rack. **Yield:**
15 servings.

Chocolate-Cola Frosting

QUICK!

½ cup butter or margarine
¼ cup plus 2 tablespoons
   cola-flavored carbonated
   beverage
3 tablespoons cocoa
1 (16-ounce) package powdered
   sugar, sifted
1 teaspoon vanilla extract
1 cup chopped pecans, toasted

• **Combine** first 3 ingredients in a large
saucepan; cook over medium heat, stirring constantly, until butter melts. (Do
not boil.) Remove from heat; add powdered sugar and vanilla, stirring until
smooth. Stir in chopped pecans. **Yield:**
about 2¼ cups.

Meredith Bennett
Joiner, Arkansas

PEANUT BUTTER-FUDGE CAKE

QUICK!

*Whether you serve it as an after-school
snack or for dessert, this recipe is sure
to be a favorite of kids of all ages.*

2 cups all-purpose flour
1 teaspoon baking soda
2 cups sugar
1 cup butter or margarine
¼ cup cocoa
1 cup water
½ cup buttermilk
2 large eggs, lightly beaten
1 teaspoon vanilla extract
1½ cups creamy peanut butter
Chocolate Frosting

• **Combine** first 3 ingredients in a large
bowl; set aside.
• **Melt** butter in a heavy saucepan over
medium heat; stir in cocoa. Add water,
buttermilk, and eggs, stirring well.
• **Cook,** stirring constantly, until mixture boils. Remove from heat; add to
flour mixture, stirring until smooth. Stir
in vanilla. Pour batter into a greased and
floured 13- x 9- x 2-inch pan.
• **Bake** at 350° for 20 to 25 minutes or
until a wooden pick inserted in center
comes out clean. Cool in pan on a wire
rack 10 minutes. Carefully spread
peanut butter over warm cake. Cool
completely.
• **Spread** Chocolate Frosting over
peanut butter; cut into squares. **Yield:**
20 to 25 servings.

Chocolate Frosting

QUICK!

1 (16-ounce) package powdered
   sugar, sifted
¼ cup cocoa
½ cup butter or margarine
⅓ cup buttermilk
1 teaspoon vanilla extract

• **Place** sugar in a bowl; set aside.
• **Bring** cocoa, butter, and buttermilk to
a boil in a small saucepan over medium
heat, stirring constantly. Pour hot mixture over sugar, stirring until smooth.
Stir in vanilla. **Yield:** 2½ cups.

Marian T. Talley
Huntsville, Alabama

MAPLE NUT CAKE

1 cup shortening
½ cup firmly packed brown sugar
1 cup maple syrup
2 large eggs
2½ cups all-purpose flour
2 teaspoons baking powder
½ teaspoon baking soda
½ teaspoon salt
2 teaspoons ground nutmeg
½ cup hot water
½ cup sherry
1 cup chopped pecans, toasted
Maple Frosting
12 to 15 pecan halves

• **Beat** shortening at medium speed
with an electric mixer until fluffy; gradually add brown sugar, beating well. Add
maple syrup and eggs, beating until
blended.
• **Combine** flour and next 4 ingredients
in a bowl; add to shortening mixture alternately with hot water and sherry, beginning and ending with flour mixture.
Beat at low speed until blended after
each addition. Stir in 1 cup chopped
pecans. Pour batter into a greased and
floured 13- x 9- x 2-inch pan.
• **Bake** at 350° for 30 minutes or until a
wooden pick inserted in center comes
out clean. Cool cake completely in pan
on a wire rack.
• **Spread** Maple Frosting on top of cake;
place a pecan half on each serving.
Yield: 12 to 15 servings.

Maple Frosting

QUICK!

¼ cup butter or margarine,
   softened
2¼ cups sifted powdered sugar,
   divided
2 to 3 tablespoons milk
½ teaspoon maple extract

• **Beat** butter at medium speed with an
electric mixer until creamy; gradually
add 1 cup powdered sugar, beating well.
Add remaining 1¼ cups powdered
sugar and milk, beating until mixture is
spreading consistency. Stir in flavoring.
Yield: 1 cup.

Sara Beebee
Kennesaw, Georgia

BEERQUICK SUGAR CAKE

QUICK!

4 cups biscuit mix
½ cup instant potato flakes
¼ cup sugar
¼ cup instant nonfat dry milk
       powder
2 large eggs, lightly beaten
1 (12-ounce) can beer, at room
       temperature
3 tablespoons vegetable oil
1 cup butter or margarine,
       melted
2 cups firmly packed brown sugar
1¼ teaspoons ground cinnamon

• **Combine** first 4 ingredients in a large bowl, and make a well in center of dry ingredients.
• **Combine** eggs, beer, and oil; add to dry ingredients, stirring just until dry ingredients are moistened.
• **Spoon** batter into a greased 15- x 10- x 1-inch jellyroll pan; let stand 10 minutes.
• **Combine** butter, brown sugar, and cinnamon; spread half of butter mixture on top of cake.
• **Bake** at 350° for 15 minutes. Remove cake from oven; spread with remaining butter mixture. Bake 10 additional minutes. Serve immediately. **Yield:** 15 to 18 servings.

Laura Greene Knapp
Cary, North Carolina

MORAVIAN SUGAR CAKE

2 (¼-ounce) envelopes active dry
       yeast
½ teaspoon sugar
½ cup warm water (105° to 115°)
1 cup butter or margarine, melted
       and divided
¾ cup water
½ cup sugar
¼ cup instant potato flakes
2 tablespoons instant nonfat dry
       milk powder
½ teaspoon salt
2 large eggs
3 cups all-purpose flour
1 cup firmly packed brown
       sugar
1 teaspoon ground cinnamon

• **Combine** first 3 ingredients in a 1-cup liquid measuring cup, and let stand 5 minutes.
• **Combine** yeast mixture, ½ cup melted butter, ¾ cup water, and next 5 ingredients in a large mixing bowl. Add 1 cup flour; beat at low speed with an electric mixer 2 minutes. Stir in enough remaining 2 cups flour to make a soft dough.
• **Cover** and let rise in a warm place (85°), free from drafts, 45 minutes or until doubled in bulk.
• **Punch** dough down; spread in a greased 15- x 10- x 1-inch jellyroll pan. Cover and let rise in a warm place (85°), free from drafts, 30 minutes.
• **Make** shallow indentations in dough at 1-inch intervals, using the handle of a wooden spoon. Drizzle with remaining ½ cup butter.
• **Combine** brown sugar and cinnamon; sprinkle over dough.
• **Bake** at 375° for 12 to 15 minutes. Cut into squares. **Yield:** 15 servings.

Eddie McGee
King, North Carolina

NANNY'S FAMOUS COCONUT-PINEAPPLE CAKE
(pictured on cover)

Jeannie won first prize in the dessert category of the Southern Living *Celebrated Holiday Recipe Contest with this cake. It beat out more than 500 other sweets. Have a taste of our Dessert of the Year.*

1 (15¼-ounce) can crushed
       pineapple in juice,
       undrained
1½ cups butter or margarine,
       softened
3 cups sugar
5 large eggs
½ cup lemon-lime soft drink *
3 cups cake flour, sifted
1 teaspoon lemon extract
1 teaspoon vanilla extract
Pineapple Filling
Cream Cheese Frosting
1 (6-ounce) package frozen
       shredded coconut, thawed
Garnish: fresh mint sprig

• **Grease** bottom and sides of three 9-inch round cakepans; line bottoms with wax paper. Grease and flour wax paper.
• **Drain** pineapple, reserving ¾ cup juice. Remove ¼ cup reserved pineapple juice for Cream Cheese Frosting, and reserve crushed pineapple for Pineapple Filling.
• **Beat** butter at medium speed with an electric mixer until creamy; gradually add sugar, beating well. Add eggs, one at a time, beating until blended after each addition.
• **Combine** ½ cup reserved pineapple juice and soft drink. Add flour to butter mixture alternately with juice mixture, beginning and ending with flour. Beat at low speed until blended after each addition. Stir in flavorings. Pour batter into prepared cakepans.
• **Bake** at 350° for 25 to 30 minutes or until a wooden pick inserted in center comes out clean. Remove from pans immediately; cool on wire racks.
• **Spread** ¾ cup Pineapple Filling between each cake layer, and spread remaining filling on top of cake, spreading to within ½ inch of edges on all layers. Spread Cream Cheese Frosting on sides of cake, and pipe border around top, if desired. Sprinkle coconut on sides and border, and garnish, if desired. **Yield:** 1 (3-layer) cake.

* For lemon-lime soft drink, we used 7-Up. Its specific level of carbonation makes the layers rise beautifully.

Pineapple Filling

QUICK!

2 cups sugar
¼ cup cornstarch
1 cup reserved drained crushed
       pineapple
1 cup water

• **Stir** together sugar and cornstarch in a saucepan. Stir in pineapple and water.
• **Cook** over low heat, stirring occasionally, 15 minutes or until very thick. Cool. **Yield:** 3 cups.

Cream Cheese Frosting

QUICK!

½ cup butter, softened
1 (3-ounce) package cream cheese, softened
1 (16-ounce) package powdered sugar, sifted
1 teaspoon vanilla extract
3 to 4 tablespoons reserved pineapple juice

● **Beat** butter and cream cheese at medium speed with an electric mixer until blended. Gradually add powdered sugar, vanilla, and enough pineapple juice to make frosting a good spreading consistency, mixing well. **Yield:** 2 cups.

Erma Jean (Jeannie) Reese
Warrenton, Georgia

LANE CAKE

1 cup unsalted butter, softened
2 cups sugar
3½ cups all-purpose flour
1 tablespoon baking powder
¼ teaspoon salt
1 cup milk
8 egg whites
Lane Cake Filling

● **Beat** butter in a large mixing bowl at medium speed with an electric mixer until creamy; gradually add sugar, beating well.
● **Combine** flour, baking powder, and salt; add to butter mixture alternately with milk, beginning and ending with flour mixture. Beat at low speed after each addition until blended.
● **Beat** egg whites at high speed until stiff peaks form. Stir one-third of egg whites into batter; gently fold in remaining egg whites. Spoon into three greased and floured 9-inch round cakepans.
● **Bake** at 325° for 25 minutes or until a wooden pick inserted in center comes out clean. Cool in pans on wire racks 10 minutes; remove from pans, and let cool completely on wire racks.
● **Spread** Lane Cake Filling between layers, and on top and sides of cake. **Yield:** 1 (3-layer) cake.

Lane Cake Filling

12 egg yolks
1½ cups sugar
¾ cup unsalted butter, melted
1½ teaspoons vanilla extract
½ cup bourbon
1½ cups finely chopped pecans
1½ cups finely chopped raisins
1½ cups flaked coconut

● **Beat** egg yolks at medium speed with an electric mixer 3 minutes; gradually add sugar, beating until blended. Beat 3 minutes. Gradually add butter; beat at low speed until blended.
● **Pour** mixture into top of a double boiler; bring water to a boil. Cook, stirring constantly, 20 minutes or until mixture thickens and candy thermometer registers 185°. Remove from heat; stir in vanilla and remaining ingredients. Cool slightly. **Yield:** 5 cups.

Chefs Edna Lewis and Scott Peacock
Atlanta, Georgia

LUSCIOUS LEMON CAKE

8 egg yolks
¾ cup butter or margarine, softened
1¼ cups sugar
2½ cups sifted cake flour
1 tablespoon baking powder
¼ teaspoon salt
¾ cup milk
1 teaspoon grated lemon rind
1 teaspoon fresh lemon juice
1 teaspoon vanilla extract
Lemon Frosting
Garnishes: lemon wedges, fresh mint leaves

● **Beat** egg yolks at high speed with an electric mixer 4 minutes or until thick and pale. Set aside.
● **Beat** butter at medium speed with an electric mixer until creamy; gradually add sugar, beating well. Add egg yolks, beating well.
● **Combine** flour, baking powder, and salt; add to butter mixture alternately with milk, beginning and ending with flour mixture. Mix after each addition. Stir in lemon rind, juice, and vanilla.

● **Spoon** batter into three greased and floured 8-inch round cakepans. Bake at 375° for 18 to 20 minutes or until a wooden pick inserted in center comes out clean. Cool in pans on wire racks 10 minutes; remove from pans, and cool completely on wire racks.
● **Spoon** about 1 cup Lemon Frosting into a decorating bag fitted with a large tip, and set aside. Spread remaining Lemon Frosting between layers and on top and sides of cake. Pipe 8 rosettes around top edge of cake, and garnish, if desired. Chill until serving time. **Yield:** 1 (3-layer) cake.

Lemon Frosting

QUICK!

1 cup butter or margarine, softened
2 teaspoons grated lemon rind
⅓ cup fresh lemon juice
8 cups sifted powdered sugar
1 to 2 tablespoons half-and-half (optional)

● **Beat** butter at medium speed with an electric mixer until creamy; stir in lemon rind and juice. (Mixture will appear curdled.) Gradually add sugar; beat at high speed 4 minutes or until spreading consistency. Gradually add half-and-half, if necessary. **Yield:** 4 cups.

Shelby W. Adkins
Penhook, Virginia

Peaches-and-Cream Cake

PEACHES-AND-CREAM CAKE
(pictured at left)

"When I started candying flowers 15 years ago, I thought it was the most wonderful thing in the world. They make a dessert special," says Marion.

1 cup unsalted butter, softened
2 cups sugar
6 large eggs
3 cups soft wheat flour
1 teaspoon baking powder
½ teaspoon baking soda
1 teaspoon salt
1 cup buttermilk
2 teaspoons vanilla extract
1 to 2 teaspoons sugar
1 cup chopped pecans, toasted
¾ cup sugar
4 egg whites
⅛ teaspoon cream of tartar
Pinch of salt
Peach Filling
Butter Whip Frosting
Candied and plain pansies

• **Beat** butter in a large mixing bowl at medium speed with an electric mixer until creamy; gradually add 2 cups sugar, beating well. Add eggs, one at a time, beating until blended after each addition.
• **Combine** flour and next 3 ingredients; add to butter mixture alternately with buttermilk, beginning and ending with flour mixture. Beat at low speed until blended after each addition. Stir in vanilla.
• **Pour** batter into two greased and floured 10-inch round cakepans or springform pans.
• **Bake** at 325° for 30 to 35 minutes or until a wooden pick inserted in center comes out clean. Cool in pans on wire racks 10 minutes; remove cake layers from pans, and let cool completely on wire racks.
• **Grease** a 10-inch springform pan; line bottom of pan with aluminum foil. Grease foil; sprinkle foil and sides of pan with 1 to 2 teaspoons sugar. Set aside.
• **Position** knife blade in food processor bowl; add pecans and ¾ cup sugar. Process until pecans are ground,

stopping once to scrape down sides; set aside.
• **Combine** egg whites, cream of tartar, and pinch of salt; beat at high speed with an electric mixer until soft peaks form. Fold in pecan mixture, and spread in prepared pan.
• **Bake** at 250° for 1 hour and 30 minutes to 1 hour and 45 minutes or until thoroughly dry. Cool completely in pan on a wire rack, and carefully remove from pan.
• **Place** 1 cake layer on a cake plate; spread cake layer with half of Peach Filling. Spread 1 cup Butter Whip Frosting over filling, and top with meringue layer.
• **Spread** remaining filling over meringue layer, and spread 1½ cups frosting over filling; top with remaining cake layer. Spread top and sides of cake with remaining frosting, as desired. Chill 2 to 3 hours; decorate with pansies. **Yield:** 1 (10-inch) cake.

Note: To make candied pansies, sprinkle 2 envelopes unflavored gelatin over 2 cups warm water; stir with a wire whisk until gelatin dissolves. Dip pansies into gelatin mixture, shaking to remove excess; sprinkle all sides of pansies with superfine sugar, covering completely. Place pansies on baking sheets; let stand 30 minutes or until dry and firm.

Peach Filling

1¾ cups dried peaches
1½ cups water
¼ cup sugar
2 tablespoons light corn
   syrup

• **Combine** dried peaches and water in a medium saucepan, and bring to a boil. Cover, remove from heat, and let stand 30 minutes or until peaches are soft.
• **Add** sugar and syrup; bring to a boil. Reduce heat, and simmer 30 minutes or until most of liquid evaporates; remove from heat.
• **Position** knife blade in food processor bowl; add peach mixture. Process until mixture is smooth, stopping once to scrape down sides; cool. **Yield:** 2 cups.

Butter Whip Frosting
QUICK!

To enhance the peach flavor of this spectacular cake, this classic buttercream frosting boasts two flavorings – vanilla and almond.

1¼ cups unsalted butter,
   softened
2 (16-ounce) packages powdered
   sugar, sifted
2 teaspoons vanilla extract
¼ teaspoon almond extract
1½ cups whipping cream

• **Combine** butter, 1 cup powdered sugar, and flavorings; beat at medium speed with an electric mixer until blended.
• **Add** remaining powdered sugar to butter mixture alternately with whipping cream, beating well after each addition. Beat at high speed until mixture is smooth and spreading consistency. **Yield:** about 6 cups.

Marion Sullivan
Charleston, South Carolina

ITALIAN CREAM CAKE

This cake is sure to win raves from your family – as it did in our Test Kitchens.

½ cup butter or margarine, softened
½ cup shortening
2 cups sugar
5 large eggs, separated
1 tablespoon vanilla extract
2 cups all-purpose flour
1 teaspoon baking soda
1 cup buttermilk
1 cup flaked coconut
Nutty Cream Cheese Frosting
Garnishes: toasted pecan halves, chopped pecans

• **Beat** butter and shortening in a large mixing bowl at medium speed with an electric mixer until creamy; gradually add sugar, beating well. Add egg yolks, one at a time, beating until blended after each addition. Add vanilla; beat until blended.
• **Combine** flour and soda; add to butter mixture alternately with buttermilk, beginning and ending with flour mixture. Beat at low speed until blended after each addition. Stir in coconut.
• **Beat** egg whites until stiff peaks form; fold into batter. Pour batter into three greased and floured 9-inch round cakepans.
• **Bake** at 350° for 25 minutes or until a wooden pick inserted in center comes out clean. Cool in pans on wire racks 10 minutes; remove from pans, and let cool completely on wire racks.
• **Spread** Nutty Cream Cheese Frosting between layers and on top and sides of cake. Garnish, if desired. **Yield:** 1 (3-layer) cake.

Nutty Cream Cheese Frosting

QUICK!

1 cup chopped pecans
1 (8-ounce) package cream cheese, softened
½ cup butter or margarine, softened
1 tablespoon vanilla extract
1 (16-ounce) package powdered sugar, sifted

• **Place** pecans in a shallow pan; bake at 350° for 5 to 10 minutes or until toasted, stirring occasionally. Cool.
• **Beat** cream cheese, butter, and vanilla at medium speed with an electric mixer until creamy. Add sugar, beating at low speed until blended. Beat at high speed until smooth; stir in pecans. **Yield:** about 4 cups.

Donna Willcut
Pryor, Oklahoma

WHIPPED CREAM CAKE

This petite cake is perfect for luncheons, anniversary dinners, teas, or birthday parties. Plan on it serving 6 to 8. And if you want a decorator look without the trouble of a homemade cake, follow the baking and assembling directions here, using 1 (18.25-ounce) package white cake mix and 2 (16-ounce) containers vanilla ready-to-spread frosting.

1 cup whipping cream
2 large eggs
1 cup sugar
1 teaspoon vanilla extract
1½ cups sifted cake flour
2 teaspoons baking powder
¼ teaspoon salt
Buttercream Frosting

• **Grease** three 6- x 2-inch round cakepans; line with wax paper. Grease and flour wax paper; set aside.
• **Beat** whipping cream with a wire whisk until foamy; set aside.
• **Beat** eggs with a wire whisk until foamy; stir in sugar and vanilla extract. Gradually stir whipping cream into egg mixture.
• **Combine** flour, baking powder, and salt; fold into whipping cream mixture. Pour batter into prepared pans.
• **Bake** at 350° for 18 minutes or until a wooden pick inserted in center comes out clean. Cool in pans on wire racks 10 minutes; remove from pans, and let cool completely on wire racks.
• **Spread** 2½ cups Buttercream Frosting between layers and on top and sides of cake.
• **Spoon** about 1 cup frosting into a decorating or heavy-duty, zip-top plastic bag fitted with a No. 5 round tip; pipe curly lines over top and sides of cake. Do not overlap lines.
• **Spoon** remaining frosting into a decorating or heavy-duty, zip-top plastic bag fitted with a No. 2B large basketweave tip; pipe a ruffle around base of cake. **Yield:** 1 (3-layer) cake.

Note: If you have only one 6- x 2-inch round cakepan, bake layers one at a time. Cover the remaining batter and set aside while each layer bakes. Wash, dry, and prepare pan again before baking each remaining layer.

Buttercream Frosting

QUICK!

1½ cups butter
1 (16-ounce) package powdered sugar, sifted
2 tablespoons milk
1 teaspoon vanilla extract

• **Beat** butter at medium speed with an electric mixer until creamy; gradually add sugar, beating until light and fluffy. Add milk and vanilla, beating to spreading consistency. **Yield:** about 4 cups.

Helen Walker
Edmond, Oklahoma

CAMEO CAKE

1½ cups butter
¾ cup water
1 (4-ounce) bar white chocolate, broken into pieces *
1½ cups buttermilk
4 large eggs, lightly beaten
1½ teaspoons vanilla extract
3½ cups all-purpose flour, divided
1 cup chopped pecans, toasted
2¼ cups sugar
1½ teaspoons baking soda
White Chocolate-Cream Cheese Frosting
Garnishes: crystallized violas with leaves, shaved white chocolate, or toasted chopped pecans

• **Combine** butter and water in a medium saucepan; bring to a boil over medium heat, stirring occasionally.

Remove from heat. Add white chocolate, stirring until chocolate melts. Stir in buttermilk, eggs, and vanilla; set aside.

• **Combine** ½ cup flour and 1 cup pecans, stirring to coat; set aside.

• **Combine** remaining 3 cups flour, sugar, and soda in a large bowl; gradually stir in white chocolate mixture. Fold in pecan mixture. (Batter will be thin.) Pour into three greased and floured 9-inch round cakepans.

• **Bake** at 350° for 20 to 25 minutes or until a wooden pick inserted in center comes out clean. Cool in pans on wire racks 10 minutes; remove from pans, and let cool completely on wire racks.

• **Spread** White Chocolate-Cream Cheese Frosting between layers and on top and sides of cake. Store cake in refrigerator. Garnish, if desired. **Yield:** 1 (3-layer) cake.

White Chocolate-Cream Cheese Frosting

QUICK!

1 (4-ounce) bar white chocolate *
1 (8-ounce) package cream cheese, softened
1 (3-ounce) package cream cheese, softened
⅓ cup butter or margarine, softened
6½ cups sifted powdered sugar
1½ teaspoons vanilla extract

• **Melt** white chocolate in a heavy saucepan over low heat, stirring constantly. Remove from heat; cool 10 minutes, stirring occasionally.

• **Beat** cream cheese and butter at medium speed with an electric mixer until creamy. Gradually add white chocolate, beating constantly until blended. Gradually add powdered sugar, beating until smooth. Stir in vanilla. **Yield:** about 5 cups.

* For white chocolate, we used Ghirardelli Classic White Confection.

CHOCOLATE CHIFFON CAKE WITH COFFEE BUTTERCREAM

Make-ahead tip: Bake and freeze the cake layers up to 3 months ahead. Assemble a few hours before serving.

6 (1-ounce) squares bittersweet chocolate, chopped
¾ cup water
1 cup butter, softened
2 cups sugar
4 large eggs
2 teaspoons vanilla extract
2½ cups sifted cake flour
2 teaspoons baking soda
⅛ teaspoon salt
1½ cups sour cream
Coffee Buttercream
Chocolate-covered coffee beans

• **Combine** chocolate and water in a heavy saucepan; cook over low heat, stirring constantly, until melted.

• **Beat** butter at medium speed with an electric mixer until creamy; gradually add sugar, beating well. Add eggs, one at a time, beating after each addition. Add chocolate mixture and vanilla; beat 1 minute or just until combined.

• **Combine** flour, soda, and salt; add to chocolate mixture alternately with sour cream, beginning and ending with flour mixture. Mix at low speed just until blended after each addition. Pour batter into three greased and floured 9-inch round cakepans.

• **Bake** at 350° for 25 to 30 minutes or until a wooden pick inserted in center comes out clean. Cool in pans on wire racks 10 minutes; remove from pans, and let cool completely on wire racks.

• **Spread** Coffee Buttercream between layers and on top and sides of cake. Arrange coffee beans on top of cake. **Yield:** 1 (3-layer) cake.

Coffee Buttercream

QUICK!

4 to 5 tablespoons instant coffee granules
3 tablespoons hot water
1 cup butter, softened
6 cups sifted powdered sugar

• **Dissolve** coffee granules in water.

• **Beat** butter at medium speed with an electric mixer until creamy; gradually add coffee mixture and sugar, beating until blended. **Yield:** 2½ cups.

Susan Curtin
Birmingham, Alabama

APPLESAUCE CAKE

¾ cup shortening
2 cups sugar
3 large eggs
3 cups all-purpose flour
1½ teaspoons baking soda
½ teaspoon salt
1 teaspoon ground cinnamon
½ teaspoon ground cloves
¼ teaspoon ground nutmeg
1½ cups applesauce
1 cup raisins
1 cup chopped walnuts or pecans

• **Beat** shortening at medium speed with an electric mixer 2 minutes or until fluffy. Gradually add sugar, beating 5 to 7 minutes. Add eggs, one at a time, beating just until yellow disappears.

• **Combine** flour and next 5 ingredients; add to shortening mixture alternately with applesauce, beginning and ending with flour mixture. Beat at low speed just until blended after each addition. Stir in raisins and chopped nuts.

• **Pour** batter into a greased and floured 12-cup Bundt pan.

• **Bake** at 350° for 1 hour or until a wooden pick inserted in center comes out clean, shielding with aluminum foil after 45 minutes to prevent excessive browning.

• **Cool** cake in pan on a wire rack 10 to 15 minutes; remove from pan, and let cool completely on wire rack. **Yield:** 1 (10-inch) cake.

Virginia Cookery, Past and Present
Olivet Episcopal Church Women
Franconia, Virginia

APPLE-WALNUT CAKE

1 cup butter or margarine,
    softened
2 cups sugar
2 large eggs
1 tablespoon vanilla extract
2 cups sifted cake flour
1 teaspoon baking powder
¼ teaspoon salt
1 (8-ounce) carton sour cream
1 cup peeled, finely chopped
    apple
1 cup finely chopped walnuts
2 tablespoons brown sugar
½ teaspoon ground cinnamon
Cream Cheese Glaze

• **Beat** butter at medium speed with an electric mixer until creamy; gradually add 2 cups sugar, beating well. Add eggs, one at a time, beating after each addition. Stir in vanilla.

• **Combine** flour, baking powder, and salt. Add flour mixture to butter mixture alternately with sour cream, beginning and ending with flour mixture. Mix at low speed just until blended after each addition. Pour half of batter into a greased and floured 12-cup Bundt pan.

• **Combine** apple and next 3 ingredients; spoon over batter in pan, leaving a ½-inch border around center and outer edges. Add remaining batter.

• **Bake** at 350° for 50 to 55 minutes or until a wooden pick inserted in center comes out clean. Cool in pan on a wire rack 10 minutes. Remove from pan; cool completely on wire rack.

• **Drizzle** with Cream Cheese Glaze. Store cake in refrigerator. **Yield:** 1 (10-inch) cake.

Cream Cheese Glaze

QUICK!

1 (3-ounce) package cream cheese,
    softened
2 to 2½ teaspoons milk
1 teaspoon vanilla extract
Dash of salt
1½ cups sifted powdered sugar

• **Beat** cream cheese in a small mixing bowl at medium speed with an electric mixer until creamy. Add milk, vanilla,

and salt, and beat until smooth. Gradually add powdered sugar, beating until smooth. **Yield:** 1 cup.

Louise W. Mayer
Richmond, Virginia

ORANGE CAKE
(pictured on opposite page)

½ cup butter, softened
2 cups sugar
7 large eggs, separated
3 cups sifted cake flour
1 tablespoon baking powder
¼ teaspoon salt
½ cup fresh orange juice
½ cup water
1 teaspoon vanilla extract
Orange Glaze
Candied Orange Zest

• **Beat** butter at medium speed with an electric mixer about 2 minutes or until creamy. Gradually add sugar, beating 5 to 7 minutes.

• **Beat** egg yolks lightly; add to butter mixture, beating until well blended.

• **Combine** flour, baking powder, and salt; add to butter mixture alternately with orange juice and water, beginning and ending with flour mixture. Beat at low speed with an electric mixer until blended after each addition. Stir in vanilla.

• **Beat** egg whites at high speed with an electric mixer until foamy; reduce speed to medium, and beat until stiff peaks form. Fold egg white into batter; spoon batter into a greased and floured 12-cup Bundt pan or 10-inch tube pan.

• **Bake** at 350° for 40 minutes or until a wooden pick inserted in center comes out clean. Immediately place pan on a double layer of damp cloth towels; press towels around sides of pan, and let stand 10 to 15 minutes. Remove cake from pan, and let cool completely on a wire rack.

• **Spoon** Orange Glaze over cake; top with Candied Orange Zest. **Yield:** 1 (10-inch) cake.

Orange Glaze

2 large oranges
2 cups sugar
1 tablespoon cornstarch
⅓ cup lemon juice
8 egg yolks, lightly beaten
½ cup butter, softened

• **Squeeze** juice from oranges, and pour through a wire-mesh strainer into a 1-cup liquid measuring cup, straining out any seeds. Measure 1 cup orange juice; reserve remaining orange juice for another use.

• **Combine** sugar and cornstarch in a small saucepan; add lemon juice and 1 cup orange juice, stirring well with a wire whisk. Cook over low heat, stirring constantly, until sugar dissolves (about 10 minutes).

• **Stir** about one-fourth of hot mixture into yolks; add to remaining hot mixture, stirring constantly. Cook over low heat, stirring constantly, 10 minutes or until mixture is thickened. Remove from heat; add softened butter, stirring until well blended. Cool; cover and chill. **Yield:** 3½ cups.

Candied Orange Zest

2 large oranges
1 cup water
½ cup sugar
Sugar (optional)

• **Remove** zest (orange part only) from oranges, using a zester, being careful not to remove white pith. Cut zest into 2-inch strips.

• **Combine** water and ½ cup sugar in a small saucepan; Bring to a boil over medium heat. Reduce heat to low; stir in rind, and cook 15 to 20 minutes or until candy thermometer registers 220°.

• **Remove** zest strips from syrup with a slotted spoon, and spread in a single layer on wax paper to cool.

• **Sprinkle** with additional sugar, if desired. **Yield:** 1 cup.

Sissy Nash and Kathy Nash Cary
Louisville, Kentucky

Orange Cake

CHOCOLATE-SPICE POTATO CAKE

1 cup butter or margarine, softened
2 cups sugar
4 large eggs
2 cups all-purpose flour
2 teaspoons baking powder
1 teaspoon ground cinnamon
1 teaspoon ground cloves
1 teaspoon ground nutmeg
¼ cup cocoa
½ cup milk
⅔ cup instant potato flakes
1 cup (6 ounces) semisweet chocolate morsels
1 cup chopped pecans

• **Beat** butter at medium speed with an electric mixer about 2 minutes or until creamy; gradually add sugar, beating 5 to 7 minutes. Add eggs, one at a time, beating just until yellow disappears.
• **Combine** flour and next 5 ingredients; add to butter mixture alternately with milk, beginning and ending with flour mixture. Set batter aside.
• **Prepare** potato flakes according to package directions. Add mashed potato to batter, and beat until blended. Stir in chocolate morsels and pecans. Pour batter into a greased and floured 10-inch tube pan.
• **Bake** at 350° for 1 hour and 20 minutes or until a wooden pick inserted in center comes out clean. Cool in pan on a wire rack 10 minutes; remove from pan, and let cool completely on wire rack. **Yield:** 1 (10-inch) cake.

Anna Rucker
Norfolk, Virginia

CANDY BAR CAKE

3 (2.15-ounce) chocolate-coated caramel and creamy nougat bars, chopped *
1 cup butter, softened and divided
2 cups sugar
4 large eggs
1 teaspoon vanilla extract
3 cups all-purpose flour
½ teaspoon baking soda
1 cup buttermilk
1 cup chopped pecans

• **Combine** candy bars and ½ cup butter in a heavy saucepan; cook over medium heat, stirring constantly, until candy bars melt. Set aside.
• **Beat** remaining ½ cup butter at medium speed with an electric mixer about 2 minutes or until creamy. Gradually add sugar, beating at medium speed 5 to 7 minutes. Add eggs, one at a time, beating just until yellow disappears. Stir in vanilla.
• **Combine** flour and soda; add to butter mixture alternately with buttermilk, beginning and ending with flour mixture. Mix at low speed just until blended after each addition. Stir in candy bar mixture and pecans.
• **Pour** batter into a greased and floured 10-inch tube pan. Bake at 325° for 1 hour and 25 minutes or until a wooden pick inserted in center of cake comes out clean. Cool in pan 15 minutes on a wire rack. Remove from pan, and let cool completely on wire rack. **Yield:** 1 (10-inch) cake.

* For the chocolate-coated caramel and creamy nougat bars, we used Milky Way candy bars.

Marie Bilbo
Meadville, Mississippi

GRANDMOTHER'S FRUITCAKE

Bake a bit of history. Grandmother's Fruitcake has been in Catherine's family for 150 years.

4 cups all-purpose flour, divided
1 pound chopped dates
1 pound candied citron
1 pound chopped pecans
1 pound dried figs, coarsely chopped
1 (15-ounce) package raisins
1 (10-ounce) package currants
1 cup butter or margarine, softened
2 cups sugar
12 large eggs, lightly beaten
1 cup milk
¾ cup light corn syrup
2 teaspoons baking soda
1 teaspoon baking powder
2 teaspoons ground nutmeg
2 teaspoons ground cinnamon
2 teaspoons ground allspice
1 cup brandy
30 pecan halves (optional)
Brandy
6 red candied cherry halves (optional)

• **Make** a liner for a 10-inch tube pan by drawing an 18-inch circle on brown paper (not recycled). Cut out circle; set pan in center, and draw around base of pan and inside tube. Remove pan, and fold circle into eighths, with lines on the outside.
• **Cut** off pointed tip of triangle along line. Unfold paper; cut along folds to the outside line. Place liner in pan; grease and set aside. Repeat procedure for second tube pan.
• **Combine** ½ cup flour, dates, and next 5 ingredients in a large bowl, tossing gently to coat. Set aside.
• **Beat** butter in a large mixing bowl at medium speed with an electric mixer until creamy; gradually add sugar, beating mixture well. Add eggs, beating until blended after each addition. Add milk and corn syrup, mixing well.
• **Combine** remaining 3½ cups flour, baking soda, and next 4 ingredients; add to butter mixture alternately with 1 cup brandy, beginning and ending with flour mixture. Mix at low speed after

each addition until blended. Pour over fruit mixture; stir well. Spoon batter evenly into prepared pans. Place pecan halves in flower designs on top of batter, if desired.

● **Bake** at 350° for 1 hour or until a wooden pick inserted in center comes out clean. Remove from oven; cool completely in pans on wire racks.

● **Remove** cakes from pans; peel paper from cakes, and discard. Wrap cakes in brandy-soaked cheesecloth; store in airtight containers in a cool place. Pour a small amount of brandy over cakes each week for at least 1 month. Before serving, place cherry halves in center of pecan flowers, if desired. **Yield:** 2 (5-pound) cakes.

Catherine Maddux
Memphis, Tennessee

NO-BAKE FRUITCAKE

For gifts, cut each loaf lengthwise into fourths. Wrap in plastic wrap; then in decorative paper. Tie ends with ribbon.

1 (16-ounce) package round buttery crackers
1 pound red and green candied cherries
1 pound candied pineapple, chopped
1 (15-ounce) package golden raisins
4 cups chopped pecans, toasted
1 cup chopped walnuts, toasted
1 (7-ounce) can flaked coconut
1 (12-ounce) can evaporated milk
1 pound large marshmallows

● **Line** three 9- x 5- x 3-inch loafpans with heavy-duty plastic wrap; set aside. Place 1 stack crackers in a large heavy-duty, zip-top plastic bag; finely crush crackers, using a meat mallet or rolling pin. Place cracker crumbs in a large bowl. Repeat procedure with remaining crackers.

● **Add** cherries and next 5 ingredients to crumbs, tossing gently to coat.

● **Combine** evaporated milk and marshmallows in a heavy saucepan; cook over medium heat, stirring constantly, until marshmallows melt. Pour over fruit mixture, and stir well. Spoon mixture evenly into prepared pans, pressing firmly.

● **Cover** and store in refrigerator 3 days. Remove from pans; wrap in heavy-duty plastic wrap, and then aluminum foil. Store in the refrigerator. **Yield:** 3 (2½-pound) cakes.

Lois Edwards
Sparta, North Carolina

CHOCOLATE FRUITCAKES

1 cup butter or margarine
6 (1-ounce) squares semisweet chocolate
1¼ cups sugar
3 large eggs
1 cup all-purpose flour
¼ teaspoon salt
1 cup red candied cherries, cut in half
1 cup green candied pineapple, cut into ½-inch wedges
¾ cup walnut halves
¾ cup pecan halves
Garnishes: red candied cherries, smilax leaves

● **Melt** butter and chocolate in a heavy saucepan over low heat, stirring often. Remove from heat; cool 15 minutes.

● **Stir** in sugar. Add eggs, one at a time, stirring well after each addition. Add flour and salt, stirring until blended. Stir in cherries and next 3 ingredients. Spoon mixture into four greased and floured 5- x 3- x 2-inch loafpans.

● **Bake** at 350° for 35 minutes or until a wooden pick inserted in center comes out clean. Cool in pans on wire racks 10 minutes; remove from pans, and cool on wire racks.

● **Wrap** in heavy-duty plastic wrap; chill 8 hours before cutting. Garnish, if desired. **Yield:** 4 (12-ounce) loaves.

Note: To make a less rich chocolate fruitcake, reduce butter to ½ cup and chocolate to 4 (1-ounce) squares.

Leslie Coles Walker
Chesapeake, Virginia

SMOOTHEST SOUTHERN POUND CAKE

1 cup butter or margarine, softened
3 cups sugar
3 cups sifted cake flour
¼ teaspoon baking soda
6 large eggs
1 (8-ounce) carton sour cream
1 teaspoon vanilla extract

● **Beat** butter at medium speed with an electric mixer (not a handheld one) about 2 minutes or until creamy. Gradually add sugar, beating at medium speed 5 to 7 minutes. Combine cake flour and baking soda, and add to butter mixture 1 cup at a time. (Batter will be extremely thick.)

● **Separate** eggs; add yolks to batter, and mix well. Stir in sour cream and vanilla.

● **Beat** egg whites until stiff, and fold into batter.

● **Spoon** into a greased and floured 12-cup Bundt or 10-inch tube pan. Bake at 300° for 2 hours or until a wooden pick inserted in center comes out clean. (You may also spoon batter into two 9- x 5- x 3-inch loafpans; bake at 300° for 1½ hours or until a wooden pick inserted in center comes out clean.) Cool in pan on a wire rack 10 to 15 minutes. Remove from pan; cool completely on wire rack. **Yield:** 1 (10-inch) cake or 2 loaves.

Note: Standard Mixing Method: If you are using a handheld mixer or prefer a conventional pound cake method, here's the procedure we suggest.

● **Beat** butter at medium speed with an electric mixer about 2 minutes or until creamy. Gradually add 3 cups sugar, beating at medium speed 5 to 7 minutes. Add eggs, one at time, beating just until yellow disappears.

● **Combine** cake flour and baking soda; add to butter mixture alternately with sour cream, beginning and ending with flour mixture. Mix at lowest speed just until mixture is blended after each addition. Stir in vanilla. Bake as directed.

Chip Smith
Houston, Texas
and Paul Frederick
Huntsville, Alabama

POUND CAKE

Vegetable cooking spray
All-purpose flour
½ cup corn oil margarine,
    softened
⅔ cup sugar
⅓ cup fat-free egg substitute
2½ cups sifted cake flour
½ teaspoon baking powder
¼ teaspoon baking soda
¼ teaspoon salt
1 (8-ounce) carton low-fat vanilla
    yogurt
1 tablespoon vanilla extract
¾ teaspoon almond extract

• **Coat** bottom of a 9- x 5- x 3-inch loaf-pan with cooking spray; dust with flour, and set aside.
• **Beat** margarine at medium speed with an electric mixer until creamy. Gradually add sugar; beat well. Add egg substitute; beat until blended.
• **Combine** flour and next 3 ingredients; add to margarine mixture alternately with yogurt, beginning and ending with flour mixture. Mix just until blended after each addition. Stir in flavorings.
• **Spoon** batter into prepared pan. Bake at 350° for 1 hour and 5 minutes or until a wooden pick inserted in center comes out clean. Cool in pan on a wire rack 10 minutes; remove cake from pan, and let cool completely on wire rack. **Yield:** 18 servings.

Mrs. Abner Belcher
Americus, Georgia

♥ Per serving: Calories 143
Fat 5.3g Cholesterol 1mg
Sodium 66mg

AZTEC POUND CAKE

1 cup butter, softened
1 tablespoon grated orange rind
2 cups sugar
6 large eggs, separated
2 cups all-purpose flour
1 cup yellow cornmeal
½ teaspoon baking soda
¼ teaspoon salt
1 (8-ounce) carton sour cream
1 teaspoon vanilla extract

• **Beat** butter and orange rind at medium speed with an electric mixer about 2 minutes or until creamy; gradually add sugar, beating well. Add egg yolks, one at a time, beating just until yellow disappears.
• **Combine** flour, cornmeal, soda, and salt; add to butter mixture alternately with sour cream, beginning and ending with flour mixture. Beat at low speed just until blended after each addition. Stir in vanilla.
• **Beat** egg whites at high speed until stiff peaks form; fold into batter. Pour batter into two greased and floured 8½-x 4½- x 3-inch loafpans.
• **Bake** at 325° for 1 hour and 5 minutes or until a wooden pick inserted in center comes out clean.
• **Cool** cakes in pans on a wire rack 10 minutes; remove from pans, and let cool completely on wire rack. **Yield:** 2 loaves.

Joy Knight Allard
San Antonio, Texas

BROWN SUGAR-RUM POUND CAKE

1½ cups butter, softened
1 (16-ounce) package light brown
    sugar
1 cup sugar
5 large eggs
¾ cup milk
¼ cup dark rum
2 teaspoons vanilla extract
3 cups all-purpose flour
1 teaspoon baking powder
¼ teaspoon salt
1 cup chopped pecans
Sweetened whipped cream
    (optional)

• **Beat** butter at medium speed with an electric mixer about 2 minutes or until creamy. Gradually add sugars, beating 5 to 7 minutes. Add eggs, one at a time, beating just until yellow disappears.
• **Combine** milk, rum, and vanilla, and set aside.
• **Combine** flour, baking powder, and salt; add to butter mixture alternately with milk mixture, beginning and ending with flour mixture. Beat at low speed just until blended after each addition. Fold in chopped pecans. Pour batter into a greased and floured 13-cup Bundt pan.
• **Bake** at 325° for 1 hour and 20 minutes or until a wooden pick inserted in center comes out clean.
• **Cool** in pan on a wire rack 10 to 15 minutes; remove from pan, and let cool completely on wire rack. Serve with sweetened whipped cream, if desired. **Yield:** 1 (10-inch) cake.

Denise Allen
Birmingham, Alabama

BLACK WALNUT POUND CAKE

1 cup butter, softened
½ cup shortening
3 cups sugar
5 large eggs
3 cups all-purpose flour
½ teaspoon baking powder
1 cup milk
½ cup black walnuts, chopped
½ teaspoon vanilla extract

• **Beat** butter and shortening at medium speed with an electric mixer about 2 minutes or until creamy. Gradually add sugar, beating at medium speed 5 to 7 minutes. Add eggs, one at a time, beating just until yellow disappears.
• **Combine** flour and baking powder; add to butter mixture alternately with milk, beginning and ending with flour mixture. Mix at low speed just until blended after each addition. Stir in walnuts and vanilla. Pour batter into a greased and floured 10-inch tube pan.
• **Bake** at 325° for 1 hour and 30 minutes or until a wooden pick inserted in center comes out clean. Cool in pan on a wire rack 10 to 15 minutes; remove from pan, and let cool completely on wire rack. **Yield:** 1 (10-inch) cake.

Note: You can freeze baked cake up to 3 months. Thaw and, if desired, reheat to serve.

BETTY'S BUTTERNUT POUND CAKE WITH CARAMEL SAUCE

1 cup butter or margarine, softened
½ cup shortening
3 cups sugar
5 large eggs
1 (5-ounce) can evaporated milk
3¼ cups all-purpose flour
¼ teaspoon salt
2 tablespoons vanilla, butter, and nut flavoring
Caramel Sauce

• **Beat** butter and shortening at medium speed with an electric mixer about 2 minutes or until creamy. Gradually add sugar, beating at medium speed 5 to 7 minutes. Add eggs, one at a time, beating just until yellow disappears.
• **Add** enough water to evaporated milk to measure 1 cup.
• **Combine** flour and salt; add to butter mixture alternately with milk mixture, beginning and ending with flour mixture. Mix at low speed just until blended after each addition. Stir in flavoring. Pour into a greased and floured 10-inch tube pan.
• **Bake** at 325° for 1 hour and 25 minutes or until a wooden pick inserted in center comes out clean. Cool in pan on a wire rack 10 to 15 minutes; remove from pan, and cool completely on wire rack. Serve with warm Caramel Sauce. **Yield:** 1 (10-inch) cake.

Note: You can bake cake in two 8½- x 4½- x 3-inch loafpans at 325° for 1 hour and 15 minutes or until a wooden pick inserted in center comes out clean.

Caramel Sauce

QUICK!

1 cup firmly packed brown sugar
1 cup whipping cream
1 cup half-and-half
3 tablespoons butter or margarine

• **Combine** all ingredients in a small heavy saucepan, and cook over low heat 45 minutes or until mixture is thickened, stirring occasionally. **Yield:** about 2 cups.

CHEESY POUND CAKE

Traditional pound cake takes on added flavor with a surprise ingredient – Cheddar cheese.

1½ cups butter, softened
1 (8-ounce) package cream cheese, softened
3 cups sugar
6 large eggs
3 cups all-purpose flour
Dash of salt
2 cups (8 ounces) finely shredded sharp Cheddar cheese
1 tablespoon vanilla extract
Apple butter (optional)

• **Beat** butter and cream cheese in a large mixing bowl at medium speed with an electric mixer about 2 minutes or until creamy. Gradually add sugar, beating at medium speed 5 to 7 minutes. Add eggs, one at a time, beating just until yellow disappears.
• **Combine** flour and salt; gradually add to butter mixture, beating at low speed just until blended after each addition. Stir in Cheddar cheese and vanilla. Pour batter into a greased and floured 10-inch tube pan.
• **Bake** at 325° for 1 hour and 45 minutes or until a wooden pick inserted in center comes out clean.
• **Cool** cake in pan on a wire rack 10 to 15 minutes; remove from pan, and let cool completely on wire rack. Serve with apple butter, if desired. **Yield:** 1 (10-inch) cake.

LaDonna Funderburk
Moultrie, Georgia

CHOCOLATE POUND CAKE

1 cup butter or margarine, softened
1 cup shortening
3 cups sugar
5 large eggs
3 cups all-purpose flour
½ teaspoon baking powder
½ teaspoon salt
¼ cup cocoa
1 cup milk
1 tablespoon vanilla extract

• **Beat** butter and shortening in a large mixing bowl at medium speed with an electric mixer about 2 minutes or until creamy. Gradually add sugar, beating at medium speed 5 to 7 minutes. Add eggs, one at a time, beating just until yellow disappears.
• **Combine** flour and next 3 ingredients; add to butter mixture alternately with milk, beginning and ending with flour mixture. Mix at low speed just until blended after each addition. Stir in vanilla. Pour batter into a greased and floured 10-inch tube pan.
• **Bake** at 325° for 1 hour and 30 minutes or until a wooden pick inserted in center of cake comes out clean. Cool in pan on a wire rack 10 to 15 minutes; remove cake from pan, and let cool completely on wire rack. **Yield:** 1 (10-inch) cake.

Louise Floyd
West Selma, Alabama

CHOCOLATE CHIP POUND CAKE

1 (18.25-ounce) yellow cake mix with pudding
1 (3.9-ounce) package chocolate instant pudding mix
½ cup sugar
¾ cup vegetable oil
¾ cup water
4 large eggs
1 (8-ounce) carton sour cream
1 cup (6 ounces) semisweet chocolate morsels
Sifted powdered sugar

• **Combine** first 3 ingredients in a large mixing bowl, stirring with a wire whisk to remove large lumps. Add oil and next 3 ingredients, stirring until smooth. Stir in chocolate morsels. Pour batter into a greased and floured 12-cup Bundt pan.
• **Bake** at 350° for 1 hour or until a wooden pick inserted in center comes out clean.
• **Cool** cake in pan on a wire rack 10 minutes; remove from pan, and let cool completely on wire rack.
• **Sprinkle** with sifted powdered sugar. **Yield:** 1 (10-inch) cake.

Becky DeWare
The Woodlands, Texas

CUTE-AS-A-BUTTON CHERRY POUND CAKE
(pictured at left)

This pound cake takes about 2 hours to bake, and the results are well worth the effort.

1 cup butter or margarine, softened
½ cup shortening
3 cups sugar
6 large eggs
1 (6-ounce) jar red maraschino cherries, drained and chopped
½ teaspoon almond extract
½ teaspoon vanilla extract
3¾ cups all-purpose flour
¼ teaspoon salt
¾ cup milk
Cream Cheese Frosting
Garnish: 1 (4-ounce) package melt-away mints *

• **Beat** butter and shortening at medium speed with an electric mixer about 2 minutes or until creamy. Gradually add sugar, beating at medium speed 5 to 7 minutes. Add eggs, one at a time, beating just until yellow disappears. Stir in cherries and flavorings.
• **Combine** flour and salt; add to the butter mixture alternately with milk, beginning and ending with the flour mixture. Mix at low speed just until blended after each addition. Pour batter into a greased and floured 10-inch tube pan.
• **Bake** at 300° for 1 hour and 45 minutes to 2 hours or until a wooden pick inserted in center comes out clean. Cool in pan on a wire rack 10 minutes; remove from pan, and let cool completely on wire rack.
• **Frost** top and sides of cake with Cream Cheese Frosting. Garnish, if desired. **Yield:** 1 (10-inch) cake.

* For melt-away mints, we used Smooth 'n Melty Petite Mints by Guittard Chocolate Company.

Cream Cheese Frosting
QUICK!

1 (8-ounce) package cream cheese, softened
½ cup butter, softened
1 (16-ounce) package powdered sugar, sifted
1 teaspoon vanilla extract

• **Combine** cream cheese and butter, beating until creamy. Add sugar and vanilla; beat until light and fluffy. **Yield:** 3 cups.

Carolyn McDaniel
York, South Carolina

BANANA POUND CAKE

1 cup shortening
½ cup butter, softened
3 cups sugar
5 large eggs
3 ripe bananas, mashed
3 tablespoons milk
2 teaspoons vanilla extract
3 cups all-purpose flour
1 teaspoon baking powder
½ teaspoon salt

• **Beat** shortening and butter at medium speed with an electric mixer about 2 minutes or until creamy. Gradually add sugar, beating at medium speed 5 to 7 minutes. Add eggs, one at a time, beating just until yellow disappears.
• **Combine** banana, milk, and vanilla.
• **Combine** flour, baking powder, and salt; add to shortening mixture alternately with banana mixture, beginning and ending with flour mixture. Beat at low speed just until blended after each addition. Pour batter into a greased and floured 10-inch tube pan.
• **Bake** at 350° for 1 hour and 20 minutes or until a wooden pick inserted in center comes out clean.
• **Cool** cake in pan on a wire rack 10 to 15 minutes; remove from pan, and let cool completely on wire rack. **Yield:** 1 (10-inch) cake.

Janet Bean
Charlotte, North Carolina

EGGNOG-PECAN POUND CAKE

1 cup butter or margarine, softened
½ cup vegetable oil
3 cups sugar
6 large eggs
3 cups all-purpose flour
1 teaspoon baking powder
1 tablespoon ground mace
1½ cups refrigerated eggnog
1 teaspoon vanilla extract
1 teaspoon lemon extract
2 cups coarsely chopped pecans

• **Beat** butter and vegetable oil at medium speed with an electric mixer about 2 minutes. Gradually add sugar, beating at medium speed 5 to 7 minutes. Add eggs, one at a time, beating just until yellow disappears.
• **Combine** flour, baking powder, and mace; add to butter mixture alternately with eggnog, beginning and ending with flour mixture. Mix at low speed just until blended after each addition. Stir in flavorings; fold in chopped pecans. Pour batter into a greased and floured 10-inch tube pan.
• **Bake** at 350° for 1 hour and 15 minutes or until a wooden pick inserted in center comes out clean; cover cake loosely with aluminum foil after 45 minutes to prevent excessive browning. Cool cake in pan on a wire rack 10 to 15 minutes; remove from pan, and let cool completely on wire rack. **Yield:** 1 (10-inch) cake.

Sharon Griffin Squire
Little Rock, Arkansas

IRISH CREAM AND COFFEE POUND CAKE

1½ cups butter or margarine, softened
3 cups sugar
6 large eggs
1½ tablespoons instant coffee granules
¼ cup hot water
½ cup Irish cream liqueur
4 cups all-purpose flour
1 teaspoon vanilla extract
1 teaspoon almond extract
Irish Cream Glaze
2 to 3 tablespoons sliced almonds, toasted

● **Beat** butter at medium speed with an electric mixer about 2 minutes or until creamy. Gradually add sugar, beating 5 to 7 minutes. Add eggs, one at time, beating just until yellow disappears.
● **Dissolve** coffee granules in hot water; stir in liqueur.
● **Add** flour to butter mixture alternately with coffee mixture, beginning and ending with flour mixture. Mix at low speed just until blended after each addition. Stir in flavorings.
● **Pour** batter into a greased and floured 13-cup Bundt pan. Bake at 300° for 1 hour and 40 minutes or until a wooden pick inserted in center comes out clean. Cool in pan on a wire rack 10 to 15 minutes; remove from pan, and let cool 30 minutes on wire rack. Brush with glaze; sprinkle with almonds. Cool completely. **Yield:** 1 (10-inch) cake.

Irish Cream Glaze

QUICK!

1 teaspoon instant coffee granules
2 tablespoons hot water
1½ tablespoons Irish cream liqueur
⅔ cup sifted powdered sugar

● **Dissolve** coffee granules in hot water; add liqueur and powdered sugar, stirring until blended. **Yield:** about ½ cup.

Note: You can freeze glazed cake up to 1 month.

H. W. Asbell
Tallahassee, Florida

LEMONY POUND CAKE

1 cup vegetable oil
2½ cups sugar
1 cup buttermilk
4 egg whites
1 large egg, lightly beaten
1 teaspoon vanilla extract
1 teaspoon butter flavoring
½ teaspoon lemon extract
3 cups all-purpose flour
¼ teaspoon baking soda
¼ teaspoon salt

● **Beat** oil and sugar at medium speed with an electric mixer 2 minutes.
● **Combine** buttermilk and next 5 ingredients, stirring until blended.
● **Combine** flour, soda, and salt; add to oil mixture alternately with buttermilk mixture, beginning and ending with flour mixture. Beat at low speed just until blended after each addition. Pour batter into a greased and floured 10-inch tube pan.
● **Bake** at 325° for 1 hour or until a wooden pick inserted in center comes out clean.
● **Cool** cake in pan on a wire rack 10 to 15 minutes; remove from pan, and let cool completely on wire rack. **Yield:** 1 (10-inch) cake.

Pretty and Pink Pound Cake Loaf: Prepare batter; divide into thirds. Spread 1 portion into a greased and floured 9- x 5- x 3-inch loafpan. Stir ¼ cup seedless raspberry jam and, if desired, 2 drops of red liquid food coloring into second portion; spread gently over first layer. Spoon remaining batter over top. Bake at 325° for 1 hour and 35 minutes or until a wooden pick inserted in center comes out clean. **Yield:** 1 loaf.

Joseph L. Whitten
Odenville, Alabama

ORANGE-PECAN POUND CAKE

1 cup butter or margarine, softened
1 cup sugar
3 large eggs
1½ teaspoons grated orange rind
½ teaspoon grated lemon rind
¼ teaspoon orange extract
½ cup finely chopped pecans
2 cups all-purpose flour, divided
½ teaspoon baking powder
⅛ teaspoon salt
⅓ cup milk
Garnishes: orange and lemon rind strips, pecan halves

● **Beat** butter at medium speed with an electric mixer about 2 minutes or until creamy. Gradually add sugar, beating at medium speed 5 to 7 minutes. Add eggs, one at a time, beating just until yellow disappears. Stir in grated rinds and orange extract.
● **Combine** pecans and ¼ cup flour; set aside. Combine remaining 1¾ cups flour, baking powder, and salt; add to butter mixture alternately with milk, beginning and ending with flour mixture. Mix at low speed just until blended after each addition; stir in floured pecans.
● **Pour** batter into a greased and floured 9- x 5- x 3-inch loafpan. Bake at 325° for 1 hour and 5 minutes or until a wooden pick inserted in center comes out clean. Cool in pan on a wire rack 10 to 15 minutes; remove from pan, and let cool completely on wire rack. Garnish, if desired. **Yield:** 1 loaf.

Gayle Nicholas Scott
Chesapeake, Virginia

TRIPLE-MINT ICE CREAM ANGEL DESSERT

1 (10-inch) angel food cake
4 cups chocolate-mint ice cream, softened and divided
2 cups pink peppermint ice cream, softened
Whipped Cream Frosting
Chocolate-Mint Sauce

● **Split** cake horizontally into 4 equal layers. Place bottom cake layer on a serving plate; spread top of layer with half of chocolate-mint ice cream to within ½ inch from edge. Top with second cake layer; cover and freeze 45 minutes or until firm. Spread second cake layer with pink peppermint ice cream. Add third cake layer; cover and freeze 45 minutes or until firm. Spread third layer with remaining chocolate-mint ice cream, and top with remaining cake layer; cover and freeze until firm.
● **Spread** Whipped Cream Frosting on top and sides of cake. Cover and freeze until firm or up to 12 hours, if desired; let stand at room temperature 15 to 20 minutes before serving. Serve with Chocolate-Mint Sauce. **Yield:** 1 (10-inch) cake.

Whipped Cream Frosting
QUICK!

3 cups whipping cream
3 tablespoons powdered sugar
1½ teaspoons vanilla extract

● **Beat** whipping cream at low speed with an electric mixer until thickened; add sugar and vanilla, beating until firm peaks form. **Yield:** 6 cups.

Chocolate-Mint Sauce
QUICK!

¾ cup half-and-half
1 (10-ounce) package mint chocolate morsels
1½ cups miniature marshmallows
¼ teaspoon salt
1 teaspoon vanilla extract

● **Heat** half-and-half in a small heavy saucepan over low heat. Stir in chocolate morsels, marshmallows, and salt; cook, stirring constantly, until chocolate morsels and marshmallows melt. Remove from heat; stir in vanilla. **Yield:** 1½ cups.

Note: Dip knife in hot water to make cutting cake easier.

Jan Carlton
Virginia Beach, Virginia

ANGEL CAKE SURPRISE

1 (10-inch) angel food cake
½ cup semisweet chocolate morsels
3 cups whipping cream, divided
1 tablespoon Chambord or other raspberry-flavored liqueur *
¼ cup sifted powdered sugar
Garnishes: grated semisweet chocolate, fresh raspberries

● **Slice** off top one-third of cake; set aside. Using a sharp knife, hollow out center of remaining cake, leaving a 1-inch shell; reserve cake pieces for another use. Place cake shell on serving plate, and set aside.
● **Melt** chocolate morsels in a small heavy saucepan over low heat until smooth, stirring often; remove from heat, and let cool.
● **Beat** 1 cup whipping cream until firm peaks form; fold in liqueur and melted chocolate. Spoon into cake shell; place top one-third of cake over filling, pressing firmly.
● **Beat** remaining 2 cups whipping cream until foamy; add powdered sugar, beating until firm peaks form. Spread sweetened whipped cream over top and sides of cake; cover and chill up to 8 hours. Garnish, if desired. Yield: 1 (10-inch) cake.

* Substitute 1 tablespoon Cointreau or other orange-flavored liqueur for Chambord, if desired.

Louise Jackson
Shreveport, Louisiana

ORANGE ANGEL FOOD CAKE

One taste of this updated standby proves that fat-free desserts can be terrific.

1 cup sugar
½ cup water
2 tablespoons orange liqueur
½ teaspoon lemon juice
15 orange sections
10 egg whites
1 teaspoon cream of tartar
¼ teaspoon salt
1½ cups sugar
¾ cup all-purpose flour
1 teaspoon vanilla extract
1 (18-ounce) jar orange marmalade
½ cup sifted powdered sugar

● **Combine** first 4 ingredients in a heavy saucepan; cook over medium-high heat, stirring constantly, 5 minutes or until a candy thermometer registers 200°. Remove from heat.
● **Dip** orange sections, one at a time, into syrup, and place on parchment paper until cool.
● **Beat** egg whites, cream of tartar, and salt at high speed with an electric mixer until foamy. Gradually add 1½ cups sugar, 2 tablespoons at a time, beating until stiff peaks form and sugar dissolves (2 to 4 minutes). Gradually fold in flour, ¼ cup at a time; fold in vanilla.
● **Line** a 15- x 10- x 1-inch jellyroll pan with parchment paper; spread marmalade over paper. Pour batter over marmalade.
● **Bake** at 325° for 25 minutes; cool in pan on a wire rack. Sprinkle with powdered sugar. Invert onto a large cutting board or baking sheet; peel off parchment paper, and cut cake into circles with a 2½-inch round cutter. Serve with orange sections. **Yield:** 5 servings.

Sara Quattlebaum
Columbia, South Carolina

♥ Per serving: Calories 287
Fat 0.2g Cholesterol 0mg
Sodium 79mg

CHOCOLATE CAKE ROLLS

Vegetable cooking spray
4 large eggs
½ cup water
1 (18.25- or 18.5-ounce) package
    Swiss chocolate, devil's food,
    or fudge cake mix
2 to 4 tablespoons cocoa

• **Coat** two 15- x 10- x 1-inch jellyroll pans with cooking spray; line with wax paper, and coat with cooking spray. Set aside.
• **Beat** eggs in a large mixing bowl at medium-high speed with an electric mixer 5 minutes. Add water, beating at low speed until blended. Gradually add cake mix, beating at low speed until moistened. Beat at medium-high speed 2 minutes. Divide batter in half, and spread batter evenly into prepared pans. (Layers will be thin.)
• **Bake** each cake at 350° on the middle rack in separate ovens for 13 minutes or until cake springs back when lightly touched in the center. (If you don't have a double oven, bake one pan at a time, setting one pan aside.)
• **Sift** 1 to 2 tablespoons cocoa in a 15- x 10-inch rectangle on a cloth towel; repeat with second towel. When cakes are done, immediately loosen from sides of pans, and turn each out onto a prepared towel. Peel off wax paper. Starting at narrow end, roll up each cake and towel together; place cakes, seam side down, on wire racks. Cool cakes completely. Use cake rolls for Chocolate-Cranberry Roulage, Chocolate-Orange Roulage, or Mint-Chocolate Roulage. **Yield:** 2 cake rolls.

CHOCOLATE-ORANGE ROULAGE

2 cups whipping cream
5 to 6 tablespoons Grand Marnier
    or other orange-flavored
    liqueur, divided *
1 tablespoon finely grated
    orange rind
Chocolate Cake Rolls (see recipe
    at left)
Cocoa
Chocolate-Orange Sauce
Garnish: orange rind curls

• **Beat** whipping cream at medium-high speed with an electric mixer until soft peaks form. Fold in 2 to 3 tablespoons Grand Marnier and orange rind; set aside.
• **Unroll** cake rolls; brush each lightly with remaining 2 to 3 tablespoons Grand Marnier. Spread each cake with half of whipped cream mixture. Reroll cakes without towels; place, seam side down, on a baking sheet. Cover and freeze at least 1 hour or up to 3 months.
• **Dust** cakes with cocoa, and cut into slices. Serve with Chocolate-Orange Sauce. Garnish if desired. **Yield:** 2 filled cake rolls (5 to 6 servings each).

* Substitute 5 to 6 tablespoons frozen orange juice concentrate, thawed and undiluted, for liqueur.

Chocolate-Orange Sauce

QUICK!

¾ cup half-and-half
2 cups (12 ounces) semisweet
    chocolate morsels
1½ cups miniature marshmallows
¼ teaspoon salt
¼ cup Grand Marnier or other
    orange-flavored liqueur *

• **Heat** half-and-half in a heavy saucepan over low heat. Stir in chocolate morsels, marshmallows, and salt. Cook over low heat, stirring constantly, until chocolate and marshmallows melt. Remove from heat; stir in Grand Marnier. Cool. **Yield:** 2 cups.

* Substitute ¼ cup frozen orange juice concentrate, thawed and undiluted, for liqueur.

CHOCOLATE-CRANBERRY ROULAGE
(pictured at right)

1 (12-ounce) carton cranberry-
    orange crushed fruit
¾ cup cranberry juice cocktail
2 tablespoons powdered sugar
1½ tablespoons cornstarch
4 to 5 tablespoons crème de cassis
    or other black currant-flavored
    liqueur, divided *
2 cups whipping cream
Chocolate Cake Rolls (see recipe
    at far left)
Cocoa
Garnishes: fresh cranberries, fresh
    mint sprigs

• **Combine** first 4 ingredients in container of an electric blender or food processor; process until smooth, stopping several times to scrape down sides.
• **Pour** mixture into a small saucepan; bring to a boil over medium heat, stirring constantly. Boil 1 minute, stirring constantly. Stir in 2 tablespoons crème de cassis. Cool.
• **Beat** whipping cream at medium-high speed with an electric mixer until soft peaks form. Fold in ⅔ cup cranberry mixture; cover and chill the remaining cranberry mixture for garnish.
• **Unroll** cake rolls; brush each lightly with remaining 2 to 3 tablespoons crème de cassis. Spread each cake with half of whipped cream mixture. Reroll cakes without towels; place, seam side down, on a baking sheet. Cover and freeze cakes at least 1 hour or up to 3 months.
• **Dust** cakes with cocoa, and cut into 1- to 2-inch slices. Spoon remaining cranberry mixture evenly onto dessert plates. Top each with a cake slice. Garnish, if desired. **Yield:** 2 filled cake rolls (5 to 6 servings each).

* Substitute 4 to 5 tablespoons cranberry juice cocktail for crème de cassis.

Chocolate-Cranberry Roulage

MINT-CHOCOLATE ROULAGE

2 cups whipping cream
5 to 6 tablespoons green crème de
    menthe, divided *
Chocolate Cake Rolls (see recipe
    on page 90)
Cocoa
Chocolate-Mint Sauce
Garnishes: whipped cream, fresh
    mint sprigs

• **Beat** 2 cups whipping cream at medium-high speed with an electric mixer until soft peaks form. Fold in 2 to 3 tablespoons crème de menthe; set aside.
• **Unroll** cake rolls; brush lightly with remaining 2 to 3 tablespoons crème de menthe. Spread each cake with half of whipped cream mixture. Reroll cakes without towels; place, seam side down, on a baking sheet. Cover and freeze at least 1 hour or up to 3 months.
• **Dust** cakes with cocoa, and cut into slices. Serve with Chocolate-Mint Sauce. Garnish, if desired. **Yield:** 2 filled cake rolls (5 to 6 servings each).

* Substitute 1½ teaspoons mint extract and 5 drops of green liquid food coloring for crème de menthe in the whipped cream. Omit brushing cake rolls with crème de menthe.

Chocolate-Mint Sauce

QUICK!

¾ cup half-and-half
1 (10-ounce) package mint
    chocolate morsels
1½ cups miniature marshmallows
¼ teaspoon salt
1 teaspoon vanilla extract

• **Heat** half-and-half in a small heavy saucepan over low heat. Stir in chocolate morsels, marshmallows, and salt; cook, stirring constantly, until chocolate morsels and marshmallows melt. Remove from heat, and stir in vanilla. Cool. **Yield:** 2 cups.

EASY PUMPKIN SWIRL

3 large eggs
1 cup sugar
⅔ cup canned pumpkin
¾ cup biscuit mix
2 teaspoons ground cinnamon
1 teaspoon pumpkin pie spice
1 cup chopped pecans
2 to 3 tablespoons powdered sugar
1 (8-ounce) package cream cheese,
    softened
⅓ cup butter or margarine,
    softened
1 cup sifted powdered sugar
1 teaspoon vanilla extract

• **Grease** bottom and sides of a 15- x 10- x 1-inch jellyroll pan; line with wax paper, and grease wax paper. Set aside.
• **Beat** eggs at high speed with an electric mixer until thick and pale. Gradually add 1 cup sugar, beating until soft peaks form and sugar dissolves (2 to 4 minutes). Fold in pumpkin.
• **Combine** biscuit mix and spices; fold into pumpkin mixture, and spread evenly into prepared pan. Sprinkle with chopped pecans. Bake at 375° for 13 to 15 minutes.
• **Sift** 2 to 3 tablespoons powdered sugar in a 15- x 10-inch rectangle on a cloth towel. When cake is done, immediately loosen from sides of pan, and turn out onto sugared towel. Carefully peel off wax paper. Starting at narrow end, roll up cake and towel together, and cool cake completely on a wire rack, seam side down.
• **Beat** cream cheese and butter at medium speed with an electric mixer until creamy; add 1 cup powdered sugar and vanilla, beating well. Unroll cake; spread with cream cheese mixture, and reroll without towel. Place on a serving plate, seam side down; cover and chill at least 2 hours. **Yield:** 1 filled cake roll (5 to 6 servings).

Ernestine Jones
Gore Springs, Mississippi

PINEAPPLE UPSIDE-DOWN CAKE ROLL

1 (20-ounce) can crushed
    pineapple in juice, undrained
1 (2.25-ounce) package sliced
    almonds, toasted
¼ cup butter or margarine
¾ cup firmly packed brown
    sugar
3 large eggs
1 cup sugar
¼ cup warm water
1 teaspoon vanilla extract
1 cup all-purpose flour
1 teaspoon baking powder
¼ teaspoon salt
¼ cup sifted powdered sugar,
    divided
Gingered Crème Chantilly

• **Drain** pineapple, pressing between layers of paper towels; set aside.
• **Reserve** 1 tablespoon sliced almonds; chop remaining almonds, and set aside.
• **Melt** butter in a small saucepan over medium-low heat. Add brown sugar, and cook, stirring constantly, 1 minute or until blended; stir in pineapple. Spread evenly in a lightly greased 15- x 10- x 1-inch jellyroll pan; sprinkle with chopped almonds. Set aside.
• **Beat** eggs in a large mixing bowl at medium-high speed with an electric mixer 3 minutes; gradually add 1 cup sugar, beating well after each addition. Add warm water and vanilla; beat 5 minutes or until thick and creamy.
• **Combine** flour, baking powder, and salt; sprinkle over batter, and fold into batter. Pour evenly over pineapple mixture, spreading to edges of pan.
• **Bake** at 375° for 13 minutes or until cake springs back when lightly touched in center. Cool in pan on a wire rack 5 minutes; loosen from sides of pan with a knife.
• **Sift** 3 tablespoons powdered sugar in a 15- x 10-inch rectangle on a cloth towel; turn cake out onto sugar. Starting at narrow end, roll up cake (without towel), and place, seam side down, on wire rack to cool completely.
• **Transfer** to a serving platter; sprinkle lightly with remaining 1 tablespoon powdered sugar. Top with reserved sliced almonds; serve with Gingered

Crème Chantilly. **Yield:** 1 filled cake roll (5 to 6 servings).

Gingered Crème Chantilly

QUICK!

You'll find crystallized ginger on your grocer's spice rack.

1 cup whipping cream
2 tablespoons powdered sugar
3 tablespoons minced crystallized ginger

● **Beat** whipping cream until foamy; gradually add powdered sugar, beating until soft peaks form. Fold in ginger. **Yield:** 2 cups.

Corile W. Wilhelm
Terra Alta, West Virginia

TOFFEE-PECAN ROULAGE

Vegetable cooking spray
4 large eggs
½ cup water
1 (18.25- or 18.5-ounce) package yellow cake mix
¼ cup almond brickle chips
¼ cup finely chopped pecans, toasted
2 to 4 tablespoons powdered sugar
2 cups whipping cream
2 tablespoons powdered sugar
4 to 6 tablespoons praline liqueur, divided *
Powdered sugar
Praline Sauce
Garnishes: whipped cream, toasted pecan halves

● **Coat** two 15- x 10- x 1-inch jellyroll pans with cooking spray. Line with wax paper; coat with cooking spray.
● **Beat** eggs in a mixing bowl at medium-high speed with an electric mixer 5 minutes. Add water, beating at low speed until blended. Gradually add cake mix, beating at low speed until moistened. Beat at medium-high speed 2 minutes. Fold in brickle chips and chopped pecans. Divide batter in half, and spread evenly into prepared pans. (Layers will be thin.)

● **Bake** each cake at 350° on the middle rack in separate ovens for 13 minutes or until cake springs back when lightly touched in the center. (If you don't have a double oven, bake one pan at a time, setting one pan aside.)
● **Sift** 1 to 2 tablespoons powdered sugar in a 15- x 10-inch rectangle on a cloth towel; repeat with second towel. When cakes are done, immediately loosen from sides of pans, and turn each out onto a sugared towel. Peel off wax paper. Starting at narrow end, roll up each cake and towel together; place, seam side down, on wire racks to cool completely.
● **Beat** whipping cream at medium-high speed with an electric mixer until foamy; gradually add 2 tablespoons powdered sugar, beating until soft peaks form. Fold in 2 to 3 tablespoons praline liqueur.
● **Unroll** cakes; brush each lightly, using remaining 2 to 3 tablespoons liqueur. Spread each cake with half of whipped cream mixture. Reroll cakes without towels; place, seam side down, on a baking sheet. Cover and freeze at least 1 hour or up to 3 months.
● **Dust** cakes with additional powdered sugar. Cut into 1- to 2-inch slices; spoon warm Praline Sauce evenly onto dessert plates. Top each with a cake slice. Garnish, if desired. **Yield:** 2 filled cake rolls (5 to 6 servings each).

* Substitute 2 tablespoons vanilla extract for praline liqueur. Use 1 tablespoon in whipped cream, and brush cakes with a mixture of 1 tablespoon vanilla plus 2 teaspoons water.

Praline Sauce

QUICK!

1 cup firmly packed brown sugar
½ cup half-and-half
½ cup butter or margarine
½ cup finely chopped pecans, toasted
½ teaspoon vanilla extract

● **Combine** first 3 ingredients; bring to a boil over medium heat, stirring constantly. Boil 1 minute, stirring constantly. Remove from heat; stir in pecans and vanilla. **Yield:** about 2 cups.

CHOCOLATE-ALMOND PETITS FOURS

¾ cup butter or margarine, softened
2 (8-ounce) cans almond paste
1½ cups sugar
8 large eggs
1½ cups all-purpose flour
1 (12-ounce) can apricot filling
Chocolate Ganache
6 ounces white chocolate, melted (optional)

● **Grease** bottom and sides of two 15- x 10- x 1-inch jellyroll pans, and line with wax paper; grease and flour wax paper. Set aside.
● **Beat** butter and almond paste at medium speed with an electric mixer until creamy. Gradually add sugar, beating well. Add eggs, one at a time, beating after each addition. Stir in flour.
● **Spread** batter evenly into prepared pans. Bake at 400° for 8 to 10 minutes. Cool in pans on wire racks.
● **Turn** cake out onto a flat surface; remove wax paper, and spread with apricot filling. Top with remaining cake, and cut with a 1½-inch round cutter.
● **Place** small cakes on a wire rack in a large shallow pan. Using a squeeze bottle, coat top and sides with warm Chocolate Ganache. (Spoon up excess frosting that drips through rack; reheat and refill bottle, and use to continue frosting cakes.) Chill cakes 10 minutes. Pipe dots on frosted cakes with white chocolate, if desired. **Yield:** 3½ dozen.

Chocolate Ganache

QUICK!

1½ cups whipping cream
24 (1-ounce) squares semisweet chocolate, chopped

● **Heat** whipping cream in a heavy saucepan over low heat. Add chocolate, stirring until smooth. (Mixture thickens as it cools; reheat over low heat, if necessary.) **Yield:** 3 cups.

Note: Freeze Chocolate-Almond Petits Fours up to 3 months.

Shannon Stansell-Boykin
Birmingham, Alabama

Chocolate-Raspberry Shortcake

CHOCOLATE-RASPBERRY SHORTCAKE
(pictured at left)

½ cup butter or margarine,
    softened
1¼ cups sugar
2 large eggs, separated
1¼ cups sifted cake flour
2 teaspoons baking powder
¼ teaspoon salt
⅓ cup cocoa
⅔ cup milk
1 teaspoon vanilla extract
2 tablespoons seedless raspberry
    jam
2 tablespoons Chambord or
    other raspberry-flavored
    liqueur
2 cups whipping cream
¼ cup sifted powdered sugar
3 cups fresh raspberries
Garnish: fresh mint sprigs

● **Grease** two 9-inch round cakepans; line with wax paper, and grease wax paper. Set aside.
● **Beat** butter at medium speed with an electric mixer 2 minutes or until creamy; gradually add sugar, beating well. Add egg yolks, one at a time, beating until blended after each addition.
● **Combine** flour and next 3 ingredients; add to butter mixture alternately with milk, beginning and ending with flour mixture. Beat at low speed until blended after each addition. Stir in vanilla.
● **Beat** egg whites at high speed with an electric mixer until stiff peaks form; gently fold into batter. Pour batter into prepared pans.
● **Bake** at 350° for 18 minutes or until a wooden pick inserted in center comes out clean. Cool in pans on wire racks 10 minutes. Remove from pans; cool completely on wire racks.
● **Cook** jam in a small saucepan over low heat until melted; stir in liqueur. Set jam mixture aside.
● **Beat** whipping cream at medium speed with an electric mixer until foamy; gradually add powdered sugar, beating until soft peaks form.
● **Place** 1 cake layer on a serving plate; brush with half of jam mixture. Arrange half of raspberries over jam. Spread half of whipped cream over raspberries.

● **Top** with remaining cake layer, and brush with remaining jam mixture. Spread remaining whipped cream over jam mixture; arrange remaining raspberries on top of shortcake. Garnish, if desired. **Yield:** 10 servings.

Mattie Scott
Birmingham, Alabama

PEAR SHORTCAKES

2 cups apple juice, divided
6 firm ripe pears, peeled and
    chopped
1 cup sugar
3 tablespoons lemon juice
½ teaspoon ground nutmeg
¼ teaspoon ground cinnamon
⅛ teaspoon ground cloves
1½ tablespoons cornstarch
½ cup slivered almonds,
    toasted
2 teaspoons grated lemon rind
8 Orange-Pecan Scones (see
    recipe on page 45)
1 cup whipping cream, whipped

● **Combine** 1¾ cups apple juice, chopped pears, and next 5 ingredients in a large saucepan; bring to a boil. Cook 10 to 12 minutes or until pear is tender. Remove pear from liquid, reserving liquid. Set pear aside. Bring liquid to a boil; reduce heat, and cook until liquid is reduced to 1 cup.
● **Combine** remaining ¼ cup apple juice and cornstarch; stir into reduced mixture. Bring to a boil, stirring constantly. Boil 1 minute, stirring constantly. Remove from heat. Stir in pear, almonds, and lemon rind; cool.
● **Split** scones; place bottom half on serving plates, and top with pear mixture, half of whipped cream, and remaining scone halves. Dollop each with remaining whipped cream. **Yield:** 8 servings.

ORANGE-STRAWBERRY SHORTCAKE

2 pints fresh strawberries, sliced
2 (11-ounce) cans mandarin
    oranges, drained
½ cup sugar
1½ tablespoons Triple Sec or
    other orange-flavored liqueur
2 cups biscuit mix
1 tablespoon sugar
1½ teaspoons ground cinnamon
⅔ cup milk
2 cups whipping cream
½ cup sifted powdered sugar
¼ cup sour cream

● **Combine** first 4 ingredients, stirring until sugar dissolves. Cover and chill 2 hours.
● **Combine** biscuit mix and next 3 ingredients; stir with a fork until dry ingredients are moistened. Turn out onto a lightly floured surface; knead 4 or 5 times. Place on a lightly greased baking sheet; press into a 7- x ¾-inch round.
● **Bake** at 425° for 15 minutes or until done. Carefully remove from pan; cool on a wire rack.
● **Beat** whipping cream until foamy; gradually add powdered sugar, beating until soft peaks form. Add sour cream, and beat until stiff peaks form.
● **Split** biscuit round in half horizontally. Place bottom half on a serving dish. Drain fruit, reserving 2 tablespoons liquid. Spoon two-thirds of fruit on bottom round; drizzle with reserved liquid. Spoon half of whipped cream mixture over fruit. Add top biscuit round. Top with remaining fruit and whipped cream mixture. **Yield:** 8 servings.

Joyce Ogletree
Newnan, Georgia

LEMON CHEESECAKE

¾ cup graham cracker crumbs
2 tablespoons sugar
1 tablespoon ground cinnamon
1 tablespoon butter or margarine,
    softened
5 (8-ounce) packages cream
    cheese, softened
1⅔ cups sugar
5 large eggs
⅛ teaspoon salt
1½ teaspoons vanilla extract
¼ cup lemon juice

• **Combine** first 3 ingredients; stir well, and set aside.
• **Grease** bottom and sides of a 10-inch springform pan with butter. Add crumb mixture; tilt pan to coat sides and bottom. Chill.
• **Beat** cream cheese at medium speed with an electric mixer until creamy; gradually add 1⅔ cups sugar, beating well at high speed. Add eggs, one at a time, beating well after each addition. Stir in salt, vanilla, and lemon juice; pour mixture into prepared crust.
• **Bake** at 300° for 1 hour and 20 minutes. (Center may be soft but will set when chilled.) Cool in pan on a wire rack; cover and chill 8 hours. **Yield:** 1 (10-inch) cheesecake.

Dale Safrit
Columbus, Ohio

LEMON DELIGHT CHEESECAKE

1 cup graham cracker crumbs
3 tablespoons sugar
2 tablespoons margarine,
    melted
3 (8-ounce) packages fat-free
    cream cheese, softened
¾ cup sugar
2 tablespoons all-purpose flour
3 tablespoons lemon juice
¾ cup fat-free egg substitute
1 (8-ounce) carton lemon nonfat
    yogurt
**Garnishes: lemon slices, fresh
    mint sprigs**

• **Combine** first 3 ingredients; press in bottom of a 9-inch springform pan.

• **Combine** cream cheese, ¾ cup sugar, and flour; beat at medium speed with an electric mixer until fluffy. Gradually add lemon juice and egg substitute, beating well. Add yogurt, beating well; pour into prepared pan. Cover loosely with aluminum foil.
• **Bake** at 350° for 1 hour or until set. Remove from oven, and immediately run a knife around edge of pan to release sides. Cool cheesecake completely in pan on a wire rack. Cover and chill at least 8 hours.
• **Remove** sides of pan. Garnish, if desired. **Yield:** 6 servings.

Note: For a crisper crust, prebake crust at 350° for 6 to 8 minutes.

Lynette Granade
Mobile, Alabama

♥ Per serving: Calories 402
Fat 6.6g Cholesterol 22mg
Sodium 894mg

CHEESECAKE WITH
RASPBERRY-LEMON SAUCE

Vegetable cooking spray
¾ cup graham cracker crumbs,
    divided
3 (8-ounce) packages nonfat
    cream cheese, softened
1½ cups sugar, divided
1 cup fat-free egg substitute
1 tablespoon grated lemon rind
1 teaspoon vanilla extract
4 egg whites
⅓ cup nonfat sour cream
1 (12-ounce) package frozen
    unsweetened raspberries,
    thawed
1 teaspoon grated lemon rind
1½ teaspoons fresh lemon juice

• **Coat** bottom and sides of a 9-inch springform pan with cooking spray; sprinkle with ½ cup graham cracker crumbs, and set aside.
• **Beat** cream cheese at medium speed with an electric mixer until creamy. Gradually add ¾ cup sugar, beating well. Add egg substitute, 1 tablespoon lemon rind, and vanilla, beating until blended.

• **Beat** egg whites at high speed until soft peaks form; gently fold into cream cheese mixture. Pour batter into prepared pan.
• **Bake** at 350° for 45 minutes or until lightly browned.
• **Combine** ¼ cup sugar and sour cream; spread over cheesecake, and sprinkle with remaining ¼ cup graham cracker crumbs.
• **Bake** at 450° for 5 minutes. Remove from oven; let cool completely. Gently run a knife around edge of pan to release sides; cover and chill at least 4 hours.
• **Combine** raspberries and remaining ½ cup sugar in a small saucepan; cook over medium-low heat, stirring constantly, until sugar dissolves. Pour mixture through a wire-mesh strainer into a bowl, discarding solids. Stir in 1 teaspoon grated lemon rind and lemon juice. Serve sauce with cheesecake. **Yield:** 8 servings.

Sandi Pichon
Slidell, Louisiana

♥ Per serving: Calories 308
Fat 1.4g Cholesterol 15mg
Sodium 542mg

KEY LIME CHEESECAKE
WITH STRAWBERRY-BUTTER
SAUCE

2 cups graham cracker crumbs
¼ cup sugar
½ cup butter or margarine,
    melted
3 (8-ounce) packages cream
    cheese, softened
1¼ cups sugar
6 large eggs, separated
1 (8-ounce) carton sour cream
1½ teaspoons grated lime
    rind
½ cup Key lime juice
Strawberry-Butter Sauce

• **Combine** first 3 ingredients in a small bowl, stirring well. Firmly press mixture in bottom and 1 inch up sides of a buttered 9-inch springform pan.
• **Bake** crust at 350° for 8 minutes; let cool in pan on a wire rack.

• **Beat** cream cheese at medium speed with an electric mixer until creamy; gradually add 1¼ cups sugar, beating well. Add egg yolks, one at a time, beating after each addition. Stir in sour cream, lime rind, and lime juice.

• **Beat** egg whites at high speed until stiff peaks form; fold into cream cheese mixture. Pour batter into prepared crust.

• **Bake** at 350° for 1 hour and 5 minutes; turn oven off. Partially open oven door; let cheesecake cool in oven 15 minutes. Remove from oven, and immediately run a knife around edge of pan to release sides.

• **Cool** completely in pan on a wire rack; cover and chill 8 hours. Serve with Strawberry-Butter Sauce. **Yield:** 1 (9-inch) cheesecake.

Strawberry-Butter Sauce
QUICK!

1¼ cups fresh strawberries, hulled
¼ cup butter or margarine, melted
½ cup sifted powdered sugar
1½ teaspoons grated lime rind

• **Position** knife blade in food processor bowl; add strawberries. Process until smooth, stopping once to scrape down sides. Stir in butter and remaining ingredients. **Yield:** 1 cup.

Nita and Harold Norman
Coral Gables, Florida

PIÑA COLADA CHEESECAKE

1⅔ cups fine dry breadcrumbs
¼ cup sugar
½ cup butter or margarine, melted
4 (8-ounce) packages cream cheese, softened
¾ cup sugar
4 large eggs
1 (15¼-ounce) can crushed pineapple, drained
1 (15-ounce) can cream of coconut
1 (8-ounce) carton sour cream
2 tablespoons cornstarch
1 teaspoon vanilla extract
1 teaspoon rum flavoring
1 teaspoon lemon juice
Topping

• **Combine** breadcrumbs, ¼ cup sugar, and butter; press in bottom and 1 inch up sides of a 10-inch springform pan. Bake at 350° for 10 to 12 minutes. Cool on a wire rack.

• **Beat** cream cheese in a large mixing bowl at medium speed with an electric mixer until creamy. Gradually add ¾ cup sugar, beating well. Add eggs, one at a time, beating after each addition. Stir in pineapple and next 6 ingredients; spoon into crust.

• **Bake** at 350° for 1 hour and 20 minutes; turn oven off. Sprinkle topping over cheesecake; return to oven. Leave in oven with door closed 1 hour; cool to room temperature on a wire rack. Cover and chill. **Yield:** 1 (10-inch) cheesecake.

Topping
QUICK!

¼ cup butter or margarine
½ cup flaked coconut
½ cup finely chopped almonds
¼ cup sugar

• **Melt** butter in a small saucepan over medium heat; add coconut and remaining ingredients, and cook until coconut and almonds are golden, stirring often. **Yield:** about 1 cup.

PUMPKIN CHEESECAKE

Try a twist on traditional pumpkin pie at your next holiday get-together. A crisp gingersnap crust cradles a rich pumpkin filling, while clouds of sweetened whipped cream blanket the top.

1¼ cups gingersnap crumbs (25 to 30 cookies)
3 tablespoons butter or margarine, melted
3 (8-ounce) packages cream cheese, softened
1¼ cups sugar, divided
1 tablespoon vanilla extract
6 large eggs, separated
2 (16.25-ounce) cans pumpkin pie mix
2 large eggs, lightly beaten
1 cup whipping cream
1 tablespoon powdered sugar

• **Combine** cookie crumbs and butter; press in bottom and 1 inch up sides of a lightly greased 12-inch springform pan. Set aside.

• **Beat** cream cheese at medium speed with an electric mixer until smooth; add 1 cup sugar and vanilla, beating until creamy. Stir in 6 egg yolks. Pour 2½ cups mixture into prepared crust; set aside.

• **Add** pumpkin pie mix and 2 eggs to remaining cream cheese mixture, stirring well; set aside.

• **Beat** egg whites at high speed until foamy. Add remaining ¼ cup sugar, 1 tablespoon at a time, beating until stiff peaks form and sugar dissolves (2 to 4 minutes). Fold into pumpkin mixture; pour over cream cheese mixture in crust.

• **Bake** at 300° for 1½ hours. Turn oven off, and gently run a knife around edge of pan to release sides. Let stand in oven with door partially open for 1½ hours. Remove sides of pan; cover and chill cheesecake.

• **Beat** whipping cream and powdered sugar at high speed until soft peaks form; spread on sides of cheesecake. **Yield:** 1 (12-inch) cheesecake.

Sudi Swirles and Jan Hryharrow
Durham, North Carolina

LUCY'S APRICOT PRALINE TORTE

1 (16-ounce) loaf pound cake
1 cup apricot preserves
Praline Buttercream
Sifted powdered sugar

• **Cut** cake horizontally into 3 layers.
• **Melt** preserves in a saucepan over low heat. Spread half of preserves over bottom layer of cake. Spread half of Praline Buttercream over preserves; place second cake layer on top of buttercream. Repeat procedure with remaining preserves and buttercream; top with remaining cake layer. Sprinkle with powdered sugar. **Yield:** 10 to 12 servings.

Praline Buttercream

½ cup unsalted butter, softened
2½ cups sifted powdered sugar
2 to 3 tablespoons whipping cream
½ cup Praline Powder
1 teaspoon vanilla extract

• **Beat** butter in a small mixing bowl at medium speed with an electric mixer until creamy; gradually add sugar, beating mixture well. Beat in whipping cream, and fold in Praline Powder and vanilla. **Yield:** 2 cups.

Praline Powder

2 tablespoons butter
¼ cup sugar
¾ cup almonds, chopped and toasted

• **Cook** butter and sugar in a small saucepan over medium heat until sugar melts and turns a light caramel color (mixture will separate), stirring occasionally. Remove from heat, and stir in almonds.
• **Pour** onto a greased aluminum foil-lined baking sheet, and cool. Break into chunks.
• **Position** knife blade in food processor bowl; add chunks of praline mixture, and process until finely crushed. **Yield:** 1 cup.

The Texas Experience
Richardson Woman's Club
Richardson, Texas

CARAMEL-SWEET POTATO TORTE

6 large eggs, separated
1⅓ cups mashed cooked sweet potato
¾ teaspoon ground cinnamon
½ teaspoon ground nutmeg
¼ teaspoon ground cloves
1½ teaspoons vanilla extract
¾ cup chopped pecans
¾ cup chopped dates
¾ cup crushed round buttery crackers
½ teaspoon cream of tartar
¾ cup sugar
Caramel Whipped Cream Filling
Garnish: pecan halves

• **Line** three 8-inch round cakepans with wax paper; grease and flour wax paper.
• **Beat** egg yolks, sweet potato, and next 4 ingredients at medium speed with an electric mixer until smooth. Stir in pecans, dates, and cracker crumbs.
• **Beat** egg whites and cream of tartar at high speed until foamy. Add sugar, 2 tablespoons at a time, beating until soft peaks form and sugar dissolves. Fold into yolk mixture.
• **Bake** at 350° for 25 minutes or until a wooden pick inserted in center comes out clean.
• **Cool** in pans on wire racks 10 minutes. Remove from pans, peeling off wax paper; cool on wire racks.
• **Spread** filling between layers and on top of cake. Garnish, if desired. Cover and chill 3 to 4 hours. **Yield:** 10 servings.

Caramel Whipped Cream Filling

2 tablespoons butter
1 tablespoon all-purpose flour
⅔ cup firmly packed brown sugar
⅓ cup light corn syrup
2 tablespoons half-and-half
1½ cups whipping cream

• **Melt** butter in a heavy saucepan over low heat; whisk in flour until smooth. Cook 1 minute, whisking constantly. Stir in brown sugar and corn syrup; cook 5 minutes, whisking constantly.
• **Remove** from heat; cool 15 minutes. Gradually whisk in half-and-half.
• **Beat** cream until soft peaks form; fold into mixture. **Yield:** about 4 cups.

CHOCOLATE-ALMOND TORTE

3 shortbread finger cookies, crushed *
1 cup sugar
⅓ cup walnut pieces
3 tablespoons slivered almonds
1 (8-ounce) package semisweet chocolate squares, chopped
½ cup butter, cut into pieces
1 tablespoon amaretto
4 large eggs
1 cup whipping cream
2 tablespoons powdered sugar

• **Press** crushed cookies evenly in bottom of a buttered 8-inch springform pan; set aside.
• **Position** knife blade in food processor bowl, and add 1 cup sugar, walnuts, and almonds; process until ground, stopping once to scrape down sides. Transfer mixture to a bowl; set aside.
• **Combine** chocolate and butter in a 1-quart liquid measuring cup; microwave at MEDIUM (50% power) 3 to 4 minutes or until melted, stirring after each minute. Let mixture stand 15 minutes.
• **Stir** liqueur into nut mixture. Add eggs, one at a time, stirring just until blended after each addition. Stir in chocolate mixture. Pour over crushed cookies in pan.
• **Bake** at 325° for 35 to 40 minutes or until set; cool completely. Remove sides from pan.
• **Beat** whipping cream and powdered sugar until soft peaks form, and serve with torte. **Yield:** 6 to 8 servings.

* For shortbread finger cookies, we used Walker Shortbread Fingers.

Note: You can chill torte. Remove from refrigerator 30 minutes before serving.
Liz Lorber
Atlanta, Georgia

At right: *Candy Bar Brownies (page 112)*

ALABAMA FUDGE-PECAN CHEWIES

Make these treats up to 2 days before serving or bake them ahead and freeze. Store them in the freezer up to 3 months.

1 (14-ounce) can sweetened
    condensed milk
2 cups (12 ounces) semisweet
    chocolate morsels
¼ cup butter or margarine
1 cup all-purpose flour
½ cup chopped pecans
1 teaspoon vanilla extract
60 pecan halves

• **Combine** first 3 ingredients in a heavy saucepan; cook over medium-low heat, stirring constantly, until chocolate and butter melt. Remove from heat.
• **Stir** in flour, chopped pecans, and vanilla.
• **Drop** by teaspoonfuls onto ungreased cookie sheets. Press a pecan half into the center of each cookie.
• **Bake** at 350° for 7 minutes. (Do not overbake.) Transfer cookies to wire racks to cool. **Yield:** 5 dozen.

Jane Boswell
Birmingham, Alabama

RICH DATE-NUT CHOCOLATE CHIP COOKIES

½ cup butter or margarine,
    softened
¾ cup firmly packed brown sugar
1 large egg
1 tablespoon vanilla extract
¾ cup chopped dates
1 cup all-purpose flour
½ teaspoon baking soda
¼ teaspoon baking powder
¼ teaspoon salt
2 cups (12 ounces) semisweet
    chocolate morsels
¾ cup coarsely chopped walnuts
½ cup flaked coconut

• **Beat** butter at medium speed with an electric mixer until fluffy; gradually add brown sugar, beating well. Add egg and vanilla, mixing well. Stir in dates; let stand 5 minutes. Beat at high speed 3 minutes.
• **Combine** flour and next 3 ingredients; gradually add to butter mixture, mixing well. Gently stir in morsels, walnuts, and coconut.
• **Drop** dough by level tablespoonfuls onto lightly greased cookie sheets.
• **Bake** at 350° for 10 to 12 minutes or until lightly browned. Transfer to wire racks to cool. **Yield:** 3 dozen.

Beverly Garver
Anderson, South Carolina

CHUNKY MACADAMIA NUT-WHITE CHOCOLATE COOKIES

½ cup butter or margarine,
    softened
¾ cup firmly packed brown
    sugar
2 tablespoons sugar
1 large egg
1½ teaspoons vanilla extract
2 cups all-purpose flour
¾ teaspoon baking soda
½ teaspoon baking powder
⅛ teaspoon salt
1 cup (6 ounces) vanilla-milk
    morsels or 1 (6-ounce) package
    white chocolate-flavored
    baking bars, cut into chunks
2 (3.5-ounce) jars macadamia
    nuts, coarsely chopped

• **Beat** butter at medium speed with an electric mixer until fluffy; gradually add sugars, beating well. Add egg and vanilla, mixing well.
• **Combine** flour and next 3 ingredients; gradually add to butter mixture, mixing well. Stir in morsels and nuts.
• **Drop** by rounded teaspoonfuls onto lightly greased cookie sheets.
• **Bake** at 350° for 8 to 10 minutes or until lightly browned. Transfer to wire racks to cool. **Yield:** 5 dozen.

Elizabeth S. Evins
Atlanta, Georgia

DOUBLE-CHOCOLATE COOKIES

QUICK!

1 (18.25-ounce) package devil's
    food cake mix with pudding
½ cup vegetable oil
2 large eggs
1 cup (6 ounces) semisweet
    chocolate morsels

• **Combine** first 3 ingredients, and beat at medium speed with an electric mixer until blended. Stir in chocolate morsels.
• **Drop** dough by rounded teaspoonfuls about 2 inches apart onto ungreased cookie sheets.
• **Bake** at 350° for 10 minutes. Cool cookies on cookie sheets 5 minutes; transfer to wire racks to cool completely. **Yield:** 3 dozen.

Marie Davis
Charlotte, North Carolina

ORANGE CRINKLES

QUICK!

To celebrate Halloween, add pumpkin faces to these bright orange cookies, using brown decorating frosting and assorted candies.

1 (18.25-ounce) package orange
    cake mix
½ cup vegetable oil
2 large eggs
2 teaspoons grated orange rind

• **Combine** all ingredients in a large bowl, stirring mixture well.
• **Drop** dough by rounded teaspoonfuls 2 inches apart onto ungreased cookie sheets.
• **Bake** at 350° for 12 minutes or until lightly browned. Cool on cookie sheets 1 minute; transfer to wire racks to cool completely. **Yield:** 3 dozen.

Marie Davis
Charlotte, North Carolina

CATS' TONGUES

These crisp, slightly sweet cookies are long and thin and resemble their name in shape.

¼ cup unsalted butter, softened
⅓ cup sugar
2 egg whites
⅛ teaspoon vanilla extract
⅓ cup all-purpose flour
Pinch of salt

● **Beat** butter at medium speed with an electric mixer until creamy; gradually add sugar, beating well. Add egg whites and vanilla, beating just until blended.
● **Combine** flour and salt; gradually add to butter mixture, beating just until blended after each addition.
● **Drop** by level teaspoonfuls onto greased cookie sheets; pull a knife through batter until each cookie is about 5 inches long (1 end will be wider).
● **Bake** at 425° for 4 to 5 minutes or until edges are lightly browned. Immediately remove from cookie sheets, and let cool on wire racks. **Yield:** 2½ dozen.

Note: If cookies harden on cookie sheets, return them to oven briefly to soften.
Chefs Edna Lewis and Scott Peacock
Atlanta, Georgia

BASIC BUTTER COOKIE DOUGH

1 cup butter or margarine,
   softened
½ cup firmly packed brown sugar
½ cup sugar
1 large egg
3½ cups all-purpose flour
2 teaspoons baking powder
½ teaspoon salt
2 tablespoons milk
2 teaspoons vanilla extract

● **Beat** butter in a large mixing bowl at medium speed with an electric mixer until creamy. Gradually add sugars, beating well. Add egg, beating well.
● **Combine** flour, baking powder, and salt; add to butter mixture alternately with milk, beginning and ending with flour mixture. Beat at low speed after each addition until mixture is blended. Stir in vanilla.
● **Divide** dough into 2 equal portions; wrap each portion in plastic wrap to prevent drying out. Chill. Proceed with cookie instructions of choice. **Yield:** 2¼ pounds.

Note: You can freeze this cookie dough, but cookies made from thawed dough may be drier than if baked immediately.
Ellender Mills
Raleigh, North Carolina

SPICE THINS

½ teaspoon ground ginger
½ teaspoon ground cinnamon
¼ teaspoon ground nutmeg
½ Basic Butter Cookie Dough
   recipe (see recipe at left)
2 (2-ounce) squares vanilla-
   flavored candy coating,
   melted
Ground cinnamon

● **Stir** or knead first 3 ingredients into Basic Butter Cookie Dough.
● **Shape** dough into 1-inch balls, and place on lightly greased cookie sheets. Dip a flat-bottom glass into flour, and flatten balls to ¼-inch thickness.
● **Bake** at 350° for 10 minutes or until lightly browned. Transfer to wire racks to cool.
● **Drizzle** candy coating over cookies; sprinkle with cinnamon. **Yield:** 2½ dozen.

PEANUT BUTTER SHORTBREAD

⅔ cup creamy peanut butter
½ Basic Butter Cookie Dough
   recipe (see recipe at left)
36 milk chocolate kisses,
   unwrapped

● **Knead** peanut butter into Basic Butter Cookie Dough until smooth and well blended.
● **Shape** dough into 1-inch balls, and place on lightly greased cookie sheets.

Make an indentation in center of each ball with thumb or spoon handle.
● **Bake** at 350° for 12 minutes or until lightly browned. Immediately press chocolate kiss in center of each cookie. Remove to wire racks to cool. **Yield:** 3 dozen.

SCOTTISH SHORTBREAD

Agnes, a native of Scotland, shares her mother's recipe for Scottish Shortbread.

1 cup butter, softened
1 cup margarine, softened
1 cup sifted powdered sugar
4 cups all-purpose flour
½ teaspoon baking powder
¼ teaspoon salt

● **Beat** butter and margarine at medium speed with an electric mixer until creamy; gradually add powdered sugar, beating well.
● **Combine** flour, baking powder, and salt; add to butter mixture. Mix at low speed until well blended.
● **Turn** dough out onto a well-floured surface; knead 10 times.
● **Shape** on a large cookie sheet into a 15- x 10-inch rectangle. Pierce dough with a fork at 2-inch intervals.
● **Bake** at 300° for 1 hour or until shortbread is golden. Cut immediately into 2½- x 1-inch pieces. Cool on cookie sheet 10 minutes; transfer to a wire rack to cool completely. **Yield:** 5 dozen.
Agnes Hunter Dauphinée
Trussville, Alabama

JAVA SHORTBREAD COOKIES

1 cup butter or margarine, softened
2 teaspoons instant coffee granules
½ cup sifted powdered sugar
2 cups all-purpose flour
3 ounces vanilla-flavored candy coating, melted
½ cup chopped pecans

• **Beat** butter and coffee granules in a mixing bowl at medium speed with an electric mixer until creamy; gradually add powdered sugar, beating well. Stir in flour.
• **Shape** dough into 3-inch logs; place on an ungreased cookie sheet.
• **Bake** at 350° for 8 minutes or until lightly browned. Transfer to wire racks to cool.
• **Dip** both ends of cookies into candy coating, and then into chopped pecans. Place on wax paper until set. **Yield:** 2½ dozen.

Wendy V. Kitchens
Charlotte, North Carolina

FINIKIA

Pronounced fin-EE-key-ah, these cookies are similar to shortbread.

1 cup sugar
1 cup vegetable oil
1 cup orange juice
½ cup butter, softened
1 tablespoon ground cinnamon
4 teaspoons baking powder
1 teaspoon baking soda
6 to 6½ cups all-purpose flour
Honey Syrup
3 cups ground walnuts

• **Combine** first 5 ingredients in a large mixing bowl, and beat at medium speed with an electric mixer until well blended. Gradually add baking powder, baking soda, and enough flour to make a medium dough (dough should not stick to your hands).
• **Turn** dough out onto a lightly floured surface, and knead several times.

• **Shape** dough into 1¼-inch balls, and flatten each into a 3- x 1-inch oval. Place on ungreased cookie sheets.
• **Bake** at 350° for 20 minutes or until lightly browned. Transfer to wire racks to cool.
• **Dip** cookies into hot Honey Syrup with a slotted spoon; roll in ground walnuts, and place on wire racks to cool. **Yield:** 4¼ dozen.

Honey Syrup

QUICK!

2 cups sugar
1 cup water
1 cup honey
2 tablespoons lemon juice

• **Combine** sugar and water in a saucepan, and bring to a boil over medium heat. Reduce heat, and simmer 10 minutes.
• **Add** honey and lemon juice, stirring well; return to a boil. Reduce heat, and simmer 5 minutes. **Yield:** 2¾ cups.

Mary Pappas
Richmond, Virginia

LEMON CRISPS

QUICK!

1 (18.25-ounce) package lemon cake mix with pudding
1 cup crisp rice cereal
½ cup butter or margarine, melted
1 large egg

• **Combine** all ingredients, stirring mixture well.
• **Shape** dough into 1-inch balls; place about 2 inches apart on ungreased cookie sheets.
• **Bake** at 350° for 9 minutes or until edges are golden. Cool on cookie sheets 1 minute; transfer to wire racks to cool completely. **Yield:** 4 dozen.

Marie Davis
Charlotte, North Carolina

GINGER COOKIES

Eloise has been making 1,500 of these delicious cookies each Christmas for almost 50 years. "I am confident that I have made at least 50,000 of these," she reports. Her cookies are so popular that the neighborhood kids call her the "Ginger Cookie Lady."

1½ cups shortening
2 cups sugar
2 large eggs
½ cup molasses
4 cups all-purpose flour
2 teaspoons baking soda
1 teaspoon ground cinnamon
1 teaspoon ground cloves
1 teaspoon ground ginger
Sugar

• **Combine** first 9 ingredients in a large mixing bowl; beat at medium speed with an electric mixer until blended.
• **Shape** into 1-inch balls, and roll in additional sugar. Place on greased cookie sheets, and flatten slightly with a flat-bottomed glass.
• **Bake** at 375° for 8 to 10 minutes. Transfer to wire racks to cool. **Yield:** 7 dozen.

Eloise Pope
Milton, West Virginia

COFFEE NUGGETS

Make-ahead tip: Bake and freeze cookies up to 3 months in advance or store in an airtight container at room temperature a couple of days before serving.

2 tablespoons instant coffee granules
1 cup butter or margarine, softened
⅓ cup sifted powdered sugar
2 cups all-purpose flour
1 cup finely chopped pecans
2 teaspoons vanilla extract
Sifted powdered sugar

• **Crush** coffee granules into a fine powder, using a mortar and pestle or back of a spoon; set coffee powder aside.

• **Beat** butter at medium speed with an electric mixer until creamy; gradually add ⅓ cup powdered sugar, beating well. Add coffee powder, flour, pecans, and vanilla, mixing until blended. Cover and chill at least 1 hour.

• **Shape** dough into 1-inch balls; place on ungreased cookie sheets.

• **Bake** at 350° for 12 minutes or until lightly browned. Transfer to wire racks; cool 10 minutes. Roll in additional powdered sugar; cool completely on wire racks. Roll in powdered sugar again, if desired. **Yield:** 3½ dozen.

Katharine Reinke
Baltimore, Maryland

DOUBLE-CHOCOLATE SUGAR COOKIES

2 cups (12 ounces) semisweet
   chocolate morsels, divided
1 cup butter or margarine,
   softened
1 cup sugar
1 large egg
2 tablespoons milk
1 teaspoon vanilla extract
3 cups all-purpose flour
1 teaspoon baking powder
½ teaspoon baking soda
½ teaspoon salt
½ cup sugar

• **Melt** 1 cup semisweet chocolate morsels in a heavy saucepan over low heat. Set aside.

• **Beat** butter at medium speed with an electric mixer until fluffy; gradually add 1 cup sugar, beating well. Add egg, milk, and vanilla, mixing well. Add melted morsels, mixing until blended.

• **Combine** flour and next 3 ingredients; gradually add to butter mixture, mixing well. Stir in remaining 1 cup chocolate morsels.

• **Shape** dough into balls, 1 tablespoon at a time; roll balls in ½ cup sugar. Place on lightly greased cookie sheets.

• **Bake** at 400° for 8 to 10 minutes. (Cookies will be soft and will firm up as they cool.) Transfer to wire racks to cool. **Yield:** 4½ dozen.

Jill D. Abell
Snellville, Georgia

FUDGE PUDDLES

½ cup butter or margarine,
   softened
½ cup creamy peanut butter
½ cup sugar
½ cup firmly packed brown sugar
1 large egg
½ teaspoon vanilla extract
1¼ cups all-purpose flour
¾ teaspoon baking soda
½ teaspoon salt
Fudge Filling
2 tablespoons chopped peanuts

• **Beat** butter and peanut butter in a large mixing bowl at medium speed with an electric mixer until creamy; gradually add sugars, beating well. Add egg and vanilla, mixing well.

• **Combine** flour, baking soda, and salt; add to butter mixture, mixing well. Cover and chill 1 hour.

• **Shape** dough into 48 (1-inch) balls. Place in lightly greased miniature (1¾-inch) muffin pans. Bake at 325° for 12 to 14 minutes or until lightly browned. Cool in pans on wire racks 5 minutes. Carefully remove cookies from pans, and let cool completely on wire racks.

• **Spoon** warm Fudge Filling into a heavy-duty, zip-top plastic bag; seal. Snip a tiny hole in one corner of bag; pipe a small amount of filling in center of each cookie. Sprinkle with peanuts. Cool. Filled cookies may be frozen up to 8 months. **Yield:** 4 dozen.

Fudge Filling

QUICK!

1 (14-ounce) can sweetened
   condensed milk
1 cup milk chocolate morsels
1 cup (6 ounces) semisweet
   chocolate morsels
1 teaspoon vanilla extract

• **Combine** all ingredients in a heavy saucepan; cook over low heat until chocolate morsels melt, stirring often. **Yield:** 2 cups.

Note: Heat any remaining Fudge Filling over low heat; serve over pound cake.

Barbara Ritchie
Waynesboro, Virginia

CARAMEL-FILLED CHOCOLATE COOKIES

1 cup butter or margarine,
   softened
1 cup sugar
1 cup firmly packed brown sugar
2 large eggs
2¼ cups all-purpose flour
¾ cup cocoa
1 teaspoon baking soda
2 teaspoons vanilla extract
1 cup finely chopped pecans,
   divided
1 tablespoon sugar
1 (8-ounce) package chewy
   caramels in milk chocolate

• **Beat** butter at medium speed with an electric mixer until creamy. Gradually add sugars, beating well. Add eggs, beating well.

• **Combine** flour, cocoa, and soda; add to butter mixture, mixing well. Stir in vanilla and ½ cup chopped pecans. Cover and chill 1 hour.

• **Combine** remaining ½ cup pecans and 1 tablespoon sugar; set aside. Divide dough into 2 portions; work with 1 portion at a time, keeping remaining portion chilled. Gently press 1 tablespoon cookie dough around each candy, forming a ball. Dip 1 side of cookie in pecan mixture. Place, pecan side up, 2 inches apart on ungreased cookie sheets. Bake at 375° for 8 minutes. (Cookies will look soft.) Let cool 1 minute on cookie sheets. Transfer to wire racks to cool. **Yield:** about 3 dozen.

Krista Kiger
Winston-Salem, North Carolina

ITALIAN CINNAMON STICKS

¾ cup sugar
½ cup walnuts, ground
1 teaspoon ground cinnamon
1 cup butter or margarine,
    softened
1 (8-ounce) package cream cheese,
    softened
2½ cups all-purpose flour
1 large egg, lightly beaten

• **Combine** first 3 ingredients; set aside.
• **Beat** butter and cream cheese at medium speed with an electric mixer until creamy; gradually add flour, mixing until well blended.
• **Shape** dough into a ball; wrap in plastic wrap, and chill 30 minutes.
• **Divide** dough in half; place 1 portion between two sheets of lightly floured wax paper, and roll into a 10-inch square (about ⅛ inch thick). Brush with egg; sprinkle with half of sugar mixture. Cut into 5- x ½-inch strips; twist strips, and place on ungreased baking sheets. Repeat procedure with remaining dough, egg, and sugar mixture.
• **Bake** at 350° for 10 to 12 minutes or until golden. Transfer to wire racks to cool. **Yield:** about 6½ dozen.

Ellie Wells
Lakeland, Florida

PEPPERMINT ROUNDS

1 cup butter or margarine,
    softened
½ cup sugar
1 large egg
1 teaspoon vanilla extract
2½ cups all-purpose flour
½ teaspoon salt
1 cup regular oats, uncooked
⅓ cup hard peppermint candy,
    crushed
Powdered sugar
Frosting

• **Beat** butter at medium speed with an electric mixer until creamy; gradually add sugar, beating well. Add egg and vanilla, beating well.
• **Combine** flour and salt; add to butter mixture. Stir in oats and peppermint

candy. Cover and chill 1 hour. Divide dough in half.
• **Roll** each portion to ⅛-inch thickness on a surface dusted with powdered sugar. Cut with a 2½-inch cookie cutter; place on greased and foil-lined cookie sheets.
• **Bake** at 350° for 8 minutes; transfer to wire racks to cool.
• **Spread** cookies with white frosting. Before frosting sets, drizzle lines of pink frosting across top of each cookie. Carefully draw a wooden pick through lines of frosting for a scalloped pattern. **Yield:** 4 dozen.

Frosting

QUICK!

4 cups sifted powdered sugar
¼ to ½ cup half-and-half
Dash of salt
1 teaspoon peppermint extract
Red liquid food coloring

• **Combine** first 4 ingredients, stirring until smooth. (Add additional half-and-half for desired consistency.)
• **Remove** ¼ cup frosting, and stir in 1 or 2 drops of red food coloring for pink frosting. **Yield:** 1½ cups.

Out of Our League
Junior League of Greensboro,
North Carolina

LEMON THYME COOKIES

1 cup butter or margarine,
    softened
1½ cups sugar
2 large eggs
2½ cups all-purpose flour
2 teaspoons cream of tartar
½ teaspoon salt
½ cup chopped fresh lemon thyme

• **Beat** butter at medium speed with an electric mixer until creamy; gradually add sugar, beating well. Add eggs, one at a time, beating until blended after each addition.
• **Combine** flour, cream of tartar, and salt; gradually add to butter mixture. Beat at low speed until blended after each addition. Stir in lemon thyme.

• **Shape** dough into 2 (10-inch) rolls; wrap each in wax paper, and chill at least 2 hours.
• **Unwrap** dough; cut each roll into ½-inch-thick slices, and place on lightly greased cookie sheets.
• **Bake** at 350° for 10 minutes. Transfer to wire racks to cool. **Yield:** 3½ dozen.

MEMORY BOOK COOKIES
(pictured at right)

1 cup butter or margarine,
    softened
2 cups firmly packed brown sugar
2 large eggs
1 teaspoon vanilla extract
3½ cups all-purpose flour
1 teaspoon baking soda
½ teaspoon salt
1 cup chopped pecans

• **Beat** butter at medium speed with an electric mixer until creamy; gradually add sugar, beating well. Add eggs and vanilla; mix well.
• **Combine** flour, soda, and salt; gradually add to butter mixture, mixing well. Stir in pecans.
• **Shape** dough into two 16-inch rolls; wrap in wax paper, and chill at least 4 hours.
• **Unwrap** and cut into ⅓-inch slices; place on ungreased cookie sheets.
• **Bake** at 375° for 6 to 8 minutes. Transfer to wire racks to cool. **Yield:** 8 dozen.

Note: You can freeze dough up to 3 months. Slice dough while frozen, and bake as directed.

Kitty Cromer
Anderson, South Carolina

Memory Book Cookies

CHOCOLATE CHIP-CINNAMON BISCOTTI

⅓ cup butter or margarine, softened
½ cup firmly packed brown sugar
½ cup sugar
1 tablespoon instant coffee or espresso granules
2 large eggs
2 cups all-purpose flour
1½ teaspoons baking powder
⅛ teaspoon salt
½ teaspoon ground cinnamon
1 cup chopped walnuts or pecans
1 cup semisweet chocolate mini-morsels
2 (2-ounce) squares vanilla-flavored candy coating, melted

• **Combine** first 4 ingredients in a large mixing bowl; beat at medium speed with an electric mixer until light and creamy. Add eggs, one at a time, beating until blended.
• **Combine** flour and next 3 ingredients; add to butter mixture, stirring until blended. Fold in nuts and chocolate morsels. Divide dough in half.
• **Shape** each portion of dough into a 10- x 2-inch log on a lightly greased cookie sheet.
• **Bake** at 350° for 25 minutes or until firm. Let cool on cookie sheet 5 minutes. Transfer logs to wire racks to cool completely.
• **Cut** each log diagonally into ½-inch-thick slices with a serrated knife, using a gentle sawing motion. Place slices on ungreased cookie sheets.
• **Bake** at 350° for 10 minutes; turn cookies over, and bake 10 additional minutes. Transfer to wire racks to cool.
• **Dip** 1 side of each cookie into candy coating; chill until set. **Yield:** 2½ dozen.

Carol Y. Chastain
San Antonio, Texas

CHOCOLATE-HAZELNUT BISCOTTI

For the same number of calories as a rice cake, you can have a slice of biscotto.

2 large eggs
⅔ cup sugar
1 tablespoon Frangelico or other hazelnut-flavored liqueur
2 cups sifted cake flour
1½ teaspoons baking powder
¼ teaspoon salt
1½ tablespoons cocoa
⅔ cup hazelnuts, chopped and toasted
Vegetable cooking spray

• **Beat** eggs at medium speed with an electric mixer until foamy. Gradually add sugar, beating at high speed until mixture is thick and pale. Add liqueur, beating until blended. Combine flour and next 3 ingredients; fold into egg mixture. Fold in nuts. Cover and chill 30 minutes.
• **Coat** a cookie sheet with cooking spray. Divide dough into 3 portions, and spoon portions 2 inches apart onto cookie sheet.
• **Shape** each portion of dough into an 8- x 1½-inch strip. Cover and chill 30 minutes; reshape dough, if necessary.
• **Bake** at 375° for 20 minutes or until lightly browned. Transfer to wire racks to cool. Cut diagonally into ½-inch-thick slices. Lay slices flat on cookie sheet. Bake at 375° for 5 minutes; turn slices over, and bake 5 additional minutes. Transfer to wire racks to cool. **Yield:** 3½ dozen.

Andy Lorber
Atlanta, Georgia

♥ Per cookie: Calories 50
Fat 1.7g Cholesterol 11mg
Sodium 17mg

FRUITCAKE BISCOTTI

Here's a fresh look at tradition – the flavors of fruitcake in a crunchy cookie. But don't worry about that old stigma. These are so good, there's no chance they'll still be hanging around after the New Year.

½ cup butter or margarine, softened
2 cups sugar
4 large eggs
1½ teaspoons grated lemon rind
½ teaspoon vanilla extract
¼ teaspoon almond extract
5 cups all-purpose flour
2 teaspoons baking soda
1 teaspoon baking powder
½ teaspoon salt
¾ cup whole blanched or slivered almonds, coarsely chopped
¾ cup dried cranberries
¾ cup dried tart cherries
½ cup candied orange rind

• **Beat** butter at medium speed with an electric mixer until creamy; gradually add sugar, beating well. Add eggs, one at a time, beating after each addition. Add rind and flavorings, mixing well.
• **Combine** flour and next 3 ingredients in a bowl; add to butter mixture, beating just until dry ingredients are moistened.
• **Turn** dough out onto a lightly floured surface; lightly flour hands, and knead in almonds, cranberries, cherries, and orange rind. Divide dough in half.
• **Shape** each portion into a 14- x 2-inch log on a lightly greased cookie sheet. Flatten logs slightly.
• **Bake** at 325° for 30 to 35 minutes or until golden. Cool on cookie sheet 5 minutes. Transfer to a wire rack to cool.
• **Cut** each log diagonally into ½-inch-thick slices with a serrated knife, using a gentle sawing motion. Place slices on ungreased cookie sheets.
• **Bake** at 325° for 10 minutes; turn cookies over, and bake 10 additional minutes. Transfer to wire racks to cool. **Yield:** 3½ dozen.

Note: If you can't find dried cranberries and cherries, substitute raisins, dates, or chopped dried apricots.

Cindy Briscoe
Birmingham, Alabama

RAISIN BARS

1 cup all-purpose flour
¼ cup sugar
⅓ cup butter or margarine
2 large eggs
1 cup sugar
2 tablespoons all-purpose flour
½ teaspoon baking powder
¼ teaspoon salt
1 tablespoon grated orange rind
2 tablespoons orange juice
¾ cup raisins, chopped
½ cup flaked coconut
2 teaspoons orange juice
2 teaspoons lemon juice
1½ teaspoons butter or
    margarine, softened
1 cup sifted powdered sugar

● **Combine** 1 cup flour and ¼ cup sugar; cut in ⅓ cup butter with pastry blender until mixture is crumbly. Press mixture in bottom of a lightly greased 9-inch square pan.
● **Bake** at 350° for 15 minutes.
● **Combine** eggs and next 8 ingredients, stirring until blended. Pour over crust.
● **Bake** at 350° for 20 to 25 minutes.
● **Combine** 2 teaspoons orange juice, lemon juice, and 1½ teaspoons butter in a small bowl; beat at medium speed with an electric mixer until smooth. Gradually add powdered sugar, beating until smooth. Pour mixture over hot layer. Cool in pan on a wire rack. Cut into bars. Freeze in an airtight container up to 3 months, if desired. **Yield:** about 3 dozen.

Three Rivers Cookbook I
Child Health Association
Sewickley, Pennsylvania

GOOEY TURTLE BARS

QUICK!

½ cup butter, melted
1½ cups vanilla wafer crumbs
2 cups (12 ounces) semisweet
    chocolate morsels
1 cup pecan pieces
1 (12-ounce) jar caramel topping

● **Combine** butter and wafer crumbs in a 13- x 9- x 2-inch baking pan; press in bottom of pan. Sprinkle with chocolate morsels and pecans.
● **Remove** lid from caramel topping; microwave at HIGH 1 to 1½ minutes or until hot, stirring after 30 seconds. Drizzle over pecans.
● **Bake** at 350° for 12 to 15 minutes or until morsels melt; cool in pan on a wire rack. Chill at least 30 minutes; cut into squares. **Yield:** 2 dozen.

PEANUT BUTTER-JAM BARS

½ cup butter or margarine,
    softened
½ cup sugar
½ cup firmly packed brown
    sugar
½ cup chunky peanut butter
1 large egg
1 teaspoon vanilla extract
1¼ cups all-purpose flour
¾ teaspoon baking soda
½ teaspoon baking powder
2 cups peanut butter morsels,
    divided
1 cup strawberry jam

● **Beat** butter at medium speed with an electric mixer until creamy; gradually add sugars, beating well. Add peanut butter, egg, and vanilla, mixing well.
● **Combine** flour, soda, and baking powder; gradually add to butter mixture, mixing well. Reserve 1 cup dough.
● **Stir** 1 cup peanut butter morsels into remaining dough; press in bottom of a 13- x 9- x 2-inch pan. Spread jam evenly over dough. Crumble reserved dough over jam, and sprinkle with remaining peanut butter morsels.
● **Bake** at 325° for 40 minutes or until golden. Cool completely in pan on a wire rack, and cut into bars. Cookies may be frozen up to 3 months. **Yield:** about 3 dozen.

Patty Flowers
Midland, Texas

MISSISSIPPI MUD

2 cups sugar
1½ cups all-purpose flour
½ cup cocoa
2 teaspoons baking powder
½ teaspoon salt
1 cup butter or margarine, melted
4 large eggs, lightly beaten
1 cup chopped pecans, divided
3 cups miniature marshmallows
Chocolate Frosting

● **Combine** first 5 ingredients in a large bowl. Add butter and eggs, stirring until smooth. Stir in ½ cup pecans. Pour mixture into a greased and floured 13- x 9- x 2-inch pan.
● **Bake** at 350° for 25 to 30 minutes or until a wooden pick inserted in center comes out clean. Immediately sprinkle marshmallows over top; return to oven, and bake 1 additional minute. Remove from oven; spread marshmallows on top. Let stand 5 minutes.
● **Spread** Chocolate Frosting evenly over marshmallows, and sprinkle with remaining ½ cup pecans. Cool completely in pan on a wire rack, and cut into squares. **Yield:** 2 dozen.

Chocolate Frosting

QUICK!

1 (16-ounce) package powdered
    sugar, sifted
⅓ cup cocoa
½ cup butter or margarine, melted
⅓ cup evaporated milk
1 teaspoon vanilla extract

● **Combine** all ingredients in a large mixing bowl; beat at medium speed with an electric mixer until dry ingredients are moistened. Beat mixture at high speed until spreading consistency. **Yield:** 2½ cups.

Note: If marshmallows do not spread easily after 1 minute in oven, do not bake longer. Let stand 1 to 2 minutes to soften.

Dee Elkins
Little Rock, Arkansas

GERMAN CHOCOLATE CHESS SQUARES

1 (18.25-ounce) package German chocolate cake mix with pudding
1 large egg, lightly beaten
½ cup butter or margarine, melted
1 cup chopped pecans
1 (8-ounce) package cream cheese, softened
2 large eggs
1 (16-ounce) package powdered sugar, sifted

• **Combine** first 4 ingredients in a large bowl, stirring until dry ingredients are moistened. Press in bottom of a greased 13- x 9- x 2-inch pan; set aside.
• **Combine** cream cheese, 2 eggs, and 1 cup sifted powdered sugar; beat at medium speed with an electric mixer until blended. Gradually add remaining powdered sugar, beating well. Pour over chocolate layer, spreading evenly.
• **Bake** at 350° for 40 minutes. Cool in pan on a wire rack, and cut into squares. **Yield:** 4 dozen.

Barbara Sutton
Portsmouth, Virginia

RICH BROWNIES

QUICK!

1 (10¼-ounce) package fudge brownie mix
½ cup miniature marshmallows
½ cup semisweet chocolate morsels
½ cup chopped pecans

• **Prepare** brownie mix according to package directions, folding marshmallows, chocolate morsels, and pecans into batter. Spread batter evenly in a greased 8-inch square pan.
• **Bake** at 350° for 24 minutes or until done. Cool in pan on a wire rack; cut into squares. **Yield:** 16 brownies.

TRIPLE DECKER BROWNIES

1½ cups quick-cooking oats, toasted
1 cup all-purpose flour
1 cup firmly packed brown sugar
½ teaspoon baking soda
¼ teaspoon salt
¾ cup butter or margarine, melted
2 (1-ounce) squares unsweetened chocolate
½ cup butter or margarine
1½ cups sugar
2 large eggs
1⅓ cups all-purpose flour
½ teaspoon baking powder
¼ teaspoon salt
½ cup milk
1 teaspoon vanilla extract
1 cup chopped pecans
Chocolate Frosting

• **Combine** first 5 ingredients in a large bowl; add ¾ cup melted butter, stirring well. Press mixture in bottom of two greased 8-inch square pans. Bake at 350° for 10 minutes.
• **Melt** chocolate and ½ cup butter in a large heavy saucepan over low heat; remove from heat. Add 1½ cups sugar and eggs, mixing well.
• **Combine** 1⅓ cups flour, baking powder, and ¼ teaspoon salt; add to chocolate mixture alternately with milk. Stir in vanilla and pecans. Spread over crust, and bake at 350° for 20 to 25 minutes. Cool in pans on wire racks. Spread with Chocolate Frosting. Cut into 2-inch squares. **Yield:** 32 brownies.

Chocolate Frosting

QUICK!

2 (1-ounce) squares unsweetened chocolate
¼ cup butter or margarine
3 cups sifted powdered sugar
2 teaspoons vanilla extract
3 to 4 tablespoons hot water

• **Melt** chocolate and butter in a heavy saucepan over low heat; remove from heat. Stir in powdered sugar, vanilla, and 1 tablespoon water. Stir in additional water until desired spreading consistency. **Yield:** 1½ cups.

NO-BAKE BROWNIES

QUICK!

2 cups (12 ounces) semisweet chocolate morsels
1 (12-ounce) can evaporated milk, divided
3 cups vanilla wafer crumbs
2 cups miniature marshmallows
1 cup chopped pecans
1 cup sifted powdered sugar
½ teaspoon salt

• **Combine** chocolate morsels and 1 cup evaporated milk in a heavy saucepan; cook over low heat until morsels melt, stirring occasionally. Set chocolate mixture aside.
• **Combine** wafer crumbs and remaining 4 ingredients in a large bowl; stir until blended. Reserve ½ cup chocolate mixture. Stir remaining chocolate mixture into crumb mixture. Press in a well-greased 9-inch square pan.
• **Combine** reserved ½ cup chocolate mixture and 2 teaspoons evaporated milk; spread over crumb mixture. (Reserve remaining evaporated milk for another use.) Cover and chill. Cut into squares. **Yield:** 3 dozen.

Jane Tutwiler
Birmingham, Alabama

CANDY BAR BROWNIES
(pictured on page 101)

4 large eggs, lightly beaten
2 cups sugar
¾ cup butter or margarine, melted
2 teaspoons vanilla extract
1½ cups all-purpose flour
½ teaspoon baking powder
¼ teaspoon salt
⅓ cup cocoa
4 (2.07-ounce) chocolate-coated caramel-peanut nougat bars, coarsely chopped *
3 (1.55-ounce) milk chocolate bars, finely chopped

• **Combine** first 4 ingredients in a large bowl; stir well.
• **Combine** flour and next 3 ingredients; stir into sugar mixture. Fold in chopped nougat bars.

• **Spoon** into a greased and floured 13- x 9- x 2-inch pan; sprinkle with chopped milk chocolate bars. Bake at 350° for 30 to 35 minutes. Cool in pan on a wire rack; cut into squares. **Yield:** 2½ dozen.

✻ For chocolate-coated caramel-peanut nougat bars, we used Snickers.

Mardee Johnson
Winston-Salem, North Carolina

MACADAMIA-FUDGE DESIGNER BROWNIES

2½ cups sugar
1½ cups butter or margarine
5   (1-ounce) squares unsweetened chocolate
6   large eggs, lightly beaten
2   cups all-purpose flour
1   cup coarsely chopped macadamia nuts or almonds
Fudge Frosting
Garnish: chopped macadamia nuts

• **Combine** sugar, butter, and chocolate in a large saucepan; cook over low heat until chocolate melts, stirring often. Remove from heat; cool 10 minutes.
• **Stir** in eggs, flour, and nuts. Pour mixture into a greased and floured 13- x 9- x 2-inch pan.
• **Bake** at 350° for 30 to 35 minutes. Cool in pan on a wire rack.
• **Pour** Fudge Frosting over top; chill 15 minutes, and cut into squares. Garnish, if desired. **Yield:** 4 dozen.

Fudge Frosting

QUICK!

1   cup whipping cream
12 (1-ounce) squares semisweet chocolate

• **Heat** whipping cream in a medium saucepan over medium heat; add chocolate, stirring until smooth. Remove from heat, and cool to room temperature. **Yield:** 2½ cups.

Daisy Cook
Tyler, Texas

RASPBERRY BROWNIES

QUICK!

½   cup butter or margarine, softened
1   cup sugar
2   large eggs
2   (1-ounce) squares unsweetened chocolate, melted
¾   cup all-purpose flour
1   cup chopped walnuts
⅓   cup raspberry jam

• **Beat** butter at medium speed with an electric mixer until soft and creamy; gradually add sugar, beating well. Add eggs and melted chocolate, mixing well. Add flour, mixing well; stir in walnuts.
• **Spoon** half of batter into a greased and floured 9-inch square pan. Spread jam over batter; top with remaining batter. Bake at 350° for about 28 to 30 minutes. **Yield:** 3 dozen brownies.

Mrs. Harland J. Stone
Ocala, Florida

TURTLE CANDIES

2   cups (12 ounces) semisweet chocolate morsels
64 pecan halves (about 1¼ cups)
28 caramels, unwrapped
2   tablespoons whipping cream

• **Microwave** chocolate morsels in a glass bowl at HIGH for 1½ minutes, stirring after 1 minute. Stir until smooth; cool until slightly thickened.
• **Drop** chocolate by tablespoonfuls onto a wax paper-lined baking sheet, shaping into 16 (1½-inch) circles. Reserve remaining chocolate. Arrange 4 pecans over each circle of chocolate, and chill until firm.
• **Place** caramels and whipping cream in a glass bowl. Microwave at HIGH 2 minutes or until caramels melt; stir after 1 minute. Let stand 4 minutes or until slightly thickened. Spoon caramel mixture evenly over pecans.
• **Microwave** remaining chocolate at HIGH 1 minute, stirring after 30 seconds; quickly spread chocolate over caramel mixture. Chill until firm. **Yield:** 16 candies.

PEANUT CLUSTERS

QUICK!

2   cups peanut butter morsels or butterscotch morsels
1   cup (6 ounces) semisweet chocolate morsels
1   (12-ounce) can salted peanuts

• **Combine** peanut butter morsels and chocolate morsels in a heavy saucepan; cook over low heat until morsels melt, stirring often. Remove from heat; add peanuts, stirring to coat.
• **Drop** by rounded teaspoonfuls onto wax paper. Cool completely, and store in an airtight container at room temperature. **Yield:** about 4 dozen.

Judy Hughes
Indian Harbour Beach, Florida

MICROWAVE TOFFEE

QUICK!

½   cup finely chopped pecans
½   cup butter or margarine
1   cup sugar
1   teaspoon salt
¼   cup water
¾   cup semisweet chocolate morsels
¼   cup finely chopped pecans

• **Sprinkle** ½ cup pecans in a 9-inch circle on a greased cookie sheet; set aside.
• **Coat** top 2 inches of a 2½-quart glass bowl with butter; place remaining butter in bowl. Add sugar, salt, and water (do not stir.) Microwave at HIGH 11 minutes or until mixture just begins to turn light brown; pour over pecans. Sprinkle with morsels; let stand 1 minute. Spread morsels over sugar mixture, and sprinkle with ¼ cup chopped pecans. Cover and chill until firm. Break into bite-size pieces. **Yield:** 1 pound.

Jan Ramsey
Quitaque, Texas

Chocolate Pralines;
Basic Pralines;
Orange Pralines

BASIC PRALINES
(pictured at left)

Vegetable cooking spray
1½ cups sugar
¾ cup firmly packed brown
    sugar
¼ cup plus 2 tablespoons
    butter
½ cup milk
1½ cups chopped pecans

• **Lightly** coat a few sheets of wax paper with cooking spray; set aside.
• **Combine** 1½ cups sugar and remaining ingredients in a heavy 3-quart saucepan. Bring to a boil over medium heat, stirring constantly. Boil, uncovered, stirring constantly, 1 to 2 minutes or until a candy thermometer registers 220°. (You may need to lower the heat with a thinner saucepan, and rely on a candy thermometer instead of a timer.)
• **Remove** from heat, and beat with a wooden spoon 4 to 6 minutes or just until mixture begins to thicken. Working rapidly, drop by tablespoonfuls onto prepared wax paper; let stand until firm. **Yield:** 2½ dozen.

Orange Pralines: Add 2½ to 3 tablespoons Cointreau or other orange-flavored liqueur before cooking.

Café au Lait Pralines: Add 1½ tablespoons instant coffee granules before cooking.

Mocha Pralines: Add 1½ to 2 tablespoons instant coffee granules and ½ cup semisweet chocolate morsels before cooking.

Chocolate-Peanut Butter Pralines: Add ½ cup semisweet chocolate morsels and ¼ cup creamy peanut butter before cooking.

Peanut Butter Pralines: Add 2 tablespoons creamy peanut butter before cooking, and stir 1 teaspoon vanilla into cooked mixture before beating.

Chocolate-Mint Pralines: Add 5 (½-ounce) chocolate-covered peppermint patties before cooking.

Hot Spicy Pralines: Add ½ teaspoon ground red pepper before cooking.

Bourbon Pralines: Add 3 tablespoons bourbon before cooking.

Chocolate Pralines: Add 2 (1-ounce) squares unsweetened chocolate before cooking.

Vanilla Pralines: Stir 1 teaspoon vanilla extract into cooked mixture before beating.

Joe Cahn
New Orleans School of Cooking and
General Store in Jax Brewery
New Orleans, Louisiana

BITTERSWEET TRUFFLES

½ cup butter or margarine
¾ cup cocoa
1 (14-ounce) can sweetened
    condensed milk
1 teaspoon vanilla extract
Cocoa

• **Melt** butter in a heavy saucepan over low heat; stir in ¾ cup cocoa. Stir in milk until smooth. Cook over medium heat, stirring constantly, until thickened and smooth (about 3 minutes). Remove from heat; stir in vanilla. Pour into a greased 8-inch square pan.
• **Cover** and chill 3 hours or until firm.
• **Shape** mixture into 1¼-inch balls; roll in additional cocoa. Place balls in miniature paper baking cups. Store in an airtight container in the refrigerator up to 1 week. **Yield:** 3 dozen.

Rublelene Singleton
Scotts Hill, Tennessee

ORANGE-PECAN TRUFFLES

8 (1-ounce) squares semisweet
    chocolate
⅓ cup butter or margarine
½ cup orange marmalade
½ cup chopped pecans, toasted
2 tablespoons orange-flavored
    liqueur *
1 cup finely chopped pecans

• **Combine** chocolate squares and butter in top of a double boiler; bring water to a boil. Reduce heat to low; cook until chocolate melts, stirring occasionally.
• **Remove** from heat; stir in marmalade, ½ cup chopped pecans, and liqueur. Cool slightly; cover and chill until firm (at least 2 hours).
• **Shape** truffle mixture into ¾-inch balls, and roll in 1 cup finely chopped pecans. (Truffle mixture tends to stick to hands.) Place truffles in paper or foil bonbon cups.
• **Store** candy in airtight containers in refrigerator up to 3 weeks or freeze up to 12 months. Serve cold. **Yield:** 3 dozen.

* You can substitute 2 tablespoons of orange juice for liqueur.

Louise W. Mayer
Richmond, Virginia

MICROWAVE CHOCOLATE FUDGE

QUICK!

3 cups semisweet chocolate
      morsels
1 (14-ounce) can sweetened
      condensed milk
¼ cup butter or margarine, cut
      into pieces
1 cup chopped walnuts

• **Combine** first 3 ingredients in a 2-quart glass bowl. Microwave at MEDIUM (50% power) 4 to 5 minutes, stirring at 1½-minute intervals.
• **Stir** in chopped walnuts, and pour mixture into a buttered 8-inch square dish. Cover and chill at least 2 hours. Cut into squares. **Yield:** 2 pounds.

Suzan L. Wiener
Spring Hill, Florida

DIAMOND FUDGE

QUICK!

1 cup (6 ounces) semisweet
      chocolate morsels
1 cup creamy peanut butter
½ cup butter or margarine
1 cup sifted powdered sugar

• **Combine** first 3 ingredients in a saucepan; cook over low heat, stirring constantly, just until mixture is smooth. Remove from heat. Add powdered sugar, stirring until smooth.
• **Spoon** into a buttered 8-inch square pan; cover and chill until firm. Let stand at room temperature about 10 minutes before cutting into squares. Store in refrigerator. **Yield:** 1½ pounds.

A Centennial Sampler
The American Association of University
Women of Elkins, West Virginia

FOUR-CHIPS FUDGE

¾ cup butter or margarine
1 (14-ounce) can sweetened
      condensed milk
3 tablespoons milk
2 cups (12 ounces) semisweet
      chocolate morsels
1 (11½-ounce) package milk
      chocolate morsels
1 (10-ounce) package peanut
      butter-flavored morsels
1 cup butterscotch-flavored
      morsels
1 (7-ounce) jar marshmallow
      cream
1½ teaspoons vanilla extract
½ to 1 teaspoon almond extract
1 pound walnuts, coarsely chopped

• **Melt** butter in a heavy Dutch oven over low heat; stir in condensed milk and milk. Add all morsels; cook, stirring constantly, until smooth. Remove from heat; stir in marshmallow cream and flavorings. Stir in walnuts.
• **Spoon** into a buttered 15- x 10- x 1-inch jellyroll pan; spread evenly. Cover and chill; cut into squares. Store in an airtight container in the refrigerator. **Yield:** 5 pounds.

Annie Grace
Walkertown, North Carolina

MINT FUDGE

2 cups sugar
⅓ cup cocoa
Pinch of salt
⅔ cup milk
2 tablespoons light corn syrup
¼ cup butter or margarine
¼ teaspoon peppermint extract
1 cup sifted powdered sugar
3 to 4 teaspoons milk
3 drops of peppermint extract
1 or 2 drops of green liquid food
      coloring

• **Combine** first 5 ingredients in a heavy 3-quart saucepan; bring mixture to a boil over medium heat, stirring constantly. Cover and boil 3 minutes.
• **Remove** lid, and cook until sugar mixture reaches soft ball stage or candy

thermometer registers 234°. Remove from heat; cool 10 minutes.
• **Add** butter and ¼ teaspoon peppermint extract; beat until mixture thickens and begins to lose its gloss.
• **Pour** mixture into a buttered 8-inch square pan or dish. Cool and cut into squares.
• **Place** squares at least ½-inch apart on a wax-paper lined baking sheet; set aside.
• **Combine** powdered sugar and remaining 3 ingredients, stirring until blended.
• **Place** mixture in a heavy-duty, zip-top plastic bag; seal. Snip a tiny hole in one corner of bag; drizzle over fudge. **Yield:** 1¼ pounds.

WHITE CHOCOLATE-COFFEE FUDGE

2 cups sugar
⅔ cup evaporated milk
½ cup butter or margarine
12 large marshmallows
1 tablespoon instant coffee
      granules
Pinch of salt
1 (6-ounce) package white
      chocolate-flavored baking bar,
      chopped
1 cup chopped pecans or walnuts
1 teaspoon vanilla extract

• **Combine** first 6 ingredients in a large saucepan. Cook over medium-low heat, stirring constantly, until mixture comes to a boil.
• **Cover**, reduce heat, and simmer 5 minutes; remove from heat.
• **Add** baking bar and remaining ingredients; stir until chocolate melts. Spoon into a buttered 8-inch square pan, spreading evenly. Cool and cut into squares. **Yield:** 2 pounds.

At right: Berry Napoleon (page 121)

DESSERTS

ORANGE BAKED APPLES WITH COOKIE CRUMBS

6 medium cooking apples (about
   2¼ pounds)
¼ cup unsweetened apple juice
1 tablespoon lemon juice
1 (4-inch) stick cinnamon, broken
   in half
⅓ cup orange marmalade
6 small gingersnaps, crushed

• **Core** apples, starting at stem end, to, but not through, opposite end. Peel top third of each apple.
• **Place** apples in an 11- x 7- x 1½-inch baking dish; add apple juice, lemon juice, and cinnamon stick to baking dish. Cover.
• **Bake** at 350° for 30 minutes. Uncover and spoon marmalade evenly into center of each apple; sprinkle with crushed gingersnaps. Bake 10 additional minutes or until apples are tender. **Yield:** 6 servings.

Beth Workman
Greensboro, North Carolina

CHAMPAGNE ORANGES

½ cup sugar
½ cup orange marmalade
1½ cups champagne *
8 large navel oranges, peeled and
   sectioned
½ cup slivered almonds,
   toasted

• **Combine** sugar and orange marmalade in a small saucepan; cook over medium heat until sugar dissolves, stirring often. Remove from heat, and let cool slightly.
• **Combine** sugar mixture, champagne, and orange sections, stirring gently. Cover and chill 8 hours. To serve, spoon orange sections into individual compotes or dessert dishes, and sprinkle evenly with toasted almonds. **Yield:** 8 servings.

* Substitute 1½ cups sparkling white grape juice for champagne.

Louise Bainter
Grove, Oklahoma

GINGER-ORANGE BAKED FRUIT

6 cups pitted prunes, cut in half
6 cups frozen sliced peaches,
   thawed and drained
1½ cups raisins
3 cups orange juice
1 (18-ounce) jar orange
   marmalade
1 tablespoon ground ginger
1 (3½-ounce) can flaked coconut,
   toasted

• **Layer** first 3 ingredients in a lightly greased 13- x 9- x 2-inch baking dish.
• **Combine** orange juice, marmalade, and ginger; pour over fruit.
• **Bake**, uncovered, at 350° for 45 to 50 minutes or until bubbly; sprinkle with coconut. Serve with a slotted spoon. If desired, bake fruit as directed, omitting coconut; spoon into individual compotes, and sprinkle with coconut. **Yield:** 18 to 20 servings.

Joel Allard
San Antonio, Texas

MIXED FRUIT COMPOTE

½ cup dried pitted prunes
½ cup dried apricot halves
1 cup apple juice
1 (2-inch) stick cinnamon
1 tablespoon grated orange
   rind
1 navel orange, peeled, sectioned,
   and chopped
1 grapefruit, peeled, sectioned,
   and chopped
1 Granny Smith apple, peeled,
   cored, and chopped
1 banana, sliced
⅓ cup orange juice
1 to 2 tablespoons brown sugar
3 tablespoons chopped walnuts,
   toasted

• **Combine** prunes and apricots in a small bowl; set aside.
• **Combine** apple juice and cinnamon stick in a small saucepan; cook over medium heat until hot, and pour over fruit mixture. Cover and let stand 8 hours.

• **Remove** and discard cinnamon stick; add orange rind and next 6 ingredients, tossing gently. Sprinkle with walnuts. **Yield:** 6 to 8 servings.

Dairy Hollow House
Eureka Springs, Arkansas

HONEYED PEACHES 'N' CREAM

The subtle tang and nutty hint of the luxuriously thick sauce adds flattering flavor notes to this ginger-spiced dessert.

¼ cup Chambord or other
   raspberry-flavored liqueur
2 tablespoons honey
1 teaspoon lemon juice
½ teaspoon ground ginger
4 cups sliced fresh or frozen
   peaches, thawed
Crème Fraîche Sauce or vanilla ice
   cream
2 tablespoons slivered almonds,
   toasted (optional)

• **Combine** first 4 ingredients in a bowl; add peaches, tossing gently. Cover and chill 2 hours.
• **Spoon** mixture into individual dessert dishes; top with Crème Fraîche Sauce or vanilla ice cream. Sprinkle with almonds, if desired, and serve immediately. **Yield:** 6 servings.

Crème Fraîche Sauce

QUICK!

⅓ cup sour cream
⅓ cup whipping cream
2 tablespoons powdered
   sugar

• **Combine** all ingredients; cover and chill 8 hours. **Yield:** ⅔ cup.

Louise Jackson
Shreveport, Louisiana

CARAMEL PEACHES

Four simple ingredients and one baking dish make this caramelized peach dessert a must-try recipe. Fresh peaches are our first choice, but when they're not in season, substitute frozen peach slices.

6 large peaches, peeled and sliced *
3 tablespoons sugar
¼ cup butter or margarine, cut into small pieces
1 cup whipping cream

• **Place** peaches in a lightly greased 11- x 7- x 1½-inch baking dish; sprinkle with sugar, and dot with butter.
• **Bake** at 400° for 25 to 30 minutes or until tender and liquid is slightly thickened, stirring once. Stir in whipping cream; bake 15 additional minutes, stirring every 5 minutes. Cool on a wire rack 15 minutes; serve warm. **Yield:** 4 to 6 servings.

* You can substitute 6 cups frozen sliced peaches, thawed, for fresh.

PEACH MELBA MERINGUES WITH BUTTERMILK CUSTARD SAUCE

4 egg whites
¼ teaspoon cream of tartar
1 cup sugar
Buttermilk Custard Sauce
5 cups sliced fresh peaches
1 cup fresh raspberries
Raspberry Sauce

• **Beat** egg whites and cream of tartar at high speed with an electric mixer until foamy. Add sugar, 1 tablespoon at a time, beating until stiff peaks form and sugar dissolves (2 to 4 minutes).
• **Drop** mixture, ½ cup at a time, onto a baking sheet lined with parchment paper; shape with a spoon to resemble shallow bowls.
• **Bake** at 250° for 1 hour. Turn oven off, and let stand in oven 1½ hours. Remove from oven, and cool completely; remove from paper.
• **Pour** Buttermilk Custard Sauce evenly onto serving plates; top with meringue shells. Spoon peaches and raspberries into shells.
• **Place** ¼ cup Raspberry Sauce in a heavy-duty, zip-top plastic bag; seal. Snip a tiny hole in one corner of bag; squeeze small circles of sauce onto Buttermilk Custard Sauce around shells. Pull a wooden pick through circles in several directions to make a design.
• **Drizzle** remaining sauce over fruit; serve immediately. **Yield:** 8 servings.

❤ Per serving: Calories 344
Fat 3.8g Cholesterol 113mg
Sodium 127mg

Buttermilk Custard Sauce

QUICK!

3 cups buttermilk
¾ cup sugar
1 tablespoon cornstarch
4 egg yolks, lightly beaten
1 teaspoon vanilla extract

• **Combine** first 4 ingredients in a heavy saucepan, whisking until blended. Bring to a boil over medium heat, whisking constantly; cook 1 minute, whisking constantly. Remove from heat; stir in vanilla. Cover and chill. **Yield:** 3 cups.

Raspberry Sauce

QUICK!

1 (12-ounce) package frozen unsweetened raspberries, thawed and undrained
2 tablespoons sugar
2 tablespoons Framboise or other raspberry-flavored liqueur
1 teaspoon cornstarch
1 tablespoon cold water

• **Combine** first 3 ingredients in container of an electric blender; process until smooth, stopping once to scrape down sides. Pour through a wire-mesh strainer into a small saucepan, pressing with back of a spoon; discard seeds.
• **Combine** cornstarch and water; stir until smooth. Stir into raspberry mixture in pan. Bring to a boil over medium heat; boil 1 minute, stirring constantly. **Yield:** 1 cup.

Susan H. Clark
Greer, South Carolina

PEAR-BLUE CHEESE GRATIN

¼ cup sugar
1 tablespoon all-purpose flour
1 teaspoon cornstarch
1 large egg
1 egg yolk
1 cup half-and-half
2 tablespoons butter or margarine
½ teaspoon vanilla extract
2 tablespoons cream cheese, softened
3 tablespoons crumbled blue cheese, softened
1 (8½-ounce) can pear halves, drained
2 to 3 tablespoons sifted powdered sugar
¼ cup walnuts, chopped
¼ cup gingersnap crumbs

• **Combine** first 3 ingredients in a small bowl; set aside. Beat egg and egg yolk in a small mixing bowl at high speed with an electric mixer until thick and pale; add sugar mixture, beating until blended. Set aside.
• **Cook** half-and-half in a small saucepan over medium heat until hot (do not boil). Gradually stir about one-fourth of hot liquid into egg mixture; add to remaining hot mixture, stirring constantly with a wire whisk. Cook over low heat, stirring constantly, until thickened. Remove from heat; stir 1 minute. Transfer to a bowl; stir in butter and vanilla. Cover and chill at least 2 hours or overnight.
• **Combine** cream cheese and blue cheese; beat at medium speed with an electric mixer until smooth. Fold into chilled mixture; spoon evenly into four lightly greased 4-inch gratin dishes or 10-ounce custard cups. Place an inverted pear half in each; sprinkle with powdered sugar. Place gratins in a 9-inch square pan; broil 5½ inches from heat (with electric oven door partially opened) 1½ minutes or until lightly browned. Combine walnuts and gingersnap crumbs; sprinkle evenly over gratins. Broil 30 to 40 additional seconds. Serve warm. **Yield:** 4 servings.

Pear en Croûte

PEARS EN CROÛTE
(pictured at left)

2 (15-ounce) packages
    refrigerated piecrusts
5 or 6 firm ripe pears, unpeeled
    (about 2 pounds)
1 egg yolk
1 tablespoon water
Caramel Sauce
Garnish: fresh mint leaves

• **Unfold** piecrusts, one at a time; place on a lightly floured surface, and roll each into a 10-inch square. Cut each square into 1-inch strips. Starting at bottom of pear, carefully begin wrapping with 1 pastry strip, overlapping strip ¼ inch as you cover pear. Continue wrapping by moistening ends of strips with water and joining to previous strip until pear is completely covered. Repeat procedure with remaining pears and pastry strips.
• **Place** pears on a baking sheet. Combine egg yolk and water; brush evenly on pastry. Bake at 350° for 1 hour or until tender.
• **Spoon** 2 to 3 tablespoons Caramel Sauce onto each dessert plate; top with a pear. Garnish, if desired. **Yield:** 5 or 6 servings.

Note: To make ahead, wrap pears in pastry; cover tightly with plastic wrap, and chill 8 hours. Remove plastic wrap; brush with egg yolk mixture, and bake as directed.

Caramel Sauce
QUICK!

1 (12-ounce) jar caramel ice cream
    topping
1 (14-ounce) can sweetened
    condensed milk
¼ cup Cointreau or other orange-
    flavored liqueur
2 tablespoons lemon juice

• **Combine** caramel topping and milk in top of a double boiler; bring water to a boil. Reduce heat to low; cook, stirring constantly, until smooth. Stir in Cointreau and lemon juice. **Yield:** 2½ cups.

Jane Micol Schatzman
Winston-Salem, North Carolina

BERRY NAPOLEONS
(pictured on page 117)

Edged with a pool of Strawberry Sauce or served plain, Berry Napoleons are the perfect finish to a summer meal.

Vegetable cooking spray
1½ cups quick-cooking oats,
    uncooked
½ cup butter or margarine,
    melted
¾ cup sugar
1 teaspoon all-purpose flour
1 teaspoon baking powder
1 large egg, lightly beaten
½ cup chopped pecans
1 teaspoon vanilla extract
¾ cup semisweet chocolate
    morsels
1½ tablespoons Chambord or
    other raspberry-flavored
    liqueur
1 tablespoon butter or margarine
2 cups whipping cream
¼ cup sifted powdered sugar
1 pint fresh blackberries or
    raspberries
Garnish: fresh berries
Strawberry Sauce (optional)

• **Cover** baking sheets with aluminum foil, and coat with cooking spray. Set aside.
• **Combine** oats and ½ cup melted butter in a bowl; stir in ¾ cup sugar, flour, and baking powder. Add egg, pecans, and vanilla, stirring until blended.
• **Drop** mixture by rounded teaspoonfuls 2 inches apart into 36 mounds onto prepared cookie sheets.
• **Bake** at 325° for 12 minutes or until lightly browned. Allow to cool completely on cookie sheets. Remove from foil, and place cookies on wax paper.
• **Combine** chocolate morsels, liqueur, and 1 tablespoon butter in a small saucepan; cook over low heat, stirring constantly, until chocolate morsels and butter melt.
• **Spoon** mixture into a heavy-duty, zip-top plastic bag; seal. Snip a tiny hole in one corner of bag, and gently squeeze bag to drizzle chocolate over cooled cookies. Let cookies stand until chocolate is firm.

• **Beat** whipping cream until foamy; gradually add powdered sugar, beating until soft peaks form. Set aside ¾ cup whipped cream.
• **Place** 1 cookie on each serving plate. Pipe or dollop ½-inch layer of whipped cream onto each cookie; top with berries. Top each with a second cookie, and repeat procedure. Top with remaining cookies. Pipe or dollop with reserved ¾ cup whipped cream; top each with a berry. If desired, spoon about 1 tablespoon Strawberry Sauce around 1 side of napoleon. Garnish, if desired. **Yield:** 12 servings.

Strawberry Sauce
QUICK!

1 (10-ounce) package frozen
    strawberries
1 tablespoon cornstarch

• **Puree** strawberries in blender.
• **Pour** mixture through a wire-mesh strainer into a small saucepan, pressing with back of a spoon. Discard seeds.
• **Add** cornstarch to juice. Bring mixture to a boil over medium heat, stirring constantly. Boil 1 minute. Cool before serving. **Yield:** 1 cup.

Mrs. Carl W. Terry
Huntsville, Alabama

PEANUT BUTTER AND CHOCOLATE NAPOLEONS

1   cup creamy peanut butter
1   (8-ounce) package cream cheese, softened
½   cup sugar
1   teaspoon vanilla extract
½   cup whipping cream, whipped
24 chocolate wafers
3   (1-ounce) squares semisweet chocolate, melted
¼   cup milk
Chocolate Sauce

• **Combine** first 4 ingredients in a large mixing bowl; beat at medium speed with an electric mixer until blended. Fold in whipped cream. Reserve ½ cup peanut butter mixture.
• **Pipe** or spoon one-fourth of remaining peanut butter mixture evenly onto 6 chocolate wafers. Top each with a second chocolate wafer; pipe or spoon another one-fourth of peanut butter mixture evenly onto the wafers. Repeat procedure with a third wafer and another one-fourth of peanut butter mixture, and top with remaining wafers. Pipe or dollop with remaining one-fourth of peanut butter mixture; chill.
• **Spoon** melted chocolate into a heavy-duty, zip-top plastic bag; seal. Snip a tiny hole in one corner of bag. Pipe chocolate to form an overlapping leaf design onto six dessert plates. Chill plates until chocolate is firm. For each chocolate garnish, pipe remaining melted chocolate onto wax paper in overlapping leaf designs; chill until chocolate is firm.
• **Combine** ½ cup reserved peanut butter mixture and milk.
• **Spoon** peanut butter mixture and Chocolate Sauce inside piped design on prepared plates. Use a wooden pick to spread sauces to edges of the leaves. Arrange napoleons on plates. Top each napoleon with a chocolate garnish. Serve immediately. **Yield:** 6 servings.

Chocolate Sauce

QUICK!

½   cup whipping cream
2   tablespoons sugar
3   (1-ounce) squares semisweet chocolate
½   teaspoon vanilla extract

• **Combine** whipping cream and sugar in a small saucepan over low heat. Add chocolate, and cook, stirring constantly, until chocolate melts. Remove from heat, and stir in vanilla. **Yield:** ¾ cup.

HELLO DOLLY DESSERT

2   cups graham cracker crumbs
¼   cup sugar
2   tablespoons ground cinnamon
½   cup butter or margarine, melted
2½ cups chopped pecans
2   cups (12-ounces) semisweet chocolate morsels
2   (6-ounce) packages white chocolate, finely chopped *
1   (14-ounce) package flaked coconut
1   (14-ounce) can sweetened condensed milk

• **Combine** first 3 ingredients; stir in butter. Press in bottom and 1 inch up sides of a 10-inch springform pan.
• **Layer** with chopped pecans, chocolate morsels, white chocolate, and coconut; press down firmly. Pour condensed milk evenly over coconut.
• **Bake** at 350° for 40 to 45 minutes. Cool 10 minutes in pan on a wire rack. Run a knife around edge to release sides; remove sides of pan. Cool completely on wire rack. Slice and reheat before serving. **Yield:** 12 to 15 servings.
Concho Confetti Cafe and Catering
San Angelo, Texas

* For white chocolate, we used Nestle's Baking Bars and Baker's Premium White Chocolate. We tried white chocolate morsels, but the layers didn't stay together.

CARAMEL FONDUE

QUICK!

3   (14-ounce) packages caramels, unwrapped
⅓ to ½ cup milk
1   (8-ounce) container cream cheese

• **Combine** caramels, ⅓ cup milk, and cream cheese in a Dutch oven; cook over low heat, stirring constantly, until mixture is smooth. Add additional milk if mixture is too thick for dipping. Spoon into a fondue pot or chafing dish. Serve with fruit or cake. **Yield:** 4 cups.
Carolyn Look
El Paso, Texas

CHOCOLATE PLUNGE

QUICK!

2   cups light corn syrup
1½ cups whipping cream
3   (12-ounce) packages semisweet chocolate morsels

• **Combine** corn syrup and whipping cream in a heavy saucepan; bring mixture to a boil.
• **Remove** from heat; add chocolate morsels, stirring until smooth. Spoon into a fondue pot or chafing dish. Serve with fruit or cake. **Yield:** 7 cups.
Mary Pappas
Richmond, Virginia

WHITE CHOCOLATE FONDUE

QUICK!

1   pound vanilla-flavored candy coating
½   cup half-and-half
2   tablespoons brandy

• **Melt** coating in a heavy saucepan over low heat, stirring constantly. Gradually add half-and-half, stirring constantly until blended. Stir in brandy.
• **Serve** at room temperature with fresh strawberries. **Yield:** 2 cups.
Ann Ruff
Bellaire, Texas

CHOCOLATE POTS DE CRÈME

QUICK!

Luscious Chocolate Pots de Crème boast just 4 ingredients and require only a saucepan and a few utensils to make.

1 cup (6 ounces) semisweet
    chocolate morsels
1 cup whipping cream
½ cup half-and-half
2 egg yolks

● **Combine** first 3 ingredients in a heavy saucepan; cook over low heat, stirring constantly, until chocolate melts.
● **Beat** egg yolks until thick and pale. Gradually stir about one-fourth of hot mixture into yolks; add to remaining hot mixture, stirring constantly.
● **Cook** over low heat, stirring constantly, 2 minutes or until mixture thickens slightly. Spoon into individual pots de crème cups or custard cups. Cover and chill. **Yield:** 4 to 6 servings.

Mrs. C. M. Conklin II
Dallas, Texas

CHOCOLATE-ALMOND SILK PUDDING

QUICK!

4 cups skim milk
½ cup amaretto
1½ cups sugar
½ cup cocoa
½ cup cornstarch
1½ teaspoons vanilla extract

● **Combine** milk and liqueur in a heavy saucepan; cook over medium heat until hot (do not boil).
● **Sift** sugar, cocoa, and cornstarch together in a large heavy saucepan; add hot milk mixture, whisking until smooth. Bring to a boil over medium heat; boil 1 minute. Stir in vanilla.
● **Pour** into 10 custard cups; cover with wax paper, and chill. **Yield:** 5 cups.

Sandi Pichon
Slidell, Louisiana

♥ Per ½-cup serving: Calories 210
Fat 0.7g Cholesterol 4mg
Sodium 59mg

FUDGY CHOCOLATE PUDDING

2 (4-ounce) bars dark sweet
    chocolate bars
⅔ cup strongly brewed coffee
1 cup sugar
1 cup butter
4 large eggs
½ cup whipping cream
1 tablespoon powdered sugar

● **Combine** chocolate and coffee in top of a double boiler; bring water to a boil. Reduce heat to low; cook until chocolate melts, stirring occasionally. Gradually whisk in 1 cup sugar. Add butter, 1 tablespoon at a time, whisking until butter melts.
● **Whisk** eggs until thick and pale. Gradually stir about one-fourth of hot mixture into eggs; add to remaining hot mixture, whisking constantly. Pour into six 6-ounce greased custard cups, and place cups in a 13- x 9- x 2-inch pan. Add hot water to pan to depth of 1 inch. Cover pan with aluminum foil.
● **Bake** at 350° for 45 minutes or until set. Remove from pan; cool on a wire rack. Cover and chill at least 8 hours.
● **Beat** whipping cream at high speed with an electric mixer until foamy; gradually add powdered sugar, beating until soft peaks form. Pipe or dollop onto pudding. **Yield:** 6 servings.

W. N. Cottrell II
New Orleans, Louisiana

LEMON-PEAR PUDDING

3 large pears, peeled and thinly
    sliced
¼ cup sugar
¼ cup fresh lemon juice
1 cup self-rising flour
¾ cup firmly packed brown sugar
1 teaspoon grated lemon rind
½ cup butter or margarine
Whipped cream

● **Combine** first 3 ingredients; place in a greased 8-inch square baking dish.
● **Combine** flour, brown sugar, and lemon rind; cut in butter with pastry blender until mixture is crumbly, and sprinkle evenly over pear mixture.

● **Bake** at 400° for 30 to 35 minutes. Serve warm with whipped cream. **Yield:** 6 servings.

Wylene B. Gillespie
Gallatin, Tennessee

BUTTERMILK BREAD PUDDING WITH BUTTER-RUM SAUCE

QUICK!

1 (16-ounce) loaf unsliced French
    bread
¼ cup butter or margarine
1 quart buttermilk
1 cup raisins
2 large eggs, lightly beaten
1⅓ cups firmly packed light brown
    sugar
1 tablespoon vanilla extract
Butter-Rum Sauce

● **Tear** bread into 1-inch pieces; reserve 7½ cups. Reserve remaining bread for another use.
● **Melt** butter in a 13- x 9- x 2-inch pan in 350° oven.
● **Combine** 7½ cups bread pieces, buttermilk, and raisins in a bowl; set aside.
● **Combine** eggs, brown sugar, and vanilla, whisking well.
● **Add** egg mixture to bread mixture, stirring gently. Pour into pan of melted butter.
● **Bake** at 350° for 1 hour. Serve warm or cold with Butter-Rum Sauce. **Yield:** 10 to 12 servings.

Butter-Rum Sauce

QUICK!

½ cup butter or margarine,
    softened
½ cup sugar
1 egg yolk
¼ cup water
3 tablespoons rum

● **Combine** first 4 ingredients in a small saucepan, stirring well.
● **Cook** over medium heat until sugar dissolves and sauce begins to thicken (about 10 minutes). Gently stir in rum. **Yield:** ¾ cup.

Marie Davis
Charlotte, North Carolina

DURFEE'S BREAD PUDDING

1 (16-ounce) loaf French bread
½ cup raisins
6 large eggs, lightly beaten
4 cups milk
1½ cups sugar
2 tablespoons butter or margarine,
   melted
½ teaspoon almond extract
¼ teaspoon vanilla extract
⅓ cup slivered almonds,
   toasted

• **Cut** bread into 1¼-inch-thick slices; place in a single layer in a lightly greased 13- x 9- x 2-inch baking dish. Sprinkle with raisins.
• **Combine** eggs and next 5 ingredients in a large bowl, stirring until blended. Pour egg mixture over bread, and let stand 30 minutes.
• **Sprinkle** almonds over egg mixture; place dish in a large pan. Add hot water to pan to depth of 1 inch.
• **Bake** at 350° for 45 minutes or until a knife inserted in center comes out clean, shielding with aluminum foil after 30 minutes to prevent excessive browning. Serve warm with whipped cream. **Yield:** 12 to 15 servings.

Odile Besseau and Durfee Bedsole
The Taylor House
Marshall, Texas

BREAD PUDDING WITH WHISKEY SAUCE

1 (16-ounce) loaf French bread
3 cups milk
1 cup cream sherry
3 large eggs, beaten
2 cups sugar
2 tablespoons butter, melted
2 tablespoons vanilla extract
1 cup raisins
2 tablespoons butter or margarine,
   melted
½ cup honey
Whiskey Sauce

• **Break** bread into small chunks, and place in a large bowl. Add milk and sherry; let stand 10 minutes. Stir until thoroughly mixed.

• **Combine** eggs, sugar, 2 tablespoons butter, and vanilla; add to bread mixture, stirring well. Stir in raisins.
• **Spoon** mixture into a lightly greased 11- x 7- x 1½-inch baking dish. Combine 2 tablespoons butter and honey; pour over pudding. Bake at 350° for 45 minutes or until set. Serve with warm Whiskey Sauce. **Yield:** 10 to 12 servings.

Whiskey Sauce

QUICK!

1 cup sugar
1 cup milk
½ cup butter
2 tablespoons cornstarch
¼ cup cold water
½ cup bourbon

• **Combine** sugar, milk, and butter in a heavy saucepan; cook over low heat until sugar dissolves and butter melts.
• **Combine** cornstarch and water; add to butter mixture. Add bourbon, and bring to a boil over medium heat; cook 1 minute. **Yield:** 2¾ cups.

Julie and Cliff Collins
French Quarter
New Orleans, Louisiana

CREOLE BREAD PUDDING SOUFFLÉ

½ cup butter or margarine,
   softened
1 cup sugar
5 large eggs
2 cups whipping cream
1 tablespoon vanilla extract
⅛ teaspoon ground cinnamon
¼ cup raisins
12 (1-inch-thick) slices French
   bread
1 tablespoon butter or margarine
1½ tablespoons sugar
6 large eggs, separated
½ cup sugar
½ cup sifted powdered sugar
Whiskey Sauce

• **Beat** ½ cup butter at medium speed with an electric mixer until creamy; gradually add 1 cup sugar, beating well. Add eggs, one at a time, beating after

each addition. Gradually add cream, mixing well. Stir in vanilla, cinnamon, and raisins. Pour mixture into a lightly greased 13- x 9- x 2-inch pan.
• **Arrange** bread slices in pan over cream mixture; let stand 10 minutes. Turn bread slices over; let stand 10 minutes. Cover pan with aluminum foil; place in a larger shallow pan. Pour hot water to depth of 1 inch into larger pan. Bake at 350° for 40 minutes. Remove foil, and bake 10 additional minutes. Place 2½ cups baked bread mixture in a large bowl; set aside. Reserve remainder for another use. (For a quick dessert, reheat remainder, and serve with leftover Whiskey Sauce.)
• **Grease** a 1½-quart soufflé dish with 1 tablespoon butter; coat bottom and sides of dish with 1½ tablespoons sugar, and set aside.
• **Combine** egg yolks and ½ cup sugar in top of a double boiler; place over simmering water, and beat at high speed with an electric mixer 4 minutes or until mixture thickens. Add yolk mixture to bread mixture in bowl, and beat at medium speed until smooth. Set aside.
• **Beat** egg whites at high speed with an electric mixer until foamy. Gradually add powdered sugar, beating until stiff peaks form; fold into bread mixture. Pour into prepared soufflé dish. Bake at 375° for 40 minutes; serve with warm Whiskey Sauce. **Yield:** 6 to 8 servings.

Whiskey Sauce

QUICK!

1 cup sugar
1 cup whipping cream
⅛ teaspoon ground cinnamon
1 tablespoon butter or margarine
1½ teaspoons cornstarch
¼ cup cold water
1 tablespoon bourbon

• **Combine** first 4 ingredients in a heavy saucepan. Cook over medium heat until sugar dissolves, stirring often.
• **Combine** cornstarch and water; stir into cream mixture, and bring to a boil, stirring constantly. Boil 1 minute, stirring constantly. Remove from heat, and stir in bourbon. **Yield:** 1⅔ cups.

Commander's Palace
New Orleans, Louisiana

TIRAMISÙ

Tiramisù literally means "pick me up" in Italian. Try it with mascarpone or with our reduced-fat substitute.

1 (3-ounce) package vanilla pudding mix
2 cups skim milk
1 cup mascarpone cheese *
2¾ cups reduced-fat frozen whipped topping, thawed and divided
1 loaf angel food cake
1½ teaspoons instant coffee granules
½ cup hot water
¼ cup brandy
¼ cup Kahlúa or other coffee-flavored liqueur
Garnish: cocoa

• **Combine** pudding mix and milk in a saucepan; bring to a boil over medium heat, stirring constantly. Remove from heat; pour pudding into a mixing bowl, and cool.
• **Add** mascarpone cheese to pudding; beat at low speed with an electric mixer until smooth. Fold in 1¾ cups whipped topping, and set aside.
• **Slice** cake in half horizontally. Cut each layer vertically into 16 equal rectangles, and set aside.
• **Dissolve** coffee granules in hot water; stir in brandy and Kahlúa. Brush over tops and bottoms of cake pieces.
• **Line** bottom and sides of a 3-quart trifle bowl or soufflé dish with half of cake pieces; cover with half of pudding mixture. Repeat procedure with remaining cake pieces and pudding mixture. Cover and chill 8 hours.
• **Spread** remaining 1 cup whipped topping over Tiramisù, and garnish, if desired. Cover and chill. **Yield:** 12 servings.

✳ Mascarpone cheese is a soft, buttery Italian cheese made from fresh cream. You can find it in the gourmet section at large supermarkets.

❤ Substitute 1 (8-ounce) package reduced-fat cream cheese, 3 tablespoons reduced-fat sour cream, and 2 tablespoons skim milk for mascarpone. With this substitution, you'll save 5.4 fat grams and 46 calories per serving.

Lucy Susan Barrett
Birmingham, Alabama

❤ Per serving: Calories 257
Fat 11.1g Cholesterol 18mg
Sodium 174mg

SWEET POTATO FLAN

2 medium sweet potatoes (1¾ pounds) *
¾ cup sugar
2 (14-ounce) cans sweetened condensed milk
2 cups milk
10 large eggs
1 teaspoon ground cinnamon
½ teaspoon ground allspice
¼ teaspoon ground cloves
1 teaspoon vanilla extract
Garnish: toasted coconut

• **Pierce** sweet potatoes several times with a fork; place on a baking sheet.
• **Bake** at 375° for 1 hour or until done; cool to touch. Peel sweet potatoes, and mash. Set aside 1 cup mashed sweet potato; reserve any remaining sweet potato for another use.
• **Sprinkle** sugar in a 10-inch round cakepan; place over medium heat, and cook, shaking pan constantly, until sugar melts and turns a light golden brown. Cool. (Caramelized sugar may crack slightly as it cools.)
• **Combine** ½ cup mashed sweet potato, 1 can sweetened condensed milk, 1 cup milk and half of next 5 ingredients in container of an electric blender; process until smooth, stopping once to scrape down sides. Pour sweet potato mixture into a large bowl.
• **Repeat** procedure; add sweet potato mixture to bowl, stirring well with a wire whisk.
• **Pour** mixture over caramelized sugar in cakepan; cover with aluminum foil, and place cakepan in a larger shallow pan. Add hot water to larger pan to depth of ½ inch.
• **Bake** at 325° for 1 hour and 15 minutes or until a knife inserted in center comes out clean. Remove pan from water, and uncover; cool on a wire rack 30 minutes.
• **Cover** and chill at least 8 hours.
• **Run** a knife around edge of flan to loosen; invert onto a serving plate. Garnish, if desired. **Yield:** 1 (10-inch) flan.

✳ Substitute 1 cup canned mashed sweet potatoes for fresh.

W. N. Cottrell
New Orleans, Louisiana

FLAN DE QUESO

½ cup sugar
1 (14-ounce) can sweetened condensed milk
1 (8-ounce) package cream cheese, cubed and softened
4 large eggs
3 slices white bread, torn
1 cup water
⅔ cup evaporated milk
3 tablespoons butter or margarine, melted
1 teaspoon vanilla extract

• **Sprinkle** sugar in a 9-inch round cakepan; place over medium heat, and cook, shaking pan occasionally, until sugar melts and turns a light golden brown. Cool. (Caramelized sugar may crack slightly as it cools.)
• **Combine** condensed milk and remaining 7 ingredients in container of an electric blender; process until smooth, stopping once to scrape down sides. Pour over caramelized sugar.
• **Place** cakepan in a larger shallow pan. Add hot water to larger pan to depth of 1 inch.
• **Bake**, uncovered, at 350° for 55 minutes or until a knife inserted in center of flan comes out clean.
• **Remove** cakepan from water; cool on a wire rack at least 30 minutes.
• **Run** a knife around edge of flan to loosen; invert flan onto a serving plate. Cool. **Yield:** 6 servings.

Note: You can also caramelize sugar on a gas cooktop, stirring to speed caramelization.

Myrna M. Ruiz
Marietta, Georgia

Basic Crèmes Brûlée

BASIC CRÈME BRÛLÉE
(pictured at left)

2 cups whipping cream
5 egg yolks
½ cup sugar
1 tablespoon vanilla extract
½ cup firmly packed light brown
    sugar
Garnishes: fresh raspberries,
    fresh mint sprigs

• **Combine** first 4 ingredients; stir with a wire whisk until sugar dissolves and mixture is smooth. Pour evenly into 5 (5- x 1-inch) round individual baking dishes; place dishes in a large roasting pan or a 15- x 10- x 1-inch jellyroll pan. Add hot water to pan to depth of ½ inch.
• **Bake** at 275° for 45 to 50 minutes or until almost set. Cool custards in water in pan on a wire rack. Remove from pan; cover and chill at least 8 hours.
• **Sprinkle** brown sugar evenly over each custard; place custards in pan.
• **Broil** 5½ inches from heat (with electric oven door partially opened) until sugar melts. Let stand 5 minutes to allow sugar to harden. Garnish, if desired. **Yield:** 5 servings.

Berry Crème Brûlée: Place 8 to 10 fresh blackberries or raspberries in each baking dish; pour custard mixture over berries. Proceed as directed in basic recipe, baking 45 minutes.

Chocolate Crème Brûlée: Combine 4 (1-ounce) squares semisweet chocolate and ½ cup whipping cream from basic recipe in a small heavy saucepan; cook over low heat, stirring constantly, until chocolate melts. Add remaining 1½ cups whipping cream; reduce vanilla to 1 teaspoon. Proceed as directed in basic recipe, baking 55 minutes. For a Chocolate-Raspberry version, place 8 to 10 fresh raspberries in each baking dish, add custard, and increase baking time to 1 hour and 5 minutes.

Double Raspberry Crème Brûlée: Reduce vanilla to 1 teaspoon; add 1 additional egg yolk and 1½ tablespoons Framboise or other raspberry-flavored liqueur to custard mixture. Place 8 to 10 fresh raspberries in each baking dish; pour custard mixture over berries. Proceed as directed in basic brûlée recipe, baking 55 minutes.

Ginger Crème Brûlée: Reduce vanilla to 1 teaspoon; add 2 tablespoons grated fresh ginger to custard mixture. Proceed as directed in basic brûlée recipe, baking 1 hour and 5 minutes.

Orange Crème Brûlée: Reduce vanilla to 1 teaspoon; add 1 additional egg yolk, 2 tablespoons grated orange rind, and 2 tablespoons Grand Marnier or other orange-flavored liqueur to custard mixture. Proceed as directed in basic brûlée recipe, baking 1 hour.

Peppermint Crème Brûlée: Reduce vanilla to 1 teaspoon; add 1 additional egg yolk and 3 tablespoons peppermint schnapps. Proceed as directed in basic recipe, baking 50 minutes. Substitute 5 hard peppermint candies, crushed, for brown sugar; broil as directed.

White Chocolate-Macadamia Nut Crème Brûlée: Combine 4 ounces white chocolate and ½ cup whipping cream from basic brûlée recipe in a heavy saucepan; cook over low heat, stirring constantly, until chocolate melts. Add remaining 1½ cups whipping cream; reduce vanilla to 1 teaspoon. Proceed as directed in basic brûlée recipe. Place 1 tablespoon chopped macadamia nuts, toasted, in each baking dish; pour custard over nuts. Bake as directed 1 hour and 10 minutes.

GOAT CHEESE CUSTARD

1 large egg
⅓ cup sugar
1 teaspoon cornstarch
1½ teaspoons lemon juice
1 teaspoon vanilla extract
3 (5.3-ounce) containers creamy
    goat cheese
¼ cup milk
1 (16-ounce) package frozen
    strawberries, thawed
¼ cup amaretto
2 tablespoons sugar

• **Combine** first 5 ingredients in a large bowl, whisking until smooth.
• **Whisk** goat cheese and milk until smooth; add to egg mixture, whisking until smooth.
• **Pour** into four lightly greased 6-ounce custard cups, and place cups in a 9-inch square pan. Add hot water to pan to depth of 1 inch.
• **Bake** at 375° for 10 minutes; reduce oven temperature to 325°, and bake 35 additional minutes or until almost set. Transfer to a wire rack to cool. Cover and chill 8 hours.
• **Combine** strawberries, liqueur, and 2 tablespoons sugar in container of an electric blender or food processor; process until smooth, stopping once to scrape down sides. Pour through a wire-mesh strainer into a bowl, pressing with back of a spoon; discard seeds. Cover and chill.
• **Spoon** ¼ cup strawberry sauce on each serving plate; unmold custards onto plates. **Yield:** 4 servings.

Note: Serve leftover strawberry sauce over ice cream.

CHOCOLATE TRUFFLE MOUSSE WITH RASPBERRY SAUCE

8 (1-ounce) squares semisweet
   chocolate
¼ cup light corn syrup
¼ cup butter or margarine
2 egg yolks, lightly beaten
1 cup whipping cream, divided
2 tablespoons powdered sugar
½ teaspoon vanilla extract
Garnish: chocolate curls
Raspberry Sauce

• **Combine** first 3 ingredients in a heavy saucepan; cook over low heat, stirring constantly, until chocolate melts.
• **Combine** yolks and ¼ cup cream. Gradually stir about ½ cup chocolate mixture into yolk mixture; add to remaining chocolate mixture, stirring constantly. Cook over medium-low heat 1 minute or until a thermometer registers 160°. Remove from heat; cool to room temperature.
• **Beat** remaining ¾ cup whipping cream until foamy; gradually add powdered sugar, beating until soft peaks form. Stir in vanilla.
• **Stir** ½ cup whipped cream mixture into chocolate mixture; fold in remaining cream mixture. Spoon into four stemmed glasses; cover and chill at least 8 hours. Garnish, if desired. Serve with Raspberry Sauce. **Yield:** 4 servings.

Raspberry Sauce
QUICK!

1 (10-ounce) package frozen
   raspberries, thawed
2 teaspoons cornstarch
⅓ cup light corn syrup

• **Place** raspberries in container of an electric blender; process 1 minute or until smooth, stopping once to scrape down sides. Pour mixture through a wire-mesh strainer into a small saucepan, discarding seeds. Add cornstarch, stirring well; stir in corn syrup.
• **Cook** over medium heat, stirring constantly, until mixture boils. Boil 1 minute, stirring constantly. Remove from heat; cool. **Yield:** 1⅓ cups.
Nancy Williams
Starkville, Mississippi

PEPPERMINT CANDY MOUSSE

8 ounces hard peppermint candies
   (about 2 cups)
½ cup half-and-half
1 envelope unflavored gelatin
1 tablespoon cold water
1½ cups whipping cream
Chocolate sauce

• **Place** candies in a heavy-duty, zip-top plastic bag; seal bag, and crush until the consistency of powder, using a meat mallet or rolling pin.
• **Combine** powdered candies and half-and-half in a small saucepan. Cook mixture over low heat, stirring constantly, about 10 minutes or until candy dissolves. (Remove and discard any undissolved candy.) Set warm peppermint mixture aside.
• **Sprinkle** gelatin over 1 tablespoon cold water in a large bowl; let stand 1 minute. Add warm peppermint mixture, stirring until gelatin dissolves (about 2 minutes). Cool.
• **Beat** whipping cream until soft peaks form. Gently fold into peppermint mixture. Pour mixture into a lightly oiled 4-cup mold.
• **Cover** and chill at least 8 hours. Unmold onto a serving plate. Serve with Chocolate Sauce. **Yield:** 6 to 8 servings.
Rublelene Singleton
Scotts Hill, Tennessee

VANILLA SOUFFLÉS WITH VANILLA CRÈME SAUCE

This top-rated dessert is one of our most requested recipes.

Vegetable cooking spray
Sugar
1½ tablespoons butter or
   margarine
1½ tablespoons all-purpose
   flour
6 tablespoons half-and-half
2 tablespoons sugar
2 large eggs, separated
1 tablespoon vanilla extract
1 tablespoon sugar
Sifted powdered sugar
Vanilla Crème Sauce

• **Coat** the bottom and sides of two 6-ounce baking dishes with cooking spray; sprinkle with sugar. Set aside.
• **Melt** butter in a small saucepan over medium heat; add flour, stirring until mixture is smooth. Cook 1 minute, stirring constantly.
• **Add** half-and-half, stirring constantly; stir in 2 tablespoons sugar. Cook over medium heat, stirring constantly, until thickened. Remove from heat; set aside.
• **Beat** egg yolks until thick and pale. Gradually stir about half of hot mixture into egg yolks; add to remaining hot mixture, stirring constantly. Cook over medium heat 2 minutes; stir in vanilla. Cool 15 to 20 minutes.
• **Beat** egg whites at high speed with an electric mixer until foamy. Gradually add 1 tablespoon sugar, beating until soft peaks form. Gradually fold egg whites into half-and-half mixture. Spoon into prepared baking dishes.
• **Bake** at 350° for 25 minutes or until puffed and set. Sprinkle with powdered sugar, and serve immediately with Vanilla Crème Sauce. **Yield:** 2 servings.

Vanilla Crème Sauce
QUICK!

½ cup sugar
1 teaspoon cornstarch
½ teaspoon vanilla extract
1 cup whipping cream
4 egg yolks

• **Combine** first 3 ingredients in a heavy saucepan; gradually stir in whipping cream. Cook over low heat, stirring constantly, until sugar dissolves. Set aside.
• **Beat** egg yolks until thick and pale. Gradually stir about half of hot whipping cream mixture into yolks; add to remaining hot mixture, stirring constantly. Cook over medium heat, stirring constantly, until thickened.
• **Pour** through a wire-mesh strainer into a small bowl, discarding lumps. Cover and store in refrigerator up to 3 days. Serve with Vanilla Soufflés, fresh fruit, pound cake, or ice cream. **Yield:** 1½ cups.

LEMON SOUFFLÉ

We used Wilton meringue powder in this soufflé. Look for it in crafts stores, cake-decorating supply stores, or at Wal-Mart.

1   tablespoon butter or margarine
2   tablespoons sugar
2   envelopes unflavored gelatin
½   cup cold water
1   teaspoon sugar
1   tablespoon grated lemon rind
¾   cup lemon juice
⅓   cup meringue powder
1½ cups sugar, divided
1   cup water
2   cups whipping cream
1   (2-ounce) package slivered almonds, toasted and chopped
Garnish: Candied Lemon Peel

• **Cut** a piece of wax paper long enough to fit around a 2-quart soufflé dish, allowing a 1-inch overlap; fold paper lengthwise into thirds. Lightly butter one side of paper and soufflé dish. Wrap paper around outside of dish, buttered side against dish, allowing it to extend 3 inches above rim; secure with tape. Sprinkle sides of dish with 2 tablespoons sugar.
• **Sprinkle** gelatin over cold water in a saucepan; let stand 1 minute. Add 1 teaspoon sugar; cook over low heat, stirring until gelatin dissolves. Stir in lemon rind and juice. Set aside.
• **Combine** meringue powder, 1 cup sugar, and water in a large bowl. Beat at high speed with an electric mixer 5 minutes. Gradually add remaining ½ cup sugar, and beat at high speed 5 minutes or until stiff peaks form. Fold in gelatin mixture.
• **Beat** whipping cream until soft peaks form. Fold into gelatin mixture.
• **Pour** into prepared dish, and chill 8 hours.
• **Remove** collar, gently pat chopped almonds around sides of soufflé. Garnish, if desired. **Yield:** 8 to 10 servings.

Candied Lemon Peel

1   large lemon
2   tablespoons light corn syrup
1   tablespoon sugar

• **Peel** lemon, and cut rind into ¼-inch-wide strips. Reserve peeled lemon for another use.
• **Combine** lemon rind and corn syrup in a small saucepan, and bring to a boil over medium heat; reduce heat, and cook 3 to 4 minutes.
• **Toss** lemon rind with sugar to coat; spread on wax paper to dry. **Yield:** about ⅓ cup.

Barbara Crowe
Birmingham, Alabama

SOUFFLÉ AU CHOCOLAT COINTREAU

Bill prefers to whip egg whites by hand, but this recipe works just fine using a mixer, too. You can cut this recipe in half to serve 6.

Butter or margarine
2   tablespoons sugar
¼   cup butter or margarine
2   cups (12 ounces) semisweet chocolate morsels
¼   cup Cointreau or other orange-flavored liqueur
12 large eggs, separated
1½ cups sifted powdered sugar
1   teaspoon ground cinnamon
1   teaspoon cream of tartar
Powdered sugar
Chocolate Cream
Garnish: orange rind strips

• **Cut** a piece of aluminum foil long enough to fit around a 2¾-quart soufflé dish or straight-sided casserole, allowing a 1-inch overlap; starting from one long side, fold foil into thirds. Lightly butter one side of foil and dish. Wrap foil around outside of dish, buttered side against dish, allowing it to extend 3 inches above rim to form a collar; secure with string or masking tape. Add 2 tablespoons sugar, tilting prepared dish to coat sides. Set aside.
• **Combine** ¼ cup butter and chocolate morsels in top of a double boiler; bring water to a boil. Reduce heat to low; cook until chocolate and butter melt, stirring often. Remove from water; cool 5 minutes. Stir in Cointreau. Set aside.
• **Beat** egg yolks; gradually add pow-

dered sugar, beating until mixture is thick and pale. Stir in chocolate mixture and cinnamon. Set aside.
• **Beat** egg whites and cream of tartar in a large mixing bowl at high speed with an electric mixer until stiff peaks form. Gently stir 1½ cups egg white mixture into chocolate mixture.
• **Fold** remaining egg white mixture into chocolate mixture. Pour into prepared soufflé dish.
• **Bake** at 375° for 50 to 55 minutes. Sprinkle with powdered sugar, and remove collar. Serve immediately with Chocolate Cream. Garnish, if desired. **Yield:** 12 servings.

Chocolate Cream

QUICK!

1   cup whipping cream
1   tablespoon sifted powdered sugar
1½ teaspoons cocoa

• **Beat** all ingredients at medium speed with an electric mixer until soft peaks form. **Yield:** 2 cups.

Bill Gilchrist
Birmingham, Alabama

WATERMELON GRANITA

Granita is an Italian fruity, icy dessert. We consider it a snow cone for adults.

4   cups cubed watermelon, seeded
½   cup sugar
2   tablespoons lemon juice

• **Combine** all ingredients in container of an electric blender or food processor; process until smooth and sugar dissolves, stopping once to scrape down sides.
• **Pour** into an 8-inch square pan. Cover and freeze 2 hours or until almost firm, stirring occasionally.
• **Remove** from freezer 5 minutes before serving; stir, if necessary. Serve immediately. **Yield:** 4 to 6 servings.

Donna Presley
Perrytown, Arkansas

CINNAMON ICE CREAM SOMBREROS

4 cups milk
1 teaspoon vanilla extract
¼ cup ground cinnamon
1⅓ cups sugar
12 egg yolks
1 cup whipping cream
1 (8-ounce) package semisweet chocolate
8 ounces premium white chocolate baking squares
Chocolate Sauce
Cornmeal Sombreros
Garnish: fresh strawberry fans

● **Combine** first 3 ingredients in a saucepan; bring to a boil over medium heat, stirring occasionally. Remove from heat; cover and let stand 15 minutes.
● **Combine** sugar and egg yolks in a large mixing bowl; beat at high speed with an electric mixer 3 minutes or until thick and pale. Gradually stir about one-fourth of hot mixture into yolks; add to remaining hot mixture, stirring constantly. Cook over low heat until mixture reaches 185° (about 3 minutes). Remove from heat; set saucepan in ice. Stir in whipping cream; cover and chill.
● **Pour** mixture into freezer container of a 1-gallon hand-turned or electric freezer. Freeze according to manufacturer's instructions. Spoon ice cream into a 13- x 9- x 2-inch pan; cover and freeze 8 hours.
● **One** hour before assembling, scoop ice cream into 10 balls, and place on a baking sheet. Cover with plastic wrap, and immediately return to freezer.
● **Melt** semisweet chocolate in a small saucepan over low heat, stirring until smooth. Place a 14- x 10-inch piece of wax paper on a cloth towel, and spread melted chocolate evenly into a 12- x 8-inch rectangle. Make "waves" of chocolate by loosely gathering towel crosswise under wax paper. Let chocolate harden; peel off wax paper. Break or cut chocolate into 3- x 2-inch pieces, and freeze until ready to serve. Repeat procedure with white chocolate.
● **To** serve, spoon warm Chocolate Sauce onto dessert plates. Place Cornmeal Sombreros on sauce, and fill with ice cream balls. (Reserve remaining sombreros for another use.) Position chocolate pieces around ice cream. Garnish, if desired. **Yield:** 10 servings.

Chocolate Sauce
QUICK!

1 cup whipping cream
2½ cups semisweet chocolate morsels
¼ cup butter or margarine
2 tablespoons sugar
1 teaspoon vanilla extract

● **Place** whipping cream in a saucepan; bring to a boil over medium heat. Remove from heat; add chocolate morsels and remaining ingredients, stirring until smooth. Cover and chill. Just before serving, cook over low heat until warm. **Yield:** 2½ cups.

Cornmeal Sombreros

¾ cup all-purpose flour
⅓ cup yellow cornmeal
3 tablespoons sugar
1 teaspoon salt
¾ cup milk
½ cup water
3 large eggs
1 tablespoon butter or margarine, melted
Vegetable cooking spray
8 cups vegetable oil

● **Combine** first 4 ingredients in container of an electric blender; process 1 minute. Add milk and next 3 ingredients; process 25 seconds, stopping once to scrape down sides. Transfer batter to a bowl; cover and chill at least 1 hour or overnight.
● **Coat** bottom of a 5-inch crêpe pan or small nonstick skillet with cooking spray; place over medium heat just until hot, not smoking. Pour 3 tablespoons batter into pan, and quickly tilt pan in all directions so batter covers pan in a thin film. Cook about 1 minute or until crêpe can be shaken loose from pan. Flip crêpe, and cook about 30 seconds.
● **Place** crêpes on a towel to cool. Stack between layers of wax paper to prevent sticking. Repeat until all batter is used. Freeze crêpes, if desired. (Thaw crêpes before frying.)
● **Pour** oil into a Dutch oven; heat to 375°. Spray a tortilla or "bird's nest" frying basket with cooking spray. Arrange 1 crêpe in bottom basket; place smaller basket on top, and secure with clip. Completely immerse basket in hot oil; fry crêpe until golden (about 1 minute). Remove from oil, and unclip frying basket. Gently turn out sombrero onto paper towels. Repeat procedure with remaining crêpes. **Yield:** 15 sombreros.

Libby and Jim Collet
Dallas, Texas

FRENCH TOAST BANANA SPLITS
(pictured at right)

3 large eggs
½ cup whipping cream
½ cup Frangelico
1½ to 2 teaspoons ground cinnamon
1 teaspoon vanilla extract
½ cup sugar
2 large bananas, sliced
2 teaspoons unsalted butter
6 croissants
1 (5-ounce) jar hot fudge topping
1 quart vanilla ice cream
½ cup chopped hazelnuts, toasted

● **Whisk** together eggs and whipping cream. Stir in liqueur, cinnamon, and vanilla. Pour into a shallow dish.
● **Place** sugar in a separate shallow dish; dredge banana in sugar.
● **Melt** butter in a nonstick skillet over medium heat; add banana, and cook until lightly browned, turning once. Remove from skillet, and keep warm.
● **Cut** croissants in half horizontally; dip in egg mixture, coating well. Cook in skillet over medium heat, 3 or 4 halves at a time, until lightly browned, turning once. Place on individual serving plates.
● **Remove** lid from hot fudge topping; microwave topping at HIGH 1 minute, stirring after 30 seconds.
● **Top** croissants with ice cream; drizzle with topping. Spoon bananas over top, and sprinkle with toasted hazelnuts. Serve immediately. **Yield:** 6 servings.

Caroline Kennedy
Lighthouse Point, Florida

French Toast Banana Splits

LOLLAPALOOZA

This crazy, mixed-up name perfectly describes this fudge sundae that begins with an awesome brownie.

¼ cup butter or margarine
1 cup (6 ounces) semisweet chocolate morsels
¾ cup sugar
⅔ cup all-purpose flour
¼ teaspoon baking powder
¼ teaspoon salt
2 large eggs, lightly beaten
½ teaspoon vanilla extract
½ cup chopped pecans
½ cup semisweet chocolate morsels
Ice cream
Easy Hot Fudge Sauce

● **Combine** butter and 1 cup chocolate morsels in a heavy saucepan. Cook over low heat, stirring constantly, until chocolate and butter melt. Remove from heat.
● **Add** sugar and next 5 ingredients, stirring until blended. Stir in pecans and ½ cup chocolate morsels.
● **Spread** mixture into a lightly greased 8-inch square pan.
● **Bake** at 350° for 30 minutes or until center is set. Cool in pan on a wire rack.
● **Cut** into squares, and serve with ice cream and warm Easy Hot Fudge Sauce. **Yield:** 16 servings.

Easy Hot Fudge Sauce
QUICK!

2 cups (12 ounces) semisweet chocolate morsels
1 (12-ounce) can evaporated milk
1 cup sugar
1 tablespoon butter or margarine
1 teaspoon vanilla extract

● **Combine** first 3 ingredients in a heavy saucepan.
● **Cook** over medium heat, stirring constantly, until chocolate melts and mixture comes to a boil.
● **Add** butter and vanilla, stirring until butter melts. **Yield:** 3 cups.

Cheryl Welch
Everyday Gourmet
Jackson, Mississippi

MINT-CHOCOLATE CHIP ICE CREAM SQUARES

3 cups cream-filled chocolate sandwich cookie crumbs (about 30 cookies, crushed)
¼ cup butter or margarine, melted
½ gallon mint-chocolate chip ice cream, slightly softened
1 (5-ounce) can evaporated milk
½ cup sugar
1½ (1-ounce) squares unsweetened chocolate
1 tablespoon butter or margarine
1 (12-ounce) carton frozen whipped topping, thawed
1 cup chopped pecans, toasted
Garnish: fresh mint sprigs

● **Combine** cookie crumbs and ¼ cup butter. Press in bottom of a lightly greased 13- x 9- x 2-inch pan; freeze.
● **Spread** ice cream evenly over crust; freeze until firm.
● **Combine** evaporated milk and next 3 ingredients in a small heavy saucepan. Bring to a boil over low heat, stirring constantly with a wire whisk. Cook, stirring constantly, 3 to 4 minutes or until thickened. Cool to room temperature.
● **Spread** chocolate mixture over ice cream; top with whipped topping, and sprinkle with pecans. Cover and freeze until firm. To serve, let stand at room temperature 10 minutes, and cut into squares. Garnish, if desired. **Yield:** 15 servings.

CARAMEL-TOFFEE BOMBE

1⅓ cups gingersnap cookie crumbs (about 20 cookies)
¼ cup butter or margarine, melted
1 quart vanilla ice cream, softened
4 (1.4-ounce) English toffee-flavored candy bars, crushed
Praline Sauce

● **Line** a 2-quart bowl with heavy-duty plastic wrap. Set aside.
● **Combine** cookie crumbs and butter; press mixture into prepared bowl. Combine ice cream and crushed candy, and spoon into bowl. Cover and freeze at least 8 hours.

● **To** serve, let bowl stand at room temperature 5 minutes; invert onto a serving plate. Carefully remove bowl and plastic wrap. Cut into wedges, and serve immediately with warm Praline Sauce. **Yield:** 10 to 12 servings.

Praline Sauce
QUICK!

½ cup firmly packed brown sugar
½ cup half-and-half
¼ cup butter or margarine
¼ cup slivered almonds, toasted and chopped
1 teaspoon vanilla extract

● **Combine** first 3 ingredients in a small saucepan; bring mixture to a boil over medium heat, stirring occasionally. Boil 2 minutes, stirring occasionally. Remove from heat; stir in almonds and vanilla. **Yield:** 1 cup.

Paula McCollum
Springtown, Texas

BANANAS GLACÉ
QUICK!

⅓ cup light rum
⅓ cup apricot preserves
2 tablespoons butter or margarine
2 large firm bananas
Vanilla ice cream
Garnishes: dried apricot halves, fresh mint leaves

● **Combine** first 3 ingredients in a small skillet; cook over medium heat until butter melts, stirring often.
● **Peel** bananas, and cut in half lengthwise. Cut each half into 6 pieces; add to skillet.
● **Cook** over low heat until thoroughly heated, stirring occasionally. Serve banana mixture immediately over vanilla ice cream; garnish, if desired. **Yield:** 4 servings.

Rita W. Cook
Corpus Christi, Texas

At right: *Macadamia Nut French Toast (page 147)*

EGGS AND CHEESE

*Lump Crab
Hash With Three-
Pepper Hollandaise;
Morrison House
Brioche, page 68*

LUMP CRAB HASH WITH THREE-PEPPER HOLLANDAISE
(pictured at left)

This recipe gets its title from the blend of pink, green, and white peppercorns in the hollandaise sauce. If you don't have a peppercorn blend, substitute black pepper.

1 large red potato, peeled and cubed
1 medium-size sweet potato, peeled and cubed
1 large red bell pepper
1 pound fresh jumbo lump crabmeat
2 tablespoons butter
1 cup chopped purple onion
1 large tomato, peeled, seeded, and chopped
2 green onions, chopped
¾ teaspoon salt
¾ teaspoon pepper
8 poached eggs
Three-Pepper Hollandaise

• **Cook** potato in boiling water to cover 4 to 5 minutes or until almost tender; drain and set aside.
• **Place** bell pepper on an aluminum foil-lined baking sheet.
• **Broil** pepper 5½ inches from heat (with electric oven door partially opened) about 5 minutes on each side or until pepper looks blistered.
• **Place** pepper in a plastic bag; seal and let stand 10 minutes to loosen skin. Peel pepper; remove and discard seeds. Coarsely chop pepper, and set aside.
• **Drain** crabmeat, removing any bits of shell; set aside.
• **Melt** butter in a skillet or Dutch oven over medium-high heat; add potato and 1 cup onion, and cook, stirring constantly, until onion is tender.
• **Add** crabmeat, bell pepper, tomato, and next 3 ingredients; cook until thoroughly heated. Spoon hash onto individual serving plates; place poached eggs onto hash, and top with Three-Pepper Hollandaise. **Yield:** 4 servings.

Three-Pepper Hollandaise
QUICK!

3 egg yolks, lightly beaten
⅓ cup dry white wine
1 tablespoon lemon juice
1 teaspoon Worcestershire sauce
1 teaspoon freshly ground mixed peppercorns
1 cup butter, melted

• **Combine** first 5 ingredients in top of a double boiler; bring water to a boil. Reduce heat to low; cook, stirring constantly with a wire whisk, 4 minutes or until a thermometer registers 160°. Remove from heat immediately.
• **Add** butter in a thin stream, whisking until blended. **Yield:** 1 cup.

Chef Ken Vedrinski
Woodlands Resort and Inn
Summerville, South Carolina

BELL PEPPER FRITTATA

3 cloves garlic, minced
1 large purple onion, sliced
2 red bell peppers, cut into thin strips
1 yellow bell pepper, cut into thin strips
3 tablespoons olive oil, divided
2 yellow squash, thinly sliced
2 zucchini, thinly sliced
½ pound fresh mushrooms, sliced
6 large eggs
¼ cup whipping cream
2½ to 3 teaspoons salt
2 teaspoons freshly ground pepper
8 slices sandwich bread, cubed
1 (8-ounce) package cream cheese, cubed
2 cups (8 ounces) shredded Swiss cheese

• **Cook** first 4 ingredients in 1 tablespoon oil in a large skillet until tender. Drain and pat dry; set aside.
• **Cook** squash and zucchini in 1 tablespoon oil in skillet until tender. Drain and pat dry; set aside.
• **Cook** mushrooms in remaining 1 tablespoon oil in skillet until tender. Drain and pat dry; set aside.

• **Whisk** together eggs and next 3 ingredients in a large bowl; stir in vegetables, half of bread cubes, cream cheese, and Swiss cheese. Press remaining bread cubes in bottom of a lightly greased 10-inch springform pan, and place on a baking sheet. Pour vegetable mixture into pan.
• **Bake** at 325° for 1 hour, covering with aluminum foil after 45 minutes to prevent excessive browning. Serve warm. **Yield:** 8 servings.

Yvonne M. Greer
Mauldin, South Carolina

POTATO-BACON FRITTATA

3 tablespoons butter or margarine
2 cups frozen potatoes with onions and peppers *
6 large eggs
2 tablespoons milk
¼ teaspoon salt
¼ teaspoon pepper
1 cup (4 ounces) shredded Cheddar cheese
6 slices bacon, cooked and crumbled
Garnish: diced fresh tomato or picante sauce

• **Melt** butter in a 10-inch nonstick skillet over medium heat; add frozen potatoes, and cook 10 minutes or until browned.
• **Combine** eggs and next 3 ingredients, stirring with a wire whisk; pour over potatoes. As mixture starts to cook, gently lift edges of frittata with a spatula, and tilt pan so uncooked portion flows underneath. If center remains uncooked, carefully turn frittata over, and cook 5 minutes or until center is done.
• **Place** frittata on serving platter, and sprinkle with shredded cheese. Cover with aluminum foil; let stand 5 minutes.
• **Sprinkle** with crumbled bacon; garnish, if desired. Serve immediately. **Yield:** 6 servings.

* For potatoes with onions and peppers, we used Potatoes O'Brien.

Judi Grigoraci
Charleston, West Virginia

FRESH VEGETABLE FRITTATA

1 large red bell pepper, chopped
1 cup sliced fresh mushrooms
1½ cups (6 ounces) shredded
      Swiss cheese, divided
¼ pound asparagus, cut into
      1-inch pieces
7 large eggs, lightly beaten
½ cup mayonnaise
½ teaspoon salt
2 tablespoons chopped fresh basil

• **Layer** pepper, mushrooms, and half of cheese in a lightly greased 9½-inch deep-dish pieplate. Top with asparagus and remaining cheese.
• **Combine** eggs and remaining 3 ingredients; pour evenly over cheese. Bake at 375° for 35 minutes or until a knife inserted in center comes out clean. Let stand 5 minutes. Serve warm or at room temperature. **Yield:** 8 servings.

Martha Johnston
Birmingham, Alabama

GOLDEN CHEESE-SHIITAKE OMELET

2 ounces fresh shiitake mushrooms
2 tablespoons butter, divided
1 small onion, finely chopped
⅔ cup cottage cheese
4 large eggs, lightly beaten
¼ teaspoon salt
¼ teaspoon freshly ground pepper

• **Remove** stems from mushrooms; discard. Cut caps into thin slices.
• **Melt** 1 tablespoon butter in a nonstick skillet over medium heat. Add mushrooms and onion; cook, stirring constantly, until tender. Transfer to a bowl, and stir in cottage cheese. Wipe skillet.
• **Combine** eggs, salt, and pepper; beat with a fork. Melt remaining butter, rotating pan to coat bottom. Add egg mixture. As mixture starts to cook, gently lift edges with a spatula, and tilt pan so uncooked portion flows underneath.
• **Spoon** mushroom mixture evenly onto half of omelet; fold omelet in half. Serve immediately. **Yield:** 2 servings.

Mariet Van den Munckh of Vedder
Dublin, Georgia

DILL-CHEESE-HAM OMELET
QUICK!

6 large eggs, lightly beaten
¼ cup milk
¼ teaspoon curry powder
½ teaspoon dried dillweed
2 teaspoons Worcestershire sauce
Vegetable cooking spray
½ cup chopped green onions
½ cup chopped cooked ham
½ cup (2 ounces) shredded
      Cheddar cheese
¼ cup (1 ounce) shredded Havarti
      cheese

• **Combine** first 5 ingredients; set aside.
• **Coat** a 10-inch omelet pan or nonstick skillet with cooking spray; add green onions, and cook over medium heat until tender.
• **Add** egg mixture. As mixture starts to cook, gently lift edges with a spatula, and tilt pan so uncooked portion flows underneath. Top with ham and cheeses.
• **Cover** and cook 3 minutes or until set. Fold in half; serve immediately. **Yield:** 4 servings.

Tom Maze
Petersburg, Virginia

SHRIMP AND CHEESE OMELET
QUICK!

2 large eggs
1 tablespoon water
1 tablespoon butter or margarine
3 tablespoons shredded Monterey
      Jack cheese
¼ cup coarsely chopped cooked
      shrimp
1 tablespoon sliced green
      onions
2 teaspoons chopped fresh
      parsley

• **Whisk** together eggs and 1 tablespoon water; set aside.
• **Heat** an 8-inch omelet pan or nonstick skillet over medium heat. Add butter, and rotate pan to coat. Add egg mixture. As mixture starts to cook, gently lift edges with a spatula, and tilt pan so uncooked portion of egg mixture flows underneath.

• **Sprinkle** half of omelet with cheese and next 3 ingredients; fold in half. Serve immediately. **Yield:** 1 serving.

❤ To reduce fat and cholesterol, substitute ½ cup fat-free egg substitute and 1 egg white, vegetable cooking spray, and reduced-fat Monterey Jack cheese for eggs, butter, and cheese, respectively.

THREE-CHEESE SOUFFLÉS
(pictured at right)

The subtle blend of Parmesan, Cheddar, and cream cheeses makes this a soufflé you won't soon forget.

2 tablespoons grated Parmesan
      cheese
4 large eggs, separated
1 cup (4 ounces) shredded sharp
      Cheddar cheese
1 (3-ounce) package cream cheese,
      cubed
⅓ cup half-and-half
¼ cup grated Parmesan cheese
½ teaspoon onion salt
½ teaspoon dry mustard
¼ teaspoon ground red pepper

• **Sprinkle** 2 tablespoons Parmesan cheese evenly into five buttered individual soufflé dishes or 6-ounce custard cups. Set aside.
• **Beat** egg whites at high speed with an electric mixer until stiff.
• **Combine** egg yolks, Cheddar cheese, and remaining 6 ingredients in container of an electric blender; process 30 seconds or until smooth. Process at high speed 10 to 15 seconds; pour into a bowl. Gently fold in egg whites; pour into prepared dishes. Seal in aluminum foil, and freeze up to 1 week.
• **Unwrap** soufflés, and place in an 8-inch square pan. Add hot water to pan to depth of 1 inch.
• **Bake** at 400° for 10 minutes; reduce oven temperature to 350°, and bake 20 to 25 additional minutes or until puffed and golden. Serve immediately. **Yield:** 5 servings.

Note: If not freezing soufflés, bake as directed at 350° for 20 to 25 minutes.

Three-Cheese Soufflés

CHILE-CHEESE SOUFFLÉS

¼ cup butter or margarine
¼ cup all-purpose flour
1¾ cups milk
¾ cup (3 ounces) shredded sharp
    Cheddar cheese
¾ cup (3 ounces) shredded
    Monterey Jack cheese
1 (4.5-ounce) can chopped green
    chiles, drained
1 teaspoon salt
6 large eggs, separated

• **Melt** butter in a heavy saucepan over low heat; add flour, whisking until smooth. Cook 1 minute, whisking constantly. Gradually add milk, and cook over medium heat, whisking constantly, until thickened and bubbly.
• **Add** cheeses, chiles, and salt, stirring until cheeses melt.
• **Beat** egg yolks at medium speed with an electric mixer until thick and pale. Gradually stir about one-fourth of hot mixture into yolks; add to remaining hot mixture, stirring constantly. Bring to a boil; remove from heat.
• **Beat** egg whites at high speed until stiff but not dry; gently fold into cheese mixture. Pour into nine buttered individual soufflé dishes or 6-ounce custard cups. Seal in aluminum foil, and freeze up to 1 week.
• **Unwrap** soufflés, and place in a 13- x 9- x 2-inch pan. Add hot water to pan to depth of 1 inch.
• **Bake** at 400° for 10 minutes; reduce oven temperature to 350°, and bake 25 additional minutes or until puffed and golden. Serve immediately. **Yield:** 9 servings.

Note: If not freezing soufflés, bake as directed at 350° for 25 minutes.

QUICHE CASSEROLE

QUICK!

6 slices whole wheat bread, torn
¼ teaspoon garlic powder
1 (26-ounce) carton frozen quiche
    filling with ham, thawed
1 medium-size red bell pepper, cut
    into rings

• **Place** bread evenly in a lightly greased 11- x 7- x 1½-inch baking dish; set aside.
• **Stir** garlic powder into quiche filling; pour over bread.
• **Bake** at 400° for 20 minutes; top with pepper rings, and bake 5 additional minutes. Let casserole stand 5 minutes before serving. **Yield:** 4 to 6 servings.

SUNDAY EGG CASSEROLE

2 tablespoons butter or margarine
4 tablespoons dry sherry, divided
1 pound fresh mushrooms, sliced
1 (10¾-ounce) can cream of
    chicken soup, undiluted
1 (8-ounce) carton sour cream
2 tablespoons all-purpose flour
½ teaspoon salt
½ teaspoon pepper
1 tablespoon finely chopped onion
1 (2-ounce) jar chopped pimiento,
    drained
1 (10-ounce) package frozen
    English peas, thawed and
    drained
14 hard-cooked eggs, cut
    lengthwise into 4 wedges
1 (8-ounce) can sliced water
    chestnuts, drained
1 cup fresh breadcrumbs (2 slices
    bread)
1 tablespoon butter or margarine,
    melted

• **Melt** 2 tablespoons butter in a large skillet; add 2 tablespoons sherry and mushrooms, and cook over medium heat 5 minutes or until mushrooms are tender. Drain well; set aside.
• **Combine** remaining 2 tablespoons sherry, soup, and next 6 ingredients in a medium saucepan. Cook 2 minutes or until mixture is bubbly; stir in mushrooms and peas.

• **Arrange** egg wedges and water chestnuts in bottom of a lightly greased 13- x 9- x 2-inch baking dish. Pour soup mixture evenly over top.
• **Combine** breadcrumbs and melted butter. Sprinkle over soup mixture.
• **Bake** at 375° for 20 minutes or until top is golden. **Yield:** 6 to 8 servings.

Brenda Russell
Signal Mountain, Tennessee

EGGS BAKED IN MUSHROOM SAUCE

1 pound fresh mushrooms, sliced
¼ cup butter or margarine,
    melted
3 tablespoons all-purpose flour
2 cups whipping cream
1 egg yolk, lightly beaten
1 teaspoon beef-flavored bouillon
    granules
1 tablespoon grated onion
2 tablespoons chopped fresh
    parsley
¼ teaspoon salt
¼ teaspoon pepper
⅛ teaspoon dried thyme
8 large eggs
Grated Parmesan cheese
4 English muffins, halved and
    toasted

• **Cook** mushrooms in melted butter in a large saucepan over medium heat 5 minutes, stirring constantly; remove mushrooms with a slotted spoon, and set aside. Add flour to drippings in saucepan, stirring until smooth. Cook, stirring constantly, 1 minute.
• **Combine** whipping cream and next 3 ingredients. Gradually add to flour mixture; cook over medium heat, stirring constantly, until mixture is thickened and bubbly. Stir in reserved mushrooms, parsley, and next 3 ingredients.
• **Pour** into a lightly greased 13- x 9- x 2-inch baking dish. Make 8 indentations in mushroom mixture, and break an egg into each. Sprinkle each with Parmesan cheese, and bake at 350° for 7 to 8 minutes. Serve over English muffin halves. **Yield:** 8 servings.

Sally B. Harris
Tarboro, North Carolina

LAYERED VEGETABLE CHEESECAKE

1⅓ cups dry breadcrumbs
⅓ cup butter or margarine, melted
2 (8-ounce) packages Neufchâtel cheese, softened
2 large eggs
⅓ cup all-purpose flour
1 (8-ounce) carton sour cream
¼ cup minced onion
¼ teaspoon salt
¼ teaspoon ground white pepper
¾ cup shredded carrot
¾ cup diced green bell pepper
¾ cup diced red bell pepper
Cucumber-Dill Sauce
Garnishes: cucumber slices, fresh dill sprigs

● **Combine** breadcrumbs and butter; press in bottom and 1 inch up sides of a 9-inch springform pan. Set aside.
● **Beat** cheese at high speed with an electric mixer until fluffy. Add eggs, one at a time, beating well after each addition. Add flour and next 4 ingredients; beat until blended.
● **Pour** about one-fourth of cheese mixture into prepared pan; sprinkle with carrot. Top with one-third remaining cheese mixture; sprinkle with green bell pepper. Top with half of remaining cheese mixture; top with red bell pepper. Top with remaining cheese mixture.
● **Bake** at 300° for 1 hour or until set. Turn oven off, and partially open oven door; leave cheesecake in oven 1 hour. Remove from oven; cool completely in pan on a wire rack. Cover and chill. Serve with Cucumber-Dill Sauce. Garnish, if desired. **Yield:** 6 to 8 servings.

Cucumber-Dill Sauce

QUICK!

1 (8-ounce) carton plain yogurt
⅓ cup mayonnaise or salad dressing
½ cup chopped unpeeled cucumber
¼ teaspoon salt
¼ teaspoon dried dillweed

● **Combine** all ingredients, stirring well. Cover and chill. **Yield:** 1½ cups.

GARLICKY HAM AND SPINACH GRITS

1 head garlic
2 to 3 teaspoons olive oil
4 ounces thinly sliced country ham, cut into ¼-inch strips
1 tablespoon peanut or vegetable oil
3 cups chicken broth
1 cup quick-cooking grits
½ cup butter or margarine
¼ teaspoon salt
¼ teaspoon pepper
1 cup milk
4 large eggs
1 cup (4 ounces) shredded Swiss cheese
1 (10-ounce) package frozen chopped spinach, thawed and well drained
¼ cup grated Parmesan cheese

● **Cut** off flat end of garlic head, and spread apart whole cloves, leaving tight outer covering intact. Trim pointed end so head will sit flat. Place garlic head, trimmed end down, in a garlic roaster or on a sheet of aluminum foil.
● **Drizzle** with olive oil; cover with lid or wrap in aluminum foil.
● **Bake** at 350° for 1 hour or until golden. Cool.
● **Squeeze** out pulp from each clove.
● **Position** knife blade in food processor bowl, and add garlic pulp. Process until smooth, stopping often to scrape down sides. Set aside.
● **Cook** ham in peanut oil in a skillet over medium-high heat, stirring constantly, until browned. Drain on paper towels, and set aside.
● **Bring** broth to a boil in a large saucepan; stir in grits. Cook over medium heat 3 to 5 minutes or until thick, stirring often. Remove from heat.
● **Stir** in garlic puree, butter, salt, and pepper.
● **Combine** milk and eggs; add to grits mixture, stirring well. Fold in ham, Swiss cheese, and spinach.
● **Grease** an 11- x 7- x 1½-inch baking dish or eight 10-ounce custard cups. Sprinkle bottom and sides of baking dish or cups with Parmesan cheese, coating well. Spoon grits mixture evenly into baking dish or cups.

● **Bake** at 350° for 45 minutes (35 minutes for cups) or until puffed and firm. Serve immediately. **Yield:** 8 servings.

Note: To freeze Garlicky Ham and Spinach Grits, prepare as directed, but do not bake. Cover unbaked grits with aluminum foil, and freeze. To serve, thaw in refrigerator; remove from refrigerator, and let stand 30 minutes. Bake as directed.

CHRISTMAS MORNING STRATA

1 pound ground pork sausage
2 teaspoons prepared mustard
6 slices white sandwich bread, crusts removed
2 cups (8 ounces) shredded Swiss cheese
1½ cups milk
3 large eggs, lightly beaten
½ teaspoon Worcestershire sauce
⅛ teaspoon salt
⅛ teaspoon pepper
⅛ teaspoon ground nutmeg

● **Brown** sausage in a skillet over medium heat, stirring until it crumbles; drain well. Stir in mustard.
● **Fit** bread in a greased 11- x 7- x 1½-inch baking dish; top with sausage mixture and cheese.
● **Combine** milk and remaining 5 ingredients; pour over bread mixture. Cover and chill 8 hours.
● **Bake**, uncovered, at 350° for 50 minutes or until set. **Yield:** 6 servings.

Karen Belle
Lovettsville, Virginia

HAM AND EGGS CRESCENT PIZZA

1 (8-ounce) can refrigerated
   crescent rolls
¼ cup chopped onion
1 tablespoon butter or margarine,
   melted
1 cup finely chopped cooked
   ham
1 cup (4 ounces) shredded Swiss
   cheese
4 large eggs, lightly beaten
½ cup milk
½ teaspoon salt
¼ teaspoon pepper
1 tablespoon chopped fresh or
   frozen chives

• **Unroll** crescent rolls, and place in an ungreased 13- x 9- x 2-inch pan. Press crescent rolls ½ inch up sides to form a crust; seal perforations. Bake on lower rack of oven at 375° for 5 minutes, and set aside.
• **Cook** onion in butter in a small skillet over medium heat, stirring constantly, until crisp-tender; stir in ham, and spoon evenly over dough. Sprinkle with cheese.
• **Combine** eggs and next 3 ingredients; pour over cheese. Sprinkle with chives.
• **Bake** at 350° for 25 to 30 minutes or until set. Serve immediately. **Yield:** 6 to 8 servings.

Mrs. Ezra Sanders
Obion, Tennessee

JALAPEÑO CHEESE PIE

This is a good recipe for the flavor-timid.
The heat of the peppers is soothingly
coated with cheese. Stir in chicken or
sausage for an easy brunch dish.

1 (11.5-ounce) jar whole jalapeño
   peppers, drained
4 cups (16 ounces) shredded
   Cheddar cheese
6 large eggs, lightly beaten

• **Cut** peppers in half lengthwise; remove and discard seeds. Rinse with cold water; drain on paper towels. Mince peppers.

• **Sprinkle** half of cheese in a lightly greased 11- x 7- x 1½-inch pan; top with peppers and remaining cheese. Pour eggs over top.
• **Bake** at 350° for 30 to 40 minutes or until lightly browned and set. Cool 5 to 10 minutes, and cut into squares. **Yield:** 12 servings.

Adapted from
Cooking Texas Style
Candy and Sandra Marquez
San Antonio, Texas

SPINACH PIE WITH MUENSTER CRUST

3 (10-ounce) packages frozen
   chopped spinach, thawed
2 (6-ounce) packages Muenster
   cheese slices
1 small onion, finely chopped
1 cup reduced-fat cottage cheese
3 large eggs, lightly beaten
⅓ cup grated Parmesan cheese
½ teaspoon salt
¼ teaspoon pepper
Garnish: pimiento strips

• **Drain** spinach well, pressing between layers of paper towels, and set spinach aside.
• **Cut** 2 or 3 cheese slices into small triangles, and reserve for top of pie. Cover bottom and sides of a lightly greased 9-inch pieplate with remaining Muenster slices, overlapping cheese as needed.
• **Combine** spinach, onion, and next 5 ingredients; spoon into cheese-lined pieplate.
• **Bake** at 350° for 45 minutes or until set. Top with reserved cheese triangles. Cool 10 minutes before serving. Garnish, if desired. **Yield:** 6 to 8 servings.

Michelle Stockhaus
Lorton, Virginia

SPINACH PIE PARMA

2 cups garlic-onion croutons,
   crushed
¼ cup butter or margarine,
   melted
1 pound fresh spinach, torn *
¼ cup water
3 large eggs, lightly beaten
1 cup small-curd cottage cheese
¼ cup freshly grated Parmesan
   cheese
¼ cup chopped onion
2 tablespoons sour cream
2 or 3 cloves garlic, pressed
½ teaspoon salt
⅛ teaspoon ground red pepper
4 ounces Monterey Jack cheese,
   cut into ¼-inch cubes
2 tablespoons freshly grated
   Parmesan cheese

• **Combine** croutons and butter, stirring well; press into bottom of an 8-inch square baking dish.
• **Combine** spinach and ¼ cup water in a skillet; cover and cook over medium heat 4 minutes or until wilted. Drain well on paper towels.
• **Combine** spinach, eggs, and next 7 ingredients, stirring well; stir in Monterey Jack cheese, and spoon over prepared crust.
• **Bake** at 350° for 35 minutes or until knife inserted in center comes out clean. Sprinkle with 2 tablespoons Parmesan cheese, and let stand 5 minutes. **Yield:** 6 servings.

✳ Substitute 1 (10-ounce) package frozen chopped spinach, thawed and well drained, for fresh.

TORTILLA PIE

QUICK!

1 (16-ounce) can refried beans
1 teaspoon chili powder
½ teaspoon ground cumin
8 (8-inch) flour tortillas
½ (16-ounce) jar chunky salsa
2 (4-ounce) cartons guacamole
1 (8-ounce) package shredded
    Mexican cheese blend
Garnishes: fresh cilantro sprigs,
    sour cream

● **Combine** first 3 ingredients in a small bowl, stirring well; set aside.
● **Place** 1 tortilla in a lightly greased 9-inch round cakepan; spread with half of bean mixture, and top with another tortilla. Spread with half of salsa, and top with another tortilla. Spread with half of guacamole, and top with another tortilla. Sprinkle with half of cheese, and top with another tortilla.
● **Repeat** layers with remaining ingredients, ending with cheese; cover with aluminum foil.
● **Bake** at 350° for 20 minutes or until thoroughly heated. Cut pie into wedges; garnish, if desired. **Yield:** 6 servings.

CREAM CHEESE QUICHE

½ (15-ounce) package
    refrigerated piecrusts
1 tablespoon butter or margarine
¼ cup chopped onion
1 (8-ounce) package cream cheese,
    cubed
¾ cup milk
4 large eggs, lightly beaten
1 cup finely chopped cooked ham
1 (2-ounce) jar diced pimiento,
    undrained
¼ teaspoon dried dillweed
⅛ teaspoon pepper

● **Fit** piecrust into a 9-inch quiche dish according to package directions; prick bottom and sides with a fork.
● **Bake** piecrust at 425° for 12 minutes; set aside.
● **Melt** butter in a small saucepan over medium-high heat; add onion, and cook until tender. Add cream cheese and

milk; cook over low heat, whisking until cream cheese melts. Gradually whisk about one-fourth of hot mixture into eggs; add to remaining hot mixture, whisking constantly. Whisk in ham and remaining 3 ingredients; pour mixture into prepared crust.
● **Bake** at 350° for 35 to 40 minutes or until set. **Yield:** 6 to 8 servings.

MEXICALI QUICHE WITH AVOCADO TOPPING

6 (6-inch) corn tortillas
½ pound ground hot pork
    sausage
¼ cup finely chopped onion
1 tablespoon chili powder
1 teaspoon ground cumin
3 large eggs, lightly beaten
1 (4.5-ounce) can chopped green
    chiles, undrained and divided
1½ cups half-and-half
½ teaspoon salt
⅛ teaspoon pepper
1½ cups (6 ounces) shredded
    Monterey Jack cheese, divided
Avocado Topping

● **Pour** water to depth of 2 inches into a large skillet. Bring to a boil; remove from heat.
● **Dip** each tortilla in water to soften; drain on paper towels. Place tortillas in six lightly greased 10-ounce custard cups; set aside.
● **Cook** sausage and next 3 ingredients in skillet over medium heat until meat is browned, stirring until it crumbles; drain and set aside.
● **Combine** eggs, half of green chiles, half-and-half, salt, and pepper in a large bowl; stir in sausage mixture.
● **Spoon** half of egg mixture evenly into tortilla shells; sprinkle with half of cheese. Pour remaining egg mixture evenly over cheese.
● **Bake** at 350° for 20 minutes. Sprinkle with remaining half of cheese, and bake 5 additional minutes.
● **Remove** from oven, and let stand 5 minutes. Remove from custard cups, and sprinkle with remaining green chiles. Serve with Avocado Topping. **Yield:** 6 servings.

Avocado Topping

QUICK!

1 avocado, mashed
1 tomato, peeled, seeded, and
    chopped
1 clove garlic, minced
1 to 2 tablespoons lime juice

● **Combine** all ingredients in a small bowl. **Yield:** 1½ cups.

Note: To make quiche in a 9-inch deep-dish pieplate, soften 8 corn tortillas in boiling water as directed; place in lightly greased pieplate, overlapping and extending tortillas about ½ inch over edge. Spoon half of egg mixture into shell; sprinkle with half of cheese, and spoon remaining egg mixture over cheese. Bake at 350° for 30 minutes. Sprinkle with remaining cheese; bake 5 additional minutes. Remove from oven; let stand 5 minutes. Sprinkle with remaining green chiles. Serve with Avocado Topping. **Yield:** 6 servings.

TEX-MEX EGG BURRITOS

QUICK!

1 pound ground hot pork sausage
12 large eggs, lightly beaten
1 (4.5-ounce) can chopped green
    chiles, drained
8 (8-inch) flour tortillas, warmed
Picante sauce
Shredded Cheddar cheese
Sliced jalapeño peppers (optional)

● **Brown** sausage in a large skillet, stirring until it crumbles; drain. Add eggs and chiles to sausage.
● **Cook**, without stirring, over medium heat until mixture begins to set on bottom. Draw a spatula across bottom of pan to form large curds. Continue cooking until eggs are thickened but still moist; do not stir constantly.
● **Spoon** egg mixture evenly down center of tortillas; top each with picante sauce, cheese, and jalapeño peppers, if desired. Fold opposite sides over filling. Serve immediately. **Yield:** 8 servings.

Georgana McNeil
Houston, Texas

EGGNOG FRENCH TOAST

QUICK!

1½ cups refrigerated eggnog
½ teaspoon freshly grated nutmeg
8 (1-inch-thick) slices French
    bread
2 tablespoons butter or margarine
Rum Syrup

• **Combine** eggnog and nutmeg in a shallow dish. Place bread slices in dish, turning to coat.
• **Melt** butter in a large skillet. Remove bread slices from eggnog mixture, allowing excess to drain. Cook in skillet 3 minutes on each side or until golden. Serve immediately with Rum Syrup. **Yield:** 4 servings.

Rum Syrup

QUICK!

1 cup pure maple syrup
2 tablespoons butter or margarine
2 tablespoons light rum or
    ½ teaspoon rum extract

• **Combine** all ingredients in a saucepan; cook over low heat until heated, stirring often. **Yield:** 1¼ cups.

Hugh Montgomery
Birmingham, Alabama

STUFFED FRENCH TOAST

Texans Gail Drago and Ann Ruff discovered this wonderful recipe when researching their book, Texas Historic Inns Cookbook.

1 (8-ounce) package cream cheese,
    softened
¼ cup crushed pineapple
½ cup chopped pecans, toasted
1 (16-ounce) loaf French bread
4 large eggs
1 cup whipping cream
1 teaspoon ground ginger
½ teaspoon vanilla extract
1 (12-ounce) jar apricot preserves
½ cup orange juice

• **Beat** cream cheese and pineapple at medium speed with an electric mixer until mixture is light and fluffy; stir in pecans.
• **Cut** bread into 12 (1½-inch-thick) slices; cut a pocket through top crust of each slice. Stuff each slice evenly with cream cheese mixture.
• **Combine** eggs and next 3 ingredients, stirring well with a wire whisk. Dip bread slices in egg mixture, coating all sides.
• **Cook** on a lightly greased griddle over medium-high heat 3 minutes on each side or until golden.
• **Combine** preserves and orange juice in a saucepan; cook over low heat, stirring constantly, until preserves are melted. Serve with hot French toast. **Yield:** 6 servings.

Annie's Bed and Breakfast
Big Sandy, Texas

BRUNCH POPOVER PANCAKE

4 large eggs, lightly beaten
1 cup milk
1 cup all-purpose flour
¼ teaspoon salt
⅓ cup butter or margarine, melted
3 tablespoons orange marmalade
3 tablespoons butter or margarine
1 tablespoon lemon juice
1 (16-ounce) package frozen sliced
    peaches, thawed and drained
1 cup frozen blueberries, thawed

• **Place** a well-greased 12-inch cast-iron skillet in a 425° oven for 5 minutes.
• **Combine** first 5 ingredients, stirring with a wire whisk until blended.
• **Remove** skillet from oven. Pour batter into hot skillet.
• **Bake** at 425° for 20 to 25 minutes. (This pancake resembles a giant popover and will fall quickly after removing from oven.)
• **Combine** marmalade, 3 tablespoons butter, and lemon juice in a saucepan; bring to a boil. Add peaches, and cook over medium heat 2 to 3 minutes, stirring constantly.
• **Spoon** mixture on top of baked pancake. Sprinkle with blueberries. **Yield:** 4 servings.

Bunny Campbell
Gainesville, Florida

ARKANSAS GERMAN-BAKED PANCAKE

Innkeeper Crescent Dragonwagon published this recipe and hundreds more in her book, The Dairy Hollow House Cookbook.

3 large eggs
¾ cup milk
½ teaspoon vanilla extract
¾ cup all-purpose flour
½ teaspoon salt
1½ tablespoons butter or
    margarine
Apple Filling
Sifted powdered sugar
Whipped cream

• **Heat** a 12-inch cast-iron skillet in a 450° oven for 5 minutes.
• **Combine** first 3 ingredients in a mixing bowl; beat at medium speed with an electric mixer until smooth. Add flour and salt; beat 5 minutes.
• **Melt** butter in skillet; pour batter into hot skillet.
• **Bake** at 450° for 15 minutes; reduce oven temperature to 350°, and bake 8 additional minutes or until puffed and browned. Remove from oven; spoon warm Apple Filling over pancake (pancake will deflate). Sprinkle with powdered sugar, and dollop with whipped cream. Cut into wedges, and serve immediately. **Yield:** 4 servings.

Apple Filling

QUICK!

¼ cup butter or margarine
4 large Granny Smith apples,
    cored and sliced
¼ cup honey

• **Melt** butter in a large skillet over medium-high heat; add apple, and cook, stirring constantly, 12 minutes or until tender. Stir in honey; cook just until thoroughly heated. **Yield:** 4 servings.

Dairy Hollow House
Eureka Springs, Arkansas

At right: *Crab-Stuffed Lobster Tail (page 168) and Blue Cheese-Walnut Stuffed Fillet (page 187)*

FISH AND SHELLFISH

m
eve
at

1½
1 lar
2 tal
  c
1 tal
1 tal
  l
1 tea
¾ te
½ te
½ te
¼ te
⅛ te
¾ cu
Vege
Garn

Tarta

• Arr
x 9- x
minu
utes
testec
set as
• Con
in a la
• Sha
with
paper
• Pou
skille
medi
side c
towe
tartar
servin

✱ Sub
raise

4 (8-in
1 pou
  mi
¼ teas
¼ teas
¼ cup
Vegetal
Sour cr
Sliced
Lime w

● Wrap
● Bake
thoroug
● Sprin
lightly
sauce.
with co
● Cook
medium
on each
when t
from ba
● Spoo
tortillas
onions
tortillas
Yield: 4

HON

1 (2-i
3 gree
½ cup
4 clov
1 pou
  tr
4 (6-o
  fil
¼ cup
⅓ cup
  sa
⅓ cup
⅓ cup
2 teas

● Peel
Cut gr
set gin
● Pour
skillet;

OVEN-FRIED CATFISH

QUICK!

*Try this recipe using any type
of whitefish fillets.*

¾ cup crushed corn flakes cereal
¾ teaspoon celery salt
¼ teaspoon onion powder
¼ teaspoon paprika
Dash of pepper
Vegetable cooking spray
4 (6-ounce) skinless farm-raised
   catfish fillets, halved

● **Combine** first 5 ingredients; set aside.
Spray all sides of fish with cooking
spray, and coat with corn flake mixture.
Arrange fillets in a single layer on a baking sheet coated with cooking spray.
Spray tops of fillets with cooking spray.
● **Bake** at 350° for 30 minutes or until
fish flakes easily when tested with a
fork. **Yield:** 4 servings.

Note: After trying Chef Chris Dupont's
Molasses Catfish at his Cafe Dupont in
Springville, Alabama, we adapted his
creamy molasses sauce recipe to serve
with this Oven-Fried Catfish. For a special touch, add 2 tablespoons chopped
toasted pecans to the corn flake mixture
in the recipe above, and proceed as directed. While the fish bakes, combine ¾
cup dry white wine and ¼ cup molasses. Cook 15 minutes or until mixture
reduces to ⅓ cup. Stir in 2 tablespoons
whipping cream. Spoon sauce evenly
over catfish fillets. This sauce will add 5
fat grams and 100 calories to the nutritional analysis (below) of each serving,
but it's worth the indulgence.

*Edith Askins
Greenville, Texas*

♥ Per serving: Calories 247
Fat 8.7g Cholesterol 77mg
Sodium 673mg

GRAND LAGOON STUFFED FLOUNDER

Crabmeat Stuffing
6 (1-pound) whole flounder,
   dressed
⅓ cup butter or margarine,
   melted
3 tablespoons lemon juice

● **Spoon** Crabmeat Stuffing evenly into
each fish cavity. Place fish in a lightly
greased 15- x 10- x 1-inch jellyroll pan.
● **Combine** butter and lemon juice; drizzle over fish.
● **Bake** at 350° for 25 minutes or until
fish flakes easily when tested with a
fork. **Yield:** 6 servings.

Crabmeat Stuffing

1 green bell pepper, finely
   chopped
½ cup finely chopped onion
2½ tablespoons finely chopped
   celery
½ (16-ounce) package saltine
   crackers, crushed
½ pound fresh crabmeat, drained
   and flaked
1½ teaspoons salt
1½ teaspoons pepper
2 large eggs
1 cup mayonnaise or salad
   dressing
¼ cup Worcestershire sauce
¼ cup prepared mustard
2 tablespoons lemon juice

● **Combine** first 7 ingredients in a large
bowl; set aside.
● **Combine** eggs and remaining 4 ingredients; stir into crabmeat mixture.
Yield: 5 cups.

Note: Use any leftover Crabmeat Stuffing to stuff peeled and butterflied jumbo
shrimp (baked as directed for flounder)
or shaped into croquettes and browned
in hot oil.

Bay Leaves
*Junior Service League of
Panama City, Florida*

OVEN-FRIED FISH

QUICK!

*The key to a crispy coating when
oven-frying is to bake the fish at a high
temperature. A fifty-fifty combination of
cornmeal and fine, dry breadcrumbs
enhances the crunchiness of the coating.*

¼ cup cornmeal
¼ cup fine, dry breadcrumbs
½ teaspoon salt
½ teaspoon paprika
¼ teaspoon dried dillweed
⅛ teaspoon pepper
1 pound fish fillets, cut into 1-inch
   strips *
⅓ cup milk
3 tablespoons butter or margarine,
   melted
Garnishes: lemon halves tied in
   cheesecloth, fresh flat-leaf
   parsley sprigs

● **Combine** first 6 ingredients in a shallow dish. Dip fillets in milk, and dredge
in cornmeal mixture. Place in a lightly
greased 13- x 9- x 2-inch pan, and drizzle
with butter.
● **Bake** fillets at 450° for 10 minutes or
until fish flakes easily when tested with
a fork. Garnish, if desired. **Yield:** 4 to 6
servings.

* For fish fillets, we used grouper and
orange roughy.

*Louise Ellis
Talbott, Tennessee*

MONTEGO BAY GRILLED FISH WITH CARIBBEAN SALSA

3 tablespoons chopped fresh
    cilantro
1 roasted jalapeño pepper,
    chopped (see note)
2 tablespoons fresh lime juice
1 tablespoon minced garlic
1 tablespoon minced fresh
    ginger
Vegetable cooking spray
4 grouper or amberjack fillets
    (about 1½ pounds)
Caribbean Salsa

• **Combine** first 5 ingredients; set aside.
• **Coat** a grill tray with cooking spray, and place on grill rack. Heat, covered with grill lid, over hot coals (400° to 500°) 10 minutes. Place fish on grill tray.
• **Cook**, covered with grill lid, 10 minutes. Turn fish, and spread with cilantro mixture. Cook, covered with grill lid, 10 minutes or until fish flakes easily when tested with a fork. Serve with Caribbean Salsa. **Yield:** 4 servings.

Caribbean Salsa

1 large ripe banana, chopped
½ cup finely chopped red bell
    pepper
½ cup finely chopped green bell
    pepper
½ cup chopped fresh cilantro
3 green onions, finely chopped
1 roasted jalapeño pepper,
    chopped (see note)
1 tablespoon minced fresh
    ginger
2 tablespoons brown sugar
3 tablespoons fresh lime juice
1 tablespoon olive oil
¼ teaspoon salt
⅛ teaspoon pepper

• **Combine** all ingredients, tossing gently to coat; cover and chill 2 hours. **Yield:** 2½ cups.

Note: To roast jalapeños, place on an aluminum foil-lined baking sheet. Broil 5½ inches from heat (with electric oven door partially opened) about 5 minutes on each side or until blistered. Place in a heavy-duty, zip-top plastic bag; seal and let stand 10 minutes to loosen skins. Peel peppers, and remove and discard seeds.

GARLIC-BASIL MARINATED GROUPER

QUICK!

5 pounds grouper fillets
Garlic-Basil Marinade
Vegetable cooking spray
Garnish: fresh parsley sprigs

• **Arrange** fish in a large shallow dish; pour Garlic-Basil Marinade over fish. Cover and chill 1 hour.
• **Remove** fish from marinade, discarding marinade. Arrange fish in a grill basket coated with cooking spray.
• **Cook**, covered with grill lid, over medium coals (300° to 350°) 9 minutes on each side or until fish flakes easily when tested with a fork. Garnish, if desired, and serve immediately. **Yield:** 10 servings.

Garlic-Basil Marinade

QUICK!

¾ cup olive oil
½ cup tomato sauce
¼ cup balsamic vinegar
4 cloves garlic, crushed
¼ cup chopped fresh basil
1 teaspoon salt
1 teaspoon ground red pepper

• **Combine** all ingredients in a small bowl. **Yield:** 1⅔ cups.

Jim and Jane Bowyers
Maitland, Florida

HOT SPICY GROUPER

QUICK!

4 (4-ounce) grouper or snapper
    fillets
¼ cup lemon juice
2 tablespoons water
2 tablespoons hot sauce
1 tablespoon vegetable oil
2 teaspoons grated fresh ginger
½ teaspoon salt
Vegetable cooking spray
1 tablespoon sesame seeds,
    toasted
1 tablespoon chopped fresh
    parsley

• **Place** grouper in a shallow dish; set aside.
• **Combine** lemon juice and next 5 ingredients; divide marinade in half.
• **Cover** and chill 1 portion. Pour remaining portion over fish, turning to coat. Cover with aluminum foil. Chill 1 hour, turning fish occasionally.
• **Remove** fish from marinade, discarding marinade.
• **Arrange** fish in a single layer in a grill basket coated with cooking spray. Cook, covered with grill lid, over hot coals (400° to 500°) 5 minutes on each side or until fish flakes easily when tested with a fork, basting with reserved marinade.
• **Transfer** fish to a serving plate; sprinkle with sesame seeds and parsley. **Yield:** 4 servings.

Penny Caughfield
Cocoa, Florida

♥ Per serving: Calories 155
Fat 5.9g   Cholesterol 42mg
Sodium 393mg

*Pan-Fried Grouper
With Vanilla
Wine Sauce*

PAN-FRIED GROUPER WITH VANILLA WINE SAUCE
(pictured at left)

1 cup boiling water
1 fish-flavored bouillon cube
1 cup dry white wine
2 tablespoons chopped onion
1 vanilla bean, cut in half
     lengthwise and divided
⅓ cup all-purpose flour
¼ teaspoon salt
¼ teaspoon pepper
1 (2½-pound) grouper fillet
¼ cup butter or margarine,
     divided
2 tablespoons all-purpose flour
⅓ cup whipping cream
⅛ teaspoon salt
Garnish: fresh chives

● **Combine** first 4 ingredients and half of vanilla bean in a saucepan; bring to a boil, stirring until bouillon cube dissolves. Boil 10 minutes or until mixture is reduced to ¾ cup. Pour mixture through a wire-mesh strainer into a 1-cup liquid measuring cup, discarding solids, and set broth mixture aside.
● **Position** knife blade in food processor bowl; add remaining half of vanilla bean. Process until finely chopped. Add ⅓ cup flour, ¼ teaspoon salt, and pepper; process 10 seconds.
● **Cut** fillet into 6 equal portions. Coat each portion evenly with flour mixture; shake off excess.
● **Melt** 2 tablespoons butter in a heavy skillet; add fish, and cook 3 minutes on each side or until fish flakes easily when tested with a fork. Remove fish to a serving platter, and keep warm.
● **Melt** remaining 2 tablespoons butter in a heavy saucepan over low heat; add 2 tablespoons flour, stirring until smooth. Cook 1 minute, stirring constantly. Gradually add reserved reduced broth mixture; cook over medium heat, stirring constantly, until mixture is thickened.
● **Stir** in whipping cream and ⅛ teaspoon salt; cook over medium heat until thoroughly heated.
● **Pour** sauce over grouper. Garnish, if desired. **Yield:** 6 servings.

Kim McCully
Knoxville, Tennessee

WINE-HERB HALIBUT STEAK
QUICK!

3 tablespoons butter or
     margarine
4 (1-inch-thick) halibut steaks
½ cup dry white wine
1 tablespoon lemon juice
¼ teaspoon dried basil
¼ teaspoon dried oregano
¼ teaspoon salt
¼ teaspoon pepper
¼ teaspoon paprika

● **Melt** butter in a large skillet over medium heat. Arrange halibut steaks in a single layer, and cook 3 to 4 minutes on each side.
● **Add** wine and lemon juice; sprinkle basil and remaining 4 ingredients over steaks. Cover, reduce heat, and simmer 8 to 10 minutes or until fish flakes easily when tested with a fork. Serve with pan drippings. **Yield:** 4 servings.

Carrie Treichel
Johnson City, Tennessee

MIDDLE EASTERN MAHIMAHI
QUICK!

1 tablespoon butter or margarine
1 cup sliced green onions
½ cup finely chopped yellow bell
     pepper
2 teaspoons minced garlic
1½ cups currant jelly
¼ cup water
1 teaspoon ground cinnamon
1 teaspoon ground cumin
½ teaspoon ground red pepper
½ teaspoon lemon juice
2 bay leaves
6 mahimahi steaks (3 pounds)
1½ cups finely chopped tomato
1 teaspoon paprika
½ teaspoon seasoned salt

● **Melt** butter in a medium skillet over medium-high heat; add green onions and next 9 ingredients, and cook 2 minutes, stirring occasionally. Remove from heat; set aside.
● **Place** fish steaks in a lightly greased 13- x 9- x 2-inch baking dish; pour green onion mixture evenly over fish steaks.

Top with chopped tomato, and sprinkle evenly with paprika and seasoned salt.
● **Bake** at 425° for 20 to 30 minutes or until fish flakes easily when tested with a fork. Remove and discard bay leaves. Serve fish steaks immediately. **Yield:** 6 servings.

Marion Hall
Knoxville, Tennessee

QUICK FISH FILLETS
QUICK!

This quick and easy recipe results in fantastic fish from the oven or microwave.

1 pound orange roughy fillets
¼ cup fine, dry breadcrumbs
1 teaspoon chopped fresh
     parsley
½ teaspoon paprika
¼ cup plain yogurt
1 teaspoon prepared mustard
Vegetable cooking spray
Lemon wedges

● **Cut** orange roughy into serving-size pieces.
● **Combine** breadcrumbs, parsley, and paprika in a shallow dish.
● **Combine** yogurt and mustard. Dip fillets in yogurt mixture, and dredge in breadcrumb mixture; place in a 9-inch square baking dish coated with cooking spray.
● **Bake** at 450° for 20 minutes or microwave, covered with a paper towel, at HIGH 4 minutes or until fish flakes easily when tested with a fork. Serve with lemon wedges. **Yield:** 2 servings.

Laura Morris
Bunnell, Florida

PESTO-CRUSTED ORANGE ROUGHY

QUICK!

Try this flavorful herbed crust on any mild-flavored fish like cod, catfish, snapper, or grouper.

2 tablespoons pesto
½ cup fine, dry breadcrumbs
¼ teaspoon pepper
4 (4-ounce) orange roughy
    fillets
Vegetable cooking spray

● **Combine** pesto, breadcrumbs, and pepper in a shallow dish. Dredge fillets in breadcrumb mixture, and place in an 11- x 7- x 1½-inch baking dish coated with cooking spray. Coat fillets with cooking spray.
● **Bake** at 400° for 15 minutes or until fish flakes easily when tested with a fork. **Yield:** 4 servings.

♥ Per serving: Calories 190
Fat 7g Cholesterol 24mg
Sodium 274mg

STEAMED ORANGE ROUGHY WITH HERBS

QUICK!

This unbelievably simple recipe has so much flavor you won't need to reach for the salt shaker.

½ cup fresh parsley sprigs
½ cup fresh chives
½ cup fresh thyme sprigs
½ cup fresh rosemary sprigs
2 (8-ounce) orange roughy
    fillets *
Fresh lemon slices

● **Arrange** half of herbs in bottom of a steaming basket. Top with fillets and remaining herbs.
● **Cover** and steam fillets 7 minutes or until fish flakes easily when tested with a fork. Serve with lemon slices. **Yield:** 4 servings.

* Substitute any mild-flavored fish for orange roughy in this recipe. Try cod,

grouper, snapper, or farm-raised catfish. And don't limit yourself to the herbs we suggest; use any fresh herb you have available.

♥ Per serving: Calories 79
Fat 0.8g Cholesterol 23mg
Sodium 72mg

FILLETS TOMATILLO

QUICK!

1 cup finely chopped fresh
    tomatillo (4 large tomatillos)
¼ cup finely chopped onion
¼ cup finely chopped celery
2 tablespoons chopped green bell
    pepper
1 clove garlic, minced
2 teaspoons olive oil
¼ cup clam juice or chicken
    broth
2 tablespoons canned chopped
    green chiles
2 tablespoons lime juice
½ teaspoon chopped fresh
    cilantro
½ teaspoon ground cumin
¼ teaspoon dried oregano
⅛ teaspoon salt
⅛ teaspoon ground red pepper
4 (4-ounce) orange roughy
    fillets
Vegetable cooking spray

● **Cook** first 5 ingredients in olive oil in a medium skillet over medium-high heat 5 minutes, stirring constantly.
● **Add** clam juice and next 7 ingredients; cover, reduce heat, and cook 15 minutes, stirring occasionally. Set aside, and keep warm.
● **Arrange** fish in a grill basket coated with cooking spray. Cook, covered with grill lid, over medium-hot coals (350° to 400°) 7 to 8 minutes on each side or until fish flakes easily with a fork. Serve fillets with tomatillo mixture. **Yield:** 4 servings.

Ginny Munsterman
Garland, Texas

♥ Per serving: Calories 124
Fat 3.7g Cholesterol 23mg
Sodium 193mg

GRILLED SALMON STEAKS

QUICK!

2 tablespoons mayonnaise
½ teaspoon chopped fresh dill or
    ⅛ teaspoon dried dillweed
2 (1-inch-thick) salmon steaks
Garnishes: lemon halves, fresh dill
    sprigs

● **Combine** mayonnaise and dill; spread on both sides of salmon.
● **Cook**, covered with grill lid, over medium-hot coals (350° to 400°) 5 to 6 minutes on each side or to desired degree of doneness. Garnish, if desired. **Yield:** 2 servings.

Susan Nash
Birmingham, Alabama
and
Julia Rutland
Cordova, Tennessee

GRILLED HERBED SALMON STEAKS

QUICK!

8 (¾-inch-thick) salmon steaks
¾ cup dry white vermouth or dry
    white wine
¾ cup olive oil
1½ tablespoons lemon juice
1 tablespoon chopped fresh thyme
    or 1 teaspoon dried thyme
1 tablespoon chopped fresh
    marjoram or 1 teaspoon dried
    marjoram
1 tablespoon chopped fresh sage
    or 1 teaspoon rubbed sage
1 tablespoon chopped fresh
    parsley
¾ teaspoon salt
⅛ teaspoon freshly ground pepper
Garnish: fresh thyme sprigs

● **Place** salmon in two shallow dishes. Combine vermouth and next 8 ingredients; reserve ⅓ cup marinade. Pour remaining marinade over salmon; cover and chill 1 hour.
● **Remove** salmon from marinade, discarding marinade. Cook salmon, covered with grill lid, over medium-hot coals (350° to 400°) 5 to 6 minutes on

each side or until salmon flakes easily when tested with a fork, brushing often with reserved marinade. Garnish, if desired. **Yield:** 8 servings.

Note: You can broil salmon steaks 5½ inches from heat (with electric oven door partially opened) 6 to 8 minutes on each side or until fish flakes easily when tested with a fork, brushing often with reserved marinade.

The Lucullan Society
Lynchburg, Virginia

MINT-MARINATED SALMON STEAKS

Cut into the salmon steaks near the center to test for doneness. Grilling time for the steaks may vary, depending upon weather conditions.

½ cup dry white wine
¼ cup olive oil
2 cloves garlic, minced
½ teaspoon salt
¼ teaspoon pepper
1 tablespoon lemon juice
¼ cup chopped fresh mint
4 (¾-inch-thick) salmon steaks
Vegetable cooking spray

• **Combine** first 7 ingredients, stirring until blended.
• **Place** salmon steaks in a large shallow dish, and pour wine mixture over salmon. Cover and chill 2 hours, turning salmon occasionally.
• **Remove** salmon from marinade, discarding marinade.
• **Coat** grill rack or fish basket with cooking spray, and place salmon on rack or in basket.
• **Cook** salmon, covered with grill lid, over medium coals (300° to 350°) 10 minutes on each side or until done. Remove from heat; cover and chill. **Yield:** 4 servings.

SALMON FILLETS WITH SWEET CORN RELISH

QUICK!

2 tablespoons vegetable oil
2 pounds salmon fillets, cut into 8 portions
¼ teaspoon salt
Sweet Corn Relish

• **Brush** oil on skinless side of salmon; sprinkle with salt. Cook over medium-hot coals (350° to 400°) 7 minutes on each side or until fish flakes easily when tested with a fork. Serve with Sweet Corn Relish. **Yield:** 8 servings.

Sweet Corn Relish

4 or 5 ears fresh yellow corn
1 cup chopped cabbage
⅓ cup chopped onion
⅓ cup chopped green bell pepper
⅓ cup chopped red bell pepper
¼ cup sugar
1½ teaspoons dry mustard
¾ teaspoon celery seeds
¾ teaspoon mustard seeds
¾ teaspoon ground turmeric
½ to ¾ teaspoon salt
1 cup white vinegar
¼ cup water

• **Remove** and discard husks and silks from corn. Cook corn 5 minutes in boiling water to cover; drain. Cut kernels from cob.
• **Combine** corn, cabbage, and remaining ingredients in a large saucepan; bring to a boil. Cover, reduce heat, and simmer 20 minutes. Cover and chill. **Yield:** 3 cups.

Wolf Trap Farm Park
for the Performing Arts
Vienna, Virginia

GRILLED SALMON QUESADILLA WITH CUCUMBER SALSA

1 (8-ounce) salmon fillet
4 (8- to 10-inch) flour tortillas
1 cup (4 ounces) shredded Monterey Jack cheese
2 ounces goat cheese, crumbled
2 jalapeño peppers, seeded and sliced
Cucumber Salsa

• **Cook** salmon, covered with grill lid, over medium-hot coals (350° to 400°) 5 to 6 minutes on each side or until done. Cool; flake with a fork.
• **Spoon** flaked salmon evenly over half of each tortilla. Top evenly with cheeses and pepper slices. Fold tortillas in half.
• **Cook** tortillas in a large nonstick skillet over high heat 1 minute on each side or until tortillas are slightly browned and cheese melts. Cut each quesadilla into 3 triangles, and serve with chilled Cucumber Salsa. **Yield:** 4 servings.

Cucumber Salsa

1 large cucumber, chopped
1 clove garlic, minced
1 tablespoon finely chopped poblano chile pepper
1 tablespoon finely chopped purple onion
1 tablespoon finely chopped red bell pepper
1 tablespoon finely chopped yellow bell pepper
1 tablespoon finely chopped fresh cilantro
1 teaspoon olive oil
¼ teaspoon salt
⅛ teaspoon pepper

• **Combine** all ingredients; cover and chill. **Yield:** 1¼ cups.

Tom Nickoloff
La Paz Restaurante Cantinas
Atlanta, Georgia

SALMON IN PARCHMENT

*Serve this dish with rice or couscous
to soak up the flavorful cooking liquid.*

⅓ cup dry white wine
⅓ cup fresh lime juice
2 tablespoons chopped fresh dill
6 (4-ounce) salmon steaks
4 carrots
2 leeks
1 red bell pepper
Vegetable cooking spray
½ teaspoon salt
¼ teaspoon pepper
6 slices lime
12 fresh dill sprigs, divided

• **Combine** first 3 ingredients in a shallow dish; add salmon. Cover and chill 30 minutes.
• **Slice** carrots diagonally; thinly slice white part of leeks, and separate into rings. Thinly slice red pepper.
• **Combine** carrot, leek, and red pepper in a saucepan; add water to depth of 1 inch. Bring to a boil; boil 1 minute. Drain vegetables, and plunge into ice water to stop the cooking process; drain.
• **Cut** six 18- x 12-inch pieces of parchment paper; fold each piece in half to make a 12- x 9-inch rectangle. Trim into half heart-shaped pieces. Coat one side of each piece of parchment with cooking spray; arrange three-fourths of vegetable mixture evenly on coated sides of parchment, leaving a 1-inch border.
• **Remove** salmon from marinade, reserving marinade. Place fish over vegetables; pour 2 tablespoons reserved marinade over each steak, and sprinkle with salt and pepper. Top each with a lime slice. Place remaining vegetables on fish; top each with 1 dill sprig.
• **Bring** opposite sides of parchment together; fold edges over twice to seal, and fold pointed ends underneath packet. Place on baking sheets.
• **Bake** at 425° for 10 to 12 minutes. Cut opening in packets; top with remaining dill sprigs. **Yield:** 6 servings.

*Patricia A. Chapman
Huntsville, Alabama*

❤ Per serving: Calories 225
Fat 8.5g   Cholesterol 62mg
Sodium 273mg

SALMON BAKE WITH PECAN-CRUNCH COATING

*This pecan coating also
works well on firm fish like
grouper and amberjack.*

4 (4- to 6-ounce) salmon fillets
⅛ teaspoon salt
⅛ teaspoon pepper
2 tablespoons Dijon mustard
2 tablespoons butter, melted
1½ tablespoons honey
¼ cup soft breadcrumbs
¼ cup finely chopped pecans
2 teaspoons chopped fresh parsley
Garnishes: fresh parsley sprigs,
   lemon slices

• **Sprinkle** salmon with salt and pepper. Place fillets, skin side down, in a lightly greased 13- x 9- x 2-inch pan.
• **Combine** mustard, butter, and honey; brush on fillets.
• **Combine** breadcrumbs, pecans, and chopped parsley; spoon mixture evenly on top of each fillet.
• **Bake** at 450° for 10 minutes or until fish flakes easily. Garnish, if desired. **Yield:** 4 servings.

*Helen H. Maurer
Christmas, Florida*

SESAME-CRUSTED SALMON WITH GINGER VINAIGRETTE

1 large English cucumber, peeled
   and coarsely chopped
½ cup rice wine vinegar
⅛ teaspoon salt
2 tablespoons sugar
¼ cup water
¼ cup low-sodium soy sauce
2 tablespoons rice wine vinegar
1 tablespoon honey
1 teaspoon hot sauce
½ teaspoon ground coriander
½ teaspoon dark sesame oil
4 (4-ounce) salmon fillets
1 tablespoon sesame seeds,
   toasted
1 large English cucumber, thinly
   sliced
Ginger Vinaigrette
Garnish: fresh mint sprigs

• **Position** knife blade in food processor bowl; add chopped English cucumber. Process until smooth, stopping once to scrape down sides.
• **Line** a large wire-mesh strainer with cheesecloth or a coffee filter; pour pureed cucumber through strainer into a bowl, discarding pulp.
• **Stir** ½ cup vinegar and salt into cucumber liquid; set aside.
• **Combine** sugar and water in a saucepan; bring to a boil over medium heat, stirring often. Stir into cucumber liquid mixture; set aside.
• **Combine** soy sauce and next 5 ingredients in a small bowl; brush over salmon. Place salmon in a lightly greased 13- x 9- x 2-inch pan; sprinkle with sesame seeds.
• **Bake** fillets at 450° for 10 to 12 minutes or until fish flakes easily when tested with a fork.
• **Arrange** salmon fillets and sliced cucumber in four bowls. Spoon cucumber liquid mixture evenly into each dish. Drizzle with a small amount of Ginger Vinaigrette. Garnish, if desired. **Yield:** 4 servings.

❤ Per serving: Calories 395
Fat 23.1g   Cholesterol 63mg
Sodium 744mg

Ginger Vinaigrette
QUICK!

1 (1½-inch-long) piece fresh
   ginger, peeled
1 clove garlic
2 tablespoons rice wine vinegar
1 tablespoon low-sodium soy sauce
1 tablespoon honey
⅛ teaspoon dried crushed red
   pepper
¼ cup peanut oil
½ teaspoon dark sesame oil

• **Position** knife blade in food processor bowl; add ginger and garlic. Process until smooth.
• **Add** vinegar and next 3 ingredients; process 30 seconds. Slowly pour peanut oil and sesame oil through food chute with processor running, blending just until smooth. **Yield:** 1½ cup.

*Bacchanalia
Atlanta, Georgia*

SALMON SCALOPPINE WITH VEGETABLE CONFETTI AND PERNOD SAUCE

⅓ cup all-purpose flour
¼ teaspoon salt
¼ teaspoon pepper
1 pound salmon fillet, cut diagonally into ½-inch strips
1 leek
¼ cup butter or margarine, divided
1 carrot, scraped and cut into 2-inch thin strips
¼ cup dry white wine
¼ cup chicken broth
½ cup whipping cream
¼ teaspoon salt
⅓ cup finely chopped tomato
1½ tablespoons Pernod *

● **Combine** first 3 ingredients; dredge salmon strips in flour mixture. Set aside.
● **Wash** leek. Remove root, tough outer leaves, and dark green leaves. Cut white part of leek into thin 2-inch strips.
● **Melt** 2 tablespoons butter in a large skillet. Add leek and carrot, and cook over medium heat, stirring constantly, 2 minutes or until crisp-tender. Remove vegetables from skillet; set aside.
● **Melt** remaining 2 tablespoons butter in skillet; add salmon, and cook 2 minutes on each side. Remove from skillet, and place in a 250° oven to keep warm.
● **Add** wine and chicken broth to skillet; cook over high heat 5 minutes or until reduced to about ¼ cup.
● **Stir** in whipping cream and salt. Cook over medium-high heat 4 minutes or until sauce is thickened. Add chopped tomato and Pernod; cook 1 minute.
● **Place** salmon on serving plates; drizzle with sauce, and top with vegetables. **Yield:** 2 main-dish servings or 4 appetizer servings.

* Pernod is a yellowish, licorice-flavored liqueur.

Jean Cooper
Washington, D.C.

SMOKED SALMON

Hickory or fruitwood chips
2 teaspoons onion powder
¼ teaspoon salt
¼ teaspoon pepper
1 (1½-pound) salmon fillet with skin

● **Soak** wood chips in water at least 30 minutes.
● **Combine** onion powder, salt, and pepper; rub fillet with mixture. Cover and chill 30 minutes.
● **Prepare** charcoal fire in smoker; let burn 15 to 20 minutes.
● **Drain** chips, and place on coals. Place water pan in smoker; add water to pan to depth of fill line.
● **Place** fillet, skin side down, on upper food rack; cover with smoker lid.
● **Cook** 1½ hours or until fish flakes easily. **Yield:** 4 servings.

Sylvia D. Ellis
San Antonio, Texas

CARIBBEAN BANANA FISH

¼ teaspoon coriander seeds
¼ teaspoon lemon pepper
¼ teaspoon ground nutmeg
¼ teaspoon ground allspice
¼ teaspoon salt
¼ teaspoon pepper
Vegetable cooking spray
4 (4-ounce) red snapper fillets, skinned
¼ cup all-purpose flour
2 bananas, peeled and sliced
4 small green onions, chopped
¼ cup sweetened coconut milk
¼ cup rum

● **Crush** coriander seeds, using a mortar and pestle; add lemon pepper and next 4 ingredients, stirring well. Set aside.
● **Coat** a large nonstick skillet with cooking spray, and place over medium heat until hot.
● **Dredge** snapper fillets in flour, and arrange in hot skillet. Sprinkle half of spice mixture over fillets, and cook over medium-high heat until lightly browned. Turn fillets; sprinkle with remaining spice mixture, and cook until browned.

● **Place** banana slices over fillets, and sprinkle with chopped green onions. Add coconut milk, and cook until fish flakes easily when tested with a fork.
● **Add** rum to skillet; cover and let stand 5 minutes. **Yield:** 4 servings.

Teresa Smith
Miami, Florida

♥ Per serving: Calories 286
Fat 7.1g   Cholesterol 42mg
Sodium 224mg

SNAPPER FINGERS WITH BANANA SALSA

1½ cups crushed potato chips
¼ cup grated Parmesan cheese
1 teaspoon ground thyme
1 pound snapper or grouper fillets, cut into strips
¼ cup milk
Banana Salsa
Garnish: fresh parsley sprigs

● **Combine** first 3 ingredients in a shallow dish; dip fish in milk, and dredge in potato chip mixture. Place fish in a single layer on a greased baking sheet.
● **Bake** at 500° for 8 to 10 minutes. Serve fish with Banana Salsa. Garnish, if desired. **Yield:** 8 servings.

Banana Salsa

2 medium-size ripe bananas, chopped
½ cup chopped green bell pepper
½ cup chopped red bell pepper
3 green onions, chopped
1 tablespoon chopped fresh cilantro
2 tablespoons light brown sugar
3 tablespoons fresh lime juice
1 tablespoon vegetable oil
¼ teaspoon salt
¼ teaspoon pepper
1 small jalapeño pepper, seeded and chopped (optional)

● **Combine** first 10 ingredients. Add jalapeño pepper, if desired. Cover and chill at least 3 hours. **Yield:** 8 servings.

Nita and Harold Norman
Coral Gables, Florida

YELLOWTAIL SNAPPER WITH JULIENNE VEGETABLES

½ cup Dijon mustard
2 egg yolks
4 (6- to 8-ounce) yellowtail
   snapper fillets
1½ cups coarsely chopped
   cashews
1 tablespoon unsalted butter
1 tablespoon olive oil
Julienne Vegetables
2 tablespoons chopped shallots
½ cup orange juice
1 tablespoon fresh lime juice
¼ cup unsalted butter, melted
1 tablespoon chopped fresh
   parsley
Garnishes: lime and lemon wedges,
   fresh basil, edible flowers

• **Combine** mustard and egg yolks; brush over skinless side of fillets. Dredge coated sides in nuts; chill 10 minutes.
• **Heat** 1 tablespoon butter and oil in a large nonstick skillet; place fillets, nut side down, in skillet. Cook over medium heat 5 to 8 minutes. Carefully turn; cook 5 to 8 minutes or until fish flakes easily.
• **Arrange** Julienne Vegetables on a large platter; place fillets, nut side up, on top of vegetables. Keep warm.
• **Wipe** skillet with a paper towel; add shallot, and cook over medium heat, stirring constantly, until tender. Add juices, and bring to a boil. Cook until mixture is reduced to about 3 tablespoons. Whisk in ¼ cup melted butter, 1 teaspoon at a time. Stir in parsley. Pour over fillets; garnish, if desired. Serve immediately. **Yield:** 4 to 6 servings.

Julienne Vegetables

1 clove garlic, minced
2 tablespoons olive oil
1 sweet potato, peeled and cut
   into very thin strips
1 large carrot, scraped and cut
   into very thin strips
1 small jicama, peeled and cut into
   very thin strips
3 leeks (bulb ends only), cut into
   very thin strips
½ teaspoon salt
¼ teaspoon pepper

• **Cook** garlic in olive oil in a large skillet over medium heat, stirring constantly, until golden. Add vegetables, and cook, stirring constantly, 3 to 5 minutes or until vegetables are crisp-tender. Sprinkle with salt and pepper. **Yield:** 4 to 6 servings.

PEPPERED SNAPPER WITH CREAMY DILL SAUCE

QUICK!

4 (4-ounce) snapper fillets
2 teaspoons olive oil, divided
2 tablespoons coarsely ground
   pepper
Vegetable cooking spray
2 cups hot cooked rice (cooked
   without salt or fat)
Creamy Dill Sauce

• **Brush** snapper on both sides with 1 teaspoon olive oil; sprinkle with pepper, and gently press into fish. Cover and let stand 15 minutes.
• **Coat** a large nonstick skillet with cooking spray; add remaining 1 teaspoon olive oil, and place over medium heat. Cook fillets 3 to 5 minutes on each side or until fish flakes easily when tested with a fork. Remove from heat; keep warm.
• **Spoon** rice evenly onto serving plates; top each with a fillet. Spoon warm Creamy Dill Sauce evenly over fillets. Serve immediately. **Yield:** 4 servings.

❤ Per serving: Calories 389
Fat 11.9g Cholesterol 72mg
Sodium 1825mg

Creamy Dill Sauce

QUICK!

1 (10-ounce) container
   refrigerated reduced-calorie
   Alfredo sauce
2 tablespoons dry white wine
1 teaspoon dried dillweed

• **Combine** all ingredients in a small heavy saucepan, and stir well. Cook over medium heat, stirring constantly, until mixture is thoroughly heated. **Yield:** 1 cup.

SWORDFISH STIR-FRY

QUICK!

If you can't find cellophane noodles, substitute a package of low-fat ramen noodles minus the seasoning packet. Substitute shrimp or chicken breasts for the swordfish.

1 (4-ounce) package cellophane
   noodles
1 tablespoon cornstarch
½ cup fat-free chicken broth
3 tablespoons fresh lime juice
1 tablespoon fish sauce
1 tablespoon sugar
1 teaspoon chili puree with garlic
Vegetable cooking spray
½ pound boneless swordfish fillet,
   cut into 1-inch pieces
1 teaspoon canola oil
½ red bell pepper, thinly sliced
2 cloves garlic, pressed
1 tablespoon minced fresh ginger
1 large cucumber, peeled, seeded,
   and sliced
⅓ cup chopped green onions
¼ cup chopped fresh cilantro

• **Cook** cellophane noodles according to package directions; drain and set aside.
• **Combine** cornstarch and next 5 ingredients; set aside.
• **Coat** a large nonstick skillet with cooking spray, and place over medium-high heat until hot; add fish, and stir-fry 2 to 3 minutes or until tender. Remove fish from skillet; set aside.
• **Pour** oil into skillet; add bell pepper, garlic, and ginger, and stir-fry 1 minute. Add cucumber, and stir-fry 30 additional seconds.
• **Stir** in broth mixture; bring to a boil. Boil 1 minute. Return fish to skillet; add green onions and cilantro, stirring until coated. Serve over noodles. **Yield:** 2 servings.

Chloe Dowling
Birmingham, Alabama

❤ Per serving: Calories 457
Fat 8.7g Cholesterol 44mg
Sodium 757mg

SWORDFISH WITH CASHEW AND CRACKED PEPPER CRUST

QUICK!

1½ cups cashews
2 tablespoons cracked pepper
4 (8-ounce) swordfish steaks
2 tablespoons olive oil
Garnish: fresh basil sprigs

• **Position** knife blade in food processor bowl; add cashews, and process until ground, stopping once to scrape down sides. Combine cashews and pepper in a shallow dish; coat both sides of swordfish with mixture.

• **Pour** oil into a large skillet; place over medium heat until hot. Add swordfish, and cook 10 minutes on each side or until fish flakes easily when tested with a fork. Garnish, if desired. Serve with hot cooked grits, green beans, mushrooms, and bell pepper strips. **Yield:** 4 servings.

Chef Chris McDonald
Atlanta Fish Market
Atlanta, Georgia

ORANGE-GINGER MARINATED SWORDFISH STEAKS

QUICK!

10 (8-ounce) swordfish steaks
    (about 1 inch thick)
1½ cups tomato-based barbecue
    sauce
1 cup white wine
2 tablespoons grated orange rind
1 cup orange juice
¼ cup soy sauce
2 tablespoons finely chopped fresh
    ginger
4 cloves garlic, minced
Vegetable cooking spray
Garnishes: fresh parsley sprigs,
    orange slices

• **Arrange** fish in a large shallow dish. Combine barbecue sauce and next 6 ingredients; pour marinade over fish. Cover and chill at least 2 hours or up to 24 hours, turning occasionally.

• **Remove** fish from marinade, discarding marinade. Place fish in grill baskets coated with cooking spray.

• **Cook,** covered with grill lid, over medium coals (300° to 350°) 10 minutes on each side. Garnish, if desired, and serve immediately. **Yield:** 10 servings.

Abby and Bill Myers
Jacksonville, Florida

GRILLED TROUT

You can substitute any fresh herb for the tarragon in this recipe.

¼ cup olive oil
¼ cup fresh tarragon
¼ cup lemon juice
½ teaspoon salt
2 (2-pound) dressed trout
4 sprigs fresh tarragon
1 lemon, sliced
Vegetable cooking spray

• **Combine** olive oil and tarragon in a small saucepan. Cook over very low heat 20 minutes; pour mixture through a wire-mesh strainer, discarding solids.

• **Combine** oil mixture, lemon juice, and salt, whisking to blend. Brush half of mixture inside each trout. Place 2 sprigs tarragon and 2 lemon slices inside each trout.

• **Place** trout in a large baking dish. Pour remaining oil mixture over trout. Cover and chill 2 hours.

• **Place** trout in a grill basket coated with cooking spray. Cook, covered with grill lid, over hot coals (400° to 500°) 5 minutes on each side or until fish flakes easily when tested with a fork. **Yield:** 4 servings.

♥ Per serving: Calories 233
Fat 11.6g Cholesterol 83mg
Sodium 185mg

Baked Trout: Prepare trout as directed, and bake at 350° for 30 minutes or until fish flakes easily when tested with a fork. Do not turn trout during baking.

CLASSIC TROUT AMANDINE

QUICK!

A perfect marriage – delicate trout with buttery almonds and a rich sauce.

2 cups milk
2 teaspoons salt, divided
2 dashes of hot sauce
6 trout fillets
¾ cup all-purpose flour
½ teaspoon pepper
1¼ cups butter or margarine,
    divided
1 tablespoon olive oil
½ cup sliced almonds
2 tablespoons lemon juice
2 teaspoons Worcestershire sauce
¼ cup chopped fresh parsley

• **Combine** milk, 1 teaspoon salt, and hot sauce in a 13- x 9- x 2-inch dish; add fillets, turning to coat. Cover and chill 2 hours. Drain, discarding marinade.

• **Combine** flour and pepper in a shallow dish.

• **Melt** ¼ cup butter in a large skillet over medium heat; add oil. Dredge fillets in flour mixture; add to skillet, and cook 2 minutes on each side or until fish flakes easily when tested with a fork. Remove to a serving platter; keep warm.

• **Combine** remaining 1 cup butter and almonds in a saucepan; cook over medium heat until almonds are lightly browned. Add remaining 1 teaspoon salt, lemon juice, and Worcestershire sauce; cook 2 minutes. Remove from heat; stir in parsley. Pour almond mixture over fillets, and serve immediately. **Yield:** 6 servings.

Debbie Slatter
Kenner, Louisiana

STUFFED RAINBOW TROUT

¼ cup butter or margarine
½ cup finely chopped onion
½ cup finely chopped celery
¼ cup chopped fresh parsley
1 clove garlic, minced
½ teaspoon salt
¼ teaspoon dried tarragon
⅛ teaspoon lemon pepper
3 cups Italian bread cubes
1 large egg, lightly beaten
1 tablespoon dry white wine
4 (8- to 10-ounce) whole farm-
    raised trout, dressed
½ teaspoon salt
1 tablespoon lemon juice
1 tablespoon soy sauce
½ cup all-purpose flour
2 slices bacon, cut in half
Garnishes: lemon slices, fresh
    parsley sprigs

● **Melt** butter in a large skillet over medium heat; add onion and celery, and cook, stirring constantly, until tender. Remove from heat; stir in parsley and next 4 ingredients. Add bread cubes; toss gently. Combine egg and white wine; stir into bread mixture. Spread evenly in an 11- x 7- x 1½-inch baking dish; set aside.
● **Rinse** trout; pat dry. Sprinkle inside of fish evenly with ½ teaspoon salt. Combine lemon juice and soy sauce; brush inside of fish, reserving remaining lemon juice mixture. Dredge fish in flour. Place over stuffing, overlapping slightly. Drizzle with reserved lemon juice mixture. Place bacon over trout. Cover and bake at 350° for 45 minutes. Uncover and bake 15 additional minutes. Garnish, if desired, and serve immediately. **Yield:** 4 servings.

The Colonel's Lady
Gatlinburg, Tennessee

TROUT FILLETS WITH CAPERS

QUICK!

If you're watching your sodium intake, capers are not for you. But their pungency adds loads of flavor and no fat.

½ cup all-purpose flour
¼ teaspoon salt
½ teaspoon pepper
1 teaspoon paprika
4 (6-ounce) trout fillets
1 tablespoon olive oil
¼ cup fresh lemon juice
¼ cup capers, undrained

● **Combine** first 4 ingredients in a shallow dish; dredge fillets in mixture.
● **Pour** olive oil in a large nonstick skillet; place over medium heat. Add fillets, and cook 3 minutes; turn fillets, and cook 1 additional minute. Add lemon juice and capers; cover and remove from heat. Let stand 3 to 5 minutes or until fish flakes easily when tested with a fork.
● **Transfer** fillets to a serving platter; spoon sauce over fillets, and serve immediately. **Yield:** 4 servings.

Carrie Easley
Dallas, Texas

♥ Per serving: Calories 297
Fat 9.4g Cholesterol 97mg
Sodium 863mg

SEARED TUNA STEAKS ON MIXED GREENS WITH LEMON-BASIL VINAIGRETTE

This recipe works with shrimp, too.

4 (4-ounce) tuna steaks
1 tablespoon reduced-sodium
    Cajun seasoning
Vegetable cooking spray
8 cups mixed salad greens
Lemon-Basil Vinaigrette
Garnish: finely chopped red bell
    pepper

● **Sprinkle** tuna steaks evenly with Cajun seasoning.
● **Coat** grill rack with cooking spray; place on grill over medium-hot coals (350° to 400°). Place tuna on rack.
● **Cook**, covered with grill lid, 5 minutes on each side or to desired degree of doneness.
● **Cover** and chill at least 8 hours.
● **Combine** salad greens and half of Lemon-Basil Vinaigrette, tossing gently; arrange on four plates. Top each with a tuna steak, and drizzle evenly with remaining vinaigrette. Garnish, if desired. **Yield:** 4 servings.

♥ Per serving: Calories 189
Fat 5.1g Cholesterol 51mg
Sodium 59mg

Lemon-Basil Vinaigrette

QUICK!

2 lemons, peeled, sectioned, and
    finely chopped
2 tablespoons white wine vinegar
1 tablespoon vegetable oil
1 tablespoon fresh basil leaves,
    finely chopped
¼ teaspoon cracked black
    pepper
¼ teaspoon hot sauce

● **Combine** all ingredients in a jar. Cover tightly; shake vigorously. **Yield:** ½ cup.

Sally Koch
Metairie, Louisiana

TUNA STEAKS WITH TARRAGON BUTTER

QUICK!

2 tablespoons butter or margarine, softened
¼ teaspoon lemon juice
½ teaspoon minced fresh tarragon or ¼ teaspoon dried tarragon
2 (½-pound) tuna steaks (about ¾ inch thick)
¼ teaspoon salt
¼ teaspoon freshly ground pepper
1 tablespoon olive oil

• **Combine** first 3 ingredients in a bowl; shape into a 1-inch-thick log; cover and chill until firm.
• **Sprinkle** tuna with salt and pepper on all sides. Heat olive oil in a nonstick skillet over medium heat; cook tuna 5 minutes on each side or to desired degree of doneness. Slice tarragon butter, and serve with tuna. **Yield:** 2 servings.

BROILED TUNA WITH ROSEMARY

QUICK!

4 (4-ounce) tuna steaks
½ cup dry white wine
1 tablespoon lemon juice
1½ teaspoons fresh rosemary
½ teaspoon garlic powder
½ teaspoon dried oregano
¼ teaspoon salt
⅛ teaspoon pepper
Vegetable cooking spray
Garnish: fresh rosemary sprigs

• **Place** tuna steaks in a large heavy-duty, zip-top plastic bag. Combine wine and next 6 ingredients; pour over steaks. Seal bag, and chill 1½ hours, turning bag occasionally.
• **Remove** steaks, discarding marinade. Place steaks on a rack coated with cooking spray; place rack in broiler pan. Broil 4 to 5 inches from heat (with electric oven door partially opened) 3 to 4 minutes on each side or until done. Garnish, if desired. **Yield:** 4 servings.

❤ Per serving: Calories 165
Fat 5.5g Cholesterol 42mg
Sodium 88mg

GRILLED FLORIDA TUNA

QUICK!

½ cup mayonnaise or salad dressing
1 tablespoon lime juice
1 clove garlic, pressed
½ teaspoon ground red pepper
½ teaspoon ground cumin
4 (½-inch-thick) tuna steaks (about 1 pound)

• **Combine** first 5 ingredients. Brush on steaks. Cook, covered with grill lid, over medium coals (300° to 350°) 5 to 7 minutes on each side to desired degree of doneness. **Yield:** 4 servings.

INLAND GRILLED TUNA

QUICK!

¼ cup soy sauce
1 tablespoon maple syrup
1 tablespoon prepared horseradish
4 (6-ounce) tuna steaks
Vegetable cooking spray

• **Combine** first 3 ingredients in a shallow dish; add tuna, turning to coat. Cover tuna, and chill 1 hour, turning occasionally.
• **Remove** tuna from marinade; discard marinade. Coat grill rack with cooking spray.
• **Place** tuna on rack over medium-hot coals (350° to 400°); cook tuna, covered with grill lid, 2 minutes on each side or to desired degree of doneness. **Yield:** 4 servings.

Joel Knox
Inland Seafood Company
Atlanta, Georgia

YELLOWFIN TUNA WITH CORN, PEPPER, AND TOMATO SALSA

Spice up sweet peppers, corn, tomatoes, and tuna with a Scotch bonnet pepper. It may look like a tiny bell pepper, but zowee, it packs a powerful punch.

1 red bell pepper
1 yellow bell pepper
4 ears fresh corn
2 large tomatoes, seeded and chopped
1 Scotch bonnet pepper, seeded and chopped ✻
2 tablespoons ground cumin
½ teaspoon salt
¼ teaspoon ground white pepper
Hickory chips
4 tuna steaks (about 2 pounds)
1 tablespoon olive oil
2 to 3 teaspoons cracked black pepper
½ to 1 teaspoon dried thyme
Garnishes: mixed salad greens, whole chile peppers

• **Place** bell peppers on a baking sheet; bake at 425° for 5 minutes. Cool. Remove and discard seeds; chop peppers.
• **Cut** corn from cob. Cook in boiling water to cover 3 minutes. Drain; cool.
• **Combine** chopped bell pepper, corn, tomato, and next 4 ingredients. Cover and chill.
• **Soak** hickory chips in water 30 minutes. Prepare charcoal fire on one side of grill; let burn until coals are white. Drain hickory chips, and place on hot coals.
• **Brush** tuna steaks with oil; sprinkle with black pepper and thyme.
• **Cook** tuna steaks, without grill lid, directly over hot coals 2 minutes on each side. Transfer tuna steaks to opposite side of grill, and cook indirectly, covered with grill lid, 5 to 7 minutes or to desired degree of doneness.
• **Spoon** salsa onto serving plates, and top with tuna steaks. Garnish, if desired. Serve immediately. **Yield:** 4 servings.

✻ Substitute your favorite hot chile pepper or skip the pepper altogether.

Chef Mark Rodriguez
Jordan's Grove
Maitland, Florida

CREAMED CHIPPED TUNA

QUICK!

Instead of the usual jar of dried beef, open a can of tuna for this convenient entrée.

4 frozen puff pastry shells *
3 tablespoons butter or margarine
¼ cup finely chopped onion
3 tablespoons all-purpose flour
2 cups milk
2 (6-ounce) cans solid white tuna
    in spring water, drained and
    flaked
2 hard-cooked eggs, sliced
1 cup (4 ounces) shredded Swiss
    cheese
½ cup frozen English peas,
    thawed
¼ teaspoon salt
½ teaspoon freshly ground
    pepper
1 tablespoon finely chopped fresh
    parsley

● **Bake** pastry shells according to package directions; set aside.
● **Melt** butter in a heavy saucepan over low heat; add onion, and cook, stirring constantly, 2 minutes or until onion is tender.
● **Stir** in flour; cook 1 minute, stirring constantly. Gradually add milk, stirring constantly with a wire whisk. Cook, stirring constantly, until mixture is thickened and bubbly.
● **Stir** in tuna and next 5 ingredients, and cook, stirring constantly, until cheese melts.
● **Spoon** tuna mixture over pastry shells; sprinkle with parsley. **Yield:** 4 servings.

* Substitute 4 slices toast, cut in half, for pastry shells.

Carol Richard
Birmingham, Alabama

SMOKED FISH HASH

4 cups finely chopped peeled
    potato
2½ cups flaked smoked fish
    (about ¾ pound)
6 slices bacon, cooked and
    crumbled
2 tablespoons chopped onion
2 tablespoons chopped fresh
    parsley
⅛ teaspoon pepper
⅓ cup vegetable oil
½ cup water
Paprika

● **Combine** first 6 ingredients; set aside.
● **Heat** oil in a heavy nonstick skillet; stir in potato mixture. Add water; cover, reduce heat, and simmer 7 minutes. Uncover and cook 8 to 10 minutes or until browned, stirring occasionally.
● **Spoon** into a serving dish; sprinkle with paprika. Serve immediately. **Yield:** 6 servings.

Frank Lawlor
Sebastian, Florida

FISH-STUFFED POTATOES

6 medium baking potatoes
½ cup butter or margarine,
    melted
1 (5-ounce) can evaporated milk
2 teaspoons salt
½ teaspoon black pepper
¼ teaspoon ground red pepper
2 cups flaked smoked fish (about
    ½ pound)
1 cup (4 ounces) shredded
    Cheddar cheese
3 tablespoons finely chopped
    greens onions or chives
Paprika

● **Scrub** potatoes. Wrap each potato in aluminum foil; bake at 400° for 1 hour or until done. Cut potatoes in half lengthwise; carefully scoop out pulp, leaving ¼-inch shells intact.
● **Combine** potato pulp, butter, and next 4 ingredients. Stir in flaked fish, cheese, and green onions. Stuff shells with potato mixture, and sprinkle evenly with paprika.

● Place stuffed shells on a baking sheet. Bake at 350° for 10 minutes or until thoroughly heated. **Yield:** 6 servings.

Frank Lawlor
Sebastian, Florida

CRAB-STUFFED POTATOES

6 large baking potatoes
Vegetable oil
½ cup butter or margarine,
    softened
½ cup sour cream
1 cup (4 ounces) shredded
    Cheddar cheese
½ teaspoon salt
½ teaspoon Old Bay seasoning
¼ teaspoon pepper
½ pound fresh lump crabmeat *
¼ cup finely sliced green
    onions
2 tablespoons fine, dry
    breadcrumbs
¼ teaspoon paprika
¼ teaspoon Old Bay seasoning

● **Wash** potatoes, and rub skins with vegetable oil. Prick each potato several times with a fork. Bake at 400° for 1 hour or until potatoes are done. Let potatoes cool.
● **Cut** a 1-inch lengthwise strip from top of each potato. Carefully scoop out potato pulp, leaving a ¼-inch shell intact; mash pulp.
● **Combine** potato pulp, butter, and next 5 ingredients. Drain crabmeat, removing any bits of shell. Gently stir crabmeat and green onions into potato pulp mixture. Stuff shells with potato mixture; place on a baking sheet. Sprinkle with breadcrumbs, paprika, and ¼ teaspoon Old Bay seasoning. Bake stuffed potatoes at 425° for 15 minutes. **Yield:** 6 servings.

* You can substitute one 6-ounce can lump crabmeat, drained, for ½ pound fresh lump crabmeat.

Sandra Rhodes Potter
Cambridge, Maryland

CRABMEAT KAREN

1 cup finely chopped fresh
   mushrooms
¾ cup finely chopped green
   onions
1 large egg, lightly beaten
¼ cup whipping cream
½ teaspoon salt
¼ teaspoon ground white
   pepper
¼ teaspoon ground red pepper
1 pound fresh lump crabmeat
1 cup soft breadcrumbs
White Wine Sauce
3 (17¼-ounce) packages frozen
   puff pastry sheets, thawed
2 large eggs, lightly beaten
Garnishes: cherry tomatoes, fresh
   parsley sprigs

• **Combine** first 7 ingredients. Drain crabmeat, removing any bits of shell. Add crabmeat and breadcrumbs to mushroom mixture, tossing gently. Set aside.
• **Begin** preparing White Wine Sauce. While it is simmering, roll puff pastry to ⅛-inch thickness. Cut 12 "crabs" from pastry with a 7- x 4-inch crab-shaped cookie cutter, if available. If not, make separate paper pattern pieces, cutting the body portion about 7 x 4 inches. Cut two patterns for the claws, one about 5 x 2 inches and the other about 2 x 1 inches.
• **Placing** pattern pieces separately on the pastry, cut 12 body portions and 24 of each claw section with pastry wheel or knife. Spoon reserved crabmeat mixture evenly onto six body portions, leaving a ½-inch border on all sides. Brush edges with beaten eggs; top with remaining six body portions, pinching edges to seal. Place on a baking sheet, brushing with beaten eggs; set aside.
• **Attach** 1 longer claw section to each shorter claw section, pressing edges to seal. Brush edges of 12 "claws" with beaten eggs; top with remaining claws, pressing edges to seal. Place on a baking sheet; brush with beaten eggs. Bake "crabs" and "claws" at 375° for 20 minutes or until golden.
• **Spoon** 3 tablespoons White Wine Sauce into center of each plate. Place a warm "crab" in the center; arrange a "claw" on each side. Garnish, if desired. Serve immediately. **Yield:** 6 servings.

White Wine Sauce

¼ cup chopped shallots
½ cup dry white wine
2 teaspoons fish-flavored bouillon
   granules
2 cups boiling water
½ bunch fresh parsley
3 bay leaves
1 sprig fresh thyme
1 stalk celery, cut into pieces
2 black peppercorns
½ cup whipping cream
1½ tablespoons cornstarch
1 tablespoon water
⅛ teaspoon salt
⅛ teaspoon ground white
   pepper

• **Combine** shallot and wine in a small saucepan; bring to a boil. Reduce heat, and simmer 5 minutes or until reduced by one-third.
• **Dissolve** bouillon in boiling water; set aside.
• **Cut** a 14-inch square of cheesecloth; place parsley and next 3 ingredients in center. Tie with string. Add to wine mixture with bouillon and peppercorns. Bring to a boil, reduce heat, and simmer, uncovered, 20 minutes.
• **Pour** liquid through a large wire-mesh strainer into a bowl, reserving broth. Discard vegetables and herbs.
• **Combine** broth and whipping cream in saucepan; bring to a boil, reduce heat, and simmer, uncovered, 10 minutes. Combine cornstarch and water, stirring until smooth. Gradually stir into whipping cream mixture; cook 1 minute, stirring constantly. Stir in salt and white pepper. **Yield:** 1¼ cups.

Note: Check gourmet kitchen shops for a crab-shaped cookie cutter.

Arnaud's
New Orleans, Louisiana

CRAB IMPERIAL

1 pound fresh lump crabmeat
¼ cup butter or margarine
3 tablespoons all-purpose flour
1½ cups half-and-half
2 teaspoons chopped fresh
   parsley
1½ teaspoons dry mustard
¾ teaspoon salt
1 tablespoon lemon juice
2 teaspoons prepared horseradish
1 teaspoon Worcestershire
   sauce
1 cup soft breadcrumbs
2 tablespoons butter or margarine,
   melted

• **Drain** crabmeat, removing any bits of shell; set aside.
• **Melt** ¼ cup butter in a large heavy saucepan over low heat; add flour, stirring until mixture is smooth. Cook 1 minute, stirring constantly. Gradually add half-and-half; cook over medium heat, stirring constantly, until thickened and bubbly.
• **Stir** in parsley and next 5 ingredients; add crabmeat, stirring gently. Spoon into greased baking shells.
• **Combine** breadcrumbs and 2 tablespoons butter; sprinkle evenly over crabmeat mixture.
• **Bake** at 350° for 30 minutes or until bubbly. **Yield:** 6 servings.

Jane Maloy
Wilmington, North Carolina

CHESAPEAKE BAY CRAB CAKES

1 pound lump crabmeat
1 large egg
4 saltine crackers, crushed
1½ teaspoons dried parsley flakes
¾ teaspoon Old Bay seasoning
½ teaspoon Worcestershire sauce
3 or 4 drops of hot sauce
⅛ teaspoon freshly ground pepper
3 tablespoons mayonnaise or salad
    dressing
3 tablespoons mayonnaise or salad
    dressing
½ teaspoon Old Bay seasoning
Paprika
Tartar Sauce

• **Drain** crabmeat, removing any bits of shell.
• **Combine** egg and next 7 ingredients; stir in crabmeat.
• **Shape** into 6 (3-inch) patties. Place on a lightly greased baking sheet.
• **Combine** 3 tablespoons mayonnaise and ½ teaspoon Old Bay seasoning; spread evenly on crab cakes. Sprinkle with paprika.
• **Bake** at 350° for 20 minutes or until golden. (Do not overbake.) Serve with Tartar Sauce. **Yield:** 6 servings.

Tartar Sauce

QUICK!

1 cup mayonnaise or salad
    dressing
1 teaspoon Dijon mustard
1½ tablespoons finely chopped
    fresh parsley
1½ tablespoons chopped capers
1 hard-cooked egg, finely chopped
1 tablespoon sweet pickle relish
1 tablespoon chopped fresh chives

• **Combine** all ingredients; cover and chill. **Yield:** 1 cup.

Susan Smith
Easton, Maryland

GULF COAST CRAB CAKES
(pictured at right)

1 tablespoon butter or margarine
1 clove garlic, minced
1 tablespoon finely chopped red
    bell pepper
2 teaspoons finely chopped onion
1½ teaspoons finely chopped
    green bell pepper
1½ teaspoons finely chopped
    yellow bell pepper
1½ tablespoons all-purpose flour
⅓ cup whipping cream
1 pound fresh lump crabmeat
1¼ cups soft breadcrumbs,
    divided
½ finely chopped serrano chile
    pepper
1 egg yolk
2 teaspoons chopped fresh chives
1 teaspoon dry mustard
1 teaspoon stone-ground mustard
1 teaspoon lemon juice
½ teaspoon salt
¼ teaspoon pepper
¼ cup butter or margarine,
    divided
Vegetable oil
1 corn tortilla, cut into thin
    strips
Lime-Saffron Sauce
Mango Slaw
Garnish: fresh cilantro sprigs

• **Melt** 1 tablespoon butter in a large skillet over medium heat; add garlic and next 4 ingredients, and cook 3 minutes, stirring often. Stir in flour; cook 3 minutes, stirring constantly. Gradually add whipping cream, and cook, stirring constantly, until thickened. Remove from heat.
• **Drain** crabmeat, removing any bits of shell. Stir crabmeat, ¼ cup breadcrumbs, chile pepper, and next 7 ingredients into red pepper mixture. Cover and chill 3 to 4 hours.
• **Shape** crabmeat mixture into 10 (2-inch) patties; dredge in remaining 1 cup breadcrumbs.
• **Melt** 2 tablespoons butter in a large skillet over medium heat; add half of patties, and cook until golden, turning once. Drain on paper towels. Repeat procedure with remaining 2 tablespoons butter and patties. Set aside.

• **Wipe** skillet with paper towels.
• **Pour** oil to depth of 1 inch into skillet. Fry tortilla strips in hot oil over medium-high heat until golden. Drain on paper towels. Set aside.
• **Spoon** Lime-Saffron Sauce onto plates, and arrange crab cakes and Mango Slaw on sauce. Top with tortilla strips, and garnish, if desired. **Yield:** 5 servings.

Lime-Saffron Sauce

1 cup dry white wine
Pinch of saffron
½ teaspoon butter or margarine
1 small shallot, finely chopped
3 tablespoons lime juice
2 tablespoons whipping cream
½ cup butter, cut into pieces
¼ teaspoon salt

• **Combine** wine and saffron in a saucepan; bring to a boil. Remove from heat; let stand 30 minutes.
• **Melt** ½ teaspoon butter in a large skillet over medium heat; add shallot, and cook, stirring constantly, until tender. Add wine mixture and lime juice; cook over medium heat until mixture is reduced to ¼ cup.
• **Stir** in whipping cream, and cook until mixture is reduced to ¼ cup. Remove from heat; add ½ cup butter and salt, stirring until butter melts. **Yield:** about ¾ cup.

Mango Slaw

1 cup finely shredded red cabbage
1 cup peeled, chopped mango
1 medium tomato, chopped
1 serrano chile pepper, finely
    chopped
1 green onion, chopped
⅓ cup chopped fresh cilantro
3 tablespoons lime juice
1 teaspoon olive oil
⅛ teaspoon salt
⅛ teaspoon pepper

• **Combine** all ingredients; cover and chill at least 2 hours. Serve with a slotted spoon. **Yield:** 3 cups.

Chef Bruce Auden
BIGA
San Antonio, Texas

Rm 1050   440-231-0255
                    B,T

~~Old Dutch~~

~~gingersnaps~~
CRAB CAKE

HELPING PAWS

Hot sauce

Mayo   Cracker meal — sprinkle
eggs - beaten   Parsley
dry mustard   crab meat - lump

Bake 375°   till brownish

salsa + eggplant mix

Helping Paws, Inc.

P.O. Box 634 Hopkins, MN 55343

PH 952.988.9359 FAX 952.988.9296

www.helpingpaws.org

Gulf Coast Crab Cakes

CRAB-STUFFED LOBSTER TAILS

(pictured on page 149)

Have lobsters steamed at your supermarket to save time.

2 quarts water
2 tablespoons salt
2 (1½- to 1¾-pound) live lobsters
½ pound fresh lump crabmeat
1 clove garlic, minced
1 tablespoon chopped fresh parsley
2 tablespoons freshly grated Parmesan cheese
2 tablespoons fine, dry breadcrumbs
¼ teaspoon salt
¼ teaspoon Old Bay seasoning
¼ teaspoon pepper
2 tablespoons butter, melted
1 teaspoon lemon juice
Garlic-Butter Sauce
Garnishes: lemon halves, fresh flat-leaf parsley sprigs

• **Combine** water and 2 tablespoons salt in a large Dutch oven; bring to a boil. Plunge lobsters, head first, into boiling water; return to a boil. Cover, reduce heat, and simmer 10 minutes; drain and let cool.
• **Break** off large claws and legs. Crack claw and leg shells, using a seafood or nut cracker; remove meat, and set aside. Break off tail. Cut top side of tail shell lengthwise, using kitchen shears. Cut through center of meat and remove vein. Leave meat in shell. Rinse and set aside.
• **Drain** crabmeat, removing any bits of shell. Combine crabmeat, garlic, and next 8 ingredients; toss gently. Spoon mixture into lobster tail. Place on a baking sheet.
• **Bake** at 400° for 12 minutes or until thoroughly heated. Serve with Garlic-Butter Sauce and claw and leg meat. Garnish, if desired. **Yield:** 2 servings.

Garlic-Butter Sauce

QUICK!

½ cup butter
2 tablespoons whipping cream
2 tablespoons lemon juice
1 clove garlic, minced

• **Melt** butter in a saucepan over low heat; add whipping cream, and cook 1 minute, stirring constantly. Stir in lemon juice and garlic. **Yield:** ⅔ cup.

CRAWFISH ÉTOUFFÉE

Seafood markets sell frozen, peeled crawfish tails harvested in Louisiana or China. You can substitute peeled shrimp, but the color won't be as intense.

½ cup butter or margarine
1 large onion, chopped
¼ cup finely chopped celery
¼ cup chopped green bell pepper
2 cloves garlic, minced
1 pound peeled crawfish tails
1 teaspoon salt
½ teaspoon ground black pepper
½ teaspoon onion powder
¼ teaspoon ground white pepper
½ teaspoon hot sauce
1½ tablespoons all-purpose flour
¾ cup water
½ cup finely chopped green onions
¼ cup finely chopped fresh parsley
Hot cooked rice

• **Melt** butter in a large skillet over medium heat. Add onion and next 3 ingredients, and cook 5 minutes, stirring constantly.
• **Stir** in crawfish and next 5 ingredients; cook 5 minutes. Stir in flour; cook 2 minutes, stirring constantly.
• **Stir** in water gradually; cook over low heat 20 minutes, stirring occasionally.
• **Stir** in green onions and parsley; cook 3 minutes. Serve over rice. **Yield:** 4 to 6 servings.

Jude Theriot
Lake Charles, Louisiana

PAN-FRIED GRITS WITH CREAMED OYSTERS

3 cups whipping cream
¼ teaspoon salt
⅛ teaspoon pepper
2 medium leeks
2 (10-ounce) containers Standard oysters, undrained
1 clove garlic, minced
1 shallot, finely chopped
3 tablespoons butter or margarine, melted
8 shiitake mushroom caps, thinly sliced
Pan-Fried Grits
Garnish: thin strips fresh spinach leaves

• **Combine** first 3 ingredients in a heavy saucepan; bring to a boil over medium heat. Reduce heat to low, and simmer, uncovered, 35 to 40 minutes or until whipping cream mixture is reduced to 1½ cups, stirring occasionally. Cover and set aside.
• **Wash** leeks, and cut white part into thin strips; set aside. Reserve green tops for another use.
• **Drain** oysters, reserving ½ cup liquid; set aside.
• **Cook** garlic and shallot in butter in a large skillet over medium-high heat, stirring constantly, until tender.
• **Add** leeks and mushrooms, and cook 2 to 3 minutes or until vegetables are tender, stirring often. Add oysters and reserved liquid, and cook 3 to 5 minutes or until oysters begin to curl. Add reserved whipping cream mixture, and cook until thoroughly heated, stirring occasionally.
• **To** serve, place 2 triangles of Pan-Fried Grits on each plate; top with oyster mixture. Garnish, if desired. **Yield:** 6 servings.

Pan-Fried Grits

8 cups water
2 teaspoons salt
¼ cup butter or margarine
2 cups quick-cooking yellow grits, uncooked
2 large eggs, divided
⅓ to ½ cup butter or margarine, divided

- **Combine** first 3 ingredients in a Dutch oven; bring to a boil. Stir in grits; bring to a boil over medium heat. Reduce heat, and cook 4 to 5 minutes, stirring occasionally.
- **Beat** 1 egg with a fork. Gradually stir about one-fourth of hot mixture into beaten egg; add to remaining hot mixture, stirring constantly.
- **Pour** grits mixture into a buttered 15- x 10- x 1-inch jellyroll pan; cover and chill 8 hours. Cut chilled grits into 6 (5-inch) squares, and cut each square into 2 triangles.
- **Beat** remaining egg in a shallow dish. Dip each grits triangle in beaten egg. Melt half of remaining butter in a large skillet. Add as many grits triangles as will fit, and cook on each side until golden. Repeat procedure with remaining grits triangles and butter. **Yield:** 12 triangles.

Jeff Tuttle
Pawleys Island, South Carolina

SCALLOPED OYSTERS
QUICK!

1 quart oysters, undrained
5 cups crushed round buttery
    crackers, divided
½ teaspoon salt
½ teaspoon ground red pepper
2 teaspoons Worcestershire sauce
2 cups half-and-half
¼ cup unsalted butter, cut into
    pieces

- **Drain** oysters, reserving 3 tablespoons liquid.
- **Place** half of cracker crumbs in a greased 13- x 9- x 2-inch baking dish. Arrange oysters over crumbs; sprinkle with salt, pepper, and Worcestershire sauce. Top with remaining crumbs; drizzle with reserved oyster liquid and half-and-half. Top with butter.
- **Bake** at 400° for 30 minutes. **Yield:** 8 servings.

Sissy Nash and Kathy Nash Cary
Louisville, Kentucky

WILD RICE AND OYSTERS

6 cups chicken broth
2 (6-ounce) packages wild rice
½ cup butter or margarine, melted
    and divided
2 quarts oysters, drained
1 pound fresh mushrooms, sliced
½ cup chopped celery
½ cup chopped onion
½ cup all-purpose flour
1 cup chicken broth
1 cup whipping cream
1 to 1½ tablespoons curry
    powder
1 teaspoon onion powder
1 teaspoon dried thyme
½ teaspoon salt
¼ teaspoon pepper
¼ teaspoon hot sauce
½ cup chopped fresh parsley

- **Bring** 6 cups chicken broth to a boil in a large saucepan. Add rice; cover tightly, and simmer 50 to 60 minutes. (Drain rice after cooking if all chicken broth is not absorbed; discard broth.) Toss rice with 2 tablespoons melted butter. Set aside.
- **Cook** oysters, mushrooms, celery, and onion in 2 tablespoons butter in a large skillet over medium heat until edges of oysters begin to curl, stirring occasionally. Drain well, and set aside.
- **Pour** remaining 4 tablespoons butter into a large heavy saucepan or Dutch oven; add flour, stirring until smooth. Cook over low heat 1 minute, stirring constantly. Gradually add 1 cup chicken broth and whipping cream; cook over medium heat, stirring constantly, until mixture is thickened and bubbly. Stir in curry powder and next 5 ingredients. Add wild rice and oyster mixtures, stirring well.
- **Spoon** mixture into a lightly greased 3½-quart casserole. Bake, uncovered, at 350° for 30 minutes or until bubbly. Sprinkle with parsley. **Yield:** 10 to 12 servings.

Kreis Beall
The Inn at Blackberry Farm
Walland, Tennessee

SEARED SCALLOPS WITH TOMATO-MANGO SALSA
QUICK!

Scallops should smell sweet, not fishy. They cook very quickly and will become tough and chewy if overcooked.

1 medium tomato, finely chopped
¾ cup finely chopped mango
3 tablespoons finely chopped
    purple onion
2 tablespoons finely chopped fresh
    basil
2 tablespoons red wine vinegar
1 tablespoon capers
1 tablespoon olive oil
12 sea scallops
¼ teaspoon salt
¼ teaspoon pepper
¼ avocado, sliced
Garnish: fresh basil sprigs

- **Combine** first 6 ingredients. Cover and chill salsa at least 30 minutes.
- **Heat** olive oil in a skillet over medium-high heat until hot. Add scallops; cook 3 minutes or until scallops are white, turning once. Remove scallops from skillet; sprinkle with salt and pepper.
- **Arrange** scallops, salsa, and avocado slices evenly on plates. Garnish, if desired. **Yield:** 2 servings.

Note: You can thread scallops on skewers and grill. Cook, covered with grill lid, over hot coals (400° to 500°) 3 to 5 minutes on each side or until scallops are white.

Joe R. Farralt
Muskogee, Oklahoma

♥ Per serving: Calories 246
Fat 11.2g Cholesterol 30mg
Sodium 782mg

Grilled Orange Scallops With Cilantro-Lime Vinaigrette

GRILLED ORANGE SCALLOPS WITH CILANTRO-LIME VINAIGRETTE
(pictured at left)

1 cup orange juice
3 tablespoons chopped fresh basil
18 sea scallops *
1 head Bibb lettuce
4 cups mixed baby lettuces
Cilantro-Lime Vinaigrette
30 yellow pear-shaped cherry
    tomatoes
30 pear-shaped cherry tomatoes
2 cucumbers, cut into thin strips
Garnishes: fresh basil sprigs, thin
    orange rind strips

• **Combine** orange juice and basil in a dish; add scallops, tossing to coat.
• **Cover** and chill about 1 hour. Uncover and drain, discarding marinade.
• **Cook** scallops, covered with grill lid, over hot coals (400° to 500°) 3 to 5 minutes on each side or until scallops are white.
• **Place** lettuces in a bowl; drizzle with Cilantro-Lime Vinaigrette, and toss gently to combine.
• **Arrange** lettuces on individual plates, and top with scallops, tomatoes, and cucumber. Garnish, if desired. Serve immediately. **Yield:** 6 servings.

* Substitute 30 large shrimp, peeled with tails intact, for sea scallops.

Note: Cook scallops directly on grill rack, but if your rack openings are too large, cook them in a grill basket or threaded on skewers.

♥ Per serving: Calories 324
Fat 11g Cholesterol 52mg
Sodium 272mg

Cilantro-Lime Vinaigrette
QUICK!

¼ cup sugar
¼ cup extra-virgin olive oil
2 tablespoons lime juice
2 tablespoons rice wine vinegar
1 clove garlic, minced
1 shallot, minced
1½ teaspoons fresh cilantro, finely
    chopped

• **Combine** all ingredients in a jar. Cover jar tightly, and shake vigorously. **Yield:** ¾ cup.

Penny Caughfield
Cocoa, Florida

SCALLOPS IN VERMOUTH-CREAM SAUCE
QUICK!

1 pound sea scallops
2 tablespoons all-purpose flour
2 tablespoons butter or margarine
¼ cup dry vermouth
½ cup whipping cream
¼ teaspoon salt
⅛ teaspoon pepper

• **Coat** scallops with flour. Melt butter in a large skillet over medium heat; add scallops. Cook 3 to 4 minutes or until scallops are white, stirring occasionally. Remove scallops from skillet.
• **Add** vermouth to skillet, stirring to loosen particles that cling to bottom. Bring to a boil; cook 3 minutes or until reduced by half. Stir in whipping cream, salt, and pepper; reduce heat to low. Add scallops; cook just until thoroughly heated. **Yield:** 2 main-dish servings or 4 appetizer servings.

Elaine C. Heintz
Staunton, Virginia

STUFFED SHRIMP WITH HOLLANDAISE SAUCE

24 unpeeled jumbo fresh shrimp
¼ cup butter, divided
1 medium onion, finely chopped
½ red bell pepper, finely chopped
½ green bell pepper, finely
    chopped
2 cloves garlic, minced
½ cup fine, dry breadcrumbs
2 tablespoons Cajun seasoning
1 large egg, lightly beaten
⅓ cup mayonnaise
1 pound frozen crawfish tails,
    thawed and chopped
2 tablespoons lemon juice
2 tablespoons dry white wine
Hollandaise Sauce

• **Peel** shrimp, leaving tails intact; devein shrimp, if desired. Butterfly shrimp by making a deep slit down back of each from large end to tail, cutting to, but not through, inside curve of shrimp. Set aside.
• **Melt** 2 tablespoons butter in a large saucepan; add onion and next 3 ingredients. Cook over medium-high heat until vegetables are tender, stirring often. Stir in breadcrumbs and seasoning; set aside.
• **Combine** egg, mayonnaise, and crawfish; stir into onion mixture.
• **Stuff** slit in each shrimp with about 3 tablespoons crawfish mixture; arrange on an aluminum foil-lined 15- x 10- x 1-inch jellyroll pan.
• **Melt** remaining 2 tablespoons butter in a small saucepan; add lemon juice and wine. Drizzle over shrimp.
• **Bake** shrimp at 400° for 20 minutes. Serve with Hollandaise Sauce. **Yield:** 6 to 8 servings.

Hollandaise Sauce

1 cup fat-free egg substitute
½ teaspoon salt
¼ cup lemon juice
1 cup butter, softened and
    divided
1 teaspoon grated lemon rind

• **Combine** egg substitute and salt in a heavy saucepan; cook over medium heat, stirring constantly with a wire whisk. Gradually add lemon juice, beating constantly with a wire whisk.
• **Remove** from heat; add ½ cup butter, 2 tablespoons at a time, beating well after each addition. (The butter should not simply melt; it should be worked into the sauce mixture with whisk.)
• **Pour** mixture into container of an electric blender. With blender on high, drop remaining ½ cup butter, 2 tablespoons at a time, into blender. Blend mixture until smooth; stir in lemon rind.
• **Return** to saucepan to keep warm, and place pan in larger pan filled with hot water. **Yield:** 2 cups.

Dick and Inez Thompson
Bay St. Louis, Mississippi

PHYLLO PIZZA

8 sheets frozen phyllo pastry,
    thawed
Butter-flavored cooking spray *
10 unpeeled large fresh shrimp
1 tablespoon olive oil
1 tablespoon lemon juice
¼ teaspoon salt
⅛ teaspoon pepper
1 (8-ounce) package cream cheese,
    softened
1 (4-ounce) package feta cheese
1 teaspoon dried tarragon
3 cherry tomatoes, cut into
    wedges
½ small green bell pepper, cut into
    thin strips
½ small red bell pepper, cut into
    thin strips
¼ cup sliced ripe olives
2 tablespoons butter, melted
1 teaspoon minced garlic

● **Place** 1 phyllo sheet in a 15- x 10- x 1-inch jellyroll pan coated with cooking spray; keep remaining phyllo sheets covered with a slightly damp towel until ready to use. Coat phyllo sheet in pan with cooking spray. Layer remaining phyllo sheets on first sheet, spraying each with cooking spray. Roll phyllo edges toward center, forming a 15- x 7-inch rectangle. Spray edges of phyllo with cooking spray, and prick bottom of crust with a fork.
● **Bake** phyllo at 400° for 5 minutes. Remove from oven, and gently press down center; bake 5 additional minutes, and let cool.
● **Peel** shrimp, and devein, if desired; slice shrimp in half lengthwise. Cook shrimp in olive oil in a skillet over medium heat 1 minute, stirring constantly. Add lemon juice, salt, and pepper. Set aside.
● **Combine** cheeses; spread on phyllo crust, and sprinkle with tarragon. Top with shrimp, tomato, bell pepper strips, and olives. Combine butter and garlic; drizzle over pizza.
● **Bake** at 400° for 10 minutes. Serve hot. **Yield:** 4 to 6 servings.

* Substitute ⅔ cup melted butter for cooking spray brushed on phyllo pastry sheets.

SHRIMP ENCHILADAS IN TOMATILLO SAUCE

Green chile sauce makes a spicy substitution for the tomatillo sauce in this recipe.

1 pound unpeeled large fresh
    shrimp
1 large onion, finely chopped
2 teaspoons olive oil
1 tablespoon all-purpose flour
1½ cups reduced-sodium chicken
    broth
1 (12-ounce) can tomatillo
    sauce
1 teaspoon ground cumin
½ teaspoon dried oregano
8 corn tortillas
1½ cups (6 ounces) shredded
    reduced-fat Monterey Jack
    cheese
½ cup nonfat sour cream

● **Peel** shrimp, and devein, if desired. Set shrimp aside.
● **Cook** onion in olive oil in a large nonstick skillet over medium-high heat, stirring constantly, until onion is tender. Add flour, stirring until smooth; cook 1 minute.
● **Stir** in chicken broth and next 3 ingredients; cook 15 minutes or until mixture is thickened.
● **Add** shrimp; cook 5 minutes or until shrimp turn pink. Remove from heat, and cool slightly.
● **Dip** corn tortillas in shrimp mixture; place on a flat surface. Place 3 or 4 shrimp in center of each tortilla, using a slotted spoon; sprinkle each with about 1 tablespoon cheese, and roll tightly.
● **Place** tortillas, seam side down, in a lightly greased 11- x 7- x 1½-inch baking dish. Pour remaining shrimp mixture over top, and sprinkle with remaining cheese.
● **Cover** and bake at 350° for 15 minutes. Uncover and bake 10 minutes or until cheese melts. Serve with sour cream. **Yield:** 4 servings.

Karl Harvey
Baton Rouge, Louisiana

♥ Per serving: Calories 360
Fat 13.3g Cholesterol 114mg
Sodium 438mg

QUESADILLAS WITH SHRIMP AND BRIE

1 medium-size purple onion,
    sliced
2 tablespoons vegetable oil,
    divided
6 (6-inch) flour tortillas
1 (15-ounce) Brie cheese
½ pound cooked shrimp, peeled,
    deveined, and coarsely
    chopped
Papaya Salsa

● **Cook** onion in 1 tablespoon oil in a skillet over medium-high heat, stirring constantly, until tender. Set aside.
● **Heat** tortillas according to package directions.
● **Trim** rind from Brie, and discard; thinly slice Brie. Place Brie slices on half of each tortilla. Top evenly with onion and shrimp; fold in half, and set aside.
● **Brush** skillet with remaining 1 tablespoon oil; cook 2 quesadillas at a time over medium heat about 1 minute or until lightly browned, turning once.
● **Cut** each into 4 wedges; serve with Papaya Salsa. **Yield:** 6 servings.

Papaya Salsa

1 ripe papaya, chopped
1 small ripe avocado, chopped
3 scallions, chopped
½ red bell pepper, finely
    chopped
½ jalapeño pepper, seeded and
    finely chopped
2 tablespoons chopped fresh
    cilantro
Juice of 1 lime

● **Combine** all ingredients; cover and chill. **Yield:** 2½ cups.

Jean Cooper
Washington, D.C.

SHRIMP WITH GIN AND GINGER

QUICK!

1½ pounds unpeeled large fresh
    shrimp (about 28)
3 tablespoons butter or margarine
2 cloves garlic, minced
2 tablespoons minced fresh ginger
⅓ cup gin
2 small carrots, cut into thin
    strips
2 small stalks celery, cut into thin
    strips
1 leek, cut into thin strips
4 fresh snow pea pods, cut into
    thin strips
¼ teaspoon salt
½ cup whipping cream

• **Peel** shrimp, and devein, if desired.
Set aside.
• **Melt** butter in a skillet over medium
heat; add shrimp, and cook, stirring constantly, until shrimp turn pink (about 2
to 3 minutes). Remove shrimp, reserving drippings in skillet; set aside, and
keep warm.
• **Cook** garlic and ginger in reserved
drippings over medium heat 1 minute,
stirring constantly.
• **Add** gin, stirring to loosen browned
particles that cling to bottom. Stir in carrot and remaining 5 ingredients; cook
over medium heat 5 minutes.
• **Stir** in shrimp; serve immediately.
Yield: 4 servings.

Kathy Ruiz
Houston, Texas

CREAMED SHRIMP ON
PECAN-CORNMEAL ROUNDS

1 pound unpeeled medium-size
    fresh shrimp
¼ cup butter or margarine
½ cup chopped onion
½ cup chopped red or green bell
    pepper
1 (10¾-ounce) can cream of
    mushroom soup, undiluted
½ cup water
¼ teaspoon ground black pepper
⅛ teaspoon ground red pepper
Pecan-Cornmeal Rounds
Garnish: fresh parsley sprigs

• **Peel** shrimp, and devein, if desired; set
aside.
• **Melt** butter in a heavy skillet over
medium-high heat; add onion and
chopped pepper. Cook 2 minutes or
until vegetables are crisp-tender. Stir in
soup and next 3 ingredients. Bring to a
boil, stirring constantly. Add shrimp; reduce heat, and simmer 10 minutes or
until shrimp turn pink.
• **Place** a plain Pecan-Cornmeal Round
on each serving plate; top with shrimp
mixture and a pecan-topped round. Garnish, if desired. **Yield:** 4 servings.

Pat Gindrup
Conroe, Texas

Pecan-Cornmeal Rounds

¾ cup plus 2 tablespoons butter,
    softened
1½ cups all-purpose flour
½ cup yellow cornmeal
2 tablespoons sugar
¾ teaspoon salt
1 egg, lightly beaten
¾ cup chopped pecans
4 pecan halves

• **Beat** butter at medium speed with an
electric mixer until creamy. Add flour
and next 4 ingredients; mix at low speed
until blended. Stir in chopped pecans.
Wrap dough in plastic wrap; chill 1 hour.
• **Turn** dough out onto a lightly floured
surface. Roll to ½-inch thickness. Cut
into 8 shapes with a 3-inch daisy-shaped
or round cutter. Place on a lightly
greased baking sheet. Press a pecan half
in center of half the rounds.
• **Bake** at 350° for 20 minutes or until
rounds are lightly browned; remove
from pan, and cool on wire racks. **Yield:**
8 rounds.

Edith Askins
Greenville, Texas

SHRIMP AND PEPPER
SOFT TACOS

¾ pound unpeeled medium-size
    fresh shrimp
2 cloves garlic, minced
1 tablespoon olive oil
½ teaspoon ground cumin
1 large onion, chopped
2 tomatoes, chopped
1 Anaheim chile pepper, seeded
    and minced
1 jalapeño pepper, seeded and
    minced
¼ cup chopped fresh cilantro
¼ teaspoon salt
4 (8-inch) flour tortillas
Fresh lime wedges
Shredded Monterey Jack cheese
    with peppers
Sour cream

• **Peel** shrimp, and devein, if desired.
• **Cook** garlic in oil in a large skillet over
medium heat, stirring constantly, until
tender; add shrimp and cumin, and cook
about 1 minute, stirring constantly. Remove shrimp, and set aside.
• **Add** onion to skillet; cook, stirring
constantly, until tender. Add shrimp,
tomato, and peppers; cook until thoroughly heated. Remove from heat, and
stir in cilantro and salt.
• **Spoon** ¾ cup shrimp mixture in center of each tortilla; squeeze lime wedges
over shrimp mixture, and top with
cheese and sour cream. Fold tortillas in
half. **Yield:** 4 servings.

Julia Hardie Kaczvinsky
Ruston, Louisiana

*Classic Charleston
Breakfast Shrimp*

CLASSIC CHARLESTON BREAKFAST SHRIMP
(pictured at left)

1 pound unpeeled medium-size
    fresh shrimp
2 tablespoons lemon juice
¼ teaspoon salt
⅛ teaspoon ground red
    pepper
¼ cup finely chopped onion
⅓ cup finely chopped green bell
    pepper
3 tablespoons melted bacon
    drippings
2 tablespoons all-purpose flour
¾ cup Shrimp Stock or chicken
    broth
Creamy Grits
Garnishes: green bell pepper strips,
    fresh lemon slices

• **Peel** and devein shrimp. Combine shrimp, lemon juice, salt, and red pepper in a small bowl; set aside.
• **Cook** onion and green bell pepper in bacon drippings in a large skillet over medium-high heat about 10 minutes, stirring constantly. Sprinkle flour over vegetables; cook, stirring constantly, about 2 minutes or until flour begins to brown. Add shrimp and Shrimp Stock; cook, stirring constantly, 2 to 3 minutes or until shrimp turn pink and gravy is smooth. Add water or additional stock, if gravy is too thick. Serve immediately over Creamy Grits. Garnish, if desired. **Yield:** 2 servings.

Note: If you make the Shrimp Stock, use the fresh shrimp left over from the stock to make Classic Charleston Breakfast Shrimp.

Shrimp Stock

2 pounds unpeeled medium-size
    fresh shrimp with heads
3 quarts water
1 large carrot
2 stalks celery, quartered
1 medium onion, quartered
½ cup fresh thyme sprigs
½ cup fresh parsley sprigs
½ cup fresh basil leaves
½ cup fresh oregano sprigs
1 tablespoon dried savory

• **Remove** heads, and peel shrimp; place heads and shells in a large Dutch oven. Reserve shrimp for another use. Add water and remaining ingredients; bring to a boil. Reduce heat, and simmer, uncovered, 45 minutes.
• **Pour** mixture through a wire-mesh strainer into a container, discarding solids. Reserve desired amount of stock, and freeze remaining stock for another use. **Yield:** 8 cups.

Creamy Grits

2 cups water
2 tablespoons butter or margarine
½ cup regular or stone-ground
    grits, uncooked
1 cup half-and-half or whipping
    cream, divided

• **Bring** water and butter to a boil in a heavy saucepan. Stir in grits; return to a boil over medium heat. Reduce heat, and cook 10 minutes or until thickened, stirring occasionally. Stir in ½ cup half-and-half; simmer 10 minutes, stirring occasionally. Add remaining ½ cup half-and-half; simmer 10 minutes, stirring occasionally. **Yield:** 2 servings.
Adapted from Hoppin' John's
Lowcountry Cooking
(Bantam)

SPICY SHRIMP AND SAUSAGE OVER CREAMY GRITS WITH TASSO GRAVY

1½ pounds Italian sausage
1½ pounds unpeeled medium-size
    fresh shrimp
2 tablespoons unsalted butter
Tasso Gravy
¼ cup whipping cream
Creamy Grits
¼ cup chopped fresh parsley

• **Prick** sausage several times with a fork; place on a rack in broiler pan. Bake at 350° for 20 minutes, turning after 10 minutes; set aside.
• **Peel** and devein shrimp; cook in butter in a large skillet 3 to 5 minutes or until shrimp turn pink. Add sausage and 2½ cups Tasso Gravy; cook over medium heat 1 to 2 minutes. Stir in whipping cream; cook until thoroughly heated. If mixture is too thick, thin with water or chicken broth.
• **Spoon** about 1 cup Creamy Grits into each shallow bowl; spoon shrimp-sausage mixture over grits. Sprinkle with parsley; serve with remaining Tasso Gravy. **Yield:** 8 to 10 servings.

Tasso Gravy

¼ cup butter
½ cup all-purpose flour
3 (10½-ounce) cans condensed
    chicken broth, undiluted
3 ounces tasso, chopped (about
    ¾ cup) *

• **Melt** butter in a heavy saucepan over low heat; add flour, stirring until smooth. Cook over low heat, stirring constantly, 3 to 5 minutes or until lightly browned. Gradually add broth to mixture; cook over medium heat, stirring constantly with a whisk, until thickened. Bring to a boil; reduce heat, and simmer 10 to 15 minutes, stirring occasionally. Stir in tasso. **Yield:** 3¾ cups.

* Tasso is cured pork or beef that has been seasoned with Cajun spices and smoked. You can substitute 3 ounces smoked, boneless pork loin, cubed, and ½ teaspoon hot sauce for tasso.

Creamy Grits

6 (10½-ounce) cans condensed
    chicken broth, undiluted
2½ cups coarsely ground regular
    white grits, uncooked
1 cup whipping cream
½ teaspoon ground white pepper

• **Bring** chicken broth to a boil in a large heavy Dutch oven; stir in grits. Bring mixture to a boil. Cover, reduce heat, and simmer 25 minutes or until broth is absorbed and grits are soft, stirring often. Stir in whipping cream and pepper; cook 20 minutes over low heat, stirring often. **Yield:** about 10 cups.
Chef Donald Barickman
Magnolias
Uptown/Down South Restaurant
Charleston, South Carolina

CREAMY SHRIMP AND NOODLES

1 pound unpeeled medium-size
   fresh shrimp
6 ounces fettuccine, uncooked
2 tablespoons butter or margarine
1 small red bell pepper, cut into
   strips
1¼ cups milk
2 (0.6-ounce) envelopes cream of
   chicken-flavored instant soup
   mix
½ cup frozen English peas
3 tablespoons grated Parmesan
   cheese
¼ teaspoon garlic powder

• **Peel** shrimp, and devein, if desired; set aside.
• **Cook** fettuccine according to package directions; drain and set aside.
• **Melt** butter in a large skillet over medium-high heat; add shrimp and red bell pepper. Cook 3 minutes, stirring constantly.
• **Combine** milk and soup mix; add to shrimp mixture. Stir in peas, cheese, and garlic powder. Bring to a boil; reduce heat and simmer 5 minutes or until thickened, stirring often. Toss with fettuccine. Serve immediately. **Yield:** 3 to 4 servings.

Carolyne M. Carnevale
Ormond Beach, Florida

SHRIMP CREOLE

¼ cup vegetable oil or bacon
   drippings
¼ cup all-purpose flour
1½ cups chopped onion
1 cup chopped green onions
1 cup chopped celery
1 cup chopped green bell pepper
2 cloves garlic, minced
1 (16-ounce) can chopped
   tomatoes, undrained
1 (8-ounce) can tomato sauce
1 (6-ounce) can tomato paste
1 cup water
1½ teaspoons salt
1 teaspoon black pepper
½ teaspoon ground red pepper
2 or 3 bay leaves
1 tablespoon lemon juice
1 teaspoon Worcestershire sauce
⅛ teaspoon hot sauce
5 pounds unpeeled jumbo fresh
   shrimp
½ cup finely chopped fresh
   parsley
Saffron Rice
Garnish: fresh parsley sprigs

• **Combine** oil and flour in a cast-iron skillet; cook over medium heat, stirring constantly, until roux is chocolate-colored (about 15 minutes). Stir in onion and next 4 ingredients; cook 15 minutes, stirring often.
• **Transfer** roux mixture to a large Dutch oven; add tomatoes and next 10 ingredients. Bring to a boil; cover, reduce heat, and simmer 1 hour, stirring occasionally.
• **Peel** and devein shrimp; add shrimp to tomato mixture, and simmer 10 to 15 minutes or until shrimp turn pink. Remove and discard bay leaves. Sprinkle with finely chopped parsley; serve over Saffron Rice. Garnish, if desired. **Yield:** 14 servings.

Saffron Rice

7 cups water
2 tablespoons butter or margarine
2 (10-ounce) packages saffron
   yellow rice mix

• **Bring** water and butter to a boil in a large saucepan; stir in yellow rice mix.

Cover, reduce heat, and simmer 20 minutes or until water is absorbed and rice is tender. **Yield:** 8 cups.

Note: Make Shrimp Creole 1 day in advance, and store in the refrigerator. To serve, reheat over medium heat, stirring occasionally (do not boil).

Ethel Banta
Natchez, Mississippi

TANGY HONEYED SHRIMP

1½ pounds unpeeled large fresh
   shrimp
3 tablespoons peanut oil
2 teaspoons minced garlic
1 teaspoon minced fresh ginger
1 (10½-ounce) can condensed
   chicken broth, undiluted
1 tablespoon cornstarch
2 tablespoons honey
2 tablespoons ketchup
1 tablespoon white vinegar
1 tablespoon rice wine or dry
   sherry
1 tablespoon soy sauce
⅛ teaspoon dried crushed red
   pepper
1 tablespoon sesame oil
2 green onions, cut into 1-inch
   pieces and shredded
1 teaspoon chopped fresh cilantro
Rice Timbales
Garnish: fresh cilantro sprigs

• **Using** a small knife, cut back of shrimp along vein line under running water; remove shell and vein, keeping tail intact. Drain on paper towels.
• **Pour** peanut oil around top of a preheated wok, coating sides; heat at high (400°) for 1 minute. Add drained shrimp, garlic, and ginger. Cook, stirring constantly, about 8 minutes or until shrimp turn pink.
• **Combine** broth and next 7 ingredients, stirring until smooth. Add to shrimp mixture, stirring constantly.
• **Bring** mixture to a boil; cook 1 minute. Stir in sesame oil, green onions, and chopped cilantro; cook until thoroughly heated. Serve immediately with Rice Timbales. Garnish, if desired. **Yield:** 3 to 4 servings.

Rice Timbales

2 cups water
½ teaspoon salt
1 cup long-grain rice, uncooked

● **Combine** water and salt in a heavy saucepan; bring to a boil. Gradually add rice, stirring constantly. Cover, reduce heat, and simmer 20 minutes or until water is absorbed and rice is tender.
● **Press** hot rice into four oiled 6-ounce custard cups. Immediately invert onto serving plates. Keep warm. **Yield:** 4 servings.

SEAFOOD RISOTTO

1 pound unpeeled medium-size
    fresh shrimp
½ pound fresh sea scallops
1 pound fresh squid *
1 pound fresh unshelled mussels
1 pound fresh unshelled clams
6 cloves garlic, minced
¼ cup olive oil
½ cup dry white wine
¼ cup lemon juice
4 sprigs fresh thyme, finely
    chopped
4 sprigs fresh oregano, finely
    chopped
Risotto
Lettuce leaves
2½ tablespoons Gremolata
½ teaspoon finely ground sea
    salt
½ teaspoon freshly ground
    pepper

● **Peel** shrimp, and devein, if desired; set aside. Cut sea scallops in half crosswise; set aside.
● **Rinse** squid under cold water. Cut into ½-inch slices, and set aside.
● **Remove** "beards" from mussels. Scrub mussels and clams thoroughly with a brush to remove grit; set aside.
● **Cook** garlic in olive oil in a large skillet over medium heat 2 to 3 minutes, stirring constantly. Add shrimp and scallops; cook, stirring constantly, 2 to 3 minutes or until shrimp turn pink. Remove shrimp and scallops with a slotted spoon; set aside.
● **Cook** squid in skillet over medium heat 2 to 3 minutes, stirring constantly; remove with a slotted spoon, and set aside.
● **Add** mussels, clams, wine, and next 3 ingredients to skillet. Bring to a boil over high heat. Cover and cook, shaking pan often, 3 to 5 minutes or until shells open. Remove and discard unopened shells.
● **Add** shrimp, scallops, and squid. Cook over medium heat until thoroughly heated.
● **Remove** seafood with a slotted spoon, reserving liquid. Stir liquid into cooked Risotto. Place Risotto on a lettuce-lined serving plate, and top with seafood mixture. Sprinkle with 2½ tablespoons Gremolata, salt, and pepper, and serve immediately. **Yield:** 12 servings.

＊ Substitute 1 pound sea scallops or shrimp.

Risotto

⅓ cup olive oil
¼ cup butter or margarine
1 large onion, chopped
4 cups Arborio rice (short grain),
    uncooked
1 cup dry white wine
2 pounds Roma tomatoes, peeled,
    seeded, and chopped
8 cups hot chicken broth
2½ tablespoons Gremolata

● **Heat** olive oil and butter in a Dutch oven over medium heat. Add onion; cook 2 to 3 minutes, stirring constantly. Add rice, stirring to coat well. Stir in wine, and cook until wine is absorbed. Stir in tomato; cook 2 minutes, stirring constantly. Reduce heat to medium-low.
● **Add** about 1 cup hot chicken broth; cook, stirring constantly, until liquid is absorbed. Repeat procedure, using remaining chicken broth, adding 1 cup at a time allowing liquid to be absorbed after each addition, stirring constantly. (This process will take about 1 hour.)
● **Stir** Gremolata into rice mixture. **Yield:** 12 servings.

Gremolata

6 cloves garlic, minced
½ cup finely chopped fresh
    flat-leaf parsley
¼ cup grated lemon rind

● **Combine** all ingredients in a small bowl. **Yield:** ⅓ cup.

Liz Lorber
Atlanta, Georgia

MISS HANNAH'S CASSEROLE

5 cups water
1½ pounds unpeeled medium-size
    fresh shrimp
3¼ cups water
½ teaspoon salt
1 cup regular grits, uncooked
2 large eggs, lightly beaten
¼ cup milk
2 cloves garlic, minced
1½ cups (6 ounces) shredded
    Cheddar cheese, divided
Garnish: chopped fresh parsley

● **Bring** 5 cups water to a boil; add shrimp, and cook 3 to 5 minutes or until shrimp turn pink. Drain well; rinse with cold water. Peel shrimp, and devein, if desired; set aside.
● **Bring** 3¼ cups water and salt to a boil in a medium saucepan; stir in grits. Cover, reduce heat, and simmer 10 minutes. Remove from heat.
● **Combine** eggs and milk; gradually stir into grits. Stir in shrimp, garlic, and 1 cup cheese.
● **Spoon** into a lightly greased 11- x 7- x 1½-inch baking dish. Sprinkle with remaining ½ cup cheese. Bake at 350° for 30 minutes. Let stand 5 minutes. Garnish, if desired. **Yield:** 6 servings.

The Gullah House Restaurant
St. Helena Island, South Carolina

SHRIMP AND RICE CASSEROLE

6 cups water
2 pounds unpeeled medium-size
    fresh shrimp
2 tablespoons butter or margarine
1 cup chopped celery
1 cup chopped onion
1 cup long-grain rice, cooked
1 cup milk
1 (10¾-ounce) can cream of
    mushroom soup, undiluted
1 (8-ounce) can whole water
    chestnuts, drained and
    chopped
½ cup mayonnaise or salad
    dressing
1 teaspoon dried parsley flakes
¼ teaspoon salt
½ teaspoon pepper
Chopped fresh parsley (optional)

• **Bring** water to a boil; add shrimp, and
cook 3 to 5 minutes or until shrimp turn
pink. Drain well; rinse with cold water.
Peel shrimp, and devein, if desired.
• **Melt** butter in a large skillet over
medium-high heat; add celery and
onion, and cook, stirring constantly,
until tender. Stir in shrimp, cooked rice,
and next 7 ingredients. Spoon mixture
into a lightly greased 2-quart casserole.
• **Bake** at 350° for 30 minutes or until
bubbly. Sprinkle with parsley, if desired.
Yield: 6 servings.

Lona B. Shealy
Leesville, South Carolina

SPICY SHRIMP CASSEROLE

2 pounds unpeeled medium-size
    fresh shrimp
3 cups cooked long-grain-and-wild
    rice mix
1 cup (4 ounces) shredded
    longhorn Cheddar cheese
1 (10¾-ounce) can cream of
    mushroom soup, undiluted
1 tablespoon butter or margarine
½ cup chopped green onions
2 teaspoons Worcestershire sauce
½ teaspoon dry mustard
½ teaspoon freshly ground
    pepper
¼ cup milk
1 teaspoon Cajun seasoning
Garnishes: green onions, peeled
    cooked shrimp

• **Peel** shrimp, and devein, if desired.
• **Combine** rice, shrimp, cheese, and
soup in a bowl.
• **Melt** butter in a large skillet over
medium-high heat, and add chopped
green onions; cook, stirring constantly,
until tender.
• **Stir** cooked green onions, Worcestershire sauce, and next 4 ingredients into
rice mixture. Spoon mixture into a
lightly greased 11- x 7- x 1½-inch or 2-
quart baking dish.
• **Bake** at 375° for 45 minutes. Garnish,
if desired. **Yield:** 6 servings.

Judy Grimes
Brandon, Mississippi

PAELLA CASSEROLE

½ pound chorizo or Italian link
    sausage, sliced
1 (2½- to 3-pound) broiler-fryer,
    cut up
1 medium onion, chopped
1 medium-size green bell pepper,
    seeded and chopped
1 medium-size red bell pepper,
    chopped
2 cloves garlic, minced
2 medium tomatoes, chopped
1 (10-ounce) package yellow
    saffron rice mix, uncooked
3½ cups water
1 pound unpeeled medium-size
    fresh shrimp
1 (10-ounce) package frozen
    English peas, thawed

• **Brown** sausage in a large Dutch oven
over medium heat. Remove sausage, reserving drippings in Dutch oven; set
sausage aside.
• **Add** chicken pieces to reserved drippings, and cook until browned, turning
once. Remove chicken, reserving drippings in Dutch oven; set chicken aside.
• **Cook** onion, peppers, and garlic in
drippings. Cook, stirring constantly,
until tender. Stir in tomato.
• **Add** rice mix and 3½ cups water;
bring to a boil. Stir in sausage.
• **Spoon** mixture into a lightly greased
4-quart paella pan or baking dish.
Arrange chicken pieces on top.
• **Cover** casserole, and bake at 375° for
30 minutes.
• **Peel** shrimp, and devein, if desired; set
aside.
• **Remove** casserole from oven; top
with shrimp and peas. Cover and bake
at 375° for 30 additional minutes or until
chicken is done. **Yield:** 8 servings.

Barbara Dryden
Pollock, Louisiana

*At right: Beef With Tomatoes and Arti-
chokes (page 187), Mock Caesar Salad
(page 303), and Creamy Fettuccine (page
218)*

SPICY NEW YORK STRIP ROAST

1 (1¾-pound) New York strip
   steak (about 3 inches
   thick)
1 teaspoon dried thyme
1 teaspoon dried oregano
1 teaspoon dried rosemary
¼ teaspoon salt
¼ teaspoon freshly ground black
   pepper
¼ teaspoon ground red
   pepper
1 tablespoon olive oil

• **Trim** excess fat from steak.
• **Combine** thyme and next 5 ingredients in a small bowl; crush with back of a spoon. Pat mixture evenly on both sides of steak. Chill.
• **Heat** olive oil in a heavy cast-iron or ovenproof skillet over medium-high heat; add steak, and cook 3 minutes on each side.
• **Bake** at 450° for 20 to 25 minutes or to desired degree of doneness. Remove from oven; cover with aluminum foil, and let stand 10 minutes. To serve, cut steak into thin slices. **Yield:** 4 to 6 servings.

Margot Hahn
Washington, D.C.

EYE-OF-ROUND ROAST WITH FRUITED ONION MARMALADE

1 (2- to 3-pound) eye-of-round
   roast
1 teaspoon salt
½ teaspoon pepper
½ cup all-purpose flour
2 tablespoons vegetable oil
2 to 3 cloves garlic, sliced
1 (14½-ounce) can beef broth
1 (12-ounce) bottle dark beer
Fruited Onion Marmalade

• **Sprinkle** roast with salt and pepper; dredge in flour.
• **Cook** roast in hot oil in a Dutch oven over medium heat until browned on all sides.
• **Add** garlic, broth, and beer; bring to a boil. Cover, reduce heat, and simmer

1½ hours or until tender. Serve with Fruited Onion Marmalade. **Yield:** 6 to 8 servings.

Fruited Onion Marmalade

1 tablespoon butter or margarine
1 tablespoon light brown sugar
2 onions, sliced
1 (8-ounce) package chopped
   dried fruit
1 cup beef broth
1½ teaspoons apple cider
   vinegar
¼ teaspoon ground ginger

• **Cook** butter and brown sugar in a large skillet over medium-low heat, stirring constantly, until sugar dissolves. Stir in sliced onion, and cook 20 minutes or until onion is tender, stirring mixture occasionally.
• **Stir** in chopped dried fruit and remaining ingredients.
• **Cover,** reduce heat, and simmer 20 minutes or until fruit is tender. **Yield:** about 2 cups.

MUSTARD GREENS-STUFFED TENDERLOIN
(pictured at right)

1 (16-ounce) package frozen
   chopped mustard greens
3 tablespoons butter or margarine,
   divided
1 cup thinly sliced green
   onions
¾ pound country ham slices
1 cup soft breadcrumbs
¼ teaspoon ground red pepper
1 (3- to 4-pound) trimmed beef
   tenderloin
¼ teaspoon ground black
   pepper
2 to 3 tablespoons cracked black
   pepper
1 tablespoon all-purpose flour
1 cup beef broth
½ cup dry red wine
¼ teaspoon ground black pepper
Garnish: fresh mustard greens

• **Cook** greens according to package directions; drain. Press between layers of

paper towels to remove excess moisture; transfer to a large bowl.
• **Melt** 1 tablespoon butter in a skillet; add green onions, and cook until tender, stirring often. Add to greens.
• **Melt** remaining 2 tablespoons butter in skillet; add ham, and cook over medium-high heat 4 minutes, turning once. Remove ham from skillet, reserving drippings in skillet; chop ham. Stir ham, breadcrumbs, and red pepper into greens.
• **Preheat** oven to 500°.
• **Make** a lengthwise cut down center of tenderloin, cutting to, but not through, bottom. Starting from center cut, slice horizontally toward 1 side, stopping ½ inch from edge. Repeat on opposite side. Unfold meat so that it's flat. Place between two pieces of heavy-duty plastic wrap. Flatten to ½-inch thickness, using a meat mallet or rolling pin.
• **Sprinkle** ¼ teaspoon ground black pepper over tenderloin; spread with greens mixture. Roll up, jellyroll fashion, starting with a long side; secure with heavy string at 4-inch intervals.
• **Press** cracked pepper on tenderloin, and place seam side down on a lightly greased rack in a roasting pan. Place tenderloin in oven, and reduce oven temperature to 350°.
• **Bake** 40 minutes or until meat thermometer inserted in thickest portion registers 145° (medium-rare) to 160° (medium). Cover loosely with aluminum foil, and let stand 15 minutes.
• **Stir** flour into reserved ham drippings in skillet; cook over medium-low heat, stirring constantly, 4 to 5 minutes or until caramel-colored.
• **Add** broth and wine gradually, and cook over medium-low heat, stirring constantly, until gravy is thickened and bubbly. Stir in ¼ teaspoon ground black pepper.
• **Slice** tenderloin, and garnish, if desired. Serve with gravy. **Yield:** 8 to 10 servings.

Mustard Greens-Stuffed Tenderloin

PAN-ROASTED FILLET OF BEEF WITH BLUE CHEESE SAUCE

Though not for the calorie conscious, a splurge of creamy, pungent Blue Cheese Sauce is a great way to add pizzazz to your favorite steak.

1 (2-pound) trimmed beef
    tenderloin
½ teaspoon salt
½ teaspoon freshly ground
    pepper
1 tablespoon vegetable oil
Vegetable cooking spray
Blue Cheese Sauce

● **Sprinkle** tenderloin with salt and pepper; rub with oil. Cover and chill up to 8 hours.
● **Brown** tenderloin in a hot cast-iron skillet coated with cooking spray about 1 minute on each side. Transfer tenderloin to a rack coated with cooking spray, reserving drippings in skillet; place rack in broiler pan. (Set skillet aside to make sauce.)
● **Bake** at 450° for 18 minutes or until a meat thermometer inserted in thickest portion registers 145° (medium-rare) or 160° (medium).
● **Remove** tenderloin from oven, and let stand 5 minutes. Cut tenderloin into 4 equal portions.
● **Spoon** warm Blue Cheese Sauce evenly onto four serving plates, and top each with a portion of tenderloin. **Yield:** 4 servings.

Blue Cheese Sauce

3 tablespoons unsalted butter,
    softened
2 ounces crumbled blue cheese
2 cups beef broth
1 carrot, scraped and coarsely
    chopped
1 stalk celery, coarsely chopped
3 cloves garlic, chopped
3 tablespoons Madeira or port
    wine
⅓ cup half-and-half

● **Combine** butter and crumbled blue cheese; shape into 4 portions, and chill until firm.

● **Combine** beef broth, carrot, and celery in a small saucepan. Bring to a boil; reduce heat, and simmer 5 to 7 minutes or until broth is reduced to ½ cup. Remove and discard vegetables; set broth aside.
● **Cook** garlic and Madeira in a skillet over medium heat 2 minutes. Add broth, and cook 3 to 5 minutes or until mixture is reduced to ½ cup. Gradually stir in half-and-half, and cook 5 minutes or until sauce is light brown. Remove sauce from heat; set aside up to 1 hour, if desired. Just before serving, reheat sauce over low heat.
● **Add** blue cheese mixture to warm sauce, 1 portion at a time, stirring until sauce is smooth. Pour sauce through a wire-mesh strainer into a small bowl, pressing with back of a spoon. **Yield:** about 1 cup.

CHUTNEYED BEEF TENDERLOIN

4 cups low-sodium beef broth
1 carrot, scraped and chopped
1 onion, quartered
1 stalk celery, chopped
1 (8-ounce) jar chutney, finely
    chopped
1 teaspoon salt
½ teaspoon coarsely ground
    pepper
1 tablespoon butter or margarine,
    softened
1 (5- to 6-pound) beef tenderloin,
    trimmed
Wine Reduction Sauce
3 tablespoons butter
½ teaspoon chopped fresh
    thyme or ¼ teaspoon dried
    thyme

● **Combine** first 4 ingredients in a saucepan; bring to a boil over medium heat. Reduce heat, and simmer, uncovered, 40 minutes or until mixture is reduced to about 1½ cups. Pour mixture through a wire-mesh strainer into a bowl, reserving vegetables; set broth aside.
● **Position** knife blade in food processor bowl; add vegetables. Process until smooth. Set aside.

● **Combine** chutney and next 3 ingredients, stirring until smooth. Spread half of chutney mixture over all surfaces of tenderloin. Place tenderloin on a rack in a shallow roasting pan.
● **Bake** at 450° for 20 minutes. Remove from oven, and spread remaining half of chutney mixture on tenderloin. Bake 10 to 20 additional minutes or until a meat thermometer inserted in thickest portion registers 145° (medium-rare) or 160° (medium). Remove meat from pan, and let stand 15 minutes before slicing.
● **Remove** rack from pan.
● **Add** reserved broth to pan, and place pan over burners. Bring broth mixture to a boil over medium heat, stirring to loosen browned particles that cling to bottom. Pour broth mixture into a saucepan; add vegetable mixture and Wine Reduction Sauce.
● **Bring** sauce mixture to a boil; reduce heat, and simmer 5 minutes, stirring often. Whisk in 3 tablespoons butter, 1 tablespoon at a time. Stir in thyme. Serve sauce with tenderloin. **Yield:** 12 servings.

Wine Reduction Sauce

1 (750-milliliter) bottle Cabernet
    Sauvignon
3 cloves shallots, minced
1 bay leaf
3 or 4 sprigs fresh thyme

● **Combine** all ingredients in a large saucepan. Bring mixture to a boil over medium heat; reduce heat, and simmer, uncovered, until liquid is reduced to about 1 cup (about 40 minutes).
● **Pour** sauce mixture through a wire-mesh strainer into a measuring cup, pressing with back of a spoon. Discard solids. **Yield:** 1 cup.

Jan Downs
Shreveport, Louisiana

BARBECUED BEEF TENDERLOIN

Mesquite or hickory chips
1 (3½- to 4-pound) beef
    tenderloin, trimmed
½ teaspoon salt
½ teaspoon pepper
1 cup Barbecue Sauce

• **Soak** mesquite chips in water 30 minutes.
• **Prepare** charcoal fire in smoker; let burn 20 minutes. Place mesquite chips on coals. Place water pan in smoker; add water to pan to depth of fill line.
• **Sprinkle** tenderloin with salt and pepper. Place on food rack. Cover with smoker lid. Cook 30 minutes.
• **Baste** tenderloin with 1 cup Barbecue Sauce. Cover and cook 1½ to 2 hours or until a meat thermometer inserted in thickest portion registers 145° (medium-rare) or 160° (medium). Serve with additional Barbecue Sauce. **Yield:** 12 servings.

Barbecue Sauce

QUICK!

2 (16-ounce) cans tomato sauce
1¼ cups ketchup
½ cup steak sauce
¼ cup lemon juice
¼ cup honey

• **Combine** all ingredients in a large saucepan.
• **Bring** to a boil; reduce heat, and simmer 30 minutes, stirring occasionally. Store remaining sauce in refrigerator up to 1 week or freeze up to 1 month. **Yield:** 5 cups.

King Ranch
Kingsville, Texas

BLUE CHEESE-WALNUT STUFFED FILLETS

(pictured on page 149)

QUICK!

Lightly toasting the walnuts brings out their fragrance, enhances their subtle flavor, and makes them crisper. Be sure the walnuts you use are plump and meaty; shriveled nutmeats are past their prime.

¼ cup crumbled blue cheese
2 tablespoons finely chopped
    walnuts, toasted
2 teaspoons half-and-half
2 (1-inch-thick) beef tenderloin
    steaks (6 ounces each)
2 tablespoons butter or
    margarine
1 clove garlic, minced
3 green onions, finely chopped
⅓ cup Madeira

• **Combine** first 3 ingredients. Cut a pocket into side of each steak. Spoon blue cheese mixture evenly into steak pockets. Set aside.
• **Melt** butter in a medium skillet over medium-high heat; add garlic and green onions, and cook, stirring constantly, until tender. Remove garlic mixture, reserving butter in skillet; set garlic mixture aside.
• **Cook** steaks in skillet over medium-high heat 7 minutes on each side or to desired degree of doneness. Remove steaks, reserving drippings in skillet. Add wine to drippings, and cook 1 to 2 minutes or until reduced by half. Stir in garlic mixture; spoon over steaks. **Yield:** 2 servings.

Wanda Sanders Randall
Birmingham, Alabama

BEEF WITH TOMATOES AND ARTICHOKES

(pictured on page 181)

QUICK!

2 (1¼-inch-thick) beef tenderloin
    steaks (filet mignon)
Marinade
½ cup oil-packed dried tomatoes,
    undrained
1½ tablespoons finely chopped
    green onions
1 clove garlic, finely chopped
1 (14-ounce) can artichoke hearts,
    drained and quartered
¼ teaspoon dried basil

• **Place** steaks in an 8-inch square dish. Drizzle Marinade evenly over steaks; cover and chill 8 hours, turning steaks several times. Drain steaks, discarding Marinade.
• **Cook** steaks, without grill lid, over medium-hot coals (350° to 400°) 4 to 5 minutes on each side or to desired degree of doneness. Set steaks aside, and keep warm.
• **Drain** tomatoes, reserving 1 tablespoon oil from tomatoes in a large skillet. Chop tomatoes; set aside.
• **Cook** green onions and garlic in reserved oil in skillet over medium-high heat 2 minutes, stirring constantly. Add tomato, artichoke hearts, and basil; cook 5 minutes, stirring often. Thinly slice steaks, and serve with tomato mixture. **Yield:** 2 servings.

Marinade

QUICK!

1 tablespoon olive oil
2 teaspoons red wine vinegar
1 tablespoon finely chopped
    onion
1 clove garlic, minced
½ teaspoon mustard
¼ teaspoon dried basil
¼ teaspoon dried rosemary
⅛ teaspoon salt
⅛ teaspoon pepper

• **Combine** all ingredients in a small bowl. **Yield:** 3 tablespoons.

GINGERED
TENDERLOIN STEAK

QUICK!

For its full flavor, look for ginger that has smooth skin. Wrinkled skin means it's dry and less flavorful.

¼ teaspoon salt
1 teaspoon pepper
1 tablespoon minced fresh ginger
2 cloves garlic, minced
2 (8-ounce) beef tenderloin steaks
      (1½ inches thick)
1 tablespoon butter
1 tablespoon vegetable oil
⅓ cup dry white wine
1 jalapeño pepper, seeded and
      minced

● **Combine** first 4 ingredients; rub on all sides of steaks. Cover and chill 2 hours.
● **Melt** butter and oil in a heavy skillet over medium-high heat; add steaks, and cook 4 minutes on each side or to desired degree of doneness. Remove steaks from skillet, and keep warm.
● **Add** wine and jalapeño pepper to skillet; cook 2 minutes, stirring constantly. Pour over steaks. **Yield:** 2 servings.

MESQUITE-GINGER BEEF
WITH FRESH FRUIT RELISH

QUICK!

3 tablespoons balsamic vinegar
2 teaspoons ground red pepper
2 teaspoons mesquite-flavored
      barbecue seasoning
2 teaspoons brown sugar
2 teaspoons minced fresh
      ginger
2 cloves garlic, minced
3 tablespoons sesame oil
4 (1¼-inch-thick) beef tenderloin
      steaks (4 to 6 ounces each)
1 tablespoon canola oil
Fresh Fruit Relish
**Garnish: fresh watercress
      sprigs**

● **Combine** first 7 ingredients in a shallow dish or heavy-duty, zip-top plastic bag; add steaks. Cover or seal, and chill 1½ hours, turning steaks occasionally.

● **Remove** steaks from marinade, discarding marinade.
● **Pour** canola oil into a heavy nonstick skillet; place over medium heat until hot. Add steaks, and cook 4 to 6 minutes on each side or to desired degree of doneness. Serve with Fresh Fruit Relish. Garnish, if desired. **Yield:** 4 servings.

Fresh Fruit Relish

QUICK!

1 cup finely chopped mango
½ cup finely chopped fresh
      pineapple
¼ cup chopped red bell pepper
¼ cup finely chopped green bell
      pepper
3 tablespoons thinly sliced green
      onions
3 tablespoons chopped fresh
      watercress
¼ teaspoon dry mustard
2 teaspoons balsamic vinegar
2 teaspoons fresh lime juice

● **Combine** all ingredients; cover and chill. Serve with a slotted spoon. **Yield:** 2 cups.

Mary Louise Lever
Rome, Georgia

FILET MIGNON WITH
MUSHROOM SAUCE

4 (4-ounce) beef tenderloin
      steaks
¼ teaspoon salt
¼ teaspoon freshly ground pepper
½ teaspoon dried thyme
Vegetable cooking spray
2 shallots, finely chopped
1 cup sliced fresh mushrooms
½ cup Red Wine Garlic Sauce
¼ cup fat-free beef broth
¼ teaspoon salt

● **Sprinkle** steaks with ¼ teaspoon salt, pepper, and thyme. Place steaks on a rack coated with cooking spray; place rack in broiler pan.
● **Broil** steaks 5½ inches from heat (with electric oven door partially opened) 2 to 3 minutes on each side or to desired degree of doneness. Remove

steaks from oven, and wrap in aluminum foil to keep warm; set aside.
● **Cook** shallot in a large skillet coated with cooking spray over medium heat, stirring constantly, until tender. Stir in mushrooms, and cook 1 to 2 minutes. Add Red Wine Garlic Sauce, beef broth, and ¼ teaspoon salt; cook 2 to 3 minutes. Serve over steaks. **Yield:** 4 servings.

♥ Per serving: Calories 214
Fat 8.4g   Cholesterol 71mg
Sodium 366mg

Red Wine Garlic Sauce

1 (750-milliliter) bottle dry red
      wine
1 head garlic, crushed (about 12
      cloves)

● **Combine** wine and garlic in a large saucepan; simmer 45 minutes or until mixture is reduced to about 1 cup.
● **Pour** mixture through a wire-mesh strainer into a small container, discarding garlic. Store sauce in refrigerator up to 1 week or freeze up to 3 months. **Yield:** 1 cup.

Note: You can serve this slow-simmered, fat-free sauce over cooked mushrooms, beef, chicken, pork, or firm-fleshed fish like tuna or swordfish.

FILLET OF BEEF WITH
RED PEPPER BUTTER

QUICK!

⅓ cup butter, softened
¼ cup finely chopped red bell
      pepper
¾ teaspoon seasoned salt
¼ to ½ teaspoon ground red
      pepper
2 (2½-inch-thick) beef tenderloin
      steaks

● **Combine** first 4 ingredients, stirring well. Shape into 4 (2-inch) rounds on a wax paper-lined baking sheet; cover and chill 1 hour or until firm.
● **Place** beef tenderloin steaks on a rack in broiler pan.

- **Broil** 5½ inches from heat (with electric oven door partially opened) 6 minutes. Turn steaks over, and top each with a butter round.
- **Broil** 6 to 7 additional minutes (with electric oven door partially opened) or until meat thermometer inserted in thickest portion registers 145° (medium-rare), 160° (medium), or to desired degree of doneness. Turn steaks over, and transfer to a serving platter; top with remaining butter rounds. **Yield:** 2 servings.

Kira F. Giffin
Houston, Texas

BEEF AND SHRIMP STIR-FRY

1   cup beef broth
1   cup chicken broth
1   tablespoon chopped green
      onions
1   tablespoon soy sauce
1   bay leaf
3   black peppercorns
½   teaspoon dried thyme
⅛   teaspoon dried oregano
1   tablespoon cornstarch
1½ tablespoons cold water
½   pound unpeeled medium-size
      fresh shrimp
1   tablespoon olive oil
½   pound beef tenderloin, cut into
      1-inch strips
¾   cup fresh broccoli flowerets
½   cup sliced zucchini
½   red bell pepper, cut into thin
      strips
½   cup snow pea pods
½   cup sliced fresh mushrooms
Hot cooked rice

- **Combine** first 8 ingredients in a medium saucepan, and bring to a boil; reduce heat, and simmer, uncovered, 30 minutes. Remove from heat, and pour liquid through a wire-mesh strainer into a 2-cup liquid measuring cup, discarding solids. Return broth mixture to saucepan.
- **Combine** cornstarch and water, stirring until smooth; stir into broth mixture, and bring to a boil. Cook 1 minute; remove from heat. Set aside.
- **Peel** and devein shrimp; set aside.

- **Pour** oil around top of preheated wok, coating sides; heat at medium-high (375°) for 2 minutes. Add shrimp, beef, and broccoli; cook 1 to 2 minutes, stirring constantly. Add zucchini and next 3 ingredients; cook 2 minutes, stirring constantly. Add broth mixture, and cook until thoroughly heated. Serve over rice. **Yield:** 4 servings.

Sue-Sue Hartstern
Louisville, Kentucky

FLAVORFUL FLANK STEAK

1   tablespoon butter or margarine
¼   cup chopped onion
1   clove garlic, minced
½   teaspoon chili powder
½   cup tomato sauce
2   tablespoons white vinegar
1   tablespoon honey
¼   teaspoon salt
¼   teaspoon pepper
1   (1½-pound) flank steak (¾ inch
      thick)

- **Melt** butter in a medium saucepan over medium-high heat; add onion, garlic, and chili powder, and cook, stirring constantly, until onion is tender.
- **Stir** in tomato sauce and next 4 ingredients; bring to a boil. Reduce heat, and simmer 5 minutes or until slightly thickened; cool.
- **Make** ¼-inch-deep cuts on both sides of steak; place steak in a shallow dish or heavy duty, zip-top plastic bag. Pour tomato sauce mixture over steak, turning to coat. Cover or seal, and chill at least 2 hours and up to 8 hours.
- **Cook** steak, without grill lid, over medium-hot coals (350° to 400°) about 7 minutes on each side or to desired degree of doneness. To serve, slice diagonally across grain. **Yield:** 4 servings.

Karen Peacock
Black Mountain, North Carolina

MARINATED FLANK STEAK

QUICK!

Cutting grilled flank steak diagonally across the grain into thin strips helps keep the slices of meat tender.

1   cup vegetable oil
½   cup soy sauce
⅓   cup red wine vinegar
¼   cup lemon juice
3   tablespoons Worcestershire
      sauce
2   tablespoons Dijon mustard
1   teaspoon freshly ground
      pepper
1   large onion, sliced
1   clove garlic, minced
2   (1-pound) flank steaks

- **Combine** first 9 ingredients in a shallow dish or a large heavy-duty, zip-top plastic bag; add steaks. Cover or seal, and chill 8 to 12 hours, turning steaks occasionally.
- **Remove** steaks and onion slices from marinade, discarding marinade. Wrap onion in heavy-duty aluminum foil.
- **Cook** steaks and onion, covered with grill lid, over medium-hot coals (350° to 400°) about 15 minutes or to desired degree of doneness, turning steaks and onion occasionally.
- **Cut** steaks diagonally across grain into thin strips; serve with onion slices. **Yield:** 4 to 6 servings.

Karen Dibble
Dallas, Texas

Plum Good Fajitas

PLUM GOOD FAJITAS
(pictured at left)

1 (16-ounce) can purple plums in heavy syrup, undrained
½ cup butter or margarine
1 large onion, chopped
1 (6-ounce) can frozen lemonade concentrate, thawed and undiluted
½ cup chili sauce
¼ cup soy sauce
1 tablespoon dry mustard
1 teaspoon ground ginger
1 teaspoon Worcestershire sauce
2 drops of hot sauce
8 (8-inch) flour tortillas
1 red bell pepper, cut into strips
1 green bell pepper, cut into strips
1 large onion, sliced
2 (1-pound) flank steaks
Sliced green onions
Sour cream or guacamole
Garnish: fresh cilantro sprigs

• **Drain** plums, reserving syrup; remove pits from plums. Place plums and syrup in container of an electric blender; process until smooth, stopping once to scrape down sides. Set plum puree aside.
• **Melt** butter in a saucepan over medium-high heat; add chopped onion, and cook, stirring constantly, until tender. Stir in puree, lemonade concentrate, and next 6 ingredients. Bring sauce to a boil; reduce heat, and simmer 15 minutes.
• **Heat** tortillas according to package directions; keep warm.
• **Place** peppers and sliced onion in a greased grill basket. Place basket and steaks on grill rack; baste with sauce. Cook, without grill lid, over hot coals (400° to 500°), 10 minutes on each side or to desired degree of doneness, basting often.
• **Cut** steaks diagonally across grain into thin strips.
• **Serve** steak and grilled vegetables in tortillas; top with green onions and sour cream or guacamole. Garnish, if desired. **Yield:** 8 servings.

Mary Tom Harper
Corpus Christi, Texas

JAVA FAJITAS

Brewed coffee gives these fajitas their unique flavor.

⅓ cup tomato paste
1¼ cups strongly brewed coffee
½ cup Worcestershire sauce
1 tablespoon sugar
2 teaspoons ground red pepper
1 teaspoon ground black pepper
3 tablespoons fresh lime juice
1 tablespoon vegetable oil
2 (1½-pound) flank steaks
24 (10-inch) flour tortillas
Pico de Gallo
Garnishes: fresh cilantro sprigs, lime wedges, serrano chile peppers, avocado slices

• **Combine** first 8 ingredients in a shallow dish or large heavy-duty, zip-top plastic bag; add steaks. Cover or seal; chill 8 hours, turning occasionally.
• **Remove** steaks from marinade, reserving marinade.
• **Cook** steaks, covered with grill lid, over hot coals (400° to 500°) about 6 minutes on each side or to desired degree of doneness.
• **Cut** steaks diagonally across grain into thin slices; keep warm.
• **Bring** marinade to a boil; boil 10 to 15 minutes or until reduced to 1 cup.
• **Place** steak down center of tortillas; drizzle with marinade. Top with Pico de Gallo. Roll up; serve immediately. Garnish, if desired. **Yield:** 12 servings.

♥ Per serving: Calories 590
Fat 20.7g Cholesterol 62mg
Sodium 1038mg

Pico de Gallo

2 medium tomatoes, chopped
½ onion, chopped
3 serrano chile peppers, chopped
½ cup fresh cilantro, chopped
¼ teaspoon salt
¼ teaspoon ground white pepper
2 tablespoons lemon juice

• **Combine** all ingredients. Cover and chill at least 3 hours. **Yield:** 3 cups.

Janie Baur
Spring, Texas

BLACKENED 'N' PEPPERED STEAK
QUICK!

This recipe generates plenty of pepper-scented smoke, so you may want to cook outdoors. We seared the steaks in an iron skillet over a propane cooker (like one used for a fish fry; you can purchase one at a hardware store). You can also prepare the steaks with the fan on in a well-ventilated kitchen.

4 (1½-inch-thick) New York strip steaks
¾ cup whole black peppercorns, crushed
¼ cup olive oil
¼ cup butter or margarine
1 cup chopped green onions
3 cups dry red wine
1 (3½-ounce) jar capers, drained

• **Trim** all visible fat from steaks; cut steaks in half crosswise. Dredge in peppercorns, coating all sides of steaks. Set aside.
• **Pour** olive oil in a large cast-iron skillet; place on burner of a propane cooker. Heat until hot, following manufacturer's instructions. Brown steaks on each edge in skillet. Cook 4 minutes on each side or to desired degree of doneness. Remove steaks to serving plate; keep warm. Discard drippings.
• **Melt** butter in skillet; add green onions, and cook 1 minute, stirring constantly. Add wine and capers; cook until liquid is reduced to 1½ cups. Serve with steak. **Yield:** 8 servings.

Note: Do not leave skillet unattended. Hot oil and wine can ignite. If mixture ignites, immediately cover skillet with a large lid to extinguish flames, and reduce heat.

Dave Christy
Pine Mountain, Georgia

GRECIAN SKILLET RIB EYES

QUICK!

*This olive-feta topping works
great on chicken and lamb, too.*

1½ teaspoons garlic powder
1½ teaspoons dried basil, crushed
1½ teaspoons dried oregano,
    crushed
½ teaspoon salt
⅛ teaspoon pepper
2 (1-inch-thick) rib-eye steaks
    (1¾ to 2 pounds)
1 tablespoon olive oil
1 tablespoon fresh lemon juice
2 tablespoons crumbled feta
    cheese
1 tablespoon chopped kalamata or
    ripe olives

• **Combine** first 5 ingredients; rub onto
all sides of steaks.
• **Pour** oil into a large nonstick skillet;
place over medium heat until hot. Add
steaks, and cook 10 to 14 minutes or to
desired degree of doneness, turning
once. Sprinkle with lemon juice; top
with cheese and olives. **Yield:** 2 to 4
servings.

Fran Yuhas
Scotrun, Pennsylvania

GRILLADES AND BAKED
CHEESE GRITS

4½ pounds round steak
2 teaspoons salt
2 teaspoons pepper
Vegetable oil
⅔ cup all-purpose flour
2 cups chopped onion
1½ cups chopped green bell
    pepper
½ cup chopped green onions
½ cup chopped celery
½ cup chopped fresh parsley
4 cloves garlic, minced
2 (14½-ounce) cans stewed
    tomatoes, undrained
1 teaspoon dried thyme
3 bay leaves
2 cups water
Garnish: fresh parsley sprigs
Baked Cheese Grits

• **Cut** meat into serving-size pieces;
sprinkle with salt and pepper.
• **Pour** ½ cup oil into a Dutch oven. Fry
steak in hot oil over medium-high heat
until browned (about 2 minutes on each
side). Remove to platter, and repeat
until all meat is browned.
• **Measure** pan drippings; add enough
oil to drippings to measure ⅔ cup;
return to Dutch oven. Add flour; cook
over medium heat, stirring constantly,
10 minutes or until roux is caramel-
colored.
• **Stir** in onion and next 5 ingredients;
cook over medium heat until tender;
stirring often. Add tomatoes and next 3
ingredients, stirring well.
• **Return** meat to Dutch oven. Bring to a
boil; cover, reduce heat, and simmer 1½
hours, stirring occasionally. Remove
and discard bay leaves.
• **Transfer** mixture to a serving dish;
garnish, if desired. Serve with Baked
Cheese Grits. **Yield:** 12 servings.

Baked Cheese Grits

5 cups boiling water
1 teaspoon salt
⅔ cup quick-cooking yellow grits,
    uncooked
⅔ cup quick-cooking white grits,
    uncooked
1 (15½-ounce) can yellow
    hominy, undrained
½ cup butter or margarine
2 cups (8 ounces) shredded sharp
    Cheddar cheese
½ cup grated Parmesan cheese

• **Bring** water and salt to a boil in a
heavy Dutch oven; stir in grits. Return to
a boil; reduce heat, and cook 4 to 5 minutes, stirring occasionally.
• **Stir** in hominy, butter, and Cheddar
cheese; spoon into a lightly greased 13-
x 9- x 2-inch baking dish. Sprinkle with
Parmesan cheese.
• **Bake** at 350° for 45 minutes or until
set. **Yield:** 12 servings.

Wilder Selman
New Orleans, Louisiana

PEANUTTY BEEF
STIR-FRY

QUICK!

1¼ pounds lean boneless top
    sirloin steak
3 tablespoons reduced-sodium
    soy sauce
2 to 3 tablespoons brown
    sugar
2 tablespoons creamy peanut
    butter
2 teaspoons lemon juice
½ teaspoon garlic powder
¼ teaspoon dried crushed red
    pepper
¼ teaspoon ground black
    pepper
2 teaspoons sesame or vegetable
    oil
1 medium-size red bell pepper,
    cut into 1-inch pieces
4 green onions, cut into 1-inch
    pieces
Hot cooked rice
Garnish: chopped peanuts

• **Trim** fat from steak, and slice steak diagonally across grain into ⅛-inch strips;
set aside.
• **Combine** soy sauce and next 6 ingredients, stirring with a whisk until
blended; set aside.
• **Pour** oil around top of a preheated
nonstick wok or large skillet, coating
sides; heat at medium-high (375°) 1
minute. Add steak strips; cook 2 minutes, stirring constantly. Add red bell
pepper and green onions; cook 2 minutes, stirring constantly. Stir in soy
sauce mixture; cover and cook 3 minutes or until thoroughly heated. Serve
over rice. Garnish, if desired. **Yield:** 4
servings.

INDIVIDUAL MEAT LOAVES

1½ pounds lean ground beef
½ pound hot ground pork
    sausage
1 small onion, finely chopped
1 teaspoon salt
¼ teaspoon pepper
½ teaspoon poultry seasoning
2 tablespoons Worcestershire
    sauce
5 slices white bread
2 large eggs
½ cup milk
1½ cups soft breadcrumbs
1½ cups chili sauce
½ cup boiling water
Garnish: fresh parsley sprigs

● **Combine** first 7 ingredients; set meat mixture aside.
● **Remove** crust from bread, and reserve for another use; cut bread into cubes. Combine bread cubes, eggs, and milk in a large mixing bowl; beat at medium speed with an electric mixer until smooth. Stir in meat mixture, and shape into 6 individual loaves; roll each loaf in breadcrumbs.
● **Place** in a lightly greased 13- x 9- x 2-inch pan. Spread chili sauce over loaves. Pour boiling water into dish. Bake, uncovered, at 350° for 1 hour. Transfer loaves to a serving platter; garnish, if desired. **Yield:** 6 servings.

Leanne Baker
Johnson City, Tennessee

MEAT LOAF WITH CHUNKY TOMATO SAUCE

1 pound ground chuck
1 medium onion, chopped
1 medium-size green bell pepper, chopped
2 cloves garlic, minced
¾ cup quick-cooking oats, uncooked
½ cup ketchup
2 large eggs, lightly beaten
1 tablespoon steak sauce
¼ teaspoon salt
¼ teaspoon seasoned salt
¼ teaspoon pepper
Chunky Tomato Sauce

● **Combine** all ingredients except Chunky Tomato Sauce; press meat mixture into a 9- x 5- x 3-inch loafpan or shape into a loaf, and place on a rack in broiler pan.
● **Bake** at 350° for 50 to 60 minutes or until done. Serve with Chunky Tomato Sauce. **Yield:** 4 servings.

Chunky Tomato Sauce

QUICK!

1 (14½-ounce) can diced tomatoes, undrained
1 (5½-ounce) can spicy vegetable juice
½ cup chopped celery
½ cup chopped green bell pepper
½ cup chopped onion
½ teaspoon garlic powder
1 teaspoon dried basil
1 teaspoon dried marjoram
1 teaspoon dried oregano
1 teaspoon dried parsley flakes

● **Combine** all ingredients in a large saucepan, stirring well; bring mixture to a boil. Reduce heat, and simmer 15 minutes, stirring sauce occasionally. **Yield:** 2 cups.

Kathy Rogers
Cary, North Carolina

INDIVIDUAL BARBECUED BEEF LOAVES

½ cup ketchup
⅓ cup cider vinegar
3 tablespoons brown sugar
1 teaspoon beef-flavored bouillon granules
1½ pounds lean ground beef
1 cup fine, dry breadcrumbs
2 tablespoons finely chopped onion
½ teaspoon salt
¼ teaspoon pepper
1 cup evaporated milk

● **Combine** first 4 ingredients in a saucepan, stirring well; cook mixture over medium heat, stirring constantly, until bouillon granules dissolve. Set barbecue sauce aside.

● **Combine** beef and remaining 5 ingredients, stirring until mixture is thoroughly blended.
● **Shape** mixture into 6 loaves; place loaves in a lightly greased 11- x 7- x 1½-inch baking dish. Spoon barbecue sauce over loaves.
● **Bake** at 350° for 45 minutes. Serve immediately. **Yield:** 6 servings.

Peggy C. Brown
Winston-Salem, North Carolina

SPINACH MEAT LOAF

We added the steak sauce to Ann's recipe; it helps to keep the meat loaf moist.

2 large eggs, lightly beaten
1½ pounds ground round
½ cup regular oats, uncooked
½ cup wheat germ
½ cup shredded carrot
¼ cup chopped onion
1 (10-ounce) package frozen chopped spinach, thawed and well drained
½ cup milk
1 teaspoon salt
½ teaspoon pepper
½ cup steak sauce

● **Combine** all ingredients except steak sauce, stirring well; shape into a 9- x 5- x 3-inch loaf, and place on a lightly greased rack in broiler pan.
● **Bake** at 350° for 40 minutes. Spread steak sauce over meat loaf; bake 20 additional minutes or until a meat thermometer inserted in center registers 160°. **Yield:** 6 to 8 servings.

Ann Birkmire
Sharon, Massachusetts

MEATBALL KABOBS

1½ pounds ground chuck
1 cup regular oats, uncooked
1 large egg, lightly beaten
1 teaspoon curry powder
1 teaspoon Worcestershire
    sauce
1 (4¾-ounce) jar pimiento-stuffed
    olives, drained
16 cherry tomatoes
2 medium-size green bell peppers,
    quartered
8 new potatoes, cooked
8 mushrooms
¼ cup barbecue sauce
Vegetable cooking spray
Barbecue sauce

• **Combine** first 5 ingredients; divide meat mixture into 24 equal portions. Shape each portion into a ball around an olive.
• **Alternate** meatballs, tomatoes, green pepper, potatoes, and mushrooms on six 14-inch skewers. Brush with ¼ cup barbecue sauce.
• **Coat** food rack with cooking spray; place rack on grill over medium-hot coals (350° to 400°), and place kabobs on rack.
• **Cook**, covered with grill lid, 10 minutes or until done, turning once. Serve with additional barbecue sauce. **Yield:** 4 to 6 servings.

Peggy Huffstetler
Lebanon, Tennessee

QUICKER ENCHILADAS

QUICK!

1 pound ground chuck
1 small onion, chopped
1 (10¾-ounce) can cream of
    mushroom soup, undiluted
2 (4.5-ounce) cans chopped
    green chiles, undrained and
    divided
8 (8-inch) flour tortillas
1 (8-ounce) package shredded
    colby-Monterey Jack cheese
    blend, divided
1 (10¾-ounce) can Cheddar
    cheese soup, undiluted
Salsa

• **Brown** ground chuck and onion in a large skillet, stirring until meat crumbles; drain. Stir in mushroom soup and 1 can green chiles.
• **Spoon** ½ cup beef mixture down center of each tortilla; sprinkle each with 2½ tablespoons cheese blend. Roll up tortillas, and place each, seam side down, in a lightly greased 13- x 9- x 2-inch baking dish. Pour Cheddar cheese soup over tortillas.
• **Drain** remaining can green chiles; sprinkle chiles and remaining ¾ cup cheese over soup.
• **Cover** and bake at 350° for 20 minutes; uncover and bake 5 additional minutes. Serve enchiladas with salsa. **Yield:** 4 servings.

Mrs. Joe Ford
Hamlin, Texas

SAUSAGE AND BEAN DINNER

QUICK!

If you're serving a crowd, spoon this entrée over hot cooked rice or pasta.

1 pound reduced-fat smoked
    sausage, cut into ¼-inch slices
1 large green bell pepper, chopped
1 medium onion, chopped
1 tablespoon vegetable oil
2 (14½-ounce) cans stewed
    tomatoes, undrained
1 (16-ounce) can pink beans,
    drained
1 (16-ounce) can pinto beans,
    drained
1 (15-ounce) can Great Northern
    beans, drained
½ teaspoon garlic powder

• **Brown** sausage in a Dutch oven over medium-high heat; remove sausage, and set aside. Discard drippings.
• **Cook** pepper and onion in oil in Dutch oven over medium heat, stirring constantly, until tender.
• **Add** cooked sausage, tomatoes, and remaining ingredients. Bring mixture to a boil; reduce heat, and simmer 30 minutes. **Yield:** 6 servings.

Michele C. Harrington
Chesapeake, Virginia

SAUSAGE-VEGETABLE SKILLET

QUICK!

Kielbasa sausage is usually sold precooked, but brown the sausage in the skillet anyway – it brings out its smoky flavor.

1 tablespoon butter or margarine
1 pound kielbasa sausage, cut into
    ½-inch slices
1 head cauliflower, broken into
    flowerets
3 zucchini, thinly sliced
3 carrots, scraped and thinly
    sliced
1 medium onion, thinly sliced
½ teaspoon salt
¼ teaspoon pepper
1 cup (4 ounces) shredded
    Monterey Jack cheese

• **Melt** butter in a 12-inch skillet over medium-high heat; add sausage, and cook until browned, stirring often. Remove with a slotted spoon, reserving drippings in skillet; set sausage aside.
• **Add** cauliflower and next 3 ingredients to skillet; cook, stirring constantly, 5 minutes or until crisp-tender. Stir in salt and pepper; cover, reduce heat, and simmer 5 minutes. Stir in sausage; cook just until thoroughly heated.
• **Spoon** mixture into individual baking dishes, and sprinkle with cheese. Cover and let stand until cheese melts. **Yield:** 6 servings.

Betty Levine
Loudon, Tennessee

CREOLE LIVER

QUICK!

2 tablespoons all-purpose flour
½ teaspoon dried thyme
¼ teaspoon pepper
1 pound thinly sliced beef liver
2 tablespoons vegetable oil
1 medium onion, chopped
1 large green bell pepper,
  chopped
1 clove garlic, pressed
1 (14.5-ounce) can diced
  tomatoes, undrained
1 bay leaf
½ teaspoon salt
Hot cooked grits

• **Combine** first 3 ingredients in a shallow dish; dredge liver in flour mixture.
• **Cook** liver in hot oil in a large skillet over medium-high heat until browned, turning once. Remove liver, reserving drippings in skillet.
• **Add** onion, bell pepper, and garlic to drippings, and cook until tender, stirring often. Add liver, tomatoes, bay leaf, and salt; cover, reduce heat, and simmer 10 minutes. Remove and discard bay leaf. Serve over grits. **Yield:** 4 servings.

Debbie E. Ipock
Charlotte, North Carolina

AMARETTO-LIME VEAL

QUICK!

4 slices bacon, chopped
⅓ cup sliced almonds
Vegetable oil
1 pound (¼-inch-thick) veal
  cutlets
¼ teaspoon salt
½ teaspoon coarsely ground
  pepper
½ cup all-purpose flour
½ cup amaretto
1½ tablespoons fresh lime juice
½ cup sliced green onions
¼ cup butter or margarine

• **Cook** bacon in a large skillet until crisp; remove bacon, reserving drippings in skillet. Set bacon aside.
• **Add** almonds to drippings, and cook over medium heat, stirring constantly, until lightly browned; remove almonds, reserving drippings in skillet. Drain almonds on paper towels; set aside.
• **Add** oil to drippings to make ¼ cup; set aside.
• **Sprinkle** cutlets evenly with salt and pepper; dredge in flour. Heat 2 tablespoons drippings mixture in skillet; add half of cutlets, and cook 1 minute on each side or until lightly browned. Remove to a serving dish; keep warm. Repeat procedure with remaining 2 tablespoons drippings mixture and cutlets. Drain excess drippings from skillet.
• **Add** amaretto, lime juice, and green onions to skillet; bring to a boil, deglazing skillet by scraping particles that cling to bottom. Boil 2 minutes, stirring often. Remove from heat; add butter, 1 tablespoon at a time, stirring until butter melts. Stir in almonds, and spoon over cutlets. Sprinkle with bacon. **Yield:** 4 servings.

VEAL CUTLETS WITH LEEKS AND ZINFANDEL CREAM

QUICK!

Wrap leftover leek tops in cheesecloth and use them to flavor soups.

3 leeks
3 tablespoons all-purpose flour
¾ teaspoon salt
½ teaspoon freshly ground
  pepper
1 pound veal cutlets
3 tablespoons olive oil, divided
½ cup white Zinfandel
½ cup whipping cream

• **Remove** and discard green tops from leeks. Cut white portions diagonally into thin slices; set aside.
• **Combine** flour, salt, and pepper in a shallow bowl; dredge cutlets in flour mixture.
• **Cook** cutlets in 2 tablespoons hot oil in a large skillet 2 minutes on each side or until golden. Transfer cutlets to a serving platter, and keep warm.
• **Cook** leeks in remaining 1 tablespoon olive oil in skillet 1 minute; add wine, and cook 1 minute or until most of liquid evaporates, stirring often.
• **Add** whipping cream to leek mixture, and cook, stirring constantly, about 2 minutes or until mixture is reduced by half. Serve with veal. **Yield:** 4 servings.

Louise W. Mayer
Richmond, Virginia

STUFFED VEAL CUTLETS

6 (4-ounce) veal cutlets
6 slices prosciutto (about
  5 ounces)
4 ounces fontina cheese, cut into
  5 strips
¼ teaspoon salt
¼ teaspoon pepper
½ cup all-purpose flour
1 tablespoon butter or margarine,
  melted
1 tablespoon vegetable oil
1 cup dry white wine
Hot cooked spaghetti

• **Place** cutlets between two sheets of heavy-duty plastic wrap, and flatten to ⅛-inch thickness, using a meat mallet or rolling pin.
• **Wrap** a prosciutto slice around each cheese strip, and place in center of each cutlet. Fold ends of veal cutlets over prosciutto and cheese; fold sides over, and secure with a wooden pick.
• **Sprinkle** veal with salt and pepper, and dredge in flour. Brown on all sides in butter and oil in a heavy skillet. Remove veal from skillet; set aside, and keep warm.
• **Add** wine to skillet; boil until wine is reduced by half. Return veal to skillet; cover and simmer 5 minutes. Serve over spaghetti. **Yield:** 6 servings.

Sue-Sue Hartstern
Louisville, Kentucky

LEMON VEAL

The long cooking time tenderizes this lean cut of veal, and infuses it with the flavors of rosemary, lemon, and wine.

1 tablespoon all-purpose flour
1 teaspoon beef-flavored bouillon
    granules
½ teaspoon paprika
½ teaspoon chopped fresh
    parsley
¼ teaspoon dried rosemary
⅛ teaspoon pepper
½ pound boneless round rump
    veal, trimmed and cut into
    1-inch cubes
Vegetable cooking spray
2 medium carrots, scraped and
    cut into thin strips
¼ cup dry white wine
¼ cup water
1 tablespoon lemon juice
2 cups hot cooked rice (cooked
    without salt or fat)

• **Combine** first 6 ingredients in a heavy-duty, zip-top plastic bag; add veal; seal bag, and shake to coat.
• **Coat** a nonstick skillet with cooking spray; place over medium heat until hot. Add veal, and cook, stirring constantly, until lightly browned.
• **Add** carrot and next 3 ingredients to veal in skillet; bring to a boil, stirring constantly. Cover, reduce heat, and simmer 40 minutes. Serve over rice. **Yield:** 2 servings.

Terri Cohen
North Potomac, Maryland

❤ Per serving: Calories 472
Fat 7.3g Cholesterol 100mg
Sodium 577mg

VEAL MEAT LOAF

2 pounds ground veal *
½ cup soft breadcrumbs
⅓ to ½ cup finely chopped green
    or red bell pepper
3 large eggs
1½ teaspoons salt
¼ teaspoon finely chopped fresh
    thyme or ⅛ teaspoon dried
    thyme
¼ teaspoon finely chopped fresh
    or dried rosemary
¼ teaspoon pepper
1¼ cups thinly sliced fresh
    mushrooms
Vegetable cooking spray

• **Combine** first 8 ingredients; stir in mushrooms.
• **Divide** meat mixture into 6 equal portions; place each portion in a 4- x 2½- x 1½-inch loafpan coated with cooking spray. Place loafpans in a shallow baking pan.
• **Bake** at 350° for 25 to 30 minutes or until done. Let stand 5 minutes. **Yield:** 6 servings.

* Substitute 2 pounds ground pork for ground veal.

Note: For 1 large loaf, place meat mixture in a 7½- x 3- x 2-inch loafpan coated with cooking spray. Bake at 350° for 1 hour and 5 minutes or until done. Let stand 5 minutes.

Prime Time Cafe
Disney MGM Studios
Lake Buena Vista, Florida

MARINATED RACK OF LAMB

4 (6- to 8-rib) lamb rib roasts,
    trimmed (about 8 pounds)
1 cup dry white vermouth
1 cup steak seasoning sauce *
3 tablespoons garlic powder
2 tablespoons dried Italian
    seasoning
Garnish: fresh parsley sprigs

• **Place** lamb in a large shallow dish or large heavy-duty, zip-top plastic bags.

• **Combine** vermouth and next 3 ingredients; pour 1 cup marinade over lamb. Cover and chill remaining marinade. Cover dish or seal bags, and chill 8 hours, turning lamb often.
• **Remove** meat from marinade, discarding marinade. Place lamb, fat side up, on a rack in a shallow roasting pan.
• **Bake** at 325° for 1 hour and 15 minutes or until a meat thermometer inserted in thickest portion registers 150° (medium-rare), basting often with reserved marinade. Garnish, if desired. **Yield:** 12 servings.

* For steak seasoning sauce, we used Dale's. Substitute 1 cup any brand of soy sauce-based marinade.

Note: Remove lamb from oven at 160° if you desire medium doneness or at 170° (well doneness).

Helen Shores Lee
Birmingham, Alabama

GRILLED LEG OF LAMB

1 head garlic
1 (6- to 7-pound) leg of lamb,
    trimmed
1 (750-milliliter) bottle dry red
    wine
¼ cup olive oil
1 tablespoon dried oregano
1 tablespoon dried rosemary
2 teaspoons paprika

• **Peel** garlic; cut 5 cloves into thin slices, and crush remaining cloves.
• **Make** 1-inch-deep cuts into lamb, using a small paring knife; insert a garlic slice into each cut. Place lamb in a large shallow dish.
• **Combine** crushed garlic, wine, and remaining 4 ingredients; reserve 1 cup wine mixture in the refrigerator. Pour remaining wine mixture over lamb; cover and marinate in refrigerator 8 hours, turning occasionally.
• **Remove** lamb from marinade, discarding marinade. Insert meat thermometer in thickest portion, making sure it does not touch fat or bone.
• **Cook** lamb over low coals under 300° for 1½ hours, or until thermometer

registers 145°, turning and basting with reserved wine mixture every 15 minutes. Remove lamb from heat; cover and let stand 30 minutes or until thermometer registers 150° (medium-rare). **Yield:** 8 servings.

Michael Spanos
Birmingham, Alabama

GRILLED LAMB WITH MANGO SALSA

Occasionally you can find boneless leg of lamb; if you can't, ask your butcher to remove the bone from a leg of lamb.

1 teaspoon cumin seeds
1 teaspoon coriander seeds
1 cup olive oil
½ cup dry white wine
¼ cup tequila
2 tablespoons fresh lime juice
2 tablespoons minced fresh garlic
2 tablespoons chopped fresh cilantro
2 jalapeño peppers, seeded and finely chopped
½ teaspoon salt
½ teaspoon freshly ground pepper
1 (4- to 4½-pound) boneless leg of lamb
Mango Salsa
Garnish: fresh cilantro sprigs

● **Cook** cumin seeds in a heavy skillet, stirring constantly, until browned; remove from heat, and crush. Repeat procedure with coriander seeds.
● **Combine** crushed cumin and coriander seeds, olive oil, and next 8 ingredients in a large heavy-duty, zip-top plastic bag or a large shallow dish. Add lamb, turning to coat. Seal bag or cover dish, and chill 8 hours, turning occasionally.
● **Cook** lamb, without grill lid, over medium-hot coals (350° to 400°) about 40 minutes or until meat thermometer inserted in thickest portion of meat registers 150° (medium-rare) or to desired degree of doneness, turning meat once.
● **Cut** lamb into thin slices; serve with Mango Salsa. Garnish, if desired. **Yield:** 8 servings.

Mango Salsa

4 medium mangoes, peeled and chopped
⅓ cup chopped fresh cilantro
¼ cup chopped celery
¼ cup finely chopped green onions
¼ cup chopped yellow or red bell pepper
1 jalapeño pepper, seeded and minced
¼ cup honey
¼ cup olive oil
2 tablespoons fresh lime juice
¼ teaspoon salt

● **Combine** first 6 ingredients in a small bowl. Combine honey and remaining 3 ingredients; pour over mango mixture. Toss gently to coat; cover and chill 30 minutes. **Yield:** about 4 cups.

Sue Sims
San Angelo, Texas

ROLLED LAMB ROAST

1 clove garlic, sliced
1 tablespoon chopped fresh parsley
1 teaspoon salt
½ teaspoon pepper
½ teaspoon chopped fresh thyme
1 (5-pound) lamb shoulder, boned
2 tomatoes, chopped
2 onions, chopped
1 green bell pepper, chopped
3 tablespoons olive oil
8 small turnips, peeled
½ cup Madeira
2 bay leaves

● **Combine** first 5 ingredients; sprinkle over lamb. Top with half of chopped vegetables. Roll roast, starting at shortest end; tie securely.
● **Pour** oil in a large Dutch oven; place over medium-high heat until hot. Brown lamb in hot oil about 20 minutes. Add remaining half of chopped vegetables, turnips, wine, and bay leaves.
● **Cover** and bake at 325° for 2 hours and 15 minutes or until meat thermometer inserted in thickest portion registers

150° (medium-rare). Remove and discard bay leaves. **Yield:** 10 servings.

Irma Seidensticker
Comfort, Texas

LEG OF LAMB WITH HUNTER SAUCE

1 (5-pound) leg of lamb
3 cloves garlic, thinly sliced
3 tablespoons Dijon mustard
1 tablespoon chopped fresh rosemary
2 teaspoons cracked pepper
Hunter Sauce

● **Cut** small slits in lamb with a sharp knife; insert garlic slices into slits. Place lamb in a large shallow dish.
● **Combine** mustard, rosemary, and pepper; spread over lamb. Cover and chill at least 1 and up to 2 days. Remove lamb from refrigerator, and place in a roasting pan; let stand at room temperature 30 minutes.
● **Bake** at 450° for 15 minutes; reduce oven temperature to 350°, and bake 1 additional hour or until meat thermometer inserted in thickest portion registers 145°. Remove from oven; cover lamb loosely with aluminum foil, and let stand 20 minutes or until thermometer registers 150° (medium-rare). Serve with Hunter Sauce. **Yield:** 8 to 10 servings.

Hunter Sauce

QUICK!

½ cup firmly packed brown sugar
½ cup ketchup
¼ cup butter or margarine
¼ cup apple jelly
3 tablespoons lemon juice
1 teaspoon ground cinnamon
½ teaspoon ground allspice
½ teaspoon pepper
¼ teaspoon ground cloves

● **Combine** all ingredients in a medium saucepan; cook over low heat, stirring until smooth. **Yield:** 1⅓ cups.

Sissy Nash and Kathy Nash Cary
Louisville, Kentucky

GRILLED LAMB WITH SWEET PEPPER RELISH

Lightly grill an extra red or yellow bell pepper or two with the lamb. Cut off the top, remove and discard the seeds, and use as a container to serve Sweet Pepper Relish.

4 (8-ounce) lamb rib sections
    (2 ribs per section)
¼ teaspoon salt
¼ teaspoon garlic powder
¼ teaspoon pepper
½ teaspoon chopped fresh
    basil
½ teaspoon chopped fresh
    rosemary
Sweet Pepper Relish
Garnish: fresh herbs

• **Trim** fat from rib sections, and set lamb aside.
• **Combine** salt, garlic powder, and pepper; sprinkle evenly over lamb. Press basil and rosemary evenly onto lamb rib sections.
• **Cook**, covered with grill lid, over medium-hot coals (350° to 400°) 12 minutes on each side or until meat thermometer inserted in thickest portion registers 150° (medium-rare) to 160° (medium).
• **Serve** lamb with Sweet Pepper Relish. Garnish, if desired. **Yield:** 4 servings.

Sweet Pepper Relish

2 red bell peppers, cut into thin
    strips
2 yellow bell peppers, cut into thin
    strips
¾ cup firmly packed brown sugar
8 serrano chile peppers, seeded
    and cut into thin strips

• **Combine** all ingredients in a small bowl, stirring gently. Cover relish mixture, and chill 8 hours.
• **Place** relish mixture in a small saucepan; bring to a boil over medium-low heat, stirring constantly. Reduce heat, and simmer 40 minutes, stirring often. Remove from heat, and let cool completely. **Yield:** 1 cup.

Gert Rausch
Austin, Texas

ROSEMARY-MARINATED LAMB KABOBS

Cubes of lamb soak up the vibrant flavors of orange juice, lime juice, and soy and teriyaki sauces. Green onions, rosemary, garlic, and black peppercorns further pique the palette of the marinade.

½ cup orange juice
¼ cup lime juice
¼ cup soy sauce
2 tablespoons teriyaki sauce
¼ cup finely chopped green
    onions
2 teaspoons dried rosemary
1 teaspoon minced garlic
5 to 7 black peppercorns
1 pound lean lamb, cut into 1-inch
    cubes
2 to 4 green bell peppers,
    quartered
1 large purple onion, cut into 8
    slices
1 navel orange, cut into 8
    slices
Hot cooked rice

• **Combine** first 8 ingredients in a shallow container or heavy-duty, zip-top plastic bag. Add lamb; cover or seal, and chill 8 hours, turning once.
• **Drain** lamb, discarding marinade. Arrange lamb on skewers. Place green bell pepper and onion in a grilling basket. Cook lamb and vegetables, covered with grill lid, over hot coals (400° to 500°) 10 minutes, turning often.
• **Place** orange slices on grill rack, and cook just until thoroughly heated, turning slices once.
• **Serve** lamb, vegetables, and orange slices over rice. **Yield:** 4 servings.

Alex Saied
Hoover, Alabama

DIJON-ROSEMARY LAMB CHOPS

QUICK!

¼ cup Dijon mustard
8 lamb chops (4 pounds)
1 tablespoon dried rosemary,
    crushed
All-purpose flour
2 tablespoons olive oil
1 cup dry white wine, divided
½ cup whipping cream
Salt and pepper

• **Spread** mustard over lamb chops; sprinkle evenly with rosemary. Dredge chops in flour, shaking off excess flour.
• **Pour** oil into a large skillet; place over medium-high heat until hot. Add chops, and cook until browned, turning once. Reduce heat to medium; cover and cook 10 minutes.
• **Turn** chops over, and add ¼ cup dry white wine. Cook 10 additional minutes or to desired degree of doneness. Remove from skillet, and keep warm.
• **Add** remaining ¾ cup wine to pan drippings, stirring to loosen browned particles that cling to bottom.
• **Cook** 10 minutes or until liquid is reduced to about 1 cup, stirring occasionally. Add whipping cream; simmer 2 minutes. Season with salt and pepper to taste. Serve sauce with lamb chops. **Yield:** 4 servings.

Chef J. R. Contway
Bentwood Country Club
San Angelo, Texas

SAGE LAMB CHOPS

QUICK!

Lamb chops from the microwave? We were pleasantly surprised.

1 tablespoon red wine vinegar
1 teaspoon dark brown sugar
½ teaspoon rubbed sage
⅛ teaspoon garlic powder
⅛ teaspoon salt
⅛ teaspoon pepper
4 (1-inch-thick) lamb chops

• **Combine** first 6 ingredients in a 9-inch pieplate or microwave-safe dish. Add chops, turning to coat; arrange chops with bones toward center of dish. Cover and chill 2 to 3 hours.

● **Microwave** at MEDIUM-HIGH (70% power) 3 to 5 minutes or until chops are pink in the center (do not overcook). Cover with aluminum foil; let stand 3 minutes. **Yield:** 2 servings.

LaJuan Coward
Jasper, Texas

GREEK MEAT LOAF

Leftovers taste luxurious drizzled with yogurt sauce and stuffed inside pita bread.

2½ pounds lean ground lamb
1 large onion, diced
1 green bell pepper, diced
½ cup quick-cooking oats, uncooked
¼ cup chopped fresh parsley
2½ teaspoons dried oregano
2 teaspoons chopped fresh mint or ½ teaspoon dried mint flakes
2 teaspoons pepper
½ teaspoon salt
1 (8-ounce) can tomato sauce
2 large eggs, lightly beaten

● **Combine** all ingredients in a large bowl; shape mixture into a loaf, and place in a lightly greased 9- x 5- x 3-inch loafpan.
● **Bake** at 350° for 1½ hours or until meat thermometer inserted in center registers 160°, and serve immediately. **Yield:** 8 servings.

Toni Reed Rashid
Birmingham, Alabama

CROWN PORK ROAST WITH CRANBERRY-PECAN STUFFING

1 tablespoon salt
1 tablespoon pepper
2 teaspoons dried thyme
1 (16-rib) crown pork roast, trimmed
2 cups Cranberry-Pecan Stuffing
¼ cup butter or margarine
⅓ cup all-purpose flour
2 (14½-ounce) cans chicken broth
2 tablespoons Grand Marnier or other orange-flavored liqueur *
2 tablespoons grated orange rind
¼ teaspoon salt
¼ teaspoon pepper
Garnishes: kumquat leaves, sugared kumquats, grape clusters, crabapples

● **Combine** first 3 ingredients; rub over all sides of roast.
● **Fold** a piece of aluminum foil into an 8-inch square; place on a rack in a roasting pan. Place roast, bone ends up, on foil-lined rack.
● **Bake** at 350° for 1 hour.
● **Spoon** 2 cups Cranberry-Pecan Stuffing into center of roast; cover with a 12-inch square of heavy-duty foil, and fold over tips of ribs.
● **Bake** at 350° for 1½ hours or until a meat thermometer inserted in thickest portion registers 160°. Remove foil; let roast stand 15 minutes before slicing.
● **Pour** pan drippings into a skillet; add butter, and cook over medium heat until butter melts. Add flour, whisking until smooth; cook, whisking constantly, until caramel-colored.
● **Stir** in chicken broth and next 4 ingredients; cook, whisking constantly, until smooth and thickened. Serve with roast. Garnish, if desired. **Yield:** 12 servings.

* You can substitute an equal amount of orange juice for liqueur.

Note: To make sugared fruit, sprinkle 4 envelopes unflavored gelatin over 4 cups warm water; stir with a wire whisk until gelatin dissolves. Dip fruit into gelatin mixture, shaking to remove excess; sprinkle all sides of fruit with

superfine sugar, covering completely. Place on baking sheets; let stand 30 minutes or until dry and firm.

Cranberry-Pecan Stuffing

You can make the stuffing ahead. Place it in a large bowl; cover and chill until ready to bake. If not preparing a roast, spoon all stuffing into two lightly greased 11- x 7- x 1½-inch baking dishes; bake as directed.

2 cups dried cranberries
1 cup Grand Marnier or other orange-flavored liqueur *
2 pounds mild ground pork sausage
4 cups coarsely chopped celery
1½ cups chopped onion
½ cup butter or margarine
2 (14½-ounce) cans chicken broth
1 teaspoon salt
½ teaspoon pepper
1 teaspoon dried thyme
2 (6-ounce) packages pork stuffing mix
2 tablespoons grated orange rind
2 cups chopped pecans

● **Combine** cranberries and liqueur in a small saucepan; bring to a boil over medium-high heat. Remove from heat, and set aside.
● **Brown** sausage in a large skillet, stirring until it crumbles; drain, reserving 2 tablespoons drippings in skillet. Set sausage aside.
● **Cook** celery and onion in drippings over medium-high heat 10 minutes, stirring constantly. Add butter and next 4 ingredients; cook, stirring constantly, 3 minutes or until butter melts.
● **Combine** cranberry mixture, sausage, stuffing mix and seasoning packet, orange rind, and pecans in a large bowl, stirring well.
● **Spoon** 2 cups stuffing mixture into roast; spoon remainder of stuffing mixture into a lightly greased 13- x 9- x 2-inch baking dish.
● **Cover** and bake at 350° for 20 minutes; uncover and bake 10 additional minutes or until lightly browned. **Yield:** 12 servings.

SAUSAGE-STUFFED PORK RIB ROAST

1 (3- to 5-pound) center-cut pork
   rib roast (8 bone)
½ to 1 pound smoked sausage
¼ cup butter, softened
2 tablespoons red port wine
2 tablespoons cane syrup
2 tablespoons muscadine jelly
¼ cup minced garlic
1 tablespoon chopped fresh
   tarragon
1 tablespoon chopped fresh
   thyme
1 tablespoon chopped fresh
   basil
1 tablespoon chopped fresh
   rosemary
1 teaspoon salt
1 teaspoon pepper
10 pearl onions
1 cup chicken broth
Brown Sauce
Muscadine jelly
Garnish: fresh rosemary sprigs

• **Push** a boning knife through center of pork roast, making a slit from end to end. Cut sausage the length of roast; prick sausage at ½-inch intervals, and insert into slit in roast. Place the stuffed roast in a lightly greased roasting pan.
• **Combine** butter and next 3 ingredients; spread over roast.
• **Combine** garlic and next 6 ingredients; sprinkle over roast. Add onions and chicken broth to roasting pan.
• **Cover** and bake at 350° for 45 minutes. Uncover and bake 15 to 20 additional minutes or until meat thermometer registers 160°. Remove roast, reserving 1 cup pan drippings for Brown Sauce. Serve roast with Brown Sauce and additional muscadine jelly. Garnish, if desired. **Yield:** 8 servings.

Brown Sauce

QUICK!

2 tablespoons butter
2 tablespoons all-purpose flour
2½ cups beef broth
1 cup reserved pan drippings
2 tablespoons muscadine jelly
1 tablespoon tomato sauce
¼ cup red port wine

• **Melt** butter in a heavy saucepan over medium heat, and add flour, stirring until smooth. Cook 1 minute, stirring constantly. Gradually stir in broth and 1 cup reserved pan drippings.
• **Bring** to a boil, stirring constantly, and cook until slightly thickened. Stir in jelly, tomato sauce, and port.
• **Pour** through a fine wire-mesh strainer into a container for a smoother consistency, if desired. **Yield:** 3½ cups.

Chef John Folse
Lafitte's Landing
Donaldsonville, Louisiana

APRICOT-PECAN STUFFED PORK LOIN

The bourbon sauce for this roast requires "flaming" on the cooktop before pouring over the pork and baking. This is to burn off the alcohol and to prevent the sauce from flaming in the oven. (Beware: Skipping this step could mean a call to the fire department.)

1½ cups dried apricots halves
½ cup pecans
1 clove garlic
½ teaspoon salt
¼ teaspoon pepper
2 tablespoons dried thyme, divided
¼ cup molasses, divided
¼ cup peanut or vegetable oil,
   divided
1 (5-pound) rolled boneless pork
   loin roast, well trimmed
1 cup bourbon
1 cup chicken broth
¼ cup whipping cream
¼ teaspoon salt

• **Position** knife blade in food processor bowl; add first 5 ingredients, and process until coarsely chopped. Add 1 tablespoon thyme, 1 tablespoon molasses, and 2 tablespoons oil; process until mixture is finely chopped.
• **Remove** pork loin halves from elastic net. (There should be 2 pieces.) Trim excess fat. Make a cut lengthwise down center of each piece, cutting to, but not through, bottom. Starting from center cut, slice horizontally toward 1 side, stopping ½ inch from edge. Repeat on opposite side. Unfold meat so that it's flat. Repeat with other loin half.
• **Flatten** to ½-inch thickness, using a meat mallet or rolling pin. Repeat with remaining loin half.
• **Spread** apricot mixture evenly on top of pork. Roll each loin half, separately, jellyroll fashion, starting with long side. Secure with string, and place seam side down in a shallow roasting pan. Brush with remaining 2 tablespoons oil; sprinkle with remaining 1 tablespoon thyme.
• **Bring** remaining 3 tablespoons molasses, bourbon, and chicken broth to a boil in a large saucepan. Remove from heat. Carefully ignite bourbon mixture with a long match. When flames die, pour over pork roasts.
• **Bake** at 350° for 1 to 1½ hours or until meat thermometer inserted in thickest portion registers 160°. Remove pork from pan, reserving drippings in pan, and keep pork warm.
• **Add** whipping cream and salt to drippings in pan, and cook over medium-high heat, stirring constantly, until slightly thickened.
• **Slice** pork, and serve with sauce. **Yield:** 10 servings.

FRUITCAKE-STUFFED PORK LOIN

Fruitcake breaks tradition as a delicious stuffing for this elegant entrée.

⅓ cup chopped onion
1 clove garlic, minced
1 tablespoon olive oil
3 cups crumbled fruitcake
1 (5-pound) rolled boneless pork
   loin roast
¼ teaspoon salt
¼ teaspoon pepper
2 tablespoons dried thyme, divided
1 cup apple juice
1 cup chicken broth
¼ cup bourbon
¼ cup honey
2 tablespoons butter or margarine
2 tablespoons all-purpose flour
2 tablespoons bourbon
¼ cup whipping cream
Garnishes: fresh grapes, kumquats,
   fresh thyme sprigs, canned
   crabapples

- **Cook** onion and garlic in olive oil in a skillet over medium-high heat, stirring constantly, until tender. Remove skillet from heat; add fruitcake, and stir well.
- **Remove** pork loin from elastic net. (There should be 2 pieces.) Trim excess fat. Make a cut lengthwise down the center of each piece, cutting to, but not through, bottom. Starting from center cut of each piece, slice horizontally toward 1 side, stopping ½ inch from edge. Repeat on opposite side. Unfold each piece of meat so that it lies flat.
- **Flatten** to ½-inch thickness, using a meat mallet or rolling pin.
- **Sprinkle** salt, pepper, and 1 tablespoon thyme evenly over pork. Sprinkle fruitcake mixture evenly over pork.
- **Roll** each loin half, jellyroll fashion, starting with long side. Secure with string, and place seam side down in a shallow roasting pan.
- **Pour** apple juice and chicken broth around rolled pork loins in pan.
- **Combine** ¼ cup bourbon and honey. Brush lightly over rolled pork loins. Sprinkle with remaining 1 tablespoon thyme.
- **Bake** at 350° for 50 minutes or until meat thermometer inserted in thickest portion registers 160°, basting with bourbon mixture every 20-minutes. Remove pork loins from pan, reserving pan drippings. Place pork on a serving platter, and keep warm.
- **Pour** pan drippings into a saucepan; bring to a boil, and cook 10 to 15 minutes until mixture is reduced to 1 cup. Set aside.
- **Melt** butter in a small heavy saucepan over low heat; add flour, stirring until smooth. Cook 1 minute, stirring constantly. Gradually add reduced drippings and 2 tablespoons bourbon; cook over medium heat, stirring constantly, until mixture thickens and boils. Remove from heat; stir in whipping cream. Serve with sliced pork. Garnish, if desired. **Yield:** 10 servings.

ROLLED PORK WITH RHUBARB SAUCE

A honeyed glaze of rhubarb and raspberries balanced with tangy apple cider vinegar and mustard tops this pork roast. Snippets of fresh rosemary and thyme provide fragrant flavor contrast.

1 **(3-pound) rolled boneless pork loin roast**
2 **tablespoons chopped fresh rosemary, divided**
2 **tablespoons chopped fresh thyme, divided**
3 **cloves garlic, cut into fourths**
Olive oil-flavored cooking spray
2 **cups fresh or frozen sliced rhubarb, thawed**
1 **(10-ounce) jar seedless raspberry preserves**
⅔ **cup honey**
2 **tablespoons apple cider vinegar**
½ **teaspoon dry mustard**
¼ **teaspoon ground cloves**
Garnishes: fresh rosemary and thyme sprigs

- **Remove** string from pork roast; trim fat. Sprinkle half of chopped rosemary and thyme on top of half of pork roast; place other half of roast on top, and tie at 2-inch intervals with heavy string.
- **Place** roast in a shallow roasting pan. Cut 12 small slits in roast; insert garlic pieces. Sprinkle with remaining chopped rosemary and thyme, and coat with cooking spray.
- **Bake** at 325° for 1 hour.
- **Combine** rhubarb and next 5 ingredients in a saucepan; bring to a boil over medium heat. Reduce heat, and simmer 10 minutes; cool slightly.
- **Position** knife blade in food processor bowl; add rhubarb mixture, and pulse 4 times or until smooth, stopping once to scrape down sides. Reserve ⅔ cup mixture. Brush roast with remaining mixture.
- **Bake** roast 20 additional minutes or until meat thermometer inserted in thickest portion registers 160°. Let roast stand 10 minutes. Serve with reserved rhubarb mixture. Garnish, if desired. **Yield:** 10 servings.

ROASTED PORK LOIN

You'll love what the garlic-ginger marinade does for this tender pork.

½ **cup soy sauce**
¼ **cup vegetable oil**
2 **tablespoons molasses**
1 **tablespoon ground ginger**
2 **teaspoons dry mustard**
6 **cloves garlic, minced**
1 **(4- to 5-pound) rolled boneless pork loin roast**

- **Combine** first 6 ingredients in a bowl, stirring with a wire whisk until blended.
- **Remove** pork loin halves from elastic net. (There should be 2 pieces.) Trim excess fat from pork. Place pork in a shallow dish or heavy-duty, zip-top plastic bag; pour soy sauce mixture over pork, turning to coat. Cover and chill at least 8 hours.
- **Remove** pork loin from marinade, reserving marinade. Bring marinade to a boil; set aside. Place pork loin halves together, and secure with string. Place in a greased roasting pan.
- **Bake** at 325° for 2 hours or until meat thermometer inserted in thickest portion registers 160°, brushing with marinade during first hour of cooking. **Yield:** 10 to 12 servings.

Myrna M. Ruiz
Marietta, Georgia

HONEY-ROASTED PORK

1 (2- to 3-pound) boneless pork
    loin roast
¼ cup honey
2 tablespoons Dijon mustard
2 tablespoons mixed or black
    peppercorns, crushed
½ teaspoon dried thyme,
    crushed
½ teaspoon salt
Garnishes: fresh watercress, apple
    and orange slices

• **Place** roast on a lightly greased rack in
shallow roasting pan.
• **Combine** honey and next 4 ingredients; brush about half of mixture over
roast.
• **Bake** at 325° for 1 hour; brush with
remaining honey mixture. Bake 30 additional minutes or until a meat thermometer inserted in thickest portion
registers 160°. Garnish, if desired. **Yield:**
8 servings.

Janie Wallace
Seguin, Texas

ROAST PORK LOIN WITH APPLES AND MUSHROOMS

1 (3-pound) rolled boneless pork
    loin roast, well trimmed
1 teaspoon dried thyme
¼ teaspoon salt
¼ teaspoon pepper
⅓ cup apple cider
2 tablespoons dry white vermouth
1 cup chicken broth
1 cup whipping cream
3 tablespoons butter or margarine,
    divided
3 small cooking apples, peeled,
    cored, and cut into eighths
¾ pound fresh mushrooms, sliced
Garnish: fresh thyme sprigs

• **Sprinkle** pork roast with seasonings,
and place in a lightly greased 13- x 9- x
2-inch baking pan. Bake at 450° for 20
minutes; reduce oven temperature to
325°, and bake 1 hour and 15 minutes or
until a meat thermometer registers 160°.
Transfer roast to platter; let stand 10
minutes before slicing.

• **Place** baking pan over medium heat;
add apple cider, stirring to loosen any
particles that cling to bottom. Add vermouth, chicken broth, and whipping
cream. Bring mixture to a boil; cook 15
minutes or until thickened, stirring
often. Remove from heat.
• **Melt** 1½ tablespoons butter in a large
skillet; add apple, and cook until golden,
turning once. Remove from skillet; set
aside, and keep warm. Melt remaining
1½ tablespoons butter in skillet over
medium heat; add mushrooms, and
cook until tender. Stir in cream mixture,
and cook over low heat until thoroughly
heated.
• **Place** 3 slices of pork roast on individual plates; spoon about ¼ cup sauce
over meat, and serve with apple slices.
Garnish, if desired. **Yield:** 8 servings.

Ouida Hamilton
Birmingham, Alabama

TROPICAL PORK LOIN

2 (15-ounce) cans sliced mangoes,
    drained
1 small onion, chopped
2 cloves garlic, minced
½ cup honey
⅓ cup soy sauce
¼ cup chopped crystallized ginger
¾ cup lemon-lime carbonated
    beverage
1 (2½- to 3-pound) boneless pork
    loin roast, well trimmed
¼ cup flaked coconut, toasted

• **Position** knife blade in food processor bowl; add mangoes. Process until
smooth, stopping once to scrape down
sides. Pour 2 cups mango puree into a
large shallow dish or heavy-duty, zip-top
plastic bag; chill remaining puree.
• **Add** onion and next 5 ingredients to
dish or bag, stirring well; add roast,
turning to coat. Cover or seal, and chill 6
to 8 hours, turning roast occasionally.
• **Remove** roast, reserving ½ cup marinade. Place roast on a rack in lightly
greased broiler pan; pour reserved ½
cup marinade over roast.
• **Bake** at 325° for 1½ hours or until a
meat thermometer inserted in thickest
portion registers 160°.

• **Broil** 5½ inches from heat (with electric oven door partially opened) 5 minutes or until lightly browned. Remove
roast to a serving platter, and keep
warm; reserve ¼ cup drippings in
broiler pan.
• **Add** remaining mango puree to reserved pan drippings; cook over
medium heat until sauce is thoroughly
heated, stirring occasionally.
• **Sprinkle** coconut over roast; serve
with sauce. **Yield:** 8 servings.

Nita and Harold Norman
Coral Gables, Florida

GRANDMA RUTH'S GRILLED PORK LOIN

Bottled Italian dressing makes the
marinade for this pork loin so easy.

1 (3- to 4-pound) boneless pork
    loin roast
1 (8-ounce) bottle Italian dressing
1 cup dry white wine
3 cloves garlic, minced
10 black peppercorns
Vegetable cooking spray

• **Pierce** roast at 1-inch intervals with a
fork; set aside. (Piercing allows marinade to penetrate the meat better.)
• **Combine** dressing and next 3 ingredients in a large heavy-duty, zip-top plastic
bag. Reserve ½ cup wine mixture in refrigerator for basting during grilling.
• **Add** roast to remaining wine mixture
in bag; seal bag, and chill 8 hours, turning occasionally.
• **Remove** roast from marinade, discarding marinade.
• **Coat** a grill rack with cooking spray,
and place over medium-hot coals (350°
to 400°); place roast on rack.
• **Cook**, covered with grill lid, 35 minutes or until meat thermometer inserted
in thickest portion registers 160°, turning and basting with reserved ½ cup
wine mixture after 20 minutes. **Yield:** 8
to 10 servings.

Diane Buescher
Jackson, Missouri

HONEY-GRILLED PORK LOIN

An Asian blend of honey, sesame oil, soy sauce, garlic, and ginger imparts character to the pork. If you prefer, have your butcher butterfly the roast for you to simplify preparation.

1 (3-pound) boneless pork loin roast
⅔ cup soy sauce
1 teaspoon ground ginger
3 cloves garlic, crushed
¼ cup firmly packed brown sugar
⅓ cup honey
1½ tablespoons sesame oil
Vegetable cooking spray

• **Trim** fat from roast. Butterfly roast by making a lengthwise cut, cutting to within ½ inch of other side, and open roast. Place in a shallow dish or large heavy-duty, zip-top plastic bag.
• **Combine** soy sauce, ginger, and garlic, stirring well; pour over roast. Cover or seal, and chill at least 3 hours, turning roast occasionally.
• **Remove** roast from marinade, discarding marinade; set aside.
• **Combine** brown sugar, honey, and sesame oil in a small saucepan; cook over low heat, stirring constantly, until sugar dissolves.
• **Coat** grill rack with cooking spray. Brush roast with honey mixture. Cook, without grill lid, over medium-hot coals (350° to 400°) 20 to 25 minutes or until meat thermometer registers 160°, turning twice and basting often. **Yield:** 10 to 12 servings.

SPINACH AND BACON STUFFED PORK TENDERLOIN

½ cup finely chopped onion
1 clove garlic, minced
Vegetable cooking spray
1 cup sliced fresh mushrooms
1 (10-ounce) package frozen chopped spinach, thawed and drained
4 slices bacon, cooked and crumbled
1 tablespoon Dijon mustard
¼ teaspoon salt
¼ teaspoon pepper
2 (¾-pound) pork tenderloins, trimmed
2 tablespoons Dijon mustard
2 teaspoons dried rosemary, crushed
1 teaspoon dried oregano
1 teaspoon dried thyme
1 teaspoon pepper
¼ teaspoon salt
½ cup dry white wine

• **Cook** onion and garlic in a large non-stick skillet coated with cooking spray over medium heat, stirring constantly, until vegetables are tender. Add mushrooms; cook 3 minutes, stirring constantly. Stir in spinach and next 4 ingredients; set aside.
• **Slice** each pork tenderloin lengthwise down center, cutting to, but not through, bottom. Place between sheets of heavy-duty plastic wrap; pound into a 12- x 8-inch rectangle.
• **Spoon** half of spinach mixture over 1 tenderloin; spread to within ½ inch of sides. Roll tenderloin, jellyroll fashion, starting with short side. Tie with heavy string at 1½-inch intervals. Repeat procedure with remaining tenderloin and spinach mixture.
• **Combine** 2 tablespoons mustard and next 5 ingredients; spread evenly over tenderloins. Place seam side down in a shallow baking pan coated with cooking spray. Add wine to pan.
• **Bake** at 325° for 45 minutes. Let stand 10 minutes; remove strings. Cut into ½-inch slices. **Yield:** 6 servings.

♥ Per serving: Calories 227
Fat 7.6g Cholesterol 88mg
Sodium 504mg

GRILLED PORK TENDERLOIN WITH APPLES, CELERY, AND POTATOES

6 small new potatoes (10 ounces)
⅓ cup chopped purple onion
Vegetable cooking spray
2 Granny Smith apples, chopped
⅓ cup dry white wine
2 (10-ounce) pork tenderloins, trimmed
¼ teaspoon salt
¼ teaspoon freshly ground pepper
1 shallot, finely chopped
1 tablespoon olive oil
2 stalks celery, thinly sliced
1 tablespoon chopped fresh rosemary
⅔ cup white wine vinegar
2 tablespoons sugar
1 tablespoon chopped fresh parsley

• **Bake** potatoes at 350° for 20 minutes or until tender; cool. Cut potatoes into quarters; set aside.
• **Cook** onion in a saucepan coated with cooking spray over medium heat until tender. Add apple and wine; bring to a boil. Reduce heat, and simmer 10 minutes. Remove from heat, and set aside.
• **Sprinkle** pork with salt and pepper.
• **Cook** pork, covered with grill lid, over medium-hot coals (350° to 400°) about 15 to 20 minutes or until meat thermometer inserted in thickest portion registers 160°, turning once.
• **Cook** shallot in olive oil in a large non-stick skillet over medium-high heat, stirring constantly, until lightly browned. Stir in potato, apple mixture, celery, and rosemary. Cook 1 minute or until thoroughly heated. Place on serving plates, top with sliced pork, and keep warm.
• **Add** vinegar and sugar to skillet, stirring to dissolve sugar and scraping any particles that cling to bottom. Cook 3 to 5 minutes or until reduced by half.
• **Drizzle** over sliced pork and apple; sprinkle with chopped parsley. **Yield:** 4 servings.

*Chefs' Café
Atlanta, Georgia*

♥ Per serving: Calories 446
Fat 20.1g Cholesterol 101mg
Sodium 255mg

GRILLED PORK TENDERLOIN

QUICK!

½ cup soy sauce
½ cup dry sherry or orange juice
2 tablespoons brown sugar
1 teaspoon ground ginger
2 cloves garlic, pressed
2 (¾-pound) pork tenderloins

• **Combine** first 5 ingredients in a shallow dish or heavy-duty, zip-top plastic bag. Add tenderloins; cover dish or seal bag, and chill 8 hours, turning often.
• **Remove** tenderloins from marinade, discarding marinade.
• **Cook** tenderloins, covered with grill lid, over hot coals (400° to 500°) 12 to 15 minutes or until a meat thermometer inserted in thickest portion registers 160°, turning once.
• **Cut** into slices. **Yield:** 4 to 6 servings.
Cathy Robinson
Columbia, South Carolina

HONEY-MUSTARD PORK TENDERLOIN

QUICK!

2 (¾-pound) pork tenderloins, trimmed
Vegetable cooking spray
¼ cup honey
2 tablespoons apple cider vinegar
1 tablespoon Dijon mustard
½ teaspoon paprika

• **Place** tenderloins on a rack coated with cooking spray; place rack in broiler pan, and set aside.
• **Combine** honey and remaining 3 ingredients; spoon one-third of honey mixture over tenderloins, and set remaining honey mixture aside.
• **Bake** at 350° for 30 minutes or until a meat thermometer inserted in thickest portion registers 160°, basting occasionally with honey mixture. Cut tenderloins into thin slices. **Yield:** 6 servings.
Marie Davis
Charlotte, North Carolina

♥ Per serving: Calories 183
Fat 4.3g   Cholesterol 64mg
Sodium 121mg

APPLE-MUSHROOM PORK TENDERLOIN

2 (¾-pound) pork tenderloins, trimmed *
¾ cup all-purpose flour
½ teaspoon salt
¼ teaspoon pepper
Vegetable cooking spray
1 clove garlic, minced
1 cup sliced fresh mushrooms
¾ cup frozen apple juice concentrate, thawed and undiluted

• **Cut** each tenderloin crosswise into 6 medallions. Place medallions, cut side down, between two sheets of heavy-duty plastic wrap; flatten each medallion to ¼-inch thickness, using a meat mallet or rolling pin.
• **Combine** flour, salt, and pepper; coat pork slices with flour mixture.
• **Coat** a large nonstick skillet with cooking spray; place skillet over medium heat until hot.
• **Arrange** pork in skillet, and cook until browned on both sides.
• **Remove** pork from pan; set aside. Add garlic and mushrooms; cook 30 seconds, stirring constantly. Add apple juice concentrate and pork; simmer 3 minutes until thoroughly heated. **Yield:** 6 servings.

* You can substitute 6 skinned and boned chicken breast halves for pork tenderloins.

♥ Per serving: Calories 275
Fat 4.2g   Cholesterol 74mg
Sodium 253mg

PORK MEDAILLONS WITH PORT WINE AND DRIED CRANBERRY SAUCE

Port wine is a sweet, fortified wine that balances with the tartness of the dried cranberries, orange rind, and balsamic vinegar in this dish.

1 large red bell pepper
1 teaspoon olive oil
1 medium-size purple onion, finely chopped
2 shallots, finely chopped
2 tablespoons minced fresh ginger
½ cup port wine
⅓ cup balsamic vinegar
2 tablespoons sugar
1 ripe pear, peeled and chopped
2 teaspoons grated orange rind
½ cup dried cranberries
1 cup fat-free chicken broth
2 tablespoons fresh thyme leaves
¼ teaspoon ground red pepper
2 (1-pound) pork tenderloins, trimmed
½ teaspoon salt
½ teaspoon freshly ground pepper
Garnish: fresh thyme sprigs

• **Place** red bell pepper on an aluminum foil-lined baking sheet. Bake at 500° for 20 minutes or until skin looks blistered, turning once.
• **Place** pepper immediately into a heavy-duty, zip-top plastic bag; seal and let stand 10 minutes to loosen skin. Peel pepper; remove and discard seeds. Cut pepper into strips; set aside.
• **Pour** oil into a large skillet; place over medium heat until hot. Add onion and shallot, and cook 10 minutes, stirring often.
• **Add** ginger and next 3 ingredients; bring to a boil. Reduce heat, and simmer 10 minutes or until liquid is reduced by three-fourths, stirring often.
• **Add** pepper strips, pear, and next 5 ingredients; simmer 10 minutes or until pear is tender, stirring occasionally. Remove from heat; keep warm.
• **Cut** each tenderloin into 8 slices. Place each slice between two sheets of heavy-duty plastic wrap, and flatten slightly with a meat mallet or rolling pin.

Sprinkle each side of slices with salt and pepper; arrange in a single layer on a rack in broiler pan.

• **Broil** 5½ inches from heat (with electric oven door partially opened) 3 minutes on each side or until meat thermometer inserted in thickest portion registers 160°. Garnish, if desired, and serve with sauce. **Yield:** 8 servings.

Ray Overton
Roswell, Georgia

♥ Per serving: Calories 254
Fat 9g Cholesterol 66.1mg
Sodium 204mg

PORK SCALOPPINE MARSALA

QUICK!

Imported from Italy, Marsala is a fortified wine with a rich, smoky flavor that can range from sweet to dry. The dry Marsala in this pork recipe enhances the simple, straightforward flavors of butter and freshly ground pepper.

2 (¾-pound) pork tenderloins
½ cup all-purpose flour
¼ cup butter or margarine, divided
1⅓ cups dry Marsala *
2 teaspoons beef-flavored bouillon granules
⅛ teaspoon freshly ground pepper
Hot cooked rice

• **Cut** each tenderloin into 6 (2-ounce) medaillons. Place pork, cut side down, between two sheets of heavy-duty plastic wrap; flatten to ¼-inch thickness, using a meat mallet or rolling pin.
• **Dredge** pork in flour. Cook half of pork medaillons in 2 tablespoons butter in a large skillet over medium heat about 2 minutes on each side or until lightly browned. Remove from skillet; keep warm. Repeat procedure with remaining 2 tablespoons butter and pork medaillons. Pour off excess butter, if necessary, leaving pan drippings.
• **Add** Marsala, bouillon granules, and pepper to skillet, and simmer mixture 3 to 4 minutes.

• **Return** pork medaillons to skillet; cover and simmer 2 minutes. Serve with rice. **Yield:** 6 servings.

* Substitute 1¼ cups dry white wine plus 2 tablespoons brandy for dry Marsala.

Mike Singleton
Memphis, Tennessee

EASY PORK PARMIGIANA

QUICK!

Using your favorite brand of spaghetti sauce makes quick work of this classic Italian dish. Buy grated and shredded cheeses to cut preparation time even further.

1 large egg
1 tablespoon water
2 tablespoons grated Parmesan cheese
⅓ cup Italian-seasoned breadcrumbs
4 (1¼-inch-thick) slices pork tenderloin (about 8 ounces)
2 tablespoons vegetable oil
1 cup spaghetti sauce
½ cup (2 ounces) shredded mozzarella cheese

• **Combine** egg and water; set aside.
• **Combine** Parmesan cheese and breadcrumbs; set aside.
• **Place** each piece of pork between two sheets of heavy-duty plastic wrap; flatten to ¼-inch thickness, using a meat mallet or rolling pin.
• **Dip** pork in egg mixture, and dredge in crumb mixture.
• **Cook** pork slices in hot oil in a large skillet over medium heat just until browned, turning once. Arrange pork in a lightly greased 8-inch square baking dish; top with spaghetti sauce.
• **Bake** at 350° for 25 minutes; top with mozzarella cheese. Bake 5 additional minutes. **Yield:** 4 servings.

Linda Sutton
Winston-Salem, North Carolina

PORK PICCATA

QUICK!

This pork-inspired version of the timeless Italian veal dish boasts the traditional ingredients of lemon juice and chopped parsley, but adds a twist by including capers and serving the mixture on a bed of fettuccine.

2 (¾-pound) pork tenderloins
½ cup all-purpose flour
½ teaspoon salt
¼ teaspoon pepper
3 tablespoons olive oil, divided
½ cup dry white wine
½ cup lemon juice
3 tablespoons butter or margarine
¼ cup chopped fresh parsley
1½ tablespoons capers
Hot cooked fettuccine
Garnishes: lemon slices, fresh parsley sprigs

• **Cut** each tenderloin into 6 (2-ounce) medaillons. Place, cut side down, between two sheets of heavy-duty plastic wrap; flatten to ¼-inch thickness, using a meat mallet or rolling pin.
• **Combine** flour, salt, and pepper; dredge pork in flour mixture.
• **Cook** half of pork in 1½ tablespoons oil in a large skillet over medium heat about 2 minutes on each side or until lightly browned. Remove from skillet; keep warm. Repeat procedure with remaining 1½ tablespoons oil and pork.
• **Add** wine and lemon juice to skillet; cook until thoroughly heated. Add butter, chopped parsley, and capers, stirring until butter melts.
• **Arrange** pork over pasta; drizzle with wine mixture. Garnish, if desired. Serve immediately. **Yield:** 6 servings.

KUNG PAO PORK

QUICK!

Dried crushed red pepper turns up the heat in this stir-fry favorite.

1 small red bell pepper
½ small onion
¾ pound lean pork
¼ cup soy sauce, divided
¼ cup water
2 tablespoons lemon juice
2 tablespoons sugar
2 teaspoons cornstarch
¼ teaspoon dried crushed red
    pepper
2 tablespoons olive oil
2 cloves garlic, minced
¼ cup unsalted roasted peanuts
Hot cooked rice

• **Cut** bell pepper and onion into 1-inch pieces; set aside. Cut pork into ½-inch cubes; drizzle with 2 tablespoons soy sauce.
• **Combine** remaining 2 tablespoons soy sauce, water, and next 4 ingredients, stirring until blended; set aside.
• **Pour** olive oil around top of a preheated wok or large skillet, coating sides; heat at medium-high (375°) 2 minutes. Add pork and garlic, and stir-fry 3 minutes or until lightly browned. Add bell pepper and onion; stir-fry 3 minutes or until vegetables are tender.
• **Add** soy sauce mixture; stir-fry 2 minutes or until thickened. Stir in peanuts, and serve over rice. **Yield:** 3 servings.

Sandra Enwright
Winter Park, Florida

APRICOT-MUSHROOM STUFFED PORK CHOPS

Ask your butcher to cut pockets in the pork chops – it's one less thing you'll have to worry about.

4 tablespoons butter or margarine,
    divided
1 (8-ounce) package sliced fresh
    mushrooms
⅓ cup chopped onion
⅓ cup chopped celery
1 cup soft breadcrumbs
½ cup dried apricot halves,
    chopped
½ cup chopped fresh parsley
½ teaspoon rubbed sage
8 (1-inch-thick) center-cut pork
    loin chops, cut with pockets
2 teaspoons salt
1 teaspoon freshly ground pepper
1 cup dry white wine
1½ tablespoons cornstarch
2 tablespoons cold water

• **Melt** 2 tablespoons butter in a large skillet over medium-high heat; add mushrooms, onion, and celery, and cook, stirring constantly, 5 minutes or until tender. Stir in breadcrumbs and next 3 ingredients; remove from heat.
• **Sprinkle** both sides and pocket of each pork chop with salt and pepper. Spoon vegetable mixture evenly into pockets, and secure with wooden picks.
• **Melt** remaining 2 tablespoons butter in skillet; add chops, and cook until browned, turning once. Place chops in a lightly greased roasting pan or large shallow baking dish; add white wine.
• **Cover** and bake at 350° for 45 minutes or until done. Remove from pan; discard wooden picks. Keep chops warm.
• **Remove** and discard fat from pan drippings; place 1½ cups drippings in a small saucepan.
• **Combine** cornstarch and water, stirring until smooth; stir into reserved drippings.
• **Cook** over medium heat, stirring constantly, until mixture thickens and boils. Boil 1 minute, stirring constantly. Remove from heat; serve with chops. **Yield:** 8 servings.

Margert Stewart
Murfreesboro, Tennessee

BONELESS PORK CHOPS WITH ANCHO CREAM SAUCE
(pictured at right)

4 (½-inch-thick) boneless pork
    loin chops
¼ teaspoon salt
¼ teaspoon pepper
4 slices bacon
Vegetable cooking spray
¼ cup Ancho Base
¾ cup whipping cream

• **Sprinkle** chops with salt and pepper. Wrap 1 slice bacon around each chop; secure with wooden picks, if desired.
• **Coat** food rack with cooking spray; place on grill over medium coals (300° to 350°). Place pork chops on rack, and cook, covered with grill lid, 8 minutes on each side or until done.
• **Combine** ¼ cup Ancho Base and whipping cream in a saucepan, whisking until smooth. Bring to a boil over medium heat, whisking constantly. Reduce heat, and simmer, whisking constantly, 5 minutes or until thickened.
• **Spoon** Ancho Cream Sauce onto plates; top each with a pork chop. Serve immediately. **Yield:** 4 servings.

Ancho Base

3 dried ancho chile peppers
4 ounces dried tomatoes
3 tablespoons minced garlic
½ cup chopped onion
4 beef-flavored bouillon cubes
1 tablespoon dried oregano
1 tablespoon brown sugar
2 tablespoons Worcestershire
    sauce
¼ cup tomato paste
1½ cups water

• **Combine** all ingredients in a saucepan. Bring to a boil over medium heat; reduce heat, and simmer 10 minutes, stirring occasionally. Cool 15 minutes.
• **Position** knife blade in food processor bowl; add pepper mixture. Process until smooth, stopping often to scrape down sides. Chill up to 1 week or freeze up to 3 months. **Yield:** 2¼ cups.

Chef Ron Brannon
Austin Central Markets Cooking School
Austin, Texas

Boneless Pork Chops With
Ancho Cream Sauce

Cassoulet

CASSOULET
(pictured at left)

1 pound dried Great Northern
      beans
2½ quarts water
½ pound salt pork with skin
3 cloves garlic, crushed
1 onion
2 carrots, scraped and cut in half
2 stalks celery, cut in half
1 teaspoon dried thyme
1 bay leaf
1 (6- to 7-pound) chicken
1 teaspoon salt
2 teaspoons freshly ground
      pepper
1 pound andouille sausage, cut
      into 2-inch pieces *
2 pounds boneless center-cut pork
      chops
1 medium onion, chopped
4 cloves garlic, minced
1 cup dry white wine
1 (14.5-ounce) can diced
      tomatoes, undrained
½ teaspoon dried thyme
2 teaspoons freshly ground
      pepper
1 cup fresh French breadcrumbs
¼ cup chopped fresh parsley

• **Sort** and wash beans; place in an 8-quart ovenproof Dutch oven. Cover with water 2 inches above beans; let soak 8 hours. Drain.
• **Add** 2½ quarts water to beans; stir in salt pork and next 6 ingredients. Bring to a boil; cover and cook 2 hours or until beans are tender, adding water if necessary. Remove and discard salt pork, onion, carrot, celery, and bay leaf; set beans aside.
• **Place** chicken in a roasting pan; sprinkle with salt and 2 teaspoons pepper.
• **Bake** at 350° for 2 hours or until meat thermometer inserted in meaty portion of thigh registers 180°; cool completely, reserving 3 tablespoons drippings. Cut chicken into serving-size pieces; set aside.
• **Cook** sausage in a skillet over medium-high heat until browned; remove sausage, reserving drippings in skillet. Set sausage aside.
• **Add** pork chops to skillet, and cook until browned on both sides; remove

pork chops, reserving drippings in skillet. Set pork chops aside.
• **Add** reserved chicken drippings to skillet. Add chopped onion and minced garlic, and cook over medium-high heat, stirring constantly, until tender. Add wine, and cook 6 minutes or until reduced by half.
• **Add** tomatoes, ½ teaspoon thyme, and 2 teaspoons pepper; stir into beans.
• **Spoon** half each of beans, sausage, chicken, and pork chops into a Dutch oven; repeat layers with remaining ingredients. Sprinkle with breadcrumbs.
• **Bake** at 325° for 1½ hours. Sprinkle with parsley. **Yield:** 8 to 10 servings.

✱ Substitute any spicy smoked sausage for andouille.

BARBECUED COUNTRY-STYLE RIBS

Thanks to Mildred Bickley of Bristol, Virginia, we have Rollin Johnson's recipe for ribs. He served these at family gatherings for decades.

1 small onion, finely chopped
1 cup finely chopped celery
1½ tablespoons bacon
      drippings
1 (15-ounce) can tomato sauce
¾ cup honey
½ cup water
¼ cup dry red wine
2 tablespoons lemon juice
2 tablespoons Worcestershire
      sauce
1 teaspoon salt
½ teaspoon pepper
¼ teaspoon garlic powder
1 cup water
2 tablespoons white vinegar
4 pounds boneless country-style
      pork ribs *

• **Cook** onion and celery in bacon drippings in a large saucepan over medium-high heat, stirring constantly, until tender. Add tomato sauce and next 8 ingredients. Bring mixture to a boil; reduce heat, and simmer 1 hour, stirring occasionally. Reserve 1½ cups tomato sauce mixture.

• **Combine** water and vinegar in a spray bottle.
• **Cut** ribs apart; cook, covered with grill lid, over medium coals (300° to 350°) 1 to 1½ hours or until done, spraying with vinegar solution and turning ribs occasionally. Baste with remaining 1 cup tomato sauce mixture after 30 minutes. Serve with reserved 1½ cups tomato sauce mixture. **Yield:** 8 servings.

✱ You can substitute 4 pounds bone-in country-style pork ribs. Cook as directed. **Yield:** 6 servings.

Rollin Johnson
Bristol, Virginia

GINGER PORK RIBS

1 tablespoon butter or margarine
1 medium onion, chopped
1 cup ginger marmalade or
      preserves
¼ cup soy sauce
2½ tablespoons honey
2½ tablespoons dry sherry
1 tablespoon grated fresh
      ginger
1 tablespoon grated orange rind
4 to 5 pounds baby-back pork
      ribs

• **Melt** butter in a large skillet over medium-high heat; add onion, and cook, stirring constantly, until tender. Add marmalade and next 5 ingredients; cook over medium heat, stirring constantly, until thoroughly heated.
• **Arrange** ribs in a shallow dish; pour ginger mixture over ribs. Cover and chill at least 8 hours.
• **Remove** ribs from marinade, discarding marinade. Place ribs on a rack in a roasting pan.
• **Bake** at 350° for 45 minutes or until tender. **Yield:** 4 servings.

Note: You can find ginger marmalade at specialty supermarkets.

Mike Singleton
Memphis, Tennessee

GAME POT PIE WITH PARMESAN CRUST

This hearty three-meat stew works just as well out of the crust and spooned over hot biscuits or cornbread.

4 cloves garlic, minced
1 small shallot, minced
¼ cup olive oil
1 pound boneless venison, cut into 1-inch pieces
1 pound boneless rabbit, cut into 1-inch pieces
1 pound boneless duck breasts, cut into 1-inch pieces
1 cup dry red wine
1 cup crème de cassis or other black currant-flavored liqueur
½ cup dried apricot halves, chopped
¼ teaspoon salt
¼ teaspoon pepper
1 bay leaf
4 cups Venison Stock (see recipe on page 378)
1 small turnip, peeled and chopped
1 medium carrot, scraped and chopped
1 cup chopped rutabaga
1 cup pearl onions, peeled
1 medium-size red potato, cut into ½-inch cubes
½ cup fresh shiitake mushrooms, sliced (3 whole)
1 (15½-ounce) can white beans, rinsed and drained
1½ teaspoons fresh thyme leaves
1½ teaspoons chopped fresh chives
1½ teaspoons chopped fresh parsley
Whipped Celery Potatoes (see recipe on page 398)
Parmesan Crust

● **Cook** garlic and shallot in olive oil in a large Dutch oven over medium-high heat, stirring constantly, until tender.
● **Add** venison, rabbit, and duck; cook, stirring constantly, until meat is browned. Stir in wine and next 5 ingredients. Bring mixture to a boil; reduce heat, and simmer 30 minutes.

● **Stir** in Venison Stock and next 6 ingredients. Bring to a boil; reduce heat, and simmer 30 minutes or until vegetables are tender. Add beans and next 3 ingredients; cook until mixture is thoroughly heated. Remove and discard bay leaf.
● **Ladle** into bowls. Pipe or dollop Whipped Celery Potatoes into 4 rosettes evenly spaced around rim of each bowl. Top each with Parmesan Crust. **Yield:** 8 servings.

Parmesan Crust

12 sheets frozen phyllo pastry, thawed
½ cup butter or margarine, melted
¾ cup grated Parmesan cheese

● **Place** 1 sheet of pastry on a large cutting board, keeping remaining pastry covered with a slightly damp towel until ready to use. Brush pastry sheet with butter, and sprinkle with 1 tablespoon Parmesan cheese. Repeat procedure 2 times, layering pastry, butter, and cheese.
● **Cut** 2 (6- to 8-inch) circles from stacked pastry, and place on a lightly greased baking sheet. Lightly grease bottom of a second baking sheet, and place on top of pastry circles to keep phyllo flat during baking.
● **Bake** at 350° for 10 minutes or until golden. Cool crusts on baking sheet on a wire rack.
● **Repeat** procedure 3 times, using remaining pastry, butter, and cheese. **Yield:** 8 crusts.

Chef David Everett
Dining Room at Ford's Colony
Williamsburg, Virginia

SANTA FE SPANISH RABBIT

A rich tomato sauce tenderizes and flavors extra-lean rabbit. Bill serves this game dish with black beans and rice.

¼ cup all-purpose flour
¼ teaspoon freshly ground pepper
1 (3-pound) rabbit, cleaned and cut into pieces
2 to 4 tablespoons olive oil
1 small onion, chopped
1 stalk celery, chopped
2 cloves garlic, minced
1 cup dry white wine
1 (10¾-ounce) can condensed beef broth, undiluted
4 medium tomatoes, coarsely chopped
⅓ cup ripe olives, cut in half
⅓ cup green olives, cut in half
1 to 2 tablespoons chopped fresh oregano
Garnish: roasted red bell pepper slices

● **Combine** flour and ground pepper in a large, heavy-duty, zip-top plastic bag; add rabbit, shaking to coat.
● **Brown** rabbit in olive oil in a large Dutch oven over medium-high heat; remove rabbit, reserving drippings in Dutch oven.
● **Cook** onion, celery, and garlic in drippings over medium heat, stirring constantly, 3 minutes or until tender. Add wine, and simmer until liquid is reduced by half (about 15 minutes).
● **Stir** in beef broth; bring to a boil. Reduce heat; add rabbit, tomato, olives, and oregano.
● **Simmer**, stirring occasionally, 30 minutes or until rabbit is tender. (For a thicker sauce, remove rabbit, and keep warm. Continue simmering sauce until thickened.) Garnish, if desired. **Yield:** 4 servings.

Bill Hall
Nashville, Tennessee

At right: *Late-Night Pasta Chez Frank*
(page 223)

PASTA, GRAINS, AND RICE

BOURBON-PECAN ALFREDO

QUICK!

6 ounces linguine, uncooked
2 tablespoons butter or margarine
3 cloves garlic, minced
¾ cup bourbon, divided
1 cup whipping cream
1 cup freshly grated Parmesan
     cheese
½ cup pecan pieces, toasted
2 tablespoons chopped parsley

• **Cook** linguine according to package directions; drain and keep warm.
• **Melt** butter in a skillet over medium-high heat; add garlic, and cook, stirring constantly, until tender.
• **Add** ½ cup bourbon, and cook 3 to 5 minutes, stirring constantly. Stir in whipping cream and cheese. Cook over low heat, stirring constantly, until cheese melts. Gradually stir in remaining ¼ cup bourbon; stir in pecans and parsley. Pour over pasta; toss. Serve immediately. **Yield:** 2 main-dish servings or 4 side-dish servings.

Megen McCully
Knoxville, Tennessee

LINGUINE WITH
RED PEPPER SAUCE

8 ounces linguine, uncooked
Vegetable cooking spray
2 tablespoons olive oil
6 cups chopped red bell pepper
3 cloves garlic, crushed
½ cup balsamic vinegar or red
     wine vinegar
⅔ cup chopped fresh basil
½ teaspoon salt
¼ teaspoon pepper

• **Cook** linguine according to package directions, omitting salt or fat; drain and keep warm.
• **Coat** a nonstick skillet with cooking spray; add olive oil, red bell pepper, and garlic. Cook over low heat 30 minutes, stirring occasionally.
• **Place** mixture in container of an electric blender or food processor. Add vinegar and remaining 3 ingredients to container; process until smooth,

stopping once to scrape down sides. Spoon over linguine. Serve immediately. **Yield:** 4 servings.

♥ Per serving: Calories 337
Fat 8.9g   Cholesterol 0mg
Sodium 304mg

PESTO PRIMAVERA

Ruth captures the season's freshness with this vegetable-packed dish.

3 quarts water
1 cup sliced carrot
1 cup dried tomatoes, cut into
     fourths
1 (16-ounce) package linguine
2 yellow squash, cut into thin
     strips
1 red bell pepper, cut into thin
     strips
⅓ cup Ruth's Pesto
Toasted pine nuts

• **Bring** water to a boil in a large Dutch oven; add carrot, tomato, and linguine; cook 8 minutes.
• **Add** squash and bell pepper; cook 2 minutes. Drain well, and stir in ⅓ cup Ruth's Pesto. Sprinkle with pine nuts; serve immediately. **Yield:** 8 servings.

Ruth's Pesto

QUICK!

4 cups loosely packed fresh basil
     leaves
1½ cups olive oil
1 cup freshly grated Parmesan
     cheese
½ cup pine nuts, toasted
3 cloves garlic
¼ teaspoon pepper

• **Combine** all ingredients in container of an electric blender or food processor; process until smooth, stopping once to scrape down sides. **Yield:** 2 cups.

Note: Freeze pesto in 2-tablespoon portions in sections of ice cube trays. Allow 1 cube per 2 ounces pasta.

Ruth Davidon
Arlington, Virginia

TRAVELING LINGUINE WITH
ROASTED VEGETABLES
(pictured at right)

Although this pasta recipe was designed to cook over a campfire while "roughing it," you're sure to enjoy it equally as much when prepared in the comfort of your own kitchen.

2 yellow squash, cut into
     chunks
2 zucchini, cut into chunks
1 purple onion, quartered
1 small eggplant, unpeeled and
     cut into chunks
1 red bell pepper, quartered
⅓ cup butter or margarine
2 to 3 teaspoons dried Italian
     seasoning
½ teaspoon pepper
2 teaspoons chicken-flavored
     bouillon granules
2 quarts water
8 ounces linguine, uncooked
¼ cup grated Parmesan cheese

• **Place** first 5 ingredients on a lightly greased 24- x 18-inch piece of heavy-duty aluminum foil; dot with butter, and sprinkle with Italian seasoning and pepper. Seal securely.
• **Cook** over hot coals (400° to 500°) 20 to 30 minutes or until vegetables are tender. Remove from heat, and keep sealed.
• **Combine** bouillon granules and 2 quarts water in a stockpot; cover and place in hot coals. Bring to a boil; add linguine, and cook until tender. Drain. Top with vegetables; sprinkle with cheese. **Yield:** 2 to 3 servings.

C. M. Rodes
Louisville, Kentucky

Traveling Linguine With Roasted Vegetables

ARTICHOKE AND SHRIMP LINGUINE

QUICK!

8 ounces linguine, uncooked
1 pound unpeeled medium-size fresh shrimp
¼ cup olive oil
3 cloves garlic, minced
½ teaspoon dried crushed red pepper
1 (14-ounce) can artichoke hearts, drained and quartered
½ cup ripe olives, sliced
¼ cup fresh lemon juice
⅛ teaspoon salt
⅛ teaspoon pepper
½ cup grated Parmesan cheese

• **Cook** linguine according to package directions; drain and keep warm.
• **Peel** shrimp, and devein, if desired.
• **Heat** oil in a skillet over medium-high heat; add shrimp, garlic, and red pepper, and cook, stirring constantly, 5 minutes or until shrimp turn pink.
• **Stir** in artichoke hearts and next 4 ingredients. Add to pasta, and sprinkle with cheese. **Yield:** 3 to 4 servings.

Ann Winniford
Dallas, Texas

SAUTÉED SHRIMP AND PASTA

8 ounces linguine, uncooked
2 pounds unpeeled medium-size fresh shrimp
1 small onion, chopped
2 cloves garlic, minced
1 tablespoon hot sesame oil
6 plum tomatoes, peeled and chopped
1 teaspoon dried oregano
½ teaspoon salt
½ teaspoon dried basil
½ teaspoon freshly ground pepper
¼ cup chopped fresh parsley
¼ cup kalamata olives, sliced
¼ cup lemon juice
2 ounces crumbled feta cheese

• **Cook** linguine according to package directions; drain and keep warm.

• **Peel** shrimp, and devein, if desired.
• **Cook** onion and garlic in oil in a large skillet until tender, stirring often. Stir in tomato and next 4 ingredients; cook 3 minutes, stirring constantly. Add shrimp, and cook 3 minutes or until shrimp turn pink, stirring occasionally.
• **Stir** in parsley, olives, and lemon juice; cook just until thoroughly heated. Serve over linguine; sprinkle with cheese. **Yield:** 4 servings.

Carol Barclay
Portland, Texas

♥ Per serving: Calories 449
Fat 10.6g Cholesterol 185mg
Sodium 708mg

PASTA WITH PEANUT SAUCE

QUICK!

Be sure to use dark sesame oil in this recipe. It has a more intense sesame taste than light sesame oil, and it stands up well to the peanut and pepper flavor accents of this pasta dish.

8 ounces spaghetti, uncooked
12 green onions
3 yellow squash
1 red bell pepper
1 tablespoon dark sesame oil
1 tablespoon minced garlic
¼ cup creamy peanut butter
¼ cup reduced-sodium soy sauce
3 tablespoons lime juice
1 tablespoon sugar
1 teaspoon dried crushed red pepper

• **Cook** spaghetti according to package directions, omitting salt and fat; drain and keep warm.
• **Cut** white portion of green onions into 2-inch pieces; reserve green tops for another use. Cut squash in half lengthwise; cut halves into slices. Remove and discard seeds from red pepper, and cut red pepper into thin strips.
• **Cook** vegetables in a saucepan in boiling water to cover 3 minutes; drain vegetables, and set aside.

• **Pour** oil into a large skillet; place over medium heat until hot. Add garlic; cook 1 minute, stirring constantly. Add peanut butter, stirring until smooth. Stir in soy sauce and next 3 ingredients.
• **Add** vegetables to skillet, and toss gently to coat; remove vegetables from skillet with a slotted spoon.
• **Add** spaghetti to sauce in skillet, tossing to coat; transfer to a serving platter, and top with vegetables. Serve immediately. **Yield:** 4 servings.

Bruce Messer
Middlesboro, Kentucky

♥ Per serving: Calories 400
Fat 13g Cholesterol 0mg
Sodium 577mg

LEMON-GARLIC PASTA

QUICK!

2 tablespoons butter or margarine
2 tablespoons olive oil
4 to 5 cloves garlic, minced
¼ cup lemon juice
¼ teaspoon salt
½ to 1 teaspoon pepper
8 ounces thin spaghetti, cooked
⅓ cup chopped fresh parsley

• **Melt** butter in a large skillet over medium-high heat; add olive oil and minced garlic. Cook 1 minute, stirring constantly. Add lemon juice, salt, and pepper.
• **Bring** to a boil; pour mixture over pasta. Add parsley; toss gently. Serve immediately. **Yield:** 4 servings.

Nina Page Winkler
Orlando, Florida

LATE-NIGHT PASTA CHEZ FRANK

(pictured on page 217)

6   cloves garlic, pressed
2   tablespoons olive oil
4   jalapeño peppers or other chile
    peppers, seeded and minced
8   plum tomatoes, chopped
½   teaspoon salt
⅓ to ½ cup chopped fresh basil
1   (8-ounce) package spaghettini
    or vermicelli, cooked
Freshly grated Parmesan
    cheese
Garnish: fresh basil sprigs

• **Cook** garlic in oil in a large nonstick skillet over medium heat, stirring constantly, 1 to 2 minutes or until golden. Add pepper, and cook 1 minute, stirring constantly.
• **Add** tomato and salt; cook 3 minutes or until thoroughly heated. Stir in chopped basil. Serve immediately over pasta, and sprinkle with Parmesan cheese. Garnish, if desired. **Yield:** 2 to 3 servings.

Chef Frank Stitt
Highlands Bar & Grill
Birmingham, Alabama

CHICKEN-VEGETABLE SPAGHETTI

4   skinned and boned chicken
    breast halves, cut into 2-inch
    strips
2   tablespoons olive oil
3   medium zucchini, cut in half
    lengthwise and sliced (about
    1 pound)
1   large green bell pepper, coarsely
    chopped
½   pound fresh mushrooms,
    sliced
¼   cup chopped onion
1   clove garlic, minced
1   (30-ounce) jar spaghetti
    sauce
2   cups (8 ounces) shredded
    mozzarella cheese, divided
12 ounces spaghetti, uncooked
2   tablespoons chopped fresh
    parsley

• **Cook** chicken in oil in a large skillet over medium-high heat, stirring constantly, until no longer pink. Drain and set aside, reserving 1 tablespoon drippings in skillet.
• **Add** zucchini and next 4 ingredients to skillet; cook over medium heat, stirring constantly, until crisp-tender.
• **Stir** in chicken and spaghetti sauce; cook until thoroughly heated, stirring occasionally. Stir in 1 cup cheese; cook until cheese melts, stirring often.
• **Cook** spaghetti according to package directions; drain. Arrange on a large platter; top with sauce mixture, and sprinkle with remaining 1 cup cheese and parsley. **Yield:** 4 to 6 servings.

Yvonne M. Greer
Mauldin, South Carolina

CASSEROLE SPAGHETTI

*As one parent stated during
taste testing of this recipe,
"Kids will vacuum up this recipe."*

1½ pounds ground chuck
1   green bell pepper, chopped
1   large onion, chopped
½   cup chopped celery
2   cloves garlic, crushed
1   (10¾-ounce) can cream of
    mushroom soup, undiluted
¾   cup water
1   (16-ounce) can tomatoes,
    undrained and chopped
2   tablespoons chili powder
½   teaspoon salt
¼   teaspoon pepper
1   (8-ounce) package spaghetti
2   ounces sharp Cheddar cheese,
    cut into ½-inch cubes
1   (5-ounce) jar pimiento-stuffed
    olives, drained
¾   cup (3 ounces) shredded sharp
    Cheddar cheese

• **Cook** first 5 ingredients in a Dutch oven, stirring until meat crumbles; drain well, and return meat mixture to Dutch oven.
• **Stir** in soup and next 5 ingredients.
• **Bring** to a boil over medium heat. Cover, reduce heat, and simmer 1 hour, stirring occasionally.

• **Cook** spaghetti according to package directions; drain.
• **Stir** spaghetti, cheese cubes, and olives into meat sauce. Spoon mixture into a lightly greased 11- x 7- x 1½-inch baking dish.
• **Cover** and bake at 325° for 20 minutes or until thoroughly heated. Sprinkle with ¾ cup shredded cheese, and bake, uncovered, 10 additional minutes. **Yield:** 6 to 8 servings.

Note: You can prepare Casserole Spaghetti ahead, omitting shredded cheese. Cover and chill 8 hours. Remove from refrigerator; let stand at room temperature 30 minutes. Cover and bake at 325° for 45 minutes or until thoroughly heated. Uncover and sprinkle with shredded cheese; bake 10 additional minutes.

QUICK CHICKEN AND PASTA

QUICK!

2   quarts water
½   teaspoon salt
4   ounces vermicelli, uncooked
¾   cup frozen English peas
⅓   cup Italian salad dressing
1   cup chopped cooked chicken
¼   teaspoon sweet red pepper
    flakes
2   tablespoons grated Parmesan
    cheese

• **Combine** water and salt in a large saucepan; bring to a boil. Add vermicelli and peas. Return to a boil; reduce heat, and cook 10 minutes. Drain and set aside.
• **Heat** salad dressing in saucepan. Add chopped chicken and red pepper flakes, and cook 2 minutes, stirring constantly. Add reserved pasta mixture, and cook until thoroughly heated. Sprinkle with Parmesan cheese, tossing mixture well. **Yield:** 2 servings.

Jennifer Shupe
Raleigh, North Carolina

*Bow Ties, Black Beans,
and Key Limes*

BOW TIES, BLACK BEANS, AND KEY LIMES
(pictured at left)

6 ounces bow tie pasta, uncooked
   (2½ cups)
4 cloves garlic, minced
2 tablespoons olive oil
⅓ cup fresh Key lime juice
¼ cup dry sherry
1 cup sliced green onions
½ pound plum tomatoes, peeled
   and chopped
1 (15-ounce) can black beans,
   rinsed and drained
½ teaspoon salt
¼ teaspoon freshly ground pepper
2 teaspoons grated Key lime rind
¼ cup chopped fresh flat-leaf
   parsley
Garnish: fresh flat-leaf parsley
   sprigs

• **Cook** pasta according to package directions; drain and keep warm.
• **Cook** garlic in oil in a skillet over medium-high heat, stirring constantly, 2 minutes or until tender. Add lime juice and sherry; cook over high heat 5 minutes or until reduced to ¼ cup.
• **Add** green onions and chopped tomato; cook over medium heat 5 to 8 minutes, stirring occasionally.
• **Stir** in beans and next 3 ingredients; pour over pasta, tossing to coat. Sprinkle with chopped parsley, and garnish, if desired. Serve immediately. **Yield:** 3 servings.

Mike Adams
Naples, Florida

PEPPERY PASTA

3 pounds ripe plum tomatoes,
   peeled and quartered
8 green onions, thinly sliced
8 cloves garlic, minced
1 tablespoon olive oil
2 small sweet banana peppers,
   thinly sliced
⅓ cup chopped fresh oregano or
   2 tablespoons dried oregano
¼ cup chopped fresh basil or 1½
   teaspoons dried basil
½ teaspoon sea or table salt
8 green onions, thinly sliced
3 yellow bell peppers, cut into thin
   strips
3 red or orange bell peppers, cut
   into thin strips
3 tablespoons chopped fresh or
   1 tablespoon dried oregano
1 tablespoon olive oil
10 to 12 crimini or button
   mushrooms, coarsely chopped
1 teaspoon sea or table salt
1 teaspoon dried crushed red
   pepper
1 (16-ounce) package mostaccioli
   pasta
8 ounces fontina or mozzarella
   cheese, shredded

• **Position** knife blade in food processor bowl; add one-third of tomato. Pulse 5 or 6 times or until finely chopped. Remove tomato from processor bowl, and set aside. Repeat procedure twice.
• **Cook** 8 green onions and garlic in 1 tablespoon olive oil in a large heavy saucepan, stirring constantly, 10 minutes or until tender.
• **Stir** in tomato, banana pepper, and next 3 ingredients.
• **Bring** mixture to a boil over medium heat, stirring constantly; reduce heat, and simmer, uncovered, 1 hour, stirring occasionally. Remove from heat; keep tomato mixture warm.
• **Cook** 8 green onions, bell pepper strips, and 3 tablespoons fresh oregano in 1 tablespoon olive oil in a large skillet over medium heat, stirring constantly, 12 to 15 minutes or until vegetables are crisp-tender. Add mushrooms, 1 teaspoon salt, and crushed red pepper; cook about 7 minutes or until mushrooms are tender, stirring often.

• **Cook** pasta according to package directions; drain and place on a large serving platter.
• **Pour** tomato mixture over pasta; spoon mushroom mixture over sauce, and sprinkle with shredded cheese. **Yield:** 8 servings.

Joelle Diorio
Orlando, Florida

ORZO PRIMAVERA
QUICK!

3 quarts water
1 teaspoon salt
2 cups orzo, uncooked
1 pound fresh asparagus, cut into
   1-inch pieces
3 cloves garlic, minced
½ cup chopped red bell pepper
1 tablespoon olive oil
1 teaspoon butter or margarine,
   melted
1 cup frozen English peas, thawed
½ cup chicken broth
1 teaspoon grated lemon rind
¼ teaspoon ground white pepper
½ cup freshly grated Parmesan
   cheese

• **Combine** water and salt in a large Dutch oven; bring to a boil. Add orzo, and cook 5 minutes. Add asparagus, and cook 4 minutes. Drain and set mixture aside in a large serving bowl.
• **Cook** garlic and red bell pepper in oil and butter in Dutch oven over medium heat, stirring constantly, 1 minute or until crisp-tender. Add peas; cook 1 minute, stirring constantly. Add chicken broth, lemon rind, and white pepper; bring to a boil, and cook 1 minute.
• **Add** vegetable mixture to orzo mixture, tossing well. Sprinkle with Parmesan cheese. Serve immediately. **Yield:** 6 to 8 servings.

Note: Orzo is a rice-shaped pasta.
Preserving Our Italian Heritage
Sons of Italy Florida Foundation of Tampa

PASTA POTPOURRI

QUICK!

4 ounces penne or rigatoni,
     uncooked
1 teaspoon sesame oil
1½ tablespoons olive oil
1½ tablespoons sesame oil
1 small purple onion, chopped
2 medium carrots, scraped and
     diagonally sliced
2 medium zucchini, halved
     lengthwise and sliced
2 cloves garlic, pressed
1½ teaspoons grated ginger
½ teaspoon dried crushed red
     pepper
2 tablespoons soy sauce
2 teaspoons rice wine vinegar
1 tablespoon freshly grated
     Parmesan cheese
2 teaspoons chopped fresh
     cilantro

• **Cook** pasta according to package directions; drain and toss with 1 teaspoon sesame oil. Set aside.
• **Pour** olive oil and 1½ tablespoons sesame oil around top of a preheated wok, coating sides; heat at medium-high (375°) 1 minute. Add onion and carrot; cook, stirring constantly, 2 minutes or until onion is tender.
• **Add** zucchini and next 3 ingredients; cook 1 minute, stirring constantly.
• **Stir** in cooked pasta, soy sauce, and vinegar; cook 1 minute or until thoroughly heated.
• **Transfer** to a serving dish; sprinkle with cheese and cilantro. **Yield:** 4 to 6 servings.

Note: To create a quick main dish, add leftover chopped cooked chicken, beef, or pork.

Nan Rasor
San Antonio, Texas

HOT BROWN PASTA CASSEROLES

QUICK!

8 ounces penne pasta, uncooked
     (2½ cups)
6 ounces sliced cooked ham, cut
     into ½-inch strips
6 ounces sliced smoked turkey,
     cut into ¼-inch strips
1 (10¾-ounce) can Cheddar
     cheese soup, undiluted
½ cup milk
¼ teaspoon pepper
8 slices tomato
8 slices bacon, cooked
¼ cup freshly grated Parmesan
     cheese

• **Cook** pasta according to package directions; drain. Combine pasta, ham, and turkey in a bowl.
• **Combine** soup, milk, and pepper; stir into pasta mixture. Spoon into four lightly greased individual baking dishes; top with tomato slices.
• **Bake** at 350° for 15 minutes. Top with bacon slices, sprinkle with cheese; bake 5 additional minutes or until thoroughly heated. Serve immediately. **Yield:** 4 servings.

Lillian Harris
Mayfield, Kentucky

BASIL-CHEESE PASTA

QUICK!

1 (12-ounce) package rotini
2 cloves garlic, minced
2 tablespoons olive oil
1 (3-ounce) package cream cheese,
     softened
½ cup cottage cheese
⅓ cup grated Parmesan cheese
½ cup dry white wine
½ cup chopped fresh basil

• **Cook** rotini according to package directions, and drain well. Set aside, and keep warm.
• **Cook** garlic in oil in a skillet over medium-high heat 1 minute, stirring constantly. Add cheeses; reduce heat and cook, stirring constantly, until blended.

• **Stir** in wine and basil; cook 3 minutes or until mixture is slightly thickened, stirring often. Spoon over rotini. **Yield:** 4 servings.

Betty Rabe
Plano, Texas

ZITI WITH SAUSAGE AND BROCCOLI

QUICK!

1 pound Italian link sausage
2 cloves garlic, crushed
½ teaspoon dried crushed red
     pepper
1 teaspoon olive oil
2 (14.5-ounce) cans diced
     tomatoes, undrained
8 ounces ziti pasta, uncooked
2 cups broccoli flowerets
½ cup freshly grated Romano or
     Parmesan cheese

• **Cut** sausage diagonally into ½-inch-thick slices. Cook sausage in a large nonstick skillet over medium-high heat until browned; remove sausage, and set aside. Wipe skillet with paper towels.
• **Cook** garlic and red pepper in oil in skillet, stirring constantly, until lightly browned; add tomatoes, and cook until thoroughly heated. Remove from heat; keep warm.
• **Cook** pasta according to package directions, adding broccoli during last 5 minutes of cooking time. Drain and toss gently with sausage mixture and cheese. Serve immediately. **Yield:** 3 servings.

Candace Reed
Dallas, Texas

SAUSAGE-STUFFED SHELLS

½ (12-ounce) package jumbo
     pasta shells (about 20)
1 pound mild Italian link
     sausage
1 large egg, lightly beaten
¾ cup Italian-seasoned
     breadcrumbs
1 (30-ounce) jar spaghetti
     sauce
¼ cup grated Parmesan cheese

- **Cook** pasta shells according to package directions; drain and set aside.
- **Remove** and discard casings from sausage. Brown sausage in a large skillet, stirring until it crumbles; drain.
- **Combine** sausage, egg, and breadcrumbs in skillet; set aside.
- **Spread** 1 cup spaghetti sauce in bottom of a lightly greased 13- x 9- x 2-inch baking dish. Spoon sausage mixture into shells, and place in baking dish. Pour remaining sauce over stuffed shells.
- **Cover** and bake at 350° for 15 minutes; sprinkle with Parmesan cheese, and bake, uncovered, 5 additional minutes or until thoroughly heated. **Yield:** 4 to 6 servings.

Note: To make ahead, store stuffed shells in the refrigerator, without sauce or cheese, at least 8 hours. Assemble shells and sauce in baking dish as directed, and let stand at room temperature 30 minutes. Cover and bake at 350° for 20 minutes; sprinkle evenly with Parmesan cheese, and bake, uncovered, 5 additional minutes or until thoroughly heated.

Christine Johnston
Bossier City, Louisiana

RAVIOLI WITH CREAMY PESTO SAUCE

QUICK!

1 cup whipping cream
1 (2.82-ounce) jar pesto
1 (3-ounce) jar capers, drained (optional)
2 (9-ounce) packages refrigerated cheese-filled ravioli, uncooked
2 tablespoons pine nuts, toasted

- **Combine** whipping cream and pesto in a saucepan; add capers, if desired. Cook over low heat until thoroughly heated, stirring often.
- **Cook** pasta according to package directions, and drain. Toss pasta with sauce, and sprinkle with toasted pine nuts. Serve immediately. **Yield:** 4 to 6 servings.

CREAMY MACARONI AND CHEESE

2 quarts water
1 teaspoon salt
1 (8-ounce) package elbow macaroni
4 cups (16 ounces) shredded Cheddar or Jarlsberg cheese
1 (8-ounce) carton sour cream
1 cup mayonnaise
2 tablespoons chopped onion
1 cup cheese crackers, crushed
Garnish: green onion fan

- **Bring** water and salt to a boil in a large Dutch oven; stir in macaroni. Return to a rapid boil, and cook 8 to 10 minutes or until tender; drain. Rinse with cold water; drain.
- **Combine** macaroni, cheese, and next 3 ingredients. Spoon into a lightly greased 11- x 7- x 1½-inch baking dish; sprinkle with crushed crackers.
- **Bake** at 325° for 30 to 35 minutes, and garnish, if desired. **Yield:** 6 to 8 servings.

♥ To reduce fat and calories, substitute nonfat sour cream, fat-free mayonnaise, and reduced-fat Cheddar cheese.

Nat Holland
Columbia, South Carolina

MUSHROOM-MACARONI CASSEROLE

2 quarts water
1 teaspoon salt
1 (8-ounce) package elbow macaroni
1 (10¾-ounce) can cream of mushroom soup, undiluted
1 cup mayonnaise
2 cups (8 ounces) shredded sharp Cheddar cheese
1 (4-ounce) can sliced mushrooms, drained
1 (2-ounce) jar diced pimiento, drained (optional)
¾ cup crushed round buttery crackers (about 15 crackers)
1 tablespoon butter, melted

- **Bring** water and salt to a boil in a large Dutch oven; stir in macaroni. Return to a rapid boil, and cook 8 to 10 minutes or until tender; drain. Rinse with cold water; drain.
- **Combine** macaroni, soup, and next 3 ingredients; add pimiento, if desired. Spoon into a lightly greased 2-quart casserole. Combine cracker crumbs and butter; sprinkle evenly over macaroni mixture.
- **Bake** at 300° for 30 minutes or until mixture is thoroughly heated. **Yield:** 6 to 8 servings.

Melba Edwards-Johnson
Sunset Beach, North Carolina

SAUSAGE AND NOODLE CASSEROLE

1 (8-ounce) package medium egg noodles
1 (16-ounce) package mild ground pork sausage
1 (10¾-ounce) can cream of chicken soup, undiluted
1 (8-ounce) carton sour cream
½ cup crumbled blue cheese
1 (4½-ounce) jar sliced mushrooms, drained
1 (2-ounce) jar diced pimiento, drained
2 tablespoons finely chopped green bell pepper
½ cup soft breadcrumbs
1 tablespoon butter or margarine, melted

- **Cook** noodles according to package directions; drain and set aside.
- **Brown** sausage in a large nonstick skillet, stirring until it crumbles; drain and set aside.
- **Combine** soup, sour cream, and blue cheese in a large saucepan; cook over medium heat, stirring constantly, until cheese melts.
- **Add** noodles, sausage, mushrooms, pimiento, and green pepper, tossing to coat. Spoon mixture into a lightly greased 11- x 7- x 1½-inch baking dish.
- **Combine** breadcrumbs and butter; sprinkle over casserole.
- **Bake** at 350° for 30 minutes. **Yield:** 6 servings.

Claudia Barnes
Birmingham, Alabama

VEGETABLE-NOODLE KUGEL

Traditionally, kugel is served as a side dish on the Jewish Sabbath. Our version adds carrot and zucchini to the baked pudding.

1 (8-ounce) package medium egg noodles
1 onion, chopped
2 carrots, scraped and coarsely shredded
1 zucchini, coarsely shredded
1 tablespoon vegetable oil
1 (16-ounce) carton sour cream
1 (12-ounce) carton cottage cheese
1 teaspoon dried rosemary, crushed
½ teaspoon salt
¾ teaspoon pepper
¼ cup grated Parmesan cheese

• **Cook** noodles according to package directions; drain.
• **Cook** onion, carrot, and zucchini in hot oil in a large skillet until tender; stir in noodles, sour cream, and next 4 ingredients. Spoon into a lightly greased 2-quart baking dish.
• **Cover** and bake at 350° for 25 minutes; sprinkle with Parmesan cheese, and bake, uncovered, 5 additional minutes. **Yield:** 6 to 8 servings.

LASAGNA SUPREME

12 lasagna noodles, uncooked
1 pound ground beef
1 small onion, chopped
1 clove garlic, minced
2 (6-ounce) cans tomato paste
1 (16-ounce) can whole tomatoes, undrained and chopped
1½ cups water
1 tablespoon dried basil
1 teaspoon salt
½ teaspoon dried rosemary
2 bay leaves
2 large eggs, lightly beaten
2 cups ricotta cheese
1 (8-ounce) carton sour cream
2 tablespoons dried parsley flakes or ¼ cup chopped fresh parsley
½ teaspoon salt
¼ teaspoon pepper
1 cup (4 ounces) shredded Cheddar cheese
½ cup grated Parmesan cheese
½ cup grated Romano cheese
2 (8-ounce) packages mozzarella cheese slices

• **Cook** lasagna noodles according to package directions. Drain well, and set aside.
• **Cook** ground beef, onion, and garlic in a large skillet over medium heat until meat is browned and onion is tender, stirring until meat crumbles. Drain well. Wipe pan drippings from skillet with a paper towel.
• **Combine** tomato paste and next 6 ingredients in skillet; return meat mixture to skillet. Bring mixture to a boil, stirring occasionally; reduce heat, and simmer, uncovered, 1 hour and 15 minutes, stirring often. Remove and discard bay leaves.
• **Combine** eggs and next 5 ingredients; set aside.
• **Arrange** 4 lasagna noodles in bottom of a lightly greased 13- x 9- x 2-inch baking dish. Layer with one-third each of meat mixture, egg mixture, and Cheddar, Parmesan, and Romano cheeses. Repeat layers twice.
• **Bake**, uncovered, at 375° for 30 to 35 minutes or until bubbly. Arrange mozzarella cheese slices over top of lasagna;

bake 5 additional minutes. Let stand 10 minutes. **Yield:** 8 to 10 servings.

Note: To freeze half of lasagna, prepare half of lasagna in an 8-inch square baking dish, and bake as directed above. Prepare remaining half of lasagna in an 8-inch square aluminum pan; freeze, unbaked, up to 2 months. To bake, thaw in refrigerator 24 hours; let stand at room temperature 30 minutes. Bake at 375° for 35 to 40 minutes; add mozzarella cheese slices, and bake 5 additional minutes.

Betty Beske
Arlington, Virginia

GOURMET WHITE LASAGNA

8 lasagna noodles, uncooked
1 pound ground beef
½ pound ground pork sausage
1 cup chopped onion
½ cup chopped celery
1 clove garlic, minced
2 teaspoons dried basil
1 teaspoon dried oregano
½ teaspoon dried Italian seasoning
½ teaspoon salt
1 cup half-and-half
1 (3-ounce) package cream cheese, softened
½ cup dry white wine
2 cups (8 ounces) shredded Cheddar cheese
1½ cups (6 ounces) shredded Gouda cheese
1 (12-ounce) carton small-curd cottage cheese
1 large egg, lightly beaten
2 cups (8 ounces) shredded mozzarella cheese

• **Cook** noodles according to package directions; drain and set aside.
• **Cook** ground beef and next 4 ingredients in a large skillet, stirring until meats crumble; drain. Stir in basil and next 5 ingredients. Stir in wine and Cheddar and Gouda cheeses; cook, stirring constantly, until cheeses melt. Set aside.
• **Combine** cottage cheese and egg; set aside.

• **Arrange** half of noodles in a lightly greased 13- x 9- x 2-inch baking dish; top with half each of meat mixture, cottage cheese mixture, and mozzarella cheese. Repeat layers with remaining meat mixture, cottage cheese mixture, and mozzarella cheese.

• **Bake**, uncovered, at 350° for 40 minutes; let stand 10 minutes before serving. **Yield:** 6 servings.

Mrs. Larry Coppernoll
Linden, North Carolina

MICROWAVE LASAGNA

QUICK!

1 pound ground beef
1 (28-ounce) jar spaghetti sauce
½ cup water
1½ cups cottage cheese
1 large egg, lightly beaten
1½ teaspoons pepper
8 lasagna noodles, uncooked
1 (10-ounce) package frozen chopped spinach, thawed
2 cups (8 ounces) shredded mozzarella cheese
½ cup grated Parmesan cheese

• **Crumble** beef in a 2-quart bowl. Microwave at HIGH 4 minutes or until browned, stirring once; drain. Stir in spaghetti sauce and water.

• **Combine** cottage cheese, egg, and pepper.

• **Spread** ½ cup meat sauce in a 13- x 9- x 2-inch baking dish. Top with half each of uncooked noodles, cottage cheese mixture, spinach, meat sauce, and mozzarella cheese. Repeat layers with remaining half of noodles, cottage cheese mixture, spinach, meat sauce, and mozzarella cheese; cover with heavy-duty plastic wrap.

• **Microwave** at HIGH 8 minutes; microwave at MEDIUM (50% power) 30 to 32 minutes or until noodles are tender, turning dish occasionally.

• **Sprinkle** with Parmesan cheese; cover and let stand 15 minutes before serving. **Yield:** 6 servings.

Queever Bronssard
New Iberia, Louisiana

CHICKEN LASAGNA FLORENTINE

6 lasagna noodles, uncooked
1 (10-ounce) package frozen chopped spinach, thawed
2 cups chopped cooked chicken
2 cups (8 ounces) shredded Cheddar cheese
⅓ cup finely chopped onion
¼ to ½ teaspoon freshly ground nutmeg
1 tablespoon cornstarch
½ teaspoon salt
¼ teaspoon pepper
1 tablespoon soy sauce
1 (10¾-ounce) can cream of mushroom soup, undiluted
1 (8-ounce) carton sour cream
1 (4.5-ounce) jar sliced mushrooms, drained
⅓ cup mayonnaise or salad dressing
1 cup freshly grated Parmesan cheese
Butter-Pecan Topping

• **Cook** noodles according to package directions; drain and set aside.

• **Drain** spinach well, pressing between layers of paper towels.

• **Combine** spinach, chicken, and next 11 ingredients in a large bowl; stir well.

• **Arrange** 2 noodles in a lightly greased 11- x 7- x 1½-inch baking dish. Spread half of chicken mixture over noodles. Repeat procedure with remaining noodles and chicken mixture. Sprinkle with Parmesan cheese and Butter-Pecan Topping.

• **Cover** and bake at 350° for 55 to 60 minutes or until hot and bubbly. Let stand 15 minutes before cutting. **Yield:** 8 servings.

Butter-Pecan Topping

QUICK!

2 tablespoons butter or margarine
1 cup chopped pecans

• **Melt** butter in a skillet over medium heat; add pecans, and cook 3 minutes. Cool completely. **Yield:** 1 cup.

CHICKEN LASAGNA

1 (8-ounce) package medium egg noodles
½ cup butter or margarine
½ cup all-purpose flour
1 teaspoon dried basil
1 teaspoon salt
½ teaspoon pepper
4 cups chicken broth
4 cups chopped cooked chicken
1 (24-ounce) carton cottage cheese
1 large egg, lightly beaten
2 cups (8 ounces) shredded mozzarella cheese
¾ cup freshly grated Parmesan cheese

• **Cook** noodles according to package directions; drain and set aside.

• **Melt** butter in a large saucepan over medium heat; stir in flour and next 3 ingredients. Cook 1 to 2 minutes, stirring constantly.

• **Add** chicken broth, stirring until smooth; bring to a boil. Reduce heat, and simmer 5 to 8 minutes or until mixture is thickened and bubbly. Stir in chicken, and remove from heat.

• **Combine** cottage cheese and egg in a bowl, stirring well.

• **Spoon** one-third chicken mixture into a lightly greased 13- x 9- x 2-inch baking dish. Top with half each of noodles, cottage cheese mixture, and mozzarella cheese. Repeat layers, ending with chicken mixture. Sprinkle with Parmesan cheese.

• **Bake** at 350° for 1 hour. **Yield:** 8 servings.

Yvonne M. Greer
Mauldin, South Carolina

CRABMEAT LASAGNA

6 lasagna noodles, uncooked
¼ cup butter or margarine
1 cup shredded carrot
½ cup finely chopped celery
½ cup finely chopped onion
⅓ cup chopped yellow bell pepper
⅓ cup chopped red bell pepper
3 cloves garlic, minced
1 teaspoon coriander seeds, crushed
1 (8-ounce) carton plain yogurt
¼ cup chopped fresh cilantro
¼ teaspoon salt
⅛ teaspoon ground white pepper
⅛ teaspoon ground nutmeg
1 pound fresh lump crabmeat
2 cups (8 ounces) shredded mozzarella cheese
2 cups (8 ounces) shredded process American cheese

● **Cook** noodles according to package directions; drain.
● **Melt** butter in a large skillet over medium-high heat; add carrot and next 6 ingredients. Cook 4 to 5 minutes or until vegetables are tender, stirring often.
● **Combine** yogurt and next 4 ingredients in a bowl; stir in vegetable mixture.
● **Drain** crabmeat, removing any bits of shell. Add to yogurt mixture, and toss.
● **Combine** shredded cheeses.
● **Arrange** 3 lasagna noodles in bottom of a lightly greased 13- x 9- x 2-inch baking dish; top with half of crabmeat mixture, and sprinkle with half of cheese mixture. Repeat layers with remaining noodles and crabmeat mixture.
● **Cover** and bake at 350° for 30 minutes or until thoroughly heated. Sprinkle with remaining cheese mixture, and bake, uncovered, 5 additional minutes. **Yield:** 6 servings.

Carolene and Richard Martinez
Natchez, Mississippi

VEGETABLE LASAGNA

Sunny serves any leftover slices of this garden-fresh favorite chilled. "It's even better the second day," she says.

10 lasagna noodles, uncooked
2 cups sliced fresh mushrooms
1 cup grated carrot (about 1 large)
½ cup chopped onion
1 tablespoon olive oil
1 (15-ounce) can tomato sauce
1 (12-ounce) can tomato paste
1 (4¼-ounce) can chopped ripe olives, drained
1 (4.5-ounce) can chopped green chiles, undrained
1½ teaspoons dried oregano
2 cups cottage cheese
1 (10-ounce) package frozen chopped spinach, thawed and well drained
4 cups (16 ounces) shredded Monterey Jack cheese
1 (3-ounce) package refrigerated grated Parmesan cheese

● **Cook** noodles according to package directions. Drain and set aside.
● **Cook** mushrooms, carrot, and onion in olive oil over medium-high heat, stirring constantly, until tender. Stir in tomato sauce and next 4 ingredients.
● **Place** half of cooked lasagna noodles in a greased 13- x 9- x 2-inch baking dish or pan. Layer with half each of cottage cheese, spinach, tomato sauce mixture, Monterey Jack cheese, and Parmesan cheese. Repeat layers.
● **Bake** at 375° for 45 minutes or until bubbly. Let stand 10 minutes before serving. **Yield:** 8 servings.

Sunny Tiedemann
Bartlesville, Oklahoma

LEMON COUSCOUS

QUICK!

1 tablespoon grated lemon rind
2 tablespoons fresh lemon juice
1 tablespoon butter or margarine
⅛ teaspoon salt
1 cup chicken broth
⅔ cup couscous, uncooked
2 tablespoons pecan pieces, toasted
2 tablespoons chopped fresh parsley
2 tablespoons finely chopped red bell pepper
Garnishes: fresh mint sprigs, lemon slices

● **Combine** first 5 ingredients in a saucepan; bring to a boil over medium-high heat. Add couscous, stirring well; cover, remove from heat, and let stand 10 minutes. Stir in pecans, parsley, and bell pepper. Garnish, if desired. **Yield:** 2 servings.

GARLIC AND HERB CHEESE GRITS

QUICK!

Serve this flavorful 10-minute side dish with grilled or broiled beef or chicken.

4 cups fat-free chicken broth
1 cup quick-cooking grits, uncooked
1 (5-ounce) package light garlic-and-herb soft, spreadable cheese
¼ teaspoon freshly ground pepper

● **Bring** broth to a boil in a medium saucepan over high heat; gradually stir in grits. Cook, stirring constantly, 5 to 7 minutes or until thickened.
● **Remove** from heat, and stir in cheese and pepper. Serve immediately. **Yield:** 5 cups.

♥ Per ¾-cup serving: Calories 161
Fat 4.1g   Cholesterol 12mg
Sodium 112mg

GRITS AND GREENS

If you don't have stone-ground grits on hand or can't find them at your grocery store, substitute regular grits.

1 cup whipping cream
4 cups chicken broth, divided
1 cup stone-ground grits,
      uncooked
¼ to ½ cup milk
1 pound fresh collard greens
¼ cup butter or margarine
1 to 1½ cups freshly grated
      Parmesan cheese
¼ to ½ teaspoon freshly ground
      pepper
Garnish: chopped cooked bacon or
      cubed cooked ham

• **Combine** whipping cream and 3 cups chicken broth in a large saucepan. Bring to a boil, and gradually stir in grits.
• **Cook** over medium heat until mixture returns to a boil; cover, reduce heat, and simmer 25 to 30 minutes, stirring often. Gradually add milk, if necessary, for desired consistency.
• **Remove** and discard stems and any discolored spots from greens. Wash greens thoroughly; drain and cut into ½-inch strips.
• **Combine** greens and remaining 1 cup chicken broth in a large skillet; bring to a boil. Cover, reduce heat, and simmer 5 minutes or until greens are tender. Drain and plunge into ice water to stop the cooking process. Drain well on paper towels.
• **Add** butter, cheese, and pepper to grits, stirring until butter and cheese melt. Stir in greens.
• **Cook**, stirring constantly, until thoroughly heated. Garnish, if desired. **Yield:** 6 to 8 servings.

Marion Sullivan
Charleston, South Carolina

CHEESE GRITS WITH GREEN CHILES

6 cups water
1½ cups quick-cooking grits,
      uncooked
2 teaspoons salt
1 teaspoon paprika
1 teaspoon ground red pepper
3 large eggs
4 cups (16 ounces) shredded sharp
      Cheddar cheese
1 (4.5-ounce) can chopped green
      chiles, undrained

• **Bring** water to a boil in a saucepan; stir in grits and salt. Return to a boil; cover, reduce heat, and simmer 10 minutes or until thickened, stirring often. Stir in paprika and ground red pepper.
• **Beat** eggs in a large bowl. Gradually stir about one-fourth of hot grits mixture into eggs; add to remaining hot grits mixture, stirring constantly.
• **Stir** in cheese and chiles; pour into a greased 11- x 7- x 1½-inch baking dish.
• **Bake** at 325° for 45 minutes or until set. Serve immediately, or spoon into 10 lightly greased (6-ounce) custard cups; cool. Invert onto a greased baking sheet; remove cups.
• **Bake** at 300° for 5 minutes or until heated. **Yield:** 8 to 10 servings.

Note: For grits with more fire, substitute 5 pickled jalapeño peppers, unseeded and chopped, for the green chiles. For milder grits, use ½ (4.5-ounce) can chopped green chiles, undrained.

Jean Andrews
Red Hot Peppers *(Macmillan)*

HOT TOMATO GRITS

2 slices bacon, chopped
2 (14½-ounce) cans chicken broth
½ teaspoon salt
1 cup quick-cooking grits, uncooked
2 large ripe tomatoes, peeled and
      chopped
2 tablespoons canned chopped
      green chiles
1 cup (4 ounces) shredded
      Cheddar cheese

• **Cook** bacon in a large heavy saucepan until crisp, reserving drippings in pan. Gradually add broth and salt, and bring to a boil.
• **Stir** in grits, tomato, and chiles; return to a boil, stirring often. Reduce heat; simmer 15 to 20 minutes, stirring often.
• **Stir** in cheese; cover and let stand 5 minutes. **Yield:** 6 servings.

Lucy S. Wheaton
Birmingham, Alabama

SKILLET POLENTA SQUARES

Serve this enhanced version of polenta as a first course or side dish.

2 cups water
2 cups chicken broth
1 cup white cornmeal
½ cup whipping cream
1 cup (4 ounces) shredded
      Monterey Jack cheese with
      peppers
White cornmeal
Vegetable oil
Salsa
Garnish: fresh cilantro sprigs

• **Bring** water and broth to a boil in a saucepan; gradually whisk in 1 cup cornmeal. Return to a boil; reduce heat, and cook 5 minutes, stirring constantly.
• **Add** whipping cream, and cook 20 minutes, stirring often. Stir in cheese.
• **Spoon** mixture into a lightly greased 9-inch square pan. Cover and chill at least 2 hours or until firm.
• **Cut** into 3-inch squares, and dredge in cornmeal.
• **Pour** oil to depth of ½ inch into a large heavy skillet. Fry polenta in hot oil over medium heat 2 minutes on each side or until golden. Drain on paper towels. Serve immediately with salsa. Garnish, if desired. **Yield:** 9 servings.

*Spoonbread Grits With Savory
Mushroom Sauce*

SPOONBREAD GRITS WITH SAVORY MUSHROOM SAUCE
(pictured at left)

1 (14½-ounce) can chicken broth
½ cup quick-cooking grits, uncooked
¼ cup butter or margarine
1 cup milk
1 cup buttermilk
3 large eggs, lightly beaten
1 cup yellow cornmeal
1 teaspoon baking powder
1 teaspoon salt
¼ teaspoon baking soda
⅛ teaspoon ground red pepper (optional)
Savory Mushroom Sauce
Garnish: fresh thyme sprigs

• **Bring** broth to a boil in a large saucepan; stir in grits. Reduce heat, and simmer 5 to 7 minutes or until thickened, stirring occasionally. Stir in butter and next 3 ingredients.
• **Combine** cornmeal and next 4 ingredients; stir into grits mixture. Pour mixture into a lightly greased 11- x 7- x 1½-inch baking dish.
• **Bake** at 425° for 45 minutes or until lightly browned. Cut into triangles, if desired, and serve with Savory Mushroom Sauce; garnish, if desired. **Yield:** 4 to 6 servings.

Savory Mushroom Sauce
QUICK!

2 tablespoons butter or margarine
3 (3½-ounce) packages fresh shiitake mushrooms, sliced
1 clove garlic, minced
2 tablespoons all-purpose flour
¼ cup dry white wine
1 cup chicken broth
½ teaspoon salt
¼ teaspoon pepper

• **Melt** butter in a skillet; add mushrooms and garlic, and cook until tender, stirring often. Remove mushrooms with a slotted spoon, reserving drippings in skillet.
• **Whisk** flour into reserved drippings until smooth. Cook, whisking constantly, until lightly browned. Gradually add wine and broth; cook over medium heat, whisking constantly, until thickened and bubbly. Stir in salt and pepper. Add mushrooms, and cook, stirring constantly, until thoroughly heated. **Yield:** 2 cups.

Mrs. Charles DeHaven
Owensboro, Kentucky

SOUTHWESTERN GRITS CAKES

4 cups water
1 teaspoon salt
1 cup quick-cooking grits, uncooked
½ cup chopped green onions
1 (4.5-ounce) can chopped green chiles, drained
2 tablespoons diced pimiento, drained
⅛ teaspoon hot sauce
2 tablespoons butter or margarine, divided
1 (15-ounce) can black beans, rinsed and drained
1 (8-ounce) jar picante sauce
1 medium tomato, seeded and chopped
2 tablespoons chopped fresh cilantro

• **Bring** water and salt to a boil in a medium saucepan. Stir in grits; return to a boil over medium heat, stirring constantly. Cover, reduce heat, and simmer 5 minutes. Remove from heat; stir in green onions and next 3 ingredients.
• **Pour** mixture into a buttered 9-inch square pan; cover and chill 3 hours or until firm. Invert pan to remove grits; cut grits into 4 squares. Cut each square into 2 triangles.
• **Heat** 1 tablespoon butter over medium heat; add 4 triangles, and cook 5 to 7 minutes on each side or until lightly browned. Gently transfer to a serving platter; keep warm. Repeat with remaining butter and triangles.
• **Combine** black beans and picante sauce in a small saucepan; cook over medium heat until thoroughly heated, stirring often. Spoon over grits cakes; sprinkle with chopped tomato and cilantro. Serve immediately. **Yield:** 4 servings.

Note: You can bake grits cakes (or triangles) at 350° for 7 minutes or broil 5½ inches from heat (with electric oven door partially opened) 7 minutes on 1 side. (Do not turn.)

Janice Elder
Charlotte, North Carolina

RICE WITH SPRING VEGETABLES

Substitute Swiss or Parmesan cheese for the fontina and Gruyère cheeses.

2 tablespoons unsalted butter
1 small onion, finely chopped
1 clove garlic, chopped
1½ cups Arborio rice, uncooked
½ cup 1-inch fresh asparagus pieces
½ cup small Sugar Snap peas
½ cup finely chopped leek
½ cup thinly sliced carrot
3 (14½-ounce) cans chicken or vegetable broth
1 teaspoon chopped fresh mint
2 ounces prosciutto or cooked ham, cut into thin strips
⅓ cup grated Parmesan cheese
½ cup (2 ounces) shredded fontina cheese
2 ounces grated Gruyère cheese
¼ teaspoon freshly ground pepper
Pinch of ground nutmeg
Garnishes: fresh flat-leaf parsley and thyme sprigs

• **Melt** butter in a large skillet over medium-low heat; add onion and garlic, and cook, stirring constantly, 10 minutes or until tender.
• **Stir** in rice and next 5 ingredients; cook over medium-high heat 25 minutes, stirring often.
• **Add** mint; cook 5 minutes or until liquid is absorbed and rice is tender, stirring often.
• **Stir** in prosciutto and next 5 ingredients; garnish, if desired. **Yield:** 3 main-dish servings or 6 appetizer servings.

Jerry Mauri
Baltimore International Culinary College
Baltimore, Maryland

SPANISH RICE

3 tablespoons vegetable oil
2 cups long-grain rice, uncooked
2 large green bell peppers,
     chopped
2 large celery stalks, chopped
2 medium onions, finely
     chopped
2 teaspoons cumin seeds,
     crushed
1 to 1½ teaspoons salt
½ teaspoon pepper
¼ teaspoon garlic powder
6 cups water
1 (8-ounce) can tomato sauce

• **Heat** oil over medium-high heat in a heavy Dutch oven; add rice and next 7 ingredients, and cook until rice is browned, stirring often.
• **Stir** in water and tomato sauce; bring to a boil. Reduce heat to medium; cover and cook 25 minutes or until rice is tender. **Yield:** 8 to 10 servings.

King Ranch
Kingsville, Texas

BAKED RICE

1 cup wild rice, uncooked
1½ cups brown rice, uncooked
1 tablespoon butter or margarine
1 (10½-ounce) can condensed
     beef broth
2½ to 3 cups water
3 tablespoons butter or margarine
1 (8-ounce) package mushrooms,
     sliced
2 carrots, scraped and finely
     chopped
1 bunch green onions, sliced
1 (8-ounce) can sliced water
     chestnuts, drained
¼ teaspoon salt
¼ cup dry white vermouth
     (optional)
2 tablespoons cold butter or
     margarine, cut into small
     pieces

• **Place** wild rice in a large bowl; add water to depth of 1 inch above rice. Cover and let stand at least 8 hours. Drain rice. Rinse and drain again.

• **Combine** wild rice, brown rice, 1 tablespoon butter, beef broth, and 2½ cups water in a large heavy saucepan.
• **Bring** to a boil; cover, reduce heat, and simmer about 45 minutes or until water is absorbed and rice is tender. (Add additional water to prevent sticking or burning, if necessary.)
• **Melt** 3 tablespoons butter in a large heavy skillet. Add mushrooms and next 3 ingredients; cook over medium heat until all liquid is absorbed (about 3 minutes), stirring often.
• **Stir** vegetables and salt into rice mixture, and spoon into a lightly greased 13- x 9- x 2-inch baking dish.
• **Drizzle** with vermouth, if desired, and dot with butter; cover.
• **Bake** at 350° for 40 minutes or until thoroughly heated. **Yield:** 12 servings.

Note: To make ahead, prepare casserole, omitting vermouth and butter. Cover and chill overnight. Remove from refrigerator, and let stand at room temperature 30 minutes. To serve, add vermouth, if desired, and butter, and bake at 350° for 50 minutes or until thoroughly heated. To prepare casserole without soaking wild rice, cook wild rice as directed on package.

PECAN-LEMON WILD RICE

3 cups chicken broth
1½ tablespoons lemon rind,
     divided
1 tablespoon fresh lemon juice
1 tablespoon butter or margarine
1 cup wild rice, uncooked
½ cup chopped pecans, toasted
¼ cup chopped fresh parsley
3 tablespoons chopped green
     onions

• **Combine** broth, 2¼ teaspoons lemon rind, lemon juice, and butter in a medium saucepan. Bring to a boil; stir in rice. Cover, reduce heat, and simmer 50 to 60 minutes or until liquid is absorbed and rice is tender. Stir in pecans, remaining 2¼ teaspoons lemon rind, parsley, and green onions. **Yield:** 4 to 6 servings.

Sandi Pichon
Slidell, Louisiana

WILD RICE CASSEROLE

2 (6-ounce) packages long-grain-
     and-wild rice mix
1 (8-ounce) jar process cheese
     spread
1 (8-ounce) can sliced water
     chestnuts, drained
1 (6-ounce) jar sliced mushrooms,
     drained
1 (2-ounce) jar diced pimiento,
     drained
1 (2.8-ounce) can French fried
     onions, crushed

• **Cook** rice mix according to package directions.
• **Stir** in cheese spread and next 3 ingredients. Spoon into a lightly greased 11- x 7- x 1½-inch baking dish.
• **Cover** and bake at 325° for 20 minutes; uncover and sprinkle with crushed onions.
• **Bake**, uncovered, 10 additional minutes. **Yield:** 8 servings.

June Smith
Covington, Georgia

MIAMI RICE

QUICK!

1⅓ cups orange juice
1½ cups water
1 (10-ounce) package yellow rice
1 cup chopped dates

• **Bring** orange juice and water to a boil in a saucepan; stir in rice.
• **Cover**, reduce heat, and simmer 25 minutes or until liquid is absorbed and rice is tender. Stir in chopped dates. **Yield:** 8 servings.

Nita and Harold Norman
Coral Gables, Florida

At right: *Spicy Blueberry Pie (page 238)*

PIES AND PASTRIES

APPLE-BOURBON PIE

"I started making desserts when I was 10 years old. My first was a yellow cake from a baking powder recipe booklet. My uncle wants that cake each year for our reunion. Now, my recipe inspiration comes from travels to bed-and-breakfast and country inns." – Eugenia

½ cup raisins
½ cup bourbon
3 pounds cooking apples
¾ cup sugar
2 tablespoons all-purpose flour
1 teaspoon ground cinnamon
¼ teaspoon salt
⅛ teaspoon ground nutmeg
½ cup chopped pecans or walnuts, toasted
1 (15-ounce) package refrigerated piecrusts
2 teaspoons apricot preserves, melted
1 tablespoon buttermilk
1 tablespoon sugar

• **Combine** raisins and bourbon, and let soak at least 2 hours.
• **Peel** apples, and cut into ½-inch slices; arrange apple slices in a steamer basket over boiling water. Cover and steam 10 minutes or until apple slices are tender.
• **Combine** ¾ cup sugar and next 4 ingredients in a large bowl; add apple slices, raisin mixture, and pecans, stirring to combine.
• **Fit** 1 piecrust into a 9-inch pieplate according to package directions; brush preserves over piecrust. Spoon apple mixture into piecrust.
• **Roll** remaining piecrust to press out fold lines; cut with a 3-inch leaf-shaped cutter. Mark veins on leaves with a pastry wheel or sharp knife. Arrange pastry leaves over apple mixture; brush leaves with buttermilk, and sprinkle pie with 1 tablespoon sugar.
• **Bake** at 450° on lower rack of oven 15 minutes. Shield edges of pie with strips of aluminum foil to prevent excessive browning. Reduce oven temperature to 350°, and bake 30 to 35 additional minutes. **Yield:** 1 (9-inch) pie.

Eugenia W. Bell
Lexington, Kentucky

MEXICAN APPLE PIE

1½ cups sugar
2 cups water
½ cup butter or margarine, melted
4 cups peeled, chopped Golden Delicious apples (about 1½ pounds)
2 teaspoons ground cinnamon
10 (6-inch) flour tortillas
Whipped cream
Ground cinnamon (optional)

• **Combine** sugar and water in a saucepan; cook over medium heat, stirring constantly, until sugar melts. Set aside.
• **Place** butter in a 13- x 9- x 2-inch baking dish; set aside.
• **Combine** apples and 2 teaspoons cinnamon, stirring to coat.
• **Place** about ½ cup apple mixture down center of each tortilla. Roll up, and place seam side down in baking dish. Pour sugar mixture over top of tortillas, and cover with aluminum foil.
• **Bake** at 350° for 30 minutes.
• **Uncover** and bake 25 to 30 minutes. Let stand 10 minutes. Serve warm with whipped cream; sprinkle with additional cinnamon, if desired. **Yield:** 10 servings.

Diane Dawson Martin
Summerville, Georgia

SPICY BLUEBERRY PIE
(pictured on page 237)

Discover the thrill of picking your own blueberries. Enjoy them by the handful or, even better, served under a hot, flaky crust in this easy-to-make pie.

¾ cup sugar
¼ cup firmly packed brown sugar
½ cup all-purpose flour
½ teaspoon ground cinnamon
¼ teaspoon ground allspice
5 cups fresh blueberries
1 tablespoon lemon juice
1 tablespoon butter or margarine, melted
1 (15-ounce) package refrigerated piecrusts
1 tablespoon milk
1 teaspoon sugar

• **Combine** first 8 ingredients, tossing gently.
• **Fit** 1 piecrust into a 9-inch pieplate according to package directions. Spoon blueberry mixture into pastry shell.
• **Roll** remaining piecrust to ⅛-inch thickness; cut into 6 (2½-inch-wide) strips. Arrange strips in a lattice design over filling; fold edges under, and crimp. Brush pastry with milk; sprinkle with 1 teaspoon sugar.
• **Bake** at 400° for 40 to 45 minutes or until golden, shielding edges with strips of aluminum foil during last 20 minutes of baking to prevent excessive browning. **Yield:** 1 (9-inch) pie.

Nan Ferguson
Atlanta, Georgia

LEMONY CHERRY PIE
(pictured at right)

2 (16-ounce) cans pitted tart red cherries, undrained
1 cup sugar
3 tablespoons cornstarch
2 tablespoons butter or margarine
1 tablespoon lemon juice
⅛ teaspoon red liquid food coloring (optional)
Pastry for double-crust 9-inch pie

• **Drain** cherries, reserving ½ cup juice. Set both aside.
• **Combine** sugar and cornstarch in a large saucepan; stir in reserved cherry juice. Cook over medium heat, stirring constantly, until mixture comes to a boil; boil 1 minute, stirring constantly. Remove from heat, and stir in cherries, butter, lemon juice, and, if desired, food coloring; cool.
• **Roll** half of pastry to ⅛-inch thickness on a lightly floured surface. Place in a 9-inch pieplate; trim off excess pastry along edges. Pour cherry mixture into pastry shell.
• **Roll** remaining pastry to ⅛-inch thickness; cut into ½-inch strips. Arrange in lattice design over cherries; trim strips even with edges. Make shaped cutouts with remaining pastry. Moisten edge of piecrust with water, and gently press cutouts around edges. Bake at 375° for 30 to 35 minutes. **Yield:** 1 (9-inch) pie.

Lemony Cherry Pie

CRANBERRY-PECAN PIE

1 (15-ounce) package refrigerated
   piecrusts
1 teaspoon all-purpose flour
3½ cups fresh or frozen
   cranberries, divided
½ cup raisins, divided
¾ cup chopped pecans
1½ cups sugar
3 tablespoons all-purpose flour
¼ cup light corn syrup
1 teaspoon grated orange rind
Garnish: fresh or frozen cranberries

• **Unfold** 1 piecrust, and press out fold lines; sprinkle with 1 teaspoon flour, spreading over surface. Place piecrust, floured side down, in a 9-inch pieplate; fold edges under, and flute. Set aside.
• **Roll** remaining piecrust to press out fold lines; cut with a 3¾-inch leaf-shaped cutter, and mark veins, using a pastry wheel or sharp knife. Drape leaves over small balls of aluminum foil on an ungreased baking sheet. Bake at 350° for 7 minutes; remove foil balls, and bake 3 additional minutes. Let cool.
• **Position** knife blade in food processor bowl, and add 1¾ cups cranberries and ¼ cup raisins. Pulse 5 or 6 times or until coarsely chopped, stopping once to scrape down sides. Transfer to a large bowl. Repeat procedure with remaining 1¾ cup cranberries and ¼ cup raisins.
• **Combine** cranberry mixture, pecans, and next 4 ingredients; spoon into pastry shell. Bake at 350° for 20 minutes; cover edges of pastry with strips of aluminum foil to prevent excessive browning, and bake 20 additional minutes. Let cool on a wire rack. Arrange pastry leaves around edges, and garnish, if desired. **Yield:** 1 (9-inch) pie.

KENTUCKY MINCEMEAT PIE

1 (23-ounce) can mincemeat pie
   filling
1 (8-ounce) can crushed
   pineapple, drained
2 cups sliced cooking apples
1 (15-ounce) package refrigerated
   piecrusts
1 tablespoon sugar

• **Combine** first 3 ingredients in a large bowl; set aside.
• **Fit** 1 piecrust into a 9-inch pieplate according to package directions. Spoon mincemeat mixture into piecrust.
• **Roll** remaining piecrust to press out fold lines; cut with a 3-inch leaf-shaped cutter. Mark veins on leaves with a pastry wheel or sharp knife. Arrange pastry leaves over mincemeat mixture; sprinkle pie with sugar.
• **Bake** at 425° for 30 to 32 minutes or until golden. Shield edges of pie with strips of aluminum foil after 12 minutes to prevent excessive browning. **Yield:** 1 (9-inch) pie.

Betty Lee Long
Chapel Hill, North Carolina

SPIRITED MINCE PIE

¾ cup raisins
3 tablespoons brandy *
1 (15-ounce) package refrigerated
   piecrusts
1 teaspoon all-purpose flour
1 (29-ounce) jar mincemeat
1 large cooking apple, cored and
   finely chopped
1 cup chopped walnuts
¼ cup firmly packed brown
   sugar
1 teaspoon grated lemon or orange
   rind
1 tablespoon fresh lemon juice

• **Combine** raisins and brandy in a large bowl; let stand 2 hours.
• **Unfold** 1 piecrust, and press out fold lines; sprinkle with flour, spreading over surface. Place piecrust, floured side down, in a 9-inch pieplate; fold edges under, and flute. Set aside.
• **Combine** raisin mixture, mincemeat, and remaining 5 ingredients; spoon into pastry shell.
• **Roll** remaining piecrust on a lightly floured surface to press out fold lines; cut with a 3¼-inch leaf-shaped cutter, and mark veins, using a pastry wheel or sharp knife. Roll pastry scraps into balls. Arrange leaves and balls on top of filling as desired.
• **Bake** at 375° for 10 minutes; cover edges with strips of aluminum foil to

prevent excessive browning, and bake 25 additional minutes. Cool on a wire rack. **Yield:** 1 (9-inch) pie.

* Substitute orange juice for brandy.
Robert W. Nolen
Falls Church, Virginia

ELIZABETH AND PHOEBE'S FRESH PEACH PIE
(pictured at right)

QUICK!

"Betty Edge was my college roommate. I named this pie after her daughters. Assemble it at the last minute so the crust will remain crisp," Marion advises.

¼ cup unsalted butter, softened
1 cup sifted powdered sugar
1 tablespoon brandy
1 baked 9-inch pastry shell
6 large fresh peaches, peeled and
   sliced
3 tablespoons fresh lemon
   juice
¼ cup sugar
1½ cups whipping cream
3 tablespoons sifted powdered
   sugar
1 teaspoon vanilla extract

• **Beat** butter at medium speed with an electric mixer until creamy; gradually add 1 cup powdered sugar and brandy, beating well. Spread in bottom of pastry shell; chill.
• **Combine** peaches, lemon juice, and ¼ cup sugar; cover and chill.
• **Beat** whipping cream at high speed with an electric mixer until foamy; gradually add 3 tablespoons powdered sugar and vanilla, beating until soft peaks form. Cover and chill.
• **Drain** peaches; arrange over butter mixture. Dollop whipped cream mixture over peaches; serve immediately. **Yield:** 1 (9-inch) pie.

Marion Sullivan
Charleston, South Carolina

*Elizabeth and Phoebe's
Fresh Peach Pie*

BACKYARD PEAR PIE

4 large pears, peeled, cored, and
    thinly sliced
¼ to ⅓ cup lemon juice
3 tablespoons butter or margarine
½ cup firmly packed brown sugar
½ cup sugar
1 teaspoon ground cinnamon
½ teaspoon salt
½ teaspoon ground nutmeg
2 tablespoons all-purpose flour
1 (15-ounce) package refrigerated
    piecrusts
1 teaspoon all-purpose flour

• **Combine** first 8 ingredients in a large
saucepan; cook over medium heat
about 12 minutes or until pears are tender, stirring occasionally.
• **Gradually** sprinkle in 2 tablespoons
flour, stirring constantly; cook, stirring
constantly, about 2 minutes or until
slightly thickened.
• **Unfold** 1 piecrust, and press out fold
lines; sprinkle with 1 teaspoon flour,
spreading over surface. Place piecrust,
floured side down, in a 9-inch pieplate;
spoon pear mixture into pastry shell.
• **Roll** remaining piecrust on a lightly
floured surface to press out fold lines;
place over pear mixture. Fold edges
under, and crimp. Cut slits in top crust
to allow steam to escape. Bake at 350°
for 45 minutes. **Yield:** 1 (9-inch) pie.

Chip Smith
Houston, Texas
and
Paul Frederick
Huntsville, Alabama

GINGER-PEAR PIE

1 unbaked 9-inch pastry shell
1 cup gingersnap crumbs
¼ cup firmly packed brown sugar
1 tablespoon all-purpose flour
½ teaspoon ground cinnamon
⅛ teaspoon salt
¼ cup butter or margarine,
    softened
5 medium pears, peeled, cored,
    and thinly sliced (about 2½
    pounds)
1 medium pear (optional)
1 tablespoon finely chopped
    pecans (optional)

• **Bake** pastry shell at 450° for 9 to 11
minutes; set aside.
• **Combine** gingersnap crumbs and next
5 ingredients. Layer half of pear slices in
pastry shell; sprinkle half of gingersnap
mixture over pears. Repeat procedure
with remaining pears and gingersnap
mixture. Cover loosely with aluminum
foil, and bake at 375° for 40 minutes. Uncover and bake 10 additional minutes, if
you do not plan to garnish.
• **To** garnish, peel optional pear; cut
in half, leaving stem intact in 1 half.
Remove core; thinly slice half of pear
with stem, cutting to, but not through,
stem end. Reserve half without stem for
other use. After baking pie 40 minutes,
fan and arrange pear half with stem
on pie; sprinkle with pecans. Bake, uncovered, 10 additional minutes. **Yield:** 1
(9-inch) pie.

LaJuan Coward
Jasper, Texas

PEAR-MACADAMIA PIE

Grated lemon rind adds a
subtle hint of citrus to the tender
pastry crust of this rich pie.

Hint-of-Citrus Pastry *
½ cup pear preserves
2 tablespoons Frangelico or other
    hazelnut-flavored liqueur
⅔ cup macadamia nuts
½ cup sugar
1½ tablespoons all-purpose flour
¼ cup butter or margarine,
    softened
1 large egg
2½ pounds ripe pears, peeled,
    cored, and thinly sliced

• **Prepare** pastry; set aside, and keep
pastry warm.
• **Combine** preserves and Frangelico in
a small heavy saucepan; cook over
medium heat, stirring constantly, until
warm. Pour mixture through a wire-
mesh strainer into a small bowl, discarding solids. Gently brush a thin layer
of glaze over warm pastry, reserving remaining glaze.
• **Position** knife blade in food processor bowl; add nuts, sugar, and flour.
Process until ground. Add butter and
egg; process until smooth. Spread mixture evenly over pastry, and freeze 15
minutes.
• **Arrange** pear slices over nut mixture;
bake at 350° for 30 minutes. Cover
loosely with aluminum foil, and bake 40
additional minutes or until pears are
tender and golden. Remove from oven;
immediately brush pears with reserved
glaze. Cool. **Yield:** 1 (10-inch) pie.

Hint-of-Citrus Pastry

1½ cups all-purpose flour
¼ cup sugar
1 teaspoon grated lemon rind
⅛ teaspoon salt
3 tablespoons butter
3 tablespoons shortening
6 to 7 tablespoons cold water

• **Combine** first 4 ingredients in a bowl;
cut in butter and shortening with pastry
blender until mixture is crumbly. Sprinkle cold water, 1 tablespoon at a time,

evenly over surface; stir with a fork until dry ingredients are moistened. Shape into a ball; cover and chill.

• **Roll** pastry to ⅛-inch thickness on a lightly floured surface. Gently place in a 10-inch pieplate; trim off excess pastry along edges. Fold edges under, and crimp; bake at 350° for 5 minutes. **Yield:** 1 (10-inch) pastry shell.

* Substitute ½ of a 15-ounce package refrigerated piecrusts, if desired. Unfold 1 piecrust, and lightly roll to fit a 10-inch pieplate. Sprinkle with 1 teaspoon flour, spreading over surface. Place piecrust, floured side down, in a 10-inch pieplate; fold edges under, and crimp. Bake piecrust as directed.

Men's Gourmet
Raleigh, North Carolina

MAMA'S PUMPKIN PIE

Mary, who shared this recipe, usually makes pastry from scratch, but we give you the easy way out here with refrigerated piecrusts. We use them a lot in our own homes.

½ (15-ounce) package
   refrigerated piecrusts
1¾ cups canned pumpkin
1¾ cups sweetened condensed
   milk
2 large eggs, lightly beaten
⅔ cup firmly packed light brown
   sugar
2 tablespoons sugar
1¼ teaspoons ground cinnamon
½ teaspoon salt
½ teaspoon ground ginger
½ teaspoon ground nutmeg
¼ teaspoon ground cloves

• **Fit** piecrust into a 9-inch pieplate according to package directions; fold edges under, and crimp.
• **Combine** pumpkin and remaining 9 ingredients in a large bowl; beat at medium speed with an electric mixer 2 minutes. Pour pumpkin mixture into prepared piecrust.
• **Bake** at 425° for 15 minutes. Reduce oven temperature to 350°; bake 50 additional minutes or until a knife inserted

in center comes out clean. Cool on a wire rack. **Yield:** 1 (9-inch) pie.

Note: You should always store pumpkin pie in the refrigerator.

Mary White
Birmingham, Alabama

SWEET POTATO PIE

Serve this pie chilled with low-fat vanilla ice cream for a cooling dessert.

1 (14½-ounce) can mashed sweet
   potatoes
¾ cup milk
¾ cup firmly packed brown
   sugar
2 large eggs
1 tablespoon butter or margarine,
   melted
½ teaspoon salt
½ teaspoon ground cinnamon
1 unbaked 9-inch pastry shell

• **Combine** all ingredients except pastry shell in container of an electric blender; process until smooth, stopping once to scrape down sides. Pour into pastry shell.
• **Bake** at 400° for 10 minutes. Reduce oven temperature to 350°, and bake 35 additional minutes or until a knife inserted in center comes out clean, shielding edges with aluminum foil after 20 minutes to prevent excessive browning. **Yield:** 1 (9-inch) pie.

Jerry Mauri
Baltimore International Culinary College
Baltimore, Maryland

PINEAPPLE-GRITS PIE

If you think grits are only for breakfast or as a receptacle for redeye gravy, this recipe will make you think again.

2 cups water
½ cup quick-cooking grits,
   uncooked
¼ teaspoon salt
1 (8-ounce) can crushed
   pineapple, drained
½ (8-ounce) package cream
   cheese, softened
3 large eggs
1 cup sugar
½ cup milk
¼ teaspoon vanilla extract
2 (9-inch) graham cracker
   crusts

• **Bring** water to a boil in a saucepan; add grits and salt, and return to a boil. Cover, reduce heat to low, and cook 5 minutes, stirring occasionally. Remove from heat.
• **Combine** grits, crushed pineapple, and cream cheese in container of an electric blender, and process until smooth, stopping once to scrape down sides. With blender running, add eggs, one at a time.
• **Add** sugar, milk, and vanilla, and process until smooth, stopping once to scrape down sides. Pour pineapple mixture evenly into crusts.
• **Bake** at 300° for 1 hour or until mixture is set; cool on a wire rack. **Yield:** 2 (9-inch) pies.

Pineapple-Coconut Chess Pie

PINEAPPLE-COCONUT CHESS PIE
(pictured at left)

1½ cups sugar
3 tablespoons cornmeal
2 tablespoons all-purpose flour
¼ teaspoon salt
4 large eggs, lightly beaten
1 teaspoon vanilla extract
¼ cup butter or margarine, melted
1 (15¼-ounce) can crushed pineapple, well drained
1 (3½-ounce) can flaked coconut
1 unbaked 9-inch pastry shell

● **Combine** first 4 ingredients in a large bowl; add eggs and vanilla, stirring until blended. Stir in butter, pineapple, and coconut; pour into unbaked pastry shell.
● **Bake** at 350° for 1 hour or until set, covering with aluminum foil after 40 minutes to prevent excessive browning. Cool pie on a wire rack. **Yield:** 1 (9-inch) pie.

Joy Knight Allard
San Antonio, Texas

CHOCOLATE-PECAN CHESS PIE

1¼ cups sugar
¼ cup cocoa
1 tablespoon all-purpose flour
1 tablespoon cornmeal
Pinch of salt
¾ cup chopped pecans
4 large eggs, lightly beaten
½ cup milk
1 tablespoon vanilla extract
1 unbaked 9-inch deep-dish pastry shell

● **Combine** first 5 ingredients in a medium bowl; stir in pecans.
● **Combine** eggs, milk, and vanilla, and stir into sugar mixture; pour into pastry shell.
● **Bake** at 350° for 45 minutes or until set. Cool on a wire rack. **Yield:** 1 (9-inch) pie.

Nuttin' 'Cept Pecan Pies
Charles Wallace
Austin, Texas

LEMON-PECAN PIE

1 unbaked 9-inch deep-dish pastry shell
4 large eggs, lightly beaten
6 tablespoons butter or margarine, softened
1 cup light corn syrup
½ cup firmly packed brown sugar
2 teaspoons grated lemon rind
¼ cup lemon juice
3 tablespoons all-purpose flour
1¼ cups coarsely chopped pecans
Whipped cream

● **Bake** pastry shell at 450° for 5 to 7 minutes. Remove from oven, and let cool completely.
● **Combine** eggs and next 6 ingredients; stir in pecans, and pour into prepared crust.
● **Bake** at 350° for 40 minutes, shielding edges with strips of aluminum foil after 25 minutes to prevent excessive browning. Cool on a wire rack. Serve with whipped cream. **Yield:** 1 (9-inch) pie.

Nuttin' 'Cept Pecan Pies
Charles Wallace
Austin, Texas

OLD PECAN STREET SPECIAL

4 large eggs, lightly beaten
1 cup light corn syrup
⅔ cup sugar
3 tablespoons butter or margarine, melted
1 tablespoon vanilla extract
1½ cups coarsely chopped pecans
1 unbaked 9-inch deep-dish pastry shell

● **Combine** first 5 ingredients; stir in chopped pecans, and pour into pastry shell.
● **Bake** at 350° for 50 to 55 minutes. Let pie cool on a wire rack. **Yield:** 1 (9-inch) pie.

Nuttin' 'Cept Pecan Pies
Charles Wallace
Austin, Texas

BUTTERMILK-COCONUT PIE

3 large eggs, lightly beaten
1½ cups sugar
½ cup flaked coconut
½ cup buttermilk
½ cup butter or margarine, melted
2 tablespoons all-purpose flour
1 teaspoon vanilla extract
1 unbaked 9-inch deep-dish pastry shell

● **Combine** first 7 ingredients; pour into pastry shell.
● **Bake** at 350° for 45 minutes; shield with aluminum foil after 25 minutes to prevent excessive browning, if necessary. **Yield:** 1 (9-inch) pie.

Barbara and Tommy Glenn
Huntsville, Alabama

MAGNOLIA PIE

This go-with-everything buttermilk pie is sure to please. If desired, top with your favorite fresh berries.

1½ cups sugar
¼ cup all-purpose flour
⅓ cup butter or margarine, softened
3 large eggs
1 cup buttermilk
1 teaspoon vanilla extract
½ teaspoon lemon extract
1 unbaked 9-inch pastry shell
Garnishes: whipped cream, lemon slices

● **Combine** first 3 ingredients; beat at medium speed with an electric mixer until blended. Add eggs, buttermilk, and flavorings. Beat at low speed until blended. Pour into pastry shell.
● **Bake** at 325° for 1 hour or until a knife inserted in center comes out clean. Cool on a wire rack. Garnish, if desired. **Yield:** 1 (9-inch) pie.

Mrs. H. W. Walker
Richmond, Virginia

QUICK 'N' EASY CUSTARD PIE

QUICK!

2 cups milk
3 large eggs
½ cup sugar
¾ teaspoon vanilla extract
¼ teaspoon freshly grated
    nutmeg
Dash of salt
1 unbaked 9-inch pastry shell
Freshly grated nutmeg

● **Heat** milk in a medium saucepan until hot. (Do not boil.)
● **Combine** eggs and sugar; beat at high speed with an electric mixer until thickened. Add vanilla, ¼ teaspoon nutmeg, and salt; beat until blended. Gradually stir in hot milk, stirring constantly. Pour into pastry shell; sprinkle with additional nutmeg.
● **Bake** on lower rack of oven at 400° for 25 minutes or until a knife inserted in center of pie comes out clean. Cool completely on a wire rack; cover and chill at least 2 hours before serving. **Yield:** 1 (9-inch) pie.

Claudine M. Moore
Lenoir, North Carolina

WEIDMANN'S BLACK BOTTOM PIE

1½ cups gingersnap crumbs
    (about 26 cookies)
⅓ cup butter or margarine,
    melted
½ cup sugar
¼ cup cornstarch
2 cups milk
4 large egg yolks, beaten
1 teaspoon vanilla extract
1 (1-ounce) square unsweetened
    chocolate
1 envelope unflavored gelatin
2 tablespoons cold water
1 tablespoon meringue powder
¼ cup cold water
½ cup sugar, divided
2 tablespoons bourbon
¾ cup whipping cream,
    whipped
Grated unsweetened chocolate

● **Combine** gingersnap crumbs and butter, and press mixture in bottom and up sides of a 9-inch pieplate.
● **Bake** at 375° for 6 to 8 minutes; cool completely.
● **Combine** ½ cup sugar, cornstarch, and milk in a heavy saucepan. Cook over medium heat, stirring constantly, 8 to 10 minutes or until mixture thickens and boils. Boil 1 minute, stirring constantly. Remove from heat.
● **Stir** about one-fourth of hot mixture gradually into yolks; add to remaining hot mixture, stirring constantly. Stir in vanilla.
● **Melt** chocolate in a small heavy saucepan over low heat, stirring often; set aside.
● **Sprinkle** gelatin over 2 tablespoons cold water; let stand 1 minute. Add gelatin to milk mixture in saucepan. Cook over low heat, stirring until gelatin dissolves (about 2 minutes).
● **Add** 1 cup milk mixture to melted chocolate, stirring with a wire whisk until smooth. Spread over crust. Cool remaining milk mixture.
● **Beat** meringue powder, ¼ cup cold water, and 2 tablespoons sugar at high speed with an electric mixer 5 minutes. Gradually add remaining 6 tablespoons sugar, beating until stiff peaks form (about 3 minutes).
● **Fold** remaining milk mixture and bourbon into meringue mixture; spread over chocolate mixture in crust. Cover and chill pie at least 4 hours.
● **Spread** whipped cream over pie; sprinkle with grated chocolate. **Yield:** 1 (9-inch) pie.

Weidmann's Restaurant
Meridian, Mississippi

CHOCOLATE CREAM PIE

1¼ cups sugar
½ cup all-purpose flour
¼ cup cocoa
Dash of salt
4 egg yolks
2 cups milk
¼ cup butter or margarine
1 teaspoon vanilla extract
1 baked 9-inch pastry shell
Meringue

● **Combine** first 4 ingredients in a large heavy saucepan; set aside.
● **Combine** egg yolks and milk; stir into sugar mixture. Add butter.
● **Cook** over medium heat, stirring constantly, until mixture thickens and boils. Remove from heat. Stir in vanilla. Spoon into pastry shell.
● **Spread** Meringue over hot filling, sealing to edge of pastry.
● **Bake** at 325° for 25 to 28 minutes. **Yield:** 1 (9-inch) pie.

Maryanne I. Kachelhofer
Birmingham, Alabama

Meringue

QUICK!

4 to 6 egg whites
½ to ¾ teaspoon cream of tartar
½ cup sugar
½ teaspoon vanilla extract

● **Beat** egg whites and cream of tartar at high speed with an electric mixer just until foamy.
● **Gradually** add sugar, 1 tablespoon at a time, beating until stiff peaks form and sugar dissolves (2 to 4 minutes). Add vanilla, beating well. **Yield:** enough for 1 (9-inch) pie.

CHOCOLATE-BANANA-PECAN CREAM PIE

¼ cup butter or margarine,
    softened
1 (3-ounce) package cream cheese,
    softened
1½ cups sifted powdered sugar
¼ cup whipping cream
½ teaspoon vanilla extract
3 bananas, sliced
1 (6-ounce) can pineapple juice
1 baked 9-inch pastry shell
½ cup chopped pecans, toasted
2 (1-ounce) squares semisweet
    chocolate
1 cup whipping cream
3 tablespoons powdered sugar

● **Beat** butter and cream cheese at medium speed with an electric mixer until creamy; gradually add 1½ cups powdered sugar alternately with ¼ cup whipping cream, beginning and ending with powdered sugar. Stir in vanilla. Set filling aside.

• **Toss** banana slices in pineapple juice; drain. Pat slices dry with paper towels.

• **Spoon** half of filling into pastry shell. Arrange banana slices over top of filling. Top with remaining filling, and sprinkle with pecans. Set pie aside.

• **Melt** chocolate in a heavy saucepan over low heat. Spoon into a small heavy-duty, zip-top plastic bag. Snip a tiny hole in one corner of bag; drizzle melted chocolate over pecans and filling. Set aside.

• **Beat** 1 cup whipping cream at low speed with an electric mixer until foamy; gradually add 3 tablespoons powdered sugar, beating until soft peaks form.

• **Spoon** whipped cream into a large heavy-duty, zip-top plastic bag. Snip ½ inch from corner of bag. Pipe dollops around outside edge of pie. **Yield:** 1 (9-inch) pie.

Joel Allard
San Antonio, Texas

WHITE CHOCOLATE-BANANA CREAM PIE

1 (4-ounce) bar white chocolate, finely chopped and divided *
1 cup milk
½ vanilla bean
3 tablespoons sugar
2 tablespoons cornstarch
3 egg yolks
1 tablespoon butter or margarine
2 tablespoons white crème de cacao
2 tablespoons crème de bananes
1 cup whipping cream
2 to 3 bananas, sliced
3 tablespoons lemon juice
1 baked 9-inch pastry shell
Cocoa
Garnish: strawberry fan

• **Place** half of white chocolate in top of a double boiler; place over boiling water. Cook until chocolate melts, stirring often. Pour onto an aluminum foil-lined baking sheet. Let stand at room temperature until chocolate cools and

feels slightly tacky but is not firm. (If chocolate is too hard, curls will break; if too soft, chocolate will not curl.) Pull a cheese plane across chocolate until curl forms. Repeat until chocolate is curled. Chill curls.

• **Combine** milk and vanilla bean in a small saucepan; bring to a boil. Remove and discard vanilla bean. Set hot milk aside.

• **Combine** sugar, cornstarch, and egg yolks in a heavy saucepan; gradually stir in hot milk.

• **Cook** over medium heat, stirring constantly, until mixture comes to a boil. Boil 1 minute. Remove from heat. Add butter and remaining half of white chocolate, stirring until chocolate melts. Place plastic wrap directly over surface of white chocolate mixture, and let cool completely.

• **Add** liqueurs to white chocolate mixture, stirring until smooth.

• **Beat** whipping cream until soft peaks form, and fold gently into white chocolate mixture.

• **Coat** banana slices with lemon juice; drain. Pat banana slices dry with paper towels. Gently stir into white chocolate mixture. Spoon into pastry shell. Top with white chocolate curls, and dust lightly with cocoa. Garnish, if desired. **Yield:** 1 (9-inch) pie.

* For white chocolate, we use Ghiradelli Classic White Confection.

COFFEE CREAM PIE
(pictured on page 249)

¼ cup butter or margarine
⅔ cup semisweet chocolate morsels
1⅓ cups graham cracker crumbs
½ cup sugar
3 tablespoons cornstarch
1 teaspoon instant coffee granules
¼ cup boiling water
1¼ cups milk
5 egg yolks, lightly beaten
1¾ cups whipping cream
¼ cup sifted powdered sugar
Garnish: chocolate-covered coffee beans

• **Melt** butter and chocolate morsels in a heavy saucepan over low heat. Stir in graham cracker crumbs. Firmly press into a lightly greased 9-inch pieplate. Bake at 375° for 8 minutes. Cool completely on a wire rack.

• **Combine** ½ cup sugar and cornstarch in a large heavy saucepan; set sugar mixture aside.

• **Combine** coffee granules and boiling water, stirring until coffee granules dissolve. Gradually stir coffee, milk, and egg yolks into sugar mixture.

• **Cook** over medium heat, stirring constantly, until mixture thickens and boils. Boil 1 minute, stirring constantly. Remove from heat; whisk until smooth. Place plastic wrap directly on surface of mixture; chill 1 hour.

• **Beat** whipping cream at low speed with an electric mixer until foamy; gradually add powdered sugar, beating until soft peaks form.

• **Fold** 1½ cups whipped cream into coffee mixture, reserving remaining whipped cream for topping. Spoon filling into prepared crust.

• **Pipe** or dollop remaining cream on top of pie. Chill up to 8 hours. Garnish, if desired. **Yield:** 1 (9-inch) pie.

Agnes L. Stone
Ocala, Florida

RASPBERRY CREAM PIE
(pictured on opposite page)

1 cup sugar
⅓ cup all-purpose flour
2 large eggs, lightly beaten
1⅓ cups sour cream
1 teaspoon vanilla extract
3 cups fresh raspberries
1 unbaked 9-inch pastry shell
⅓ cup all-purpose flour
⅓ cup firmly packed brown
      sugar
⅓ cup chopped pecans
3 tablespoons butter, softened
Garnishes: whipped cream, fresh
      raspberries

• **Combine** first 5 ingredients in a large bowl, stirring until smooth. Gradually fold in raspberries. Spoon into pastry shell.
• **Bake** at 400° for 30 to 35 minutes or until a knife inserted in center comes out clean.
• **Combine** ⅓ cup flour and next 3 ingredients; sprinkle over hot pie.
• **Bake** at 400° for 10 minutes or until golden. Garnish, if desired. **Yield:** 1 (9-inch) pie.

Nell Hamm
Louisville, Mississippi

Note: Do not substitute frozen raspberries for fresh in this pie.

CARAMEL PIE

This recipe is so easy and wildly delicious. If you don't own a 1-quart electric slow cooker, borrow one and make this recipe. But don't try this in a 4- or 5-quart electric slow cooker – the caramel might burn.

2 (14-ounce) cans sweetened
      condensed milk
1 (9-inch) graham cracker crust
1 (8-ounce) container frozen
      whipped topping, thawed
1 (1.4-ounce) English toffee candy
      bar, coarsely chopped

• **Pour** condensed milk into a 1-quart electric slow cooker.

• **Cover** and cook 6 to 7 hours or until mixture is the color of peanut butter, stirring mixture with a wire whisk every 30 minutes.
• **Pour** into graham cracker crust; cool. Spread whipped topping over top, and sprinkle with chopped candy bar. Cover and chill. **Yield:** 1 (9-inch) pie.

♥ To reduce fat and calories, substitute 2 (14-ounce) cans nonfat sweetened condensed milk for regular.

Note: A 1-quart slow cooker has no LOW or HIGH setting, only OFF or ON setting.

Marla Highbaugh
Louisville, Kentucky

COFFEE PIE

Make-ahead tip: This pie holds up well in the refrigerator overnight. Top it with dollops of whipped cream an hour before serving, and keep chilled until guests arrive.

1 cup water
1 tablespoon instant coffee
      granules
1 tablespoon butter or margarine
30 large marshmallows, cut into
      fourths
1 cup whipping cream, whipped
1 baked 9-inch pastry shell
½ cup chopped walnuts or pecans,
      toasted
Garnishes: whipped cream,
      chocolate-covered coffee
      beans

• **Bring** water to a boil in a heavy saucepan; add coffee granules, stirring to dissolve. Add butter and marshmallows to pan.
• **Cook** over low heat until marshmallows melt, stirring occasionally. Cool completely.
• **Fold** whipped cream into coffee mixture; spoon into pastry shell. Sprinkle evenly with walnuts. Cover and chill at least 8 hours. Garnish, if desired. **Yield:** 1 (9-inch) pie.

Jodie McCoy
Tulsa, Oklahoma

BEST-EVER LEMON MERINGUE PIE
(pictured at right)

1½ cups sugar
½ cup cornstarch
⅛ teaspoon salt
4 egg yolks
1¾ cups water
½ cup fresh lemon juice
3 tablespoons butter or margarine
1 teaspoon grated lemon rind
1 baked 9-inch pastry shell
Meringue (see recipe on page 246)

• **Combine** first 3 ingredients in a large heavy saucepan; set sugar mixture aside.
• **Combine** egg yolks, water, and juice; stir into sugar mixture. Cook over medium heat, stirring constantly, until mixture thickens and boils. Boil 1 minute, stirring constantly. Remove from heat. Stir in butter and lemon rind. Spoon into pastry shell.
• **Spread** Meringue over hot filling, sealing to edge of pastry.
• **Bake** at 325° for 25 to 28 minutes. **Yield:** 1 (9-inch) pie.

Anne Galbraith
Knoxville, Tennessee

Note: This pie is very firm with a bright yellow color. If you prefer a less firm pie with a more translucent color, substitute ⅓ cup cornstarch for ½ cup cornstarch, and cook as directed.

*Best-Ever Lemon Meringue Pie;
Coffee Cream Pie, page 247;
Raspberry Cream Pie*

MANNY AND ISA'S KEY LIME PIE

½ (15-ounce) package
   refrigerated piecrusts
1 teaspoon all-purpose flour
5 large eggs, separated
1 (14-ounce) can sweetened
   condensed milk
½ cup fresh or bottled Key lime
   juice
¼ teaspoon cream of tartar
⅓ to ½ cup sugar

• **Unfold** piecrust, and press out fold lines; sprinkle with flour, spreading over surface. Place crust, floured side down, in a 9-inch pieplate; fold edges under, and flute. Prick bottom and sides of piecrust generously with fork.
• **Bake** at 450° for 9 to 11 minutes; cool on a wire rack.
• **Combine** yolks, condensed milk, and lime juice in a heavy nonaluminum saucepan. Cook over low heat, stirring constantly, 10 minutes or until mixture thickens and boils. Pour into piecrust.
• **Beat** egg whites and cream of tartar at high speed with an electric mixer until foamy. Gradually add sugar, 1 tablespoon at a time, beating until stiff peaks form and sugar dissolves (about 2 to 4 minutes).
• **Spread** meringue over warm filling, sealing to edge of pastry.
• **Bake** at 325° for 25 to 28 minutes. **Yield:** 1 (9-inch) pie.

Manny and Isa Oritz
Manny and Isa's
Islamorada, Florida

KEY LIME PIE

Morgan's idea of an excellent evening is joining friends for a meal that's finished with this refreshing Floridian dessert.

1¾ cups graham cracker crumbs
2 tablespoons sugar
6 tablespoons butter, melted
3 large eggs, separated
1 (14-ounce) can sweetened
   condensed milk
½ cup fresh Key lime juice *
1 tablespoon lemon juice
2 teaspoons grated Key lime rind *
2 tablespoons sugar
1 cup whipping cream
1 tablespoon powdered sugar
½ teaspoon vanilla extract
Garnish: quartered lime slices

• **Combine** first 3 ingredients; press in bottom and 1 inch up sides of a 9-inch springform pan. Cover and chill at least 1 hour.
• **Whisk** egg yolks; add condensed milk and next 3 ingredients, whisking until smooth.
• **Beat** egg whites at high speed until foamy; gradually add 2 tablespoons sugar, beating until soft peaks form. Fold into yolk mixture; spoon into prepared crust.
• **Bake** at 325° for 15 to 20 minutes or until set and lightly browned. Cool on a wire rack; cover and chill 8 hours.
• **Beat** whipping cream at high speed until slightly thickened; add powdered sugar and vanilla, beating until soft peaks form.
• **Remove** sides of springform pan; dollop whipped cream around top of pie. Garnish, if desired. **Yield:** 1 (9-inch) pie.

* You can substitute regular (Persian) lime juice and lime rind for the Key lime variety.

Morgan Reeser
Miami, Florida

PUMPKIN PIE WITH MERINGUE

1 (9-inch) refrigerated piecrust
1 (16-ounce) can pumpkin
3 large eggs, separated
1 (14-ounce) can sweetened
   condensed milk
½ cup flaked coconut
¼ cup water
1 teaspoon ground cinnamon
½ teaspoon ground ginger
½ teaspoon ground nutmeg
Dash of salt
¼ teaspoon cream of tartar
½ cup sugar

• **Place** piecrust in a 9-inch pieplate; trim off excess pastry along edges. Fold edges of pastry under, and crimp. Prick bottom and sides of pastry with a fork. Bake at 425° for 5 minutes on lowest oven rack.
• **Combine** pumpkin, egg yolks, condensed milk, and next 6 ingredients; pour into piecrust. Cover edges of pastry with strips of aluminum foil to prevent excessive browning, and bake pie at 400° for 30 minutes on middle oven rack.
• **Beat** egg whites and cream of tartar at high speed with an electric mixer until foamy. Gradually add sugar, 1 tablespoon at a time, beating until stiff peaks form and sugar dissolves (2 to 4 minutes). Spread over hot filling, sealing to edge of pastry. Cover edges of pastry with strips of aluminum foil to prevent excessive browning, and bake at 325° for 25 to 28 minutes or until golden; cool on a wire rack. **Yield:** 1 (9-inch) pie.

Sandra Russell
Gainesville, Florida

LEMON PARFAIT PIE

1 cup sugar
2 tablespoons cornstarch
¼ teaspoon salt
1 tablespoon grated lemon rind
⅓ cup fresh lemon juice
3 egg yolks, lightly beaten
¼ cup butter or margarine
2 pints vanilla ice cream, softened
Graham Cracker Crust
¾ cup sugar
½ cup boiling water
¼ cup meringue powder *

● **Combine** first 5 ingredients in a heavy saucepan, stirring until blended. Add egg yolks and butter. Bring mixture to a boil over medium heat, stirring constantly. Boil 1 minute; remove from heat, and let cool.
● **Spread** half of ice cream in Graham Cracker Crust, and top with half of lemon mixture. Cover and freeze until firm. Repeat procedure with remaining ice cream and lemon mixture, and freeze until firm.
● **Combine** ¾ cup sugar and boiling water, stirring until sugar dissolves. Remove from heat, and let cool.
● **Add** meringue powder; beat at high speed with an electric mixer until stiff peaks form. Spread meringue over filling, sealing to edge of crust.
● **Bake** at 425° for 5 to 7 minutes or until golden. Serve pie immediately or return to freezer. **Yield:** 1 (9-inch) pie.

* For meringue powder, we used Country Kitchen brand.

Graham Cracker Crust
QUICK!

1¼ cups graham cracker crumbs
¼ cup sugar
⅓ cup butter or margarine, melted

● **Combine** all ingredients, and press mixture in bottom and up sides of a 9-inch pieplate.
● **Bake** at 375° for 6 to 8 minutes. Cool. **Yield:** 1 (9-inch) crust.

A Taste of Georgia
Junior Service League of Newnan, Georgia

CARAMEL-NUT CRUNCH PIE
QUICK!

Use a squeeze bottle to drizzle the hot fudge and caramel toppings on this pie. The tip of a teaspoon or a zip-top plastic bag with a corner snipped off will also work.

2 cups cream-filled chocolate sandwich cookie crumbs (about 20 cookies, crushed)
½ cup unsalted dry roasted peanuts, coarsely chopped
¼ cup butter or margarine, melted
6 (2.07-ounce) chocolate-coated caramel-peanut nougat bars *
1½ quarts vanilla ice cream, slightly softened
1 (11.75-ounce) jar hot fudge sauce, divided
1 (12-ounce) jar hot caramel sauce, divided

● **Combine** first 3 ingredients; press in bottom and up sides of a 9-inch deep-dish pieplate.
● **Bake** at 350° for 10 minutes; cool completely on a wire rack.
● **Chop** candy bars into small pieces, and reserve 2 tablespoons. Fold remaining candy into ice cream, and spread evenly into prepared crust.
● **Drizzle** with 2 tablespoons fudge sauce and 2 tablespoons caramel sauce; sprinkle with reserved candy.
● **Cover** and freeze until firm.
● **Remove** pie from freezer 20 minutes before serving. Serve with remaining fudge and caramel sauces. **Yield:** 1 (9-inch) pie.

* For chocolate-coated caramel-peanut nougat bars, we used Snickers.

Lilann Taylor
Savannah, Georgia

FROZEN CHOCOLATE BROWNIE PIE

¼ cup margarine
⅔ cup firmly packed brown sugar
½ cup fat-free egg substitute
¼ cup buttermilk
¼ cup all-purpose flour
⅓ cup cocoa
¼ teaspoon salt
1 teaspoon vanilla extract
Vegetable cooking spray
½ gallon vanilla nonfat frozen yogurt, softened
1 quart chocolate nonfat frozen yogurt, softened
¾ cup chocolate syrup
Garnishes: fresh strawberries, chocolate curls

● **Melt** margarine in a large saucepan over medium-high heat; add brown sugar, stirring with a wire whisk to blend. Remove from heat, and let cool slightly.
● **Add** egg substitute and buttermilk to pan, stirring well.
● **Combine** flour, cocoa, and salt; add to buttermilk mixture, stirring until blended. Stir in vanilla. Pour into a 9-inch springform pan lightly coated with cooking spray.
● **Bake** at 350° for 15 minutes. Cool completely in pan on a wire rack.
● **Spread** half of vanilla yogurt over brownie layer; cover and freeze until firm. Spread chocolate yogurt over vanilla yogurt; cover and freeze until firm. Top with remaining vanilla yogurt. Cover and freeze at least 8 hours.
● **Remove** sides of pan. Cut into wedges. Serve each wedge with 1 tablespoon syrup; garnish, if desired. **Yield:** 1 (9-inch) pie (12 servings).

Karen Moneyhun
Centreville, Virginia

♥ Per serving: Calories 258
Fat 4.8g Cholesterol 0mg
Sodium 205mg

FROZEN CHOCOLATE-MACADAMIA NUT PIE

1 (8-ounce) package cream cheese, softened
½ cup sugar
1 teaspoon vanilla extract
1 cup (6 ounces) semisweet chocolate morsels, melted
1½ cups macadamia nuts, finely chopped
1½ cups whipping cream
½ cup sugar
Chocolate-Macadamia Crumb Crust
Garnish: sweetened whipped cream

● **Combine** first 3 ingredients; beat at high speed with an electric mixer until smooth and creamy. Add chocolate morsels; beat at lowest speed just until blended. Stir in chopped nuts.
● **Beat** whipping cream at high speed until foamy. Gradually add sugar, beating until firm peaks form; fold into chocolate mixture. Pour into Chocolate-Macadamia Crumb Crust; cover and freeze 8 hours. Garnish, if desired. **Yield:** 1 (9-inch) pie.

Chocolate-Macadamia Crumb Crust

QUICK!

1¼ cups chocolate wafer crumbs
½ cup macadamia nuts, finely chopped
⅓ cup butter or margarine, melted

● **Combine** all ingredients, and press in bottom and up sides of a 9-inch pieplate.
● **Bake** at 350° for 8 minutes; cool. **Yield:** 1 (9-inch) piecrust.

Kim McCully
Knoxville, Tennessee

MOCHA PIE

1 (11.75-ounce) jar hot fudge sauce, divided
1 (6-ounce) chocolate-flavored crumb crust
1 pint coffee ice cream, softened
3 (2.07-ounce) chocolate-coated caramel-peanut nougat bars, chopped and divided *
1 pint chocolate ice cream, softened
¼ cup slivered almonds, toasted

● **Spread** half of fudge sauce into crumb crust; carefully spread coffee ice cream over sauce. Top with half of chopped candy bars.
● **Cover** and freeze 2 hours.
● **Spread** chocolate ice cream over candy bars; carefully spread remaining fudge sauce over ice cream. Top with remaining half of candy, and sprinkle with almonds.
● **Cover** and freeze until firm. **Yield:** 1 (9-inch) pie.

* For chocolate-coated caramel-peanut nougat bars, we used Snickers.

Sharon Dorris
Nashville, Tennessee

TURTLE PECAN PIE

3 cups chocolate wafer crumbs
½ cup butter or margarine, melted
1¼ cups semisweet chocolate morsels
1 cup evaporated milk
1 cup miniature marshmallows
⅛ teaspoon salt
1 quart vanilla ice cream, divided
1 cup pecan halves, toasted

● **Combine** chocolate crumbs and butter; press firmly in a 9-inch deep-dish pieplate, and freeze 15 minutes.
● **Combine** chocolate morsels and next 3 ingredients in a heavy saucepan. Cook over low heat, stirring constantly, until thickened and smooth. Remove from heat, and set aside.

● **Spread** 2 cups ice cream into prepared crust; cover and freeze 30 minutes. Pour half of chocolate mixture over ice cream layer; cover and freeze 30 minutes. Spread remaining ice cream over chocolate mixture; cover and freeze 30 minutes. Spread remaining chocolate mixture over ice cream, and top with pecans. Cover and freeze until firm. **Yield:** 1 (9-inch) pie.

Nuttin' 'Cept Pecan Pies
Charles Wallace
Austin, Texas

APPLE-CREAM CHEESE TART

Cream Cheese Pastry
½ (8-ounce) package cream cheese, softened
¼ cup sour cream
1 egg yolk
2 tablespoons honey
⅛ teaspoon grated lemon rind
1 large Granny Smith apple, peeled and thinly sliced
1 tablespoon apple jelly
1½ teaspoons water
½ cup whipping cream
1½ teaspoons honey
⅛ teaspoon vanilla extract

● **Roll** Cream Cheese Pastry to ⅛-inch thickness on a lightly floured surface; fit into a 7½-inch round tart pan with removable bottom. Trim excess pastry along edges; freeze 10 minutes. Line pastry with aluminum foil, and fill with pie weights or dried beans.
● **Bake** at 400° for 10 minutes. Remove weights and foil, and prick bottom of crust with a fork. Bake 10 additional minutes. Cool on a wire rack (pastry will shrink).
● **Beat** cream cheese and next 4 ingredients in a mixing bowl at medium speed with an electric mixer until smooth. Spoon into tart shell, and arrange apple slices on top.
● **Combine** apple jelly and water in a small saucepan; cook over low heat, stirring constantly, until jelly melts. Brush half of jelly mixture over apples.
● **Bake** at 400° on lower rack of oven 35 minutes. Cool on wire rack 15 minutes. Brush with remaining jelly mixture; cool.

• **Beat** whipping cream at medium speed until soft peaks form; stir in 1½ teaspoons honey and vanilla. Serve with tart. **Yield:** 1 (7½-inch) tart.

Cream Cheese Pastry

QUICK!

The food processor makes quick work of this flaky pastry.

¼ cup butter, cut up
½ (8-ounce) package cream
      cheese, cut up
1 cup all-purpose flour
¼ teaspoon salt

• **Combine** all ingredients with pastry blender or in a food processor. Shape pastry into a ball; seal in plastic wrap, and chill at least 30 minutes (pastry will be dry). **Yield:** enough for 1 (7½-inch) tart shell.

Elizabeth Berek Ellis
Austin, Texas

APRICOT-APPLE CRUMB TART

2 (6-ounce) packages dried apricot
      halves
1 (8-ounce) package dried apples *
3 cups water
¼ cup sugar
1 tablespoon all-purpose flour
½ (15-ounce) package
      refrigerated piecrusts
1 teaspoon all-purpose flour
½ cup all-purpose flour
½ cup sugar
¼ cup butter or margarine
Ice cream or sweetened whipped
      cream

• **Combine** first 3 ingredients in a large saucepan; bring mixture to a boil. Reduce heat, and simmer 30 minutes. Drain well.
• **Combine** ¼ cup sugar and 1 tablespoon flour; stir into fruit mixture. Set aside.
• **Unroll** pie crust, and press out fold lines. Fit into bottom and up sides of a 9-inch tart pan; sprinkle with 1 teaspoon flour. Spoon fruit mixture into prepared pastry shell.

• **Combine** ½ cup flour and ½ cup sugar; cut in butter with pastry blender until mixture is crumbly. Sprinkle mixture over tart.
• **Bake** at 425° for 10 minutes; reduce oven temperature to 350°, and bake 35 additional minutes or until lightly browned. Serve within 12 hours with ice cream or sweetened whipped cream, if desired. **Yield:** 1 (9-inch) tart.

∗ To create a tarter dessert, substitute 1 (6-ounce) package dried apricot halves for the dried apples.

Mrs. Carl M. Schmieg
Annandale, Virginia

KING CAKE FRUIT TART

1 (20-ounce) package refrigerated
      sliceable sugar cookie dough
1 (8-ounce) package cream cheese,
      softened
1 (3-ounce) package cream cheese,
      softened
1 cup sifted powdered sugar
1 teaspoon vanilla extract
4 to 6 kiwifruit, peeled and sliced
4 to 6 carambola (star fruit),
      sliced
1 cup blueberries
1 cup seedless purple grapes, cut
      in half
1 (8-ounce) can pineapple chunks,
      drained
¾ cup apple jelly
2 tablespoons water
¼ cup chopped pecans, toasted

• **Line** 2 (9-inch) round cakepans with 12-inch squares of aluminum foil, allowing corners to extend outside pans.
• **Cut** cookie dough into ⅛-inch-thick slices; line each prepared pan with half of slices, pressing edges of dough together to seal.
• **Bake** at 325° for 15 to 20 minutes or until lightly browned; cool completely in pans on wire racks.
• **Remove** cookie crusts from pans, using foil corners. Remove foil from crusts; place crusts on serving plates.
• **Combine** cream cheese, powdered sugar, and vanilla; beat at medium speed with an electric mixer until

smooth and fluffy. Spread evenly over each crust. Arrange kiwifruit and next 4 ingredients on top.
• **Combine** apple jelly and 2 tablespoons water in a small saucepan; cook over medium heat, stirring constantly, until jelly melts. Remove from heat, and drizzle evenly over each tart. Sprinkle with pecans. Cover and chill at least 1 hour. **Yield:** 2 (9-inch) tarts.

Jami Gaudet
Macon, Georgia

CAKY FLAKY TART
(TART LEMON TART)

A good rule of thumb: 1 medium lemon yields about 3 tablespoons of juice and 2 to 3 teaspoons zest or grated rind.

1½ cups sugar
1 tablespoon all-purpose flour
1 tablespoon cornmeal
3 large eggs
3 tablespoons butter or margarine,
      melted
3 tablespoons milk
1½ teaspoons grated lemon rind
½ cup fresh lemon juice
1 unbaked 9-inch pastry shell
Garnishes: whipped cream, fresh
      mint leaves

• **Combine** first 4 ingredients in a large bowl, stirring well. Stir in melted butter and next 3 ingredients. Pour into pastry shell.
• **Bake** at 375° for 35 minutes or until filling is set, shielding edges with strips of aluminum foil after 25 minutes to prevent excessive browning. Cool completely on a wire rack. Garnish, if desired. **Yield:** 1 (9-inch) tart.

Diane Pfeifer
Stand By Your Pan
Atlanta, Georgia

CARAMEL TURTLE-TRUFFLE TART

Sugar Cookie Crust
1½ cups semisweet chocolate morsels
¾ cup whipping cream, divided
1 (14-ounce) package caramels
3 cups chopped pecans

● **Prepare** Sugar Cookie Crust, and press in bottom and up sides of an 11-inch tart pan; prick bottom generously with a fork. Bake at 400° for 10 minutes or until golden; cool.
● **Combine** chocolate morsels and ¼ cup whipping cream in a small microwave-safe bowl; microwave on HIGH 1 to 1½ minutes until chocolate melts, stirring once. Spread 1 cup mixture evenly in bottom of baked pastry, reserving remaining chocolate mixture. Cover and chill pastry 30 minutes.
● **Combine** caramels and remaining ½ cup whipping cream in a heavy saucepan; cook over low heat, stirring constantly, until caramels melt and mixture is smooth. Stir in pecans, and spread evenly over chocolate layer.
● **Spoon** reserved chocolate mixture into a small zip-top plastic bag. (If chocolate is firm, microwave on HIGH 30 seconds or until soft.) Cut a small hole in one corner of bag; drizzle chocolate over tart. Cover and chill at least 1 hour. Let stand 30 minutes before serving. **Yield:** 1 (11-inch) tart.

Sugar Cookie Crust

QUICK!

1⅓ cups all-purpose flour
⅓ cup sugar
½ cup butter, cut into slices
1 large egg
1 teaspoon vanilla extract

● **Position** knife blade in food processor bowl; add first 3 ingredients. Process 1 minute or until mixture is crumbly. Remove food pusher. Add egg and vanilla through chute with processor running; process until mixture forms a smooth dough. **Yield:** enough pastry for 1 (11-inch) tart.

Margot Hahn
Washington, D.C.

CHOCOLATE-PECAN TART WITH CARAMEL SAUCE

2 cups pecan pieces
¼ cup firmly packed brown sugar
¼ teaspoon ground cinnamon
2 tablespoons butter or margarine, softened
2 cups (12 ounces) semisweet chocolate morsels
½ cup half-and-half
Caramel Sauce

● **Position** knife blade in food processor bowl; add pecans, and pulse 5 or 6 times or until finely chopped. Add brown sugar, cinnamon, and butter; process 30 seconds, stopping once to scrape down sides.
● **Press** pecan mixture evenly in bottom and about ½ inch up sides of a 9-inch tart pan.
● **Bake** at 325° for about 25 minutes; set aside.
● **Combine** chocolate morsels and half-and-half in a saucepan; cook over medium heat, stirring constantly, until chocolate melts and mixture is smooth. Pour into tart shell.
● **Cover** and chill at least 2 hours. Serve with warm Caramel Sauce. **Yield:** 1 (9-inch) tart.

Caramel Sauce

QUICK!

½ cup butter or margarine
1¼ cups sugar
2 cups half-and-half

● **Melt** butter in a heavy saucepan over medium heat; add sugar, and cook, stirring constantly with a wire whisk, about 10 minutes or until mixture is a deep golden brown.
● **Add** half-and-half (mixture will lump), and cook, stirring constantly, until mixture is smooth and reduced to 2¼ cups (about 10 minutes). **Yield:** 2¼ cups.

Louise Bodziony
Gladstone, Missouri

WHITE CHOCOLATE CHESS TART

½ (15-ounce) package refrigerated piecrusts
1 (4-ounce) bar white chocolate, chopped
½ cup buttermilk
3 large eggs, lightly beaten
1 tablespoon vanilla extract
1¼ cups sugar
Pinch of salt
3 tablespoons all-purpose flour
1 tablespoon cornmeal

● **Fit** 1 piecrust into a 9-inch tart pan with removable bottom according to package directions; trim edges. Line pastry with aluminum foil, and fill with pie weights or dried beans.
● **Bake** at 450° for 8 minutes. Remove weights and foil; bake 3 to 4 additional minutes. Let cool in pan on a wire rack.
● **Combine** chocolate and buttermilk in a small saucepan; cook over low heat, stirring constantly, until chocolate melts and mixture is smooth. Cool 15 minutes.
● **Combine** eggs and vanilla in a bowl; gradually stir in chocolate mixture.
● **Combine** sugar and remaining 3 ingredients; gradually add to chocolate mixture, stirring until blended. Pour mixture into piecrust.
● **Bake** at 325° for 50 minutes or until a knife inserted in center comes out clean. Cool on a wire rack. **Yield:** 1 (9-inch) tart.

BRANDIED APPLE TARTS

1 (17¼-ounce) package frozen puff pastry sheets, thawed
½ cup butter or margarine, softened
2 tablespoons sugar
1 cup sugar
6 Rome apples, thinly sliced
¼ teaspoon ground cinnamon
½ cup brandy
Vanilla ice cream

● **Cut** pastry into 6 (5-inch) circles, and place on a baking sheet. Spread evenly with butter, and sprinkle with 2 tablespoons sugar. Lightly grease bottom of another baking sheet, and place directly on pastry circles.

• **Bake** at 400° for 10 minutes or until pastry is golden. Remove to wire racks to cool.

• **Sprinkle** 1 cup sugar in a large skillet; cook over medium heat, stirring constantly, until golden. Stir in apple slices and cinnamon; cook until tender, stirring occasionally. Remove apples with a slotted spoon.

• **Stir** brandy into sugar mixture; cook 10 to 15 minutes or until thickened, stirring occasionally.

• **Place** pastry circles on individual dessert plates. Arrange apple slices on top; drizzle with brandy mixture. Top with vanilla ice cream, and serve immediately. **Yield:** 6 (5-inch) tarts.

BLACKBERRY PUDDING TARTS

1 (15-ounce) package refrigerated piecrusts
2 quarts fresh or frozen blackberries, thawed
1 cup water
1½ cups sugar
½ cup self-rising flour
¼ cup butter or margarine
2 teaspoons vanilla extract
Whipped cream

• **Unfold** 1 piecrust, and roll into a 15-inch circle on a lightly floured surface; cut into 5 (5½-inch) circles. Fit each circle into a 5-inch round tart pan with removable bottom, and place pans on a baking sheet. Prick bottom and sides of pastry with a fork. Repeat procedure with remaining piecrust. Bake at 450° for 8 minutes or until lightly browned. Remove to wire racks; cool.

• **Combine** blackberries and water in a large saucepan; bring to a boil. Reduce heat, and simmer, uncovered, 5 minutes or until blackberries are soft. Mash berries with a fork; pour through a large wire-mesh strainer into a 4-cup liquid measuring cup, discarding pulp and seeds. (Measurement should be 2 cups blackberry juice. If necessary, boil berry juice to reduce to 2 cups.)

• **Combine** sugar and flour in a medium saucepan; gradually add juice, stirring constantly until smooth. Bring to a boil over medium heat, stirring constantly. Reduce heat, and simmer, uncovered, 3 minutes or until slightly thickened. Remove from heat; stir in butter and vanilla. Spoon about ¼ cup mixture into each prepared tart shell. Cool; top with a dollop of whipped cream. **Yield:** 10 (5½-inch) tarts.

Jean King
Walnut Hill, Florida

PEAR TART

Butter-flavored cooking spray
3 sheets frozen phyllo pastry, thawed
¼ cup finely chopped blanched almonds
¼ cup fat-free egg substitute
2 tablespoons sugar
1½ cups water
2 tablespoons lemon juice
3 medium-size fresh pears
2 tablespoons sugar
¼ teaspoon ground cinnamon
1 tablespoon sliced almonds
¼ cup low-sugar apple jelly, melted

• **Coat** a 10-inch pieplate with cooking spray. Place 1 sheet of phyllo pastry over pieplate, leaving edges of phyllo overhanging; coat sheet with cooking spray. Place second sheet of phyllo on top in opposite direction, and coat with cooking spray. Top with third sheet; coat with cooking spray. Roll and fold edges loosely under themselves to form a ruffled edge, and set aside.

• **Combine** chopped almonds, egg substitute, and 2 tablespoons sugar; spread over bottom of shell.

• **Combine** water and lemon juice in a medium bowl. Peel and core pears; dip pears in lemon juice mixture, and drain well. Cut pears in half vertically; cut each half into ⅛- to ¼-inch slices, keeping slices in order as they are cut. Arrange slices over almond mixture in shape of 6 pear halves, letting slices fan out slightly.

• **Combine** 2 tablespoons sugar and cinnamon; sprinkle over pears. Coat lightly with cooking spray. Cover edges of phyllo with aluminum foil to prevent excessive browning. Bake at 400° for 35 minutes. Remove foil from edges; sprinkle sliced almonds over tart. Bake 5 additional minutes or until edges of phyllo are golden. Remove from oven; brush pears with apple jelly. **Yield:** 1 (10-inch) tart (6 servings).

♥ Per serving: Calories 168
Fat 3.8g Cholesterol 0mg
Sodium 72mg

CRAN-RASPBERRY MERINGUE TARTS

3 egg whites
¼ teaspoon cream of tartar
1 cup sugar
1 teaspoon vanilla extract
½ cup no-sugar-added raspberry-cranberry fruit spread

• **Beat** egg whites and cream of tartar at high speed with an electric mixer 1 minute. Gradually add sugar, 1 tablespoon at a time, beating until stiff peaks form and sugar dissolves (about 2 to 4 minutes). Stir in vanilla.

• **Drop** by heaping teaspoonfuls onto cookie sheets lined with unglazed brown paper. (Do not use recycled paper.) Using back of a teaspoon, make a small indentation in center of each meringue. Bake at 250° for 45 minutes; turn off heat and leave meringues in oven, with door closed, at least 2 hours.

• **Carefully** peel meringues from brown paper. Just before serving, fill each with about ½ teaspoon fruit spread. **Yield:** 50 tarts.

♥ Per tart: Calories 19
Fat 0g Cholesterol 0mg
Sodium 4mg

BOWL-ME-OVER FRESH FRUIT TARTS

1 (15-ounce) package refrigerated
   piecrusts
1 cup fresh raspberries
1 cup fresh blackberries
1 cup fresh whole strawberries
1 cup fresh or canned apricots,
   halved
2 kiwifruit, peeled and sliced
1 tablespoon sugar (optional)
Lemon Cream Sauce

• **Unfold** 1 piecrust, and roll into a 13-inch circle on a lightly floured surface; carefully tear 3 (5½-inch) circles, leaving jagged edges. Repeat procedure with remaining piecrust.
• **Place** 6 (6-ounce) custard cups upside down on a 15- x 10- x 1-inch jellyroll pan; lightly grease bottom and sides of cups. Drape a pastry circle over each cup; pinch dough to make 6 pleats, conforming pastry to shape of cup. Prick bottom and sides with a fork. Bake at 425° for 10 minutes or until lightly browned. Remove to wire racks; cool 5 minutes. Carefully remove pastry from cups; turn right side up, and cool completely on wire racks.
• **Combine** fruit in a large bowl, and add sugar, if desired; cover and chill up to 2 hours.
• **To** serve, spoon about ¾ cup fruit mixture into each tart shell. Serve with Lemon Cream Sauce. **Yield:** 6 (5½-inch) tarts.

Lemon Cream Sauce

QUICK!

1 (12-ounce) jar lemon curd
1 cup whipping cream

• **Combine** lemon curd and whipping cream, beating with a wire whisk until smooth. Cover and chill up to 24 hours before serving. **Yield:** 2 cups.

Note: Look for lemon curd, a creamy mixture of lemon juice, sugar, butter, and egg yolks, at specialty food shops and large supermarkets. Serve any extra Lemon Cream Sauce over pound cake.

MIDNIGHT DELIGHTS

Make-ahead tip: Bake and freeze up to 3 months. Dollop with whipped cream mixture before serving.

⅔ cup boiling water
2 teaspoons instant coffee
   granules
1¾ cups all-purpose flour
⅓ cup cocoa
¼ cup sugar
Dash of salt
¾ cup butter, cut into small pieces
2 cups (12 ounces) semisweet
   chocolate morsels, melted
⅔ cup sugar
2 tablespoons butter, melted
2 tablespoons milk
2 teaspoons Kahlúa or other
   coffee-flavored liqueur or
   strongly brewed coffee
2 large eggs
½ cup chopped pecans or
   walnuts
½ cup whipping cream
1 tablespoon powdered sugar

• **Combine** water and coffee granules, stirring well; let cool. Reserve 2 teaspoons coffee mixture.
• **Combine** flour and next 3 ingredients; cut in butter with pastry blender until mixture is crumbly. Sprinkle remaining coffee mixture, 1 tablespoon at a time, over flour mixture, and stir with a fork until dry ingredients are moistened.
• **Turn** dough out onto a lightly floured surface, and knead 2 or 3 times. Wrap in wax paper, and chill at least 1 hour.
• **Shape** dough into ¾-inch balls; press into lightly greased miniature (1¾-inch) muffin pans, using a tart tamper or back of a spoon. Cover and chill slightly.
• **Combine** melted chocolate and next 4 ingredients, stirring until smooth; stir in eggs and chopped pecans. Spoon 1 rounded teaspoonful mixture into each tart shell.
• **Bake** at 350° for 20 minutes. Cool in pans on wire racks 15 minutes; remove from pans, and cool completely on wire racks.
• **Combine** reserved 2 teaspoons coffee mixture, whipping cream, and powdered sugar; beat at medium speed with an electric mixer until soft peaks form.

Pipe or dollop a small amount onto each tart just before serving. **Yield:** 4 dozen.
Yetta J. Burrell
Valdosta, Georgia

BOURBON-CHOCOLATE-PECAN TARTS

Try this wonderfully rich twist on a favorite Southern dessert.

Cream Cheese Pastry
¾ cup semisweet chocolate
   morsels
3 large eggs, lightly beaten
⅓ cup sugar
3 tablespoons firmly packed light
   brown sugar
1 tablespoon all-purpose flour
¾ cup light corn syrup
¼ cup butter or margarine,
   melted
3 tablespoons bourbon
2 teaspoons vanilla extract
2 cups pecan halves
Garnishes: whipped cream, pecan
   halves, chopped pecans

• **Divide** Cream Cheese Pastry into 6 equal portions; shape each portion into a ball, and press into a 4½-inch tart pan. Sprinkle chocolate morsels into tart shells; chill 30 minutes.
• **Beat** eggs and next 7 ingredients at medium speed with an electric mixer until blended. Pour batter into tart shells, filling each half full. Arrange pecan halves over filling; drizzle with remaining filling.
• **Bake** at 350° for 30 to 35 minutes or until set; cool. Garnish, if desired. **Yield:** 6 (4½-inch) tarts.

Cream Cheese Pastry

QUICK!

1 (3-ounce) package cream cheese,
   softened
½ cup butter or margarine,
   softened
1 cup all-purpose flour

• **Beat** cream cheese and butter at medium speed with an electric mixer until smooth. Add flour, and beat at low speed until a soft dough forms. **Yield:** pastry for 6 (4½-inch) tarts.

Note: You can bake tart filling in a 9-inch tart pan fitted with pastry crust. Prepare as directed, and bake at 350° for 55 minutes or until set.

Trenda Leigh
Richmond, Virginia

TOASTY SOUTHERN PECAN TARTS

1 tablespoon butter or
   margarine
1 cup chopped pecans
⅛ teaspoon salt
1 (15-ounce) package refrigerated
   piecrusts
½ cup butter or margarine
1 cup light corn syrup
1 cup sugar
¼ teaspoon ground cinnamon
3 large eggs, beaten
1 teaspoon vanilla extract
½ teaspoon lemon juice

• **Place** 1 tablespoon butter in a large shallow pan; bake at 350° until melted. Add pecans, stirring to coat; bake 8 to 10 minutes or until toasted, stirring once. Remove from oven, and sprinkle with salt; cool.
• **Roll** 1 piecrust on a lightly floured surface to press out fold lines. Cut into rounds with a 2½-inch round cutter. Fit pastry rounds into miniature (1¾-inch) muffin pans; do not trim edges. Repeat procedure with remaining piecrust. Sprinkle toasted pecans evenly into tart shells; set aside.
• **Place** ½ cup butter in a small heavy saucepan; cook over medium heat, stirring constantly, until lightly browned (do not burn). Remove from heat; cool 10 minutes.
• **Add** corn syrup and remaining 5 ingredients to butter, stirring well; spoon evenly over pecans into tart shells.
• **Bake** at 350° for 35 to 40 minutes or until set. Cool in pans 5 minutes. Remove from pans; cool completely on wire racks. **Yield:** 4½ dozen.

Palmer Ragsdale
Rockwall, Texas

APPLE DUMPLINGS WITH MAPLE-CIDER SAUCE

3 cups all-purpose flour
1 teaspoon salt
¾ cup butter, chilled and cut into
   pieces
5 tablespoons shortening
½ cup apple cider, chilled
8 large Granny Smith apples
½ cup firmly packed brown sugar
½ cup currants
½ cup chopped walnuts
⅓ cup butter, softened
1 large egg
1 tablespoon water
4 (3-inch) sticks cinnamon, broken
   in half
Maple-Cider Sauce

• **Combine** flour and salt; cut in ¾ cup butter and shortening with pastry blender until mixture is crumbly. Sprinkle cider, 1 tablespoon at a time, evenly over surface; stir with a fork until dry ingredients are moistened. Shape into 2 (½-inch-thick) squares; cover and chill.
• **Core** each apple, leaving ½ inch intact on bottom. Peel top two-thirds of each apple; set apples aside.
• **Combine** sugar, currants, and walnuts; stir in ⅓ cup softened butter, blending well. Spoon into each apple.
• **Roll** pastry squares to ⅛-inch thickness on a floured surface; cut each square into 4 (7-inch) squares.
• **Press** 1 pastry square around each apple; remove excess pastry from bottom so apple will sit level. Reroll scraps, if desired, and cut into leaf shapes.
• **Combine** egg and water, beating lightly with a fork. Brush over apples, and attach leaf shapes, if desired.
• **Place** a cinnamon stick half in top of each apple to resemble a stem. Place apples in a lightly greased 15- x 10- x 1-inch jellyroll pan.
• **Bake** at 375° for 40 minutes. Pour Maple-Cider Sauce over apples; bake 15 minutes or until apples are tender. Place apples on a serving plate; spoon sauce around apples. **Yield:** 8 servings.

Note: Serve maple whipped cream with the apples. To make it, combine 1 cup whipping cream and 3 tablespoons maple syrup in a medium bowl, and beat at high speed with an electric mixer until soft peaks form.

Maple-Cider Sauce

QUICK!

2 teaspoons cornstarch
1½ cups apple cider
⅔ cup maple syrup
¼ cup firmly packed brown sugar
¼ cup fresh lemon juice

• **Combine** cornstarch and cider in a saucepan, stirring until smooth; add maple syrup, sugar, and lemon juice. Bring to a boil over medium-high heat; boil 1 minute. **Yield:** 2 cups.

Mildred Bickley
Bristol, Virginia

APPLE SQUARES

4 cups all-purpose flour
1 teaspoon salt
2 cups shortening
1 (8-ounce) carton sour cream
6 large cooking apples, peeled,
   cored, and sliced
1 cup sugar
½ cup firmly packed brown sugar
1½ tablespoons lemon juice
¼ cup graham cracker crumbs
¼ cup fine, dry breadcrumbs

• **Combine** flour and salt; cut in shortening with pastry blender until mixture is crumbly. Add sour cream; stir with a fork until flour mixture is moistened. Cover and chill.
• **Combine** apple and next 3 ingredients; set aside.
• **Divide** flour mixture in half; roll 1 portion into a 15- x 10-inch rectangle on wax paper. Place in an ungreased 15- x 10- x 1-inch jellyroll pan. Sprinkle with graham cracker crumbs and breadcrumbs. Arrange apple mixture over crumbs. Roll remaining pastry into a 16- x 12-inch rectangle; place over apple mixture. Fold edges under, and crimp. Bake at 375° for 1 hour. Let cool in pan on a wire rack. Cut into 2-inch squares. **Yield:** about 3 dozen.

Mary Prischak
Ladson, South Carolina

APPLE STRUDEL

1 (17¼-ounce) package frozen
   puff pastry sheets, thawed
2 tablespoons butter or margarine,
   melted and divided
¼ cup firmly packed brown
   sugar
1 teaspoon grated lemon rind
½ cup chopped pecans, divided
½ cup raisins, divided
1 (21-ounce) can apple pie filling,
   chopped

● **Roll** each sheet of pastry into a 12- x 9-inch rectangle. Brush 1 rectangle with 1 tablespoon melted butter. Combine brown sugar and lemon rind; sprinkle half of brown sugar mixture on buttered pastry. Sprinkle half of pecans and raisins over brown sugar mixture. Brush remaining 1 tablespoon melted butter over second sheet of pastry, and place on top of first sheet. Sprinkle with remaining brown sugar mixture, chopped pecans, and raisins.
● **Spoon** pie filling down 1 (12-inch) edge of pastry; starting with long side, roll up, jellyroll fashion. Place strudel, seam side down, on a lightly greased baking sheet. With a knife, make diagonal 2-inch slits in top of pastry every 1 to 2 inches. Bake strudel at 400° for 40 minutes or until golden. **Yield:** 1 (12-inch) strudel.

FRIED APRICOT PIES

1 (6-ounce) package dried apricot
   halves, chopped
1¼ cups water
½ cup sugar
½ teaspoon ground cinnamon
½ teaspoon ground nutmeg
1 tablespoon lemon or orange
   juice
1 (15-ounce) package refrigerated
   piecrusts
Vegetable oil
Powdered sugar

● **Combine** apricot and water in a small saucepan; bring to a boil. Cover, reduce heat, and simmer 20 minutes or until apricot is tender. Drain, if necessary.

● **Mash** apricot. Stir in sugar, cinnamon, nutmeg, and lemon juice; set mixture aside.
● **Unfold** 1 piecrust, and press out fold lines. Roll piecrust to ⅛-inch thickness on a lightly floured surface. Cut into 5 (5-inch) circles; stack circles between wax paper. Repeat procedure with remaining piecrust.
● **Spoon** 2 tablespoons apricot mixture on half of each circle. Moisten edges with water; fold dough over apricot mixture, pressing edges to seal. Crimp edges with a fork.
● **Pour** oil to depth of 1 inch into a large heavy skillet. Fry pies in hot oil (375°) about 2 minutes or until golden, turning once. Drain well on paper towels. Sprinkle with powdered sugar. **Yield:** 10 pies.

One of a Kind
Junior League of Mobile, Alabama

SPECIAL APRICOT PIES

1 (6-ounce) package dried apricot
   halves
¾ cup water
½ teaspoon ground nutmeg
½ teaspoon vanilla extract
½ cup butter or margarine,
   softened
4 ounces cream cheese,
   softened
1½ cups all-purpose flour
½ teaspoon salt
Glaze

● **Position** knife blade in food processor bowl; add apricots. Process until finely chopped.
● **Combine** apricots, water, nutmeg, and vanilla in a small saucepan; cook over medium heat 5 minutes, stirring constantly. Set aside.
● **Beat** butter and cream cheese at medium speed with an electric mixer until creamy. Add flour and salt, beating at low speed until dough forms a ball.
● **Roll** dough to ⅛-inch thickness on a lightly floured surface. Cut with a 2½-inch round cutter.
● **Place** about 1 teaspoon apricot mixture on half of each circle. Moisten edges with water; fold dough over apricot mixture, pressing edges to seal.

Crimp edges with a fork, and prick top of each pie; place on ungreased baking sheets. Bake pies at 350° for 18 minutes or until lightly browned. Transfer to wire racks; brush with Glaze. **Yield:** 3 dozen.

Glaze

▸**QUICK!**

1 cup sifted powdered sugar
1½ tablespoons milk
½ teaspoon vanilla extract
¼ teaspoon butter-flavored
   extract

● **Combine** all ingredients in a small bowl. **Yield:** ⅓ cup.

Carol Barclay
Portland, Texas

CRANBERRY POCKETS

1 (15-ounce) package refrigerated
   piecrusts
1 (8-ounce) carton soft cream
   cheese
⅓ cup sugar
½ cup chopped fresh cranberries
½ cup chopped pecans
1 teaspoon grated orange rind
2 tablespoons powdered sugar

● **Unfold** piecrusts, and press out fold lines. Cut each piecrust into 4 squares, discarding scraps.
● **Combine** cream cheese and next 4 ingredients; spread ¼ cup mixture onto each pastry square, leaving a ½-inch border. Moisten edges with water; fold pastry diagonally over filling, pressing edges to seal.
● **Crimp** edges with a fork. Place on lightly greased baking sheets.
● **Bake** at 350° for 15 to 18 minutes or until golden. Sprinkle with powdered sugar; serve warm or at room temperature. **Yield:** 8 servings.

Note: You can freeze unbaked pockets in airtight containers up to 1 month. Bake frozen pastries at 350° for 25 minutes or until golden.

CRANBERRY DESSERT PIZZAS

Use any leftover holiday cranberries in this recipe. (For perfect streusel stripes lay strips of wax paper on the pizzas before sprinkling the topping.)

3½ cups all-purpose flour, divided
2½ cups sugar, divided
2 teaspoons cream of tartar
1 teaspoon baking soda
½ teaspoon salt
1 cup butter or margarine, softened
2 large eggs
½ teaspoon ground cinnamon
4 cups fresh cranberries
½ cup orange juice
1 tablespoon cornstarch
¼ cup regular oats, uncooked
¼ cup firmly packed light brown sugar
2 tablespoons butter or margarine, softened
¼ cup chopped pecans

• **Combine** 3 cups flour, 1 cup sugar, cream of tartar, soda, and salt; cut in 1 cup butter with pastry blender until mixture is crumbly. Stir in eggs with a fork until dry ingredients are moistened.
• **Shape** dough into a ball. Divide dough in half, and press into two greased 12-inch pizza pans.
• **Combine** ¼ cup sugar and cinnamon; sprinkle over dough.
• **Bake** at 350° for 15 minutes.
• **Combine** 1 cup sugar, cranberries, orange juice, and cornstarch in a saucepan, stirring well; bring to a boil over medium-high heat, stirring often. Cook 10 to 12 minutes or until thickened, stirring occasionally. Spread evenly over crusts.
• **Combine** remaining ½ cup flour, remaining ¼ cup sugar, oats, and brown sugar in a bowl; cut in 2 tablespoons butter with pastry blender until mixture is crumbly. Stir in pecans.
• **Cut** narrow strips of wax paper with scissors; lay at intervals over cranberry mixture. Sprinkle topping over pizzas; remove wax paper.
• **Bake** at 350° for 12 minutes; serve warm. **Yield:** 2 (12-inch) pizzas.

Agnes L. Stone
Ocala, Florida

BAKLAVA

This dessert, pronounced BAHK-lah-vah, has a delicate flavor and texture and makes a wonderful gift. It also freezes well when stored in an airtight container.

2 cups sugar
1 cup water
¾ cup honey
2 tablespoons brandy
1 tablespoon fresh lemon juice
1 (3-inch) stick cinnamon
12 cups finely chopped pecans (3 pounds, shelled)
1 cup sugar
1 tablespoon ground cinnamon
1 teaspoon ground cloves
1 (16-ounce) package frozen phyllo pastry, thawed
1 pound unsalted butter, melted
Whole cloves

• **Combine** first 6 ingredients in a saucepan; bring to a boil over medium-high heat, stirring constantly. Immediately remove from heat; cool.
• **Combine** pecans and next 3 ingredients, stirring well.
• **Cut** phyllo sheets in half crosswise; keep covered with a slightly damp towel.
• **Brush** 2 (13- x 9- x 2-inch) pans with butter. Place 8 phyllo sheets in 1 pan, brushing each sheet with butter; top with 2 cups pecan mixture.
• **Place** 3 phyllo sheets over pecan mixture, brushing each sheet with butter; top with 2 cups pecan mixture. Repeat with 3 phyllo sheets and 2 cups pecan mixture; top with 6 phyllo sheets, brushing all but top sheet with butter.
• **Repeat** procedure with remaining phyllo sheets, butter, and pecan mixture in second pan.
• **Cut** layers diagonally into ¾-inch diamonds; brush with butter. Insert a clove in center of each diamond.
• **Bake** at 300° for 1 hour. Remove from oven; pour syrup evenly over baklava. Cool in pans on wire racks.
• **Cut** again diagonally; remove from pans, and store in airtight containers at room temperature. **Yield:** about 10 dozen.

Jeannie Sfakianos
Birmingham, Alabama

CHOCOLATE ÉCLAIRS

1 (5.1-ounce) package vanilla instant pudding mix
2½ cups milk
1¾ cups frozen whipped topping, thawed
Cream Puff Pastry
½ cup butter
⅓ cup buttermilk
3 tablespoons cocoa
1 (16-ounce) package powdered sugar, sifted

• **Whisk** together pudding mix and milk in a large bowl, and chill 5 minutes. Fold in whipped topping. Spoon into a heavy-duty, zip-top plastic bag; seal and chill.
• **Place** Cream Puff Pastry in a heavy-duty, zip-top plastic bag; seal. Cut ½ inch off one corner, making a 1-inch-wide hole. Squeeze pastry into 4½-inch-long strips, 2 inches apart, on ungreased baking sheets.
• **Bake** at 400° for 30 to 40 minutes. Transfer to wire racks to cool.
• **Bring** butter, buttermilk, and cocoa to a boil over medium heat; remove from heat. Gradually add powdered sugar; stir until smooth.
• **Cut** a ½-inch hole in 1 end of each éclair with a sharp knife. Cut ¼ inch off one corner of bag with pudding mixture, making a ½-inch-wide hole. Squeeze pudding into éclairs. Spread frosting over tops. **Yield:** 12 to 15 éclairs.

Myrna Story
Waynesboro, Mississippi

Cream Puff Pastry

QUICK!

1 cup water
½ cup butter
1 cup all-purpose flour
4 large eggs

• **Bring** water and butter to a boil over medium heat; reduce heat to low. Add flour, and beat with a wooden spoon until mixture leaves sides of pan. Remove from heat. Add eggs, one at a time, beating until mixture is smooth. **Yield:** enough for 15 éclairs.

Terry Anderson
Brooksville, Florida

COFFEE NAPOLEONS

Make-ahead tip: Bake pastry, and store in an airtight container for a day or two. Make filling and chocolate sauce the day before, and chill. Assemble just before serving.

1 (3.4-ounce) package chocolate pudding mix (not instant)
1 cup milk
2 teaspoons instant coffee granules
1 (8-ounce) package cream cheese, cut into pieces and softened
½ cup whipping cream, whipped
1 (17¼-ounce) package frozen puff pastry sheets, thawed
¼ cup whipping cream
2 teaspoons instant coffee granules
6 (1-ounce) squares semisweet chocolate, chopped
1 tablespoon powdered sugar

• **Combine** pudding mix and milk in a saucepan, stirring well; stir in 2 teaspoons coffee granules. Bring to a boil over medium heat, stirring constantly; remove from heat. Add cream cheese, stirring until smooth; cool completely.
• **Fold** whipped cream into pudding mixture; cover and chill.
• **Unfold** 1 pastry sheet on a lightly floured baking sheet. Roll into a 12-inch square. Cut into 2 (12- x 6-inch) rectangles. Cut each rectangle into 6 (6- x 2-inch) strips. Prick each strip several times with a fork. Place another baking sheet directly on top of pastry strips (to prevent overpuffing).
• **Bake** at 425° for 10 minutes. Remove top baking sheet; bake 5 additional minutes or until golden. Cool on wire racks. Repeat procedure with remaining pastry sheet.
• **Combine** ¼ cup whipping cream, 2 teaspoons coffee granules, and chocolate in a heavy saucepan; cook over low heat, stirring constantly, until chocolate melts. Cool slightly; spoon into a heavy-duty, zip-top plastic bag, and snip a tiny hole in one corner of bag. Drizzle over 12 pastry strips.
• **Pipe** or spoon filling evenly on remaining 12 pastry strips, and top evenly with chocolate-drizzled strips. Sprinkle with powdered sugar, and serve immediately. **Yield:** 12 napoleons.

CREAM PUFF TREE

A holiday Cream Puff Tree is a dazzling dessert to crown your holiday meal – it's spectacular in presentation and sensational in taste. A foil-wrapped plastic cone provides the base for the elegant Cream Puff Tree. A simple sugar mixture provides the "glue" to attach the pastry puffs to the cone. Once the tree has cooled, remove the foil-wrapped cone. (Leave cone in place if using tree as decoration.)

3 cups water
1½ cups butter
3 cups all-purpose flour
1½ teaspoons salt
12 large eggs
2 cups sugar
½ cup water
1 cup light corn syrup
Dark Chocolate Sauce
White Chocolate Sauce
Caramel Sauce
Raspberry Sauce

• **Bring** 3 cups water and butter to a boil in a large saucepan over medium-high heat; reduce heat to low.
• **Add** flour and salt, and beat with a wooden spoon until mixture leaves sides of pan. Remove from heat, and cool slightly.
• **Add** eggs, one at a time, beating until smooth.
• **Spoon** batter into a decorating bag fitted with a large star tip; pipe 1½-inch mounds, 2 inches apart, onto lightly greased baking sheets.
• **Bake** at 450° for 10 minutes; reduce oven temperature to 375°, and bake 30 additional minutes or until puffed and golden. Pierce warm puffs on 1 side with a small sharp knife to let steam escape. Let cool.
• **Cover** a 12- or 15-inch plastic foam cone with aluminum foil, and place on an 18- x 12-inch piece of foil. Lightly grease foil.

• **Combine** sugar, ½ cup water, and corn syrup in a heavy saucepan; cook over low heat, stirring constantly, until sugar melts.
• **Bring** to a boil over high heat; cook, stirring constantly, 5 minutes or until mixture is light amber. Remove from heat; cool 2 minutes or until slightly thickened.
• **Dip** bottom of each cream puff into hot sugar mixture, using tongs; press puffs onto cone, starting at bottom and working toward top. Attach more cream puffs over first layer, hiding any gaps, and evenly shaping tree. If sugar mixture hardens, cook over low heat just until it melts. (Freeze any remaining cream puffs for another use.)
• **Drizzle** any remaining sugar mixture over top of tree, allowing it to flow down sides; cool.
• **Remove** and discard cone and foil. Serve with Dark Chocolate Sauce, White Chocolate Sauce, Caramel Sauce, or Raspberry Sauce. **Yield:** 12 servings.

Note: You can drop batter by rounded tablespoonfuls rather than piping it. Recipe makes about 3 dozen puffs.

Dark Chocolate Sauce

QUICK!

¾ cup whipping cream
8 (1-ounce) squares dark sweet or semisweet chocolate
2 tablespoons light corn syrup

• **Cook** whipping cream in a small heavy saucepan over medium-low heat just until thoroughly heated, stirring often. Add chocolate and corn syrup; cook until chocolate melts, stirring often. **Yield:** 1½ cups.

White Chocolate Sauce

QUICK!

¾ cup whipping cream
8 (1-ounce) squares white chocolate or baking bar
2 tablespoons light corn syrup

• **Cook** whipping cream in a small heavy saucepan over medium-low heat just until thoroughly heated, stirring often.

• **Add** white chocolate and corn syrup; cook until chocolate melts, stirring often. **Yield:** 1½ cups.

Caramel Sauce

QUICK!

½ cup butter
1 cup sugar
½ cup whipping cream
2 teaspoons vanilla extract

• **Combine** butter and sugar in a small heavy saucepan; cook over medium heat, stirring constantly, until sugar melts.
• **Stir** in whipping cream. Bring to a boil, and cook 1 minute, stirring constantly. Stir in vanilla. **Yield:** 1¼ cups.

Raspberry Sauce

QUICK!

This ruby sauce can also be drizzled over ice cream and is especially pretty coupled with fresh berries.

2 (10-ounce) packages frozen raspberries, thawed
4 teaspoons cornstarch

• **Place** raspberries in container of an electric blender; process until smooth, stopping once to scrape down sides. Pour through a wire-mesh strainer into a small saucepan, discarding seeds. Stir in cornstarch.
• **Bring** to a boil over medium heat, stirring constantly; boil 1 minute, stirring constantly. Cool. **Yield:** 1 cup.

CAJUN FIG COBBLER

¼ cup butter or margarine
1 cup all-purpose flour
1 cup sugar
2 teaspoons baking powder
1 cup milk
1 large egg
1 teaspoon vanilla extract
2 (11-ounce) jars fig preserves

• **Place** butter in a 2-quart baking dish. Bake at 375° until butter melts. Remove from oven, and set aside.

• **Combine** flour, sugar, and baking powder in a large bowl. Add milk, egg, and vanilla, stirring until smooth. Pour batter into baking dish; spoon preserves over batter.
• **Bake** at 375° for 40 minutes, covering dish with aluminum foil after 20 minutes. Serve warm with vanilla ice cream or whipped cream. **Yield:** 8 servings.

Joshua Pucheu
Ville Platte, Louisiana

BLUEBERRY UPSIDE-DOWN COBBLER

2½ cups fresh blueberries
1½ cups water
¼ cup shortening
1½ cups sugar, divided
1 cup all-purpose flour
2 teaspoons baking powder
⅛ teaspoon salt
½ cup milk
½ teaspoon ground nutmeg
Pinch of salt
3 tablespoons butter or margarine, cut into pieces
1 tablespoon lemon juice

• **Combine** blueberries and water in a nonaluminum saucepan; bring to a boil. Boil 5 minutes; let cool. Pour mixture through a wire-mesh strainer into a bowl; reserve blueberries and juice separately.
• **Beat** shortening and 1 cup sugar in a large mixing bowl at medium speed with an electric mixer until smooth.
• **Combine** flour, baking powder, and ⅛ teaspoon salt in a bowl; add to shortening mixture alternately with milk, beginning and ending with flour mixture.
• **Pour** batter into a greased 11- x 7- x 1½-inch baking dish; spoon reserved berries over batter.
• **Combine** remaining ½ cup sugar, nutmeg, and pinch of salt; sprinkle over berries. Dot with butter.
• **Combine** reserved blueberry juice and lemon juice, and pour over top of batter.
• **Bake** at 375° for 35 to 40 minutes. **Yield:** 6 servings.

Sandra Russell
Gainesville, Florida

PEACH COBBLER

1 (15-ounce) package refrigerated piecrusts
1 teaspoon all-purpose flour
4 cups frozen sliced peaches
½ cup sugar
½ teaspoon ground cinnamon
¼ cup cornstarch
½ cup water
2 tablespoons butter or margarine, melted
1 large egg
2 tablespoons milk
1 tablespoon sugar

• **Roll** 1 piecrust into a 12-inch circle. Sprinkle flour over surface. Place crust, floured side down, in a 9½-inch quiche dish. Place peaches in crust.
• **Combine** ½ cup sugar, cinnamon, and cornstarch; sprinkle over peaches, and drizzle with water and butter.
• **Unfold** remaining piecrust, and roll on a lightly floured surface into a 12-inch circle; place over peaches. Fold edges under, and flute.
• **Cut** 6 (1-inch) slits in top of piecrust with a sharp knife.
• **Combine** egg and milk, stirring well; brush over top piecrust, and sprinkle evenly with 1 tablespoon sugar. Place on a baking sheet.
• **Bake** at 350° for 1 hour or until golden. **Yield:** 8 servings.

RASPBERRY-CHERRY COBBLER

1 (16-ounce) package frozen
  unsweetened raspberries,
  thawed
1 (16-ounce) package frozen
  no-sugar-added pitted dark
  sweet cherries, thawed
1 cup sugar
¼ cup all-purpose flour
1 tablespoon lemon juice
⅛ teaspoon ground cinnamon
Vegetable cooking spray
2 cups all-purpose flour
1 tablespoon baking powder
1 teaspoon baking soda
1 teaspoon salt
2 tablespoons sugar
¼ cup reduced-calorie margarine
¾ cup plain nonfat yogurt
¼ cup evaporated skimmed milk

• **Combine** first 6 ingredients; spoon into an 11- x 7- x 1½-inch baking dish coated with cooking spray.
• **Combine** 2 cups flour and next 4 ingredients in a large bowl; cut in margarine with pastry blender until mixture is crumbly. Add yogurt and milk, stirring with a fork until dry ingredients are moistened.
• **Turn** dough out onto a lightly floured surface, and knead about 10 times.
• **Roll** dough to ½-inch thickness; cut into 12 circles, using a 2-inch round cutter. Cut 6 diamonds from remaining dough.
• **Arrange** rounds and diamond shapes on top of fruit mixture. Bake at 425° for 20 to 25 minutes or until bubbly and golden. Remove from oven; lightly coat each biscuit with cooking spray. **Yield:** 12 servings.

♥ Per serving: Calories 225
Fat 2.7g Cholesterol 0mg
Sodium 403mg

APPLE-CHEESE CRISP

A hint of cinnamon and nutmeg brings out the fresh flavors of the apple, Cheddar cheese, and toasted almonds.

6 cups peeled, cored, and sliced
  cooking apples
1 tablespoon water
½ teaspoon lemon juice
1 cup (4 ounces) shredded
  Cheddar cheese
1 cup all-purpose flour
½ cup firmly packed brown
  sugar
2 tablespoons sugar
¼ teaspoon ground cinnamon
¼ teaspoon ground nutmeg
½ cup butter or margarine
Vanilla ice cream
Toasted sliced almonds
  (optional)

• **Arrange** apple slices in a lightly greased 8-inch square baking dish.
• **Combine** water and lemon juice; sprinkle evenly over apple slices. Top evenly with cheese.
• **Combine** flour and next 4 ingredients; cut in butter with pastry blender until mixture is crumbly. Sprinkle over cheese.
• **Bake** at 350° for 40 minutes or until tender. Serve warm topped with vanilla ice cream; sprinkle with almonds, if desired. **Yield:** 6 to 8 servings.

Valerie Stutsman
Norfolk, Virginia

STRAWBERRY-RHUBARB CRISP

3 cups fresh or frozen sliced
  rhubarb, thawed
1 quart fresh strawberries,
  mashed
2 tablespoons lemon juice
1 cup sugar
⅓ cup cornstarch
2 cups all-purpose flour
1 cup sugar
1 teaspoon baking powder
1 teaspoon baking soda
½ teaspoon salt
1 cup butter or margarine
1½ cups buttermilk
2 large eggs, lightly beaten
1 teaspoon vanilla extract
¼ cup butter or margarine,
  melted
¾ cup all-purpose flour
¾ cup sugar

• **Combine** first 3 ingredients in a saucepan; cover and cook over medium heat 5 minutes.
• **Combine** 1 cup sugar and cornstarch; gradually stir into rhubarb mixture. Bring mixture to a boil, stirring constantly; boil 1 minute. Remove from heat; set aside.
• **Combine** 2 cups flour and next 4 ingredients; cut in 1 cup butter with pastry blender until mixture is crumbly. Add buttermilk, eggs, and vanilla; stir with a fork until dry ingredients are moistened.
• **Spread** half of batter evenly in a greased 13- x 9- x 2-inch baking dish. Spoon rhubarb mixture evenly over batter, and drop remaining batter by tablespoonfuls over filling.
• **Combine** ¼ cup melted butter, ¾ cup flour, and ¾ cup sugar; sprinkle over batter.
• **Bake** at 350° for 40 to 45 minutes. Cool on a wire rack. Cut into squares. **Yield:** 15 servings.

Ellie Wells
Lakeland, Florida

At right: *Basil-Stuffed Chicken With Tomato-Basil Pasta (page 281)*

POULTRY

BAKED HEN WITH CRANBERRY PAN GRAVY

1 (5½- to 6-pound) hen
5 cups water
1 large onion, quartered
Leaves from 3 stalks celery
1 teaspoon salt
⅛ teaspoon dried thyme
1 cup frozen cranberry juice
    cocktail concentrate, thawed
    and undiluted
½ cup fresh cranberries, finely
    chopped
2½ tablespoons cornstarch
3 tablespoons cold water
Garnishes: fresh rosemary, fresh
    oregano, fresh thyme, fresh
    cranberries

• **Combine** giblets and neck from hen, 5 cups water, and next 4 ingredients in a 3-quart saucepan. Bring to a boil; cover, reduce heat, and simmer 1½ hours. Pour through a wire-mesh strainer into a container, reserving broth and discarding solids. Cover and chill broth.
• **Rinse** hen with cold water; drain and pat dry. Tie ends of legs together with string. Lift wingtips up and over back, and tuck under bird. Place hen, breast side up, in a 15- x 10- x 2-inch baking dish. Cover with foil.
• **Bake** at 325° for 3 hours; uncover and bake 30 minutes or until a meat thermometer inserted in meaty portion of thigh reaches 180°. Remove hen from dish, reserving drippings.
• **Remove** and discard fat from drippings in dish, and return 2 tablespoons drippings to dish.
• **Add** water to reserved broth to equal 1½ cups. Add broth to drippings in dish. Stir to loosen browned particles; add cranberry juice concentrate and chopped cranberries. Transfer mixture to a saucepan.
• **Bring** mixture to a boil; reduce heat, and cook, stirring occasionally, 3 to 5 minutes.
• **Combine** cornstarch and water, stirring until smooth. Stir into gravy mixture; return to a boil. Cook 1 minute, stirring constantly. Serve with hen. Garnish, if desired. **Yield:** 8 to 10 servings.

Estelle Gilbert
Stanardsville, Virginia

FORTY-CLOVES-OF-GARLIC CHICKEN

So much garlic sounds like a mistake, but it's fantastic. And true garlic lovers will welcome the rich gravy that tops this piquant chicken.

1 (2½- to 3-pound) broiler-fryer
40 cloves garlic, unpeeled
½ cup dry white wine
½ to ⅔ cup chicken broth,
    divided
½ cup whipping cream
¼ teaspoon salt
⅛ teaspoon pepper

• **Place** chicken, breast side up, on a rack in a shallow roasting pan. Place 5 garlic cloves in cavity, and arrange remaining garlic cloves around chicken.
• **Bake** at 375° for 20 minutes.
• **Pour** wine over chicken, and bake 40 minutes or until done, basting occasionally with pan juices.
• **Remove** chicken from pan, reserving garlic and pan drippings; keep chicken warm. Remove garlic cloves, and set aside.
• **Remove** and discard fat from pan drippings; add enough broth to drippings to measure ½ cup.
• **Combine** drippings mixture and whipping cream in a small saucepan. Cook over medium-high heat 2 to 3 minutes, stirring occasionally.
• **Squeeze** pulp from garlic cloves into container of an electric blender or food processor. Add 2 tablespoons broth; process until smooth, stopping once to scrape down sides. Stir garlic mixture, salt, and pepper into hot drippings mixture. Serve chicken immediately with garlic mixture. **Yield:** 4 servings.

Mrs. Harland J. Stone
Ocala, Florida

LEMON-ROASTED CHICKEN

Always roast chicken with the skin on. The skin keeps the chicken moist, and the fat won't absorb into the meat. Be sure to remove the skin before serving.

1½ teaspoons salt
2 teaspoons freshly ground pepper
2 to 3 teaspoons dried rosemary,
    crushed
1 (3-pound) broiler-fryer
1 medium lemon, cut in half

• **Combine** first 3 ingredients; set aside.
• **Loosen** skin from chicken breast by running fingers between the two; rub 1 teaspoon seasoning mixture under skin. Rub remaining seasoning mixture over outside of chicken. Place chicken in a heavy-duty, zip-top plastic bag; seal and store in refrigerator 8 hours.
• **Remove** chicken from bag. Insert lemon halves into cavity; tie ends of legs together with string. Lift wing tips up and over back, and tuck under bird. Place chicken, breast side down, in a lightly greased shallow pan.
• **Bake** at 450°, turning over every 15 minutes, for 50 minutes or until meat thermometer inserted in thickest part registers 180°. Let chicken stand 10 minutes. Remove skin before serving. **Yield:** 4 servings.

Clay Nordan
Birmingham, Alabama

♥ Per 3-ounce serving without skin:
    Breast meat: Calories 116
    Fat 2g   Cholesterol 72mg
        Sodium 719mg

    Drumstick meat: Calories 132
    Fat 3g   Cholesterol 79mg
        Sodium 734mg

    Thigh meat: Calories 150
    Fat 7g   Cholesterol 81mg
        Sodium 728mg

CREOLE CHICKEN

This dish is great for a fall leaf-raking day. It cooks for a total of 3 hours and requires you to occasionally take a break from raking to add ingredients to the pot and stir.

1 (3½-pound) broiler-fryer
2 quarts water
1 teaspoon salt
1 tablespoon butter or margarine
1 medium onion, chopped
2 cloves garlic, minced
2 (16-ounce) cans whole tomatoes, undrained and chopped
2 teaspoons curry powder
2 teaspoons dried thyme
¼ teaspoon salt
Dash of ground red pepper
1 cup currants
8 ounces blanched almonds, toasted
Hot cooked rice

● **Combine** first 3 ingredients in a large Dutch oven; bring to a boil. Cover, reduce heat, and simmer 1 hour or until tender.
● **Remove** chicken, reserving 1 cup liquid; let chicken cool. Skin, bone, and cut chicken into large chunks. Cover and chill reserved liquid and chicken.
● **Melt** butter in a large skillet over medium-high heat; add onion and garlic, and cook, stirring constantly, until crisp-tender. Add tomatoes and next 4 ingredients; cover and cook over low heat 1 hour, stirring occasionally.
● **Add** currants, almonds, and chicken; cover and cook over low heat 1 hour, adding reserved liquid as needed to prevent sticking. Serve over rice. **Yield:** 6 servings.

John Feagin
Birmingham, Alabama

SIMPLY GOOD CHICKEN CASSEROLE

1 (3-pound) broiler-fryer
1 quart water
1 teaspoon salt
1 teaspoon pepper
1 (10¾-ounce) can cream of chicken soup, undiluted
1 (10¾-ounce) can cream of celery soup, undiluted
1 (8-ounce) carton sour cream
½ teaspoon pepper
½ (16-ounce) package oval-shaped buttery crackers, crushed (2 stacks)
¼ cup butter or margarine, melted

● **Combine** first 4 ingredients in a large Dutch oven; bring to a boil. Cover, reduce heat, and simmer 1 hour or until tender. Remove chicken, and cool slightly.
● **Skin** and bone chicken; cut chicken into bite-size pieces. Combine chicken, chicken soup, and next 3 ingredients, stirring well.
● **Place** half of crushed crackers in a lightly greased 11- x 7- x 1½-inch baking dish; spoon chicken mixture over crackers. Top with remaining crackers, and drizzle with butter.
● **Bake** at 325° for 35 minutes or until lightly browned. **Yield:** 6 to 8 servings.

♥ To reduce fat and calories, substitute 6 skinned chicken breast halves, reduced-fat cream of chicken and cream of celery soups, reduced-fat sour cream, and reduced-fat buttery crackers. Reduce butter to 2 tablespoons, and coat dish and top of casserole with butter-flavored cooking spray.

Note: You can add ½ teaspoon salt for additional flavor, if desired.

Jane Harber
Decatur, Georgia

CHICKEN-SQUASH CASSEROLE

1 (2½- to 3-pound) broiler-fryer
2 pounds yellow squash, cut into ¼-inch-thick slices
½ cup water
2 large carrots, scraped and shredded
1 medium onion, finely chopped
1 (8-ounce) carton sour cream
1 (10¾-ounce) can cream of mushroom soup, undiluted
½ teaspoon salt
¼ teaspoon pepper
1½ cups chicken-flavored one-step stuffing mix ✳
¼ cup butter or margarine, melted

● **Cook** chicken in a Dutch oven in boiling water to cover 45 minutes or until tender; drain. Cool chicken; skin and bone. Cut meat into bite-size pieces.
● **Combine** squash and ½ cup water in a medium saucepan; bring to a boil. Cover, reduce heat, and simmer 8 minutes or until tender; drain between paper towels.
● **Combine** squash, carrot, and onion; toss gently, and set aside.
● **Combine** sour cream and next 3 ingredients in a large bowl. Add chicken and squash mixture to sour cream mixture, stirring to blend.
● **Spoon** mixture into a lightly greased 13- x 9- x 2-inch baking dish.
● **Combine** stuffing mix and butter; sprinkle over casserole.
● **Bake** at 350° for 25 minutes or until bubbly. **Yield:** 8 servings.

✳ For chicken-flavored one-step stuffing mix, we used Stove Top One-Step Stuffing Mix.

Dorothy Burgess
Huntsville, Texas

CHICKEN POT PIE

1 (3½-pound) broiler-fryer
2 quarts water
½ teaspoon salt
½ teaspoon pepper
1 stalk celery, cut into 2-inch
    pieces
1 medium onion, quartered
1 bay leaf
3½ cups peeled, cubed red potato
    (1½ pounds)
1 (16-ounce) package frozen
    mixed vegetables
1 cup skim milk
½ cup all-purpose flour
¾ teaspoon salt
1 teaspoon pepper
½ teaspoon poultry seasoning
Butter-flavored cooking spray
5 sheets frozen phyllo pastry,
    thawed

• **Combine** first 7 ingredients in a large Dutch oven; bring to a boil. Cover, reduce heat, and simmer 1 hour or until chicken is tender.
• **Remove** chicken, reserving broth in Dutch oven; remove and discard vegetables and bay leaf. Let chicken cool to touch; skin, bone, and cut into bite-size pieces.
• **Remove** and discard fat (oily liquid) from chicken broth, reserving 3½ cups broth.
• **Bring** reserved broth to a boil in Dutch oven. Add potato and mixed vegetables; return to a boil. Cover, reduce heat, and cook about 8 minutes or until vegetables are tender.
• **Combine** milk and flour in a jar; cover tightly, and shake vigorously. Gradually add milk mixture in a slow, steady stream to broth mixture, stirring constantly. Cook, stirring constantly, 1 minute or until thickened. Stir in ¾ teaspoon salt, 1 teaspoon pepper, poultry seasoning, and chicken.
• **Spoon** mixture into a 13- x 9- x 2-inch baking dish coated with cooking spray; set aside.
• **Place** 1 phyllo sheet horizontally on a flat surface, keeping remaining sheets covered with a slightly damp towel until ready for use. Coat sheet with cooking spray. Layer remaining 4 sheets on first sheet, coating each with cooking spray.

Place on top of baking dish, loosely crushing edges around the dish.
• **Bake** at 400° for 20 minutes. **Yield:** 8 servings.

Note: Remove fat by chilling the broth and removing congealed layer of fat or by pouring the broth through a large fat separator.

♥ Per serving: Calories 249
Fat 5.5g Cholesterol 50mg
Sodium 465mg

EASY CHICKEN DIVAN

*We liked this casserole
just as well without dotting the
top with 2 tablespoons of
butter, as recommended in
the original recipe.*

1 (3½- to 4-pound) broiler-fryer,
    cut in half
2 (10-ounce) packages frozen
    broccoli spears, thawed and
    coarsely chopped
2 (10¾-ounce) cans cream of
    chicken soup, undiluted
1 cup mayonnaise
1½ teaspoons lemon juice
¾ teaspoon curry powder
½ cup (2 ounces) shredded sharp
    Cheddar cheese
¾ cup herb-seasoned stuffing mix

• **Combine** chicken and enough water to cover in a Dutch oven; bring to a boil. Cover, reduce heat, and simmer 40 minutes or until tender. Remove chicken, reserving broth for another use. Let chicken cool. Skin, bone, and cut chicken into bite-size pieces. Set aside.
• **Place** broccoli in a lightly greased 11- x 7- x 1½-inch baking dish. Top with chicken.
• **Combine** soup and next 3 ingredients; spoon over chicken. Sprinkle with cheese and stuffing mix.
• **Bake** at 400° for 25 to 30 minutes or until thoroughly heated. **Yield:** 6 to 8 servings.

♥ To reduce fat and calories, substitute reduced-sodium, reduced-fat cream of chicken soup and reduced-fat mayonnaise for the regular products.

A Taste of Georgia
Junior Service League of Newnan, Georgia

CHICKEN IN FOIL

1 (2½-pound) broiler-fryer,
    quartered and skinned
¼ teaspoon garlic salt
⅛ teaspoon paprika
1 large onion, cut into 4 slices
1 large baking potato, cut into 8
    slices
2 carrots, scraped and cut into
    ¾-inch pieces
2 stalks celery, cut into ¾-inch
    pieces
1 (4-ounce) can sliced mushrooms,
    drained
1 (10¾-ounce) can cream of
    chicken soup, undiluted

• **Cut** 4 (24- x 18-inch) pieces of heavy-duty aluminum foil.
• **Place** a chicken quarter in center of each piece of foil; sprinkle with garlic salt and paprika.
• **Top** chicken evenly with onion and next 4 ingredients.
• **Spoon** soup evenly over each portion. Seal bundles, and place on a 15- x 10- x 1-inch jellyroll pan.
• **Bake** at 400° for 1 hour and 15 minutes or until chicken is done. **Yield:** 4 servings.

*Margaret Jahns
Tarpon Springs, Florida*

GRILLED HERBED
CHICKEN QUARTERS

*Although sherry adds a sweet
kiss to this recipe, you can
substitute less-expensive soy
sauce with good results.*

2 (0.7-ounce) envelopes Italian-
  style dressing mix *
½ cup vegetable oil
½ cup dry sherry
2 (2½- to 3-pound) broiler-fryers,
  quartered and skinned

• **Combine** first 3 ingredients in a shallow dish or heavy-duty, zip-top plastic bag; add chicken. Cover or seal, and chill 8 hours or overnight, turning chicken occasionally.
• **Remove** chicken from marinade, discarding marinade.
• **Cook**, covered with grill lid, over medium-hot coals (350° to 400°) 50 to 60 minutes or until a meat thermometer inserted in thickest part of chicken registers 180°, turning occasionally. **Yield:** 8 servings.

* For Italian-style dressing mix, we used Good Seasons.

Rita W. Cook
Corpus Christi, Texas

LEMON-HERB
GRILLED CHICKEN

1 cup vegetable oil
¾ cup lemon juice
¼ cup honey
2 tablespoons dried oregano
1 tablespoon dried rosemary
1 teaspoon salt
½ teaspoon pepper
4 cloves garlic
2 (2½- to 3-pound) broiler-fryers,
  quartered and skinned

• **Combine** all ingredients except chicken in container of an electric blender, and process mixture until smooth, stopping occasionally to scrape down sides.
• **Place** chicken in a large heavy-duty, zip-top plastic bag; pour oil mixture over chicken. Seal bag, and marinate chicken in refrigerator at least 8 hours.
• **Drain** chicken, discarding marinade.
• **Cook** chicken, covered with grill lid, over medium-hot coals (350° to 400°) about 35 minutes or until meat thermometer inserted in thickest part registers 180°, turning occasionally. **Yield:** 8 servings.

SMOKY HERB CHICKEN

Hickory or fruitwood chips
1½ teaspoons dried oregano
1 tablespoon dried rosemary
1 tablespoon dried tarragon
1 tablespoon salt
1½ teaspoons pepper
1½ teaspoons onion powder
1½ teaspoons garlic powder
1½ teaspoons paprika
6 chicken quarters
½ cup olive oil
6 sprigs fresh sage

• **Soak** wood chips in water at least 30 minutes.
• **Combine** oregano and next 7 ingredients; set dried herb mixture aside.
• **Brush** chicken with olive oil, and rub with dried herb mixture, coating all sides. Place chicken in a 15- x 10- x 1-inch jellyroll pan.
• **Broil** 5½ inches from heat (with electric oven door partially open) 10 minutes on each side.
• **Prepare** charcoal fire in smoker; let burn 15 to 20 minutes.
• **Drain** chips, and place on coals. Place water pan in smoker; add sage and water to pan to depth of fill line.
• **Place** chicken on food racks; cover with smoker lid.
• **Cook** 2½ hours or until meat thermometer inserted in thickest part registers 180°. **Yield:** 6 servings.

OUR BEST SOUTHERN
FRIED CHICKEN

3 quarts water
1 tablespoon salt
1 (2- to 2½-pound) broiler-fryer,
  cut up
1 teaspoon salt
1 teaspoon pepper
1 cup all-purpose flour
2 cups vegetable oil
¼ cup bacon drippings

• **Combine** water and 1 tablespoon salt in a large bowl; add chicken. Cover and chill 8 hours.
• **Drain** chicken; rinse with cold water, and pat dry.
• **Combine** 1 teaspoon salt and pepper; sprinkle half of mixture over all sides of chicken.
• **Combine** remaining mixture and flour in a large heavy-duty, zip-top plastic bag.
• **Place** 2 pieces of chicken in bag; seal. Shake to coat completely. Remove chicken, and repeat procedure with remaining pieces.
• **Combine** vegetable oil and bacon drippings in a 12-inch cast-iron skillet or chicken fryer; heat to 360°.
• **Add** chicken, a few pieces at a time, skin side down. Cover and cook 6 minutes; uncover and cook 9 additional minutes.
• **Turn** chicken pieces; cover and cook 6 additional minutes. Uncover and cook 5 to 9 additional minutes, turning pieces during the last 3 minutes for even browning, if necessary.
• **Drain** chicken on a paper towel-lined plate placed over a large bowl of hot water. **Yield:** 4 servings.

Note: For best results, keep the oil temperature between 300° to 325°. Also, you can substitute 2 cups buttermilk for the saltwater solution to soak the chicken pieces. Proceed as directed.

John Egerton
Nashville, Tennessee

HOT AND SPICY
CHICKEN DINNER

QUICK!

2 cups quick-cooking rice,
     uncooked
2 (10-ounce) cans diced tomatoes
     and chiles, undrained
1 (10¾-ounce) can Cheddar
     cheese soup, undiluted
1 small onion, chopped
1 teaspoon dried basil
½ teaspoon salt
⅛ teaspoon pepper
2 pounds chicken legs and thighs,
     skinned

● **Combine** all ingredients except
chicken; pour mixture into a greased
11- x 7- x 1½-inch baking dish. Arrange
chicken in dish, and cover loosely with
wax paper.
● **Microwave,** uncovered, at HIGH 15
minutes. Turn chicken pieces over.
Microwave at HIGH 11 to 15 minutes or
until done. **Yield:** 4 to 6 servings.

Note: Bake the casserole at 350° for 45
minutes.

Hettie Morgan
Shreveport, Louisiana

SWISS CHICKEN
THIGHS

8 chicken thighs, skinned (about
     3 pounds)
4 slices Swiss cheese, cut
     in half
1 (10¾-ounce) can cream of
     mushroom soup, undiluted
¼ cup skim milk
8 thin slices green bell pepper
¾ cup herb-seasoned stuffing
     mix, crushed
3 tablespoons butter, melted

● **Arrange** chicken thighs in an 8-inch
square baking dish. Top each thigh with
Swiss cheese.
● **Combine** soup and milk, stirring well;
pour over cheese. Top evenly with pepper slices.
● **Combine** stuffing mix and butter;
sprinkle over casserole.

● **Bake** at 400° for 1 hour or until done.
Yield: 4 servings.

Linda A. Bowman
Cordele, Georgia

♥ Per serving: Calories 529
Fat 22.4g   Cholesterol 236mg
Sodium 769mg

♥ To save 100 calories and 12 fat grams
per serving, substitute reduced-fat
Swiss cheese, reduced-sodium, reduced-fat cream of mushroom soup,
and reduced-calorie margarine.

CHICKEN AND DUMPLINGS
WITH HERBED BROTH

1 cup self-rising flour
1 teaspoon pepper
3 pounds chicken legs and thighs
¼ cup vegetable oil
1 medium onion, chopped
2 cloves garlic, minced
1 tablespoon self-rising flour
3 (14½-ounce) cans chicken
     broth
2 tablespoons chopped fresh basil
     or 2 teaspoons dried basil
2 tablespoons chopped fresh
     thyme or 2 teaspoons dried
     thyme
1 tablespoon chopped fresh or
     dried rosemary
½ teaspoon grated lemon rind
2 tablespoons lemon juice
2 cups self-rising flour
1 cup whipping cream
¼ cup reduced-fat sour cream
     (optional)
Garnish: fresh herb sprigs

● **Combine** 1 cup flour and pepper.
Dredge chicken in flour mixture.
● **Heat** oil in a large Dutch oven over
medium heat; add chicken, and cook
until golden, turning once. Add additional oil, if needed. Remove chicken
from Dutch oven, reserving drippings in
Dutch oven.
● **Cook** onion and garlic in drippings,
stirring constantly, until tender.
● **Add** 1 tablespoon flour, and cook 1
minute, stirring constantly; gradually
add broth, stirring constantly.

● **Add** chopped basil and next 4 ingredients; bring to a boil. Return chicken to
Dutch oven; cover, reduce heat, and
simmer 30 minutes.
● **Remove** chicken from Dutch oven,
and keep warm.
● **Combine** 2 cups flour and whipping
cream in a large bowl, stirring with a
fork (mixture will be dry and crumbly).
Gently pat mixture into 2-inch balls,
handling dough as little as possible.
● **Bring** broth mixture to a rolling boil;
add dumplings. Cover, reduce heat, and
simmer, without stirring, 7 to 10 minutes
or until dumplings are firm in center.
● **Remove** broth mixture from heat. Stir
in sour cream, if desired. Serve
dumplings and broth over chicken, and
garnish, if desired. **Yield:** 4 servings.

Note: Adding the sour cream makes
this broth creamy – like a Hungarian-
style dish. The texture is more traditional without the sour cream.

BAKED BREAST OF
CHICKEN WITH MARINATED
BERMUDA ONIONS

1 large head garlic
Olive oil
½ pound goat cheese, softened
1 tablespoon chopped fresh basil
1 tablespoon chopped fresh
     parsley
¼ teaspoon salt
⅛ teaspoon pepper
8 boned whole chicken breasts,
     with skin
Marinated Bermuda Onions

● **Chop** off bottom of garlic head, and
separate whole cloves, leaving tight
outer covering intact. Place in an 8-inch
square pan, and drizzle with olive oil.
Bake at 350° for 20 minutes. Cool and
drain; squeeze out pulp from cloves. Set
aside.
● **Position** knife blade in food processor bowl; add garlic, goat cheese, and
next 4 ingredients. Process 30 seconds
or until almost smooth, stopping occasionally to scrape down sides.
● **Loosen** skin from chicken breasts,
forming a pocket without detaching

skin. Spread 2 tablespoons cheese mixture under skin of each piece of chicken. Place in a 15- x 10- x 1-inch jellyroll pan. Bake, uncovered, at 400° for 30 minutes or until done. Serve on a bed of Marinated Bermuda Onions. **Yield:** 8 servings.

Marinated Bermuda Onions

1 **cup balsamic vinegar**
¼ **cup olive oil**
3 **cloves garlic, minced**
3 **tablespoons chopped fresh basil**
¼ **teaspoon salt**
⅛ **teaspoon pepper**
3 **large Bermuda onions, thinly sliced and separated into rings**
2 **tablespoons olive oil**

● **Combine** first 6 ingredients; pour over onions. Cover and chill 1 hour; drain.
● **Cook** onions in 2 tablespoons olive oil in a large nonstick skillet over medium-high heat, stirring constantly, 3 to 5 minutes or until crisp-tender. **Yield:** 4 cups.
Morrison House
Alexandria, Virginia

OVEN-FRIED CHICKEN

If you want to eat crispy chicken on a frequent basis, we recommend this oven-fried version. The secret is baking the chicken at a high temperature, ensuring that almost-fried crispness.

1 **quart water**
1 **teaspoon salt**
6 **chicken drumsticks**
4 **chicken breast halves, skinned**
½ **cup nonfat buttermilk**
3 **cups corn flake crumbs**
2 to 3 **teaspoons Creole seasoning**
2 **teaspoons dried Italian seasoning**
½ **teaspoon garlic powder**
⅛ **teaspoon freshly ground black pepper**
⅛ **teaspoon ground red pepper (optional)**
Vegetable cooking spray

● **Combine** water and salt in a bowl; add chicken. Cover and chill 8 hours.

● **Drain** chicken; rinse with cold water, and pat dry. Place chicken in a shallow dish; pour buttermilk over chicken, turning pieces to coat.
● **Combine** corn flake crumbs and next 4 ingredients in a large heavy-duty, zip-top plastic bag. Add red pepper, if desired. Place 2 pieces chicken in bag; seal. Shake to coat completely. Remove chicken, and repeat procedure with remaining pieces.
● **Place** coated chicken, bone side down, in a 15- x 10- x 1-inch jellyroll pan coated with cooking spray, and spray chicken with cooking spray. Place pan on lowest rack in oven.
● **Bake** at 400° for 45 minutes (do not turn). **Yield:** 6 to 8 servings.

♥ Per breast half: Calories 281
Fat 3.6g   Cholesterol 68mg
Sodium 635mg

Per drumstick: Calories 176
Fat 3.6g   Cholesterol 48mg
Sodium 427mg

SEASONED CHICKEN BAKE

8 **skinned and boned chicken breast halves**
1 **(8-ounce) bottle Italian dressing**
¾ **cup herb-seasoned stuffing mix, crushed**
¼ **cup grated Parmesan cheese**
1 **teaspoon dried parsley flakes**
¼ **teaspoon salt**
⅛ **teaspoon pepper**

● **Combine** chicken and dressing in a shallow dish; cover and chill 8 hours.
● **Remove** chicken, discarding marinade. Set chicken aside.
● **Combine** stuffing mix and remaining 4 ingredients; coat chicken with stuffing mixture. Arrange chicken in a lightly greased 15- x 10- x 2-inch baking dish.
● **Bake** at 350° for 30 minutes or until chicken is done.
● **Broil** 4 to 6 inches from heat (with electric oven door partially opened) 2 minutes. **Yield:** 8 servings.
Kaye Mabry Adams
Birmingham, Alabama

HERB-SEASONED CHICKEN BREASTS

8 **skinned and boned chicken breast halves**
1½ **cups herb-seasoned stuffing mix**
1 **tablespoon butter or margarine, melted**
¼ **cup orange juice**
Hot cooked wild rice
Sweet Orange Sauce

● **Arrange** chicken in a lightly greased 13- x 9- x 2-inch baking dish. Sprinkle with stuffing mix; drizzle with butter. Pour orange juice over chicken; cover and bake at 350° for 1 hour. Serve over wild rice with Sweet Orange Sauce. **Yield:** 8 servings.

Sweet Orange Sauce

QUICK!

1 **(6-ounce) can frozen orange juice concentrate, thawed and undiluted**
½ **cup orange marmalade**
2 **tablespoons steak sauce**

● **Combine** all ingredients in a microwave-safe container. Microwave on HIGH 6 minutes or until hot and bubbly, stirring once. **Yield:** 1⅓ cups.
Snookie and Bill Dixon
Arkadelphia, Arkansas

Pepper-Sage Chicken

PEPPER-SAGE CHICKEN
(pictured at left)

QUICK!

While the chicken marinates, wash a bunch of your favorite greens and put them on to boil. Peel, chop, and roast a few sweet potatoes, and you've got a meal your whole family will enjoy.

¼ cup water
¼ cup lemon juice
2 tablespoons white wine vinegar
2 tablespoons olive oil
2 teaspoons Dijon mustard
¼ cup chopped fresh sage
1 teaspoon cracked pepper
4 skinned and boned chicken breast halves
Vegetable cooking spray
Garnish: fresh sage sprigs

• **Combine** first 7 ingredients in a large heavy-duty, zip-top plastic bag, and add chicken. Seal and chill 1 hour, turning occasionally.
• **Remove** chicken from marinade, reserving marinade.
• **Cook** chicken in a skillet coated with cooking spray over medium-high heat until browned, turning once. Add reserved marinade, and bring to a boil. Reduce heat, and simmer 15 minutes. Slice chicken into strips. Garnish, if desired. **Yield:** 4 servings.

Patsy Bell Hobson
Liberty, Missouri

BAKED CHICKEN WITH TARRAGON SAUCE

8 skinned and boned chicken breast halves
½ teaspoon salt
¼ teaspoon pepper
3 tablespoons lemon juice
½ cup mayonnaise or salad dressing
1 cup finely chopped celery
1 teaspoon dried tarragon
1 pound fresh spinach
3 medium tomatoes, cut into wedges
Garnish: celery leaves

• **Sprinkle** chicken breasts with salt and pepper. Arrange in a lightly greased 13- x 9- x 2-inch pan; sprinkle chicken breasts with lemon juice.
• **Bake** at 375° for 20 minutes or until done. Chill 1 hour.
• **Combine** mayonnaise, celery, and tarragon; set aside.
• **Remove** stems from spinach. Wash leaves thoroughly, and pat dry. Arrange spinach on individual plates. Arrange chicken and tomato wedges on top of spinach. Spoon mayonnaise mixture over chicken. Garnish, if desired. **Yield:** 8 servings.

Note: For chicken salad, coarsely chop cooked chicken, and combine with mayonnaise mixture.

Gina Holmes
Andrews, Texas

MUSTARD CHICKEN

QUICK!

Mustard lovers will thrill to this three-ingredient recipe. Preparing a flavor-packed entrée doesn't get much easier than this.

4 skinned and boned chicken breast halves
1 (8-ounce) jar sweet brown mustard *
1 teaspoon mustard seeds

• **Place** chicken on a lightly greased rack; place rack in broiler pan.
• **Combine** mustard and mustard seeds; brush on chicken breasts. Broil 5½ inches from heat (with electric oven door partially opened) 15 to 20 minutes or until done. **Yield:** 4 servings.

* For sweet brown mustard, we used Honeycup prepared mustard.

Alice Pahl
Raleigh, North Carolina

PAPRIKA CHICKEN

QUICK!

1 tablespoon margarine
4 skinned and boned chicken breast halves
1 (10¾-ounce) can reduced-sodium cream of mushroom soup, undiluted
1 tablespoon paprika
½ teaspoon dried tarragon
½ teaspoon salt
½ teaspoon ground red pepper
⅓ cup reduced-fat sour cream
Hot cooked egg noodles
Chopped fresh parsley

• **Melt** margarine in a large nonstick skillet over medium-high heat; add chicken, and cook until browned on both sides.
• **Combine** soup and next 4 ingredients; add to skillet, turning chicken to coat. Cover and cook over medium heat 8 minutes or until chicken is done.
• **Remove** chicken; keep warm. Stir sour cream into pan drippings, and cook 1 minute.
• **Place** chicken on noodles; top with sour cream mixture. Sprinkle with parsley. **Yield:** 4 servings.

Denise Gee
Birmingham, Alabama

SALSA-TOPPED CHICKEN BREASTS

Don't let the long list of ingredients fool you. The first 10 are simply tossed together to make the salsa topping.

1 (15-ounce) can black beans, rinsed and drained
1¼ cups frozen whole kernel corn, thawed
¾ cup finely chopped purple onion
¾ cup finely chopped red bell pepper
2 jalapeño peppers, seeded and finely chopped
½ cup balsamic vinegar
¼ cup olive oil
1½ tablespoons Dijon mustard
¼ teaspoon salt
⅛ teaspoon pepper
1 tablespoon chili powder
1 teaspoon ground cumin
¼ teaspoon salt
⅛ teaspoon pepper
4 skinned and boned chicken breast halves *
1 tablespoon butter or margarine
¼ cup chopped fresh cilantro

• **Combine** first 10 ingredients; cover and chill at least 2 hours.
• **Combine** chili powder and next 3 ingredients; sprinkle over chicken.
• **Melt** butter in a nonstick skillet. Add chicken, and cook 5 to 7 minutes on each side or until done.
• **Stir** cilantro into black bean mixture. Serve over chicken. **Yield:** 4 servings.

* Substitute 4 (4-ounce) orange roughy fillets for chicken. Cook 5 minutes on each side or until fish flakes easily when tested with a fork.

*Margot Hahn
Washington, D.C.*

CHAMPAGNE-POACHED CHICKEN WITH CREAMY MUSTARD SAUCE

◀QUICK!▶

1 cup champagne or sparkling wine
½ cup chicken broth
4 skinned and boned chicken breast halves
1 cup whipping cream
1 to 2 teaspoons stone-ground mustard
¼ teaspoon ground red pepper

• **Combine** champagne and broth in a large heavy skillet; bring to a boil. Add chicken; cover, reduce heat, and simmer 10 to 12 minutes or until tender. Remove chicken from skillet; set aside.
• **Stir** whipping cream, mustard, and pepper into skillet. Cook over medium heat 8 to 10 minutes or until thickened, stirring occasionally.
• **Add** chicken to skillet, and cook until thoroughly heated. **Yield:** 4 servings.

POACHED CHICKEN BREAST WITH TURNED VEGETABLES AND CHIVE SAUCE

"Turned" vegetables, pieces of carrot and zucchini trimmed into small football shapes, give this dish a chef's signature.

2 (6-inch-long) zucchini, cut into 2-inch pieces
4 (8-inch-long) carrots, scraped and cut into 2-inch pieces
3 (10½-ounce) cans low-sodium chicken broth
2¼ cups water
½ teaspoon salt
½ teaspoon freshly ground pepper
4 (4- to 5-ounce) skinned and boned chicken breast halves
1 teaspoon chicken-flavored bouillon granules
1½ tablespoons cornstarch
3 tablespoons unsalted butter, cut into ½-inch pieces and chilled
1 teaspoon lemon juice
1 tablespoon finely chopped fresh chives
⅛ teaspoon freshly ground pepper
Garnishes: lemon twist, fresh chives

• **Cut** zucchini pieces in half lengthwise.
• **Trim** zucchini and carrot pieces to resemble football shapes, using a paring knife, and set aside.
• **Place** carrots in boiling water to cover; remove from heat, cover and let stand 10 minutes. Add zucchini; cover and let stand 5 minutes. Drain and set aside.
• **Reserve** 2 tablespoons chicken broth.
• **Combine** remaining chicken broth, water, salt, and ½ teaspoon pepper in a large Dutch oven; bring to a boil. Add chicken; reduce heat to low, and cook 5 minutes. Turn chicken, and cook 5 additional minutes.
• **Remove** 2 cups chicken broth mixture from Dutch oven; set aside.
• **Add** carrots and zucchini to Dutch oven; cover and let stand while making sauce.
• **Place** 2 cups chicken broth mixture in a 2-quart saucepan; bring to a boil over medium heat, and cook 6 to 8 minutes or until liquid is reduced to 1 cup. Reduce heat, and add bouillon granules, stirring until granules dissolve.
• **Combine** cornstarch and reserved 2 tablespoons chicken broth; gradually stir into reduced liquid. Return to a boil, and cook 1 minute, stirring constantly, or until thickened. Remove from heat; add butter pieces, one at a time, and stir with a wire whisk until butter melts. (Do not boil mixture after butter is added.)
• **Stir** in lemon juice, chopped chives, and ⅛ teaspoon pepper. Set aside.
• **Drain** chicken and vegetables; cut chicken diagonally into ½-inch-wide slices. Arrange with vegetables on serving plates; spoon sauce over chicken. Garnish, if desired. **Yield:** 4 servings.

CHICKEN À LA RUSSELL

The easy béarnaise sauce drizzled over the top of this dish ties the ingredients together nicely.

1 pound ground pork sausage with sage
¾ cup all-purpose flour
1 teaspoon dried thyme
1 teaspoon salt
1 teaspoon cracked pepper
8 skinned and boned chicken breast halves
⅓ cup vegetable oil
2 (0.9-ounce) envelopes béarnaise sauce mix
1 (14-ounce) can artichoke hearts, drained and halved
⅓ cup chopped pecans
Garnishes: pecan halves, fresh sage sprigs
Wild Rice Casserole (see recipe on page 236)

• **Brown** sausage in a large skillet, stirring until it crumbles. Drain sausage, and set aside. Discard drippings from skillet.
• **Combine** flour, thyme, salt, and pepper; dredge chicken in flour mixture.
• **Heat** oil in skillet over medium heat.
• **Add** chicken to skillet, and brown on both sides. Drain chicken, and set aside.
• **Prepare** béarnaise sauce according to package reduced-calorie directions; keep warm.
• **Spread** sausage in a lightly greased 11- x 7- x 1½ -inch baking dish. Top with chicken, artichokes, béarnaise sauce, and chopped pecans.
• **Bake** at 325° for 20 minutes or until thoroughly heated. Garnish, if desired. Serve with Wild Rice Casserole. **Yield:** 8 servings.

Irene Smith
Covington, Georgia

GREEK CHICKEN BREASTS

QUICK!

¼ cup all-purpose flour
1 tablespoon dried oregano
4 skinned and boned chicken breast halves
3 tablespoons olive oil
⅓ cup dry white wine
⅓ cup chicken broth
2 medium-size ripe tomatoes, peeled and chopped
3 tablespoons sliced ripe olives
2 tablespoons capers
2 tablespoons crumbled feta cheese

• **Combine** flour and oregano in a shallow dish; dredge chicken breasts in flour mixture.
• **Heat** olive oil in a large skillet over medium heat; add chicken breasts, and cook 10 minutes, turning once.
• **Add** wine and broth; simmer 10 to 15 minutes. Add chopped tomato, olives, and capers; cook until thoroughly heated.
• **Spoon** into serving dish; sprinkle with feta cheese. **Yield:** 4 servings

JAMAICAN JERK CHICKEN

The distinguishing flavors in Jamaican jerk seasoning are thyme, allspice, and pepper. Rub the seasoning on chicken or pork, and pan-fry or grill. (As a bonus, the seasoning is fat free.)

½ cup coarsely chopped onion
6 green onions, chopped
2 cloves garlic, coarsely chopped
1 to 2 jalapeño peppers, unseeded and coarsely chopped
2 tablespoons fresh thyme leaves
1 tablespoon light brown sugar
1 teaspoon salt
1 teaspoon freshly ground pepper
1 teaspoon ground allspice
½ teaspoon ground cinnamon
¼ teaspoon ground nutmeg
6 skinned and boned chicken breast halves or boneless pork loin chops
Vegetable cooking spray

• **Position** knife blade in food processor bowl; add first 11 ingredients, and process until blended.
• **Rub** 1 tablespoon mixture onto each chicken breast. Cover and chill 1 hour.
• **Cook** chicken in a nonstick skillet coated with cooking spray 5 to 7 minutes on each side or cook, without grill lid, over medium coals (300° to 350°) 10 minutes on each side or until chicken is done. **Yield:** 6 servings.

SMOKY CAJUN JAMBALAYA

QUICK!

1 pound andouille or Cajun-style sausage
4 skinned and boned chicken breast halves
2 tablespoons peanut oil
1 cup chopped cooked ham
2 teaspoons Cajun seasoning
1 large onion, finely chopped
1 medium-size green bell pepper, chopped
½ cup chopped celery
3 cloves garlic, minced
1 (14½-ounce) can Cajun-style stewed tomatoes, undrained
½ cup chicken broth
1 tablespoon Worcestershire sauce
½ teaspoon hot sauce
3 cups hot cooked rice
1 cup finely chopped green onions

• **Cut** sausage into ½-inch slices; cut chicken into ½-inch pieces.
• **Cook** sausage in oil in a large Dutch oven over medium-high heat 3 minutes or until browned. Add chicken, and cook, stirring constantly, 3 minutes or until browned.
• **Stir** in ham, and cook until thoroughly heated. Remove meat mixture, reserving 1 tablespoon drippings in Dutch oven. Return meat mixture to pan; stir in Cajun seasoning and next 5 ingredients. Cook 5 minutes, stirring mixture constantly.
• **Stir** in chicken broth and remaining ingredients; cook, stirring constantly, 2 minutes or until thoroughly heated. **Yield:** 6 servings.

Margaret Jones
Birmingham, Alabama

MEDITERRANEAN CHICKEN

QUICK!

4 skinned and boned chicken
      breast halves
3 tablespoons all-purpose flour
2 tablespoons olive oil
1 (14½-ounce) can chicken
      broth
¼ cup sliced ripe olives
2 tablespoons capers
⅛ teaspoon pepper
1 (14-ounce) can artichoke hearts,
      halved

• **Dredge** chicken in flour; set aside.
• **Heat** olive oil in a large skillet over medium-high heat. Add chicken, and cook 3 minutes on each side or until lightly browned.
• **Add** chicken broth and next 3 ingredients. Bring to a boil; reduce heat, and simmer 20 minutes or until thickened and bubbly.
• **Stir** in artichoke hearts, and cook until mixture is thoroughly heated. **Yield:** 4 servings.

BANANA CHICKEN WITH BLACK BEAN SAUCE

QUICK!

This unusual combination of ingredients is a delicious surprise – part southwestern, part tropical.

2 large medium-ripe bananas
1 tablespoon ground cumin,
      divided
4 skinned and boned chicken
      breast halves
2 teaspoons vegetable oil
½ cup chopped red bell
      pepper
½ cup chopped green onions
1 medium tomato, chopped
2 cloves garlic, minced
1 (11-ounce) can black bean soup,
      undiluted *
¼ teaspoon pepper
¼ teaspoon dried oregano
½ teaspoon chicken-flavored
      bouillon granules
½ cup water

• **Cut** bananas in half crosswise, and then in half lengthwise; sprinkle with ½ teaspoon cumin.
• **Sprinkle** chicken with remaining cumin; set aside.
• **Heat** oil in a large nonstick skillet over medium-high heat; add bananas, and cook until lightly browned, turning often. Transfer to a serving platter, and keep warm.
• **Add** chicken to skillet; cook 4 to 5 minutes on each side or until done. Add to bananas; keep warm.
• **Add** bell pepper and next 3 ingredients to skillet; cook, stirring constantly, 2 to 3 minutes or until almost crisp-tender.
• **Add** soup and remaining 4 ingredients; cook, stirring constantly, until thoroughly heated. Spoon over chicken and bananas. **Yield:** 4 servings.

* Substitute 1 (15-ounce) can black beans, drained, for black bean soup.

Peggy Fowler Revels
Woodruff, South Carolina

COCONUT CHICKEN WITH FRESH FRUIT

2 tablespoons butter or
      margarine
8 skinned and boned chicken
      breast halves
1 tablespoon finely chopped fresh
      ginger *
½ teaspoon salt
⅓ cup flaked coconut, toasted
      and divided
1 cup whipping cream
2 to 3 bananas, quartered
1 large papaya, peeled, seeded,
      and sliced
Garnishes: lime wedges, fresh
      flat-leaf parsley sprigs

• **Melt** butter in a large skillet over medium-high heat; add chicken, and cook 4 minutes on each side or until lightly browned. Sprinkle with ginger, salt, and half of coconut; add whipping cream. Cover and cook over low heat 10 minutes.
• **Arrange** chicken, bananas, and papaya on a large serving platter. Pour warm sauce over chicken, and sprinkle with remaining coconut. Garnish, if desired. **Yield:** 8 servings.

* Substitute ¾ teaspoon ground ginger for fresh, if desired.

A Taste of Aloha
Junior League of Honolulu, Hawaii

BRAISED CHICKEN BREAST IN LEMON CREAM SAUCE

QUICK!

⅓ cup butter or margarine,
      divided
1 (12-ounce) package fresh
      mushrooms, sliced
6 skinned and boned chicken
      breast halves
½ teaspoon salt
½ teaspoon ground white pepper
½ cup all-purpose flour
1 cup chicken broth
1 cup whipping cream
3 tablespoons lemon juice

• **Melt** 3 tablespoons butter in a large skillet over medium heat. Add sliced mushrooms, and cook until browned, stirring often. Drain mushrooms, and set aside.
• **Sprinkle** chicken breasts with salt and white pepper; dredge in flour, shaking off excess.
• **Melt** remaining butter in skillet over medium heat; add chicken, and cook about 8 minutes on each side. Remove chicken from skillet, reserving 1 tablespoon drippings in skillet. Add broth.
• **Bring** broth mixture to a boil. Cook over high heat about 15 minutes or until mixture is reduced to ⅓ cup.
• **Combine** whipping cream and lemon juice; add to broth mixture. Cook over medium heat about 5 minutes. Add mushrooms and chicken breasts.
• **Bring** sauce to a boil; reduce heat, and simmer 4 to 5 minutes or until chicken is heated, spooning sauce over chicken as it cooks. **Yield:** 6 servings.

Freida Merrell
Magnolia, Arkansas

LEMON CHICKEN

QUICK!

4 skinned and boned chicken
    breast halves
½ cup all-purpose flour
¼ cup butter or margarine
2 tablespoons minced garlic
1 cup apple juice
2 tablespoons lemon juice
½ teaspoon pepper

• **Coat** chicken with flour; set aside.
• **Melt** butter in a large skillet over medium heat; add chicken and garlic. Cook 8 minutes or until chicken is browned, turning once. Remove chicken from skillet, and keep warm.
• **Add** apple juice, lemon juice, and pepper to skillet, stirring to loosen particles that cling to bottom. Bring to a boil; cook 10 minutes or until reduced to ½ cup. Pour over chicken; serve immediately. **Yield:** 4 servings.

Marge Killmon
Annandale, Virginia

SKILLET-SEARED
ORANGE CHICKEN

¾ cup fine, dry breadcrumbs
1½ teaspoons chopped fresh
    mint
1½ teaspoons chopped fresh
    cilantro
1½ teaspoons chopped fresh
    basil
4 (5-ounce) skinned and boned
    chicken breast halves
Vegetable cooking spray
1 cup broccoli flowerets
1 cup cauliflower flowerets
1 cup sliced carrot
½ cup fresh shiitake mushrooms
¼ pound fresh spinach, torn
½ cup coarsely chopped purple
    onion
Blended Rice
Mandarin-Teriyaki Sauce

• **Combine** first 4 ingredients in a shallow dish. Dredge chicken in mixture.
• **Place** a large cast-iron skillet over medium-high heat until very hot. Remove from heat; carefully coat with cooking spray, and return to heat. Add chicken, and cook 4 to 5 minutes on each side. Remove from heat; set aside, and keep warm.
• **Arrange** broccoli and next 3 ingredients in a steamer basket over boiling water; cover and steam 8 minutes or until crisp-tender.
• **Cook** spinach in a small amount of boiling water 5 to 8 minutes or until tender; drain well.
• **Place** chicken on individual serving plates; arrange steamed vegetables, spinach, and purple onion on plates. Serve with Blended Rice and Mandarin-Teriyaki Sauce. **Yield:** 4 servings.

♥ Per serving: Calories 566
Fat 4.8g Cholesterol 60mg
Sodium 1760mg

Blended Rice

½ cup basmati rice, uncooked
½ cup wild rice, uncooked
Vegetable cooking spray
½ cup peeled, finely chopped
    plum tomato
½ cup sliced green onions
¼ cup reduced-sodium soy
    sauce

• **Cook** basmati and wild rice separately according to package directions.
• **Coat** a skillet with cooking spray; add cooked rice, tomato, green onions, and soy sauce. Cook over medium heat, stirring constantly, until thoroughly heated. **Yield:** 2½ cups.

Mandarin-Teriyaki Sauce

QUICK!

1 tablespoon cornstarch
½ cup reduced-sodium soy sauce
1 cup unsweetened pineapple juice
2 tablespoons brown sugar
1 tablespoon minced garlic
1 tablespoon minced fresh
    ginger
1 tablespoon chopped fresh
    cilantro
2 (11-ounce) cans mandarin
    oranges, drained

• **Combine** cornstarch and soy sauce, stirring until smooth. Set aside.

• **Combine** pineapple juice and next 4 ingredients in a skillet; bring to a boil over medium-high heat, stirring constantly. Stir in cornstarch mixture; boil 1 minute, stirring constantly. Remove from heat; stir in oranges, and let cool. **Yield:** 3 cups.

PGA National Resort & Spa
Palm Beach Gardens, Florida

SESAME-CRUSTED CHICKEN
WITH PINEAPPLE SALSA

½ cup sesame seeds
2 tablespoons minced fresh ginger
2 teaspoons vegetable oil
4 (4-ounce) skinned and boned
    chicken breast halves
½ teaspoon salt
Pineapple Salsa

• **Bake** sesame seeds in a shallow pan at 350° for 5 minutes or until toasted, stirring often; cool.
• **Combine** sesame seeds, ginger, and oil, stirring well.
• **Sprinkle** chicken with salt; coat with sesame seed mixture, and place on a lightly greased rack in broiler pan.
• **Bake** at 400° for 20 to 25 minutes or until tender. Top evenly with Pineapple Salsa, and serve immediately. **Yield:** 4 servings.

♥ Per serving: Calories 572
Fat 15.5g Cholesterol 196mg
Sodium 519mg

Pineapple Salsa

QUICK!

1 (15¼-ounce) can pineapple
    tidbits, drained
½ cup chopped red bell pepper
1 teaspoon grated fresh ginger
1 tablespoon fresh lime juice
Pinch of ground cloves
¼ cup chopped fresh cilantro
¼ teaspoon hot sauce

• **Combine** all ingredients in a medium bowl; cover and chill 15 minutes. **Yield:** 1½ cups.

Judy Carter
Winchester, Tennessee

Chicken With Orange, Lime, and Ginger Sauce

CHICKEN WITH ORANGE, LIME, AND GINGER SAUCE

(pictured at left)

QUICK!

2½ tablespoons reduced-calorie orange marmalade
⅛ teaspoon grated lime rind
1½ tablespoons fresh lime juice
½ tablespoon grated fresh ginger
4 (4-ounce) skinned and boned chicken breast halves

● **Combine** first 4 ingredients. Place chicken on grill, and brush with half of marmalade mixture. Cook, covered with grill lid, over medium-hot coals (350° to 400°) 6 minutes. Turn chicken, and brush with remaining marmalade mixture; cook, covered with grill lid, 6 minutes or until done. Serve with grilled vegetables, if desired. **Yield:** 4 servings.

Beth Evins
Atlanta, Georgia

♥ Per serving: Calories 191
Fat 4.0g Cholesterol 96mg
Sodium 85mg

HONEY-LIME GRILLED CHICKEN

QUICK!

½ cup honey
⅓ cup soy sauce
¼ cup lime juice
4 skinned and boned chicken breast halves

● **Combine** first 3 ingredients in a heavy-duty, zip-top plastic bag; add chicken, turning to coat. Seal bag, and chill 30 minutes.
● **Remove** chicken from marinade, discarding marinade.
● **Cook** chicken, without grill lid, over medium-hot coals (350° to 400°) 5 to 6 minutes on each side or until done. **Yield:** 4 servings.

Karen Lapidus
Hampton, Alabama

CHICKEN PROVOLONE

QUICK!

6 skinned and boned chicken breast halves
6 slices prosciutto
6 ounces shredded provolone cheese
Garnish: fresh purple basil leaf or fresh rosemary sprig

● **Cook** chicken, without grill lid, over medium coals (300° to 350°) 15 to 20 minutes, turning once.
● **Place** chicken on a baking sheet; top each breast with a prosciutto slice, and sprinkle evenly with cheese. Bake at 300° for 6 minutes. Garnish, if desired. **Yield:** 6 servings.

Randall Yearwood
Nashville, Tennessee

EASY CHICKEN JALAPEÑO

QUICK!

4 skinned and boned chicken breast halves
2 tablespoons butter or margarine, melted
½ cup jalapeño jelly

● **Place** chicken breasts between two sheets of heavy-duty plastic wrap, and flatten to ¼-inch thickness, using a meat mallet or rolling pin.
● **Cook** chicken in butter in a large skillet over medium-high heat 5 minutes on each side. Transfer to a serving platter; set aside, and keep warm. Add jelly to pan drippings; bring to a boil, stirring until smooth. Spoon over chicken. **Yield:** 4 servings.

Juanita Alexander
Bradenton, Florida

CHICKEN IN MUSTARD CREAM SAUCE

QUICK!

A splash of whipping cream blended with white wine, Dijon mustard, and green peppercorns works magic spooned over quickly browned chicken breast halves.

4 skinned and boned chicken breast halves
⅛ teaspoon pepper
1 tablespoon Dijon mustard
2 tablespoons olive oil
¼ cup whipping cream
¼ cup dry white wine
2 teaspoons Dijon mustard
1 teaspoon green peppercorns in vinegar

● **Place** chicken between two sheets of heavy-duty plastic wrap, and flatten to ¼-inch thickness, using a meat mallet or rolling pin. Sprinkle with pepper, and spread 1 side of chicken breasts with 1 tablespoon mustard. Cook chicken in hot oil in a large skillet over medium heat 10 minutes, turning often. Remove from skillet; set aside, and keep warm.
● **Combine** whipping cream and remaining 3 ingredients in skillet. Bring to a boil, and cook until mixture thickens. Spoon sauce over chicken. **Yield:** 4 servings.

Carol Durr
Pasadena, Maryland

PESTO-STUFFED CHICKEN ROLLS

6 large skinned and boned chicken
    breast halves
¼ teaspoon salt
¼ teaspoon pepper
1 (3-ounce) package cream cheese,
    softened
¼ cup pesto
½ cup finely chopped red bell
    pepper
¾ cup corn flake crumbs
½ teaspoon paprika
Vegetable cooking spray
Garnish: fresh basil sprigs

• **Place** each piece of chicken between two sheets of heavy-duty plastic wrap; flatten to ¼-inch thickness, using a meat mallet or rolling pin. Sprinkle with salt and pepper; set aside.
• **Combine** cream cheese, pesto, and red bell pepper in a small bowl, stirring with a fork until blended. Spread 2 tablespoons cheese mixture over each chicken breast; roll up lengthwise, securing with wooden picks.
• **Combine** corn flake crumbs and paprika; dredge chicken rolls in crumb mixture. Place in an 11- x 7- x 1½-inch baking dish coated with cooking spray. Cover and chill 8 hours.
• **Remove** chicken from refrigerator, and let stand at room temperature 30 minutes. Bake, uncovered, at 350° for 35 minutes; let stand 10 minutes. Remove wooden picks, and slice into 1-inch rounds. (An electric knife works best.) Garnish, if desired. **Yield:** 6 servings.

Note: To make and bake on the same day, prepare according to above directions, omitting the 8-hour chilling time.

CHICKEN BREASTS WITH PECAN-SAUSAGE STUFFING

⅓ pound ground pork sausage
⅓ cup butter or margarine
⅓ cup finely chopped celery
⅓ cup finely chopped green bell
    pepper
1 small onion, finely chopped
½ cup chopped pecans, divided
¼ teaspoon pepper
⅛ teaspoon salt
3 cups dry bread cubes (¼-inch
    pieces)
1 large egg, lightly beaten
1½ tablespoons milk
4 skinned and boned whole
    chicken breasts
1½ tablespoons butter or
    margarine, melted
3 tablespoons fine, dry
    breadcrumbs
Garnish: chopped fresh parsley

• **Brown** sausage in a Dutch oven, stirring until it crumbles. Remove from pan, and set aside; discard drippings.
• **Melt** ⅓ cup butter in Dutch oven over medium-high heat; add celery, green bell pepper, and onion. Cook, stirring constantly, until vegetables are tender.
• **Add** ⅓ cup pecans, pepper, and salt; cook 3 minutes, stirring constantly. Remove from heat; stir in sausage, bread cubes, egg, and milk. Set aside.
• **Place** each chicken breast between two sheets of heavy-duty plastic wrap, and flatten to ¼-inch thickness, using a meat mallet or rolling pin.
• **Place** chicken breasts on a flat surface. Spoon sausage mixture evenly into center of each chicken breast. Fold long sides over filling, and secure with wooden picks. Place chicken, seam side down, in a baking pan lined with aluminum foil.
• **Combine** 1½ tablespoons melted butter, remaining 2 tablespoons plus 2 teaspoons pecans, and breadcrumbs; press evenly onto chicken breasts.
• **Bake** at 350° for 30 minutes or until golden. Garnish, if desired. **Yield:** 4 servings.

Jeanne S. Hotaling
Augusta, Georgia

SPINACH-STUFFED CHICKEN IN PUFF PASTRY

4 skinned and boned chicken
    breast halves *
½ teaspoon salt
½ teaspoon pepper
1 (10-ounce) package frozen
    spinach, thawed and
    drained
¾ cup (3 ounces) shredded
    Gruyère or Swiss cheese
½ cup finely chopped prosciutto
    or cooked ham (3 ounces)
¼ teaspoon salt
⅛ teaspoon pepper
Dash of ground nutmeg
1 (17¼-ounce) package frozen
    puff pastry sheets, thawed
1 large egg, lightly beaten
1 teaspoon water
1 (0.9-ounce) package béarnaise
    sauce mix

• **Place** chicken between two sheets of heavy-duty plastic wrap, and flatten to ⅛-inch thickness, using a meat mallet or rolling pin. Sprinkle chicken with ½ teaspoon each of salt and pepper, and set aside.
• **Combine** spinach and next 5 ingredients; shape into 4 balls, placing 1 ball in center of each chicken breast. Fold chicken over spinach.
• **Roll** each sheet of puff pastry into a 12-inch square. Cut a 1-inch strip from side of each sheet, setting aside for garnish. Cut each sheet in half, making 4 (5½- x 6-inch) rectangles.
• **Place** stuffed chicken breasts in center of pastry rectangles; fold sides over chicken. Combine egg and water, and brush on pastry seams, pinching to seal. Place seam side down on a lightly greased 15- x 10- x 1-inch jellyroll pan.
• **Cut** decorative stems and leaves or desired shapes from reserved pastry strips. Brush back of cutouts with egg mixture, and arrange on chicken bundles. Chill chicken bundles and remaining egg mixture 1 hour. Brush bundles with egg mixture, and bake, uncovered, at 400° for 20 to 25 minutes or until golden.
• **Prepare** béarnaise sauce according to package directions. Spoon 2 tablespoons sauce in each of four plates; top

each with chicken bundle. Serve immediately. **Yield:** 4 servings.

* Substitute 12 (1-ounce) slices of veal scaloppine for 4 chicken breasts. Overlap 3 slices of veal, and place on each puff pastry rectangle.

Missy Wilson
Birmingham, Alabama

CHICKEN FAJITA SPUDS

2 teaspoons ground cumin
1 teaspoon dried oregano, crushed
¼ teaspoon ground red pepper
½ teaspoon salt
6 skinned and boned chicken breast halves
6 large baked potatoes
1½ cups (6 ounces) shredded Mexican-style cheese blend, divided
1 (8-ounce) carton sour cream, divided
2 tablespoons butter or margarine
3 tablespoons milk
½ teaspoon salt
¼ teaspoon ground black pepper
1 (16-ounce) jar chunky salsa
Garnishes: chopped fresh cilantro, fresh cilantro sprigs

● **Combine** first 4 ingredients; rub onto all sides of chicken. Place chicken in a lightly greased 13- x 9- x 2-inch baking dish, and let stand 15 minutes.
● **Bake** at 400° for 6 minutes on each side. Cut into strips.
● **Cut** a 1-inch-wide strip from top of each baked potato. Carefully scoop out pulp, leaving shells intact; set shells aside. Mash pulp; stir in 1 cup cheese blend, ½ cup sour cream, butter, and next 3 ingredients. Spoon into shells, and place on a baking sheet.
● **Bake** potatoes at 350° for 20 minutes. Sprinkle with remaining cheese blend, and top with chicken. Bake 5 additional minutes or until cheese melts. Serve with remaining sour cream and salsa. Garnish, if desired. **Yield:** 6 servings.

Molly Connally
Annandale, Virginia

CHICKEN ENCHILADAS VERDE

14 skinned chicken breast halves (about 7 pounds)
3 quarts water
2 tablespoons ground red pepper
1 tablespoon salt
14 fresh tomatillos
1½ cups chopped onion
3 cloves garlic, minced
2 tablespoons vegetable oil
1 teaspoon salt
¼ cup chopped fresh cilantro
4 cups (16 ounces) shredded Monterey Jack cheese, divided
1 cup vegetable oil
20 corn tortillas
Verde Sauce
8 ounces feta cheese, crumbled
Red Pepper Puree
Garnish: fresh cilantro leaves

● **Combine** first 4 ingredients in a large Dutch oven; bring to a boil. Cover, reduce heat, and simmer 35 minutes or until chicken is done. Remove chicken, discarding broth; cool. Bone and shred chicken; set aside.
● **Remove** husks from tomatillos, and cook tomatillos in a saucepan in boiling water to cover 5 minutes; drain and set aside.
● **Cook** onion and garlic in 2 tablespoons oil in Dutch oven over medium-high heat until tender, stirring often. Add tomatillos and 1 teaspoon salt. Bring to a boil; reduce heat, and simmer 5 minutes. Add chicken and cilantro; cook 10 minutes. Stir in 1 cup Monterey Jack cheese.
● **Heat** 1 cup vegetable oil in a medium skillet. Fry tortillas, one at a time, 3 or 4 seconds on each side; drain on paper towels. Dip each tortilla in Verde Sauce, coating well. Place about ½ cup chicken mixture down center of each tortilla, and roll up. Repeat procedure with each tortilla. Place tortillas, seam side down, into two 13- x 9- x 2-inch baking dishes; top with remaining sauce, spreading to cover ends of tortillas. Sprinkle with remaining 3 cups Monterey Jack cheese and feta cheese. Cover and bake at 425° for 20 to 30 minutes or until thoroughly heated. Serve with Red Pepper Puree. Garnish, if desired. **Yield:** 10 servings.

Verde Sauce

8 poblano chile peppers
32 fresh tomatillos
3 cups chicken broth, divided
1 medium onion, chopped
4 cloves garlic, minced
6 romaine lettuce leaves, torn
½ cup chopped fresh cilantro
2½ teaspoons salt

● **Wash** and dry peppers; place on an aluminum foil-lined baking sheet. Broil 5 inches from heat (with electric oven door partially opened) about 5 minutes on each side or until peppers look blistered, turning once. Immediately place in a heavy-duty, zip-top plastic bag; seal and let stand 10 minutes to loosen skins. Peel peppers, and remove seeds; set aside.
● **Remove** husks from tomatillos, and cook tomatillos in a Dutch oven in boiling water to cover 5 minutes; drain. Position knife blade in food processor bowl. Add peppers, tomatillos, 1 cup chicken broth, onion, and remaining 4 ingredients; process 20 to 30 seconds or until smooth, stopping once to scrape down sides. Transfer to a Dutch oven, and cook, over medium heat 5 minutes, stirring constantly. Slowly stir in remaining 2 cups chicken broth, and simmer until thickened (about 10 to 12 minutes). **Yield:** 6 cups.

Red Pepper Puree

5 red bell peppers
1 teaspoon salt

● **Wash** and dry peppers; place on an aluminum foil-lined baking sheet. Broil 5½ inches from heat (with electric oven door partially opened) 5 minutes on each side or until peppers look blistered, turning once. Immediately place in a heavy-duty, zip-top plastic bag; seal and let stand 10 minutes to loosen skins. Peel peppers, and remove seeds.
● **Position** knife blade in food processor bowl. Add peppers and salt; process until smooth, stopping once to scrape down sides. Cover and chill, if desired. **Yield:** 2 cups.

Libby and Jim Collet
Dallas, Texas

CHICKEN ENCHILADAS WITH TOMATILLO SAUCE

1 (6½-ounce) package 6-inch corn
    tortillas
3½ cups chopped cooked chicken
3 cups (12 ounces) shredded
    Monterey Jack cheese,
    divided
Tomatillo Sauce

• **Wrap** tortillas in aluminum foil; bake at 325° for 15 minutes or until thoroughly heated.
• **Place** about ⅓ cup chicken and ¼ cup cheese down center of each tortilla; roll up, and place seam side down in a 13- x 9- x 2-inch baking dish. Repeat procedure with each tortilla. Top with 2 cups Tomatillo Sauce. Sprinkle with remaining 1 cup Monterey Jack cheese.
• **Bake** at 350° for 15 to 20 minutes. **Yield:** 4 to 5 servings.

Tomatillo Sauce

1 pound fresh tomatillos
2 cups water
1 chicken-flavored bouillon cube
¼ cup finely chopped onion
12 to 15 cloves garlic, minced
¼ cup finely chopped fresh
    cilantro
1 tablespoon finely chopped
    jalapeño pepper
1 tablespoon finely chopped
    roasted red bell pepper
1½ tablespoons brown sugar
2 tablespoons lime juice
¼ teaspoon salt

• **Remove** and discard tomatillo husks, and wash tomatillos.
• **Combine** tomatillos, water, bouillon cube, and onion in a saucepan. Bring to a boil over medium heat; reduce heat, and simmer 50 minutes or until mixture is thickened.
• **Add** garlic and remaining ingredients; cool. **Yield:** 3 cups.

Note: Serve remaining Tomatillo Sauce over grilled chicken or fish or hot cooked pasta.

Chef Ron Brannon
Austin Central Market's Cooking School
Austin, Texas

ORIENTAL CHICKEN KABOBS

QUICK!

1½ pounds skinned and boned
    chicken breast halves, cut into
    1-inch cubes
¼ teaspoon salt
¼ teaspoon pepper
1 medium-size yellow bell pepper,
    seeded and cut into 1-inch
    pieces
1 medium-size red bell pepper,
    seeded and cut into 1-inch
    pieces
1 (15-ounce) jar baby corn,
    drained and cut in half
⅓ cup hoisin or teriyaki sauce
⅓ cup honey
1 clove garlic, pressed
½ teaspoon minced fresh ginger

• **Sprinkle** chicken evenly with salt and pepper.
• **Alternate** chicken, pepper pieces, and corn on 8 (14-inch) skewers.
• **Combine** hoisin sauce and remaining 3 ingredients; brush on kabobs.
• **Cook**, covered with grill lid, over medium-hot coals (350° to 400°) 12 minutes, turning and basting with sauce mixture. **Yield:** 4 servings.

CHICKEN AND VEGETABLE STIR-FRY

QUICK!

2 tablespoons vegetable oil
1 pound chicken breast strips
2 tablespoons water
1 (16-ounce) package broccoli
    stir-fry mix
1 purple onion, cut into strips
2 red bell peppers, cut into strips
1 (11.75-ounce) bottle stir-fry
    sauce
Hot cooked rice

• **Pour** oil around top of a preheated wok, coating sides; heat at medium-high (375°) for 2 minutes. Add chicken, and stir-fry 2 minutes or until lightly browned.
• **Add** water and vegetables, stirring gently. Cover and cook 8 minutes or until vegetables are crisp-tender, stirring once. Add sauce, and stir-fry 2 additional minutes. Serve over rice. **Yield:** 4 servings.

CHOW MEIN CHICKEN CASSEROLE

QUICK!

This clever casserole comes together quickly thanks to convenience products. A can of chow mein noodles makes a quick and crunchy topping.

1 tablespoon butter or margarine
1 small red bell pepper,
    chopped
2 cloves garlic, minced
2 (8-ounce) packages sliced fresh
    mushrooms
⅓ cup slivered almonds
3 green onions, chopped
1 (10¾-ounce) can cream of
    mushroom soup, undiluted
¾ cup mayonnaise
2 teaspoons soy sauce
3 cups chopped cooked chicken
¼ teaspoon pepper
1 (3-ounce) can chow mein
    noodles

• **Melt** butter in a large skillet over medium heat. Add bell pepper, garlic, and mushrooms; cook until tender, stirring often. Stir in almonds and next 6 ingredients; pour into a lightly greased 11- x 7- x 1½-inch baking dish. Sprinkle with chow mein noodles.
• **Bake** at 350° for 30 minutes or until bubbly. **Yield:** 6 servings.

Louise W. Mayer
Richmond, Virginia

SPAGHETTI SQUASH AND CHICKEN SKILLET CASSEROLE

3 tablespoons butter or margarine
1 cup sliced fresh mushrooms
1/3 cup chopped leeks
1/4 cup chopped celery
3 tablespoons chopped red bell pepper
3 tablespoons finely chopped fresh parsley
2 cups cooked spaghetti squash
4 skinned and boned chicken breast halves, cooked and cut into thin strips
1/4 cup crushed seasoned croutons
1/4 teaspoon salt
1/4 teaspoon seasoned pepper
1/8 teaspoon garlic powder
Pinch of dried summer savory
1/2 cup sour cream
1/2 cup (2 ounces) shredded Swiss cheese

● **Melt** butter in a large skillet over medium heat. Add mushrooms and next 4 ingredients; cook, stirring constantly, 5 minutes or until tender.
● **Add** squash and next 6 ingredients; cook 4 minutes, stirring constantly.
● **Stir** in sour cream; cook, stirring constantly, just until thoroughly heated. Remove from heat.
● **Sprinkle** with cheese. Cover and let stand 1 minute. **Yield:** 3 to 4 servings.

Spaghetti Squash Tortillas: Prepare recipe according to directions; omit chicken and cheese. Spoon onto 8 (6-inch) flour tortillas, and fold. Place seam side down in a lightly greased 11- x 7- x 1½-inch baking dish. Cover and bake at 350° for 20 minutes. Uncover; sprinkle with cheese. Bake 5 additional minutes.

Fresh Ideas For Vegetable Cooking
Georgia Massie
Seagoville, Texas

TURBAN CHICKEN CURRY

1 (7¾-pound) turban squash
3½ cups chicken broth, divided
1 cup long-grain rice, uncooked
1 (6-ounce) package chopped dried tropical fruit mix
3 green onions, cut into ½-inch pieces
2 tablespoons vegetable oil
1½ tablespoons all-purpose flour
1 tablespoon curry powder
½ teaspoon salt
¼ teaspoon ground red pepper
½ cup unsweetened coconut milk
3 cups chopped cooked chicken
¼ cup flaked coconut, toasted
½ cup cashews, toasted
Garnish: fresh cilantro sprigs

● **Remove** squash crown by cutting around it with a sharp knife angled toward the center; set crown aside. Remove and discard fiber and seeds.
● **Place** base and crown, cut sides down, in a large baking pan. Add water to pan to depth of 1 inch.
● **Bake** at 350° for 1 hour or until tender. Remove from water, reserving pan of water.
● **Bring** 2½ cups chicken broth to a boil in a medium saucepan; add rice. Cover, reduce heat, and cook 20 minutes or until liquid is absorbed and rice is tender. Stir in fruit mix; cover and set aside.
● **Cook** green onions in oil in a large skillet 3 minutes; stir in flour and next 3 ingredients. Cook 1 minute, stirring constantly. Gradually add remaining 1 cup chicken broth; cook 1 minute or until mixture is slightly thickened. Stir in coconut milk.
● **Add** rice mixture and chicken to skillet, stirring just until blended. Spoon into squash base; top with crown. Place in pan with water.
● **Bake** at 350° for 20 minutes or until thoroughly heated.
● **Set** crown to the side, and sprinkle rice mixture with coconut and cashews before serving. Garnish, if desired. **Yield:** 6 servings.

Kinsey Mills
Birmingham, Alabama

CHICKEN DUMPLING PIE

An easy blend of biscuit mix, sour cream, and milk blankets this easy-to-prepare casserole with down-home goodness. Canned ingredients and a few simple additions make this recipe a dependable one-dish meal your family is sure to enjoy.

3 cups chopped cooked chicken or turkey
2 (10¾-ounce) cans cream of chicken soup, undiluted
1 (10½-ounce) can condensed chicken broth, undiluted
1 (15-ounce) can mixed vegetables, drained
½ teaspoon poultry seasoning
2 cups biscuit mix
1 (8-ounce) carton sour cream
1 cup milk

● **Combine** first 5 ingredients in a bowl, and pour chicken mixture into a lightly greased 13- x 9- x 2-inch baking dish.
● **Combine** biscuit mix, sour cream, and milk in a medium bowl; pour over chicken mixture.
● **Bake** at 350° for 50 to 60 minutes or until topping is golden. **Yield:** 6 to 8 servings.

Lilann Taylor
Savannah, Georgia

CHICKEN POT PIE

¼ cup butter or margarine
¼ cup all-purpose flour
1½ cups chicken broth
1½ cups half-and-half
¾ teaspoon salt
½ teaspoon freshly ground
    pepper
2 tablespoons butter or margarine
1 (8-ounce) package sliced fresh
    mushrooms
1 small onion, chopped
3 stalks celery, sliced
3½ cups chopped cooked
    chicken
2 hard-cooked eggs, chopped
1 (15-ounce) package refrigerated
    piecrusts

• **Melt** ¼ cup butter in a heavy sauce-pan over low heat; add flour, stirring until smooth. Cook 1 minute, stirring constantly. Gradually add chicken broth and half-and-half; cook over medium heat, stirring constantly, until thickened and bubbly. Stir in salt and pepper; set sauce aside.
• **Melt** 2 tablespoons butter in a skillet over medium-high heat; add mush-rooms, onion, and celery, and cook, stir-ring constantly, until vegetables are tender. Drain and stir vegetable mixture, chicken, and chopped egg into sauce.
• **Fit** 1 piecrust into a 9-inch deep-dish pieplate according to package direc-tions. Spoon filling into crust; top with remaining piecrust. Trim off excess pas-try. Fold edges under, and flute. Cut slits in top.
• **Bake** at 375° for 30 to 40 minutes or until top is golden, covering edges with strips of aluminum foil after 20 minutes to prevent excessive browning. **Yield:** 6 servings.

Angie Williams
Montgomery, Alabama

CHICKEN ON EGG BREAD

Nashville cooks often rely on this dish for easy entertaining. You can substitute your favorite cornbread for the Egg Bread.

3 tablespoons butter or margarine
2 tablespoons finely chopped
    celery
2 tablespoons finely chopped
    onion
3 tablespoons all-purpose flour
2 cups chicken broth
¾ cup whipping cream
¼ teaspoon salt
Egg Bread
3 cups coarsely chopped cooked
    chicken
Freshly ground pepper

• **Melt** butter in a large skillet over medium-high heat; add celery and onion, and cook, stirring constantly, until tender.
• **Add** flour; cook, stirring constantly, 1 minute. Gradually add chicken broth, whipping cream, and salt; bring to a boil, stirring constantly. Reduce heat, and simmer until slightly thickened (about 3 minutes). Remove from heat, and keep warm.
• **Cut** Egg Bread into wedges or squares; slice in half horizontally. Top with chicken and sauce. Sprinkle with pepper. **Yield:** 6 servings.

Egg Bread

1 cup milk
1 cup water
2¼ cups yellow cornmeal, divided
3 large eggs
1 teaspoon salt
2 cups buttermilk
1 teaspoon baking soda
2 tablespoons shortening

• **Combine** milk and water in a large saucepan; bring to a boil over high heat. Reduce heat, and stir in 2 cups corn-meal. Remove from heat.
• **Beat** eggs at high speed with an elec-tric mixer until foamy; add salt, and beat until light and fluffy.
• **Combine** buttermilk and soda; add to cornmeal mixture with egg mixture, and beat until smooth.

• **Place** shortening in a 10-inch cast-iron skillet; place skillet in a 400° oven for 5 minutes. Pour melted shortening into cornmeal mixture, stirring well. Add re-maining ¼ cup cornmeal, stirring until smooth. Pour cornmeal mixture into hot skillet.
• **Bake** at 400° for 25 to 30 minutes or until firm. Remove from skillet immedi-ately. **Yield:** 6 to 8 servings.

The Nashville Cookbook
Nashville Area Home Economics
Association
Nashville, Tennessee

CHICKEN RAGOÛT WITH CHEDDAR DUMPLINGS

2 cups diagonally sliced carrot
1 cup sweet red pepper strips
3 tablespoons butter or margarine
¼ cup all-purpose flour
2 cups chicken broth
1 cup milk
1 tablespoon lemon juice
½ teaspoon salt
½ teaspoon pepper
3 cups chopped cooked chicken
1 cup frozen English peas, thawed
    and drained
2 cups biscuit mix
⅔ cup milk
¾ cup (3 ounces) shredded
    Cheddar cheese
1 (2-ounce) jar diced pimiento,
    drained

• **Arrange** sliced carrot and sweet red pepper strips in a steamer basket; place over boiling water. Cover; steam 8 min-utes or until vegetables are crisp-tender; set aside.
• **Melt** butter in a large heavy saucepan over low heat; add flour, stirring until mixture is smooth. Cook 1 minute, stir-ring constantly. Gradually add chicken broth and 1 cup milk; cook over medium heat, stirring constantly, until mixture is thickened and bubbly. Re-move from heat.
• **Stir** in lemon juice, salt, and pepper. Add chicken, steamed vegetables, and peas, stirring gently. Spoon into a lightly greased 11- x 7- x 1½-inch baking dish; set aside.

• **Combine** biscuit mix and ⅔ cup milk, stirring until dry ingredients are moistened. Stir vigorously 30 seconds. Turn out onto a lightly floured surface, and knead 4 or 5 times.

• **Roll** dough into a 12- x 9-inch rectangle. Sprinkle with cheese and pimiento, leaving a ½-inch border; roll up jellyroll fashion, starting with a long side, and turn seam side down. Cut into 1-inch-thick slices, and place over chicken mixture.

• **Bake** at 400° for 30 minutes or until golden brown. **Yield:** 6 servings.

Sue Deck
Ellenwood, Georgia

CHICKEN PACKETS

These chicken bundles are a snap to make with convenience products.

2 tablespoons olive oil
4 skinned and boned chicken breast halves, cut into 1-inch pieces
1 cup chopped onion
½ cup chopped green bell pepper
½ cup sour cream
½ (10¾-ounce) can cream of mushroom soup, undiluted
½ teaspoon garlic salt
¼ teaspoon pepper
3 (8-ounce) cans refrigerated crescent dinner rolls
1 cup (4 ounces) shredded mozzarella cheese
Garnish: fresh parsley sprigs

• **Pour** oil into a medium skillet, and place over medium-high heat until hot. Add chicken, onion, and bell pepper; cook, stirring constantly, 5 minutes or until chicken is tender. Drain.

• **Combine** chicken mixture, sour cream, and next 3 ingredients in a small bowl, stirring well.

• **Unroll** crescent rolls, and separate into 12 rectangles; press perforations to seal. Spoon 2 tablespoons chicken mixture in center of each rectangle, and sprinkle evenly with cheese. Bring corners of rectangles together and twist, pinching seams to seal; place on lightly greased baking sheets.

• **Bake** at 350° for 20 minutes or until lightly browned. Garnish, if desired. **Yield:** 1 dozen.

Note: You can freeze unbaked packets in airtight containers up to 3 days. Remove from freezer, and bake, unthawed, at 350° for 30 minutes or until lightly browned.

Cathy Ruark
Brandon, Mississippi

CHICKEN AND BLACK BEAN QUESADILLAS

The ubiquitous Tex-Mex appetizer becomes a hearty meal with main-dish ingredients.

1 tablespoon fajita seasoning
2 (4-ounce) skinned and boned chicken breast halves, cut into thin strips
Vegetable cooking spray
½ onion, cut into strips
½ green bell pepper, cut into strips
2 cloves garlic, minced
1 to 2 jalapeño peppers, minced
1 (15-ounce) can black beans, rinsed and drained
½ cup chopped fresh cilantro
4 (10-inch) flour tortillas
1½ cups (6 ounces) shredded reduced-fat Monterey Jack cheese

• **Rub** fajita seasoning on all sides of chicken; cover and chill 30 minutes.

• **Cook** chicken in a large nonstick skillet over medium-high heat, stirring constantly, 4 minutes or until done. Remove from skillet, and keep warm.

• **Coat** skillet with cooking spray; add onion and next 3 ingredients, and cook until tender, stirring often. Stir in black beans and cilantro; cook, stirring constantly, until thoroughly heated.

• **Coat** 1 side of each tortilla with cooking spray; layer chicken, vegetable mixture, and cheese evenly on uncoated side of 2 tortillas. Top with remaining tortillas, coated side up. Cook in skillet over medium heat until lightly browned,

turning once. Serve immediately. **Yield:** 2 servings.

Patty Messer
Middlesboro, Kentucky

♥ Per serving: Calories 697
Fat 22.2g Cholesterol 93mg
Sodium 911mg

SPICY CHICKEN QUESADILLAS

4 skinned and boned chicken breast halves, cut into ¼-inch-thick strips
1 (1¼-ounce) package taco seasoning mix
2½ cups (10 ounces) shredded Monterey Jack cheese
⅔ cup picante sauce
1 medium-size red bell pepper, chopped
10 (10-inch) flour tortillas
Melted butter

• **Combine** chicken and taco seasoning mix in a heavy-duty, zip-top plastic bag; toss to coat. Cover and chill 1 hour.

• **Place** chicken in a 15- x 10- x 1-inch jellyroll pan.

• **Broil** chicken 5½ inches from heat (with electric oven door partially opened) 5 minutes.

• **Cool** chicken, and cut breasts into bite-size pieces.

• **Combine** chicken, cheese, picante sauce, and red pepper; set aside.

• **Brush** 1 side of each tortilla with melted butter; place 2 tortillas, buttered side down, on a lightly greased baking sheet. Top each tortilla with about 1 cup chicken mixture, spreading to edges of tortilla. Top each with another tortilla, buttered side up.

• **Bake** at 375° for 10 minutes or until golden. Cut into wedges. Repeat with remaining tortillas and chicken mixture. Serve immediately. **Yield:** 5 main-dish servings or 30 appetizers.

Note: Cook quesadillas on the cooktop in a cast-iron skillet or on a griddle. Cook quesadillas, one at a time, 3 minutes on each side.

Amy Cromwell
Atlanta, Georgia

CHICKEN-CHILE CHEESECAKE

1⅓ cups finely crushed tortilla
    chips
¼ cup butter or margarine, melted
3 (8-ounce) packages cream
    cheese, softened
4 large eggs
1 teaspoon chili powder
1 teaspoon Worcestershire sauce
¼ teaspoon salt
3 tablespoons minced green
    onions
1½ cups finely shredded cooked
    chicken
2 (4.5-ounce) cans chopped green
    chiles, drained
1½ cups (6 ounces) shredded
    Monterey Jack cheese
1 (16-ounce) carton sour cream
1 teaspoon seasoned salt
Garnish: minced green onions
Picante sauce

● **Combine** tortilla chips and butter;
press in bottom and 1 inch up sides of a
9-inch springform pan. Set aside.
● **Beat** cream cheese at high speed with
an electric mixer until light and fluffy;
add eggs, one at a time, beating well
after each addition. Stir in chili powder
and next 3 ingredients.
● **Pour** half of cream cheese mixture
into prepared pan. Sprinkle with
chicken, chiles, and cheese; carefully
pour remaining cream cheese mixture
on top. Bake at 350° for 10 minutes; reduce oven temperature to 300°, and
bake 1 additional hour or until set. Cool
completely in pan on a wire rack.
● **Combine** sour cream and seasoned
salt, stirring well; spread evenly on top
of cheesecake. Cover and chill at least 8
hours. Garnish, if desired. Serve with picante sauce. **Yield:** 8 to 10 servings.

GRANDMA ROSE'S
CHOPPED CHICKEN LIVERS
QUICK!

*Art Meripol shares his grandmother's
recipe. Although the original uses
schmaltz – rendered chicken fat – olive
oil makes a fine substitute.*

2 tablespoons olive oil
1 pound chicken livers
2 cloves garlic, minced
1 medium onion, chopped and
    divided
1 hard-cooked egg, chopped
¼ teaspoon salt
¼ teaspoon pepper

● **Pour** oil into a large skillet; place over
medium-high heat until hot. Add livers,
garlic, and half of onion; cook, stirring
constantly, 10 minutes or until livers are
done. Remove from heat.
● **Position** knife blade in food processor bowl; add remaining onion, liver
mixture, egg, salt, and pepper. Pulse 5
times or until livers are chopped. Cover
and chill. Serve with rye or pumper-
nickel bread. **Yield:** ¾ cup.

Art Meripol
Birmingham, Alabama

FRIED CHICKEN LIVERS

1 pound chicken livers
2 cups all-purpose flour
1½ teaspoons seasoned salt
1 teaspoon pepper
1 cup buttermilk
Vegetable oil

● **Pierce** chicken livers several times
with a fork.
● **Combine** flour, salt, and pepper in a
shallow dish; dredge livers in flour mixture. Dip livers in buttermilk, and
dredge in flour mixture again.
● **Pour** oil to depth of 2 inches into a
Dutch oven or electric fryer; heat to
365°. Fry livers, a few at a time, 4 to 5
minutes or until golden. Serve immediately. **Yield:** 4 to 5 servings.

CRANBERRY-CORNBREAD
STUFFED CORNISH HENS
(pictured at right)

1 (6-ounce) package cornbread
    stuffing mix
½ cup water
½ cup thinly sliced celery
1 (8-ounce) container soft cream
    cheese with chives and onions,
    divided
½ cup fresh or frozen cranberries,
    halved
¼ cup coarsely chopped pecans
4 (1- to 1½-pound) Cornish hens
1 tablespoon vegetable oil

● **Combine** seasoning packet from stuffing mix, water, and celery in a large
saucepan; bring to a boil. Cover, reduce
heat, and simmer 5 minutes.
● **Add** ¼ cup cream cheese, stirring until
blended. Stir in stuffing mix, cranberries, and pecans. Remove from heat;
cover and let stand 5 minutes.
● **Loosen** skin from hens without totally
detaching skin; place remaining cream
cheese under skin of hens. Lightly
spoon stuffing mixture into hens; close
opening with skewers. Place hens,
breast side up, in a roasting pan; brush
with oil.
● **Bake** at 350° for 1 hour or until thermometer inserted in stuffing registers
165°. Remove skewers, and serve immediately. **Yield:** 4 servings.

Betty E. Taylor
Piqua, Ohio

Cranberry-Cornbread Stuffed
Cornish Hens

CAJUN-FRIED CORNISH HENS

You like fried chicken, right? Why not try Cajun-Fried Cornish Hens? We loved 'em. (It's nice to have a whole bird to yourself.)

3 tablespoons Cajun seasoning
1 teaspoon ground red pepper
4 (1¼-pound) Cornish hens
½ cup Italian dressing
1 cup all-purpose flour
1½ gallons vegetable oil

• **Combine** seasoning and pepper; rub over inside and outside of hens.
• **Fill** the injector needle of a bulb baster with dressing, and squirt under skin of hens. Tie legs together with one end of a 30-inch string.
• **Place** flour in a large plastic bag; add hens, one at a time, and shake to coat thoroughly.
• **Pour** oil to depth of 4 inches into a deep pot of a propane cooker; heat to 350°. Carefully lower hens into hot oil, using string.
• **Fry** 18 to 20 minutes or until meat thermometer inserted in thickest part registers 180°. Remove hens from oil, and drain on paper towels; remove string. **Yield:** 4 servings.

Denise Boudreaux Schexnayder
Houma, Louisiana

JELLY-GLAZED CORNISH HENS

3 (1½-pound) Cornish hens, split
½ teaspoon salt
¼ teaspoon pepper
1 (10½-ounce) jar jalapeño jelly
2 teaspoons grated lime rind
⅓ cup lime juice
¼ cup vegetable oil
1 tablespoon chopped fresh cilantro

• **Sprinkle** hens with salt and pepper, and place, cut side down, in a large shallow dish; set aside.
• **Melt** jelly in a small saucepan over low heat; add lime rind and remaining 3 ingredients. Pour marinade mixture over hens; cover and chill 3 hours, turning occasionally.

• **For** a charcoal grill, prepare fire, and let burn until coals are white. Rake coals to opposite sides of grill, and place a drip pan between coals. For a gas grill, light one burner, placing drip pan on opposite side.
• **Drain** hens, reserving marinade. Bring marinade to a boil; set aside. Arrange hens on food rack over drip pan. Cook, covered with grill lid, over medium-hot coals (350° to 400°) 35 minutes. Brush with marinade; cook 40 additional minutes. **Yield:** 6 servings.

CORNISH HENS À L'ORANGE

1 navel orange, sliced
6 leaves fresh basil *
2 (1½-pound) Cornish hens, split
1 teaspoon salt
1 teaspoon ground white pepper
2 teaspoons grated orange rind
2 teaspoons dried thyme
¼ cup orange juice concentrate, thawed and undiluted
¾ cup water
1 tablespoon all-purpose flour
2 tablespoons water

• **Arrange** orange slices in a single layer in a lightly greased 11- x 7- x 1½-inch baking dish; top with basil.
• **Sprinkle** hens with salt and pepper; place hens, breast side down, in dish. Sprinkle evenly with orange rind and thyme.
• **Bake** at 375° for 40 minutes.
• **Combine** orange juice concentrate and ¾ cup water. Remove hens from oven, and turn hens breast side up; pour juice mixture over hens. Increase oven temperature to 400°, and bake 20 additional minutes. Transfer hens to a serving platter, reserving drippings; keep hens warm. Pour pan drippings into a saucepan, and place over medium heat.
• **Combine** flour and 2 tablespoons water, stirring well; add to pan drippings, stirring constantly. Bring to a boil; boil 1 minute. Serve with hens. **Yield:** 2 servings.

* Substitute 4 teaspoons dried basil.
Georgie O'Neill-Massa
Welaka, Florida

CORNISH HENS TARRAGON

Marinating the split Cornish hens in a tarragon-garlic based blend of olive oil, lemon juice, soy sauce, and vermouth infuses them with lots of flavor. Tarragon sprinkled on the hens before baking refreshes the herbal element.

4 (1½-pound) Cornish hens, split
¼ cup olive oil
¼ cup fresh lemon juice
¼ cup soy sauce
¼ cup dry vermouth
2 cloves garlic, crushed
1½ teaspoons salt
½ teaspoon coarsely ground black pepper
3 teaspoons dried tarragon, divided
Vegetable cooking spray

• **Place** hens, breast side down, in a large baking dish or heavy-duty zip-top plastic bag.
• **Combine** oil and next 6 ingredients; pour over hens. Sprinkle with 1½ teaspoons tarragon; cover or seal, and store in refrigerator at least 8 hours.
• **Arrange** hens, breast side up, on a rack coated with cooking spray; place rack in broiler pan. Sprinkle remaining 1½ teaspoons tarragon over hens.
• **Bake** at 350° for 1 hour or until tender. **Yield:** 4 servings.

Lisa Conlon
Crystal River, Florida

ROASTED TURKEY WITH SAUSAGE AND WILD MUSHROOM STUFFING

1 cup butter, softened
1 tablespoon dried thyme, crushed
1 (14- to 16-pound) turkey
1 tablespoon salt
1 tablespoon pepper
Sausage and Wild Mushroom
  Stuffing
2 tablespoons soy sauce
2 tablespoons sesame oil
½ cup dry white wine
¼ cup all-purpose flour
1 (16-ounce) carton half-and-half
½ teaspoon soy sauce
½ teaspoon salt
½ teaspoon pepper
Garnish: fresh sage sprigs

• **Combine** butter and thyme; stir well.
• **Remove** giblets and neck from turkey; set aside. Rinse turkey with cold water, and pat dry. Loosen skin from breast without detaching it; carefully spread butter mixture under skin. Rub outside of turkey with 1 tablespoon salt and 1 tablespoon pepper.
• **Spoon** 4 cups Sausage and Wild Mushroom Stuffing into cavity; truss turkey, and tie ends of legs together with string. Lift wingtips up and over back, and tuck under bird. Place turkey, breast side up, in a large roasting pan; rub with 2 tablespoons soy sauce and oil.
• **Bake** at 375° for 2½ hours or until meat thermometer inserted in turkey thigh registers 180° and stuffing registers 165°, shielding turkey with aluminum foil after 1 hour and basting with pan juices every 30 minutes.
• **Cook** giblets and neck in boiling water to cover 45 minutes or until tender. Drain, reserving 1 cup broth. Chop neck meat and giblets; chill.
• **Transfer** turkey to a serving platter, reserving drippings in pan. Remove and discard fat from drippings; pour ¼ cup drippings into a heavy saucepan. Stir wine and reserved broth into roasting pan, stirring to loosen particles that cling to bottom.
• **Place** ¼ cup drippings over medium heat. Add flour, and cook, whisking constantly, until browned. Gradually add wine mixture and half-and-half; cook, whisking constantly, until bubbly. Stir in neck meat and giblets, ½ teaspoon soy sauce, ½ teaspoon salt, and ½ teaspoon pepper; simmer to desired thickness, stirring often. Serve with turkey. Garnish, if desired. **Yield:** 8 servings.

Sausage and Wild Mushroom Stuffing

½ pound ground pork sausage
½ cup butter or margarine
3 pounds mixed wild mushrooms
  (shiitake, portobello, enoki),
  sliced
1 large onion, sliced
1 bunch green onions, sliced
1 (14½-ounce) can chicken broth
1 (8-ounce) package herb-
  seasoned stuffing mix
1 poultry herb bouquet, chopped
  (see note)
½ teaspoon salt
½ teaspoon pepper

• **Brown** sausage in a large skillet, stirring until it crumbles. Drain; set aside.
• **Melt** butter in skillet; add mushrooms, onion, and green onions, and cook until tender. Stir in sausage, broth, and remaining 4 ingredients. Spoon 4 cups stuffing into cavity of turkey, if desired; place remaining stuffing in a lightly greased 13- x 9- x 2-inch baking dish.
• **Bake** at 375° for 45 minutes or until lightly browned. **Yield:** 8 to 10 servings.

Note: A poultry herb bouquet contains 2 sprigs each of fresh sage, rosemary, and thyme. Or you can substitute 1 teaspoon of each dried herb for fresh.

Sudi Swirles and Jan Hryharrow
Durham, North Carolina

DEEP-FRIED TURKEY

1 (8-ounce) bottle Caesar dressing
1 (8- to 10-pound) turkey
1 to 2 gallons vegetable oil or
  peanut oil

• **Fill** the injector needle of a bulb baster with dressing, and squirt under skin. Tie legs together with one end of a 30-inch string.
• **Pour** oil to depth of 5 to 6 inches into a deep pot of a propane cooker; heat to 325°. Carefully lower turkey into oil, using string; fry 30 minutes or until thermometer inserted into meaty portion of thigh registers 180°. (Temperature of oil drops immediately after turkey is placed in it; oil may not reach 325° again.) Remove from oil; cool slightly before slicing. **Yield:** 12 to 14 servings.

Kreis Beall
The Inn at Blackberry Farm
Walland, Tennessee

CITRUS-MARINATED TURKEY BREAST

1 (6- to 7-pound) turkey breast
1 cup orange juice
¼ cup lime juice
¼ cup olive oil
3 tablespoons apple cider vinegar
2 teaspoons salt
2 teaspoons dried oregano
1 teaspoon pepper
Garnishes: fresh sage, oregano, and
  rosemary sprigs

• **Remove** and discard skin and breast bone. Place turkey in a jumbo heavy-duty, zip-top plastic bag; set aside.
• **Combine** orange juice and next 6 ingredients in a jar; cover tightly, and shake vigorously. Reserve ½ cup marinade in refrigerator. Pour remaining marinade over turkey; seal bag. Chill 8 hours, turning turkey occasionally.
• **Remove** turkey from marinade; discard marinade.
• **Cook** turkey, covered with grill lid, over hot coals (400° to 500°) for 18 minutes on each side or until a meat thermometer inserted in thickest part registers 170°, brushing occasionally with reserved marinade. Let stand 10 minutes before slicing. Garnish, if desired. **Yield:** 8 servings.

Note: To cook turkey in oven, place on a rack in a roasting pan; bake at 325° for 1 hour and 10 minutes or until a meat thermometer registers 170°, brushing occasionally with the marinade.

Carolyn Gaskins
Cherryville, North Carolina

GRILLED MARINATED TURKEY STEAKS

1 (5-pound) bone-in turkey
    breast *
½ cup soy sauce
¼ cup vegetable oil
1 tablespoon ground ginger
1 teaspoon dry mustard
3 cloves garlic, pressed

• **Purchase** turkey breast. Ask butcher to cut in half lengthwise, and then cut each half crosswise into 1-inch-thick "steaks" resembling large pork chops.
• **Combine** soy sauce and remaining 4 ingredients; pour over turkey. Cover and chill 8 hours. Remove turkey from marinade, discarding marinade.
• **Cook** turkey, covered with grill lid, over medium-hot coals (350° to 400°) 8 to 10 minutes on each side. **Yield:** 12 servings.

* Substitute 1 (5-pound) boneless turkey breast. Cut turkey in same manner yourself.

Jesse and Violet Rhinehart
Raleigh, North Carolina

GRILLED TURKEY BREAST WITH CRANBERRY SALSA

1 (6-pound) turkey breast
1 cup cranberry juice cocktail
¼ cup orange juice
¼ cup olive oil
1 teaspoon salt
1 teaspoon pepper
¼ cup chopped fresh cilantro
3 cups frozen cranberries
½ cup honey
2 tablespoons fresh lime juice
½ cup coarsely chopped purple
    onion
2 jalapeño peppers, seeded and
    coarsely chopped
½ cup coarsely chopped dried
    apricot halves
½ cup fresh cilantro leaves
2 large oranges, peeled, seeded,
    and coarsely chopped

• **Remove** and discard skin and breast bone from turkey breast, separating breast halves; place turkey in a large heavy-duty, zip-top plastic bag.
• **Combine** cranberry juice cocktail and next 5 ingredients in a jar; cover tightly, and shake vigorously. Reserve ½ cup marinade, and chill. Pour remaining marinade over turkey. Seal bag, and chill 8 hours, turning occasionally.
• **Position** knife blade in food processor bowl; add cranberries and remaining 7 ingredients. Pulse until chopped, stopping once to scrape down sides (do not overprocess). Transfer cranberry mixture to a serving bowl; chill.
• **Remove** turkey from marinade, discarding marinade.
• **Cook** turkey, covered with grill lid, over medium-hot coals (350° to 400°), about 15 minutes on each side or until a meat thermometer inserted in thickest part registers 170°, basting occasionally with reserved marinade. Let stand 10 minutes before slicing. Serve with cranberry mixture. **Yield:** 8 servings.

Julie Downey
Houston, Texas

♥ Per serving: Calories 322
Fat 5.6g   Cholesterol 79mg
Sodium 240mg

TURKEY CUTLETS WITH SAGE GRAVY

Turkey cutlets for company? You bet. A rich, creamy sauce, well worth the calories and time invested, makes this dish fit for any special occasion.

4 (5-ounce) boneless turkey
    breast cutlets
1 tablespoon finely chopped fresh
    sage leaves or 1 teaspoon
    dried leaf sage, crumbled
¼ teaspoon salt
⅛ teaspoon pepper
⅛ teaspoon paprika
½ cup all-purpose flour
2 tablespoons butter
2 tablespoons olive oil
Sage Gravy
Garnish: fresh sage leaves

• **Place** turkey cutlets between two sheets of heavy-duty plastic wrap; flatten to ¼-inch thickness, using a meat mallet or rolling pin.
• **Combine** sage, salt, pepper, and paprika; rub evenly on each side of cutlets. Cover and chill 1 to 2 hours.
• **Dredge** cutlets in flour, and shake off excess.
• **Melt** butter in a large nonstick skillet over medium heat; add olive oil. Add cutlets; cook 3 minutes on each side or until lightly browned. Transfer cutlets to a serving plate; keep warm.
• **Reserve** drippings in skillet for Sage Gravy.
• **Serve** cutlets with Sage Gravy. Garnish, if desired. **Yield:** 4 servings.

Sage Gravy

½ cup finely chopped onion
½ cup finely chopped carrot
¼ cup finely chopped celery
1 tablespoon finely chopped
    fresh sage leaves or
    1 teaspoon dried leaf sage,
    crumbled
Reserved drippings
⅓ cup dry white wine
½ cup chicken broth
1 cup half-and-half
½ teaspoon lemon juice
½ teaspoon salt
½ teaspoon pepper
2 tablespoons cold butter, cut
    into pieces

• **Add** first 4 ingredients to reserved drippings in skillet.
• **Cook** over medium heat, stirring constantly, until onion is tender. Add wine; bring mixture to a boil, and cook until liquid in skillet is reduced to about 2 tablespoons.
• **Add** broth, and cook until liquid is reduced by half. Stir in half-and-half. Return to a boil; cook until slightly thickened.
• **Pour** mixture through a wire-mesh strainer into a bowl; discard vegetables. Return mixture to skillet. Stir in lemon juice, salt, and pepper.
• **Add** butter pieces, one at a time, stirring with a wire whisk until blended. (If butter is difficult to work into gravy, place skillet over low heat for a few seconds, being careful not to get mixture too hot.) **Yield:** 1 cup.

TURKEY CUTLETS WITH TARRAGON-MUSTARD SAUCE

QUICK!

4 turkey cutlets
1 teaspoon garlic salt
¼ teaspoon pepper
2 tablespoons olive oil
½ cup plain yogurt
2 tablespoons Dijon mustard
¼ teaspoon dried tarragon
¼ teaspoon sugar
⅛ teaspoon hot sauce

• **Sprinkle** turkey cutlets with garlic salt and pepper. Cook in hot oil in a large skillet over medium-high heat 2 minutes on each side. Remove turkey, and keep warm.
• **Combine** yogurt and remaining 4 ingredients in skillet; cook over low heat until thoroughly heated. Serve over turkey. **Yield:** 4 servings.

Cathy Darling
Grafton, West Virginia

TURKEY-BASIL PICCATA

QUICK!

2 tablespoons all-purpose flour
¼ teaspoon salt
¼ teaspoon pepper
1¾ pound turkey cutlets
2 tablespoons olive oil
4 cloves garlic, minced
1½ teaspoons dried basil or 1½ tablespoons chopped fresh basil
½ cup dry white wine
1½ tablespoons fresh lemon juice
1 lemon, sliced

• **Combine** first 3 ingredients in a shallow dish; dredge cutlets in flour mixture, shaking off excess.
• **Pour** olive oil into a large skillet; place over medium-high heat until hot. Add cutlets, and cook 1½ minutes or until done, turning once. Remove cutlets from skillet.
• **Add** garlic and basil to skillet, and cook 45 seconds, stirring to loosen particles that cling to bottom. Add wine, lemon juice, and lemon slices; cook 45

seconds, stirring constantly. Return cutlets to pan; cook just until heated. Serve immediately. **Yield:** 3 to 4 servings.

Deborah Holley
Patterson, Louisiana

EASY TURKEY SCALOPPINE

QUICK!

1 tablespoon butter or margarine
2 teaspoons lemon juice
1 large egg, lightly beaten
¼ cup Italian-seasoned breadcrumbs
2 tablespoons grated Parmesan cheese
½ teaspoon dried basil
⅛ teaspoon garlic salt
⅛ teaspoon ground black pepper
⅛ teaspoon ground red pepper
4 slices fresh turkey cutlets (about ½ pound)
⅓ cup pasta sauce

• **Place** butter in a microwave-safe bowl, and microwave at MEDIUM (50% power) 1 minute or until butter melts. Add lemon juice and egg, stirring well.
• **Combine** breadcrumbs and next 5 ingredients in a shallow dish.
• **Dip** turkey in egg mixture; dredge in breadcrumb mixture. Place in a lightly greased 8-inch square baking dish.
• **Microwave** at HIGH 4 minutes, giving dish a half-turn after 2 minutes. Spoon pasta sauce evenly over turkey. **Yield:** 2 servings.

TURKEY AND PEPPERS IN CORNBREAD CRUST

2 cups chopped cooked turkey
1 (7-ounce) jar roasted red bell peppers, drained and sliced
1 (4.5-ounce) can chopped green chiles, undrained
1 (10¾-ounce) can cream of chicken soup, undiluted
½ cup sour cream
¼ cup milk
1 teaspoon chili powder
1 (11.5-ounce) can refrigerated cornbread twists

• **Combine** all ingredients except cornbread twists. Spoon into a lightly greased 8-inch square baking dish; set aside.
• **Prepare** cornbread twists according to package directions, but do not bake. Place over turkey mixture. Cover loosely with aluminum foil.
• **Bake** at 375° for 30 minutes. Uncover and bake 10 additional minutes or until cornbread is lightly browned. **Yield:** 4 to 6 servings.

Beppy Hassey
Montgomery, Alabama

EASY TURKEY EMPANADAS

QUICK!

1 (15-ounce) package refrigerated piecrusts
2 cups cooked yellow rice
1 cup chopped smoked turkey
1 cup (4 ounces) shredded Monterey Jack cheese with peppers
½ cup sliced green onions
1 (2.25-ounce) can sliced ripe olives, drained
1 to 2 teaspoons fajita seasoning
Cornmeal
Sour cream
Picante sauce

• **Unfold** piecrusts, and press out fold lines.
• **Combine** rice and next 5 ingredients; spoon evenly onto half of each piecrust. Fold piecrusts over filling, pressing edges to seal. Crimp edges with a fork. Place on a baking sheet sprinkled with cornmeal.
• **Bake** at 400° for 25 minutes or until lightly browned. Cut in half. Serve with sour cream and picante sauce. **Yield:** 4 servings.

Sandra Stewart
Northport, Alabama

HOME-STYLE TURKEY TURNOVERS

½ cup quartered fresh mushrooms
½ cup chopped fresh green
     beans
1 small onion, finely chopped
1 clove garlic, crushed
½ teaspoon dried thyme
½ teaspoon dried rosemary
2 tablespoons vegetable oil
1 tablespoon all-purpose flour
⅓ cup whipping cream
1 cup chopped cooked turkey
¼ teaspoon salt
¼ teaspoon pepper
1 (17¼-ounce) package frozen
     puff pastry sheets, thawed

• **Cook** first 6 ingredients in oil in a skillet over medium-high heat until crisp-tender, stirring often. Add flour, and cook 1 minute, stirring constantly. Add whipping cream, and cook, stirring constantly, until thickened; remove from heat. Stir in turkey, salt, and pepper; cool 5 minutes.
• **Unfold** pastry sheets, and cut each sheet into 4 squares.
• **Spoon** turkey mixture evenly in center of each square. Brush pastry edges lightly with water; fold in half to form triangles. Press edges to seal; crimp with a fork. Place on an ungreased baking sheet.
• **Bake** at 400° for 15 minutes or until golden. **Yield:** 8 servings.

Lilann Taylor
Savannah, Georgia

DOVE AU VIN

1 cup all-purpose flour
1 teaspoon salt
1 teaspoon pepper
12 doves, dressed
⅓ cup butter or margarine
1 cup chopped celery
1 cup chopped onion
1 small green bell pepper,
     chopped
1 (10½-ounce) can beef
     consommé
½ cup dry red wine
Hot cooked egg noodles or rice

• **Combine** first 3 ingredients in a large heavy-duty, zip-top plastic bag. Add doves, a few at a time; seal bag, and shake to coat.
• **Melt** butter in a large nonstick skillet over medium-high heat; add doves, and cook until browned, turning once.
• **Place** doves in a lightly greased 13- x 9- x 2-inch baking dish. Sprinkle celery, onion, and green pepper evenly over doves; add consommé. Cover with aluminum foil.
• **Bake** at 350° for 1½ hours. Pour wine over doves; cover and bake 30 additional minutes. Serve with noodles or rice. **Yield:** 6 servings.

Party Potpourri
Junior League of Memphis, Tennessee

GAME BIRDS IN WINE MARINADE

12 skinned dove breasts
¾ cup dry red wine
¼ cup vegetable oil
¼ cup soy sauce
1 tablespoon brown sugar
2 tablespoons water
1 teaspoon dried oregano
1 teaspoon ground ginger
1 clove garlic, pressed
1 (8-ounce) can sliced mushrooms,
     undrained
1 tablespoon vegetable oil
Hot cooked rice
Garnishes: chopped fresh parsley,
     fresh whole mushrooms

• **Place** dove breasts in a large shallow dish or heavy-duty, zip-top plastic bag.
• **Combine** wine and next 8 ingredients; pour over dove, turning to coat. Cover dish, or seal bag. Chill 8 hours, turning dove occasionally. Drain, reserving marinade.
• **Brown** dove in 1 tablespoon hot oil in a small Dutch oven. Add reserved marinade. Bring to a boil; cover, reduce heat, and simmer 1 hour.
• **Remove** dove from Dutch oven, reserving liquid in pan; cool slightly. Remove and discard bones from dove; return meat to pan.
• **Bring** mixture to a boil; reduce heat, and simmer 3 minutes or until mixture

is thoroughly heated. Serve over rice. Garnish, if desired. **Yield:** 4 servings.

Jill Fortney
Fort Worth, Texas

BLACKENED DUCK BREASTS

The blackening in this recipe is best done outdoors on a propane cooker due to the heavy smoke produced. If you haven't been duck hunting lately or can't find duck breasts, use 12 skinned and boned chicken breast halves, instead. They're great, too.

3 (6-ounce) packages long-grain-
     and-wild rice mix *
2 (0.9-ounce) envelopes béarnaise
     sauce mix
12 duck breast halves, skinned
     and boned
⅓ cup butter or margarine,
     melted
3 tablespoons Cajun blackened
     seasoning
2 (14-ounce) cans artichoke
     hearts, drained
½ pound fresh mushrooms,
     sliced
1 cup dry white wine
2 cloves garlic, crushed
Garnishes: lemon slices, fresh
     parsley sprigs

• **Prepare** rice mix according to package directions; keep warm.
• **Prepare** béarnaise sauce mix according to package directions; keep warm.
• **Place** a large, greased cast-iron skillet over an outdoor propane cooker until very hot (about 10 minutes), following manufacturer's instructions.
• **Brush** duck with butter; sprinkle with seasoning, and cook in hot skillet about 4 minutes on each side or until done. Remove from skillet, and keep warm.
• **Combine** artichokes and next 3 ingredients in a heavy saucepan; cook over medium heat until mushrooms are tender, stirring occasionally.
• **To serve,** slice duck into thin strips, and place on a bed of cooked rice mix. Using a slotted spoon, spoon artichoke

mixture evenly over duck strips. Top with béarnaise sauce, and serve immediately. Garnish, if desired. **Yield:** 12 servings.

Men's Gourmet
Raleigh, North Carolina

* Substitute 12 ounces angel hair pasta, cooked according to package directions, for the long-grain-and-wild rice mix.

BAKED QUAIL WITH CORNBREAD STUFFING

12 quail
Cornbread Stuffing
12 slices bacon
¼ cup Worcestershire sauce
1 (14½-ounce) can beef broth, divided

• **Cut** a pocket on each side of quail backbone, measuring about 2 inches long and 1½ inches deep.
• **Stuff** quail pockets with unbaked Cornbread Stuffing, spooning about 1 tablespoon stuffing into each pocket. Reserve remaining Cornbread Stuffing for baking.
• **Wrap** a bacon slice around each quail; place in a roasting pan, breast side down, and drizzle evenly with Worcestershire sauce.
• **Reserve** 1¼ cups beef broth.
• **Cover** and bake at 350° for 1 hour, uncovering and basting quail with remaining beef broth every 10 minutes during the first 30 minutes of cooking time.
• **Uncover** and turn quail, breast side up. Brush with pan drippings.
• **Broil** quail, uncovered, 5 inches from heat (with electric oven door partially opened) 3 to 5 minutes or until browned. Remove quail from roasting pan, reserving drippings in a pan. Keep quail warm.
• **Add** reserved 1¼ cups beef broth to drippings, stirring to loosen browned particles that cling to bottom. Cook over high heat about 15 minutes or until liquid is reduced by one-third; skim fat from liquid. Serve quail with sauce and baked Cornbread Stuffing. **Yield:** 6 servings.

Cornbread Stuffing

2 (8½-ounce) packages cornbread muffin mix
1 pound ground pork sausage
¼ cup butter or margarine
3 cups finely chopped celery
½ cup chopped onion
½ cup chopped green onions
1 (8-ounce) package herb-seasoned stuffing mix
2 (14½-ounce) cans chicken broth
3 large eggs, lightly beaten

• **Prepare** cornbread mix according to package directions; cool and crumble in a large bowl. Set aside.
• **Brown** sausage in a large skillet, stirring until it crumbles. Drain well, and stir into cornbread.
• **Melt** butter in a large skillet, and add celery and onions. Cook over medium-high heat, stirring constantly, until tender. Stir vegetables into cornbread mixture.
• **Stir** stuffing mix, broth, and eggs into cornbread mixture. Remove 1½ cups for stuffing quail. Spoon remaining mixture into a greased 13- x 9- x 2-inch baking dish.
• **Bake** at 350° for 1 hour or until golden. **Yield:** 6 to 8 servings.

Jill Fortney
Fort Worth, Texas

MAPLE-GLAZED QUAIL WITH WHITE BEAN RAGOÛT

4 (4-ounce) dressed quail
2 medium onions, diced
1 tablespoon sugar
4 fresh mushrooms, sliced
1 teaspoon white vinegar
⅓ cup fine, dry breadcrumbs
¼ teaspoon salt
¼ teaspoon pepper
¼ teaspoon dried thyme
3 tablespoons butter or margarine, melted
White Bean Ragoût
Maple Brown Sauce

• **Remove** breast and back bones from quail; set quail aside.

• **Cook** onion in a nonstick skillet over low heat 10 minutes or until browned, stirring often; add sugar and mushrooms, and cook until tender, stirring mixture often. Stir in vinegar and next 4 ingredients.
• **Spoon** into quail cavities, and secure with wooden picks. Tuck wings under, and place, breast side up, in a buttered 2-quart casserole. Brush with melted butter.
• **Bake** at 350° for 20 minutes or until done. Serve over a bed of White Bean Ragoût; drizzle with Maple Brown Sauce. **Yield:** 2 servings.

White Bean Ragoût

1 cup dried Great Northern or navy beans
½ cup diced onion
1 bay leaf
3 tablespoons diced carrot
2 cups beef broth

• **Sort** and wash beans; drain.
• **Combine** beans and water to cover in a large saucepan; let stand 1 hour. Drain beans, and return to pan. Add onion and remaining ingredients; bring to a boil. Reduce heat, and simmer 2 hours or until beans are tender, stirring occasionally. Remove and discard bay leaf. **Yield:** 2 cups.

Maple Brown Sauce

QUICK!

1 teaspoon butter or margarine
1 teaspoon all-purpose flour
½ cup beef broth
1 tablespoon maple syrup

• **Melt** butter in a small heavy saucepan over low heat; whisk in flour until smooth. Cook 1 minute, whisking constantly. Whisk in broth; cook over medium heat, whisking constantly, 5 minutes or until thickened and bubbly. Stir in maple syrup. **Yield:** ½ cup.

Devil's Pool Restaurant
Big Cedar Lodge
Ridgedale, Missouri

ROASTED QUAIL ÉTOUFFÉE

1 medium potato, peeled and cut
    into ½-inch pieces
1 large fresh leek, chopped
4 cups loosely packed fresh
    spinach
1 tablespoon vegetable oil
½ teaspoon salt
¼ teaspoon ground black pepper
8 quail, dressed
8 large plum tomatoes
½ cup vegetable oil
½ cup all-purpose flour
1½ cups chopped onion
½ cup finely chopped green bell
    pepper
½ cup finely chopped celery
2 cloves garlic, minced
4 bay leaves
3 cups chicken broth
2 teaspoons salt
2 teaspoons fresh thyme or
    ¾ teaspoon dried thyme
1 teaspoon Worcestershire
    sauce
½ teaspoon sugar
⅓ cup chopped green onions
2 tablespoons chopped fresh
    parsley
2 teaspoons ground black pepper
½ teaspoon ground red pepper
2 teaspoons hot sauce
Soufflé Cornbread (see recipe on
    page 40)

• **Cook** potato in boiling water to cover 8 minutes or until potato is tender; drain and let cool.

• **Cook** leek and spinach in 1 tablespoon oil in a large skillet over medium heat, stirring constantly, 3 minutes or until wilted; cool.

• **Combine** potato, leek mixture, ½ teaspoon salt, and ¼ teaspoon black pepper; spoon into cavities of quail. Place 1 leg over the other, and secure with a wooden pick. Place quail and tomatoes in a large roasting pan.

• **Bake** at 400° for 45 minutes; cool tomatoes slightly. Chop tomatoes, reserving liquid; set aside.

• **Pour** ½ cup oil into a large skillet or Dutch oven; place over medium-high heat until very hot. Add flour, and cook, stirring constantly, 2 to 3 minutes or until golden (do not burn).

• **Add** 1½ cups onion and next 4 ingredients; cook 4 to 5 minutes or until onion is tender. Gradually add chicken broth, stirring constantly.

• **Add** tomato, reserved liquid, 2 teaspoons salt, and next 3 ingredients; bring to a boil. Reduce heat, and simmer, uncovered, 1 hour.

• **Stir** in green onions and next 4 ingredients. Add quail, breast side up; simmer 15 minutes. Remove and discard bay leaves. Serve quail mixture over Soufflé Cornbread. **Yield:** 8 servings.

Chef Johnny Earles
Criolla's
Destin, Florida

GRILLED QUAIL

16 quail, dressed
16 jalapeño peppers
16 slices bacon
1 (8-ounce) bottle Italian
    dressing
½ cup dry white wine
⅓ cup soy sauce
¼ cup lemon juice
¼ teaspoon pepper
Garnish: banana peppers

• **Rinse** quail thoroughly with cold water; pat dry. Place a jalapeño pepper into body cavity of each quail. Wrap 1 bacon slice around each quail, and secure with a wooden pick. Place quail in a large shallow dish.

• **Combine** Italian dressing and next 4 ingredients; pour over quail. Cover and chill 8 hours. Remove quail from dish, reserving marinade. Bring leftover marinade to a boil, and set aside.

• **Prepare** charcoal fire in one end of grill; let burn 15 to 20 minutes or until flames disappear and coals are white. Cook, covered with grill lid, on opposite end 1 hour, turning once, and basting often with marinade. Garnish, if desired. **Yield:** 8 servings.

Note: You can bake quail on a rack in a roasting pan in the oven at 350° for 1 hour, turning once, and basting often with marinade.

Bee and Michael Fitzpatrick
New Orleans, Louisiana

COUNTRY-FRIED WILD TURKEY

An overnight soak in milk tenderizes these strips of wild turkey.

3 pounds boneless wild turkey
    breast
2 to 2½ cups milk
1½ cups all-purpose flour
1 to 1¼ teaspoons salt
½ teaspoon pepper
Vegetable oil
Turkey Gravy

• **Cut** turkey into 1-inch slices; cut each slice into 3- x ½-inch strips, and place in an 11- x 7- x 1½-inch baking dish. Pour milk over strips; cover and chill 8 hours. Drain turkey, discarding milk, and set aside.

• **Combine** flour, salt, and pepper in a large heavy-duty, zip-top plastic bag. Add 6 to 8 turkey strips; seal bag, and shake to coat. Place turkey strips in a single layer on wax paper; repeat procedure with remaining turkey strips.

• **Pour** oil to depth of 2 to 3 inches in a large Dutch oven; heat to 350°. Cook turkey strips, 8 to 10 at a time, until golden. Drain on paper towels; keep warm. Repeat procedure with remaining strips. Reserve ⅓ cup drippings for Turkey Gravy. Serve turkey strips with gravy. **Yield:** 8 to 10 main-dish servings or 16 to 18 appetizer servings.

Turkey Gravy

QUICK!

⅓ cup reserved turkey drippings
⅓ cup all-purpose flour
2 cups milk
½ teaspoon salt
½ teaspoon pepper

• **Pour** reserved drippings into a heavy skillet. Stir in flour; cook over medium heat, stirring constantly, until dark golden. Gradually stir in milk; cook, stirring constantly, until thickened. Stir in salt and pepper. **Yield:** 2 cups.

Jill Fortney
Fort Worth, Texas

At right: Summer Tomato Salad (page 307)

SALADS

Holiday Cranberry Salad

HOLIDAY CRANBERRY SALAD
(pictured at left)

2 cups fresh or frozen cranberries, thawed
1 cup sugar
1 (3-ounce) package lemon-flavored gelatin
1 cup boiling water
1 cup chopped celery
1 cup chopped walnuts, toasted
Lettuce leaves
Garnishes: lemon slices, celery leaves, cranberries

• **Position** knife blade in food processor bowl; add cranberries. Process 30 seconds or until chopped.
• **Combine** cranberries and sugar in a large bowl; let stand 1 hour or until sugar dissolves.
• **Combine** gelatin and boiling water in a large bowl; stir 2 minutes or until gelatin dissolves. Chill until the consistency of unbeaten egg white.
• **Stir** cranberry mixture, celery, and walnuts into gelatin mixture. Pour into a lightly oiled 4-cup mold. Cover and chill until firm.
• **Unmold** salad onto a lettuce-lined plate. Garnish, if desired. **Yield:** 6 to 8 servings.

Sunny Tiedemann
Bartlesville, Oklahoma

ORANGE-BUTTERMILK SALAD

"This very light dish can be made the day before and is always a hit. People cannot believe it's made with buttermilk." – Juanita

1 (20-ounce) can unsweetened crushed pineapple, undrained
1 (6-ounce) package orange-flavored gelatin
2 cups buttermilk
1 (8-ounce) container frozen whipped topping, thawed
1 cup chopped pecans, toasted
Lettuce leaves

• **Bring** pineapple and liquid to a boil in a medium saucepan. Remove from heat;

stir in gelatin. Stir until gelatin dissolves; let cool.
• **Add** buttermilk to pineapple mixture; cover and chill until mixture is the consistency of unbeaten egg white. Fold in whipped topping and chopped pecans.
• **Spoon** mixture into a lightly oiled 9-cup mold; cover and chill until mixture is firm.
• **Unmold** onto a lettuce-lined plate. **Yield:** 14 to 16 servings.

Juanita B. Hutto
Richmond, Virginia

FROZEN STRAWBERRY SALAD
QUICK!

1 (8-ounce) package fat-free cream cheese product, softened
½ cup sugar
1 (8-ounce) container reduced-fat frozen whipped topping, thawed
2 cups frozen no-sugar-added whole strawberries, thawed and halved
1 (15¼-ounce) can unsweetened crushed pineapple, undrained
1½ cups sliced banana (2 medium)

• **Beat** cream cheese at medium speed with an electric mixer until creamy; gradually add sugar, beating until smooth.
• **Fold** in whipped topping and remaining ingredients; spoon into a 13- x 9- x 2-inch dish. Cover with aluminum foil.
• **Freeze** until firm. **Yield:** 12 servings.

Linda S. Zachry
Dallas, Texas

♥ Per serving: Calories 138
Fat 2.6g Cholesterol 4mg
Sodium 128mg

ALMOND-CITRUS SALAD

⅔ cup vegetable oil
2 teaspoons grated grapefruit rind
½ cup fresh grapefruit juice
1 (0.7-ounce) envelope Italian salad dressing mix
1 grapefruit
2 oranges
1 avocado, sliced
3 cups torn spinach
3 cups torn leaf lettuce
3 cups torn iceberg lettuce
½ cup sliced celery
½ cup chopped green bell pepper
¼ cup Sweet and Spicy Almonds

• **Combine** oil, grapefruit rind, grapefruit juice, and salad dressing mix in a jar; cover tightly, and shake vigorously.
• **Peel** and section grapefruit and oranges, and place in a large bowl. Add avocado and next 5 ingredients.
• **Add** dressing, tossing to coat. Sprinkle with Sweet and Spicy Almonds. **Yield:** 8 servings.

Sweet and Spicy Almonds
QUICK!

Make a double batch of these almonds to serve as an appetizer or hostess gift.

1 cup sliced almonds
1 tablespoon butter or margarine, melted
1½ teaspoons sugar
¼ teaspoon ground cumin
¼ teaspoon chili powder
⅛ teaspoon dried crushed red pepper
Pinch of salt

• **Combine** almonds and butter, stirring well. Combine sugar and remaining 4 ingredients; sprinkle over almonds, tossing to coat. Spread on a lightly greased baking sheet.
• **Bake** at 325° for 15 minutes, stirring occasionally; cool. **Yield:** 1 cup.

Nora Henshaw
Okemah, Oklahoma

CAESAR MARGARITA SALAD

A frosty salted rim frames this Caesar salad inspired by the margarita.

Lime wedges (optional)
Kosher salt (optional)
1 large head romaine lettuce, torn
1 cup (4 ounces) shredded Monterey Jack cheese
¼ cup finely chopped fresh cilantro
1 red bell pepper, cut into thin strips
Margarita Dressing
Tortilla Triangles
Garnish: lime wedges

• **Rub** rims of six chilled salad plates with lime wedges, if desired; place salt in saucer, and roll rim of each plate in salt, if desired. Set aside.
• **Combine** lettuce and next 3 ingredients in a large bowl; add Margarita Dressing, tossing gently.
• **Arrange** salad on plates, and sprinkle with Tortilla Triangles. Garnish, if desired. **Yield:** 6 servings.

Margarita Dressing

QUICK!

⅓ cup canola or safflower oil
¼ cup lime juice
2 tablespoons fat-free egg substitute
1½ tablespoons tequila
1½ teaspoons Triple Sec or other orange-flavored liqueur
1 clove garlic, minced
1 serrano chile pepper, seeded and finely chopped
¼ teaspoon salt
¼ teaspoon ground cumin

• **Combine** all ingredients in a small bowl; stir well with a wire whisk. Cover and chill. **Yield:** 1 cup.

Tortilla Triangles

QUICK!

6 (6-inch) corn tortillas, cut into small triangles
½ cup canola or vegetable oil
Kosher salt

• **Fry** tortilla triangles in hot oil in a small skillet until golden; drain on paper towels, and sprinkle immediately with kosher salt. **Yield:** 1½ cups.

GREEK CAESAR SALAD

¾ cup olive oil
¼ cup lemon juice
¼ cup fat-free egg substitute
2 cloves garlic, pressed
1 teaspoon dried oregano
¼ teaspoon salt
⅛ teaspoon pepper
1 head romaine lettuce, torn
¾ cup kalamata olives, pitted
1 small purple onion, thinly sliced
½ cup crumbled feta cheese
Pita Croutons

• **Combine** first 7 ingredients in a small bowl, stirring with a wire whisk. Cover and chill.
• **Combine** lettuce and next 3 ingredients in a large bowl; gradually add enough dressing to coat leaves, tossing gently. Sprinkle with Pita Croutons, and serve with remaining dressing. **Yield:** 6 servings.

Pita Croutons

QUICK!

2 tablespoons olive oil
1 teaspoon dried oregano
¼ teaspoon crushed garlic
Dash of salt
1 (8-inch) pita bread round, split into 2 circles

• **Combine** first 4 ingredients, and brush olive oil mixture over the inside of each pita bread circle.
• **Cut** each pita bread circle into bite-size pieces, and place on a baking sheet.
• **Bake** at 400° for 5 to 7 minutes or until golden. **Yield:** 1⅓ cups.

SOUTHERN CAESAR SALAD

Caesar comes to Dixie in this stately salad, dressed in the flavors of the South.

⅓ cup peanut oil
3 tablespoons cider vinegar
2 tablespoons fat-free egg substitute
2 tablespoons honey mustard
¼ teaspoon pepper
4 ounces thinly sliced country ham, cut into ¼-inch strips
1 tablespoon peanut oil
1 large head romaine lettuce, torn
¾ cup pecans, toasted and coarsely chopped
Honeyed Cornbread Croutons

• **Combine** first 5 ingredients, and stir well with a wire whisk. Cover and chill at least 1 hour.
• **Cook** ham in peanut oil in a skillet over medium-high heat, stirring constantly, until browned. Drain on paper towels.
• **Combine** lettuce, pecans, and ham in a large bowl; add dressing, tossing gently. Sprinkle with Honeyed Cornbread Croutons. **Yield:** 6 servings.

Honeyed Cornbread Croutons

1 (11.5-ounce) package refrigerated cornbread twists
¼ cup butter or margarine, melted
1 tablespoon honey

• **Unroll** dough; separate at perforations to form 16 strips. Place on an ungreased baking sheet.
• **Combine** butter and honey; brush on strips.
• **Bake** at 375° for 11 minutes. Transfer to wire racks to cool.
• **Cut** each strip diagonally into ½-inch slices, and place on an ungreased baking sheet.
• **Bake** at 225° for 20 minutes, stirring every 5 minutes. Cool.
• **Store** in airtight container up to 1 month. **Yield:** 4 cups.

SPINACH-APRICOT SALAD

1 cup boiling water
1 (6-ounce) package dried apricot halves
1 pound fresh spinach or 1 (10-ounce) package fresh spinach
3 tablespoons cider vinegar
3 tablespoons apricot preserves
½ cup vegetable oil
¾ cup coarsely chopped macadamia nuts, toasted

• **Pour** boiling water over apricots; let stand 30 minutes. Drain well; set aside.
• **Remove** stems from spinach; wash leaves thoroughly, and pat dry. Tear into bite-size pieces. Set aside.
• **Combine** vinegar and preserves in container of an electric blender; process until smooth, stopping once to scrape down sides. With blender on high, gradually add oil in a slow, steady stream.
• **Combine** spinach, half of apricot halves, half of nuts, and dressing, and toss gently. Sprinkle with remaining apricot halves and nuts. Serve immediately. **Yield:** 8 servings.

SPINACH SALAD WITH SAUTÉED PEARS

1 (10-ounce) package fresh spinach
1 cup water
¼ cup lemon juice
2 Bosc pears
4 slices bacon, chopped
¼ cup olive oil
1 medium onion, sliced
1 medium-size red or yellow bell pepper, sliced
1 cup white wine or red wine vinegar
2 tablespoons sugar
1 teaspoon grated orange rind
1 teaspoon dried thyme
½ teaspoon dried basil
1 teaspoon salt
½ teaspoon cracked pepper
½ to 1 teaspoon hot sauce

• **Wash** spinach, and remove and discard stems; set spinach aside.

• **Combine** water and lemon juice in a bowl; peel, core, and chop pears. Place chopped pear in lemon-water mixture, and set aside.
• **Cook** bacon in olive oil over medium-high heat in a large skillet until crisp. Add onion and pepper slices; cook 3 minutes or until tender.
• **Drain** pears; add to skillet, and cook just until tender.
• **Add** vinegar, sugar, and orange rind; bring to a boil. Remove mixture from heat, and stir in thyme and remaining 4 ingredients.
• **Place** spinach in a large bowl; add vinegar mixture, and toss gently. Serve immediately with a slotted spoon. **Yield:** 6 to 8 servings.

Chef John Folse
Lafitte's Landing
Donaldsonville, Louisiana

SPINACH SALAD WITH THE BLUES

Spoon the salad dressing on the plate, and arrange the salad on top. To shred fresh spinach, roll several leaves together. Use kitchen scissors or a sharp knife to cut the roll at ¼-inch intervals.

½ cup chopped walnuts
⅓ cup olive oil
¼ cup white wine vinegar
1 tablespoon prepared mustard
1 teaspoon sugar (optional)
1 (10-ounce) bag fresh spinach, washed, trimmed, and shredded
1 head Belgian endive, washed and trimmed
2 Red Delicious apples, cored and thinly sliced
1 (4-ounce) package crumbled blue cheese

• **Spread** walnuts in a shallow pan. Bake at 350° for 5 minutes, stirring occasionally. Set aside.
• **Combine** olive oil, vinegar, mustard, and sugar, if desired, in a jar. Cover tightly, and shake vigorously. Pour evenly onto six salad plates.

• **Arrange** spinach on top of dressing.
• **Arrange** endive leaves and thin apple slices evenly beside shredded spinach.
• **Sprinkle** with walnuts and blue cheese. **Yield:** 6 servings.

Agnes L. Stone
Ocala, Florida

GREEN BEAN, WALNUT, AND FETA SALAD

1 cup coarsely chopped walnuts
¾ cup olive oil
¼ cup white wine vinegar
1 tablespoon chopped fresh dill
½ teaspoon minced garlic
¼ teaspoon salt
¼ teaspoon pepper
1½ pounds fresh green beans
1 small purple onion, thinly sliced
1 (4-ounce) package crumbled feta cheese

• **Place** walnuts in a shallow pan, and bake at 350° for 5 to 10 minutes or until toasted, stirring occasionally; set aside.
• **Combine** oil and next 5 ingredients; cover and chill.
• **Wash** beans, trim ends, and remove strings. Cut green beans into thirds, and arrange in a steamer basket over boiling water. Cover and steam 15 minutes or until crisp-tender. Immediately plunge into cold water to stop the cooking process; drain and pat dry.
• **Combine** walnuts, beans, onion, and cheese in a large bowl; toss well. Cover and chill.
• **Pour** oil mixture over bean mixture 1 hour before serving; toss just before serving. **Yield:** 6 servings.

Judi Grant
El Paso, Texas

MARINATED BEAN SALAD

QUICK!

This salad is best made the day before you want to serve it.

1 (15.8-ounce) can great Northern beans, drained and rinsed
1 (15-ounce) can black beans, drained and rinsed
1 (15-ounce) can kidney beans, drained and rinsed
1 (8-ounce) can whole kernel corn, drained and rinsed
1 (2-ounce) jar diced pimiento, drained
1 carrot, scraped and chopped
½ cup olive oil
½ cup cider vinegar
1 clove garlic, pressed
½ teaspoon salt
½ teaspoon pepper
½ teaspoon chili powder

• **Combine** first 6 ingredients in a large bowl. Set aside.
• **Combine** olive oil and remaining 5 ingredients; pour over bean mixture. Spoon into an airtight container, and chill up to 4 days. **Yield:** 6 servings.

Toasted Appetizers: Place 1 cup Marinated Bean Salad into container of an electric blender; process until smooth, adding 1 to 2 tablespoons marinating liquid, if necessary. Spread evenly on 10 thin slices of toasted French bread; top with thin slices of mozzarella or goat cheese. Bake at 350° for 3 to 5 minutes. **Yield:** 4 appetizer servings.

BROCCOLI SALAD

½ cup raisins
2 pounds broccoli, cut into flowerets
1 cup purple seedless grapes, halved
3 green onions, thinly sliced
⅔ cup mayonnaise
2 tablespoons tarragon vinegar
¼ cup slivered almonds, toasted
8 slices bacon, cooked and crumbled

• **Soak** raisins in hot water to cover 5 minutes; drain.
• **Combine** raisins, broccoli, grapes, and green onions in a large bowl. Combine mayonnaise and vinegar; stir into broccoli mixture. Cover and chill.
• **Stir** in almonds and bacon just before serving. **Yield:** 6 to 8 servings.

Ruth J. Carnes
Victoria, Texas

CONFETTI CORN SALAD

QUICK!

2 cups fresh corn, cut from cob
¾ cup water
1 (14½-ounce) can black beans, rinsed and drained
½ cup sliced green onions
½ cup chopped red bell pepper
1 small cucumber, seeded and chopped
2 cloves garlic, minced
¼ cup chopped fresh cilantro
1 teaspoon sweet red pepper flakes
¼ teaspoon salt
¼ teaspoon ground ginger
2 tablespoons corn oil
2 tablespoons rice vinegar
1 tablespoon sesame oil
1 tablespoon lime juice

• **Combine** corn and ¾ cup water in a saucepan; bring to a boil. Cover, reduce heat, and simmer 7 to 8 minutes or just until corn is tender. Drain. Combine corn, black beans, and next 5 ingredients in a large bowl.
• **Whisk** together red pepper flakes and remaining 6 ingredients until blended; pour over corn mixture. Cover and chill at least 2 hours. **Yield:** 4 to 6 servings.

Kitty Jones
Greeneville, Tennessee

MEDITERRANEAN LENTIL SALAD

QUICK!

1 cup dried lentils
1 small onion, chopped
1 quart water
1 small red bell pepper
1 small green bell pepper
1 tomato
3 green onions
1 (2¼-ounce) can sliced ripe olives, drained
½ cup Italian dressing
2 tablespoons lemon juice
½ teaspoon pepper
1 (4-ounce) package crumbled tomato-basil feta cheese

• **Bring** first 3 ingredients to a boil in a Dutch oven; reduce heat, and simmer, partially covered, 15 to 20 minutes or just until lentils are tender. Drain.
• **Chop** bell peppers, tomato, and green onions; add to lentil mixture. Stir in olives and next 3 ingredients; cover and chill. Sprinkle with cheese; serve immediately. **Yield:** 5 cups.

Donna F. Bearden
Gibsonville, North Carolina

HOPPIN' JOHN SALAD

The mint in this Southern black-eyed pea and rice salad makes it exceptionally original.

2 cups cooked black-eyed peas
3 cups cooked long-grain rice
½ cup chopped purple onion
¼ cup chopped celery
1 jalapeño pepper, seeded and minced
¼ cup loosely packed fresh chervil or parsley
¼ cup loosely packed fresh mint
1 clove garlic
½ teaspoon salt
3 tablespoons fresh lemon juice
¼ cup olive oil
¼ teaspoon freshly ground pepper

• **Combine** first 5 ingredients in a bowl.
• **Place** herbs and garlic on a cutting board, and sprinkle evenly with salt;

finely chop herbs and garlic. Sprinkle over rice mixture, and stir gently.
● **Combine** lemon juice, olive oil, and pepper in a bowl; stir into rice mixture. **Yield:** 6 servings.

John Martin Taylor
Charleston, South Carolina
The New Southern Cook
(Bantam)

GREEN PEA SALAD

QUICK!

This recipe halves easily.

2 (16-ounce) packages frozen English peas, thawed
2 green onions, sliced
2 (8-ounce) cans sliced water chestnuts, drained
⅔ cup reduced-fat sour cream
⅔ cup reduced-fat mayonnaise
1 teaspoon freshly ground black pepper
Garnishes: sliced green onions, cashew halves

● **Combine** all ingredients except garnishes, stirring gently. Garnish, if desired. **Yield:** 8 servings.

Toni Spanos Nordan and Clay Nordan
Birmingham, Alabama

CRUNCHY SPROUT SALAD

1 (3-ounce) package chicken ramen noodle soup mix
¼ cup vegetable oil
1½ tablespoons rice wine vinegar
1 tablespoon sesame oil
1 teaspoon chili-flavored oil
1 (3.2-ounce) package enoki mushrooms
2 carrots, scraped and shredded
1 cucumber, peeled, seeded, and chopped
½ cup bean sprouts
¼ pound fresh snow pea pods, cut into thin strips
1 avocado, chopped
4 leaves radicchio or red cabbage
¼ cup sesame seeds, toasted

● **Place** noodles in a 9-inch square pan; discard seasoning packet.
● **Bake** at 375° for 7 minutes or until browned, stirring twice. Cool.
● **Combine** vegetable oil and next 3 ingredients, stirring with a wire whisk until blended.
● **Combine** half of noodles, mushrooms, and next 5 ingredients. Add oil mixture; toss gently to coat.
● **Place** radicchio on individual serving plates; spoon vegetable mixture evenly on radicchio. Sprinkle with remaining half of noodles and sesame seeds. **Yield:** 4 servings.

Daisy Trippeer
Germantown, Tennessee

TOMATO AND CUCUMBER SUMMER SALAD

¼ cup mayonnaise or salad dressing
3 tablespoons white vinegar
1 green onion, chopped
1 clove garlic, pressed
1 teaspoon sugar
½ to ¾ teaspoon salt
1 teaspoon Worcestershire sauce
½ teaspoon hot sauce
½ cup vegetable oil
1 cup chopped fresh parsley
Leaf lettuce
3 medium tomatoes, thinly sliced
2 cucumbers, thinly sliced

● **Combine** first 8 ingredients in container of an electric blender; process until smooth, stopping once to scrape down sides. With blender on high, gradually add oil in a slow, steady stream. Stir in parsley. Cover and chill.
● **Arrange** lettuce on chilled salad plates. Top with tomato slices and cucumber slices. Drizzle evenly with dressing. **Yield:** 6 to 8 servings.

SUMMER TOMATO SALAD

(pictured on page 297)

2 medium-size ripe tomatoes, sliced
8 ounces fresh mozzarella cheese or goat cheese, thinly sliced
6 large fresh basil leaves, finely chopped and divided
½ teaspoon freshly ground pepper, divided
Tarragon Vinaigrette
1 medium cucumber, thinly sliced
1 sweet onion, thinly sliced
Fresh basil leaves (optional)

● **Layer** tomato and cheese slices in a shallow dish; sprinkle with half of chopped basil and ¼ teaspoon pepper. Drizzle with ¼ cup Tarragon Vinaigrette. Top with cucumber and onion slices; sprinkle with remaining half of chopped basil and ¼ teaspoon pepper, and drizzle with remaining ¼ cup Tarragon Vinaigrette.
● **Cover** and chill 4 hours. Serve on a basil leaf-lined plate, if desired. **Yield:** 4 to 6 servings.

Note: Fresh mozzarella cheese is available at gourmet grocery stores and large supermarkets.

Tarragon Vinaigrette

QUICK!

¼ cup Tarragon Vinegar (see recipe on page 354)
¼ cup olive oil
1 tablespoon chopped fresh basil
½ teaspoon lemon juice
½ teaspoon finely chopped green onions
½ teaspoon honey
¼ teaspoon Dijon mustard

● **Combine** all ingredients in container of an electric blender; process until smooth. **Yield:** ½ cup.

Cindie Hackney
Longview, Texas

Grilled Vegetable Salad

GRILLED VEGETABLE SALAD

(pictured at left)

⅓ cup white balsamic vinegar
2 tablespoons olive oil
2 shallots, finely chopped
1 teaspoon dried Italian
   seasoning
¼ teaspoon salt
¼ teaspoon pepper
1½ teaspoons molasses
½ pound carrots, scraped
1 red bell pepper
1 yellow bell pepper
2 zucchini
2 yellow squash
1 large onion

● **Combine** first 7 ingredients in a large bowl. Set aside.
● **Cut** carrots and remaining vegetables into large pieces.
● **Add** vegetables to vinegar mixture, tossing to coat. Let stand 30 minutes, stirring occasionally.
● **Drain** vegetables, reserving vinegar mixture. Arrange vegetables in a grill basket.
● **Cook,** covered with grill lid, over medium-hot coals (350° to 400°) 15 to 20 minutes, turning occasionally.
● **Return** vegetables to reserved vinegar mixture, tossing gently.
● **Cover** and chill at least 8 hours. **Yield:** 6 servings.

Margaret Jordan
Birmingham, Alabama

♥ Per serving: Calories 103
Fat 4.9g Cholesterol 0mg
Sodium 116mg

AVOCADO-POTATO SALAD WITH HORSERADISH DRESSING

1 pound baking potatoes
3 avocados, cubed
2 medium-size red apples,
   cubed
¾ cup chopped green onions
½ cup chopped walnuts or pecans,
   toasted
1 tablespoon chopped fresh
   parsley
Horseradish Dressing

● **Cook** potatoes in boiling salted water to cover 20 to 30 minutes or until tender; drain. Cool; peel and cube.
● **Combine** potato, avocado, apple, and green onions in a large bowl; toss gently. Sprinkle with walnuts and parsley; cover and chill. Serve immediately with Horseradish Dressing. **Yield:** 6 servings.

Horseradish Dressing

QUICK!

1 (8-ounce) carton sour cream
1 tablespoon prepared horseradish
1 tablespoon lemon juice
½ teaspoon salt
½ teaspoon freshly ground pepper

● **Combine** all ingredients; cover and chill. **Yield:** 1 cup.

GREEN BEAN-RED POTATO SALAD

Leave the skins on the red potatoes for pretty color and to help them keep their shape after they're cooked.

1½ pounds round red potatoes
1 (9-ounce) package frozen whole
   green beans
2 tablespoons white vinegar
1 tablespoon sugar
¾ cup mayonnaise
2 tablespoons chopped onion
½ teaspoon dried dillweed or
   1½ teaspoons finely chopped
   fresh dill

● **Cook** potatoes in boiling salted water to cover 10 minutes or until tender.

Drain potatoes, and cool to touch. Cut into slices.
● **Cook** green beans according to package directions; drain and rinse with cold water.
● **Combine** potato slices and green beans in a bowl. Combine vinegar and remaining 4 ingredients; pour over potato mixture, and toss gently. Cover and chill 4 hours. **Yield:** 4 servings.

Linda Kirkpatrick
Westminster, Maryland

NEW POTATO SALAD

3 pounds new potatoes,
   unpeeled
⅓ cup finely chopped purple
   onion
⅓ cup olive oil
⅓ cup red wine vinegar
¼ cup stone-ground mustard
2 teaspoons sugar
½ teaspoon salt
½ teaspoon freshly ground
   pepper
½ pound thick-sliced bacon,
   cooked and crumbled
1 cup chopped fresh parsley

● **Cook** potatoes in boiling water to cover 15 minutes or until tender. Drain and cool slightly. Cut into ¼-inch slices. Combine potato and onion in a large bowl; set aside.
● **Combine** olive oil and next 5 ingredients; stir well with a wire whisk. Pour dressing over potato mixture; toss gently. Cover and chill.
● **Add** bacon and chopped parsley just before serving, and toss gently. **Yield:** 12 servings.

Rebecca and Don Farris
Dallas, Texas

Summery Chicken Salad;
Honey Angel Biscuit, page 63

SUMMERY CHICKEN SALAD

(pictured at left)

A splash of dry white wine plus a dash of curry powder infuse this fruit-studded chicken salad with unexpected flavor.

6   cups chopped cooked chicken
1¼ cups sliced celery
1   (8-ounce) can pineapple tidbits, drained
1¼ cups reduced-fat mayonnaise or salad dressing
2½ tablespoons dry white wine
¾   teaspoon salt
¾   teaspoon curry powder
2   Red Delicious apples, thinly sliced
1   cantaloupe, thinly sliced
½   pound green grapes
1   pint strawberries
1   cup blackberries
Lettuce leaves
¼   cup chopped walnuts, toasted
Garnish: celery leaves

• **Combine** first 3 ingredients in a large bowl; set aside.
• **Combine** mayonnaise and next 3 ingredients. Add to chicken mixture, tossing to coat. Cover and chill 1 to 2 hours.
• **Arrange** apples and next 4 ingredients on a lettuce-lined platter; top with chicken mixture. Sprinkle with toasted walnuts. Garnish, if desired. **Yield:** 6 servings.

Mrs. Wallace Cupit
Seminole, Florida

ROYAL CURRIED CHICKEN SALAD

½   cup sliced almonds, toasted
2   cups chopped cooked chicken
¼   cup chopped water chestnuts
½   pound seedless green grapes, halved
1   (8-ounce) can pineapple chunks, drained
½   cup chopped celery
¾   cup mayonnaise
1   teaspoon curry powder
2   teaspoons lemon juice
2   teaspoons soy sauce
2   avocados

• **Combine** first 6 ingredients; set aside.
• **Combine** mayonnaise, curry powder, lemon juice, and soy sauce in a bowl; spoon mixture over chicken mixture, and toss gently to coat. Cover and chill at least 4 hours.
• **Peel** and chop avocados; sprinkle over salad, and serve immediately. **Yield:** 6 servings.

Cindy Sullivan
Tallahassee, Florida

GRILLED CHICKEN AND FRUIT SALAD

Flavor contrasts abound in this grilled chicken salad. The sweetness of orange marmalade plays off nicely against the bold characteristics of soy sauce, raspberry vinegar, and jalapeño pepper.

¾   cup orange marmalade
3   tablespoons soy sauce
3   tablespoons lemon juice
3   teaspoons chopped fresh ginger
4   skinned and boned chicken breast halves
1   pineapple
2   medium jícamas
Vegetable cooking spray
2   cups fresh strawberry halves
1   cup fresh raspberries
Orange-Raspberry Vinaigrette
Lettuce leaves

• **Combine** first 4 ingredients; reserve ¼ cup marmalade mixture, and chill. Pour remaining mixture into a heavy-duty, zip-top plastic bag; add chicken. Seal bag, and marinate in refrigerator 8 hours, turning bag occasionally.
• **Peel**, core, and cut pineapple into spears; peel jícamas, and cut into ½-inch-thick slices. Combine reserved ¼ cup marmalade mixture, pineapple, and jícama, tossing to coat. Set aside.
• **Coat** a grill basket with cooking spray; place on grill over hot coals (400° to 500°). Remove chicken from marinade, discarding marinade.
• **Add** chicken and pineapple mixture to basket; cook, covered with grill lid, 3 minutes on each side or until chicken is done. Remove from grill, and cool.
• **Cut** chicken and jícama into thin strips; cut pineapple into bite-size pieces.
• **Combine** chicken, jícama, pineapple, strawberries, and raspberries; drizzle with Orange-Raspberry Vinaigrette, and toss gently. Serve in a lettuce-lined bowl. **Yield:** 4 servings.

Orange-Raspberry Vinaigrette

QUICK!

Always wear rubber gloves when seeding and chopping a member of the pepper family. Pepper oils contain a fiery heat that can irritate even a small cut; the oils are difficult to wash away with soap and water.

½   cup orange marmalade
¼   cup raspberry vinegar
1   medium jalapeño pepper, seeded and minced
2   tablespoons finely chopped fresh cilantro
2   tablespoons olive oil

• **Whisk** together all ingredients in a bowl. **Yield:** 1 cup.

ORIENTAL CHICKEN SALAD

3 tablespoons soy sauce
2 teaspoons grated fresh
     ginger
2 skinned and boned chicken
     breast halves
5 cups coarsely chopped mixed
     salad greens
1 cup fresh bean sprouts
1 cup fresh snow pea pods,
     trimmed
½ green bell pepper, thinly
     sliced
½ red bell pepper, thinly sliced
1 cucumber, thinly sliced
1 cup sliced green onions
1 (3-ounce) package ramen
     noodles
Oriental Salad Dressing
2 teaspoons sesame seeds,
     toasted
Spicy Peanut Sauce

● **Combine** soy sauce and ginger in a shallow dish or heavy-duty, zip-top plastic bag; add chicken. Cover or seal, and marinate in refrigerator up to 4 hours.
● **Remove** chicken from marinade, discarding marinade. Place chicken on a rack in broiler pan.
● **Broil** 4 inches from heat (with electric oven door partially opened) 7 minutes on each side or until tender. Cool slightly, and slice.
● **Combine** salad greens and next 6 ingredients. Break uncooked noodles into small pieces, and sprinkle on top; reserve seasoning packet for another use. Add ½ cup Oriental Salad Dressing, tossing to coat.
● **Arrange** chicken on top; pour remaining Oriental Salad Dressing over chicken, and sprinkle with sesame seeds. Serve with Spicy Peanut Sauce. **Yield:** 4 servings.

Oriental Salad Dressing

QUICK!

⅓ cup pineapple juice
¼ cup rice vinegar
1 tablespoon reduced-sodium soy
     sauce
2 teaspoons brown sugar
1½ teaspoons sesame oil
¼ teaspoon pepper

● **Combine** all ingredients in a small jar; cover jar tightly, and shake vigorously. **Yield:** ⅔ cup.

Spicy Peanut Sauce

QUICK!

½ cup chunky peanut butter
⅓ cup coconut milk
2 tablespoons reduced-sodium soy
     sauce
1 tablespoon grated fresh ginger
1 tablespoon sesame oil
¼ teaspoon dried crushed red
     pepper
¼ cup chicken broth

● **Combine** all ingredients in a bowl, stirring well with a wire whisk. **Yield:** 1⅓ cups.

Fran Pointer
Kansas City, Missouri

THAI CHICKEN SALAD

4 skinned and boned chicken
     breast halves
Peanut-Ginger Dressing
3 ounces vermicelli, uncooked
4 cups torn romaine lettuce
2 cups thinly sliced Chinese
     cabbage
2 medium carrots, coarsely
     shredded
1 medium cucumber, thinly
     sliced
1 large red bell pepper, cut into
     strips
¼ cup chopped fresh cilantro
Chopped peanuts (optional)
Sliced cucumber (optional)

● **Cook** chicken, without grill lid, over medium coals (300° to 350°) 15 to 20 minutes, turning once. Cut into thin strips. Combine chicken and 3 tablespoons Peanut-Ginger Dressing, tossing to coat; cover and chill 8 hours.
● **Cook** vermicelli according to package directions; drain.
● **Combine** vermicelli and 3 tablespoons Peanut-Ginger Dressing, tossing to coat. Cover and chill 8 hours.
● **Combine** romaine and next 5 ingredients, tossing well; arrange on a serving

platter. Top with vermicelli and chicken; sprinkle salad with peanuts, if desired. Arrange cucumber slices around vermicelli, if desired. Serve with remaining dressing. **Yield:** 6 servings.

Peanut-Ginger Dressing

QUICK!

½ cup rice wine vinegar
2 cloves garlic
⅓ cup creamy peanut butter
¼ cup lime juice
¼ cup chopped fresh cilantro
2 tablespoons apple cider
     vinegar
1 tablespoon honey
1 tablespoon molasses
1 tablespoon hot sauce
2 teaspoons grated fresh
     ginger
2 teaspoons soy sauce

● **Combine** all ingredients in container of an electric blender; process until smooth, stopping once to scrape down sides. **Yield:** 1½ cups.

Cindie Hackney
Longview, Texas

FRUIT AND SPICE
TURKEY SALAD

1 cup long-grain basmati brown
     rice, uncooked
1½ cups chopped cooked turkey
     breast
2 green onions, sliced
1 small Red Delicious apple,
     chopped
1 small Granny Smith apple,
     chopped
½ cup seedless green grape halves
¼ cup pecan halves, toasted
¼ cup raisins
¼ cup white wine vinegar
1½ teaspoons sugar
¼ teaspoon salt
¼ teaspoon ground cinnamon
¼ cup olive oil
Red leaf lettuce

● **Cook** brown rice according to package directions. Rinse with cold water, and drain well.

• **Combine** brown rice, turkey, and next 6 ingredients in a large bowl; set aside.
• **Combine** vinegar and next 3 ingredients. Add oil, stirring with a wire whisk. Pour over rice mixture; toss gently. Cover and chill at least 2 hours. Serve on lettuce. **Yield:** 4 to 6 servings.

SMOKED TURKEY SALAD

1 (10-ounce) package fresh spinach
1 pound smoked turkey, chopped
1 red bell pepper, cut into strips
4 green onions, diagonally sliced
½ cup walnut halves
½ cup vegetable oil
¼ cup raspberry or red wine vinegar
1 teaspoon seasoned salt
1 teaspoon dried Italian seasoning
¼ teaspoon freshly ground pepper

• **Remove** stems from spinach; wash leaves thoroughly, and pat dry. Set spinach aside.
• **Combine** turkey and next 3 ingredients in a bowl. Combine oil and remaining 4 ingredients in a jar; cover tightly, and shake vigorously. Pour over turkey mixture; toss to coat. Cover and chill.
• **Place** spinach on individual salad plates; top with turkey mixture. **Yield:** 4 servings.

Peggy Fowler Revels
Woodruff, South Carolina

ORIENTAL SALMON AND WILD RICE SALAD

1 (8-ounce) fillet salmon
⅓ cup rice wine vinegar
¼ cup orange marmalade
2 tablespoons teriyaki sauce
1 tablespoon grated fresh ginger
2 teaspoons sesame oil
1 (6-ounce) package wild rice, cooked without salt
¾ cup fresh snow pea pods
½ cup sliced green onions
½ cup finely chopped red bell pepper
Bibb lettuce leaves

• **Place** salmon in an 8-inch square dish; set aside.
• **Combine** vinegar and next 4 ingredients in a jar; cover tightly, and shake vigorously. Pour half of marinade over salmon, turning to coat well. Set remaining marinade aside.
• **Cover** salmon, and chill 1 hour.
• **Drain** salmon, discarding marinade; place salmon on a rack in broiler pan.
• **Broil** 5½ inches from heat (with electric oven door partially opened) 3 to 5 minutes on each side or until fish flakes easily when tested with a fork.
• **Separate** salmon into chunks. Cool.
• **Combine** salmon, rice, and next 3 ingredients in a large bowl; drizzle with reserved marinade, tossing gently.
• **Cover** and chill at least 3 hours. Serve on lettuce leaves. **Yield:** 5 servings.

♥ Per serving: Calories 323
Fat 6.5g Cholesterol 31mg
Sodium 389mg

BROILED SALMON SALAD

2 (6-ounce) salmon steaks
1 cup Lemon and Herb Dressing, divided
1 medium zucchini
1 medium-size yellow squash
1 carrot, scraped
½ red bell pepper
1 tablespoon chopped fresh cilantro or parsley
2 cups torn fresh spinach
2 cups torn Bibb lettuce
1 tomato, cut into wedges
1 small avocado, sliced
Garnishes: lemon twists, fresh parsley sprigs

• **Place** salmon steaks in a shallow dish; pour ¼ cup dressing over steaks. Cover and chill 1 hour, turning once.
• **Cut** zucchini and next 3 ingredients into thin strips; combine with cilantro and ¼ cup dressing, tossing gently.
• **Remove** steaks from marinade, reserving marinade. Bring marinade to a boil, and set aside.
• **Place** steaks on a lightly greased rack of broiler pan. Broil 4 inches from heat

(with electric oven door partially opened) 5 to 6 minutes; turn and brush with marinade. Broil 5 to 6 additional minutes or until fish flakes easily when tested with a fork. Cool slightly.
• **Arrange** salad greens and marinated vegetables on serving plates. Top with salmon steaks, tomato wedges, and avocado slices. Garnish, if desired, and serve with remaining dressing. **Yield:** 2 servings.

Lemon and Herb Dressing

¾ cup lemon juice
½ cup vegetable oil
1 teaspoon chopped fresh parsley
¼ teaspoon minced garlic
1½ tablespoons sugar
¾ teaspoon paprika
¾ teaspoon dried basil
½ teaspoon dried tarragon
½ teaspoon seasoned salt
⅛ teaspoon pepper

• **Combine** all ingredients in a jar; cover tightly, and shake mixture vigorously. **Yield:** 1⅓ cups.

Joyce M. Maurer
Christmas, Florida

Spinach Salad With Oysters and Red Wine Vinaigrette

SPINACH SALAD WITH OYSTERS AND RED WINE VINAIGRETTE
(pictured at left)

Wolf Hanau, of North Miami, Florida, won the 1991 Buck Briscoe Memorial Award at the National Oyster Cook-Off in Leonardtown, Maryland, with a similar version of this recipe.

1 (10-ounce) package fresh
    spinach
2 (12-ounce) containers fresh
    oysters, drained
2 egg whites, lightly beaten
1½ cups Italian-seasoned
    breadcrumbs
1½ cups vegetable oil
4 large fresh mushrooms, sliced
Red Wine Vinaigrette
1 small purple onion, thinly
    sliced
4 slices bacon, cooked and
    crumbled

• **Remove** stems from spinach; wash leaves thoroughly, and pat dry. Set aside.
• **Dip** oysters in egg white; coat with breadcrumbs. Set aside.
• **Pour** oil into a large heavy skillet; heat to 350°. Fry oysters about 1 minute on each side or until golden; drain on paper towels.
• **Place** spinach on individual plates. Arrange mushrooms evenly over spinach, and drizzle with half of Red Wine Vinaigrette. Top evenly with oysters, onion slices, and bacon. Serve immediately with remaining Red Wine Vinaigrette. **Yield:** 6 servings.

Red Wine Vinaigrette
QUICK!

¾ cup olive oil
3 tablespoons dry red wine
3 tablespoons red wine vinegar
1 tablespoon Dijon mustard
½ teaspoon sugar
½ teaspoon Worcestershire
    sauce
⅛ teaspoon pepper

• **Combine** all ingredients in container of an electric blender or food processor; process until blended. **Yield:** 1 cup.

GREEK SALAD

Jane adapted this salad from one of her favorite Florida books, The Gasparilla Cookbook. *If you dig to the bottom of the mound of vegetables, you'll discover creamy potato salad.*

2 cups water
½ pound unpeeled medium-size
    fresh shrimp
1 large head leaf lettuce
Potato Salad
1 bunch watercress, chopped
3 tomatoes, cut into wedges
1 to 2 cucumbers, peeled and cut
    into spears
½ cup crumbled feta cheese
2 avocados, cut into wedges
1 green bell pepper, cut into
    rings
1 red bell pepper, cut into rings
1 (16-ounce) jar sliced beets,
    drained
12 pitted ripe olives
8 radishes
8 green onions
6 to 8 Greek pickled peppers
¾ cup olive oil
¼ cup red wine vinegar
2 teaspoons dry mustard
1 teaspoon dried oregano

• **Bring** water to a boil; add shrimp, and cook 3 to 5 minutes or until shrimp turn pink. Drain well, and rinse with cold water. Chill. Peel shrimp, and devein, if desired. Set aside.
• **Remove** large outer leaves from lettuce, and line a large platter. Shred remaining lettuce, and arrange on lettuce-lined platter.
• **Spoon** Potato Salad in center of shredded lettuce; sprinkle with watercress. Arrange tomato and cucumber alternately around edge. Sprinkle with cheese. Top with shrimp, avocado, and next 7 ingredients.
• **Combine** olive oil and remaining 3 ingredients in a jar; cover tightly, and shake vigorously. Drizzle dressing over salad, and serve immediately. **Yield:** 20 servings.

Note: Increase shrimp to 2 pounds for 8 main-dish servings.

Potato Salad

2 pounds medium-size round red
    potatoes
1 cup finely chopped purple onion
3 tablespoons red wine vinegar
¾ to 1 cup mayonnaise
2 teaspoons salt

• **Cook** potatoes in boiling water to cover 25 to 30 minutes or until tender; drain. Let cool to touch; peel and cut into ¾-inch cubes.
• **Combine** onion and vinegar; let stand 10 minutes. Stir in mayonnaise and salt; pour over potatoes, tossing gently. Cover and chill. **Yield:** about 6 cups.

Jim and Jane Bowyer
Maitland, Florida

ALOHA SHRIMP SALAD

6 cups water
2 pounds unpeeled medium-size
    fresh shrimp
1 cup finely chopped celery
1 (20-ounce) can unsweetened
    pineapple chunks, drained
⅓ cup raisins
½ cup reduced-calorie mayonnaise
2 teaspoons curry powder
Leaf lettuce or pita bread rounds

• **Bring** water to a boil; add shrimp, and cook 3 to 5 minutes or until shrimp turn pink. Drain; rinse with cold water. Peel shrimp, and devein, if desired.
• **Combine** shrimp, celery, and next 4 ingredients. Cover and chill at least 1 hour before serving. Serve on lettuce or in pita bread. **Yield:** 3 to 4 servings.

SHRIMP AND COUSCOUS SALAD

4¼ cups water
1 lemon, sliced
1¼ pounds unpeeled large fresh
      shrimp
½ cup couscous, uncooked
½ red bell pepper, chopped
1 (14-ounce) can artichoke hearts,
      drained and coarsely
      chopped
¼ cup reduced-fat mayonnaise
⅓ cup fresh lemon juice
3 tablespoons chopped fresh dill
¼ teaspoon salt
½ teaspoon pepper

• **Combine** water and lemon slices in a
Dutch oven; bring to a boil. Add shrimp;
cook 3 to 5 minutes or until shrimp turn
pink. Drain well, discarding lemon;
rinse shrimp with cold water. Peel
shrimp, and devein, if desired. Cut
shrimp in half lengthwise. Cover and
chill.
• **Cook** couscous according to package
directions; place in a large bowl to cool.
Stir with a fork; add shrimp, bell pepper,
and artichoke hearts.
• **Combine** mayonnaise and remaining
4 ingredients, stirring well. Pour dressing over shrimp mixture, tossing to coat.
Cover and chill at least 2 hours. **Yield:** 4
servings.

Janil K. Miller
Beaufort, North Carolina

♥ Per serving: Calories 234
Fat 6.2g Cholesterol 113mg
Sodium 367mg

ASIAN SALAD DRESSING

QUICK!

1 cup vegetable oil
⅓ cup rice wine vinegar
2 tablespoons soy sauce
2 tablespoons dark sesame oil
2 teaspoons dry mustard
4 teaspoons sugar
2 teaspoons grated fresh ginger

• **Combine** all ingredients in a jar; cover
tightly, and shake vigorously. Chill.
Yield: about 1½ cups.

CURRY SALAD DRESSING

QUICK!

1 cup olive oil
¼ cup lemon juice
1 tablespoon white wine vinegar
1 tablespoon mango chutney
1 teaspoon Dijon mustard
½ teaspoon curry powder
¼ teaspoon salt
¼ teaspoon pepper

• **Combine** all ingredients in container
of an electric blender; process until
smooth, stopping once to scrape down
sides. Chill. **Yield:** 1¾ cups.

Carol Scheder
Roswell, Georgia

GREEN ONION DRESSING
(pictured on page 375)

QUICK!

4 green onions, cut into 1-inch
      pieces
1 cup vegetable oil
½ cup red wine vinegar
2 tablespoons sugar
¾ teaspoon Worcestershire
      sauce
½ teaspoon dry mustard

• **Combine** all ingredients in container
of an electric blender or food processor;
pulse 3 times or until green onions
are chopped. Chill. **Yield:** 1¾ cups.
Kim Uding
Sainte Genevieve, Missouri

LEMON-HONEY VINAIGRETTE

QUICK!

1 cup white wine vinegar
¾ cup vegetable oil
¼ cup honey
1 tablespoon grated lemon rind
3 tablespoons fresh lemon juice
1 teaspoon salt
2 cloves garlic, minced

• **Combine** all ingredients in a jar; cover
tightly, and shake vigorously. Chill.
Yield: 2 cups.

PAPAYA SEED DRESSING

*When preparing fresh papayas, don't throw
away seeds. Their peppery flavor adds
mysterious pungency to this dressing.*

1 tablespoon cornstarch
1 (7.1-ounce) can papaya nectar
½ cup sugar
½ teaspoon salt
½ teaspoon dry mustard
½ cup white wine vinegar
2 tablespoons chopped onion
3 tablespoons fresh papaya seeds

• **Combine** cornstarch and nectar in a
saucepan; bring to a boil over medium
heat, stirring constantly. Boil 1 minute,
stirring constantly; cool.
• **Combine** sugar and remaining 5 ingredients in container of an electric
blender; process until seeds resemble
coarsely ground pepper. Stir into nectar
mixture; cover and chill at least 2 hours.
Serve over mixed fruit. **Yield:** 2 cups.

♥ Per tablespoon: Calories 18
Fat 0g Cholesterol 0mg
Sodium 37mg

VANILLA VINAIGRETTE

QUICK!

¼ cup sugar
2 tablespoons white wine vinegar
2 teaspoons grated onion
½ teaspoon dry mustard
¼ teaspoon salt
¼ vanilla bean or 2 teaspoons
      vanilla extract
½ cup vegetable oil

• **Combine** first 6 ingredients in container of an electric blender; process
mixture until smooth. With blender on
high, add oil in a slow, steady stream.
Serve with fresh fruit or salad greens.
Yield: ⅔ cup.

Carol Lundy
New Tazewell, Tennessee

At right: *Grilled Chili Con Queso
Sandwiches (page 326)*

HOT TUNA MELTS

QUICK!

*If you're hooked on coffee shop
tuna salad sandwiches, you'll love
these heated versions.*

1 (6-ounce) can solid white tuna in
   spring water, drained and
   flaked
⅓ cup mayonnaise
¼ cup sliced pimiento-stuffed
   olives, drained
3 hard-cooked eggs, chopped
3 tablespoons sweet pickle relish
2 tablespoons finely chopped
   onion
2 English muffins, split and lightly
   toasted
4 slices sharp Cheddar cheese

• **Combine** first 6 ingredients, stirring
well. Spoon evenly onto muffin halves;
place on a baking sheet.
• **Broil** 5½ inches from heat (with electric oven door partially opened) 2 minutes. Top each with a cheese slice; broil
1 additional minute or until cheese
melts. **Yield:** 4 servings.

TUNA ROLL SANDWICHES

QUICK!

*Brown bag tip: Pita bread pockets
make this sandwich faster to prepare.*

1 (3-ounce) package cream cheese,
   softened
2 tablespoons mayonnaise
1 tablespoon lemon juice
½ teaspoon pepper
¼ teaspoon salt
1 (10-ounce) can solid white tuna
   in spring water, drained and
   flaked *
½ cup chopped purple onion
6 large lettuce leaves
6 (8-inch) flour tortillas

• **Combine** first 5 ingredients, stirring
until smooth; add tuna and onion, stirring well.
• **Place** lettuce on tortillas, and trim to
fit. Spoon tuna mixture onto lettuce.
Roll tortilla up, and tie with kitchen

string. (Remove string before serving.)
Serve with marinated vegetables. **Yield:**
6 servings.

* You can substitute 1 (10-ounce) can
white chicken, drained and flaked, for
the tuna.

*Edith Askins
Greenville, Texas*

SHRIMP AND EGG SALAD
SANDWICHES

2 cups water
½ pound unpeeled medium-size
   fresh shrimp
6 large hard-cooked eggs, chopped
¼ cup finely chopped green onions
2 tablespoons finely chopped
   celery
1 tablespoon chopped fresh
   parsley
2 tablespoons capers (optional)
2 teaspoons chopped fresh dill
   (optional)
3 tablespoons mayonnaise or salad
   dressing
1 teaspoon lemon juice
1 teaspoon prepared mustard
¼ teaspoon salt
¼ teaspoon hot sauce
3 English muffins, split and
   toasted
**Garnishes: fresh dill sprigs, whole
   cooked shrimp, lemon slices**

• **Bring** water to a boil; add shrimp, and
cook 3 to 5 minutes or until shrimp turn
pink. Drain well, and rinse with cold
water. Peel shrimp, and devein, if desired. Coarsely chop shrimp.
• **Combine** chopped shrimp, eggs, and
next 3 ingredients; if desired, stir in capers and chopped dill. Set mixture
aside.
• **Combine** mayonnaise and next 4 ingredients; gently fold into egg mixture.
• **Spoon** onto English muffins; garnish,
if desired. **Yield:** 6 servings.

*Virginia J. MacMillan
Summerland Key, Florida*

GRILLED SEAFOOD PO'BOY
(pictured at right)

*Grilling the seafood and using
reduced-fat mayonnaise make
this sandwich low fat.*

1 pound unpeeled medium-size
   fresh shrimp
1 (10-ounce) farm-raised catfish
   fillet
2 teaspoons Creole seasoning
¼ cup lemon juice
1 teaspoon olive oil
½ cup roasted red bell pepper
   strips
1 jalapeño pepper
½ cup reduced-fat mayonnaise
2 tablespoons Creole mustard
2 tablespoons chopped fresh
   parsley
1 clove garlic, minced
2 tablespoons sliced green onions
Vegetable cooking spray
8 slices tomato
8 lettuce leaves
4 French sandwich rolls, split and
   toasted

• **Peel** shrimp, and devein, if desired.
• **Cut** fish crosswise into 1-inch slices.
Combine shrimp and fish in a shallow
dish, and sprinkle with Creole seasoning. Cover and chill 2 hours.
• **Combine** lemon juice and oil; pour
mixture over seafood. Cover and chill
30 additional minutes.
• **Pat** red pepper strips dry. Seed and
chop jalapeño pepper. Combine red
pepper strips, jalapeño pepper, mayonnaise, and next 4 ingredients; set aside.
• **Drain** seafood, and place in a grill basket coated with cooking spray.
• **Cook,** covered with grill lid, over
medium-hot coals (350° to 400°) 7 to 10
minutes, turning once.
• **Place** seafood, tomato, and lettuce
evenly on bottom halves of rolls; spread
top halves of rolls evenly with mayonnaise mixture, and place on sandwiches. **Yield:** 4 servings.

*Clemie Barron
Panama City, Florida*

♥ Per serving: Calories 405
Fat 15g   Cholesterol 112mg
Sodium 711mg

Grilled Seafood Po'Boy

Vegetable Pizza

VEGETABLE PIZZA
(pictured at left)

QUICK!

6 (8-inch) Skillet Pizza Crusts
      (see recipe on page 62)
1½ cups reduced-fat pasta sauce
1 cup sliced fresh mushrooms
1 cup (4 ounces) shredded part-
      skim mozzarella cheese
¾ cup chopped green bell pepper
½ cup chopped onion
¼ cup sliced ripe olives, drained

• **Place** frozen pizza crusts on baking
sheets. Spread each crust with ¼ cup
pasta sauce, and sprinkle evenly with
toppings.
• **Bake** at 425° for 12 to 15 minutes or
until edges are lightly browned and
cheese melts. Cut into wedges. **Yield:** 6
servings.

Kathy Piques
Knoxville, Tennessee

♥ Per serving: Calories 391
Fat 10.3g Cholesterol 11mg
Sodium 607mg

BLAZING SUNSET PIZZA

QUICK!

⅔ cup Pesto Sauce (see recipe on
      page 345)
1 (12-inch) refrigerated pizza
      crust
2 plum tomatoes, sliced
½ red bell pepper, thinly sliced
½ yellow bell pepper, thinly sliced
½ orange bell pepper, thinly sliced
1 cup (4 ounces) shredded colby-
      Monterey Jack cheese blend
Garnish: fresh basil sprig

• **Spread** Pesto Sauce over crust; top
with tomato and next 4 ingredients.
• **Bake** at 425° for 10 minutes or until
bubbly. Garnish, if desired. **Yield:** 1 (12-
inch) pizza.

SOUTHWESTERN VEGGIE PIZZA

QUICK!

1 (10-ounce) Italian bread shell *
1 carrot, scraped and chopped
1 zucchini, sliced
1 clove garlic, minced
1 tablespoon olive oil
1 (11-ounce) jar black bean dip
½ cup salsa, drained
1 cup (4 ounces) shredded
      Monterey Jack cheese with
      peppers

• **Bake** bread shell on a baking sheet at
350° for 5 minutes; set aside.
• **Cook** carrot, zucchini, and garlic in
olive oil in a skillet over medium heat,
stirring constantly, 3 to 5 minutes or
until crisp-tender; drain.
• **Spread** bean dip over bread shell; top
with salsa and vegetables.
• **Bake** at 350° for 5 minutes; sprinkle
with cheese. Bake 5 additional minutes
or until cheese melts and pizza is thoroughly heated. **Yield:** 2 to 3 servings.

✶ For the bread shell, we used Boboli.
Susan Dosier
Birmingham, Alabama

FIVE-RING PIZZAS

QUICK!

1 (14-ounce) jar pizza sauce
1 teaspoon dried Italian seasoning
1 pound ground beef
3 (10-ounce) cans refrigerated
      biscuits
½ cup (2 ounces) shredded
      Cheddar cheese
½ cup (2 ounces) shredded
      mozzarella cheese
½ cup chopped onion (optional)
¼ cup chopped green bell pepper
      (optional)
1 (2.5-ounce) can sliced
      mushrooms, drained
      (optional)

• **Combine** pizza sauce and Italian seasoning; set aside.
• **Brown** ground beef in a large nonstick
skillet, stirring until it crumbles; drain.

• **Separate** biscuits; flatten to ¼-inch
thickness on baking sheets. Spread each
with 1 tablespoon pizza sauce mixture.
Top evenly with ground beef and
cheeses; if desired, add onion, bell pepper, and mushrooms.
• **Bake** at 400° for 10 to 12 minutes.
Yield: 30 mini pizzas.

Allison Mendoza
Arlington, Texas

THE KING HENRY PIZZA

QUICK!

*If he were alive today, Henry VIII
no doubt would have the well-known
drumstick in one hand and a slice of
this meaty pizza in the other.*

1¼ cups Traditional Pizza Sauce
      (see recipe on page 344)
1 (12-inch) refrigerated pizza
      crust
½ pound ground pork sausage,
      cooked and drained
½ (3.5-ounce) package sliced
      pepperoni
8 slices bacon, cooked and
      crumbled
1 (8-ounce) package shredded
      four-cheese blend

• **Spread** Traditional Pizza Sauce over
pizza crust, and top evenly with sausage
and remaining ingredients.
• **Bake** at 425° for 10 minutes or until
bubbly. **Yield:** 1 (12-inch) pizza.

GRANOLA MIX

2 (3-ounce) packages ramen
   noodles
4 cups regular oats, uncooked
1 (2⅛-ounce) jar sesame seeds
   (⅓ cup)
1 (3.75-ounce) package sunflower
   kernels (¾ cup)
½ cup dry-roasted peanuts
⅓ cup firmly packed brown sugar
¼ cup honey
¼ cup vegetable oil
1 teaspoon vanilla extract
½ cup raisins (optional)

• **Remove** seasoning packets from noodles, and reserve for another use; break noodles into small pieces.
• **Combine** noodles, oats, and next 3 ingredients in a large bowl; set aside.
• **Combine** brown sugar and next 3 ingredients; pour over noodle mixture, and stir well. Spread mixture evenly in a 15- x 10- x 1-inch jellyroll pan.
• **Bake** at 325° for 30 minutes or until golden, stirring every 10 minutes.
• **Stir** in raisins, if desired. Cool and store mixture in an airtight container. Serve with milk or over frozen yogurt. **Yield:** 8½ cups.

Fruit Crisp: Combine 4 cups sliced fresh peaches and 1 cup fresh or frozen blackberries or blueberries, thawed, in a 9-inch round cakepan; sprinkle with 2 tablespoons sugar and 1 cup Granola Mix. Bake at 375° for 35 minutes. Serve with frozen yogurt or ice cream. **Yield:** 6 servings.

CARAMEL CRUNCH

12 cups popped popcorn (about
   ½ cup unpopped)
1 (3-ounce) can chow mein
   noodles
1 cup dry-roasted peanuts
½ cup raisins
1½ cups firmly packed brown
   sugar
¾ cup butter or margarine
¾ cup light corn syrup
1 teaspoon ground cinnamon
½ teaspoon baking soda

• **Combine** first 4 ingredients in a lightly greased roasting pan, and set aside.
• **Combine** brown sugar and next 3 ingredients in a large saucepan; cook over medium heat, stirring constantly, 5 minutes or until mixture boils. Remove mixture from heat, and stir in soda (mixture will bubble).
• **Pour** brown sugar mixture over popcorn mixture; stir with a lightly greased long-handled spoon to coat.
• **Bake** at 250° for 1 hour, stirring every 15 minutes. Remove from oven, and immediately pour onto wax paper, breaking apart large clumps as they cool. Store in airtight containers. **Yield:** 4 quarts.

Ann Niedens
Kure Beach, North Carolina

TACO-CHEESE
ANIMAL CRACKERS

1 cup all-purpose flour
1½ cups (6 ounces) shredded
   taco-flavored Cheddar
   cheese
½ cup butter or margarine,
   softened
Paprika (optional)

• **Position** knife blade in food processor bowl; add flour, shredded cheese, and butter. Process until mixture forms a ball, stopping once to scrape down sides.
• **Wrap** dough in heavy-duty plastic wrap; chill 30 minutes.
• **Unwrap** dough, and roll to ¼-inch thickness on a lightly floured surface. Cut with 2½-inch animal-shaped cutters; place on ungreased baking sheets. Sprinkle with paprika, if desired.
• **Bake** at 375° for 10 to 12 minutes or until lightly browned; cool on wire racks. **Yield:** 3 dozen.

SOUP NUTS

Keep plenty of these little jewels on hand. They're great for snacking.

2 cups all-purpose flour
½ cup grated Parmesan cheese
1 teaspoon garlic salt
½ teaspoon dried Italian
   seasoning
3 large eggs
3 tablespoons olive oil

• **Combine** first 4 ingredients in a large mixing bowl; add eggs and oil, beating at medium speed with an electric mixer until blended.
• **Turn** dough out onto a lightly floured surface; knead lightly 3 or 4 times (dough may be crumbly). Divide dough into 6 portions. Shape each portion into a 12-inch log; cut each roll into ¼-inch-thick slices, and place on ungreased baking sheets.
• **Bake** at 375° for 12 minutes or until lightly browned. Transfer to wire racks to cool completely. **Yield:** 3 cups.

CRAN-ORANGE SURPRISE

QUICK!

1 quart orange sherbet, softened
2 cups cranberry juice cocktail
1 cup lemon-lime carbonated
   beverage

• **Combine** all ingredients. Spoon mixture into paper cups or pop molds.
• **Freeze** 1 hour.
• **Insert** a wooden craft stick into each paper cup; freeze until firm. For molds, insert base of mold into pop immediately. Freeze until firm. **Yield:** 6 cups.

Note: To make pops that are for adults only, substitute ¼ cup Grand Marnier for 1 cup lemon-lime beverage, and freeze as directed. Yield: about 5 cups.

At right: *Traditional Pizza Sauce (page 344), Roasted Garlic Sauce (page 345), and Pesto Sauce (page 345)*

SAUCES AND CONDIMENTS

QUICK STRAWBERRY FIG PRESERVES

3 cups mashed fresh figs (about 2 pounds)
1½ cups sugar
1 (3-ounce) package strawberry-flavored gelatin

● **Combine** figs and sugar in a heavy saucepan; cook over medium heat 2 minutes, stirring constantly. Gradually stir in gelatin, and cook over low heat 15 minutes, stirring constantly.
● **Spoon** preserves into hot, sterilized jars, filling to ¼ inch from top. Remove air bubbles; wipe jar rims. Cover at once with metal lids, and screw on bands.
● **Process** in boiling-water bath 5 minutes. **Yield:** 4 half-pints.

Nora Henshaw
Okemah, Oklahoma

CRANBERRY CHUTNEY

Serve with turkey or as an appetizer with gingersnaps and cream cheese.

8 (16-ounce) cans whole-berry cranberry sauce
2 cups firmly packed light brown sugar
2 cups chopped dates
2 cups currants or raisins
2 cups slivered almonds
2 cups apple cider vinegar
¼ cup minced crystallized ginger
2 teaspoons ground allspice

● **Combine** all ingredients in a large Dutch oven. Bring to a boil, stirring constantly; reduce heat, and simmer 30 minutes, stirring occasionally.
● **Cool**, place in jars, and store in refrigerator up to 2 weeks. For longer storage, pack chutney into hot, sterilized jars, filling to ½ inch from top; remove air bubbles, and wipe jar rims. Cover at once with metal lids, and screw on bands.
● **Process** in boiling-water bath 5 minutes. **Yield:** 10 pints.

Louise W. Mayer
Richmond, Virginia

BLUE-RIBBON MANGO CHUTNEY

3 large mangoes, chopped (about 2 pounds) *
1½ cups chopped onion
½ cup peeled, chopped cooking apple
½ cup raisins
1 cup apple cider vinegar
1¼ cups firmly packed brown sugar
½ cup sugar
¼ cup finely chopped fresh ginger
½ teaspoon grated lime rind
2 tablespoons fresh lime juice
1 tablespoon mustard seeds
1½ teaspoons celery seeds
¾ teaspoon salt
¼ teaspoon ground cinnamon
¼ teaspoon ground cloves

● **Combine** all ingredients in a glass bowl; cover and chill 8 hours.
● **Transfer** to a Dutch oven; bring to a boil over medium heat. Reduce heat; cook 1½ hours, stirring occasionally.
● **Divide** mango mixture into airtight containers; chill up to 1 week or freeze up to 6 months. **Yield:** 3 cups.

* Substitute 1 (26-ounce) jar mango, drained and chopped, for fresh.

Kathryn McKelvey Smith
Durham, North Carolina

PEAR CHUTNEY
(pictured on opposite page)

1 pound onions, quartered
9 cloves garlic
5 pounds firm pears, peeled, cored, and chopped
1 quart white vinegar (5% acidity)
6 cups sugar
1 (24-ounce) package raisins
½ teaspoon dry mustard
1½ cups chopped crystallized ginger
½ teaspoon ground ginger
3 tablespoons mustard seeds

● **Position** knife blade in food processor bowl; add half of onion quarters and garlic. Pulse 4 or 5 times or until onion quarters are chopped. Transfer to a

Dutch oven; repeat procedure with remaining onion quarters and garlic.
● **Add** pears and vinegar to onion mixture; bring to a boil. Reduce heat; simmer 20 to 25 minutes or until tender.
● **Add** sugar, stirring until dissolved; cook over medium heat 10 minutes, stirring occasionally. Add raisins and mustard; cook 20 minutes.
● **Add** crystallized ginger, ground ginger, and mustard seeds; cook over medium heat 10 minutes or until thickened.
● **Pour** hot mixture into hot jars, filling to ½ inch from top. Remove air bubbles, and wipe jar rims. Cover jars at once with metal lids, and screw on bands.
● **Process** in boiling-water bath 10 minutes. **Yield:** 7 pints.

Jean Graham
Wilmington, North Carolina

NANNIE'S CHOWCHOW
(pictured at right)

5½ pounds green tomatoes, chopped
2¼ pounds onions, chopped
2 pounds green bell peppers, chopped
1 pound red bell peppers, chopped
1 (5-pound) cabbage, shredded
½ cup salt
1 quart water
1½ quarts white vinegar (5% acidity)
1½ cups sugar
½ cup mustard seeds
2 tablespoons celery seeds
1 tablespoon whole allspice

● **Combine** first 5 ingredients in a large nonmetallic container. Combine salt and water; stir until salt dissolves. Pour over vegetables. Chill at least 8 hours. Drain vegetables; discard liquid.
● **Combine** vinegar and remaining 4 ingredients in a stockpot; add vegetables . Bring to a boil over medium heat; reduce heat, and simmer 10 minutes.
● **Pack** hot mixture into hot jars, filling to ½ inch from top. Remove air bubbles; wipe jar rims. Cover at once with metal lids, and screw on bands.
● **Process** in boiling-water bath 10 minutes. **Yield:** 12 pints.

Nannie's Chowchow; Spiced Apple Jelly, page 347; Apple Pie Filling in a Jar, page 350; Pear Chutney

*Thyme Mayonnaise,
Thyme-Lemon Butter*

THYME-LEMON BUTTER
(pictured at left)

Put a pat on hot-off-the-grill pork chops, steak, or fish, or use it to top a baked potato or dinner roll. You can shape the butter, slice it, and freeze. Take out a little as you need it.

2 tablespoons fresh thyme leaves
1 cup butter, softened
1 teaspoon grated lemon rind
1 tablespoon fresh lemon juice

● **Position** knife blade in food processor bowl; add thyme, and pulse 10 times. Add butter, lemon rind, and lemon juice. Process until mixture is smooth, stopping once to scrape down sides.
● **Spoon** butter mixture onto plastic wrap. Shape butter mixture into a 1-inch-diameter log by folding wrap over mixture and rolling. (Work quickly to keep butter from melting.) Seal in wrap, and chill 4 hours or store in refrigerator up to 1 week. **Yield:** about 1 cup.

THYME MAYONNAISE
(pictured at left)

QUICK!

A little fresh thyme gives oomph to regular mayonnaise in potato salad, deviled eggs, and sandwiches. You can also brush it on fish, chicken, or pork chops before broiling or grilling.

1 cup mayonnaise
2 tablespoons fresh thyme leaves, chopped

● **Combine** mayonnaise and thyme; cover and chill 1 hour or store in refrigerator up to 1 week. **Yield:** about 1 cup.

PEACH KETCHUP

1 (16-ounce) can sliced peaches in heavy syrup, undrained
½ cup finely chopped onion
½ cup white vinegar
¼ teaspoon salt
½ teaspoon ground cinnamon
¼ teaspoon ground cloves
¼ teaspoon ground allspice
¼ teaspoon ground red pepper

● **Drain** peaches, reserving syrup in a small saucepan; set peaches aside.
● **Cook** syrup over medium heat 5 to 7 minutes or until reduced to ½ cup, stirring occasionally. Add peaches, onion, and remaining ingredients; bring to a boil. Reduce heat, and simmer 45 to 50 minutes or until thickened, stirring often; cool.
● **Position** knife blade in food processor bowl; add peach mixture. Process until mixture is smooth, stopping once to scrape down sides. Transfer mixture to a serving bowl; cover and chill at least 8 hours. Serve with poultry or pork. Store leftovers in refrigerator. **Yield:** about 1¼ cups.

Carole Miller Radford
Lincolnton, Georgia

PEPPERED HONEY MUSTARD

QUICK!

This mustard is excellent with chicken or mixed into a homemade vinaigrette salad dressing.

¾ cup Dijon mustard
¼ cup honey
1 tablespoon cracked pepper
⅛ teaspoon salt
Garnish: cracked pepper

● **Combine** first 4 ingredients in a small serving bowl, stirring well. Garnish, if desired. Store leftovers in refrigerator. **Yield:** 1 cup.

SWEET CIDER MUSTARD

QUICK!

Teri serves this mustard as a dip for pretzels.

½ cup sugar
¼ cup dry mustard
Dash of salt
1 large egg
⅓ cup apple cider vinegar

● **Combine** all ingredients in container of an electric blender; process 20 seconds or until smooth, stopping once to scrape down sides. Pour mixture into a heavy saucepan.
● **Cook** over medium heat, stirring constantly, 5 minutes or until mixture is thickened; cool completely. Store leftovers in refrigerator. **Yield:** about 1 cup.

Teri Schmid
Marietta, Georgia

RASPBERRY WINE VINEGAR

3 cups fresh or frozen raspberries
2 (17-ounce) bottles white wine vinegar
1 cup sugar

● **Combine** all ingredients in a large saucepan; bring to a boil. Cover, reduce heat, and simmer 10 minutes.
● **Pour** mixture through a wire-mesh strainer lined with two layers of cheesecloth, discarding pulp.
● **Pour** into decorative jars or bottles, and seal with an airtight lid or cork. Store in refrigerator up to 6 months. **Yield:** 5 cups.

Nancy Strother
Fredericksburg, Virginia

♥ Per tablespoon: Calories 13
Fat 0.0g   Cholesterol 0mg
Sodium 1mg

TARRAGON VINEGAR

1 bunch fresh tarragon (about 14 sprigs)
7 (17-ounce) bottles champagne wine vinegar
Fresh tarragon sprigs (optional)

• **Twist** tarragon gently, and place in a large glass container. Set aside.
• **Bring** vinegar to a boil, and pour over tarragon. Cover and store in a cool, dark place at room temperature 2 weeks.
• **Pour** vinegar mixture through a wire-mesh strainer into decorative bottles, discarding solids. Add additional tarragon sprigs, if desired. Seal bottles, and store in a cool, dark place up to 6 months. **Yield:** about 16 cups.

Cindie Hackney
Longview, Texas

TOMATO-HERB VINEGAR

10 large sprigs fresh rosemary
6 large sprigs fresh basil
4 large sprigs fresh oregano
12 cloves garlic, peeled and halved
10 dried tomato halves
1 teaspoon black peppercorns
3 (32-ounce) bottles red wine vinegar
Fresh rosemary sprigs (optional)

• **Twist** stems of herbs gently, and press garlic with back of a spoon. Place herbs and garlic in a large glass container. Add tomatoes and peppercorns. Set aside.
• **Bring** vinegar to a boil, and pour over herb mixture. Cover vinegar mixture, and store in a cool, dark place at room temperature 2 weeks.
• **Pour** vinegar mixture through a large wire-mesh strainer into decorative bottles, discarding solids. Add additional fresh rosemary sprigs, if desired. Seal bottles, and store in a cool, dark place up to 6 months. **Yield:** 11 cups.

Cindie Hackney
Longview, Texas

LEMON HONEY

QUICK!

4 large eggs
2 egg yolks
2 cups sugar
1 tablespoon grated lemon rind
½ cup fresh lemon juice
¼ cup butter

• **Combine** all ingredients in a heavy saucepan; cook over low heat, stirring constantly, 10 minutes or until mixture is thickened. Let cool completely. Serve with Hazelnut Scones (recipe on page 49). Store leftover honey in refrigerator. **Yield:** 2½ cups.

Sharon McCullar
Victorian Room
Shreveport, Louisiana

LEMON-MINT SUGAR

QUICK!

2 cups sugar
3 tablespoons grated lemon rind
2 tablespoons dried mint flakes
¼ teaspoon salt

• **Combine** all ingredients; spread sugar mixture in a thin layer in a 15- x 10- x 1-inch jellyroll pan.
• **Bake** sugar mixture at 200° for 15 minutes. Cool in pan.
• **Place** sugar mixture in container of an electric blender. Process to a fine powder. Store in an airtight container up to 6 months. Serve with hot or iced tea or fresh fruit. **Yield:** 2 cups.

ORANGE SYRUP

2 cups sugar
1 tablespoon grated orange rind
½ cup fresh orange juice
⅓ cup light corn syrup
¼ cup Triple Sec or other orange-flavored liqueur
2 tablespoons butter or margarine
1 teaspoon clear vanilla extract

• **Combine** all ingredients in a heavy saucepan, and bring to a boil over medium heat. Reduce heat to low; simmer 5 minutes or until sugar dissolves, stirring occasionally.
• **Pour** through a wire-mesh strainer into a small pitcher, discarding orange rind. Serve with orange sections over ice cream or waffles. Store leftovers in refrigerator. **Yield:** 2 cups.

Beverly Justice
Columbiana, Alabama

WEAVER D'S SEASONING MIX

QUICK!

Dexter uses his mix for battered fried chicken and pork chops. This recipe is enough for about 3½ pounds of fryer pieces. Tip: Just before serving, sprinkle fried chicken or pork with seasoned salt for added zest.

3½ cups all-purpose flour
3 tablespoons garlic powder
3 tablespoons seasoned salt
3 tablespoons pepper
1 tablespoon salt

• **Combine** all ingredients; store in an airtight container. **Yield:** 4 cups.

Dexter Weaver
Weaver D's Delicious Fine Foods
Athens, Georgia

At right: *Herbed Gazpacho (page 356)*

SOUPS AND STEWS

REFRIED BEAN SOUP

This dish is so filling, you need to add only tortilla chips and salsa to round out the meal.

1 small onion, chopped
2 cloves garlic, minced
1 tablespoon vegetable oil
1 (31-ounce) can refried beans
1 (16-ounce) can diced tomatoes, undrained
1 (10-ounce) can diced tomatoes and green chiles, undrained
1 (14½-ounce) can chicken broth
2 tablespoons chopped fresh cilantro (optional)
6 corn tortillas
2 cups (8 ounces) shredded Monterey Jack cheese
1 (8-ounce) carton sour cream

● **Cook** onion and garlic in oil in a Dutch oven over medium-high heat, stirring constantly, until tender. Add beans and next 3 ingredients, stirring until smooth; bring to a boil. Reduce heat, and simmer 15 minutes. Stir in cilantro, if desired.
● **Cut** tortillas into thin strips; spread in a single layer on a baking sheet. Bake at 350° for 15 minutes or until browned, stirring every 5 minutes. Cool.
● **Ladle** soup into individual soup bowls; top with tortilla strips, cheese, and sour cream. Serve immediately. **Yield:** 7 cups.

Shirley M. Draper
Winter Park, Florida

BUTTERNUT SQUASH SOUP

1 (2½-pound) butternut squash, peeled, seeded, and cut into 1-inch chunks
3 cups water
2 medium onions, chopped
1 large red bell pepper, finely chopped
2 cloves garlic, pressed
3 tablespoons vegetable oil
1 teaspoon ground cumin
1 teaspoon ground coriander
1 teaspoon ground ginger
1 teaspoon dry mustard
1 teaspoon curry powder
½ teaspoon salt
1 cup orange juice
1 teaspoon lemon juice
⅛ teaspoon ground red pepper
¼ cup fresh goat cheese (chèvre)
¼ cup water

● **Combine** squash and 3 cups water in a large saucepan. Bring to a boil over medium-high heat; cover, reduce heat, and simmer 10 minutes or until squash is tender. Drain, reserving cooking liquid; set both aside.
● **Cook** chopped onion, chopped red bell pepper, and garlic in oil in a Dutch oven over medium-high heat, stirring constantly, 10 minutes or until tender.
● **Add** cumin and next 5 ingredients, stirring mixture well.
● **Combine** half of squash and half of cooked onion mixture in container of an electric blender; process until smooth, stopping once to scrape down sides.
● **Pour** blended squash mixture into another container. Repeat procedure with remaining squash and onion mixture, and return blended squash mixture to Dutch oven.
● **Add** orange juice, lemon juice, ground red pepper, and cooking liquid to squash mixture. Cook over medium heat, stirring constantly, until thoroughly heated.
● **Combine** cheese and ¼ cup water, stirring until mixture is smooth and consistency of sour cream. Dollop onto the center of each serving. **Yield:** 7 cups.

Fleming and Brit Pfann
Celebrity Dairy
Greensboro, North Carolina

SHERRIED MUSHROOM SOUP

2 tablespoons butter or margarine
1 small onion, chopped
¼ teaspoon garlic powder
2 (10½-ounce) cans condensed chicken broth, undiluted
3 (10¾-ounce) cans cream of mushroom soup, undiluted
1 cup milk
2 tablespoons sour cream
1 tablespoon chopped fresh parsley
1 teaspoon chopped fresh thyme
1 cup quick brown rice, uncooked
½ cup dry sherry
¼ teaspoon pepper
1 (8-ounce) package sliced fresh mushrooms
Garnish: toast points

● **Melt** butter in a 3-quart saucepan over medium-high heat; add onion and garlic powder, and cook, stirring constantly, until tender. Add broth; reduce heat, and simmer 5 minutes.
● **Combine** soup and next 4 ingredients, whisking until blended; stir into broth mixture. Add rice and next 3 ingredients; cook 20 to 30 minutes or until rice is tender and soup is thickened. Garnish, if desired. **Yield:** 8 cups.

Marilyn W. Godsey
Fort Myers, Florida

FRENCH ONION SOUP

2 tablespoons butter
Vegetable cooking spray
6 large onions, thinly sliced (3 pounds)
2 (10½-ounce) cans beef consommé, undiluted
1 (13¾-ounce) can no-salt-added, fat-free beef broth
1⅓ cups water
¼ cup dry white wine
¼ teaspoon freshly ground pepper
7 (1-inch-thick) slices French bread
¼ cup grated Parmesan cheese

● **Melt** butter in a large Dutch oven coated with cooking spray. Add onion, and cook over medium heat 5 minutes, stirring often. Add 1 can beef consommé; cook over low heat 30 minutes. Gradually add remaining 1 can beef consommé and next 4 ingredients; bring to a boil, reduce heat, and simmer, uncovered, 10 minutes.

• **Place** bread slices on a baking sheet; sprinkle with cheese. Broil 6 inches from heat (with electric oven door partially opened) until cheese is golden.

• **Ladle** soup into serving bowls, and top each serving with a toasted bread slice. **Yield:** 7 cups.

♥ Per 1-cup serving: Calories 219
Fat 5.3g Cholesterol 28mg
Sodium 798mg

MARDI GRAS SOUP

English Pea Soup
Roasted Yellow Bell Pepper Soup
Shredded red cabbage

• **Pour** ¾ cup of each soup simultaneously down the sides of 5 shallow soup bowls, taking care not to mix soups. Place shredded red cabbage on top. **Yield:** 5 servings.

English Pea Soup

6 tablespoons unsalted butter
1½ cups chopped onion
3 cups vegetable or chicken broth
2 (1-pound) packages frozen English peas
¼ teaspoon salt
⅛ teaspoon ground white pepper

• **Melt** butter in a Dutch oven over medium heat; add onion, and cook, stirring constantly, until tender. Add broth, and bring to a boil.

• **Stir** in peas, salt, and pepper; reduce heat, and simmer 5 to 10 minutes or until peas are tender. Cool slightly.

• **Position** knife blade in food processor bowl; add soup, and process until smooth, stopping once to scrape down sides.

• **Pour** soup through a wire-mesh strainer into Dutch oven, discarding solids; cook over low heat just until thoroughly heated. **Yield:** 4 cups.

Roasted Yellow Bell Pepper Soup

3 yellow bell peppers
2 tablespoons unsalted butter
½ cup chopped onion
½ cup chopped leek
¼ teaspoon salt
¼ teaspoon freshly ground pepper
1 medium-size red potato, peeled and sliced
2½ cups vegetable or chicken broth

• **Cut** peppers in half; remove and discard seeds. Place peppers, cut side down, on an aluminum foil-lined baking sheet.

• **Broil** 5½ inches from heat (with electric oven door partially opened) 5 minutes or until bell peppers look blistered.

• **Place** bell peppers in a heavy-duty, zip-top plastic bag; seal and let stand 10 minutes to loosen skins. Peel peppers, and coarsely chop; set aside.

• **Melt** butter in a Dutch oven over medium heat; add onion and next 3 ingredients. Cook, stirring constantly, 10 minutes or until vegetables are tender.

• **Add** chopped bell pepper, potato, and broth; bring to a boil. Reduce heat, and simmer 10 minutes or until potato is tender, stirring occasionally. Cool slightly.

• **Position** knife blade in food processor bowl; add soup, and process until smooth, stopping once to scrape down sides. Return to Dutch oven, and cook over low heat just until soup is thoroughly heated. **Yield:** 4 cups.

Jami Gaudet
Macon, Georgia

EASY POTATO SOUP

½ (32-ounce) package frozen hash brown potatoes
1 cup chopped onion
1 (14½-ounce) can chicken broth
2 cups water
1 (10¾-ounce) can cream of celery soup, undiluted
1 (10¾-ounce) can cream of chicken soup, undiluted
2 cups milk
Garnishes: shredded Cheddar cheese, diced cooked ham or bacon

• **Combine** first 4 ingredients in a Dutch oven; bring to a boil. Cover, reduce heat, and simmer 30 minutes. Stir in soups and milk; cook until thoroughly heated. Garnish, if desired. **Yield:** 10 cups.

Harriett Blanford
Owensboro, Kentucky

BAKED POTATO SOUP

4 large baking potatoes
⅔ cup butter or margarine
⅔ cup all-purpose flour
6 cups milk
¾ teaspoon salt
½ teaspoon pepper
4 green onions, chopped and divided
12 slices bacon, cooked, crumbled, and divided
1¼ cups (5 ounces) shredded Cheddar cheese, divided
1 (8-ounce) carton sour cream

• **Wash** potatoes, and prick several times with a fork; bake at 400° for 1 hour or until done. Let cool. Cut potatoes in half lengthwise; scoop out pulp, and set aside. Discard skins.

• **Melt** butter in a heavy saucepan over low heat; add flour, stirring until smooth. Cook 1 minute, stirring constantly. Gradually add milk; cook over medium heat, stirring constantly, until mixture is thickened and bubbly.

• **Add** potato pulp, salt, pepper, 2 tablespoons green onions, ½ cup crumbled bacon, and 1 cup cheese to saucepan. Cook until thoroughly heated, and stir in sour cream. Add extra milk, if necessary, for desired consistency. Serve with remaining green onions, bacon, and ¼ cup cheese. **Yield:** 10 cups.

LaJuan Coward
Jasper, Texas

Creamy Onion and Potato Soup

CREAMY ONION AND POTATO SOUP
(pictured at left)

QUICK!

2 tablespoons butter or margarine
2 tablespoons all-purpose flour
1 cup chopped onion
1 large clove garlic, minced
2 (14½-ounce) cans chicken broth
4 cups peeled, cubed baking potato
    (about 3 large)
½ cup sliced green onions
⅛ teaspoon salt
¼ teaspoon ground white pepper
1 cup liquid nondairy creamer or
    milk
Garnish: green onion strips

● **Melt** butter in a Dutch oven over low heat; add flour, stirring until smooth. Cook 1 minute, stirring constantly. Add onion and garlic; cook 1 minute or until onion is tender. Gradually add broth, stirring constantly.
● **Add** potato and next 3 ingredients. Bring to a boil; cover, reduce heat, and simmer 15 minutes or until potato is tender, stirring occasionally. Stir in nondairy creamer, and cook until thoroughly heated. Garnish, if desired. **Yield:** 7 cups.

Cathy Darling
Grafton, West Virginia

SWEET POTATO VELOUTÉ

A velouté is a stock-based sauce thickened with a roux (flour cooked in fat). Unlike Louisiana's medium to dark roux, this one is blond, which is easier and faster to prepare.

9 to 10 cups chicken broth
1¼ pounds sweet potatoes, peeled
    and finely chopped
1 bay leaf
1 teaspoon dried Italian seasoning
½ teaspoon ground white pepper
Dash of ground red pepper
Dash of ground nutmeg
½ cup butter or margarine
½ cup all-purpose flour
Garnishes: crème fraîche or sour
    cream, chopped fresh parsley
Fried Sweet Potato Strips

● **Combine** first 3 ingredients in a Dutch oven; bring to a boil over high heat. Reduce heat; simmer 20 minutes or until potato is tender. Remove from heat; stir in Italian seasoning and next 3 ingredients. Remove and discard bay leaf. Set aside.
● **Melt** butter in a heavy skillet over medium-high heat. Add flour, and cook, stirring constantly, 5 minutes or until light golden; stir into potato mixture.
● **Place** about one-fourth of potato mixture in container of an electric blender or food processor; process until smooth. Pour into a large bowl. Repeat procedure with remaining mixture. Return mixture to Dutch oven, and cook until thoroughly heated and slightly thickened.
● **Spoon** into soup bowls. Garnish, if desired. Top each serving with Fried Sweet Potato Strips just before serving. **Yield:** 11 cups.

Note: To make lines on soup with crème fraîche or sour cream, spoon it into a small heavy-duty, zip-top plastic bag. Snip a small hole in one corner of bag, and squeeze in straight lines onto soup. Pull a wooden pick through lines in opposite directions at intervals to create design.

Fried Sweet Potato Strips

1 large sweet potato, peeled and
    grated into long strips
1 cup vegetable oil

● **Fry** potato in hot oil in a skillet until lightly browned. (Watch carefully – the thin strips brown quickly.) Remove with a slotted spoon, and drain on paper towels. (Strips will be crisp when cooled.) **Yield:** about 1 cup.

Chefs Gary Schenk and William Wells
Juban's
Baton Rouge, Louisiana

PUMPKIN-CORN SOUP WITH GINGER-LIME CREAM

3 cups fresh or frozen corn kernels
1½ cups water
2 cloves garlic, minced
¾ teaspoon salt
½ to ¾ teaspoon ground white
    pepper
3 to 3½ cups chicken broth
3 cups cooked, mashed pumpkin *
Ginger-Lime Cream
Garnish: lime zest

● **Combine** corn and water; cover and cook over medium-high heat 10 minutes or until tender.
● **Position** knife blade in food processor bowl; add corn mixture, and process 2 minutes or until smooth, stopping once to scrape down sides. Pour mixture through a wire-mesh strainer into a bowl, discarding pulp.
● **Combine** corn mixture, garlic, salt, pepper, and 3 cups chicken broth in a Dutch oven; bring to a boil over medium-high heat. Reduce heat to low; stir in pumpkin. Simmer 10 minutes, adding additional chicken broth as necessary, stirring constantly.
● **Spoon** into individual bowls, and dollop with Ginger-Lime Cream. Garnish, if desired. **Yield:** 8 cups.

* Substitute 3 cups canned pumpkin.

Ginger-Lime Cream

¼ cup fresh lime juice
1 tablespoon grated fresh ginger
1½ teaspoons grated lime rind
½ cup whipping cream

● **Combine** lime juice and ginger in a small saucepan; cook over medium heat 2 minutes. Remove from heat; pour through a wire-mesh strainer into a small mixing bowl, discarding pulp.
● **Add** lime rind and whipping cream to juice mixture; beat at medium speed with an electric mixer until soft peaks form. **Yield:** 1 cup.

CREAMY ASPARAGUS SOUP

You can prepare the vegetable puree base ahead and store in the refrigerator up to 3 days or freeze up to 6 months. Dilute with milk, and heat to serve.

½ cup chopped onion
1 cup sliced celery
3 cloves garlic, pressed
3 tablespoons butter or margarine, melted
2 (14½-ounce) cans cut asparagus, undrained
1 (16-ounce) can sliced potatoes, drained *
1 (14½-ounce) can chicken broth
1 teaspoon white vinegar
1 teaspoon salt
½ teaspoon ground black pepper
¼ teaspoon ground red pepper
½ teaspoon dried basil
1 cup milk
½ cup sour cream (optional)
Garnish: celery leaves

● **Cook** first 3 ingredients in butter in a Dutch oven over medium-high heat, stirring constantly, until tender. Stir in asparagus and next 7 ingredients.
● **Bring** to a boil, stirring often. Reduce heat, and simmer, uncovered, 10 minutes, stirring often. Cool slightly.
● **Pour** half of mixture into container of an electric blender; process until smooth, stopping once to scrape down sides. Transfer mixture to another container. Repeat procedure.
● **Return** asparagus mixture to Dutch oven. Stir in milk; cook just until thoroughly heated (do not boil). Dollop each serving with sour cream, if desired. Garnish, if desired. **Yield:** 8 cups.

* Substitute 2 medium red potatoes, cooked, peeled, and sliced, for canned.
Sider Krison
Shreveport, Louisiana

CREAMY BUTTERNUT SOUP

4 cups cooked, mashed butternut squash
2 (14½-ounce) cans chicken broth
½ teaspoon sugar
½ teaspoon salt
¼ teaspoon pepper
1 cup whipping cream, divided
¼ teaspoon ground nutmeg

● **Combine** half of first 5 ingredients in container of an electric blender or food processor, and process until smooth, stopping once to scrape down sides; pour into a large saucepan. Repeat procedure with remaining half.
● **Bring** to a boil over medium heat; gradually stir in half of whipping cream, and cook until thoroughly heated. Remove from heat.
● **Beat** remaining whipping cream at high speed with an electric mixer until firm peaks form. Dollop on soup; sprinkle with nutmeg. **Yield:** 7 cups.

Creamy Acorn-Butternut Soup: Substitute 2 cups cooked, mashed acorn squash for 2 cups cooked, mashed butternut squash.

Acorn Squash Bowls: Cut off tops of squash; cut a thin slice from bottoms to stand squash upright. Remove seeds, and brown top of shells in a hot greased skillet.

Sandra Holmes-Kennedy
Atlanta, Texas

CREAM OF CAULIFLOWER SOUP

1 large onion
2 shallots
1 clove garlic
1 tablespoon olive oil
2 (14½-ounce) cans chicken broth
1 large cauliflower, cut into flowerets
1½ cups whipping cream
1 teaspoon salt
⅛ teaspoon ground white pepper
Garnishes: asparagus tips, cracked black pepper

● **Slice** first 3 ingredients; cook in oil in a Dutch oven until tender, stirring often. Stir in broth; bring to a boil. Add cauliflower; cook 15 minutes or until tender, stirring occasionally.
● **Process** soup in batches in container of an electric blender until smooth, stopping once to scrape down sides; return to pan. Stir in whipping cream, salt, and white pepper; cook over low heat until thoroughly heated, stirring often. Ladle into soup bowls; garnish, if desired. **Yield:** 8 cups.

Julia Rutland
Cordova, Tennessee

CREAMY KALE SOUP

Be sure to use green kale – variegated kale is better for garnishing than eating.

1¼ pounds fresh kale
2 (14½-ounce) cans chicken broth
1 cup water
1½ pounds red potatoes, chopped
1½ cups chopped cooked ham
¾ teaspoon salt
2 to 3 teaspoons pepper
1 large onion, cut in half and sliced
2 cups whipping cream
2 (15-ounce) cans white beans, rinsed and drained
2 tablespoons butter or margarine, softened
2 tablespoons all-purpose flour

● **Remove** and discard stems and discolored spots from kale; rinse with cold water, and drain. Tear into bite-size pieces; set aside.
● **Combine** broth, 1 cup water, and next 4 ingredients in a large Dutch oven; bring to a boil. Reduce heat, and simmer 20 minutes, stirring occasionally. Stir in kale and onion; simmer 20 minutes, stirring occasionally. Add whipping cream and beans; bring to a boil, stirring often.
● **Combine** butter and flour, stirring until blended. Stir into soup, and simmer 10 minutes, stirring occasionally. **Yield:** 16 cups.

Pat Pittman
Boone, North Carolina

CREAM OF MUSTARD GREEN SOUP

1 (1-pound) center-cut ham slice
   with bone
8 cups water
1 large bunch fresh mustard
   greens, washed and finely
   chopped (about 4½ cups)
¼ cup butter or margarine
2 cups chopped green onions
2 cups chopped celery
1 cup chopped onion
⅓ cup butter or margarine
⅓ cup all-purpose flour
5 cups half-and-half
½ teaspoon salt
⅛ teaspoon hot sauce

● **Combine** ham and water in a Dutch oven; bring to a boil. Cover, reduce heat, and simmer 3 hours. Remove ham, leaving liquid in Dutch oven. (Reserve ham for another use.)
● **Add** mustard greens to Dutch oven, and cook, uncovered, 1 hour, stirring occasionally. Set aside.
● **Melt** ¼ cup butter in a large skillet over medium heat; add green onions, celery, and onion, and cook, stirring constantly, until mixture is tender. Remove from heat.
● **Position** knife blade in food processor bowl; add onion mixture. Process onion mixture until smooth, stopping occasionally to scrape down sides. Set aside.
● **Melt** ⅓ cup butter in Dutch oven over low heat; gradually add flour, stirring until smooth. Cook 1 minute, stirring constantly. Gradually add half-and-half; cook over medium heat, stirring constantly, until thickened and bubbly. Stir in mustard green mixture, pureed vegetables, salt, and hot sauce. Cook just until thoroughly heated (do not boil). **Yield:** 10 cups.

CREAM OF SHIITAKE SOUP

QUICK!

½ pound fresh shiitake mushrooms
¼ cup butter or margarine
2 cups chopped onion
3 tablespoons all-purpose flour
2 (14½-ounce) cans chicken broth
2 cups whipping cream
¼ teaspoon pepper
¼ teaspoon ground nutmeg

● **Remove** stems from mushrooms; discard. Finely chop mushroom caps.
● **Melt** butter in a saucepan over medium-high heat; add chopped mushroom caps and onion, and cook, stirring constantly, until tender.
● **Add** flour; cook 1 minute, stirring constantly. Gradually add broth; cook, stirring constantly, until thickened. Remove from heat. Stir in whipping cream, pepper, and nutmeg. **Yield:** 7 cups.

Jean Hartgroves
Charlestown, West Virginia

CREAM OF ROASTED SWEET RED PEPPER SOUP

8 large red bell peppers
6 cloves garlic, minced
1 small onion, chopped
3 tablespoons butter, divided
2 (14½-ounce) cans chicken broth
2 cups dry white wine
1 bay leaf
½ teaspoon salt
¼ teaspoon pepper
2 tablespoons all-purpose flour
1½ cups whipping cream
Garnish: fresh basil, cut into strips

● **Place** peppers on an aluminum foil-lined baking sheet; broil 5½ inches from heat (with electric oven door partially opened) about 5 minutes on each side or until peppers look blistered.
● **Place** roasted peppers in a heavy-duty, zip-top plastic bag; seal and let stand 10 minutes. Peel; remove and discard stem and seeds. Set roasted peppers aside.
● **Cook** garlic and onion in 1 tablespoon butter in a Dutch oven over medium heat until crisp-tender. Add chicken broth and next 4 ingredients; bring to a

boil. Reduce heat, and simmer 30 minutes. Pour broth mixture through a large wire-mesh strainer into a large container, reserving solids. Remove and discard bay leaf. Set broth mixture aside.
● **Position** knife blade in food processor bowl; add reserved solids and peppers. Process 30 seconds or until smooth, stopping once to scrape down sides; set pepper puree aside.
● **Melt** remaining 2 tablespoons butter in Dutch oven over low heat; add flour, stirring until smooth. Cook 1 minute, stirring constantly. Gradually add broth mixture; cook over medium heat, stirring constantly, until thickened and bubbly (about 3 minutes). Stir in pepper puree. Gradually stir in whipping cream. Cook over low heat until heated. Garnish, if desired. **Yield:** 8 cups.

Nicholas Rutyna
San Antonio, Texas

CREAM OF PIMIENTO SOUP

QUICK!

1 (4-ounce) jar diced pimiento,
   undrained
2 tablespoons butter or margarine
2½ tablespoons all-purpose flour
1 (14½-ounce) can chicken broth
1½ cups half-and-half
2 teaspoons grated onion
½ teaspoon salt
¼ teaspoon hot sauce

● **Place** pimiento in container of an electric blender; process until smooth, stopping once to scrape down sides. Set aside.
● **Melt** butter in a heavy saucepan over low heat; add flour, stirring until smooth. Cook 1 minute, stirring constantly.
● **Add** chicken broth and half-and-half gradually to flour mixture; cook over medium heat, stirring constantly, until mixture is thickened and bubbly.
● **Stir** in pureed pimiento, onion, salt, and hot sauce; cook over low heat, stirring constantly, until thoroughly heated. **Yield:** 3¾ cups.

Note: You can easily double the recipe.

Eugenia W. Bell
Lexington, Kentucky

CURRIED PUMPKIN SOUP

(pictured on page 2)

QUICK!

2   tablespoons butter or margarine
1   (8-ounce) package sliced fresh
      mushrooms
½   cup chopped onion
2   tablespoons all-purpose flour
1   tablespoon curry powder
3   cups chicken broth
2   cups canned pumpkin
1   tablespoon honey
½   teaspoon salt
¼   teaspoon ground nutmeg
¼   teaspoon pepper
1   (12-ounce) can evaporated milk
Garnishes: sour cream, chopped
      fresh chives

• **Melt** butter in a large saucepan; add mushrooms and onion, and cook until tender, stirring often.
• **Stir** in flour and curry powder; gradually add chicken broth, and cook over medium heat, stirring constantly, until mixture is thickened.
• **Stir** in pumpkin and next 4 ingredients; reduce heat, and simmer 10 minutes, stirring occasionally. Stir in milk, and cook, stirring constantly, until thoroughly heated. Garnish, if desired. **Yield:** 6½ cups.

Nancy Wilson
Houston, Texas

CREAM OF TOMATO SOUP WITH LEMON BASIL

3   pounds tomatoes, cut into
      fourths
¼   cup chopped fresh lemon basil
2   tablespoons butter or margarine
2   tablespoons all-purpose flour
2   cups half-and-half
1   teaspoon sugar
1   teaspoon salt
¼   teaspoon freshly ground pepper
2   tablespoons chopped fresh
      lemon basil

• **Combine** tomato and ¼ cup lemon basil in a large heavy saucepan; bring to a boil. Reduce heat, and simmer 10 to 15 minutes or until tomato is soft.

• **Pour** mixture through a wire-mesh strainer into a bowl, pressing mixture against sides of strainer with back of a spoon; discard pulp. Set tomato liquid aside.
• **Melt** butter in saucepan over low heat; add flour, stirring until smooth. Cook 1 minute, stirring constantly. Gradually add half-and-half; cook over medium heat, stirring constantly, until mixture is thickened and bubbly.
• **Stir** in sugar, salt, and pepper; gradually stir in tomato liquid and 2 tablespoons lemon basil. Cook just until thoroughly heated (do not boil). Serve immediately. **Yield:** 5½ cups.

CHEESE VELVET SOUP

6   ounces Brie cheese
½   cup finely chopped celery
½   cup finely chopped carrot
¼   cup finely chopped onion
½   cup butter or margarine, melted
½   cup all-purpose flour
2   cups chicken broth
1   teaspoon dried thyme
1   bay leaf
½   cup whipping cream
Garnish: shredded carrot

• **Carefully** cut rind from Brie, and discard; set cheese aside.
• **Cook** celery, carrot, and onion in butter in a saucepan over medium heat, stirring constantly, until tender. Add flour, and cook over low heat 1 minute, stirring constantly. Gradually stir in broth, thyme, and bay leaf. Cook, stirring constantly, until mixture is thickened and bubbly. Add cheese, stirring until smooth. Add whipping cream, and cook until thoroughly heated. Remove and discard bay leaf; serve immediately. Garnish, if desired. **Yield:** 3 cups.

Potluck on the Pedernales
Community Garden Club of
Johnson City, Texas

HERBED CHEESE SOUP

QUICK!

¼   cup butter or margarine
3   tablespoons all-purpose flour
1   tablespoon chopped fresh chives
1½ teaspoons paprika
½   teaspoon dry mustard
¼   teaspoon salt
Dash of freshly ground pepper
2   cups chicken broth
2   cups half-and-half
8   ounces fresh goat cheese
      (chèvre), crumbled *
1   clove garlic, minced
¼   teaspoon caraway seeds, crushed
1   teaspoon dried basil
1   teaspoon dried dillweed
Garnish: fresh chives

• **Melt** butter in a large saucepan over medium-high heat. Whisk in flour and next 5 ingredients. Cook 3 minutes, whisking constantly. Gradually add broth and half-and-half, and cook, whisking constantly, until smooth.
• **Add** cheese and next 4 ingredients; reduce heat to low, and cook 10 minutes, whisking constantly. Garnish, if desired. **Yield:** 4 servings.

* Substitute 1 (8-ounce) package cream cheese, cubed, for fresh goat cheese.

Patricia Bell
Split Creek Farm
Anderson, South Carolina

MACARONI AND CHEESE SOUP

1   cup elbow macaroni, uncooked
¼   cup butter or margarine
½   cup finely chopped carrot
½   cup finely chopped celery
1   small onion, finely chopped
4   cups milk
1½ cups (6 ounces) shredded
      process American cheese
2   tablespoons chicken-flavored
      bouillon granules
½   teaspoon ground white pepper
2   tablespoons cornstarch
2   tablespoons cold water
1   (8-ounce) can whole kernel corn,
      drained
½   cup frozen English peas

- **Cook** macaroni according to package directions, omitting salt; drain well. Rinse macaroni with cold water; drain and set aside.
- **Melt** butter in a large skillet over medium-high heat; add carrot, celery, and onion, and cook, stirring constantly, 5 to 7 minutes or until tender. Remove vegetable mixture from heat; set aside.
- **Combine** milk and cheese in a heavy Dutch oven, and cook over medium heat until cheese melts, stirring often. Stir in bouillon granules and pepper.
- **Combine** cornstarch and water in a small bowl, stirring well; stir into milk mixture. Cook over medium heat, stirring constantly, until mixture thickens and comes to a boil. Boil 1 minute, stirring constantly.
- **Stir** in macaroni, vegetable mixture, corn, and peas; cook over low heat, stirring constantly, until thoroughly heated. **Yield:** 8 cups.

W. N. Cottrell II
New Orleans, Louisiana

STONE CRAB BISQUE

½ cup butter or margarine, divided
½ cup finely chopped onion
½ cup finely chopped green bell pepper
2 green onions, finely chopped
¼ cup chopped fresh parsley
1 (8-ounce) package fresh mushrooms, chopped
¼ cup all-purpose flour
2 cups milk
2 teaspoons salt
¼ teaspoon pepper
1 teaspoon hot sauce
3 cups half-and-half
2½ cups stone crab claw meat (22 medium claws) ✱
¼ cup dry sherry

- **Melt** ¼ cup butter in a Dutch oven over medium-high heat; add onion and next 4 ingredients, and cook, stirring constantly, 5 minutes or until tender. Remove from Dutch oven, and set aside.
- **Melt** remaining ¼ cup butter in Dutch oven over low heat; add flour, stirring until smooth. Cook 1 minute, stirring constantly. Gradually stir in milk. Cook over medium heat, stirring constantly, until thickened and bubbly.
- **Stir** in onion mixture, salt, and next 3 ingredients. Bring to a boil, stirring constantly; reduce heat, and gently stir in crab claw meat. Simmer 5 minutes, stirring often. Gently stir in sherry. **Yield:** 8 servings.

✱ Substitute 2½ cups flaked, back-fin crabmeat for claw meat.

Note: Stone crab is in season October 15 to May 15. You can mail-order it from Joe's Stone Crab in Miami Beach, 1-800-780-2722. The medium stone crab claws come in orders of six. Market prices vary, so call for specific prices. There's an additional charge for packing and shipping.

Nita and Harold Norman
Coral Gables, Florida

OYSTER BISQUE

QUICK!

¼ cup butter or margarine
3 cloves garlic, minced
2 shallots, finely chopped
3 tablespoons all-purpose flour
1 (8-ounce) bottle clam juice
½ cup dry sherry
¼ cup lemon juice
1 tablespoon Worcestershire sauce
⅛ teaspoon hot sauce
¼ teaspoon freshly ground pepper
1 quart whipping cream
2 (12-ounce) containers fresh oysters, drained

- **Melt** butter in a large Dutch oven over medium heat; add garlic and shallot, and cook until tender, stirring often.
- **Add** flour, and cook 1 minute. Add clam juice, sherry, and lemon juice; cook 2 to 3 minutes or until thickened and bubbly.
- **Stir** in Worcestershire sauce and next 3 ingredients; add oysters, and cook over medium heat 10 minutes or just until edges of oysters curl, stirring occasionally. **Yield:** 9 cups.

SHRIMP-CHILE BISQUE

QUICK!

2 (10¾-ounce) cans cream of shrimp soup, undiluted
3 cups milk
1 (14-ounce) can artichoke hearts, drained and chopped
½ (16-ounce) loaf mild Mexican-style process cheese spread, cubed
¼ teaspoon seasoned salt
¼ teaspoon ground white pepper
½ teaspoon Beau Monde seasoning (optional)
1 (5-ounce) package frozen cooked small shrimp
Garnishes: red bell pepper slices, fresh parsley sprigs

- **Combine** first 7 ingredients in a Dutch oven; cook over low heat until cheese melts and mixture is hot, stirring often.
- **Add** shrimp; cook 1 minute or until thoroughly heated, stirring often. Spoon into bowls, and garnish, if desired. **Yield:** 8 cups.

Note: You can prepare bisque a day ahead except adding shrimp. Reheat over low heat, stirring often. Stir in shrimp, and cook as directed.

Candy Stevens Smith
Texarkana, Texas

BELL PEPPER-CHEESE CHOWDER

⅓ cup butter or margarine
1 cup chopped red bell pepper
1 cup chopped yellow bell pepper
½ cup chopped carrot
½ cup sliced celery
½ cup chopped onion
2 cloves garlic, minced
½ cup all-purpose flour
1 quart half-and-half
2 (10½-ounce) cans condensed
    chicken broth, undiluted
1 (12-ounce) can beer
½ teaspoon dry mustard
¼ teaspoon dried rosemary,
    crushed
¼ teaspoon salt
¼ teaspoon ground red pepper
½ teaspoon freshly ground black
    pepper
2 cups (8 ounces) shredded sharp
    Cheddar cheese
Garnishes: fresh rosemary sprig,
    finely chopped red and yellow
    bell pepper

• **Melt** butter in a large Dutch oven over medium-high heat. Add chopped peppers and next 4 ingredients. Cook, stirring constantly, 5 minutes or until tender.
• **Add** flour, stirring constantly. Cook 1 minute, stirring constantly. Gradually add half-and-half, chicken broth, and beer; cook, stirring constantly, until thickened and bubbly.
• **Stir** in mustard and next 4 ingredients; gradually add cheese, stirring until cheese melts. Garnish, if desired, and serve immediately. **Yield:** 11 cups.

Elizabeth A. Crawley
New Orleans, Louisiana

OVEN-ROASTED VEGETABLE CHOWDER

1½ pounds red potatoes, cut into
    ½-inch cubes
2 large carrots, scraped and cut
    into ½-inch cubes
1 large onion, coarsely chopped
6 plum tomatoes, quartered
    lengthwise
3 (14½-ounce) cans chicken
    broth
Dash of salt (optional)
Dash of pepper (optional)

• **Combine** potato and carrot in a lightly greased aluminum foil-lined 13- x 9- x 2-inch pan. Bake at 375° for 15 minutes.
• **Stir** in onion. Place tomato at one end of pan, keeping separate from potato mixture. Bake 1 hour, stirring every 15 minutes.
• **Remove** from oven. Coarsely chop tomato; set aside.
• **Bring** broth to a boil in a large saucepan; add potato mixture. Reduce heat, and simmer 10 to 15 minutes.
• **Stir** in tomato; if desired, add salt and pepper. Serve immediately. **Yield:** about 7 cups.

Chef Marcel Desaulniers
Trellis Restaurant
Williamsburg, Virginia

SOUTHERN CORN AND BACON CHOWDER

1 pound bacon, chopped
1 large onion, thinly sliced
10 ears fresh corn
2 (14½-ounce) cans chicken broth
1 medium potato, peeled and cut
    into ½-inch cubes
2 carrots, scraped and shredded
¼ cup all-purpose flour
1½ cups milk
1½ cups half-and-half
1 tablespoon lemon juice
¼ teaspoon hot sauce
2 teaspoons salt
½ teaspoon pepper

• **Cook** bacon in a Dutch oven until crisp; remove bacon, reserving drippings. Set aside.

• **Cook** onion in 3 tablespoons reserved drippings in Dutch oven until tender; drain.
• **Cut** tips of corn kernels into a large bowl; scrape milk and remaining pulp from cobs. Add corn, broth, potato, and carrot to onion in Dutch oven.
• **Bring** to a boil; reduce heat, and simmer 10 minutes or until potato is tender. Set aside.
• **Whisk** together ⅓ cup reserved bacon drippings and flour in a 10-inch heavy skillet, and cook over medium-low heat, stirring constantly, 10 minutes or until browned. Remove from heat, and set aside.
• **Add** milk and half-and-half to vegetable mixture; cook over medium heat, whisking often, until thoroughly heated. Stir in lemon juice and next 3 ingredients. Whisk in flour mixture and three-fourths of cooked bacon.
• **Cook** until thickened, stirring often. Sprinkle with remaining bacon. **Yield:** about 14 cups.

Note: You can freeze chowder up to 1 month.

Gail Laughlin
Memphis, Tennessee

TURKEY-CORN CHOWDER

QUICK!

4 medium onions, sliced
¼ cup butter or margarine, melted
5 medium red potatoes, cubed
2 stalks celery, chopped
1 tablespoon salt
½ teaspoon pepper
1 chicken-flavored bouillon cube
2 cups water
5 cups milk
2 (15¼-ounce) cans whole kernel
    corn, drained
1 (14¾-ounce) can cream-style
    corn
1 cup half-and-half
1½ teaspoons paprika
¼ teaspoon dried thyme
3 cups chopped cooked turkey *
Chopped fresh parsley

• **Cook** onion in butter in a Dutch oven until tender, stirring often. Add cubed

potato and next 5 ingredients; bring to a boil. Cover, reduce heat, and simmer 15 minutes or until vegetables are tender.
● **Add** milk and next 6 ingredients; cook until heated. Sprinkle with parsley. **Yield:** 20 cups.

✽ You can substitute 3 cups chopped cooked chicken for turkey.
Marty Sprague
36 Best Christmas Party Ideas
Fort Worth, Texas

CLAM AND SAUSAGE CHOWDER

2 **dozen fresh clams**
2 **pounds smoked Polish sausage, thinly sliced**
1 **medium onion, chopped**
2 **cloves garlic, minced**
2 **tablespoons olive oil**
1½ **pounds red potatoes, cubed**
1 **(10-ounce) package frozen whole kernel corn, thawed**
4 **(8-ounce) bottles clam juice**
2 **cups water**
1 **teaspoon fennel seeds, crushed**
½ to 1 **teaspoon ground red pepper**
2 **(16-ounce) cans crushed tomatoes, undrained**
½ **cup chopped fresh parsley**

● **Wash** clams thoroughly, discarding any opened shells. Set aside.
● **Brown** sausage in a Dutch oven over medium heat; drain on paper towels, and set aside. Wipe pan drippings from Dutch oven.
● **Cook** onion and garlic in olive oil in Dutch oven over medium-high heat, stirring constantly, until tender. Add potato and next 5 ingredients.
● **Bring** to a boil; cover, reduce heat, and simmer 15 minutes or until potato is tender. Stir in tomatoes.
● **Remove** 2 cups potato mixture, and pour into container of an electric blender. Process until smooth, stopping once to scrape down sides. Return mixture to Dutch oven.
● **Bring** to a boil. Add clams; cover, reduce heat, and simmer 4 to 5 minutes or until clam shells open. (Discard any unopened shells.)

● **Stir** in sausage and parsley; cook until thoroughly heated. **Yield:** 12 cups.

CHILI BEAN SOUP

QUICK!

½ **pound lean ground beef**
1 **small onion, finely chopped**
1 **(15-ounce) can pinto beans, undrained**
1 **(10-ounce) can diced tomatoes and green chiles, undrained**
¼ **cup dry red wine**
2 **teaspoons chili powder**
¼ **teaspoon garlic salt**

● **Cook** beef and onion in a large skillet until browned, stirring until meat crumbles; drain well.
● **Combine** beef mixture, beans, and remaining ingredients in a 1-quart electric slow cooker.
● **Cover** and cook 3 hours. If desired, serve with a green salad and cornbread. **Yield:** 2 servings.

Note: A 1-quart slow cooker has no LOW or HIGH setting, only OFF and ON.

TACO SOUP

QUICK!

1 **pound lean ground beef**
1 **large onion, chopped**
3 **(16-ounce) cans Mexican-style chili beans, undrained**
1 **(16-ounce) can whole kernel corn, undrained**
1 **(16-ounce) can chopped tomatoes, undrained**
1 **(15-ounce) can tomato sauce**
1½ **cups water**
1 **(4.5-ounce) can chopped green chiles, undrained**
1 **(1¼-ounce) package taco seasoning mix**
1 **(1-ounce) envelope Ranch-style salad dressing mix**
Toppings: tortilla chips, shredded Cheddar cheese, shredded lettuce, chopped tomato, sour cream, chopped avocado

● **Brown** ground beef and onion in a large Dutch oven over medium-high heat, stirring until beef crumbles; drain. Stir in beans and next 7 ingredients. Bring to a boil; reduce heat, and simmer, uncovered, 15 minutes. Serve with desired toppings. **Yield:** 14 cups.

Note: You can freeze Taco Soup up to 3 months.
Bette Stevens
Texarkana, Texas

CAROLINA GUMBO

QUICK!

1 **pound lean ground beef**
1 **large onion, chopped**
1 **(16-ounce) package frozen white corn, thawed**
1 **(15½-ounce) can Great Northern beans, drained**
3 **(14½-ounce) cans stewed tomatoes, undrained**
1 **(10-ounce) package frozen sliced okra, thawed**
2 **tablespoons chili powder**
Hot cooked rice
Hot sauce (optional)

● **Brown** ground beef and onion in a Dutch oven over medium-high heat, stirring until beef crumbles. Drain, rinse with hot water, and return mixture to Dutch oven.
● **Stir** in corn and next 4 ingredients. Bring mixture to a boil over medium heat, stirring occasionally; cover, reduce heat, and simmer 20 minutes, stirring occasionally.
● **Serve** over rice. Sprinkle with hot sauce, if desired. **Yield:** 6 cups.
Dawn Poston
Elkin, North Carolina

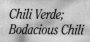

Chili Verde;
Bodacious Chili

BODACIOUS CHILI
(pictured at left)

With such a long list of ingredients, the name is obviously appropriate. But none of the items are terribly unusual or expensive, and it's easy to make. The flavor? Well, the name again applies.

2 pounds boneless beef chuck roast, cut into 1-inch cubes
2 large onions, chopped
3 stalks celery, cut into 1-inch pieces
1 large green bell pepper, coarsely chopped
1 large red bell pepper, coarsely chopped
1 cup sliced fresh mushrooms
2 jalapeño peppers, seeded and chopped
4 cloves garlic, minced
3 tablespoons olive oil
2 tablespoons cocoa
2 tablespoons chili powder
1 teaspoon ground cumin
1 teaspoon dried oregano
1 teaspoon paprika
1 teaspoon ground turmeric
½ teaspoon salt
½ teaspoon ground cardamom
¼ teaspoon pepper
1 tablespoon molasses
½ cup dry red wine
2 (16-ounce) cans whole tomatoes, undrained and chopped
1 (16-ounce) can kidney beans, drained
1 (15-ounce) can chickpeas, drained
Spicy Sour Cream Topping
Shredded Cheddar cheese

● **Cook** first 8 ingredients in olive oil in a large Dutch oven over medium-high heat, stirring constantly, until meat browns. Drain and return meat mixture to Dutch oven.
● **Stir** in cocoa and next 13 ingredients. Bring mixture to a boil; cover, reduce heat, and simmer 1½ hours, stirring occasionally. Serve chili with Spicy Sour Cream Topping and shredded cheese. **Yield:** 12 cups.

Spicy Sour Cream Topping

1 (8-ounce) carton sour cream
⅓ cup salsa
2 tablespoons mayonnaise
1 teaspoon chili powder
½ teaspoon onion powder
½ teaspoon curry powder
Dash of ground red pepper
1 tablespoon lemon juice
1 teaspoon Dijon mustard

● **Combine** all ingredients; cover and chill. **Yield:** 1⅔ cups.

Peggy Huffstetler
Lebanon, Tennessee

CINCINNATI CHILI

QUICK!

Because the meat in this chili is not browned and drained, use very lean ground beef.

2 pounds ground round
2 cups water
2 (6-ounce) cans no-salt-added tomato paste
1 large onion, finely chopped
1 clove garlic, minced
2 large bay leaves
3 tablespoons chili powder
1 tablespoon ground cumin
2 teaspoons ground allspice
1½ teaspoons ground cinnamon
1 teaspoon salt
1 teaspoon pepper
¼ teaspoon ground red pepper
1 teaspoon white wine vinegar
1 teaspoon Worcestershire sauce
Hot cooked spaghetti
Shredded Cheddar cheese
Chopped onion

● **Combine** beef and water in a 4-quart pressure cooker; stir with a fork until thoroughly blended. Stir in tomato paste and next 12 ingredients.
● **Cover** cooker with lid, and seal securely; place pressure control over vent and tube. Cook over high heat until pressure control rocks back and forth quickly. Reduce heat until pressure control rocks occasionally; cook 15 additional minutes.

● **Remove** from heat; run cold water over cooker to reduce pressure. Carefully remove lid so that steam escapes away from you.
● **Remove** and discard bay leaves. Stir chili well. Serve over hot spaghetti, and top with cheese and onion. Serve with oyster crackers. **Yield:** 6 to 8 servings.

Mary Blackmon
Lake Dallas, Texas

CHILI VERDE
(pictured on opposite page)

¾ pound beef chuck roast, cut into 1-inch cubes
¾ pound pork loin or shoulder roast, cut into 1-inch cubes
1 large onion, chopped
1 large green bell pepper, chopped
1 clove garlic, minced
2 tablespoons olive oil, divided
2 (16-ounce) cans whole tomatoes, undrained and chopped
2 (4.5-ounce) cans chopped green chiles, undrained
1 cup dry red wine
1 cup salsa
¼ cup chopped fresh cilantro
2 beef-flavored bouillon cubes
1 tablespoon brown sugar
3 tablespoons lemon juice
Hot cooked rice
Garnish: fresh cilantro sprigs

● **Combine** first 5 ingredients. Cook half of mixture in 1 tablespoon olive oil in a large Dutch oven over medium-high heat, stirring constantly, until browned. Remove from Dutch oven; set aside. Repeat procedure with remaining meat mixture and 1 tablespoon olive oil.
● **Combine** meat mixture, tomatoes, and next 7 ingredients. Bring to a boil; cover, reduce heat, and simmer 1 hour or until meat is tender, stirring occasionally. Serve over rice, and garnish, if desired. **Yield:** 11 cups.

Fran Pointer
Kansas City, Missouri

BLACK BEAN CHILI MARSALA

1 large onion, chopped
2 cloves garlic, minced
3 tablespoons vegetable oil
1 (2½-pound) boneless beef chuck
    roast, trimmed and chopped
1 (29-ounce) can tomato sauce
2 (6-ounce) cans tomato paste
1 cup Marsala *
1 cup water
2 or 3 (4-ounce) cans sliced
    mushrooms, drained
3 to 4 tablespoons chili powder
2 teaspoons seasoned salt
1 teaspoon freshly ground pepper
2 (15-ounce) cans black beans,
    undrained
Hot cooked rice
Garnish: strips of lime rind or fresh
    cilantro sprigs

• **Cook** onion and garlic in oil in a Dutch oven over medium-high heat, stirring constantly, until tender. Add chopped roast and next 8 ingredients.
• **Bring** mixture to a boil. Cover, reduce heat, and simmer 1 hour, stirring mixture occasionally.
• **Add** beans, and cook until thoroughly heated. Serve chili over rice. Garnish, if desired. **Yield:** 12 cups.

* Substitute 1 cup dry white wine plus 1½ tablespoons brandy for Marsala.

Walter C. Lund
Miami, Florida

RED CHILI STEW

1½ pounds lean beef chuck roast,
    cut into 1-inch cubes
2 cups water
3 tablespoons ground red chile
1 teaspoon salt
1 teaspoon ground oregano
1 clove garlic, pressed
3 large tomatoes, chopped

• **Combine** beef and water in a Dutch oven; bring to a boil over medium-high heat. Cover, reduce heat, and simmer 45 minutes or until meat is tender, stirring occasionally.

• **Stir** in ground chile and remaining ingredients; cook 30 additional minutes. **Yield:** 4 cups.

Rose Trujillo
Sante Fe, New Mexico

WHITE LIGHTNING TEXAS CHILI

1 pound dried navy beans
4 (14½-ounce) cans chicken broth,
    divided
1 large onion, chopped
2 cloves garlic, minced
1 tablespoon ground white
    pepper
1 tablespoon dried oregano
1 tablespoon ground cumin
1 teaspoon salt
½ teaspoon ground cloves
5 cups chopped cooked chicken
2 (4.5-ounce) cans chopped green
    chiles
1 cup water
1 jalapeño pepper, seeded and
    chopped
8 (8-inch) flour tortillas
Shredded Monterey Jack cheese
Salsa
Sour cream

• **Sort** and wash beans; place in a large Dutch oven. Cover with water 2 inches above beans. Soak 8 hours; drain beans, and return to Dutch oven. Discard liquid. Add 3 cans chicken broth, onion, and next 6 ingredients; bring to a boil. Cover, reduce heat, and simmer 2 hours or until beans are tender, stirring occasionally. Add remaining can of chicken broth, chicken, and next 3 ingredients. Cover and simmer 1 hour, stirring occasionally.
• **Make** 4 cuts in each tortilla toward, but not through, center, using kitchen shears. Line serving bowls with tortillas, overlapping cut edges of tortillas. Ladle chili into prepared bowls, and top with cheese, salsa, and sour cream. Serve immediately. **Yield:** 12 cups.

Beverly Germany
Fort Worth, Texas

BEEF STEW
(pictured at right)

1 (2¾-pound) boneless chuck
    roast *
¼ cup all-purpose flour
2 tablespoons vegetable oil
4 cups water
1 tablespoon Worcestershire
    sauce
2 teaspoons salt
1 teaspoon garlic salt
¾ teaspoon pepper
¼ teaspoon ground allspice
2 bay leaves
4 carrots, scraped
2 stalks celery
4 medium-size red potatoes
3 small onions
2 green bell peppers
3 tablespoons all-purpose flour
3 tablespoons water

• **Trim** fat from roast, and cut roast into 1-inch cubes. Place beef and ¼ cup flour in a plastic bag; seal bag, and shake vigorously to coat.
• **Pour** oil into a large Dutch oven; place over medium-high heat until hot. Add beef, and cook until browned, stirring occasionally.
• **Add** 4 cups water and next 6 ingredients; bring to a boil. Cover, reduce heat, and simmer 2 hours or until beef is tender. Remove and discard bay leaves.
• **Cut** carrots and celery into 2-inch lengths. Peel potatoes; cut potatoes and onions into eighths. Cut bell peppers into 1-inch pieces.
• **Add** carrot, celery, potato, onion, and bell pepper to beef mixture; cover and simmer 30 minutes or until vegetables are tender.
• **Combine** 3 tablespoons flour and 3 tablespoons water, stirring well; stir into stew. Bring to a boil; boil, stirring constantly, 1 minute or until thickened and bubbly. **Yield:** 6 to 8 servings.

* Substitute 2 pounds stew meat for roast.

Ann Winniford
Dallas, Texas

Beef Stew; Green Onion Dressing, page 324; Sour Cream Cornbread, page 39

REGGAE RUNDOWN

A rundown is a Jamaican dish reduced by slow cooking. This vegetable stew gets its kick from a Caribbean Scotch bonnet pepper.

1 (8-ounce) sweet potato
1 (8-ounce) baking potato
1 (14-ounce) can coconut milk
3 carrots, scraped and sliced
3 green onions, chopped
2 cloves garlic, minced
½ teaspoon salt
¼ teaspoon ground allspice
⅛ teaspoon dried thyme
1 cup peeled, chopped tomato
⅛ teaspoon minced Scotch bonnet
   or habanero pepper

• **Peel** potatoes; cut into ¾-inch cubes.
• **Bring** coconut milk to a boil in a large heavy saucepan over medium heat, stirring often; stir in potato, carrot, and next 5 ingredients. Return to a boil, stirring often; reduce heat, and simmer 7 minutes or until vegetables are almost tender, stirring often.
• **Stir** in tomato and pepper; cook 5 minutes or until thoroughly heated, stirring often. **Yield:** 4 servings.

CHICKEN STOCK

4 pounds chicken pieces
1 pound chicken wings
4 quarts water
2 onions, peeled and quartered
4 stalks celery with tops, cut into
   2-inch pieces
4 carrots, cut into 2-inch pieces
1 large bay leaf
6 sprigs fresh parsley
1 tablespoon fresh thyme or
   1 teaspoon dried thyme
6 sprigs fresh dill or ½ teaspoon
   dried dillweed
½ teaspoon black peppercorns

• **Combine** first 3 ingredients in a large stockpot; bring to a boil, skimming the surface to remove excess fat and foam.
• **Add** onion and remaining ingredients to stockpot. Return mixture to a boil; reduce heat, and simmer, uncovered, 2 hours, skimming surface to remove excess fat, if necessary. Let cool.
• **Line** a large wire-mesh strainer with a double layer of cheesecloth; place in a large bowl. Pour stock through strainer; reserve chicken for other uses, and discard remaining solids. Cool stock slightly.
• **Cover** and chill; remove and discard solidified fat from top of stock. Cover and chill stock up to 2 days or freeze up to 1 month. **Yield:** 8 cups.

BEEF STOCK

5 pounds beef or veal bones
2 large carrots, quartered
2 large onions, quartered
4 stalks celery, quartered
4 quarts water, divided
3 tablespoons tomato paste
6 to 8 sprigs fresh parsley
3 or 4 sprigs fresh thyme
4 whole cloves
½ teaspoon black peppercorns
1 bay leaf
2 cloves garlic, crushed

• **Place** first 4 ingredients in a large roasting pan; bake at 500° for 1 hour, turning occasionally.
• **Transfer** mixture to a large stockpot; discard drippings from roasting pan. Set aside.
• **Add** 1 quart water to roasting pan; bring to a boil over medium-high heat, stirring to loosen pieces that cling to bottom. Pour into stockpot; add remaining 3 quarts water, tomato paste, and remaining ingredients to stockpot.
• **Bring** to a boil; cover, reduce heat, and simmer 2 hours.
• **Line** a large wire-mesh strainer with a double layer of cheesecloth; place in a large bowl. Pour stock through strainer, discarding solids. Cool stock slightly.
• **Cover** and chill; remove and discard solidified fat from top of stock. Cover and chill stock up to 2 days or freeze up to 1 month. **Yield:** 8 cups.

VENISON STOCK

Ask your butcher or game processor to cut leg bones into smaller pieces.

5 pounds venison bones
2 (10¾-ounce) cans tomato puree
2 large carrots, scraped and
   coarsely chopped
4 stalks celery, coarsely chopped
2 large onions, coarsely chopped
2 cups dry red wine
3 quarts water
¼ teaspoon pepper
1 bay leaf
4 sprigs fresh thyme
8 sprigs fresh parsley

• **Combine** first 5 ingredients in a roasting pan; bake, uncovered, at 500° for 1 hour or until bones are well browned, turning bones over to prevent burning, if necessary. Transfer mixture to a large stockpot; set aside.
• **Add** wine to roasting pan, and bring to a boil, stirring to loosen browned particles that cling to bottom. Pour into stockpot. Add water and remaining ingredients.
• **Bring** to a boil; reduce heat, and simmer at least 3 hours.
• **Line** a large wire-mesh strainer or colander with a double layer of cheesecloth; place over a large bowl. Pour stock through strainer, discarding solids in strainer. Cool stock slightly.
• **Cover** and chill; remove and discard solidified fat from top of stock. Cover and chill stock up to 2 days or freeze up to 1 month. **Yield:** about 8 cups.

Chef David Everett
Dining Room at Ford's Colony
Williamsburg, Virginia

At right: *Skillet Zucchini Combo* *(page 409)*

VEGETABLES AND SIDE DISHES

BRANDIED CRANBERRIES

Using brandy for the liquid in this cranberry relish recipe creates a bold new flavor for a traditional favorite.

3 (12-ounce) packages fresh or
   frozen cranberries, thawed
3 cups sugar
½ cup brandy
Garnish: fresh thyme sprigs

• **Place** cranberries in a single layer in two lightly greased 15- x 10- x 1-inch jellyroll pans; pour sugar over cranberries. Cover tightly with aluminum foil.
• **Bake** at 350° for 1 hour.
• **Spoon** cranberries into a large serving bowl; gently stir in brandy. Cool. Serve cranberries chilled or at room temperature. Garnish, if desired. Store in refrigerator up to 1 week. **Yield:** 5 cups.

Carole Miller Radford
Lincolnton, Georgia

BROILED GRAPEFRUIT

QUICK!

3 large pink grapefruit
½ cup apricot preserves
1 tablespoon brown sugar
½ cup flaked coconut

• **Peel**, section, and seed grapefruit; place in four lightly greased individual baking dishes. Place dishes on a large baking sheet.
• **Combine** apricot preserves and sugar in a small bowl, stirring well; spoon over grapefruit.
• **Broil** 5½ inches from heat (with electric oven door partially opened) 2 to 3 minutes or until bubbly.
• **Sprinkle** with coconut; broil 1 additional minute or until coconut is lightly toasted. **Yield:** 4 servings.

HOT CURRIED FRUIT

This side dish doubles as a dessert when served over ice cream or pound cake.

1 (29-ounce) can pear halves,
   drained
1 (29-ounce) can peach halves,
   drained
1 (20-ounce) can pineapple
   chunks, drained
2 (17-ounce) cans apricot halves,
   drained
½ cup butter or margarine,
   softened
1 cup firmly packed brown sugar
1 tablespoon cornstarch
1½ teaspoons curry powder

• **Place** first 4 ingredients in a 13- x 9- x 2-inch baking dish.
• **Combine** butter and remaining 3 ingredients; spoon over fruit.
• **Bake** at 325° for 1 hour, basting occasionally with cooking liquid.
• **Serve** with a slotted spoon. **Yield:** 8 to 10 servings.

Note: You can prepare casserole ahead and store it in the refrigerator up to 2 days; bake according to directions just before serving.

To Market, To Market
Junior League of Owensboro, Kentucky

PINEAPPLE BAKE

Serve this sweet side dish with sliced ham, pork, chicken, or turkey.

2 (20-ounce) cans sliced pineapple
   in juice, undrained
2 cups (8 ounces) shredded sharp
   Cheddar cheese
⅔ cup sugar
⅓ cup all-purpose flour
1 cup round buttery cracker
   crumbs
¼ cup butter or margarine, melted

• **Drain** sliced pineapple, reserving ⅓ cup juice.
• **Place** pineapple in a lightly greased 11- x 7- x 1½-inch baking dish; sprinkle with cheese.

• **Combine** reserved pineapple juice, sugar, and flour; pour over cheese. Combine cracker crumbs and butter; sprinkle over flour mixture.
• **Bake** at 350° for 25 minutes or until bubbly. **Yield:** 8 servings.

Sheryl Jennings
Uvalde, Texas

HERBED ARTICHOKE SAUTÉ
(pictured at right)

10 baby artichokes
1 tablespoon olive oil
1 red bell pepper, cut into thin
   strips
1 tablespoon fresh thyme leaves
½ cup dry white wine
½ teaspoon salt
2 tablespoons chopped shallots
2 cloves garlic, minced
2 tablespoons butter

• **Hold** each artichoke by stem, and wash by plunging up and down in cold water. Cut off stem ends. Remove dark-green outer leaves from baby artichokes until light-green leaves appear. Place artichokes in a large Dutch oven; cover with water, and bring to a boil. Cook 12 to 15 minutes or until tender; drain and cool slightly.
• **Cut** artichokes in half lengthwise.
• **Cook** artichokes in oil in a large nonstick skillet over medium-high heat 2 minutes, stirring constantly. Add bell pepper strips and thyme leaves. Cook 3 additional minutes, stirring constantly. Remove artichoke mixture from skillet; set aside.
• **Combine** wine and next 3 ingredients in skillet; bring to a boil over medium-high heat. Reduce heat to low, and simmer until reduced to 2 tablespoons (about 5 minutes).
• **Stir** in butter; add artichoke mixture, and cook until thoroughly heated. **Yield:** 2 servings.

Herbed Artichoke Sauté

HAM-MUSHROOM-STUFFED ARTICHOKES

2 medium-size fresh artichokes
Lemon wedge
1½ tablespoons fresh lemon juice
1 cup sliced fresh mushrooms
1 teaspoon olive or vegetable oil
3 ounces smoked ham, cut into
     strips (about ½ cup strips)
2 tablespoons dry vermouth or
     chicken broth
¼ cup whipping cream
2 tablespoons chopped fresh
     chives
½ cup (2 ounces) shredded Swiss
     cheese

• **Hold** artichokes by stems, and wash by plunging up and down in cold water. Cut off stem end; trim about ½ inch from top of each artichoke. Remove any loose bottom leaves. With kitchen scissors, trim one-fourth off top of each outer leaf, and rub top and edges of leaves with lemon wedge to prevent discoloring.
• **Place** artichokes in a large non-aluminum Dutch oven; cover with water, and add lemon juice.
• **Bring** to a boil; cover, reduce heat, and simmer 35 minutes or until lower leaves of artichoke pull out easily. Drain and place in a baking pan.
• **Cook** mushrooms in oil in a large skillet over medium-high heat 3 minutes, stirring often. Add ham, and cook 3 minutes, stirring often. Add vermouth and whipping cream; cook 3 minutes. Remove from heat; stir in chives and cheese.
• **Spoon** mixture into and over artichokes. Broil 5½ inches from heat (with electric oven door partially opened) 3 minutes or until golden. Serve immediately. **Yield:** 2 servings.

Chef José Guiterrez
Chez Phillipe
Memphis, Tennessee

MARINATED ASPARAGUS WITH PROSCIUTTO

Prosciutto is cured Italian ham sliced paper thin. If you can't find it, ask a butcher to slice regular ham as thinly as possible.

2 pounds fresh asparagus
¾ cup vegetable oil
¼ cup white wine vinegar
2 tablespoons Dijon mustard
2 tablespoons honey
2 teaspoons dried tarragon
¼ pound prosciutto or thinly
     sliced cooked ham, cut into
     thin strips

• **Snap** off tough ends of asparagus. Remove scales from stalks with a vegetable peeler, if desired.
• **Cover** and cook asparagus in a small amount of boiling water 4 minutes or until crisp-tender; drain. Plunge into ice water to stop the cooking process; drain. Place in a shallow baking dish; set aside.
• **Combine** oil and next 4 ingredients in a jar. Cover tightly, and shake vigorously. Pour over asparagus; cover and chill at least 2 hours.
• **Remove** asparagus, reserving marinade; arrange asparagus on a serving platter. Top asparagus with prosciutto, and drizzle with reserved marinade. **Yield:** 8 servings.

Gwyneth A. Jones-Rader
Ellicott City, Maryland

ASPARAGUS WITH WARM CITRUS DRESSING
QUICK!

2 pounds fresh asparagus
½ cup butter or margarine
2 teaspoons grated lime rind
2 tablespoons fresh lime juice

• **Snap** off tough ends of asparagus. Remove scales from stalks with a vegetable peeler, if desired.
• **Place** asparagus in an 11- x 7- x 1½-inch dish. Cover tightly with heavy-duty plastic wrap, and fold back a small corner to allow the steam to escape.

• **Microwave** at HIGH 6 to 7 minutes or until crisp-tender, giving dish a half-turn after 3 minutes. Set aside.
• **Place** butter in a 2-cup liquid measuring cup; microwave at HIGH 1 minute or just until melted. Stir in lime rind and juice; pour over asparagus. **Yield:** 8 servings.

Nita and Harold Norman
Coral Gables, Florida

SESAME ASPARAGUS
QUICK!

½ pound fresh asparagus
3 tablespoons red wine vinegar
1 tablespoon dark sesame oil
1 tablespoon sesame seeds,
     toasted

• **Snap** off tough ends of asparagus. Remove scales from stalks with a vegetable peeler, if desired.
• **Cover** and cook asparagus in a small amount of boiling water 2 minutes or until crisp-tender. Drain and rinse with cold water; drain well.
• **Combine** vinegar, oil, and sesame seeds in a large heavy-duty, zip-top plastic bag; add asparagus. Seal and chill 2 hours, turning occasionally.
• **Remove** asparagus from marinade, reserving marinade. Arrange asparagus on plates; drizzle with marinade. **Yield:** 2 servings.

ASPARAGUS STIR-FRY
QUICK!

Peanut oil is recommended for stir-frying because it can stand higher temperatures than other oils before it begins to smoke or taste "off."

1½ pounds fresh asparagus
1 tablespoon peanut oil
¾ cup chicken broth, divided
1 tablespoon cornstarch
1 teaspoon sugar
2 tablespoons soy sauce
1 (2-ounce) package cashews,
     coarsely chopped and toasted
     (about ½ cup)

- **Snap** off tough ends of asparagus. Remove scales from stalks with a vegetable peeler, if desired.
- **Diagonally** cut asparagus into 1-inch pieces, and set aside.
- **Cook** asparagus in peanut oil in a large skillet over medium-high heat 2 minutes, stirring constantly. Add ¼ cup chicken broth to skillet; cover and cook 4 minutes or until asparagus is crisp-tender.
- **Combine** remaining ½ cup chicken broth, cornstarch, sugar, and soy sauce, stirring until smooth. Add to asparagus mixture, stirring constantly.
- **Bring** to a boil, and boil 1 minute, stirring constantly. Sprinkle with cashews, and serve immediately. **Yield:** 4 to 6 servings.

Kathy Sellers
Nashville, Tennessee

DILLED GREEN BEANS

QUICK!

2 pounds small fresh green
     beans, trimmed
1 cup white wine vinegar
¼ cup chopped fresh dill
3 tablespoons sugar
2 cloves garlic, crushed
½ teaspoon salt
½ teaspoon pepper

- **Place** beans in boiling water to cover; reduce heat, and simmer 8 minutes or until crisp-tender. Drain; plunge beans into ice water to stop the cooking process, and drain again. Place beans in a large shallow dish.
- **Combine** vinegar and remaining 5 ingredients, stirring until sugar dissolves; pour over beans, stirring to coat. Cover and chill 8 hours, stirring occasionally. Serve with a slotted spoon. **Yield:** 8 servings.

Irene Smith
Covington, Georgia

GREEN BEANS WITH CARAMELIZED ONIONS

2 pounds fresh green beans,
     trimmed ✱
1 pound pearl onions
¼ cup butter or margarine
¼ cup firmly packed brown sugar

- **Arrange** beans in a steamer basket over boiling water. Cover and steam 15 minutes; set aside.
- **Place** onions in boiling water 3 minutes; drain and rinse with cold water. Cut off root ends of onions; peel onions.
- **Arrange** onions in steamer basket over boiling water. Cover and steam 5 minutes; set onions aside.
- **Melt** butter in a large heavy skillet over medium heat; add sugar, and cook, stirring constantly, until bubbly. Add onions; cook 3 minutes, stirring constantly. Add beans, and cook, stirring constantly, until thoroughly heated. **Yield:** 8 servings.

✱ Substitute 2 pounds fresh brussels sprouts for beans.

Sue P. Wilson
Etowah, North Carolina

GREEN BEAN ITALIANO

1 (4½-ounce) package brown and
     wild rice mix ✱
2 tablespoons butter or margarine
1 medium onion, chopped
1 (16-ounce) carton sour cream
1 (8-ounce) package cream cheese,
     softened
3 (16-ounce) cans French-style
     green beans, drained
1 (4-ounce) jar diced pimiento,
     drained
1 (2¼-ounce) can sliced ripe
     olives, drained
1 teaspoon dried Italian seasoning
1 (8-ounce) package (2 cups)
     shredded mozzarella cheese
¼ cup grated Parmesan cheese
½ cup Italian-seasoned dried
     breadcrumbs

- **Cook** rice mix according to package directions, and set aside.

- **Melt** butter in a Dutch oven over medium-high heat. Add onion, and cook until tender, stirring often. Stir in rice, sour cream, and next 5 ingredients. Spoon mixture into a greased 13- x 9- x 2-inch baking dish.
- **Sprinkle** with mozzarella and Parmesan cheeses; top with breadcrumbs.
- **Bake** at 350° for 20 to 25 minutes until cheese is bubbly and lightly browned. **Yield:** 12 servings.

✱ For the rice, we used Success Boil-in-Bag Rice Mix for the brown and wild rice mix.

Louise W. Mayer
Richmond, Virginia

BARBECUED BEANS

½ pound ground beef
½ cup chopped onion
⅓ cup sugar
⅓ cup firmly packed brown
     sugar
½ cup barbecue sauce
¼ cup ketchup
½ teaspoon salt
½ teaspoon pepper
½ teaspoon chili powder
2 tablespoons molasses
2 teaspoons Dijon mustard
1 (15-ounce) can kidney beans,
     drained
1 (15-ounce) can butter beans,
     drained
1 (16-ounce) can pork and beans,
     undrained
10 slices bacon, cooked and
     crumbled

- **Cook** ground beef and onion in a Dutch oven, stirring until meat crumbles; drain and place in a large bowl.
- **Stir** sugar and remaining ingredients into mixture. Spoon into a lightly greased 2½-quart baking dish.
- **Bake,** uncovered, at 350° for 1 hour, stirring once. Yield: 8 to 10 servings.

Patty Renwick
Mount Airy, Maryland

BROCCOLI SOUFFLÉS

2 (10-ounce) packages frozen
   chopped broccoli, thawed
¼ cup butter or margarine
¼ cup all-purpose flour
1¼ cups milk
⅔ cup (2.6 ounces) shredded
   sharp Cheddar cheese
5 large eggs, separated
1½ teaspoons salt
¼ teaspoon minced garlic
2 tablespoons lemon juice

• **Cook** broccoli in a small amount of
boiling water 5 minutes, and drain.
• **Melt** butter in a heavy saucepan over
low heat; add flour, whisking until
smooth. Cook 1 minute, whisking constantly. Gradually add milk; cook over
medium heat, whisking constantly, until
thickened and bubbly. Add cheese, stirring until it melts. Remove from heat.
• **Beat** egg yolks at medium speed with
an electric mixer until thick and pale.
Add cooked broccoli, salt, garlic, and
lemon juice, beating until blended.
Gradually stir about one-fourth of hot
cheese mixture into yolk mixture; add
to remaining hot mixture, stirring mixture constantly.
• **Beat** egg whites at high speed until
stiff; fold one-third of egg whites into
broccoli mixture. Fold in remaining egg
whites. Pour into eight buttered individual soufflé dishes or 6-ounce custard
cups. Seal in aluminum foil, and freeze
up to 1 week.
• **Unwrap** soufflés, and place in a 13- x
9- x 2-inch pan; add hot water to pan to
depth of 1 inch.
• **Bake** at 400° for 10 minutes; reduce
heat to 350°, and bake 35 to 40 additional minutes or until puffed and
golden. Serve immediately. **Yield:** 8
servings.

Note: If not freezing soufflés, bake as
directed at 350° for 35 to 40 minutes.

BRUSSELS SPROUTS DIJON

QUICK!

⅔ cup mayonnaise or salad
   dressing
⅔ cup sour cream
¼ cup Dijon mustard
½ teaspoon garlic salt
1 tablespoon Worcestershire
   sauce
Dash of hot sauce
4 (10-ounce) packages frozen
   brussels sprouts
3 tablespoons butter or margarine,
   melted
¼ cup finely chopped pecans,
   toasted

• **Combine** first 6 ingredients in a small
saucepan; cook over low heat until
heated, stirring often. Keep warm.
• **Cook** brussels sprouts according to
package directions 5 minutes; drain.
• **Combine** brussels sprouts, butter, and
pecans, tossing to coat; serve with
sauce. **Yield:** 12 servings.

♥ To save 84 calories and 9.6 fat
grams, substitute reduced-fat mayonnaise and sour cream for the regular
versions, and reduced-calorie margarine for regular margarine. Analysis
below is for lightened version.

♥ Per serving: Calories 124
Fat 8.5g   Cholesterol 10mg
Sodium 352mg

MARINATED BRUSSELS SPROUTS

QUICK!

3 (10-ounce) packages frozen
   brussels sprouts, thawed *
½ cup olive oil
¼ cup white vinegar
1 (2-ounce) jar sliced pimiento,
   drained
2 tablespoons diced onion
2 tablespoons minced fresh
   parsley
1 teaspoon dried thyme
1 teaspoon pepper
¾ teaspoon salt

• **Cook** brussels sprouts according to
package directions, omitting salt, and
drain well.
• **Whisk** oil and remaining 7 ingredients
until blended; pour over brussels
sprouts, stirring gently to coat. Cover
and chill 2 hours. **Yield:** 8 servings.

* You can substitute 2 pounds fresh
brussels sprouts for frozen brussels
sprouts. Cook fresh brussels sprouts in
1 cup boiling water 8 minutes or until
tender.

Leisla Sansom
Alexandria, Virginia

CABBAGE-ONION-SWEET PEPPER MEDLEY
(pictured at right)

QUICK!

½ small red bell pepper
½ small yellow bell pepper
½ small green bell pepper
1 onion
2 bacon slices
2 cups shredded cabbage
3 tablespoons white vinegar
1 tablespoon vegetable oil
1 tablespoon water
1½ teaspoons brown sugar
1½ teaspoons Dijon mustard
½ teaspoon salt
½ teaspoon pepper

• **Cut** bell peppers into 2-inch-long thin
strips; chop onion, and cut bacon into 1-
inch pieces.
• **Cook** bacon in a large skillet until
crisp. Add bell pepper, onion, and cabbage, tossing gently.
• **Combine** vinegar and remaining 6 ingredients in a jar; cover tightly, and
shake vigorously. Add to vegetable mixture, stirring gently.
• **Bring** to a boil; cover, reduce heat, and
simmer 8 minutes or until cabbage is
tender, stirring occasionally. Serve immediately. **Yield:** 2 to 4 servings.

Dorothy J. Callaway
Thomasville, Georgia

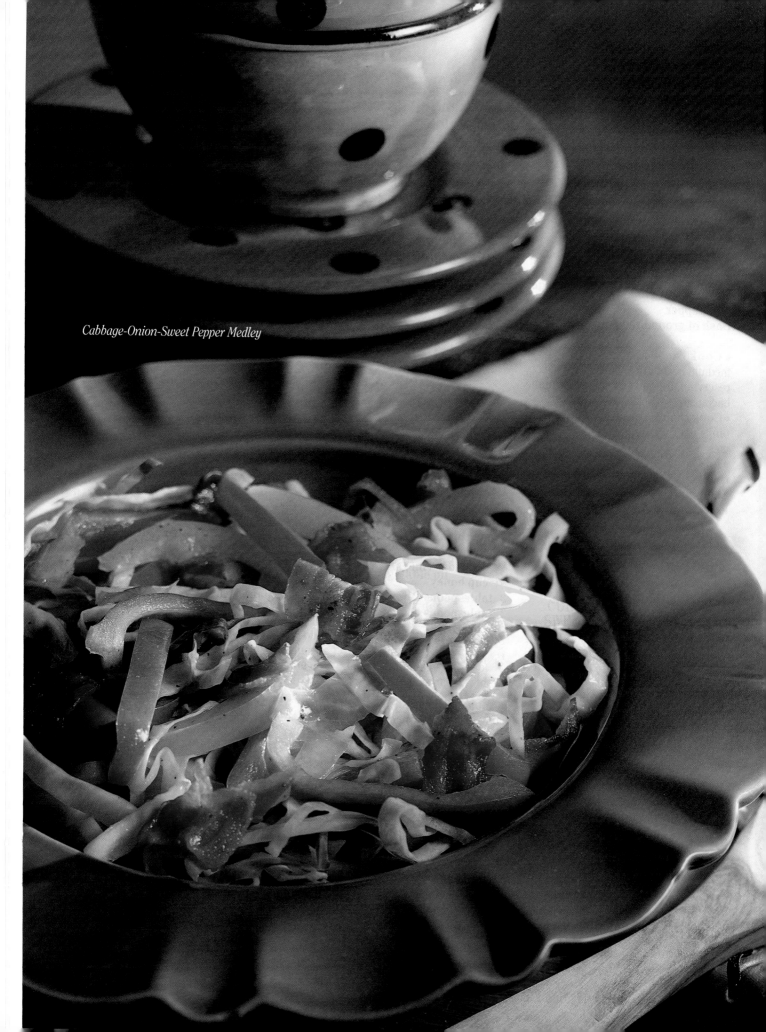

Cabbage-Onion-Sweet Pepper Medley

BALSAMIC CARAMELIZED FLORIDA SWEET ONIONS

"Caramelize" means to heat sugar until it becomes liquid or syrupy. In this recipe, the onions' natural sugar becomes caramelized while they're baking.

1 cup balsamic vinegar
2 large sweet onions, cut in half
      crosswise (about 1½ pounds)
2 tablespoons butter or margarine
1 cup walnut halves
¼ cup firmly packed brown sugar
¼ cup chopped red bell pepper
¼ cup chopped yellow bell pepper
1 to 1½ teaspoons ground red
      pepper
Garnish: fresh pineapple sage sprigs

• **Bring** vinegar to a boil in a cast-iron skillet over medium-high heat.
• **Remove** from heat; place onions, cut side down, in skillet.
• **Bake** at 400° for 55 to 60 minutes or until onions are tender and vinegar turns the color of dark chocolate.
• **Melt** butter in a skillet over medium heat. Add walnuts; cook 2 minutes, stirring often. Add sugar and next 3 ingredients; cook until bubbly, stirring often.
• **Place** an onion half, cut side up, on each plate. Sprinkle walnut mixture evenly around onions; drizzle onions with vinegar. Garnish, if desired. Serve immediately. **Yield:** 4 servings.

Note: Look for balsamic (dark, aged) vinegar next to the more common vinegars at your grocery store.

Chef Mark Rodriguez
Jordan's Grove
Maitland, Florida

GRILLED STUFFED ONIONS

1½ cups herb-seasoned stuffing mix
1 cup (4 ounces) shredded sharp
      Cheddar cheese
1 teaspoon poultry seasoning
⅓ cup butter or margarine, melted
⅓ cup hot water
6 medium-size sweet onions
Vegetable cooking spray
Garnish: fresh oregano sprigs

• **Combine** first 5 ingredients, stirring until well blended; set aside.
• **Cut** each onion into 3 horizontal slices. Spread 2 tablespoons stuffing mixture between slices, and reassemble onions. Place each onion on a 12-inch-square piece of heavy-duty aluminum foil coated with cooking spray. Bring opposite corners together, and twist foil to seal.
• **Cook**, covered with grill lid, over medium-hot coals (350° to 400°) 25 minutes or until onions are tender. Garnish, if desired. **Yield:** 6 servings.

Note: For an alternative, cover and bake onions, unwrapped, in a lightly greased 11- x 7- x 1½-inch baking dish at 350° for 1 hour or until tender.

Margaret Johns
Tarpon Springs, Florida

RATATOUILLE-STUFFED ONIONS

6 large onions, cut in half
      crosswise
1½ cups finely chopped green bell
      pepper
¾ cup peeled, finely chopped
      eggplant
¾ cup finely chopped zucchini
¾ cup thinly sliced fresh
      mushrooms
¼ cup olive oil
1½ cups peeled, seeded, chopped
      tomato
½ cup dry white wine
¼ cup tomato paste
1½ teaspoons dried thyme
1 teaspoon dried rosemary
½ teaspoon salt
½ teaspoon freshly ground
      pepper
½ teaspoon garlic powder
⅓ cup pine nuts, toasted and
      divided
2 tablespoons grated Parmesan
      cheese

• **Cut** a thin slice from bottom of onion halves, if necessary, for onions to sit upright. Scoop out onions, leaving a ½-inch-thick shell. Chop onion centers to measure 1½ cups; reserve remaining onion for another use.

• **Place** shells, upright, in a 13- x 9- x 2-inch baking dish; add hot water to dish to depth of 1 inch.
• **Cover** and bake at 400° for 35 minutes or until tender. Remove shells; drain and keep warm.
• **Cook** reserved 1½ cups chopped onion, bell pepper, and next 3 ingredients in olive oil in a large skillet over medium-high heat, stirring constantly, 3 minutes or until tender.
• **Add** tomato and next 7 ingredients; bring to a boil, stirring constantly. Reduce heat, and simmer 12 minutes or until most of liquid evaporates, stirring often. Remove from heat; stir in 3 tablespoons pine nuts.
• **Spoon** evenly into onion shells; sprinkle with cheese and remaining pine nuts. Serve immediately. **Yield:** 12 servings.

SOUTH-OF-THE-BORDER ONION RINGS
(pictured at right)

The batter's spicy sweetness stems from the unexpected – sweetened condensed milk.

2 medium onions
1 cup self-rising flour
⅓ cup self-rising cornmeal
1 large egg, lightly beaten
½ cup sweetened condensed milk
¼ cup club soda
⅓ cup minced jalapeño pepper
Vegetable oil
Salt

• **Cut** onions into ¼-inch-thick slices, and separate into rings.
• **Combine** flour and cornmeal in a bowl. Combine egg, condensed milk, and club soda; add to dry ingredients, stirring until smooth. Stir in pepper.
• **Pour** oil to depth of 3 inches into a Dutch oven; heat to 375°.
• **Dip** onion rings in batter, coating well; fry, a few rings at a time, until golden. Drain on paper towels, and sprinkle with salt. Serve immediately. **Yield:** 4 to 6 servings.

Charlotte Pierce Bryant
Greensburg, Kentucky

South-of-the-Border Onion Rings

QUICK POTATOES

QUICK!

1 tablespoon olive oil
1 large onion, chopped
2 cloves garlic, minced
½ cup chopped red bell pepper
½ teaspoon salt
¼ teaspoon pepper
¼ teaspoon hot sauce
3 cups unpeeled cubed red potato
2 tablespoons butter or margarine

● **Heat** oil in a 10-inch cast-iron skillet. Add onion and garlic; cook over medium heat, stirring constantly, until tender. Stir in bell pepper and next 3 ingredients; cook 2 minutes, stirring constantly. Add potato and butter, stir well.
● **Bake** at 400° for 20 to 30 minutes. **Yield:** 4 servings.

Pam Floyd
Birmingham, Alabama

BUTTERMILK-BASIL MASHED POTATOES

QUICK!

3½ pounds baking potatoes, peeled and cut into 1-inch cubes
1 onion, chopped
3 stalks celery, cut in half
12 cloves garlic, peeled
½ teaspoon salt
¾ cup nonfat cottage cheese
½ cup nonfat buttermilk
2 to 4 tablespoons chopped fresh basil
1 teaspoon salt
¼ teaspoon freshly ground pepper

● **Combine** first 5 ingredients in a Dutch oven; add water to cover. Bring to a boil; reduce heat, and simmer 20 minutes or until potato is tender. Drain; remove and discard celery. Mash potato mixture.
● **Position** knife blade in food processor bowl; add cottage cheese and buttermilk. Process until smooth, stopping once to scrape down sides.
● **Add** cottage cheese mixture to potato mixture; stirring mixture thoroughly until smooth. Stir in basil, 1 teaspoon salt, and pepper.

● **Cook** over low heat until heated. Serve immediately. **Yield:** 8 servings.

Ray Overton
Roswell, Georgia

♥ Per serving: Calories 205
Fat 0.3g   Cholesterol 2mg
Sodium 639mg

ROASTED GARLIC MASHED POTATOES

4 heads garlic
1 tablespoon olive oil
4 pounds baking potatoes, peeled and cut into 1-inch pieces
½ cup butter or margarine
1 cup milk
1½ teaspoons salt
½ teaspoon pepper

● **Place** garlic on a square of aluminum foil; drizzle with oil, and wrap in foil.
● **Bake** at 425° for 30 minutes; remove from oven, and set aside.
● **Cook** potato in boiling water to cover 15 to 20 minutes or until tender; drain and transfer to a mixing bowl. Add butter and remaining 3 ingredients; beat at medium speed with an electric mixer until fluffy (do not overbeat).
● **Cut** off pointed ends of garlic; squeeze pulp from garlic cloves, and stir into potato mixture. **Yield:** 8 servings.

Adelyne Smith
Dunnville, Kentucky

WHIPPED CELERY POTATOES

2 pounds Yukon Gold or red potatoes
3½ cups water
1½ teaspoons salt
1 cup butter or margarine, divided
1 cup finely chopped celery
¼ cup finely chopped onion
¼ cup milk
¼ teaspoon salt
⅛ teaspoon pepper
⅛ teaspoon ground nutmeg

● **Combine** first 3 ingredients in a large saucepan; bring to a boil. Cover and

simmer 30 to 35 minutes or until tender; drain potatoes. Cool 5 minutes; peel and place potatoes in a large mixing bowl.
● **Melt** 2 tablespoons butter in a skillet; add celery and onion. Cook, stirring constantly, 3 minutes or until tender.
● **Add** celery mixture to potatoes; beat at low speed with an electric mixer until potatoes are mashed. Add remaining butter, milk, and remaining ingredients; beat at high speed until whipped. Serve immediately. **Yield:** 6 to 8 servings.

Chef David Everett
Dining Room at Ford's Colony
Williamsburg, Virginia

THUNDERBOLT POTATOES
(pictured at right)

QUICK!

1 cup fresh yellow corn, cut from cob (about 2 ears)
2 cloves garlic, minced
2 tablespoons butter, melted
4 large baking potatoes, peeled and quartered (about 2¾ pounds)
½ to ¾ cup warm milk
1 teaspoon salt
⅛ teaspoon pepper
2 teaspoons chili powder
½ teaspoon ground cumin
1 (4.5-ounce) can chopped green chiles, undrained
Garnish: chili powder

● **Cook** corn and garlic in butter in a skillet over medium-high heat, stirring constantly, until tender; set aside.
● **Cook** potato in boiling water to cover 20 minutes or until tender; drain.
● **Combine** potato, milk, and next 4 ingredients in a mixing bowl; beat at medium speed with an electric mixer until smooth. Stir in corn mixture and chiles. Garnish, if desired. **Yield:** 4 to 6 servings.

Thunderbolt Potato Patties: Combine 2 cups leftover Thunderbolt Potatoes, 1 large egg, and 2 tablespoons all-purpose flour. Shape mixture into 8 (3-inch) patties, and dredge in ½ cup cornmeal. Cook patties in ½ cup hot oil in a large skillet until golden, turning once. **Yield:** 8 patties.

Thunderbolt Potatoes;
Thunderbolt Potato Patties

LEFTOVER POTATO PANCAKES

QUICK!

1 (16-ounce) package frozen
    whole kernel corn, thawed
1 small onion, finely chopped
½ cup chopped green onions
2 teaspoons vegetable oil
2 cups mashed potatoes
½ cup all-purpose flour
2 large eggs, lightly beaten
¾ teaspoon salt
½ teaspoon freshly ground
    pepper
Vegetable cooking spray

• **Cook** first 3 ingredients in hot oil in a large nonstick skillet over medium-high heat, stirring constantly, until vegetables are crisp-tender. Remove from heat.
• **Combine** mashed potatoes, flour, and eggs, stirring well; stir in corn mixture, salt, and pepper.
• **Coat** a large skillet with cooking spray. Place skillet over medium heat until hot. Drop mixture by rounded tablespoonfuls into skillet; cook 3 minutes on each side or until golden, wiping skillet with a paper towel as necessary. Drain; serve with salsa. **Yield:** 14 (4-inch) pancakes.

Gwen Louer
Roswell, Georgia

SOUTHWESTERN POTATO BOATS

3 baking potatoes (1½ pounds)
1 (14.5-ounce) can chili-style
    stewed tomatoes, drained
½ cup chopped purple onion
2 tablespoons chopped fresh
    cilantro
2 tablespoons minced jalapeño
    pepper
¾ teaspoon salt
¼ teaspoon pepper
1½ teaspoons vegetable oil
1½ teaspoons white vinegar
¼ teaspoon minced garlic
¼ pound bacon, cooked and
    crumbled
1 (8-ounce) package shredded
    colby-Monterey Jack cheese
    blend

• **Pierce** potatoes with a fork, and bake at 350° for 1 hour or until done. Let potatoes cool to touch.
• **Cut** potatoes in half lengthwise, and scoop out pulp, leaving ¼-inch-thick shells. Reserve pulp for another use.
• **Combine** tomatoes and next 8 ingredients; stir in bacon and cheese.
• **Bake** potato shells at 350° for 5 to 8 minutes or until lightly browned; spoon tomato mixture evenly into shells. Bake 10 to 15 additional minutes or until cheese melts. **Yield:** 6 servings.

POTATO AND RUTABAGA GRATIN

1 large rutabaga
4 medium-size red potatoes
¼ cup butter or margarine
¼ cup all-purpose flour
2 cups whipping cream
1 teaspoon salt
¼ teaspoon ground white pepper
¼ teaspoon ground red pepper
Dash of ground nutmeg
½ cup grated Parmesan cheese
Garnishes: fresh sage and rosemary
    sprigs

• **Peel**, quarter, and thinly slice rutabaga. Peel and thinly slice potatoes.
• **Melt** butter in a heavy saucepan over low heat; add flour, stirring until smooth. Cook 1 minute, stirring constantly. Gradually add whipping cream; cook over medium heat, stirring constantly, until thickened and bubbly. Stir in salt and next 3 ingredients. Set aside.
• **Sprinkle** cheese in a 10-inch cast-iron skillet lined with parchment paper or aluminum foil, and arrange half of rutabaga slices over cheese.
• **Layer** ¾ cup sauce, potato slices, and ¾ cup sauce over rutabaga. Arrange remaining rutabaga slices on top, and add remaining sauce. Cover skillet tightly with aluminum foil.
• **Bake** at 400° for 1 hour; uncover and bake 20 additional minutes. Let stand 15 minutes. Invert onto a serving platter, and garnish, if desired. To serve, cut into wedges. **Yield:** 8 servings.

Steve Oldecker
Brunswick, Georgia

DUAL POTATO GRATIN

Garlic Mashed Potatoes ∗
3 tablespoons butter or
    margarine
3 large baking potatoes, peeled
    and cut into ⅛-inch slices
Butter-flavored cooking spray
2 tablespoons grated Parmesan
    cheese
Garnish: fresh chives

• **Spoon** Garlic Mashed Potatoes evenly into four lightly greased 4-inch gratin dishes, reserving ¾ cup mashed potatoes; set aside.
• **Melt** butter in a large saucepan; add half of potato slices in a single layer, and cook 2 minutes on each side or until tender. Drain on paper towels. Repeat procedure with remaining slices.
• **Layer** potato slices around outside edges of mashed potatoes forming circles. Pipe reserved mashed potatoes in center of each dish or roll mixture into balls, placing in center.
• **Coat** gratins with cooking spray, and sprinkle evenly with Parmesan cheese. Bake at 400° for 10 minutes or until lightly browned. Garnish, if desired. **Yield:** 4 servings.

∗ You can substitute 3 cups leftover mashed potatoes.

Garlic Mashed Potatoes

3 large baking potatoes
1 teaspoon vegetable oil
2 tablespoons butter or
    margarine
¼ cup sour cream
2 cloves garlic, crushed
½ teaspoon salt
¼ teaspoon pepper

• **Scrub** potatoes, and rub evenly with vegetable oil. Bake at 400° for 1 hour or until done.
• **Cut** potatoes in half; scoop out pulp, discarding skin. Combine potato pulp, butter, and remaining ingredients in a large mixing bowl, and beat at medium speed with an electric mixer until fluffy. **Yield:** 3 cups.

Jean Carriger
Lakeland, Florida

CHEESY SCALLOPED POTATOES

2½ pounds red potatoes
3 tablespoons butter or margarine
⅓ cup chopped green onions
⅓ cup chopped red bell pepper
1 clove garlic, minced
¼ teaspoon ground red pepper
2 cups whipping cream
¾ cup milk
¾ teaspoon salt
¼ teaspoon freshly ground pepper
1 cup (4 ounces) shredded Swiss cheese
¼ cup grated Parmesan cheese

• **Cut** potatoes into ⅛-inch-thick slices; set aside.
• **Melt** butter in a Dutch oven over medium-high heat; add green onions and next 3 ingredients. Cook 2 minutes, stirring constantly. Stir in whipping cream and next 3 ingredients.
• **Add** potato slices; bring to a boil over medium heat, and cook 15 minutes or until potato slices are tender, stirring gently. Spoon into a lightly greased 11- x 7- x 1½-inch baking dish; sprinkle with cheeses.
• **Bake** at 350° for 45 minutes or until bubbly and golden. Let stand 15 minutes before serving. **Yield:** 8 servings.

Lee Wells
Knoxville, Tennessee

PEPPERY POTATO CASSEROLE

8 large potatoes, unpeeled (about 5 pounds)
¼ cup butter or margarine
1 green bell pepper, chopped
1½ tablespoons all-purpose flour
1½ cups milk
1 (6-ounce) package process cheese spread with garlic flavor
1 (6-ounce) package process cheese spread with jalapeño pepper
¼ to ½ teaspoon salt
¼ to ½ teaspoon pepper

• **Combine** potatoes and water to cover in a Dutch oven; bring to a boil over medium-high heat. Cover, reduce heat, and simmer 25 minutes or until tender; drain and cool.
• **Melt** butter in Dutch oven over medium-high heat; add chopped pepper, and cook, stirring constantly, 5 minutes or until tender. Remove pepper, reserving drippings in pan; set aside.
• **Add** flour to drippings, stirring until smooth. Cook 1 minute, stirring constantly. Gradually add milk, and cook over medium heat, stirring constantly, until mixture thickens and bubbles.
• **Stir** in cheeses, and cook, stirring constantly, until cheeses melt. Remove mixture from heat.
• **Peel** potatoes, and cut into thin slices. Layer potato in a lightly greased 13- x 9- x 2-inch baking dish, sprinkling each layer with salt, pepper, and chopped green bell pepper.
• **Spoon** cheese mixture over potato. Bake at 375° for 30 minutes or until heated. **Yield:** 8 to 10 servings.

Dianna Jolly
Harrison, Arkansas

HASH BROWN BAKE

3 cups frozen shredded potatoes
⅓ cup butter or margarine, melted
1 cup finely chopped cooked ham
1 cup (4 ounces) shredded Cheddar cheese
¼ cup finely chopped green bell pepper
2 large eggs, beaten
½ cup milk
½ teaspoon salt
¼ teaspoon pepper

• **Thaw** potato between layers of paper towels to remove excess moisture. Press potato in bottom and up sides of an ungreased 9-inch pieplate; drizzle with butter.
• **Bake** at 425° for 25 minutes or until lightly browned; cool on a wire rack 10 minutes.
• **Combine** ham, cheese, and green pepper; spoon into potato shell. Combine eggs and remaining 3 ingredients, stirring well; pour over ham mixture.
• **Bake** at 350° for 25 to 30 minutes or until set; let stand 10 minutes before serving. **Yield:** 6 to 8 servings.

Note: Assemble Hash Brown Bake ahead, omitting egg mixture, and store in refrigerator 8 hours. Let stand at room temperature 30 minutes. Combine eggs, milk, salt, and pepper; pour over ham mixture. Bake at 350° for 25 to 30 minutes.

Bernadette Colvin
Houston, Texas

CARROT HASH BROWNS

QUICK!

4 carrots, scraped and shredded
2 medium baking potatoes, peeled and shredded
½ small onion, grated
1 teaspoon salt
1 teaspoon pepper
3 tablespoons butter or margarine

• **Combine** first 5 ingredients, stirring mixture well.
• **Melt** butter in a large nonstick skillet over high heat; add carrot mixture, pressing firmly with a spatula or wooden spoon. Cook 5 to 6 minutes or until browned on bottom.
• **Invert** hash browns onto a plate; slide back into skillet. Cook 5 to 6 additional minutes or until browned on bottom.
• **Transfer** to a serving plate carefully, and cut into wedges. Serve immediately. **Yield:** 8 to 10 servings.

CARROT AND SWEET POTATO PUREE

This colorful vegetable casserole offers an excellent reason to try fresh sweet potatoes in the spring. You can make it ahead, too.

6 large sweet potatoes (about 5¾ pounds)
1½ pounds carrots, scraped and cut into 1-inch pieces
½ cup butter or margarine, divided
1½ cups water
2 tablespoons sugar
½ teaspoon salt
½ teaspoon freshly ground black pepper
½ cup lemon low-fat yogurt
½ cup nonfat sour cream
¾ teaspoon ground nutmeg
¼ teaspoon ground red pepper
Garnish: fresh mint leaves

● **Scrub** sweet potatoes, and pat dry. Prick sweet potatoes several times with a fork.
● **Microwave** at HIGH 35 to 40 minutes or until tender, rotating sweet potatoes at 10-minute intervals. Let cool to touch; peel and cut into chunks.
● **Position** knife blade in food processor bowl. Add half of sweet potatoes, and process until smooth. Transfer sweet potato to a large bowl, and repeat procedure. Set aside.
● **Combine** carrot, 1 tablespoon butter, water, and next 3 ingredients in a medium saucepan.
● **Bring** to a boil, and cook 10 to 15 minutes or until carrot is tender and liquid evaporates.
● **Position** knife blade in food processor bowl. Add carrot, remaining butter, yogurt, sour cream, nutmeg, and red pepper; process until smooth. Stir carrot mixture into sweet potato. Reserve 2 cups sweet potato mixture.
● **Spoon** remaining sweet potato mixture into a lightly greased 3-quart shallow casserole; pipe or dollop reserved sweet potato mixture around edges of casserole.
● **Bake** at 350° for 30 minutes or until thoroughly heated. Garnish, if desired. **Yield:** 12 to 14 servings.

Note: To make ahead, assemble casserole; cover and refrigerate. Remove from refrigerator, and let stand 30 minutes. Bake at 350° for 45 minutes or until thoroughly heated.

GRILLED SWEET POTATOES

QUICK!

3 medium sweet potatoes (about 2¼ pounds)
⅓ cup butter or margarine
¼ cup firmly packed brown sugar
1 tablespoon ground cinnamon

● **Wash** potatoes, and pat dry; cut in half lengthwise. Place each half in center of a 12- x 10-inch piece of aluminum foil; dot evenly with butter.
● **Combine** brown sugar and cinnamon; sprinkle evenly over potato. Wrap well, and place on food rack. Cook, without grill lid, over hot coals (400° to 500°) for 25 to 30 minutes or until done, turning foil packets once. **Yield:** 6 servings.

Bill Duke
Atlanta, Georgia

SWEET POTATO SOUFFLÉ

Attention R.E.M. fans: This home-style casserole is reportedly lead singer Michael Stipe's favorite side dish at Weaver D's.

6 small sweet potatoes (about 3 pounds)
¾ cup sugar
3 large eggs, lightly beaten
½ cup butter or margarine, melted
3 tablespoons milk
2 teaspoons ground nutmeg
2 teaspoons vanilla extract
¾ teaspoon lemon extract

● **Peel** sweet potatoes, and cut into cubes. Cook sweet potato in boiling water to cover 15 to 20 minutes or until tender; drain and mash.
● **Combine** sweet potato, sugar, and remaining ingredients, stirring until smooth. Spoon mixture into a lightly greased 11- x 7- x 1½-inch baking dish.

● **Bake** at 350° for 30 minutes or until bubbly. **Yield:** 6 to 8 servings.

Dexter Weaver
Weaver D's Delicious Fine Foods
Athens, Georgia

BRANDIED YAMS

5 large sweet potatoes (about 4¼ pounds)
¼ cup sugar
¼ to ⅓ cup brandy
3 tablespoons butter or margarine, melted
1 teaspoon salt
½ teaspoon ground nutmeg
½ teaspoon ground ginger
⅛ teaspoon pepper
1 tablespoon butter or margarine, melted
1 tablespoon grated orange rind
Garnish: orange slices

● **Cook** sweet potatoes in boiling water to cover 45 minutes or until tender; cool to touch. Peel and mash.
● **Stir** in sugar and next 6 ingredients; spoon into a greased 11- x 7- x 1½-inch baking dish. Brush with 1 tablespoon butter; sprinkle with orange rind.
● **Bake** at 350° for 25 to 30 minutes. Garnish, if desired. **Yield:** 8 servings.

Phyllis Taylor
Gillham, Arkansas

RUTABAGA WHIP

QUICK!

Mellow, earthy rutabagas join potatoes and become deliciously rich and fluffy. Even those who think they don't like rutabagas will like this.

2 pounds rutabagas, peeled and chopped
6 cups water
2 pounds baking potatoes, peeled and chopped
¼ cup butter or margarine, softened
½ cup whipping cream
1 teaspoon salt
½ teaspoon pepper

- **Combine** rutabagas and water in a Dutch oven. Bring to a boil; cook 15 minutes. Add potato; cook 15 minutes or until vegetables are tender. Drain.
- **Combine** vegetables, butter, and remaining ingredients in a large mixing bowl; beat at medium speed with an electric mixer until fluffy. **Yield:** 6 to 8 servings.

CREAMED SPINACH
QUICK!

¼ cup pine nuts
½ cup butter or margarine
2 cups whipping cream
⅔ cup grated Parmesan cheese
½ teaspoon salt
½ teaspoon freshly ground pepper
½ teaspoon freshly grated nutmeg
2 (10-ounce) packages fresh spinach, washed, trimmed, and shredded
Hot cooked grits or cornbread (optional)

- **Place** pine nuts in a shallow pan; bake at 350° for 5 minutes or until toasted, stirring occasionally. Set aside.
- **Bring** butter and whipping cream to a boil over medium-high heat; reduce heat to medium, and cook 15 minutes or until thickened, stirring often.
- **Stir** in cheese and next 3 ingredients. Add shredded spinach; cook over low heat until wilted, stirring often. Serve over grits or cornbread, if desired; sprinkle with pine nuts. **Yield:** 4 servings.

Ronda Carman
Houston, Texas

SKILLET SPINACH
QUICK!

4 slices bacon
2½ tablespoons balsamic vinegar
1 (10-ounce) package fresh spinach
2 tablespoons chopped pecans, toasted
¼ teaspoon salt
¼ teaspoon pepper
Pinch of sugar (optional)

- **Cook** bacon in a large skillet until crisp; remove bacon, reserving 1 tablespoon drippings in skillet. Crumble bacon, and set aside.
- **Add** vinegar to bacon drippings in skillet, and bring mixture to a boil over medium-high heat, stirring to loosen particles that cling to bottom.
- **Add** spinach to mixture in skillet; cook, stirring constantly, 1 to 2 minutes or until spinach is wilted. Stir in reserved bacon, pecans, salt, pepper, and sugar, if desired. Serve immediately. **Yield:** 2 servings.

Joel Allard
San Antonio, Texas

SPANAKOPITA

2 (10-ounce) packages frozen chopped spinach, thawed and drained
1 (8-ounce) package feta cheese, crumbled
1 tablespoon dried oregano
1 tablespoon dried dillweed
1 (16-ounce) package frozen phyllo pastry, thawed
⅓ cup butter or margarine, melted
Garnishes: crumbled feta cheese, tomato wedges, pepperoncini peppers, kalamata olives

- **Combine** first 4 ingredients in a bowl, stirring well.
- **Unfold** phyllo, and cut into 2 (13- x 9-inch) rectangles, keeping remaining phyllo covered with a slightly damp towel.
- **Place** 1 phyllo sheet in a buttered 13- x 9- x 2-inch baking dish; brush with melted butter. Place 1 phyllo sheet on top, allowing half of sheet to drape over one side of dish; brush portion in dish with melted butter. Repeat procedure with 15 more phyllo sheets, alternating sides of dish after each sheet so that each side of dish is covered.
- **Spread** spinach mixture evenly in dish; top with a phyllo sheet, and brush with melted butter. Fold 1 overhanging sheet on each side toward center; brush with butter. Top with a phyllo sheet; brush with butter. Repeat folding procedure with remaining overhanging phyllo sheets, topping each layer with a phyllo sheet and brushing with butter. Cut into 4 or 8 squares.
- **Bake** at 425° for 20 minutes or until lightly browned. Garnish, if desired. **Yield:** 4 main-dish servings or 8 appetizer servings.

The Cottage Inn
Eureka Springs, Arkansas

FRIED GREEN TOMATOES

4 large green tomatoes (about 2 pounds)
¼ cup sugar
¾ cup all-purpose flour
1 teaspoon salt
⅛ teaspoon pepper
3 tablespoons bacon drippings
6 tablespoons vegetable oil

- **Remove** and discard a thin slice from tops and bottoms of tomatoes; cut tomatoes into ¼-inch-thick slices.
- **Layer** tomato slices in a small deep dish, sprinkling each layer with sugar; let stand 1 hour. Drain tomato slices, reserving sugar liquid.
- **Combine** flour, salt, and pepper in a shallow dish; dredge tomato slices in mixture.
- **Heat** 1 tablespoon bacon drippings and 2 tablespoons oil in a large cast-iron skillet over medium-high heat until hot; add about one-third of tomato slices. Cook 2 to 3 minutes on each side or until golden. Drain on paper towels. Repeat procedure twice with remaining tomato slices, bacon drippings, and oil.
- **Drain** off pan drippings, reserving 1 tablespoon in skillet. Stir reserved sugar liquid until sugar dissolves. Add to drippings in skillet; bring to a boil.
- **Cook** over medium heat, stirring constantly, 1 minute or until slightly thickened. Place fried tomatoes on a serving platter, and drizzle with sugar mixture. Serve immediately. **Yield:** 4 to 6 servings.

Rose W. Roberson
Ocala, Florida

Herbed Tomato Tart

HERBED TOMATO TART

(pictured at left)

QUICK!

1 (17¼-ounce) package frozen
    puff pastry sheets, thawed
4 plum tomatoes, thinly sliced
1 teaspoon salt
1 (8-ounce) package shredded
    mozzarella cheese
1 (4-ounce) package crumbled feta
    cheese
¼ cup chopped onion
1 clove garlic, minced
¼ cup finely chopped mixed fresh
    herbs *
1 tablespoon olive oil

• **Roll** 1 pastry sheet into a 14-inch
square on a lightly floured surface; place
on an ungreased baking sheet. Cut 4 (12-
x 1-inch) strips from remaining pastry
sheet, and place along edges on top of
pastry square, forming a border. Reserve remaining pastry for another use.
• **Bake** at 400° for 10 minutes or until
golden. Transfer to a wire rack to cool.
• **Place** tomato slices in a single layer on
paper towels; sprinkle evenly with salt.
Let stand 20 minutes.
• **Place** baked pastry shell on baking
sheet; sprinkle with mozzarella cheese
and next 3 ingredients. Arrange tomato
slices in a single layer on top. Sprinkle
with herbs; drizzle with oil.
• **Bake** at 400° for 15 minutes or until
cheese melts; serve immediately. **Yield:**
4 servings.

* For the mixed fresh herbs, we combined oregano, basil, chives, sage, tarragon, rosemary, thyme, and dill. You
can substitute 1 tablespoon mixed dried
herbs for fresh.

BAKED RANCH TOMATOES

QUICK!

2 tomatoes, cut in half
Vegetable cooking spray
¼ teaspoon dried Italian seasoning
1½ tablespoons Ranch-style
    dressing
Garnish: fresh flat-leaf parsley
    sprigs

• **Place** tomato halves in an 8-inch
square pan. Coat top of halves with
cooking spray.
• **Bake** tomato halves at 350° for 16 to
20 minutes.
• **Sprinkle** with Italian seasoning, and
top evenly with dressing.
• **Broil** 3 inches from heat (with electric
oven door partially opened) 2 to 3 minutes or until tomatoes begin to brown.
Garnish, if desired. **Yield:** 4 servings.

CHILE-CHEESE STUFFED TOMATOES

QUICK!

4 medium tomatoes
½ cup sour cream
2 teaspoons all-purpose flour
1 tablespoon chopped green
    onions
½ cup (2 ounces) shredded
    Cheddar cheese
3 tablespoons canned chopped
    green chiles, drained

• **Cut** tomatoes in half horizontally;
scoop out pulp, leaving shells intact.
(Reserve pulp for another use.) Place
upside down on paper towels to drain.
• **Combine** sour cream and remaining 4
ingredients. Spoon into tomatoes. Place
in a greased 13- x 9- x 2-inch baking pan.
• **Broil** 5½ inches from heat (with electric oven door partially opened) 4 minutes or until heated. **Yield:** 8 servings.

Carol Barclay
Portland, Texas

VEGETABLE STUFFED TOMATOES

6 medium tomatoes
⅔ cup finely chopped zucchini
⅔ cup finely chopped green bell
    pepper
⅔ cup finely chopped onion
2 tablespoons olive oil
1 cup corn cut from cob
1 teaspoon sugar
¼ teaspoon salt
¼ teaspoon pepper
¼ teaspoon hot sauce

• **Cut** tops from tomatoes; chop tops,
and set aside. Scoop out pulp, leaving
shells intact; chop pulp, and set aside.
Place shells upside down on paper towels to drain.
• **Cook** zucchini, green bell pepper, and
onion in oil in a skillet over medium
heat 5 minutes, stirring constantly.
• **Stir** in chopped tomato tops and pulp,
corn, and remaining 4 ingredients.
Cover, reduce heat, and simmer 20 minutes, stirring often.
• **Spoon** into tomato shells, and place in
a shallow baking dish.
• **Bake,** uncovered, at 350° for 20 minutes. **Yield:** 6 servings.

Caroline Wallace Kennedy
Newborn, Georgia

SPINACH-TOPPED TOMATOES

1 (10-ounce) package frozen
    chopped spinach
2 teaspoons chicken-flavored
    bouillon granules
3 large tomatoes, cut in half
    crosswise
1 teaspoon salt
⅓ cup freshly grated Parmesan
    cheese
1 cup cornbread stuffing mix
½ cup butter or margarine, melted
1 large egg, lightly beaten
⅓ cup chopped onion
1 clove garlic, minced
¼ teaspoon pepper
Freshly grated Parmesan cheese

• **Cook** spinach according to package
directions, adding chicken bouillon
granules to cooking water; drain well.
• **Sprinkle** tomato with salt; place, cut
side down, on paper towels, and let
stand 15 minutes.
• **Combine** spinach, ⅓ cup Parmesan
cheese, and next 6 ingredients; set
aside.
• **Place** tomato, cut side up, on a baking
sheet. Top each tomato evenly with
spinach mixture.
• **Bake** at 350° for 15 minutes. Sprinkle
with additional Parmesan cheese; bake
5 additional minutes. **Yield:** 6 servings.

Kathy Zenor-Horine
Louisville, Kentucky

GINGERED ACORN SQUASH WITH SPICED CRANBERRY SAUCE

6 small acorn squash
1 cup water
½ cup butter or margarine
2 cloves garlic, minced
¼ cup whipping cream
1½ tablespoons minced fresh
      ginger
¾ teaspoon salt
¼ teaspoon ground white pepper
Spiced Cranberry Sauce

• **Cut** squash in half crosswise; remove and discard seeds. Place, cut side down, in a 15- x 10- x 1-inch jellyroll pan, and add 1 cup water.
• **Bake** at 350° for 1 hour or until tender; drain. Scoop pulp from bottom halves, leaving ½-inch shells; set shells aside. Scoop all pulp from remaining squash halves; mash all pulp.
• **Melt** butter in a large skillet; add garlic, and cook until tender, stirring often. Stir in squash pulp, whipping cream, and next 3 ingredients; cook over low heat, stirring constantly, until thoroughly heated.
• **Spoon** into squash shells; top and serve with Spiced Cranberry Sauce. **Yield:** 6 servings.

Spiced Cranberry Sauce

QUICK!

1 cup water
1 cup sugar
1 (3-inch) piece fresh ginger,
      peeled
1 firm pear, diced
1 teaspoon grated lemon rind
1 (12-ounce) package fresh or
      frozen cranberries
2 tablespoons fresh lemon
      juice

• **Bring** first 3 ingredients to a boil in a heavy saucepan, stirring constantly; boil 5 minutes.
• **Add** pear and lemon rind; return mixture to a boil, and cook 3 minutes, stirring occasionally. Stir in cranberries. Reduce heat, and simmer, without stirring, 3 to 5 minutes or until cranberry skins pop. Remove from heat; cool. Cover and chill.

• **Discard** ginger; cover and chill sauce up to 2 days. Stir in lemon juice just before serving. **Yield:** 2½ cups.

*Sudi Swirles and Jan Hryharrow
Durham, North Carolina*

BUTTERNUT SQUASH CASSEROLE

2 cups cooked, mashed butternut
      squash
3 large eggs
¾ cup sugar
⅓ cup butter, softened
⅓ cup milk
1 teaspoon ground ginger
½ teaspoon coconut flavoring
Crunchy Cereal Topping

• **Combine** first 7 ingredients; pour into a greased 8-inch square baking dish.
• **Bake** at 350° for 35 minutes. Sprinkle with topping; bake 10 additional minutes. **Yield:** 6 to 8 servings.

Crunchy Cereal Topping

QUICK!

1½ cups corn flake crumbs
¾ cup firmly packed brown sugar
½ cup chopped pecans
¼ cup butter or margarine, melted

• **Combine** all ingredients in a bowl. **Yield:** 2½ cups.

*Fay Redding
Gastonia, North Carolina*

HARVEST SQUASH MEDLEY

1 (1½-pound) butternut squash,
      peeled and seeded
2 sweet potatoes (about
      ¾ pound), peeled
3 tablespoons butter or margarine
¼ cup honey
¼ cup orange juice
½ teaspoon ground cinnamon
⅛ teaspoon ground nutmeg
1 tablespoon grated orange rind
2 small cooking apples, peeled,
      cored, and sliced
½ cup chopped walnuts, toasted

• **Cut** squash and sweet potatoes into ¾-inch chunks. Place in a greased 11- x 7- x 1½-inch baking dish; set aside.
• **Combine** butter and next 5 ingredients in a small saucepan. Bring to a boil over medium heat, stirring constantly; pour over squash and sweet potato.
• **Cover** and bake at 350° for 30 minutes. Uncover and stir in apple. Bake, uncovered, at 350° for 30 additional minutes or until tender. Sprinkle with walnuts. **Yield:** 6 to 8 servings.

*Valerie Stutsman
Norfolk, Virginia*

SAUTÉED CHAYOTE SQUASH WITH CILANTRO

1 (¾-pound) chayote squash, cut
      into wedges
2 tablespoons hot red chili oil
1 teaspoon chopped fresh cilantro
1 clove garlic, pressed
¼ teaspoon salt
1 cup bean sprouts

• **Cook** squash in oil in a skillet over medium-high heat, turning often, 10 minutes or until tender. Add cilantro, garlic, and salt; cook 2 minutes. Add sprouts, and serve immediately. **Yield:** 2 to 3 servings.

*Chef Siegfried Eisenberger
Broadmoor Hotel
Colorado Springs, Colorado*

ASIAN SPAGHETTI SQUASH

2 (2¼-pound) spaghetti squash
1 clove garlic
2 tablespoons sesame or olive oil
2 tablespoons vegetable oil
2 tablespoons rice wine vinegar
2 tablespoons soy sauce
1 teaspoon sugar
½ to 1 teaspoon dried crushed red
      pepper
½ cup sliced green onions
½ cup grated carrot
½ cup snow pea pods, cut
      lengthwise into thin strips
2 tablespoons sesame seeds,
      toasted

• **Cut** squash in half lengthwise; remove seeds. Place squash, cut side down, in a shallow baking dish or pan. Add water to dish to depth of ½ inch.

• **Bake** at 375° for 45 minutes or until skin is tender and strands may be easily loosened with a fork. Drain and cool slightly.

• **Position** knife blade in food processor bowl; add garlic, and process until finely chopped, scraping down sides, if necessary. Add sesame oil and next 5 ingredients. Process until blended, stopping once to scrape down sides; set garlic mixture aside.

• **Remove** spaghetti-like strands of squash, using a fork; discard shells. Combine squash, green onions, carrot, and snow peas in a large bowl. Add garlic mixture; toss gently. Sprinkle with sesame seeds. Serve immediately. **Yield:** 6 to 8 servings.

CAJUN VEGETABLE SAUTÉ

QUICK!

2 tablespoons olive oil
1 large zucchini, sliced
1 large yellow squash, sliced
1 medium onion, chopped
1 clove garlic, crushed
¼ cup chopped fresh chives
1 teaspoon Creole seasoning
½ teaspoon pepper
¼ teaspoon hot sauce

• **Heat** olive oil in a large skillet until hot; add zucchini and remaining ingredients, and toss gently. Cover, reduce heat, and cook 10 minutes or until crisp-tender. **Yield:** 3 to 4 servings.

Marie Wiker
Gaithersburg, Maryland

DILLED SUMMER SQUASH

2 tablespoons butter or margarine
2 cloves garlic, minced
2 teaspoons chopped fresh dill
6 green onions, cut into 1-inch pieces
2 yellow squash, thinly sliced
2 zucchini, thinly sliced
½ green bell pepper, sliced
⅓ cup water
¼ teaspoon salt
¼ teaspoon pepper

• **Melt** butter in a skillet; add garlic, dill, and green onions. Cook over medium-high heat 1 minute, stirring constantly. Add squash and zucchini; cook 1 minute, stirring constantly. Add bell pepper and remaining ingredients; cook 2 minutes, stirring constantly. Cover, reduce heat, and simmer 3 minutes or until crisp-tender. **Yield:** 4 servings.

Deborah D. Forster
Atascosa, Texas

SQUASH CASSEROLE

2½ pounds yellow squash, sliced *
½ cup butter or margarine
2 large eggs
¼ cup mayonnaise
1 (8-ounce) can sliced water chestnuts, drained
1 (4-ounce) jar diced pimiento, drained
½ cup chopped onion
¼ cup chopped green bell pepper
2 teaspoons sugar
1½ teaspoons salt
10 round buttery crackers, crushed (about ½ cup)
½ cup (2 ounces) shredded sharp Cheddar cheese

• **Cover** and cook squash in a small amount of boiling water 8 to 10 minutes or until tender; drain well, pressing between layers of paper towels to remove excess moisture.

• **Combine** squash and butter in a bowl; mash until butter melts. Stir in eggs and next 7 ingredients; spoon into a lightly greased shallow 2-quart baking dish. Sprinkle squash with crushed crackers.

• **Bake** at 325° for 30 minutes. Sprinkle with cheese; bake 5 additional minutes or until cheese melts. **Yield:** 8 servings.

∗ You can substitute 2½ pounds zucchini, sliced, for the squash.

Judy Frazer
Sylacauga, Alabama

VEGETABLE BURRITOS

QUICK!

1 pound fresh mushrooms, sliced
1 cup chopped onion
1 cup chopped green bell pepper
2 cloves garlic, crushed
2 teaspoons olive oil
1 (15-ounce) can kidney beans, drained
2 tablespoons finely chopped ripe olives
¼ teaspoon pepper
8 (8-inch) flour tortillas
½ cup nonfat sour cream
1 cup chunky salsa, divided
½ cup (2 ounces) shredded reduced-fat sharp Cheddar cheese
Vegetable cooking spray

• **Cook** first 4 ingredients in olive oil in a large nonstick skillet over medium-high heat, stirring constantly, until tender. Remove from heat; drain. Combine cooked vegetables, kidney beans, olives, and pepper.

• **Spoon** about ½ cup bean mixture evenly down center of each tortilla. Top evenly with sour cream, ½ cup salsa, and cheese; fold opposite sides of tortillas over filling.

• **Coat** a large nonstick skillet or griddle with cooking spray. Heat over medium-high heat until hot. Cook tortillas, seam-side down, 1 minute on each side or until thoroughly heated. Top each tortilla evenly with remaining ½ cup salsa. **Yield:** 8 servings.

Linda Askey
Birmingham, Alabama

♥ Per serving: Calories 259
Fat 6.2g Cholesterol 4mg
Sodium 443mg

MARINATED GRILLED VEGETABLES

Don't let the long ingredient list discourage you from making this delicious recipe. It's simply a variety of vegetables marinated in a vinaigrette dressing and then grilled.

½ cup balsamic vinegar
¼ cup extra-virgin olive oil
2 tablespoons dry white wine
1 tablespoon finely chopped shallot
½ tablespoon minced garlic
½ tablespoon freshly ground black pepper
1 teaspoon kosher salt
4 new potatoes, unpeeled
4 plum tomatoes, cut in half lengthwise
3 small zucchini, cut in half lengthwise
2 ears yellow corn, cut into 3-inch pieces
2 purple onions, cut into ¾-inch slices
2 fresh portobello mushrooms, quartered
1 pound fresh asparagus, trimmed
1 small eggplant, cut lengthwise into 1-inch slices
1 red bell pepper, quartered
1 yellow bell pepper, quartered
1 tablespoon chopped fresh chives
1 tablespoon chopped fresh rosemary
1 tablespoon chopped fresh parsley

• **Combine** first 7 ingredients in a large bowl; set aside.
• **Cook** potatoes in boiling water 5 minutes; drain. Cut potatoes in half.
• **Add** potato, tomato, and next 8 ingredients to vinegar mixture; toss gently to coat. Let stand about 1 hour, tossing mixture occasionally.
• **Remove** vegetables from marinade; reserving marinade.
• **Cook** vegetables, covered with grill lid, over medium-hot coals (350° to 400°) 12 to 14 minutes, turning vegetables once. Remove vegetables from grill as they are done.
• **Drizzle** remaining marinade over cooked vegetables, and arrange on serving plates.

• **Combine** chopped chives, rosemary, and parsley; sprinkle over vegetables. **Yield:** 8 servings.

Chefs' Café
Atlanta, Georgia

♥ Per serving: Calories 218
Fat 7.7g Cholesterol 0mg
Sodium 312mg

CHINESE VEGETABLE POUCHES

1 tablespoon peanut oil
1 large carrot, scraped and chopped
1 pound cabbage, chopped
2 green onions, chopped
2 tablespoons soy sauce
2 tablespoons dry sherry
½ teaspoon sugar
¼ teaspoon ground ginger
1 clove garlic, pressed
¼ cup chopped roasted cashews
1 tablespoon cornstarch
2 tablespoons water
1 teaspoon hoisin sauce (optional)
1 (16-ounce) package egg roll wrappers (12 wrappers)
12 to 36 fresh chives
3 cups peanut oil
Garnishes: green onion fan, finely chopped carrot

• **Pour** 1 tablespoon peanut oil around top of a preheated wok, coating sides; heat at high (400°) 1 minute. Add carrot, and cook 1 minute, stirring constantly. Add cabbage, and cook, stirring constantly, 5 minutes or until tender. Stir in green onions and next 6 ingredients.
• **Combine** cornstarch, water, and hoisin sauce, if desired, stirring until smooth; add to cabbage mixture. Cook, stirring constantly, 1 minute or until thickened. Let cool.
• **Spoon** evenly into centers of wrappers; moisten edges with water. Bring ends to the middle, pressing together in center. Pull ends up and out to resemble a pouch. Tie chives around centers.
• **Pour** 3 cups peanut oil into a wok; heat to 375°. Fry pouches 4 minutes or until lightly browned, turning, if necessary. Drain on paper towels. Garnish, if desired. **Yield:** 12 pouches.

STEAMED VEGETABLES WITH GARLIC-GINGER BUTTER SAUCE

1 pound small fresh asparagus
3 carrots, scraped and cut into thin strips
3 small round red potatoes, sliced
Garlic-Ginger Butter Sauce
Chopped fresh parsley
Garnish: grated orange rind

• **Snap** off tough ends of asparagus. Remove scales with a vegetable peeler, if desired. Set aside.
• **Arrange** carrot and potato in a steamer basket; place over boiling water. Cover and steam 5 minutes.
• **Add** asparagus; cover and steam 5 minutes or until crisp-tender.
• **Arrange** vegetables on plates; drizzle with Garlic-Ginger Butter Sauce, and sprinkle with parsley. Garnish, if desired. **Yield:** 4 servings.

Garlic-Ginger Butter Sauce
QUICK!

⅓ cup butter or margarine
1 tablespoon brown sugar
½ teaspoon ground ginger
¼ teaspoon grated orange rind
1 clove garlic, minced

• **Combine** all ingredients in a saucepan. Cook over medium heat, stirring until sugar dissolves. **Yield:** ⅓ cup.

CHEESY SUMMER VEGETABLES
QUICK!

1 (10-ounce) package frozen sliced okra
1 (10-ounce) package frozen whole kernel corn
2 (10-ounce) cans diced tomatoes and green chiles, undrained
1 (15-ounce) can black beans, drained and rinsed
½ teaspoon garlic powder
½ teaspoon pepper
1 cup (4 ounces) shredded reduced-fat Cheddar cheese

- **Combine** first 6 ingredients in a large saucepan. Cover and cook over medium heat 8 minutes, stirring occasionally.
- **Sprinkle** with shredded cheese just before serving. Serve with a slotted spoon. **Yield:** 6 servings.

♥ Per 1-cup serving: Calories 177
Fat 4.2g Cholesterol 12mg
Sodium 540mg

ROASTED VEGETABLES

QUICK!

4 small yellow squash, cut into
   1-inch slices
4 small zucchini, cut into 1-inch
   slices
2 large purple or sweet onions,
   quartered
2 tablespoons olive oil
2 teaspoons dried oregano
½ to ¾ teaspoon salt
½ teaspoon pepper
2 large red bell peppers, cut into
   ½-inch strips
2 large yellow bell peppers, cut
   into ½-inch strips
2 tablespoons balsamic vinegar
¼ cup chopped fresh parsley

- **Toss** first 3 ingredients with olive oil; spread in a large roasting pan, and sprinkle with oregano, salt, and pepper.
- **Bake** at 500° for 10 minutes. Add pepper strips; toss gently. Bake 10 additional minutes or until vegetables are tender and begin to char.
- **Place** in a serving bowl; cool slightly. Add vinegar and parsley; toss gently. **Yield:** 6 to 8 servings.

Ann Beckham
Macon, Georgia

TANGY MIXED VEGETABLES

QUICK!

1 (8-ounce) package sliced fresh
   mushrooms
1 green bell pepper, cut into 1-inch
   pieces
1 medium onion, chopped
1 (8-ounce) can pineapple chunks,
   undrained
4 medium carrots, scraped and
   sliced
½ teaspoon ground ginger
½ teaspoon curry powder
½ teaspoon dried basil
1 (8-ounce) can sliced water
   chestnuts, drained
1 tablespoon brown sugar
¼ teaspoon salt

- **Cook** first 3 ingredients in a large non-stick skillet 5 minutes or until tender, stirring often. Drain and set aside.
- **Drain** pineapple, reserving juice. Pour juice into skillet; set pineapple chunks aside. Add carrot and next 3 ingredients to juice; bring to a boil. Cover, reduce heat, and simmer 10 to 15 minutes or until carrot is tender.
- **Stir** in mushroom mixture, pineapple, water chestnuts, brown sugar, and salt; cook until heated. **Yield:** 4 servings.

Hilda Marshall
Bealeton, Virginia

SKILLET ZUCCHINI COMBO
(pictured on page 379)

QUICK!

3 ears fresh corn
1 onion, quartered and sliced
1 red bell pepper, cut into ½-inch
   squares
1 clove garlic, minced
2 tablespoons vegetable oil
3 medium zucchini, sliced
1 large tomato, peeled and
   chopped
2 jalapeño peppers, seeded and
   minced
1½ teaspoons chopped fresh basil
½ teaspoon dried Italian seasoning
½ teaspoon salt
¼ cup freshly grated Parmesan
   cheese

- **Cut** corn kernels from cobs, and set aside.
- **Cook** onion, bell pepper, and garlic in oil in a large skillet 5 minutes, stirring often.
- **Add** zucchini; cook 7 minutes, stirring often.
- **Add** corn, tomato, and next 4 ingredients; cover and cook over low heat 7 minutes, stirring often. Sprinkle with Parmesan cheese, and serve immediately. **Yield:** 6 side-dish servings or 3 main-dish servings.

Janice Rinks
Bluff City, Tennessee

VEGETARIAN SAUTÉ

QUICK!

1 medium onion, chopped
1 medium-size green bell pepper,
   chopped
1 medium zucchini, chopped
2 cloves garlic, minced
2 tablespoons olive oil
1 (14½-ounce) can chili-style
   stewed tomatoes, undrained
1 (15-ounce) can dark red kidney
   beans, rinsed and drained
½ teaspoon dried oregano
¼ teaspoon salt
¼ teaspoon pepper
½ cup (2 ounces) shredded
   Cheddar cheese

- **Cook** first 4 ingredients in olive oil in a large skillet over medium-high heat 5 minutes or until tender.
- **Stir** in tomatoes and next 4 ingredients; cook until heated. Sprinkle with Cheddar cheese. **Yield:** 4 servings.

Valerie Stutsman
Norfolk, Virginia

FRESH VEGETABLE SKILLET DINNER

2 tablespoons butter or margarine
1 large onion, sliced
2 medium-size yellow squash, sliced (about ½ pound)
1 large red or green bell pepper, sliced
2 large tomatoes, cut into wedges
¼ teaspoon salt
¼ teaspoon freshly ground black pepper
3 cups packed fresh spinach
1 cup (4 ounces) shredded Monterey Jack cheese

• **Melt** butter in a large skillet over medium-high heat; add onion, and cook 5 minutes, stirring often. Add squash and red or green pepper; cook 3 to 5 minutes, stirring often.
• **Add** tomato, salt, and pepper; cover, reduce heat, and simmer 5 to 10 minutes. Place spinach over mixture; cover and cook over low heat 3 additional minutes.
• **Add** shredded cheese; cover and cook 2 minutes or until spinach wilts and cheese melts. Serve immediately. **Yield:** 2 to 3 servings.

Chef Mark Abernathy
Juanita's
Little Rock, Arkansas

MEXICAN VEGETARIAN CASSEROLE

1 (15¼-ounce) can whole kernel corn, drained
1 (15-ounce) can black beans, rinsed and drained
1 (10-ounce) can whole tomatoes and green chiles
1 (8-ounce) carton sour cream
1 (8-ounce) jar picante sauce
2 cups (8 ounces) shredded Cheddar cheese
2 cups cooked rice
¼ teaspoon pepper
1 bunch green onions, chopped
1 (2¼-ounce) can sliced ripe olives
1 (8-ounce) package Monterey Jack cheese, shredded

• **Combine** first 8 ingredients; spoon into a lightly greased 13- x 9- x 2-inch baking dish. Sprinkle with green onions, olives, and Monterey Jack cheese.
• **Bake** at 350° for 50 minutes. **Yield:** 6 servings.

Margaret Monger
Germantown, Tennessee

VEGETABLE TAGINE

1 onion
1 green bell pepper
3 carrots, scraped
2 sweet potatoes
1 eggplant
4 plum tomatoes
3 zucchini
1 tablespoon olive oil
3 cloves garlic, minced
5 (16-ounce) cans fat-free chicken broth
2 tablespoons lemon juice
1 tablespoon honey
½ cup golden raisins
½ teaspoon ground cumin
½ teaspoon ground coriander
½ teaspoon ground turmeric
¼ teaspoon ground cinnamon
1 (15.5-ounce) can chickpeas, rinsed and drained
1 teaspoon salt
1 teaspoon pepper
2 tablespoons sambal oelek *

• **Chop** onion and bell pepper; cut carrots and next 4 ingredients into 2-inch pieces.
• **Cook** onion and bell pepper in oil in a Dutch oven 6 minutes or until tender, stirring often. Add garlic, and cook 1 minute, stirring often; stir in carrot, sweet potato, eggplant, tomato, broth, and next 7 ingredients. Bring to a boil over medium-high heat; cover, reduce heat, and simmer 30 minutes, stirring occasionally.
• **Stir** in zucchini, chickpeas, salt, and pepper; simmer 10 to 15 minutes or until zucchini is tender. Remove 1 cup cooking liquid; stir sambal oelek into liquid, and serve sauce with tagine. Serve over couscous. **Yield:** 4 servings.

∗ Sambal oelek is a hot chile paste. You can substitute any Asian or Mexican chile paste.

Liz Lorber
Atlanta, Georgia

♥ Per serving: Calories 205
Fat 2.8g   Cholesterol 0mg
Sodium 421mg

NANNIE'S CORNBREAD DRESSING

2 cups self-rising flour
1 cup self-rising white cornmeal
2 cups buttermilk
3 large eggs
½ cup butter or margarine, melted
Vegetable cooking spray
1 cup chopped celery
1 to 2 medium onions, chopped
1 jalapeño pepper, seeded and chopped
¼ teaspoon pepper
2 to 3 cups chicken broth
Paprika
Garnish: celery leaves

• **Combine** flour and cornmeal in a large bowl; make a well in center of mixture.
• **Combine** buttermilk, eggs, and butter, stirring well; add to dry ingredients, stirring mixture just until moistened.
• **Place** a 9-inch square pan in a 400° oven for 5 minutes or until hot. Remove pan from oven, and carefully coat with cooking spray. Spoon batter into hot pan.
• **Bake** at 400° for 25 minutes or until lightly browned. Cool in pan on a wire rack; crumble into a large bowl.
• **Add** celery, onion, jalapeño pepper, and pepper, stirring well. Stir in enough broth to make a moist, thick mixture.
• **Spoon** cornbread mixture into an 11- x 7- x 1½-inch baking dish coated with cooking spray.
• **Bake** at 350° for 20 minutes or until lightly browned. Sprinkle dressing with paprika, and garnish, if desired. **Yield:** 8 servings.

Carole Miller Radford
Lincolnton, Georgia

GREEN CHILE-CORNBREAD DRESSING

QUICK!

¼ cup butter or margarine
2 cups chopped onion
1 cup sliced celery
1 (14½-ounce) can chicken broth
1 (17-ounce) can whole kernel corn, drained
2 (4.5-ounce) cans chopped green chiles, drained
3 tablespoons chopped fresh parsley
½ teaspoon salt
½ teaspoon poultry seasoning
¼ teaspoon dried oregano
¼ teaspoon pepper
6 cups cornbread crumbs
½ cup chopped pecans, toasted

● **Melt** butter in a large Dutch oven; add onion and celery, and cook over medium-high heat, stirring constantly, until tender.
● **Stir** in broth and next 7 ingredients. Add cornbread crumbs and pecans, tossing until moistened; spoon into a greased 13- x 9- x 2-inch baking dish, and cover with aluminum foil.
● **Bake** at 350° for 30 minutes or until dressing is thoroughly heated. **Yield:** 8 to 10 servings.

Charlotte Pierce Bryant
Greensburg, Kentucky

SAUSAGE-CORNBREAD DRESSING

1 pound ground pork sausage
2 medium onions, chopped
4 stalks celery, chopped
6 cups crumbled cornbread
3 cups white bread cubes, toasted
2 teaspoons rubbed sage
¼ teaspoon salt (optional)
1 teaspoon pepper
4 cups turkey broth
2 large eggs, lightly beaten

● **Combine** sausage, onion, and celery in a large skillet; cook over medium heat, stirring until sausage crumbles. Drain well.

● **Combine** cornbread, bread cubes, sage, salt, if desired, and pepper in a large bowl; stir in sausage mixture. Add broth and eggs, stirring well. Spoon mixture into a lightly greased 13- x 9- x 2-inch baking dish.
● **Bake** at 350° for 45 minutes or until lightly browned. **Yield:** 10 to 12 servings (9 cups).

Marjorie Henson
Benton, Kentucky

GRITS DRESSING

3 cups regular grits, uncooked
1 cup all-purpose flour
1 teaspoon baking powder
¼ teaspoon baking soda
2 large eggs
4 cups buttermilk
2 tablespoons vegetable oil
1 large onion, chopped
1 cup chopped celery
2 to 4 tablespoons dried sage, crumbled
1 teaspoon baking powder
2 large eggs, lightly beaten
1 (12-ounce) can evaporated milk
2 (14½-ounce) cans chicken broth

● **Heat** a well-greased 10-inch cast-iron skillet in a 325° oven 5 minutes or until skillet is hot.
● **Combine** first 4 ingredients in a large bowl; make a well in center of mixture. Combine 2 eggs, buttermilk, and oil; add to grits mixture, stirring just until dry ingredients are moistened.
● **Remove** skillet from oven, and pour batter into skillet. Bake at 325° for 1 hour or until firm in center, but not browned. Cool and crumble.
● **Combine** crumbled grits mixture, onion, and remaining ingredients in a bowl; pour mixture into a greased 13- x 9- x 2-inch baking dish.
● **Bake** at 325° for 50 minutes or until dressing is firm. **Yield:** 10 servings.

APPLE-WALNUT STUFFING

⅓ cup butter or margarine
1 large onion, finely chopped
2 stalks celery, finely chopped
1 cup chopped red cooking apple
1 cup chopped green cooking apple
2 cups white bread cubes, toasted
1 cup chopped walnuts
2 tablespoons dried whole-leaf sage
½ teaspoon dried rosemary
½ teaspoon dried thyme
1 large egg, beaten
½ cup milk
½ teaspoon salt
¼ teaspoon pepper

● **Melt** butter in a small skillet over medium-high heat; add onion and celery, and cook, stirring constantly, until tender.
● **Combine** apple, bread cubes, and next 4 ingredients in a large bowl; stir in vegetable mixture, egg, and remaining ingredients. Spoon mixture into a lightly greased 11- x 7- x 1½-inch baking dish.
● **Bake** at 350° for 30 minutes. **Yield:** 6 servings (4½ cups).

Crown Pork Roast with Apple-Walnut Stuffing: Purchase a well-trimmed (12-rib) crown pork roast (about 7 pounds), and season it with salt and pepper. Fold a piece of aluminum foil into an 8-inch square; place on rack in roasting pan. Place roast, bone ends up, on foil-lined rack. Bake at 325° for 1 hour. Cut a piece of foil long enough to fit around ribs. Wrap foil around ribs, and fold over tips of ribs. Spoon Apple-Walnut Stuffing into center of roast, and cover with additional foil. Insert a meat thermometer into roast without touching fat or bone. Bake at 325° for 1½ hours or until thermometer registers 160°. Remove foil from roast, and let stand 15 minutes before serving. **Yield:** 12 servings.

Susie Smith
Springville, Alabama

INDEX

METRIC EQUIVALENTS

The recipes that appear in this cookbook use the standard United States method for measuring liquid and dry or solid ingredients (teaspoons, tablespoons, and cups). The information on this chart is provided to help cooks outside the U.S. successfully use these recipes. All equivalents are approximate.

METRIC EQUIVALENTS FOR DIFFERENT TYPES OF INGREDIENTS

A standard cup measure of a dry or solid ingredient will vary in weight depending on the type of ingredient. A standard cup of liquid is the same volume for any type of liquid. Use the following chart when converting standard cup measures to grams (weight) or milliliters (volume).

Standard Cup	Fine Powder (ex. flour)	Grain (ex. rice)	Granular (ex. sugar)	Liquid Solids (ex. butter)	Liquid (ex. milk)
1	140 g	150 g	190 g	200 g	240 ml
¾	105 g	113 g	143 g	150 g	180 ml
⅔	93 g	100 g	125 g	133 g	160 ml
½	70 g	75 g	95 g	100 g	120 ml
⅓	47 g	50 g	63 g	67 g	80 ml
¼	35 g	38 g	48 g	50 g	60 ml
⅛	18 g	19 g	24 g	25 g	30 ml

USEFUL EQUIVALENTS FOR LIQUID INGREDIENTS BY VOLUME

¼ tsp			=	1 ml	
½ tsp			=	2 ml	
1 tsp			=	5 ml	
3 tsp =	1 tbls	=	½ fl oz =	15 ml	
	2 tbls	= ⅛ cup =	1 fl oz =	30 ml	
	4 tbls	= ¼ cup =	2 fl oz =	60 ml	
	5⅓ tbls	= ⅓ cup =	3 fl oz =	80 ml	
	8 tbls	= ½ cup =	4 fl oz =	120 ml	
	10⅔ tbls	= ⅔ cup =	5 fl oz =	160 ml	
	12 tbls	= ¾ cup =	6 fl oz =	180 ml	
	16 tbls	= 1 cup =	8 fl oz =	240 ml	
	1 pt	= 2 cups =	16 fl oz =	480 ml	
	1 qt	= 4 cups =	32 fl oz =	960 ml	
			33 fl oz =	1000 ml	= 1 l

USEFUL EQUIVALENTS FOR DRY INGREDIENTS BY WEIGHT

(To convert ounces to grams, multiply the number of ounces by 30.)

1 oz	=	1/16 lb	=	30 g
4 oz	=	¼ lb	=	120 g
8 oz	=	½ lb	=	240 g
12 oz	=	¾ lb	=	360 g
16 oz	=	1 lb	=	480 g

USEFUL EQUIVALENTS FOR LENGTH

(To convert inches to centimeters, multiply the number of inches by 2.5.)

1 in			=	2.5 cm	
6 in	= ½ ft		=	15 cm	
12 in	= 1 ft		=	30 cm	
36 in	= 3 ft	= 1 yd	=	90 cm	
40 in			=	100 cm	= 1 m

USEFUL EQUIVALENTS FOR COOKING/OVEN TEMPERATURES

	Fahrenheit	Celcius	Gas Mark
Freeze Water	32° F	0° C	
Room Temperature	68° F	20° C	
Boil Water	212° F	100° C	
Bake	325° F	160° C	3
	350° F	180° C	4
	375° F	190° C	5
	400° F	200° C	6
	425° F	220° C	7
	450° F	230° C	8
Broil			Grill